International Handbook
of Medical Education

INTERNATIONAL HANDBOOK OF MEDICAL EDUCATION

Edited by
Abdul W. Sajid
Christine H. McGuire
Rebecca Monroe Veach
Laura R. Aziz
Linda K. Gunzburger

Foreword by George E. Miller

GREENWOOD PRESS
Westport, Connecticut • London

Library of Congress Cataloging-in-Publication Data

International handbook of medical education / edited by Abdul W. Sajid
... [et al.] ; foreword by George E. Miller.
     p.   cm.
    Includes bibliographical references and index.
    ISBN 0–313–28423–7 (alk. paper)
      1. Medical education policy—Handbooks, manuals, etc. 2. Medical
education—Handbooks, manuals, etc. I. Sajid, Abdul W.
    [DNLM: 1. Education, Medical. W 18 I647 1994]
    R737.I54 1994
    610′.71′1—dc20   93–37854
    DNLM/DLC
    for Library of Congress

British Library Cataloguing in Publication Data is available.

Library of Congress Catalog Card Number: 93–37854
ISBN: 0–313–28423–7

First published in 1994

Greenwood Press, 88 Post Road West, Westport, CT 06881
An imprint of Greenwood Publishing Group, Inc.

Printed in the United States of America

The paper used in this book complies with the
Permanent Paper Standard issued by the National
Information Standards Organization (Z39.48–1984).

10 9 8 7 6 5 4 3 2 1

Copyright Acknowledgment

The editors and publisher gratefully acknowledge permission to reprint portions of:

Sharifah Shahabudin. 1992. Medical education in Malaysia. *Teaching and Learning in Medicine*
4(2):80–82. Used with permission from Lawrence Erlbaum Associates.

R. F. Jones, 1993. *American Medical Education: Institutions, Programs and Issues.* Washington, DC:
Association of American Medical Colleges.

Contents

Illustrations

Foreword

In 1971, when Abdul Sajid embarked on his career as a medical educator, international collaboration in the field was a relatively primitive enterprise. By the time of his tragic death in 1992 he had played a major role in shaping this growing movement and was admired throughout the world for his thoughtful, constructive, and always sensitive contributions. The *International Handbook of Medical Education* is a fitting tribute to his initiative, as well as a reminder of how much remains still to be done to assure a more appropriate fit between health professions education and the health needs of both developed and developing nations.

An early effort to promote international dialogue was the 1953 First World Conference on Medical Education, held in London under the sponsorship of the World Medical Association. It attracted some 600 participants representing 127 Faculties of Medicine in 62 countries. In his opening address Sir Lionel Whitby, President of the Conference, noted: "The world . . . has become so shrunken . . . that we can no longer take a parochial view of our problems." During the ensuing days, 91 formal papers were delivered, and innumerable commentators shared information about the ways in which their institutions and nations were coping with such common problems as student selection, curriculum development, and instructional and evaluation procedures. Chicago was the venue for the 1959 Second World Conference, which was organized and conducted in a similar manner.

Seven years later, reflecting on these two events, Dr. Raymond B. Allen, President of the 1959 assembly, summarized in these words the central theme of both meetings: "The ideals of excellence--the philosophy of the first-rate end of lifelong learning--epitomized the concern of medical Faculties throughout the world. The clear call was to adapt medical education to the mounting challenge of the twentieth-century revolution in science and technology."

Although virtually no sustained action resulted from those conferences, the World Health Organization (WHO), whose primary mission is that of directing and coordinating international health work, particularly in the field of public health, was taking vigorous steps to strengthen medical schools. The major thrust was a Fellowship program that provided opportunities for faculty members, especially those in developing nations, to improve their preparation as biomedical scientists (and thus, presumably, as medical teachers). Such institution-strengthening efforts were also undertaken by many medical schools in industrialized countries through cooperative relationships with sister schools in the third world. Here, too the focus was primarily on enhancing capabilities in medical science and technology.

It was at the 1966 Third World Conference, held in New Delhi, that a subtle shift in structure and content became evident. Entitled "Medical Education in the Service of Mankind," the meeting was organized in workshop style, with introductory papers leading to small group discussions designed "to start each participant thinking about how medical education could serve the people of his nation and what he could do after his return home to help attain this end." It was further designed to emphasize that "medicine is no longer just a biological science; it is also a social science."

These themes were further developed at the 1972 Fourth World Conference in Copenhagen, where workshops addressed such topics as identifying determinants of medical education (e.g., individual and community health needs); instituting change in medical education (e.g., teaching the teacher to teach); and evaluating medical education (e.g., using the quality and quantity of medical care as criteria for such measurements). However, perhaps the most visionary action taken there was the formal establishment of the World Federation for Medical Education, intended to catalyze the betterment of medical teaching and learning through cooperative efforts among national associations of medical schools, most of which had been created during the prior two decades.

By then, the pace of educational research and development in medicine had accelerated to the point where medical schools in many parts of the world were beginning to create intramural units charged with pursuing questions of curriculum development, instructional practices, and evaluation procedures in a more organized and dispassionate manner. And the World Health Organization Division of Health Manpower Development, under the dynamic leadership of Professor Tamas Fülöp, expanded its efforts in this field by establishing a global network of health professions teacher-training centers designed to foster the introduction of educational science into the practice of medical education.

The University of Illinois Center for Educational Development (now the Department of Medical Education) was initially the most prominent of these centers, mounting long- and short-term workshops both in Chicago and on-site at distant medical schools, and a master's degree program in health professions education that is now being offered at selected foreign medical schools as well as at the Department. Soon other groups in North America and abroad were conducting similar programs. Among the most vigorous of the overseas units were the School of Medical Education at the University of New South Wales, in Australia, and the Centre for Medical Education at the University of Dundee, in Scotland.

Valuable as these efforts appeared to be, there was dawning recognition that even refined statements of educational objectives or improved use of instructional and evaluation techniques, if focused on medical science alone rather than also embracing medical service requirements, could overlook national health needs that the education of physicians was intended to serve. At a 1979 WHO conference in Jamaica, this issue was addressed by a group representing medical schools which had attempted to bridge that apparent gulf between science and service. The outcome of this gathering was another global network, one of problem based and community oriented schools, whose collaboration and mutual help system was encouraged and supported by the World Health Organization, but independently operated through a secretariat at the University of Limburg Medical School in Maastricht, The Netherlands. By 1993, 97 institutions had become full members of the Network, with others registered as associates.

Many of the contributors to this *Handbook* come from the Network's institutional membership; but all have been touched by the spirit it represents and the educational philosophy it promotes. However, they are by no means alone. There are now nearly a score of WHO Collaborating Centers addressing issues of health manpower development, several regional and global groups reflecting the concerns of particular medical specialties in educational program development (e.g., the European Academy of Teachers in General Practice and the World Organization of National Colleges, Academies and Academic Associations of General Practitioners/Family Physicians), and national and regional organizations of medical schools linked through the World Federation for Medical Education. It was the Federation that, at a 1988 World Conference, produced the Edinburgh Declaration which has become a guidepost for medical educators around the world. That organization conducted a follow-up meeting in 1993 entitled "The Changing Medical Professions: Implications for Medical Education."

Such a brief, and inevitably incomplete, historical account is intended to do no more than set the stage for what follows by highlighting the accelerating pace of international cooperative activities in medical education and the general direction in which they are moving. Although Abdul Sajid's name will not be found among the authors of those substantive chapters, his voice and his spirit must surely have been felt by all as they organized their thoughts about the field that became his world.

George E. Miller, MD

Preface

This *Handbook* is intended as a comprehensive source book and reference on the status of medical education worldwide at the close of the twentieth century. Writing in July 1991, Professor Abdul Sajid, the initiator and designer of this volume, spoke of his vision for the book as follows:

Physicians have played a prominent role in shaping health care, and their influence is in part a by-product of their professional preparation. As recently as thirty years ago, a traveler journeying around the world could understand the essentials of any country's system of medical education simply by asking which clearly defined model--French, English, or German--that country had adopted. As the world moves into the next century, however, the growing internationalization of health care is reflected in a merging of those discrete models. Nations responding to changes in political, social, and economic systems in every corner of the globe face the further challenge of reorienting their health systems and their methods of training health personnel consistent with new realities.

How the nations of the world adapt their systems of medical education to respond to shifts from disease-oriented, curative medicine to public or community-oriented preventive health care models has been a subject of discussion at recent international forums sponsored by the World Health Organization and the World Federation for Medical Education. Can "high tech" also be "high touch?" Is there a way by which we can utilize the latest technology without losing the human aspects of medicine? Can we prepare future practitioners who know how to use biomedical technology without jeopardizing human dignity? Will the physician trained in today's medical schools be a global practitioner whose skills and talents can be deployed across national boundaries? With a focus on the educational issues that cross national boundaries, the *Handbook* brings narrative perspective to these new challenges.

This reference work examines the current status of medical education around the globe, as individual nations prepare to train physicians for the medical realities of the twenty-first century. The book focuses on the forces that influence the unique characteristics of medical education in specific countries. The changing pattern of disease, the health outcomes of environmental degradation, national and international policy shifts in response to these forces and to the economics of health care constitute the context for looking at national systems for preparing human resources: admissions practices, unique models of curricula, certification standards, and the role of professional bodies and international agencies.

One major problem with the sources currently available has been the absence of comparable data across countries. A databook based solely on numbers, however, is obsolete before it reaches the market. This *Handbook* provides more than an instant-in-time snapshot of students and curricula. Rather, it delineates the directions chosen as national priorities that tomorrow's physicians will carry from their educational experiences into their practice of medicine.

To implement his vision, Dr. Sajid invited leading medical educators in each of 28 nations to prepare a chapter describing briefly the nature of the health care and medical education systems in their respective countries. To facilitate comparison across countries, regions, and topics each author was asked to comment on the following: the evolution and the current structure of the medical education system (especially as it relates to the health care delivery system), the role of national policy in shaping medical education, admission policies, undergraduate curricular structure and innovation, graduate medical education, continuing medical education, licensure and certification, the role of research in medical education, government/private sector involvement, international linkages and collaboration, and current issues and trends.

Geographic diversity constituted one important criterion for choosing the countries profiled. Although the chapters are arranged alphabetically by country, they can also be considered in terms of major regions--the Americas, Western Europe, Eastern Europe and the former USSR, the Middle East, Africa, Asia, and the Western Pacific--each of which is described by representative entries.

The education and certification of physicians within a country involves a complex interaction among political, educational, and health care delivery systems. That interaction can vary widely among countries within a geographic region (as witness the contrast between the health care delivery and medical education systems in the United States and Canada). Countries profiled within the same geographic region, therefore, represent different emphases as these systems interact and shape each other.

To demonstrate this variety of relationships among sectors, every effort was made to ensure that the countries chosen for inclusion represented different stages of economic development, alternative social and political organization, a variety of health care delivery systems, critical regional issues, and the full range of responses of the medical education community to these challenges. As this *Handbook* was being completed, the political and economic geography of the world as it had existed since the end of World War II was in flux and cartographers were hard-pressed to keep up with changing boundaries and national names. Among the 28 countries included in this *Handbook*, many are in such a transition: changing economic systems, governmental structures, alliances, and boundaries.

The chapters delineate a broad picture of the challenges confronting each country: the innovations and adaptations incorporated in each system, and the similarities, differences, parallels and lessons learned. Each of the countries included brings a valuable and often unique perspective to the *Handbook*. The book does not prescribe a preferred model of medical education; rather, it offers useful ideas and insights and invites the reader to benefit from the experiences of others.

For ease in comparing specific topics across countries, major subject headings are included in the index, and additional cross country data have been compiled in the Appendices. For readers who wish additional information on particular topics, countries, or regions, a Selected Bibliography is provided.

Many of the chapters in this volume list persons whose generous assistance the authors wish to acknowledge. For help with the manuscript as a whole, the editors wish to acknowledge Professor Sajid's many professional colleagues who assisted him in identifying authors, reviewed drafts of several of the chapters, and otherwise lent their support to completing this book. Special thanks are due to Professor Tamas Fülöp, former Director, Division of Development of Human Resources for Health, World Health Organization (WHO); Dr. Charles Boelen, Chief, Educational Development of Human Resources for Health, WHO; Professor Georges Bordage, Professor Fazil Elahi, Professor Mohan Garg, Professor Lev Sverdlow, and Dr. Silvia Santos. The book would not have been completed without the unstinting assistance of Gladys Khan, Maggie Wade, and Shelly Taylor.

Editors, Chicago
November 1993

International Handbook
of Medical Education

1

An Overview of Medical Education in the Late Twentieth Century

CHRISTINE H. MCGUIRE

The twentieth century witnessed two major worldwide revolutions in medical education. The locus, date, and nature of the precipitating event that triggered the first can be specified with precision, and its manifestations as it spread were readily visible and essentially uniform. Not so the second: no single event can be assigned responsibility for the seemingly spontaneous developments that began to appear in diverse places in the late 1950s and early 1960s, apparently in response to diffuse disappointments and disillusionments with the medical education establishment.

The first revolution was prompted by the publication in 1910 of Abraham Flexner's modest little report to his sponsors--the Carnegie Foundation--summarizing his observations of, conclusions about, and recommendations for reform in medical education. The prompt elimination of proprietary schools and the incorporation of medical education into the university system in the United States can be traced directly to Flexner's influence. The reform of the curriculum to stress the scientific basis of medicine and the implementation of that emphasis by separating instruction in the basic sciences from the clinical disciplines took root worldwide. While details of the educational system may vary from country to country, the general pattern everywhere reflects the philosophy and strategy advocated by Flexner. Even after the Flexnerian model began to be called into question in the West, it continued to be emulated by emerging institutions in the developing world, where other educational systems were regarded as inferior and as evidence of accepting second-class status for their citizens.

In contrast, the second revolution was not characterized by clear-cut origins or uniform development. Rather, following World War II, medical educators in some Western countries began to manifest concern about perceived changes in the numbers and quality of medical school applicants and to express the view that many excellent potential applicants were being seduced into the then more glamorous atomic sciences. At the same time, a new generation of medical students--older and more seasoned by their wartime experiences--increasingly questioned the seeming irrelevance of some of their studies and the medieval approach to instruction in many institutions--a revulsion most destructively expressed in the Cultural Revolution in China.

Responses to these protests were many and varied: a few institutions (e.g., McMaster University in Canada and Ben Gurion University of the Negev in Israel) pioneered radically new curricula that differed not only from traditional programs but also from each other; many institutions experimented with more limited changes (e.g., reducing or eliminating laboratory instruction, introducing elective courses, etc.), and a significant number established units of medical education to do research on, and assist in the reform of, medical education.

THE MISSION OF THE MEDICAL EDUCATION ESTABLISHMENT

Giving further impetus to reform, in 1978 the World Health Organization (WHO) adopted the Alma Ata Declaration proclaiming "Health for All by the Year 2000" as its official goal and designating "primary care" as its preferred strategy. Thus, the obvious was made explicit: namely, that it is the primary mission of any program of medical education to prepare students and house staff to function effectively in the prevailing health care delivery system so as to resolve, within the limits of existing knowledge and resources, the health needs of the population to be served.

To fulfill this mission, it is essential that those responsible for educational planning be knowledgeable about, and take account of, the following parameters: (1) the structure and requirements of the health care delivery system, (2) the health problems prevalent in the region, (3) the constraints imposed by the evolving nature of the medical profession itself, and (4) the consequent changes in the characteristics of the student population that may alter their learning requirements.

COMMON CHALLENGES

While the particular constellation of salient factors in each of the four areas listed above differs from country to country, there are certain general conditions that are shared by most.

Though the amount of health care available through the private sector on a fee-for-service basis varies from country to country, a significant amount of care in all countries is furnished, at least to some groups, either by means of direct government subsidy or through prepaid insurance programs, which are usually financed by employers, labor unions, and/or government. These health care systems face three common problems worldwide. As the application of high technology spreads, health costs are everywhere outrunning resources; there is everywhere a maldistribution among specialties and particularly between specialists and general physicians; and, even in the face of an overall oversupply of physicians in some places (e.g., Belgium, as a result of a policy of open admission to medical school; Israel, as a result of immigration), rural areas are nowhere adequately served.

Available methods for dealing with these problems necessarily vary from country to country depending on the indigenous system, but all rely to some extent on their educational institutions to motivate and to train students to practice in underserved areas. As is evident in succeeding chapters the responsiveness of the educational process to these expectations varies greatly but is nowhere completely adequate.

Threats to Health

Among the many health problems physicians are now called on to manage, the following are certain to escalate worldwide in the coming decades.

The changing age distribution of the population. Problems of an aging population now command our attention in the West, and similar trends can be anticipated in some developing countries in response to modifications in public policy and social norms, such as the "one child per family" campaign of China; alternatively, in other countries, numbers in the younger age groups are exploding in response to limited improvements in sanitation, nutrition, and immunization. These changes present new challenges to health care workers everywhere.

The HIV/AIDS pandemic. The necessity of providing sufferers of this plague with supportive therapy and of counseling them and their immediate associates is now worldwide. Of greater significance for the future, however, is the importance of prevention, a major responsibility for which necessarily falls on health care providers, particularly in African and other nonindustrialized countries, where the number of new cases is increasing most rapidly.

Substance abuse. Despite widely heralded "wars on drugs," there is very little evidence that this global scourge, or the fetal defects and neonatal addictions associated with it, are being effectively controlled anywhere; instead, young people everywhere, in all social strata, are being recruited into the illegal drug culture at younger and younger ages.

An increasingly diverse population. More and more physicians in every country must be prepared to deal with unfamiliar problems that a more heterogeneous population may present. As immigration from developing to developed nations increases and as travel between these regions expands, old plagues are spreading and diseases thought to have disappeared in some areas are once again surfacing. For example, witness the emergence in Southeast Asia and elsewhere of new strains of malaria that are resistant to all available drugs, and the resurgence in the West of tuberculosis and of certain childhood afflictions which, until recently, appeared to have been conquered. Physicians now being trained anywhere in the world will increasingly be called on to help mitigate these threats. However, such demands on physicians are not alone due to the mobility of the populations they serve; they also arise from the internationalization of medical practice that has seen an increasing number of physicians being trained in one country and practicing in another, with different health problems and unfamiliar cultural responses.

Pollution and its consequences. Given the rate at which we are poisoning our environment, overt and covert toxicoses, and the associated damage to our genetic pool, will emerge as major health problems throughout the world unless we educate our physicians to take an urgently proactive role in preventing this catastrophe, while also managing the effects of what they are unable to prevent.

Technology spiraling out of control. In the developed world current changes in the organization of work are of a magnitude that rivals the Industrial Revolution, while in other countries essentially rural societies based on a village economy are being rapidly precipitated directly into advanced urban industrialized cultures. In both cases, the associated occupational and social changes are now proceeding at a pace which increasing numbers of people find beyond their adaptive capacity. The resulting pressures, together with our failure to cope with a pyramiding technology, have created physical and emotional stresses that physicians must be prepared to help relieve.

And, though worldwide anxiety about confrontations between the major powers may have temporarily abated, covert concerns about the potential for atomic genocide may actually have been exacerbated as a consequence of nuclear proliferation among smaller nations and terrorist groups.

Even if we manage to avoid what has been called "the ultimate epidemic," the suffering associated with a worldwide resurgence of tribalism will continue to engender disabling physical, psychosomatic, and behavioral dysfunctions that, unless countered by rational statesmanship, may eventually overshadow all other health problems.

The Nature of the Medical Profession

The foregoing constitutes a very partial list of the escalating problems that current medical students must be prepared to help resolve. But they must learn how to do so within the constraints imposed by evolving medical knowledge and practice, the following aspects of which are of special relevance in educational planning:

The Knowledge Explosion. Cliché though it may have become, it is nonetheless essential to recognize that acceleration in the rate of expansion of the knowledge base has altered forever the character of the medical profession and its educational requirements. Knowledge, now doubling every five to eight years, is reliably predicted to begin shortly to double every year! The traditional practice of simply adding to an already overcrowded curriculum no longer suffices. Instead, students need to be helped to develop strategies for dealing with the sheer volume of information, concepts, principles, and skills that health providers must now have at their command.

Specialization. Everywhere, specialization and specialists are proliferating at the expense of high-quality primary care. This trend has exacerbated a number of policy issues, among the most important of which are the following: the definition of a common educational core equally suitable both as preparation for further specialized training and as preparation for direct entry into general practice; the inclusion within the core of experiences that enhance the attractiveness, and augment the skills requisite for delivery, of primary care services essential to meeting national needs; and consideration of compulsory public service in general practice in underserved areas as a requirement for the licensure of all physicians.

Diminished autonomy. In most countries of the world, physicians are increasingly subject to a variety of legislative, juridical, and bureaucratic controls, ranging from the necessity for coordination with other professionals inevitably imposed by division of labor, through the sometimes frustrating bureaucratic restrictions mandated by hospital, clinic, insurance and governmental authorities, to the constraints enforced by a mounting flurry of legislation and a crisis of litigation occurring in many Western countries, especially the United States.

Ethical dilemmas. The same inexorable march of science that has brought spectacular progress in managing health problems and made available sophisticated technologies for increasing the length and improving the quality of life, has also created new and ever more difficult moral, ethical, and philosophic dilemmas for health care providers, consideration of which can no longer be avoided in training programs.

Globalization of medical practice. In modern times, strict immigration regulations and licensure requirements have always limited the movement of professionals across national boundaries. Nonetheless, as suggested above, following World War II large numbers of former colonials sought postgraduate training in the ex-mother country and/or in the United States and Canada, where they were frequently welcomed to stay and practice to fill perceived shortages of health personnel in those countries. However, as the demand in the latter became satiated, policymakers--with self-proclaimed virtue--increasingly responded to complaints from the developing world (that it was subsidizing wealthier countries through this obvious "brain drain") by demanding that prospective trainees furnish proof of their intention to return to their respective home countries. It would seem, therefore, that mobility across national boundaries would be diminishing. But such is not the case: the proliferation of trading agreements (e.g., the European Economic Community) that facilitate the free flow of goods and, in some cases, persons across national boundaries has put implicit pressure on medical schools to meet uniform worldwide standards (see Chapter 2).

Traditional versus Western medicine. Though Western medicine is typically embraced by policymakers everywhere, some countries (notably India, China, and, to some extent, Japan) have long respected forms of Vedic, Taoist, herbal, and other indigenous modes of treatment; other countries (most notably in Africa and Central and South America) have strong cadres of native healers sought by significant numbers of the local population. Hence, in some places formal training programs of traditional lore and practice exist side by side and act in cooperation with Western educational institutions, clinics and dispensaries. Clearly, this situation requires special consideration by policymakers who must allocate resources, and by medical faculty who must prepare graduates to practice in cultures where patients may seek assistance from providers trained in other traditions.

The needs of medical students. With a few notable exceptions (e.g., Eastern Europe and the former USSR), physicians in most countries have, especially in recent decades, enjoyed not only the satisfactions of service but also the rewards of relatively high prestige and favored economic status--a fact that inevitably influences self-selection into the profession. At the same time, educational institutions throughout the world have, with very few exceptions (e.g., Belgium), been exceedingly selective in their admissions policies, typically restricting entry on the basis of very narrowly defined criteria of academic aptitude and accomplishment, particularly achievement in the "hard sciences."

In most countries of the world we are now witnessing dramatic change in these factors which weigh so heavily in the determination of student characteristics. Alterations in the nature of medical practice, as outlined above and described in succeeding chapters, have modified the satisfactions to be derived from professional practice and, therefore, the motivations of people attracted to it. Furthermore, deliberate policies have been adopted--country-wide in some instances--to create a larger applicant pool and more diverse student population by encouraging applications from members of groups who, for many reasons, had not previously been well-represented. In some countries this was evidenced by deliberate affirmative action policies to attract women, ethnic, or religious minorities, persons from economically deprived groups or rural areas, individuals with educational backgrounds in the humanities or the social and behavioral sciences, or others less typical of traditional medical schools.

Whatever the stimulus, the results are everywhere the same: medical faculties are increasingly required to evaluate applicants and to work with students whose preparation, motivations, and talents for both the study and practice of medicine may differ markedly from those of students with whom the faculty is most familiar. If the needs of these new types of students are to be met, different approaches to medical education and additional support systems (both financial and personal) are likely to be required.

RESPONSE TO CHALLENGE--UNDERGRADUATE MEDICAL EDUCATION

Typically, institutional responses to the challenges outlined above have embraced seven aspects of the educational system: (1) admission polices, (2) the content of the program, (3) the organization of the curriculum, (4) the setting for instruction, (5) the methods of instruction and assessment employed, (6) the interaction among educational, research and service functions within an institution, and (7) the relation between the institution and the external licensure authorities, accreditation bodies, and the society to be served. While the combination of responses to challenge are as varied as the patterns of challenge themselves, major trends to be reported in detail in succeeding chapters can be summarized as follows:

Admissions policies. While many institutions and some countries have established financial and academic support systems to facilitate implementation of a policy of diversity and a few places still have open admission policies, most institutions are maintaining and/or increasing selectivity.

Content of the educational program. The most common response in this area continues to be the accretion of subjects for study: not only the simple addition of new technical subjects, such as molecular biology, for example, but also, in some institutions, increased attention to the social and behavioral sciences and the expansion of both didactic and clinical instruction in public health and community medicine. However, the introduction of new subjects has only rarely been associated with the elimination of existing courses.

Organization of the curriculum. Superficially, it would appear that the duration of the undergraduate medical curriculum varies widely from country to country--being as short as three years in some places and up to seven or eight years in others. However, appearances are deceiving. If instruction in the premedical sciences, which in some countries takes place in the faculties of arts and sciences, and the year or more of supervised clinical experience usually required for licensure are both included, then the first clinical degree can be said to require at least six or seven years postsecondary practically everywhere. Equally prevalent is the traditional separation between basic and clinical sciences; indeed, in most countries the program of study is divided neatly into three discrete compartments labeled premedical (lasting one or two years), preclinical or basic sciences (usually two years in length), and clinical instruction (of two to three years duration). As noted above, in some countries premedical instruction is incorporated into a four-year university program which must be completed before admission to medical school; while in others, students are admitted directly from secondary school into a six- or seven-year program, all parts of which are conducted by the medical faculty. The year or more of supervised hospital practice typically mandated to meet licensure requirements may or may not be under the control of the medical faculty.

In most institutions the entire curriculum is organized by discipline and responsibility for instruction is located in independent departments. However, this departmental structure is gradually being replaced in a few institutions by a curriculum organized more functionally for purposes of learning in terms of organ systems and/or health problems, and many institutions are attempting to provide more integrative experiences by introducing students to patient care during the preclinical phase and by incorporating community medicine throughout the undergraduate experience.

The settings for learning. Instruction worldwide remains predominantly in medieval-like lecture halls; where it has escaped, it is most often to be found in outmoded laboratories (for the basic science disciplines) or tertiary care centers (for the clinical sciences), neither particularly relevant to the health problems and facilities most graduates will face. In response to the dissatisfactions outlined above and, more particularly, to the emphasis of the World Health Organization on primary care, a few institutions are introducing medical students to patient care settings even in the first year of medical school, expanding instruction in ambulatory settings, and, by means of various types of liaisons with practitioners and public health clinics, exposing students to a full range of community health problems.

Instructional and assessment methodologies. Lectures and oral and essay examinations still predominate everywhere in the world. However, more and more institutions are beginning to supplement, and in some cases even to supplant, lecture programs with small-group, problem-based tutorials. Less frequently, but to some extent, traditional examinations and student evaluations based on highly personal testimony are gradually being superseded in a few institutions by demonstrably more valid and reliable simulation methodologies and various other forms of performance assessment. However, perhaps due to cost and lack of available expertise, these developments are not yet widespread.

Integrated reforms. As suggested above, response to challenge has, for the most part, been piecemeal and evolutionary. However, in a few places totally innovative programs have been adopted either institutionwide or in newly created "alternate tracks" within an institution. The latter strategy seems particularly suited to well-established Faculties (e.g., Harvard University, University of New Mexico), whereas schoolwide reform appears generally more viable in newly founded or deeply troubled institutions. Fully implemented innovations differ from traditional programs in purporting to be "problem-based, student-centered, and community-oriented." In practice, however, most innovative programs incorporate only one or two of these characteristics and, with few exceptions (e.g., Suez Canal University and Ben-Gurion University of the Negev), are limited to the basic science component of the curriculum. As yet, there has been insufficient research to document the relative effectiveness of the integrated reforms that have been introduced.

The relation among educational, research, and service responsibilities. Investigators continue to document the low status accorded educational functions in evaluating medical faculty for retention and promotion, the priority given to disciplinary research in those decisions, and the low prestige of, and lack of support for, educational research. There seems little evidence of any change in this attitude.

Accreditation, licensure, and cross-licensing. Every country has some mechanism for identifying "approved" medical schools. In some, approval may rest on a centuries old charter to a university and/or Faculty; in others, it may be based on periodic visitation and detailed inspection of facilities, faculty, and programs by a committee from an officially designated body to which the government has delegated the power of accreditation; and only those who have graduated from an accredited institution can be licensed to practice. In some countries, completion of an approved program automatically confers eligibility for licensure; in others, it merely provides admission to a lengthy national examination, passage of which is necessary for independent practice.

Practitioners licensed in one country rarely have extended practice privileges in another. Aside from a few bilateral arrangements and/or special circumstances (e.g. as between the United Kingdom and Commonwealth countries), persons trained and/or licensed in one country are generally required to undertake additional training and/or examination to obtain licenses in another. However, these conditions are likely to change as multinational agreements such as the European Economic Community spread to other regions.

RESPONSE TO CHALLENGE—GRADUATE AND CONTINUING EDUCATION

Although a residency or internship may be required, nowhere is postgraduate specialty certification required to practice, and almost nowhere is participation in continuing education required to maintain either a medical license or certification as a specialist. Nevertheless, policymakers in most countries report that there are too many specialists, too few advanced training programs for primary care physicians, and too many negative incentives to enter general practice. Attempts to exercise strict controls on the specialty distribution of physicians have met with little success anywhere and are, for the most part, indirect (i.e., operating by means of limitations either on training opportunities or on employment opportunities). Such policies, as well as other arrangements with respect to specialty training and life long learning, are even more variable from country to country than are those that characterize undergraduate education. In some countries training requirements, accreditation of programs, and number of training positions are subject to detailed regulation by formally organized groups of specialists and certification as a specialist is restricted to whose who can prove they have satisfactorily completed required training and have passed national examinations administered under the auspices of recognized specialty boards; at the other extreme individuals may be designated as specialist after informal apprenticeship with physicians who are known to limit their practice to the relevant areas. In either case the training ordinarily takes place in tertiary care centers that may or may not be affiliated with a recognized medical Faculty.

Arrangements for continuing education are even more variable. In some places medical graduates and specialty societies take the leadership in providing structured programs for which some formal recognition (credit) and/or reward is provided; in others, reliance is placed almost exclusively on pharmaceutical companies with an economic interest in the content of educational programs. But, with very few exceptions, participation is everywhere voluntary.

SUPPORT FOR EDUCATIONAL REFORM

The limited responsiveness of both ministries and medical Faculties to the educational challenges outlined above and documented in succeeding chapters, can be explained in part by the restricted organizational and financial support available to assist in developing sounder programs.

Organizational Support

At the international level, the Division of Development of Human Resources for Health (formerly known as the Division of Health Manpower Development, HMD) of WHO has, in the past, exerted more significant influence in support of reform than has any other body. Under the leadership of a series of enlightened directors, most notably Tamas Fülöp, WHO-HMD developed, in collaboration with the then Office of Research in Medical Education of the University of Illinois College of Medicine, a global plan for assisting medical faculties to gain the expertise to design, implement, and evaluate more effective programs of medical education. In brief, this comprehensive plan called for establishing an International Teacher Training Center (ITTC) at the University of Illinois to train selected medical faculty from around the world who, in turn, would create Regional Teacher Training Centers (RTTCs)--one in each WHO region--whose mission it would be to train personnel for National Teacher Training Centers (NTTCs), which would then be available to train and support faculty from local institutions.

With very substantial financial, as well as organizational, support from WHO, this ambitious project was launched in the late 1960s and soon led to the establishment of a number of RTTCs (e.g., in Australia for the Western Pacific Region, and in Iran for the Eastern Mediterranean Region); NTTCs quickly followed (e.g., in Thailand and in the Philippines), and offices or departments of research in medical education became increasingly common even in individual institutions. With the exception of the RTTC at Shiraz, which fell victim to the Iranian Revolution, most of these centers continue to offer training, consultation and research services, with the centers at Dundee in Scotland and at New South Wales in Australia being among the most active internationally. In addition, McMaster University in Canada and Maastricht University in The Netherlands present frequent workshops on problem-based learning and tutorial instruction to an international clientele. More extended programs leading to a master's degree in health professions education are offered by a few institutions, most notably the Department of Medical Education at the University of Illinois and the School of Medical Education at New South Wales.

In addition to the Health Manpower Division of WHO, two other initiatives merit mention: (1) the Network of Community Oriented Educational Institutions for the Health Sciences (also established under the auspices and with the support of WHO-HMD) whose newsletters, annual international meetings, and secretariat today provide an essential service in disseminating useful information to member institutions throughout the world, about research and development in medical education; and (2) the World Federation for Medical Education, which sponsored the international invitational congress that eventuated in the Edinburgh Declaration, calling not only for reform in the content, organization, strategy and setting of medical training, but also for the promotion of dynamic, reciprocal linkages between the medical education establishment and the health care delivery system.

In addition to these more visible international organizations, some of which perform research and training as well as dissemination and publication functions, there is in most countries some kind of national association of medical schools which serves as a forum for the exchange of information about educational developments and for the recognition, presentation and dissemination of refereed educational research. Notable among these are the Nordic Federation of Medical Schools, the British Association for the Study of Medical Education (ASME), the

Australian and New Zealand Association for Medical Education (ANZME), the European Association of Medical Education (AMEE), and the Group on Educational Affairs (GEA) of the Association of American Medical Colleges (AAMC). Most professional associations in the various basic science and clinical disciplines also include a section in their annual meetings and/or journals devoted to discussion of both undergraduate teaching and specialty training. All of these continue to serve as sources of ideas and support for medical faculty interested in improving their teaching, while simultaneously affording some measure of peer recognition so important in the promotion process.

Financial Support

In most countries medical schools are primarily dependent on governmental sources for support of both research and educational functions, and in many instances, the funds available to support the latter depend entirely on enrollment, with no supplement for educational experimentation and development.

With respect to research support, public funds are typically devoted almost exclusively to the basic and clinical sciences, as is financing from pharmaceutical companies, which are primarily interested in encouraging research leading to results that may be patented and marketed and in sponsoring continuing education offerings that disseminate these results to practitioners.

Hence, with minor exceptions, such as WHO, the United States Agency for International Development (USAID), and the Asian Development Bank, institutions eager to undertake educational research and development have been forced to rely heavily on support from a variety of private foundations. Historically, these have been concentrated mainly in North America (e.g., Commonwealth, Kellogg, Robert Wood Johnson), Britain (e.g., Wellcome Trust, Neuffield Foundation) and Western Europe (e.g., Volkswagon, Smith-Kline). While such foundations have, on occasion, supported major overseas projects and often provide travel and training grants to other nationals, most private foundations that support educational research and development understandably devote most of their resources to home based projects. Thus institutions in emerging countries have had only limited access to any financial aid in the support of educational improvements.

CODA

In the following chapters, the authors describe the particular constellation of challenges prevailing in their respective countries with regard to the systemic, social, professional, and individual student needs outlined above, and the program of medical education each has developed in response to that unique set of conditions. Given the relatively limited support of and reward for educational activities reported above, perhaps the wonder is that medical education has progressed as rapidly as the following chapters would indicate.

NOTE

The author wishes to express special appreciation to her husband, Dr. Jules Masserman, who reviewed the preliminary draft of this chapter, offered many valuable suggestions that have been incorporated in it, and otherwise assisted in its preparation.

REFERENCES

In addition to the succeeding chapters which served as a primary source of information for this overview, the following general references are especially helpful resources about the current sociocultural context of medical practice and general trends in curriculum, instruction and assessment.

Curry, L., J.F. Wergin, et al. 1993. *Educating professionals*. San Francisco: Jossey-Bass.

Dinham, S.M., and F.T. Stritter. 1983. Research on professional education. In M.E. Wittock, ed., *Handbook of research in teaching*. New York: MacMillan.

Flexner, A. 1910. *Medical education in the United States and Canada: A report to the Carnegie Foundation for the Advancement of Teaching*. Bulletin no. 4. Boston: Updyke.

Hart, I.R., and R.M. Hardin. 1987. *Further developments in assessing clinical competence*. International Conference Proceedings. Montreal, Canada: Can-Heal Publications.

McGuire, C.H. 1992. Social medicine and world health. In J.H. Masserman and C.H. Masserman, eds., *Social psychiatry and world accords*, pp. 49-57. New York: Gardner Press.

---------. 1989. The curriculum for the year 2000. *Med Educ* 23:221-227.

McGuire, C.H., R.P. Foley, A. Gorr, R.W. Richards, et al., eds. 1983. *Handbook of health professions education*. San Francisco: Jossey-Bass.

Nooman, Z., H.G. Schmidt, and E.S. Ezzat, eds. 1990. *Innovation in medical education: An evaluation of its present status*. New York: Springer Publishing.

Payer, L. 1988. *Medicine and culture: Varieties of treatment in the United States, England, West Germany and France*. New York: Henry Holt.

Schmidt, H.G., M. Lipkin, et al, eds. 1989. *New directions for medical education: Problem-based learning and community-oriented medical education*. New York: Springer-Verlag.

Starr, P. 1982. *The social transformation of American medicine*. New York: Basic Books.

2

Evaluation and Change in Medical Education

MARJORIE P. WILSON

Geopolitical changes throughout the world, as well as changes in science and technology, make international exchange a necessary feature of the era of global medicine that has overtaken us. The question arises, should we have a system of standards and credentialing worldwide that is sufficiently consistent to facilitate such exchanges? At this stage, we can only identify some of the issues that would impinge on such a process and attempt to understand the role of examinations and other assessment methodologies in the overall process of physician evaluation, whether at the national or international level.

LICENSURE AND CERTIFICATION: MODELS OF EVALUATION AND ASSESSMENT

The Educational Commission for Foreign Medical Graduates (ECFMG) in the United States has some knowledge of how current requirements for licensure or registration to practice medicine vary from country to country because foreign nationals have had to meet their particular nation's requirement in order to obtain ECFMG certification. ECFMG has just completed updating its information on licensure country by country. In 1994, the World Health Organization (WHO) will confirm or modify further the information we have obtained through its periodic questionnaire in preparation for publication of the seventh edition of the *World Directory of Medical Schools.* We already know that, for a variety of reasons, there are substantial differences from country to country. Two of the major variables are (1) whether a national examination is mandatory and (2) whether a period of time in clinical training or practice is required before the license is conferred. In some countries, clinical experience is regarded as a required part of the educational process, while in others it is a mandated public service duty. In the latter case, medical education may have been subsidized by the government because of physician workforce needs, and a period of social service is required as a "payback."

In describing licensure in the United States, Thomas J. Monahan of the New York State Medical Board has said:

The practice of the medical profession is a public trust earned through a rigorous sequence of education, examination, and experience. In assuring that this public trust is appropriately carried out and to assure the public that adequate standards are applied to the delivery of medical care by physicians, a system of professional licensure exists which has two fundamental objectives: the establishment and preservation of agreed-upon standards of excellence for entry into the profession, and the protection of the public health and welfare. . . . State medical boards throughout the nation have attempted to achieve the fundamental objectives of licensure by relying upon a process that consists of three components--education, examination, and experience. (Monahan 1990, p. 35)

In the United States, medical licensure is governed by individual state medical boards. Each state board has the authority to establish standards and requirements that it believes necessary to assure competency. This system resembles medical licensure throughout the world, whereby each country determines its own criteria for medical licensure. In one sense, despite the many differences nationally and internationally in the who, what, when and how of medical licensure, the overall goals appear universal: to protect the public and the physician. In addition to protecting the public by requiring that objective criteria are met prior to the practice of medicine, the individual physician should be protected from discrimination and the arbitrary setting of standards.

Until recently, when other criteria had been met, physicians in the United States could obtain licensure at the individual state level either by passing the examinations of the National Board of Medical Examiners or by taking the Federation Licensing Examination (FLEX) given by the individual states. The new United States Medical Licensing Examination (USMLE), introduced in June 1992, was "designed to assess the examinee's understanding of and ability to apply concepts and principles that are important in health and disease and that constitute the basis of safe and effective patient care" (USMLE 1992). There are three steps in the new examination.

USMLE Step 1 assesses whether an examinee understands and can apply key concepts of basic biomedical science, with an emphasis on principles and mechanisms of health, disease and modes of therapy. Step 2 assesses whether an examinee possesses the medical knowledge and understanding of clinical science considered essential for the provision of patient care under supervision, including emphasis on health promotion and disease prevention. Step 3 will assess whether an examinee possesses the medical knowledge and understanding of biomedical and clinical science considered essential for the unsupervised practice of medicine. (USMLE 1992)

After 1994, the three steps of the USMLE will be the only route to licensure available in the United States.

Since 1958, the ECFMG has been fulfilling its responsibility to assess the readiness of graduates of foreign medical schools to enter residency or fellowship programs in the United States that are accredited by the Accreditation Council for Graduate Medical Education (ACGME) through a certification program that also includes education, examination, and credentials validation components. ECFMG has also been delegated the authority, through the United States Information Agency, to sponsor physicians coming from other countries as exchange visitors in accredited graduate medical education programs and other advanced educational opportunities in the United States. The objective of this sponsorship program is to enhance international exchange in the field of medicine and promote mutual understanding between people of the United States and other countries through this exchange of individuals, knowledge, and skills. When a graduate of a foreign medical school has met all the requirements for ECFMG certification, the candidate is eligible to apply to accredited graduate medical education programs in the United States. Through this certification program, the ECFMG provides assurances to directors of programs approved by the ACGME and to the public that the physician has met the minimum standard of eligibility to enter such programs.

To obtain ECFMG certification, graduates of foreign medical schools must have had at least four credit years in attendance at a medical school listed, at the time of the student's graduation, in the *World Directory of Medical Schools* published by the World Health Organization. They must have successfully completed the full medical curriculum prescribed by the medical school and by the country in which it is located. Furthermore, graduates of foreign medical schools must have fulfilled all the educational requirements to practice medicine in the country in which they received their medical education, and nationals of the country must also have obtained an unrestricted license or certificate of registration to practice medicine in that country. Applicants for ECFMG certification must document completion of the medical education requirement in the form of medical education credentials prescribed by the country in which the medical school is located. Medical credentials presented to the ECFMG by the candidate are sent directly to the foreign medical school(s) for validation by the appropriate officials. Finally, applicants must pass the English proficiency test and (formerly) the well-known Foreign Medical Graduate Examination in the Medical Sciences (FMGEMS), both of which are administered by ECFMG. Now, the FMGEMS has been entirely replaced by the USMLE, and satisfactory completion of Step 1 and Step 2 are required for ECFMG certification.

STANDARDS AND THE QUALITY OF MEDICAL EDUCATION

There is a growing worldwide interest in assessing all aspects of the quality of medical education. In recent years, the ECFMG has had a full schedule of discussions with representatives from individual medical schools, ministries, countries, and regions of the world about adapting its examination and credentialing process to internal evaluation standards. Just as many medical schools in the United States use the National Board examinations as an external standard for internal evaluation of students and curriculum, ECFMG has had many inquiries about a somewhat analogous process using the ECFMG medical science examinations in a similar way. Often, the dean of a medical school has asked ECFMG to provide an analysis of the performance of its students over a five to ten year period on the ECFMG medical science examinations. Until 1982, the ECFMG published such statistics on medical schools of the world. However, since then we have declined to make such information available publicly, although we have undertaken some specific studies of individual schools when requested to do so by the dean. There are many reasons for our reluctance to report such findings, but primary among them is the fact that individuals taking our examinations are often self-selected and the numbers from any given medical school are too small to be statistically significant. However, a number of schools have seemed interested in using the examinations more generally for all of their students, at least until it is possible for them to develop, within the school or within the country, a means of preparing their own examinations.

What place do examinations have in evaluation and assessment? There is the use of examinations for licensure to practice medicine in the United States and for licensure to practice medicine in other countries, the use of examinations as part of a credentialing process for exchange of physicians for advanced medical education purposes and the use of examinations for the evaluation of students while still in medical school and for the evaluation of the curriculum. All these uses have different objectives, but at times all of these examinations derive from a core examination process. One must be cautious that such a universal system not stifle innovation and creative curriculum change. However, given the tremendous demand for expertise in the development of valid and reliable examinations and the tremendous cost to achieve the outcome of excellent examination systems, the broader use and adaptation of an existing process for these multiple objectives may be a place at least to begin.

For example, since 1983 the ECFMG has made a large financial investment in the development of a clinical competence assessment examination using standardized patients (Sutnick, Ross, and Wilson 1992; Stillman, et al. 1992; Sutnick, et al. 1993). The results of this developmental work have now been offered to medical schools throughout the world for their adaptation to internal evaluation systems. Although it is doubtful that ECFMG will use this examination as part of its certification process in the near future because of logistical problems, it is a valuable instrument for evaluation of the development of clinical competence of medical students and has been adapted for use by medical schools, including translation into their own languages.

THE CALL FOR CHANGE IN MEDICAL EDUCATION

Many authors have expressed dissatisfaction with the health care delivery system and the medical education process that prepares the physicians who hold key positions in that system (Muller 1984; Willis 1988; World Federation for Medical Education 1988). In its document, *Changing Medical Education: An Agenda for Action,* (1991), the WHO suggested a coordinated series of activities intended to facilitate change in medical education in order to meet the current and future requirements of society. Citing the university's ultimate educational goal to prepare people to function properly in society, the report pointed out that in the professional context, this requires an understanding of the circumstances in which future medical graduates will function.

One of the fundamental reasons for dissatisfaction remains a general lack of competence on the part of the medical and health professions to meet new challenges: increased emphasis on the humanization of care, integrated care, more consumer participation, equal access to care, assessment of technology, cost containment, consideration of the population perspective in planning health care, protection of the environment, promotion of healthy lifestyles, etc. A new era, the search for a new paradigm that integrates all these factors, has begun. (World Health Organization 1991)

The report goes on to say that physicians of tomorrow should be able to respond better to the community than is the case today; therefore, they must possess the competencies necessary to promote healthy lifestyles and to communicate with consumers and community leaders in order to obtain their involvement, that they should also be capable of applying critically the latest technologies in the health sciences and of making decisions that take into account multifaceted issues that include ethical, financial, and other considerations, and that they will need to strike a balance between the expectations of their patients and those of society at large. The authors call national authorities, training institutions, and professional associations to initiate and support a movement that will educate the next generation and reeducate those who are now in practice to respond to the changing needs and demands of their society. They suggest that the change will occur because "the agenda for change" addresses the issue of institutional reform by opening a wide dialogue and searching for consensus among all parties concerned in the initiatives that are required in both the health care system and in medical education, and by involving them in developing appropriate strategies to achieve shared objectives.

The suggested agenda consists of three components: (1) setting standards and developing tools for assessment; (2) adopting appropriate strategies for change; and (3) implementing follow-up through worldwide monitoring (World Health Organization 1991).

At the Fifth World Conference on Medical Education held in Palm Springs, California, in 1990, the delegates to the World Medical Association accepted a proposed declaration for further review that reinforced the concept of the globalization of medical education and the medical profession, specifically citing the need for international use of standard methods of assessing professional competence and performance and for evaluating the learning process across the entire continuum of medical education. The meeting of the World Federation for Medical Education (WFME) held in August 1993 was also planned around the subject of change in medical education. These activities all focus on defining more explicitly the contemporary purpose of medical education and training for the medical profession. That purpose is clearly related to competent delivery of health and medical care to the community. A worldwide movement appears to be emerging that mandates change in medical education, an important aspect of which will be the establishment of standards and methodologies for measuring competence. Competence for what? How will competence be measured and evaluated? How will standards be set, and what standards are to be accepted? All these questions fundamental to the process, must be addressed at the local, national or international level. One can see that formal examinations play a part in standard setting and evaluation, but only a part, and it follows that licensure per se is, therefore, only one mechanism among many for quality control. However, publicly accepted licensure requirements and processes legitimize external methods of evaluation and thus can be a tremendous force for establishing and maintaining the quality of medical education, enhancing subsequent practice, and forcing the establishment of internal standards.

Change inevitably results in tensions and conflicts. Healthy organizations and enlightened societies can manage these conflicts to a constructive and effective outcome. The chapters in this book describe the evolution of medical education in countries from various parts of the world. They describe changes that have taken place in the past and some set the scene for changes to come in the future. We can all learn much from each other and we can all support each other in our struggles to enhance the health of people everywhere through improvements in medical education. The tasks will not be easy, the conflicts and tensions many, but there is a sense that the time has come for significant change and that individuals, organizations and institutions everywhere connected with the profession of medicine are ready to undertake the effort for the common good. A recent report entitled "Health Research: Essential Link to Equity and Development," from the Commission on Health Research for Development, states that our world has become a global health village generating an urgent need for mutual learning and joint action, and that every country must decide what it can contribute to the international effort to master the world's unsolved health problems (Evans 1990). To paraphrase the philosophy of the late Alan Woods in his testimony before the U.S. Congress in 1990, increasingly, the prospects of all of us for a secure and prosperous future are linked to the fortunes of other nations (Woods 1989).

REFERENCES

Evans, J. (Chair). Commission on Health Research for Development. 1990. *Health research: Essential link to equity in development.* Oxford University Press. See esp. pp. 1-136.

Monahan, T.J. 1990. State medical boards and licensing examinations. *National Board of Medical Examiners 75th anniversary: In service to medicine.* Philadelphia: National Board of Medical Examiners, p. 35.

Muller, S. (Chair). 1984. Physicians for the twenty-first century. Report of the Project Panel on the General Professional Education of the Physician and College Preparation for Medicine. *J Med Educ* 59 (11, Part 2):1-208.

Stillman, P.L., M.B. Regan, H.A. Haley, J.J. Norcini, M. Friedman, and A.I. Sutnick. 1992. The use of a patient note to evaluate clinical skills in first-year residents who are graduates of foreign medical schools. *Acad Med* 67:S57-S59.

Sutnick, A.I., L.P. Ross, and M.P. Wilson. 1992. Assessment of clinical competencies by the Foreign Medical Graduate Examination in the Medical Sciences (FMGEMS). *Teaching and Learning in Medicine* 4:150-155.

Sutnick, A.I., P.L. Stillman, J.J. Norcini, M. Friedman, M.B. Regan, R.G. Williams, E.K. Kachur, M.A. Haggerty, and M.P. Wilson. 1993. ECFMG assessment of clinical competence of graduates of foreign medical schools. *JAMA* 270:1041-1045.

United States Medical Licensing Examinations (USMLE). Office of the USMLE Secretariat. 1992. *U.S. Medical licensure statistics and current licensure requirements.* American Medical Association.

World Conference on Medical Education. World Federation for Medical Education. 1988. "Edinburgh Declaration." Edinburgh, Scotland.

Willis, D., ed. 1988. The changing character of the medical profession. *Milbank Quarterly* 66 (Supplement 2).

Woods, A. 1989. Economic growth and human progress: U.S. economic development assistance in the 21st century. In Agency for International Development, ed. *Introductory statement of the Agency for International Development's fiscal year 1990 congressional presentation* (10 January), 1 (Foreword), pp. 1-26. Washington, DC.

World Health Organization, Division of Development of Human Resources for Health. 1991. *Changing medical education: An agenda for action.* Geneva: WHO.

3

Australia

RAJA BANDARANAYAKE
PHILLIP GODWIN

Australia (officially the Commonwealth of Australia) is the smallest continent and the sixth largest country on earth. It is made up of six states and lies between the Pacific and Indian oceans in the Southern Hemisphere. The population of Australia in 1988 was estimated to be 16,470,000, with an urban-rural ratio of 86 to 14 percent. The Australian population is multicultural, and the Aborigines account for 1.1 percent of the total population.

OVERVIEW OF THE HEALTH CARE DELIVERY SYSTEM

The Australian health care system has undergone considerable change over the past decade, with health services increasingly targeted to prevention and primary care. This trend is in keeping with the primary health care strategy adopted by the World Health Organization (1978).

Health care in Australia is incorporated at all levels of government--federal, state, and local. Health services are delivered in both the public sector, through medicare and public hospitals, and the private sector, with reliance on private medical and hospital insurance. Historically, health care in Australia has evolved from a predominantly private system to a mix of public and private service delivery.

With the escalating complexity in medical science and the associated dilemmas in service delivery, the medical profession is increasingly being required to display concern for ethical, moral, and religious issues in health care.

In Australia most of the population lives in urban areas, with more than 80 percent living on the coast. Access to health care is a problem only for those people in isolated rural areas. The young and the aged tend to be large consumers of health services. The aging of the population is very important in terms of the demand for and cost of providing service. Changing environmental factors and life-style patterns impinge on the provision and delivery of services for physical and mental health.

Australian life expectancy has increased steadily during this century. In 1989, life expectancy at birth for males was 73.30 years and for females, 79.55 years, compared with 64 years for males and 69 years for females in 1935. In 1985, the infant mortality rate was 10 per 1,000 live births compared with 50 per 1,000 in 1935. The infant mortality rate in the Aboriginal population was 30 per 1,000 live births in 1984. The major cause of death in 1988 for both males and females remained ischemic heart disease, which accounted for 27.3 percent of all male deaths and 25.3 percent of all female deaths. The proportion of deaths attributable to cancer continued to increase, while the proportion due to heart disease decreased. While it is increasingly apparent that causes of death in developed countries are largely dependent on the age structure of the population, socioeconomic status is one of the major factors associated with differing rates of mortality and morbidity.

The organization and financing of health services in Australia is complex. In 1987 the Commonwealth Department of Health and the Department of Community Services were amalgamated to form the Department of Community Services and Health, which has recently been renamed the Department of Health, Housing, Local Government, and Community Services.

Each state in Australia has a health commission or department. Local government also provides health services, particularly child and maternal health care. Funding for health care is principally under the auspices of the Health Insurance Commission. Expenditure on health care has grown substantially in the last 20 years. The share of gross domestic product (GDP) spent on health care in the last 5 years has remained fairly constant, between 7.5 and 8.0 percent. Every Australian citizen is entitled to "free" medical and public hospital care funded by an income tax levy of 1.4 percent. In addition, any individual may opt to take out private insurance, which provides a choice of medical specialist and private hospital accommodation, as well as certain other specified benefits. A growing difficulty in the Australian public hospital system is escalating waiting periods for elective surgery. Nonetheless, the number of individuals with private health insurance is decreasing, with less than half the population having some private coverage.

At the local level, health services, particularly in New South Wales, are organized in Area Health Boards. These boards promote, protect, and maintain the health of the residents of that area; manage hospitals and other health services under their control; consult and cooperate with individuals and organizations concerned with health; investigate and assess health needs in their areas; and plan the future development of health services.

Approximately 25 percent of the medical work force are in salaried positions, and that number is increasing.

Consumers' expectations and demands for health care are also changing in Australia, with increasing expectations for high-quality, comprehensive care with access to a range of interventions and diagnostics. Their demands for health information and health education are increasing. There is concern that the health care system has become excessively specialized and that the use of medication and technological intervention should be reduced. These trends in the Australian health care system have definite implications for medical education at both undergraduate and postgraduate levels.

HISTORICAL BACKGROUND

Australian medical education encompasses all three phases--undergraduate, postgraduate, and continuing--in the continuum of medical education. In keeping with its historical antecedents, medical education has been closely fashioned on the British system ever since the first medical school was established in the University of Melbourne in 1862.

Significant departures from the traditional pattern of undergraduate medical education were evidenced in the latter part of this century with the opening of the last two of the ten medical schools in Flinders and Newcastle Universities. The classical division of the curriculum into premedical, preclinical, and clinical phases has been retained in all schools established in the intervening period.

Influenced significantly by the Flexner Report (Flexner 1910), a strong scientific base has continued to be the foundation on which clinical experiences are built in the latter phases of the curriculum. Until recently, all Australian medical schools sought and obtained accreditation from the General Medical Council of the United Kingdom, and changes in British medical education were closely paralleled by similar changes in Australian medical schools. It was only as recently as 1985 that a Medical Council was established in Australia with a mandate to accredit medical schools. As medical educators became more cognizant of educational theory, the following changes occurred. Boundaries between successive phases of the curriculum were blurred. Student motivation was heightened through early contact with patients in introductory clinical courses. The introduction of a varying period of elective study enabled students to pursue an area of interest under supervision; however, this was not intended as an opportunity for specialization, that being the domain of postgraduate education. Behavioral and social sciences were introduced into the curriculum and have grown over the years into a stream that threads its way through all its phases. The most dramatic change was seen when the Faculty of Medicine at the University of Newcastle introduced a problem-centered curriculum, fashioned on the pioneering effort at McMaster University in Canada but with a stronger community orientation. This remains the only medical curriculum of its kind in Australia.

Accreditation is a major force influencing change. Accreditation teams appointed by the Australian Medical Council (AMC), while ensuring that minimal standards are met, also facilitate innovation. Schools are encouraged to develop internal systems of curriculum monitoring and review, and most have responded by developing structures and strategies for evaluation. Departmental course evaluations have been a feature of the Australian medical school for some time. Changes in response to this feedback are modest and range from fine-tuning of courses at department level to more major shifts in curriculum structure. The chief impediment to change is the departmental structure of the typical medical school. As the administrative, educational, and research unit, the department is both a strength and a weakness of the system. While fostering the development of academic excellence in the discipline, it can engender isolationism and "tunnel vision." The reluctance to look beyond the department's confines to possible links with other disciplines impedes both horizontal and vertical integration. The importance of the department as the unit is encouraged by a system of resource allocation in which departmental contact time with students is the prime determinant of funding. This acts as a deterrent to change. The schools at Flinders and Newcastle have adopted a nondepartmental structure as far as the curriculum is concerned, thus averting the struggle for curriculum time commonly seen in the more conventional schools.

ROLE OF NATIONAL POLICY IN SHAPING MEDICAL EDUCATION

During the last two decades, several committees of inquiry have studied and reported on medical education in relation to national policy, socioeconomic realities, and demographic patterns (Karmel 1973; Sheldrake et al. 1978; Saint 1981; Thomson 1981; Doherty 1988). The Australian Universities Commission responded to the recommendations of the Karmel Committee (Karmel 1973) to increase the emphasis on community medicine, general practice, and geriatrics in the curriculum. Financial support was provided by the government to establish departments of community medicine and community health centers, although clinical faculty were reluctant to compromise their share of the curriculum by giving more time to the emerging discipline. In one medical school, Ewan (1985) observed that "the total amount of formal exposure to practical aspects of medical care outside the confines of the teaching hospital consisted of a 40-hour general practice elective undertaken during a vacation period." Saint (1981), in reviewing community practice teaching in medical schools, observed a "mood of torpor" in some faculties caused by economic constraint, and warned that educational stagnation could result if they did not reexamine their goals and priorities. Curricular developments in community medicine have indeed been significant over the last decade. This has been achieved partly through incorporation of community hospitals and health centers into the educational sphere, with attempts to integrate the academic health center with community health service. While most Australian medical curricula are still far from being truly community-oriented, the trend that has been created seems promising in contributing to a relevant program of medical education.

Australia's population has required the introduction of geriatric medicine as a subject in the curriculum. These courses enable the student to develop skills in managing not only the diseases that affect the elderly, but also their psychological and social problems. Other significant additions to the curriculum in response to priority health needs have been medical ethics, nutrition, alcoholism and drug dependence, and AIDS. Medical schools are also devoting greater attention to communication and counseling skills. These skills, together with the emphasis on behavioral sciences, are helping medical students achieve greater understanding of, for example, the patient with AIDS.

The most comprehensive study of the continuum of medical education in relation to long-term trends in health care, including work force considerations, was undertaken by a committee appointed by the Commonwealth Minister for

Health in 1987. The report (Doherty 1988) is an invaluable resource on Australian medical education. Many of the committee's recommendations concerning competency-based skills assessment, recertification, and assessment of overseas-trained doctors are currently the focus of concern and intense discussion. It remains to be seen whether the committee's findings will have an indirect influence in shaping the future of medical education in this country, in spite of tardiness in the direct implementation of its recommendations.

ADMISSION

Admissions are controlled by the individual medical school through a faculty selection or admissions committee. Criteria for admission are not uniform across schools. Selection is mainly based on academic performance on the examination at the end of the 12th year of schooling. The competition for places in medical school is so intense that in all but one school, intake is limited to the top 1 or 2 percent in the Higher School Certificate (or equivalent) examination. The exception is the University of Newcastle, where the top 1 to 2 percent performers are admitted directly and additional selections are made from the top 10 percent, based on performance in written psychometric tests and in a structured interview (Vinson, Cooley, and Turnbull 1979; Feletti et al. 1985). The psychometric tests are designed to assess decision making, empathy, creativity, and higher mental ability, while the interview is used to assess compatibility with the school's educational style, perseverance, tolerance of ambiguity, supportiveness to others, motivation to become a doctor, self-confidence, and communication skills. Increasing numbers of older students, especially those with other tertiary studies are also being selected. Some schools limit the use of the interview to certain categories of applicants, such as "borderline" performers, mature age students, Aboriginal students, or refugees. Some schools insist on prerequisite subjects for admission (usually English, mathematics, and chemistry).

Table 3.1 (p. 26) shows enrollment for 1991. Normally, 90 percent of students who are admitted to Australian medical schools complete their studies and receive their degrees.

In a careful analysis of medical school admissions data, the Committee of Inquiry into Medical Education and Medical Workforce (Doherty 1988) found that: (1) Australian medical students were young compared to those in other Western countries. (2) The proportion of female students increased to 40 percent in the early 1980s and has leveled off since. (3) Children whose parents are professionals or in managerial positions are overrepresented among those who apply for, and are accepted into, medical courses. (4) Students from private schools are represented in higher proportion than those from public schools, although not more so than in other Faculties of the university. (5) The various ethnic groups in pluralist Australian society were substantially reflected in the ethnic mix of Australian medical students and graduates.

Overseas students who satisfy certain minimum academic requirements are admitted to medical schools on a sponsored or fee-paying basis, subject to a predetermined quota. They are required to return to their home countries on completion of their undergraduate training.

Table 3.1
Australian Undergraduate Medical School Enrollment, Fall 1991

Medical School	Undergraduate Total	Undergraduate First Year
Sydney	1,186	246
New South Wales	985	200
Tasmania	272	48
Western Australia	665	119
Adelaide	664	126
Queensland	1,302	224
Flinders Medical Center	362	53
Melbourne	1,062	180
Monash	894	174
Newcastle	330	81
TOTAL # Medical Schools	Total Undergraduate Students	Total First Year Students
10	7,722	1,451

CURRICULAR STRUCTURE AND INNOVATION

The typical curriculum of the Australian medical school is of six years' duration and consists of premedical, preclinical, and clinical phases, though these are no longer clearly demarcated. The premedical phase includes the sciences basic to medicine, such as chemistry, physics and biology. Because in most medical schools these subjects are not stipulated prerequisites for admission, the premedical phase or a bridging science course is considered essential for the study of medicine. In some schools, the boundary between the premedical and preclinical phases is indistinct, as the premedical subjects have been integrated with or incorporated into courses conducted by the preclinical departments. The preclinical phase lasts two to three years and sometimes overlaps with the premedical phase and with the clinical phase in the latter half of the curriculum. It includes the basic medical sciences of anatomy, physiology, biochemistry, pharmacology, pathology, and microbiology. The clinical phase of the curriculum is conducted mostly in the teaching hospital, and includes medicine, surgery, pediatrics, obstetrics and gynecology, and psychiatry. In addition, instruction in community medicine occurs in both the preclinical and clinical phases, and classes are conducted both on campus and in community settings. A careful analysis of the medical curriculum of the University of New South Wales reveals that all students are introduced to four definite but overlapping streams: biomedical, behavioral, community, and clinical. Each of these streams can be traced through most of the curriculum.

Three significant departures from the typical, including a recent, radical proposal, are worth mentioning. The first is the problem-centered curriculum at the University of Newcastle medical school, where vertical integration between basic and clinical sciences is achieved through clinical problems that are sequenced through the curriculum to achieve iterative exposure to the sciences at progressively more complex levels (Engel and Clarke 1979). The second, Flinders University, achieves integration among basic, clinical, and public health knowledge through multidisciplinary courses, based partly on body systems and partly on case studies. The third--a radically different proposal, yet to be implemented--comes from three medical schools in the country where the requirement of a bachelor of science or arts degree to be completed before a student undertakes medical studies makes their curriculum more in the nature of a graduate program, bringing it closer to medical education in the United States.

The general outline of the typical curriculum has remained relatively stable over the years. Content of courses has kept pace with the expanding body of knowledge in most subjects. Course modifications have been made in response to changing health needs and priorities, either through addition of new subjects (e.g., geriatrics) or through integration of relevant content into existing courses (e.g., nutrition). Mechanisms for curricular change are closely tied to the committee structure in the school. The stimulus for change may arise from several sources: internal or external reviewers, students, faculty, members of the profession, health authorities, or the community. Submissions are discussed by a curriculum committee of senior faculty members and referred to the relevant phase or year committee. If the change is considered desirable and feasible, the curriculum committee delegates to an ad hoc committee the task of developing a detailed proposal. This is discussed by the relevant phase or year committee and the curriculum committee before being submitted to the faculty for approval. Implementation of the change (once approved) is left to the departments concerned. Where a school evaluation committee exists, it assumes responsibility for monitoring the change (Bandaranayake, Craig, and Wagner 1992).

Clinical training takes place primarily through a system of rotating clinical attachments, predominantly in tertiary care hospitals. Lectures, small group discussion, grand rounds, and clinical demonstrations complement these attachments. Because the governance of the teaching hospital is different from that of the university, there is a potential conflict over the priorities in caring for patients and teaching students (Rotem et al. 1981). Some clinical teachers are full-time university academic staff, while others are visiting and resident hospital staff. Though the latter may have conjoint appointments with the health department and the university, their primary employer is the health department, and their main concern is patient care. Nevertheless, they contribute significantly to the teaching program.

The tertiary nature of the teaching hospital precludes students from adequate exposure to primary care. Students are assigned for approximately 50 percent of their training to community hospitals and health centers and general practices, which enables them to be trained in primary and continuing care of the patient.

Australia subscribes to WHO's "Health for All by the Year 2000" policy, enunciated in the Alma Ata Declaration (World Health Organization 1978). The cornerstone of this policy being primary health care, one response was the establishment of the Better Health Commission, which recommended goals and strategies for improvements in the prevention of illness and in health awareness. The importance of a community approach in the achievement of these goals is reflected in medical education by the increasing emphasis given to community medicine and the care of the elderly in the medical curriculum.

Four Australian medical schools have medical education units staffed by trained educationists; others have professional educationists associated with them. Such individuals train faculty in new teaching techniques and advise on curriculum development and evaluation. Australian universities have recently shown an increasing tendency to consider achievements in teaching and educational development in appointments and promotion exercises. In some universities, special awards for teaching excellence have been instituted and workshops on teaching and assessment techniques help faculty to introduce innovative methods in the classroom.

GRADUATE MEDICAL EDUCATION

The period following graduation from medical school is best considered in two phases, with different objectives. First, the period of internship, which lasts one year in all states, is a period of supervised clinical practice that all graduates must satisfactorily complete before they are registered as practitioners. Second, vocational training in the appropriate specialty is undertaken by those who wish to specialize. The year of internship includes both service and training functions. The hospitals to which interns are assigned are accredited by the state medical board associated with each state health department. Interns are supervised and assessed by senior staff in these hospitals, who then report to the corresponding medical board. In an analysis of interns' work patterns, Dally, Ewan, and Pitney (1984) concluded that the time devoted to service far exceeded that given to training. The year is generally shared between the major disciplines of Medicine and Surgery and their associated subspecialties, though the importance of experience in general, rather than in specialist units, is emphasized. However, the spectrum of patients encountered in a typical teaching hospital, to which interns are most commonly assigned, is not representative of patients encountered in a district hospital to which they are often appointed after registration. Suggestions for the inclusion, in appropriate locations, of general practice, psychiatry, and community practice have not been heeded. One reason has been the reluctance to increase the period from one to two years in order to achieve a more rounded preregistration training.

Postgraduate training and examinations in specialties are conducted by professional Colleges, following British tradition. At present, fifteen such

Colleges grant specialist qualification with some larger Colleges offering training in the relevant subspecialties. Each state has its own Act for the recognition of specialists. All Colleges require the medical graduate to complete internship training before acceptance to specialty training and some require a further period of clinical service of up to two years. Training is in two parts, basic and advanced, and the trainee is required to pass an examination, usually in the basic medical sciences relevant to the specialty, before being admitted to advanced training. Training posts and programs are accredited by the College. Advanced training culminates in a final examination conducted by the specialist college. Medical schools offer academic research degrees and/or postgraduate course work degrees in some specialties. Clinical academics play a prominent role in the training and examination procedures of their respective Colleges.

In response to emerging specialties such as Occupational Medicine, new Colleges or branches of existing Colleges are created. The Committee of Inquiry into Medical Education and Medical Workforce (Doherty 1988), in expressing concern about the possible proliferation of specialties and subspecialties, pointed out the potential dangers of poor-quality programs, fragmentation, the relative neglect of overlapping but important areas of older specialties. It recommended that a small emerging specialty come under the aegis of an existing major College.

The ratio of specialists to nonspecialists (including general practitioners) is approximately 1 to 2.3. The ten most popular specialties are anesthesia, psychiatry, obstetrics and gynecology, general medicine, general surgery, diagnostic radiology, pathology, ophthalmology, pediatrics and orthopedics. However, the numbers of graduates seeking, and accepted for, specialty training do not necessarily reflect resource requirements in those fields; to some extent, numbers are limited by the availability of training positions in the specialty.

Public Health and General Practice have been emphasized in recent years and deserve special mention. Postgraduate training in the former specialty increased following the report of a review undertaken in 1986 on research and educational requirements for Public Health and Tropical Health (White 1986). Many Master of Public Health (MPH) programs admitted postgraduate students from the different health and health-related professions. Their multidisciplinary nature has the potential to enhance cooperation and collaboration in a field where teamwork is vital.

The Family Medicine Program (FMP) of the Royal Australian College of General Practitioners (RACGP) is funded by the Department of Health, Housing, Local Government, and Community Services and provides special training in general practice in the community and in hospitals. Fellowship of the College requires further examination and experience. Neither FMP nor fellowship, however, is compulsory for independent practice, unrestricted entry to which could result in an oversupply of independent practitioners. Rural practice remains neglected, however, due to a maldistribution of the independent practitioner population.

LICENSURE

The medical schools and the professional Colleges are responsible for certification of the competence of the undergraduate and postgraduate student. Licensure of the generalist or the specialist is the prerogative of the health authority in the state where the professional wishes to practice.

Cross-Licensing of Physicians

A significant number of Australia's physicians have been trained in medical schools in foreign countries. The Committee of Inquiry (Doherty 1988) estimated that there was a net gain of 4,037 medical practitioners through immigration in the 16 years before 1987. Under Australia's immigration policy, these immigrants arrive under the family reunion scheme, or the employer nomination scheme, or else come from New Zealand. A "points scheme," based on several criteria including skills and work experience, is used to determine eligibility to migrate. Most "medical migrants" come from New Zealand, the United Kingdom, and Ireland.

Foreign medical graduates (except those from New Zealand medical schools) who wish to practice medicine in Australia are now required to pass an examination conducted by the AMC before they become eligible for registration. As with Australian graduates, registration is the responsibility of the corresponding state health authority. The AMC examination is not linked to work force requirements, and there has been a sharp rise in recent years in the numbers presenting for examination, necessitating the imposition of limits. The examination consists of two parts, a multiple-choice examination and a clinical examination. These two parts must be passed in sequence, with a maximum of three attempts in each. Prerequisites for admission to the AMC examination system are permanent resident status and English language competence as assessed by a Council on Overseas Professional Qualifications. The standard of the examination is set at the level expected of an Australian medical graduate at the end of internship. No international agreements or political alliances influence standards; graduates of all foreign medical schools are treated alike, in spite of obvious differences in standards among and within countries.

At present, generalists and specialists must pass the same examination. As a result the majority of successful candidates register for general practice. A recent Working Party appointed by the AMC to review its examination procedures recommended the separate assessment of generalists and specialists, the former by the AMC, as at present, and the latter by the respective Colleges (Kerr Grant 1991). The lack of adequate training positions in medical schools and hospitals has been a constant problem in Australian medical education. The dearth of opportunities for retraining or reorientation of overseas trained doctors has been of concern to all who are interested in developing an equitable system to ensure a safe and useful contribution to Australian health care from a significant resource.

CONTINUING MEDICAL EDUCATION

An Australian Postgraduate Federation in Medicine established in 1961 is comprised of representatives from state postgraduate committees and the Australian Medical Association (AMA). It serves a coordinating role in bringing together the providers of continuing medical education (CME) and in identifying postgraduate and continuing education needs. The provision of CME is seen as the responsibility of professional Colleges, specialist societies, postgraduate committees, the AMA and medical schools. Professional Colleges vary in the quality and quantity of their CME activities. Some have national committees or boards that direct activities at state level, thereby ensuring that all members have opportunities to benefit from the programs. An example is the Royal Australian College of General Practice (RACGP), whose state medical education committees provide CME to general practitioners. In addition, those general practitioners who supervise trainees in the College's Family Medicine Program have special opportunities to participate in CME through teleconferences, satellite broadcasts, and computer access. A recent development has been the mounting of a distance education program in clinical education for supervisors in the FMP. Most Colleges see a link between quality assurance programs and CME. For example, the Royal College of Pathologists of Australia has a well established quality assurance program in all its subspecialties and sees these programs as "educative in raising and maintaining accepted standards of laboratory performance."

The Royal Australian College of Obstetricians and Gynaecologists (RACOG) introduced regulations for mandatory CME at the time it was established in 1978. At present certification as a Fellow is given for a five-year period. For continuing certification, the Fellow must provide documentary evidence of involvement in CME over the last three of the previous five years. "Cognate points" can be obtained through educator activities (publications, presentations and teaching), attendance at courses and meetings, supervised learning projects, participation in peer review/quality assurance programs and completion of self-assessment tests (RACOG 1988, pp. 642-651).

Medical schools vary in their contribution to CME. Some mount significant programs, especially if they have affiliated postgraduate medical education committees. Individual departments undertake some continuing education activities, but schools complain of difficulties in mounting organized and regular programs due to resource constraints. The main problems stem from lack of adequate coordination and the paucity of assessment of educational needs. Many activities do not reach practitioners who are not affiliated to bodies providing continuing education.

ROLE OF RESEARCH IN MEDICAL EDUCATION

The importance of research in improving the quality of teaching and clinical work is accepted by all medical schools. Preclinical and clinical faculty are required to undertake research studies as part of their academic role. Thus, all full-time faculty devote a variable proportion of their time to individual or collaborative research, often with colleagues in related specialties. The average time spent in research by the basic scientist is likely to be greater than that by the clinician. Understandably, a considerable portion of the latter's time is taken up by clinical work. However, even within a given department it is often evident that some faculty devote much of their time to teaching and others to research. These differences depend on the individual's interest in, and dedication to, one or the other role, on the opportunities available within the department, and on funding. In spite of recent attempts by many universities to reward teaching excellence, tenure and promotion decisions are largely swayed by the individual's research contribution.

Most research in medical schools is carried out with the aid of research grants from national or State bodies (such as the National Health and Medical Research Council, Australian Research Council or a state department of health), from private foundations (such as the Clive and Vera Ramaciotti Foundations), or from the university itself. Competition for these grants is extremely high. Seeding grants are given by some bodies to encourage young or new researchers by enabling them to start a project.

GOVERNMENT/PRIVATE SECTOR INVOLVEMENT

Universities in Australia are almost entirely public institutions, funded by the national government. The extent of funding to each university is determined by student numbers. Allocations to university departments are made based on the number of student contact hours. The funding of medical education, however, is more complex and variable among the states, primarily because the teaching hospitals are the responsibility of the state health department. The relationship between the state health department and medical school varies regarding source of payment of nonuniversity and university clinical teachers in a given teaching hospital. Private foundations do not fund medical education directly but rather through research and development projects and the establishment of senior academic positions in identified departments. Medical schools and departments also accrue some income from a relatively small number of sponsored or fee-paying overseas students at both the undergraduate and postgraduate levels.

INTERNATIONAL LINKAGES AND COLLABORATION

Opportunities in Australia for maintaining links with international medical education are many. The most significant of these is the overseas elective study that many medical students undertake during the clinical phase of their studies. Such periods of study, be they in one of the developing countries around Australia or in the technologically advanced Western nations, give these students different perspectives on health priorities and care and broaden their horizons. Some schools have established exchange programs for undergraduate and postgraduate students with foreign medical schools. Surrounded as it is by developing countries in Asia and the Pacific, Australia has a vigorous program of sponsorship and/or placement of students from these countries in her universities. Organizations such as the Australian International Development Assistance Bureau (AIDAB) and the Australian Universities International Development Project (IDP) actively support undergraduate and postgraduate students on an intergovernmental basis. International organizations such as WHO are also active in this respect, although more so at the graduate level. The multicultural nature of the typical Australian university, a true reflection of Australian society at large, is further enriched by this constant flow of overseas students. The sharing of experiences helps open the minds of the Australian medical students to issues in health care in the countries from which their foreign colleagues come.

Exchange of academic staff also contributes to the international flavor of curricula. Many Australian faculty undertake assignments in foreign countries to help fledgling medical schools and return with valuable experiences that they share with their students. A steady stream of academic visitors from overseas universities also contributes to the teaching programs.

The WHO Regional Center for Health Development is associated with the School of Medical Education in the University of New South Wales Faculty of Medicine. Originally established as the WHO Regional Teacher Training Center for the Western Pacific Region, it expanded its sphere of activity in the 1980s to include primary health care, community development, and management. This change was in keeping with WHO's global strategy of Health for All. The Center trains health professions educators, including medical educators, in education as a strategy for achieving the goals of the Alma Ata Declaration. Alumni of the Center are scattered in many countries of the world, where they play a vital role in human resources development and help Australia maintain its international links and reputation in health professions education.

ISSUES AND TRENDS

The medical graduates who are being prepared now will be practicing well into the twenty-first century. The importance of this fact to the medical educator is obvious. The Committee of Inquiry into Medical Education and Medical

Workforce (Doherty 1988) refrained from making predictions about what will be expected of a medical practitioner in the next century. However, it did identify certain trends that need to be reflected and emphasized in Australian medical education if it is to be responsive to the health needs of the Australian society of the future. Among the trends identified in the Report as requiring future emphasis are:

- The increasing need to cater to an aging population and disadvantaged groups, particularly regarding psychological disturbances;
- Medical ethics and an awareness of measures to be taken to avoid or reduce the effects of medical litigation;
- Health promotion, health education, and disease prevention;
- The importance of teamwork in health care, especially as, with increasing consumer awareness, the medical practitioner comes under scrutiny by the community served;
- The role of the alternate health practitioner;
- The ability to work in organizations, including the planning and management of health services;
- The management of chronic disorders, with increasing care in community settings;
- The ability to cope with increasing demands placed on the health services by AIDS and other "new" diseases;
- The mastery of new technology; and
- An increased computer literacy in all stages of medical education.

Can the medical graduate of the future meet these emerging societal needs? The answer lies partly in the responsiveness of the Australian medical school, which has, until now, shown this ability in spite of an insistence on the importance of the disciplines that comprise it. Innovative educational methods and technology will contribute significantly as the schools endeavor to meet these goals. A new orientation to health care is called for, however, in which the provider encourages consumers to take increasing responsibility for their health. In the same way a new orientation to learning is called for, in which medical students assume increasing responsibility for their continued learning, adapting to the changes that are likely to occur in a career of practice. The medical school must take the responsibility for inculcating in students the habit of self-directed learning, and continuing medical education will then receive much more attention than has hitherto been evident in Australia.

NOTE

The authors thank the Australian Medical Council, State Medical Boards, Medical Schools and Professional Colleges who provided information incorporated into this chapter.

REFERENCES

Bandaranayake, R., P. Craig, and R. Wagner. 1992. A multidimensional approach to evaluating a changing curriculum. *Annals of Community-Oriented Education* 5:159-166.

Dally, P., C. Ewan, and W.R. Pitney. 1984. Assessment of an Australian medical internship. *Medical Education* 18:181-186.

Doherty, R.L. (Chairman). 1988. *Australian medical education and workforce into the 21st Century.* Report of the Committee of Inquiry into Medical Education and Medical Workforce. Canberra: Australian Government Publishing Services.

Engel, C.E., and R.M. Clarke. 1979. Medical education with a difference. *Programmed Learning and Educational Technology* 16:72-87.

Ewan, C. 1985. Curriculum reform: Has it missed its mark? *Medical Education* 19:266-275.

Feletti, G.I., R.W. Sanson-Fisher, M. Vidler, and The Admissions Committee of the Faculty. 1985. Evaluating a new approach to selecting medical students. *Medical Education* 19:276-284.

Flexner, A. 1910. *Medical education in the United States and Canada: A report to the Carnegie Foundation for the Advancement of Teaching.* Bulletin no. 4. Boston: Updyke.

Grant, C., and H.M. Lapsley. 1987. *The Australian health care system.* Australian Studies in Health Service Administration no. 60. Kensington: University of New South Wales, School of Health Administration.

Karmel, P.(Chairman). 1973. *Expansion of medical education: Report of the Committee on Medical Schools to the Australian Universities Commission.* Canberra: Australian Government Publishing Service.

Kerr Grant, A. (Chairman). 1991. *Report of the Working Party to Review the AMC Examination.* Canberra: Australian Medical Council.

Royal Australian College of Obstetricians and Gynaecologists (RACOG). 1988. Policy on continuing certification. In Doherty (1988), Appendix 13. (Cited as RACOG.)

Rotem, A., P. Craig, K.R. Cox, and C.E. Ewan. 1981. The organization and management of medical education in Australia. *Health Policy and Education* 2:177-206.

Saint, E.G. 1981. *Review of community practice teaching in medical schools.* Report for the Commonwealth Tertiary Education Commission. Canberra.

Sheldrake, P.F., R.D. Linke, I.D. Mensh, D.I. Newble, and E.F Rosinski. 1978. *Medical education in Australia: Present trends and future prospects in Australian medical schools.* ERDC Report no. 16. Canberra: Australian Government Publishing Service.

Thomson, E. (Chairman). 1981. *Future needs for medical education in Queensland.* Report of Committee to Inquire into Future Needs and Training for Medical Practice in Queensland. Brisbane: Medical Board of Queensland.

Vinson, T., G. Cooney, and J. Turnbull. 1979. Admission to medical school: The Newcastle experiment. *Programmed Learning and Educational Technology* 16:70-87.

White, K.L. 1986. *Independent review of research and educational requirements for public health and tropical health in Australia: Australia's Bicentennial Health Initiative.* Canberra: Commonwealth Department of Health.

World Health Organization. 1978. Alma Ata Declaration. *Report of the Conference on Primary Health Care at Alma Ata, USSR, 6-12 September.* Geneva: WHO.

4

Belgium

L. Cassiers

Belgium is a small European country whose geographic location has laid it open to foreign influences throughout its history, resulting in a long-standing outward-looking tradition. The country's population is characterized by multiple philosophical and linguistic backgrounds. Belgium has both French and Dutch-speaking populations, which has created an atmosphere conducive to competition and creativity.

OVERVIEW OF THE HEALTH CARE DELIVERY SYSTEM

Belgium's health care system is based on the principle of compulsory insurance. All individuals are required to pay a percentage of their income in social insurance contributions and must register with a sickness insurance fund. The fund reimburses individual health care expenditure according to tariffs set by the national government. The sickness insurance funds are not private insurance companies in the commercial sense. They are strictly regulated by a lengthy series of statutes, and in fact, they are, to a large extent, the creatures of (and have many de facto links with) political parties and trade unions.

The doctor-patient relationship is governed by the principle of freedom of choice. Individuals consult the practitioner of their choice, while doctors are free to charge the amount they see fit. In practice, however, the surplus of medical practitioners means that the vast majority of doctors apply the scale of charges recommended by the state in order to maintain the size of their practice. The same applies to the hospitals, which are noncommercial bodies bound to the state under detailed contracts stipulating compliance with the scale of charges.

The rates of reimbursement of health care expenditure are fixed under collective agreements between the doctors' professional association, insurance funds, and the state, one of whose obligations is to underwrite any losses incurred by the system. In essence, health care is a semi-state-run system. Individuals have freedom to choose their doctor and receive virtually free treatment with no limitation on benefits, but the incomes of medical practitioners and hospitals are subject to a considerable degree of control.

Health policy in Belgium is also defined by consensus among the principal protagonists concerned within officially organized groups for formal consultations. Patients' interests are represented by the insurance funds which, to a certain extent, reflect the reality of the situation. The doctors' professional association and representatives of hospital administrative bodies represent the interests of the health care professionals. One notable shortcoming is the lack of specific representation of nursing staff. Finally, there is the third party, the state, which takes part in the consultations, both directly and indirectly, to contain spending budgets. This system of formal consultations has been in force for the past three decades. I think it fair to say that its foremost concern has been the universal provision of virtually free, high-quality curative medicine, and that it has succeeded in that aim. At the same time, these consultations have resulted in modern, well-equipped hospitals, sound bed management, and adequate financing for new techniques as they have emerged to join the armamentarium of diagnostic and therapeutic resources. Indeed, it has tended to favor specialized medicine more than general medicine. Over the past decade or so, however, this trend has slowly begun to shift because of growing interest in home care and primary or first-line medical care. Finally, preventive medicine has been relegated to a very low place in the policies introduced by the actors concerned. In fact, prevention is chiefly the result of policy decisions beyond the control of these protagonists, taken by semipublic bodies like the Institute for Epidemiological Monitoring, the AIDS Agency, the Childbirth and Childhood Charity, and other private, semipublic-funded agencies concerned with such matters as the prevention of cancer or cardiovascular disease. The policies operated by these agencies are ill-coordinated and generally underfunded.

The virtual failure to involve the Faculties of Medicine as institutions in developing this country's medical policy is also noteworthy. That observation must, however, be qualified by taking certain concrete facts into consideration. Various teams from the Schools of Public Health (or what is now called "community medicine") attached to the Faculties of Medicine have occasionally been commissioned to conduct epidemiological or economic field studies. Also, many members of the country's university teaching clinics (academic medical centers)--generally professors--sit on the various official groups responsible for framing medical policy, where they often play an important role. Nevertheless, the Faculties of Medicine are not represented as such.

Subject to these few reservations, it can be said that the system worked efficiently for almost twenty years. The situation has been steadily deteriorating over the last ten years, however. Health spending has spiraled increasingly out of control, primarily, as in other countries, because of the rising cost of health care and the aging population. The problem has been compounded by a particular combination of circumstances peculiar to this country. The reimbursement of all forms of medical treatment encourages its proliferation, often to no good purpose. This is compounded by the absence of any form of admission restrictions on the intake of medical students and qualifying practitioners. Belgium has one of the highest populations of medical practitioners in the western world (1 doctor to every 284 inhabitants). For a growing number of doctors, this means a shortage of patients, which is as detrimental to their professional expertise as it is to their ability to earn a living. It also leads to an overconsumption of medical resources, which is plunging the health system into a growing deficit. This situation is the result of political circumstances peculiar to Belgium, chief among which are the facts that the sickness insurance bodies are direct emanations of the political parties and trade unions, the doctors' association and the insurance bodies have been constantly at loggerheads for the past thirty years, and university funding is proportional to the institution's student enrollment.

HISTORICAL BACKGROUND

In Belgium, all the Faculties of Medicine form part of complete universities. Also, officially subsidized research is university-based in this country. Both these facts have greatly influenced medical education. Because medicine commingles with the other sciences, and because they take part in research as a whole, the Faculties of Medicine set great store on retaining their intellectual status as a university discipline, utterly refusing to become ordinary advanced technical colleges of applied sciences. Their purpose, evidently, is to train medical practitioners, but also simultaneously, to train a sufficient number of high-caliber researchers.

This has entailed a series of direct and indirect consequences. The first is that the two stages of medical education (preclinical and clinical) have always been treated as two parts of a whole. Clinical training constantly refers back to the basic knowledge acquired in the pre-clinical stage, which long maintained a general character, with little emphasis on the medical aspect. Therefore, until as recently as 1968, the qualification awarded at the end of the first stage was "degree in natural and medical sciences," and the curriculum included courses in botany, zoology, and comparative anatomy. A second consequence is that clinical or bedside training made only slow headway. Up to 1968, it generally accounted for no more than one of the seven years' study. Even now, when it lasts for at least two years, more attention is still paid to the theory of pathology and treatment.

Because they are part of complete universities, the Faculties of Medicine fall under the authority of the Ministry of Education, not the Ministry of Public Health. Government health officials, therefore, have little influence over the development of medical studies.

The main influences on developments in the universities and Faculties of Medicine in this country must be sought in Belgium's political peculiarities. The majority of universities, which account for three-quarters of the student population, are independent of the state. They do, however, receive government funding in proportion to their student numbers. These independent universities reflect to a marked degree the linguistic and philosophical differences that characterize the country's population; indeed, they help perpetuate those divisions. That is why Belgium has both French-and Dutch-speaking universities. Moreover, each language community has both Catholic and non-or antidenominational universities. This nurtures a high level of competition among these universities in both the recruitment of students and the search for research funding. This competition is what gives the impetus to development and modernization in medical education, far more than the direct influence of health ministry officials in the country. Each Faculty of Medicine strives to maintain its teaching and research at a high level of excellence, both to preserve the influence of its ideology and to retain the funding that will allow it to develop further.

A second element of national policy that exerts a major influence on the style of medical training is the free access to university education afforded to all those who have successfully matriculated from upper secondary education, which is itself free. Democratic considerations have made this an abiding principle in this country for the past thirty years, resulting in a substantial increase in student numbers. The same democratic principle, upheld by the trade unions and tallying with the financial interests of the universities, has so far ruled out the imposition of admission restrictions on medical studies. To all this, finally, must be added the traditionally large intake of foreign students into Belgian universities. Between 20 and 50 percent of the students in Belgian Faculties of Medicine are from other countries.

These excess student numbers have led to stricter grading standards in examinations in order to maintain at least some degree of control over the numbers of prospective medical students. Hence, only a third of those enrolled pass the first year of their first degree, and selection remains strict in subsequent years. As part of this trend, the faculties have emphasized the theoretical and basic aspects of their courses. The clinical aspect, which forms a later part of the curriculum and is harder to control, has developed only at a much slower rate. The extra subjects and examinations have increased substantially, particularly as advances in medical knowledge have progressed apace, as in other fields. Finally, high numbers of medical students have encouraged the retention of the "talk and chalk" lecture and held back the development of more modern learning techniques that require a higher teacher/student ratio. For example, no Faculty of Medicine in this country has to date contemplated using problem-solving techniques.

All in all, medical education in Belgium has made steady and considerable advances in the content of the subjects taught, which have been modernized and diversified to keep pace with progress. Thus, the teaching of theory is currently of a very high standard; clinical or bedside teaching, on the other hand, has been slower to develop. On average, it accounts for two years of the seven-year course. Finally, teaching methods have progressed very little. Audiovisual aids are naturally much employed, but self-study and personal initiative are little-used, while lecture theatres remain overcrowded.

These characteristics are doubtless destined to change rapidly in coming years. The rules being established by the European Economic Community (EEC) to allow doctors and students to move freely within Europe will be fully operational by 1995. The other states associated with Belgium are pressing for this country to apply, as they do, admission restrictions to limit the number of qualified medical practitioners. Standards of study will gradually become more uniform throughout Europe.

This brief historical account would not be complete without a reference to the teaching of specialties (stage 3) and continuing education. Both types of training have expanded over the last decade and are destined to loom larger still in medical faculty teaching.

ROLE OF NATIONAL POLICY IN SHAPING MEDICAL EDUCATION

National health policy has little direct effect on the development of medical education. Conversely, the Faculties of Medicine exert little influence on health policy. Competition for students and funds, in fact, has made Faculties keenly concerned to train doctors who are suitably equipped for the realities of patient contact. Also, clinical teaching is evidently provided by practitioners. Epidemiological or environmental changes are, therefore, rapidly passed on into the teaching of therapeutic medicine. The Faculties themselves take the initiative of maintaining the quality of the training they dispense. Thus, the aging of the population prompted the emergence of various courses in gerontology, the appearance of AIDS rapidly led to the training of specialists, who also helped train other physicians, and so on. Additionally, having the basic sciences taught by professors working in research laboratories ensures that the content of teaching is always state-of-the-art. It should also be mentioned that the exaggerated trend toward the teaching of specialties and hospital-based medicine has gradually been rectified over the past fifteen years. All Faculties have introduced "University Centres of General Medicine" where the teaching is offered by experienced general practitioners (GPs). They will assume an increasingly prominent role in medical training, especially the clinical aspects. By contrast, basic medical training remains relatively uninfluenced by the economic and preventive aspects of medicine. Faculties are aware of these shortcomings and are striving to rectify them by including these aspects in the courses. The already overburdened curriculum, however, means that too little is being achieved too slowly.

Alongside their curative medicine curricula, however, most Faculties have established research and teaching programs in various areas of public health/community medicine, such as epidemiology, health economics, management training, and training in preventive medicine. To judge by the growing numbers of students enrolling, these programs must be counted an undeniable success. Career opportunities for such specialists remain very limited in Belgium, however. Consequently, they are very much geared to issues beyond the national scope, such as the specific problems of the developing world, and they attract high proportions of foreign students.

All in all, there can be no question that medical education in Belgium is developing, but it remains heavily influenced by the relative freedom allowed to Faculties to determine their own curricula. The state, indeed, lays down only a handful of basic conditions for medical education. It prescribes a period of seven years, with annual examinations. Legislation also stipulates the major subjects that must be taught, but in very general terms. Within that framework, which is under the purview of the Education rather than the Health Ministry, the Faculties are completely free to develop their own detailed curricula. In so doing, they are guided more by advances in medical science than by national health policy decisions. Nor does the state exert any organized direct control over either the studies or the qualification conferred by the Faculties. It accepts the legal validity of the academic qualification conferred by approved universities, trusting to their quality.

One illustration of the adverse effect of this separation between medical training and the authorities responsible for national health policy can be seen in the absence of admission restrictions. Both the public authorities and the Faculties of Medicine have, in recent years, become increasingly aware of the difficulties created by this situation. Attempts to reconcile matters are being made, such as devising teaching standards for specialists, including specialists in general medicine. Cooperation with health policy makers is also taking place within the organization of continuing medical education. The trend is, therefore, toward health policymakers acquiring a greater say in the fate of medical education, but this is a slowly developing trend due to the lack of official structures for formal consultation between policymakers and the Faculties.

ADMISSION

Applicants for the first stage must hold the Belgian upper secondary school leaving certificate or university entrance certificate. Agreements exist, chiefly with other EEC countries, governing the recognition of foreign qualifications, and the Minister has power to adjudicate in disputes. These legal rules are important in determining whether students qualify for inclusion on the grant list for state subsidies. They also form part of the conditions for access to the medical profession.

Compulsory annual examinations are held throughout the university program; two sessions are held on officially prescribed dates. Students are entitled to sit both sessions in the year; should they fail at the first, therefore, they are free to re-sit the examination at the later session. Students may also repeat a year; but in the first stage, they may repeat only one of the three years.

Only those who have passed the first stage (degree in medical sciences) will be admitted to the second stage. Here again, however, mutual recognition of diplomas exists with other countries. Annual examinations are held, as in the first stage. The second stage is a four-year course, which includes two years of practical training. Unlike the practice in other European countries, no final dissertation or thesis is presented.

The studies culminate in the award by the university of the diploma of "Doctor of Medicine, Surgery and Obstetrics." The diploma is automatically validated by the state after verification that the statutory conditions mentioned above have been complied with. One or two additional years of supervised practice are required before a doctor is permitted to practice unsupervised.

It will be seen, then, that in this country, the entry requirements for medical education are prescribed by statute and compliance is assured by the state. It should be clearly understood, however, that the purpose of these rules is not to limit the number of students, but merely to ensure that they attain an adequate level of competence. Indeed, it is not in the interests of the universities and Faculties of Medicine to restrict admissions unduly, since the grants they receive from the government are proportional to their enrollment. They have, therefore, dealt with the increase in applications by adapting their teaching resources rather than restricting admissions. The result is a surplus of qualified doctors in this country. It is currently estimated that 20 to 30 percent of the doctors graduating from Belgium's Faculties of Medicine are surplus to the country's requirements, not counting the foreign students who return home after qualifying. Very recently, however (1992), the political authorities and the universities embarked on discussions about imposing admission restrictions on the intake of medical students.

Demographic Profile of Medical Students

In 1990, admission to all Belgian Faculties of Health Sciences (excluding Pharmacy) totalled 2,352, of whom over 20 percent were foreign students (Table 4.1, p. 49).

Faculty Demographics

It is quite difficult to estimate the exact population of medical teachers in the Faculties of Medicine in Belgium. The first difficulty comes from the fact that some Faculties have in their charge, not only medicine, but also health professions such as pharmacy, dentistry, public health, and kinesitherapy. Not only is the comparison between Faculties therefore difficult, but also it would be necessary, in each case, to count separately the teaching times allowed to medicine and to other branches. Further, the Faculties count many researchers and clinicians who take part in the teaching without an academic appointment. Some give occasional lectures; others are in charge of the practical training of students in basic or clinical sciences. Interns and residents also participate in clinical training and, finally, some older students act as tutors for younger students.

Taking these factors into account, it seems quite reasonable to estimate an overall average of one full-time equivalent (FTE) academic professor per 20 undergraduate medical students, with the total number of persons participating in medical teaching estimated at 1.5 FTE per undergraduate.

CURRICULAR STRUCTURE AND INNOVATION

Since the 1929 Medical Act, medical students in Belgium have followed a seven-year course divided into two stages: three years of basic sciences and four years of clinical sciences. The same statute prescribed the minimum content of the curriculum. The list of subjects has since been updated several times. Currently, the first year of studies is a foundation course concentrating on physics, chemistry, and general biology (plant and animal). Some Faculties supplement this with courses in philosophy and mathematics. The following two years deal with the study of the biological (macro-and microscopic morphology) and psychological aspects of the healthy individual, together with an introduction to the study of the diseased individual: the morphological, biochemical, physiological, and psychological aspects of general pathology. A number of Faculties also include practical nursing or preventive and social medicine courses in this first stage. The second, four-year, stage covers the theoretical and practical study of the diseased individual; it comprises lectures, clinical demonstrations and two years of clinical or bedside training. Here, the various branches are grouped by physiological systems and the emphasis is placed on training in the clinical approach as a particular method of reasoning and judgment.

Being prescribed by statute, the structure of this curriculum is quite stable. Any changes require formal consultations between deans, rectors, the Academy of Medicine, and the Ministry of Education. However, the statute prescribes only the minimum essential requirements for a registerable medical qualification. On this basis, the Faculties retain the discretion to vary the content of the core curriculum. They also enjoy considerable freedom in the choice of teaching methods. In each Faculty, an academic board consisting of the senior professors and student representatives frames the detailed curriculum. This has led a number of Faculties to radically revise their curricula over the past ten years. Among the earliest major changes was increasing the medical emphasis of the basic sciences and the length of clinical training. Much more emphasis has been placed on teaching by systems--cardiocirculatory, locomotor, digestive, and so forth--to reduce compartmentalization among specialists. At the same time, the number of oral examiners and examinations has been reduced, while cooperation with non university practitioners has been substantially increased to improve student training in what will become their daily work. Finally, specific training in general medicine has been developed in all Faculties.

GRADUATE MEDICAL EDUCATION

Despite these major efforts to rationalize university studies, student numbers are still too high and teaching methods have not developed adequately. New reforms are also emerging under pressure from EEC authorities. For the past two years, newly qualified GPs have been required to undergo one or two additional years of practical training and supervised (but paid) practice before being allowed to practice entirely unsupervised. The trend now is to consider the first six years of medical training as a general foundation, after which the new physician would specialize either in general medicine (two years) or another field (four to six years, according to the specialty (see Table 4.2, p. 51). Discussions are also in progress as to whether career-long continuous or booster training should be made compulsory. The plethora of doctors leads a great many newly qualified physicians to specialize. To preserve an appropriate balance between GPs and specialists, there is a statutory requirement that at least 40 percent of new graduates should have the opportunity to specialize. This figure is broadly respected.

LICENSURE

Newly qualified Doctors of Medicine are entitled to begin independent practice immediately on receipt of their diplomas. To qualify fully as a general practitioner, however, (and thus receive the higher rate of reimbursement from social security), they must practice for at least two years under the tutelage of an approved senior practitioner. To qualify as a specialist, they must engage in (paid) practice under the tutelage of an approved specialist for a period varying from four to six years, according to the field of specialization, and attend a specified number of courses and seminars.

At the conclusion of the specialization period, a doctor is licensed by a ministerial committee, half of whose members are doctors drawn from the Board of Specialists, the other half being professors from the Faculties of Medicine. Licensed specialists may practice their specialty unsupervised and are entitled to social security reimbursement for treatment procedures unique to their specialty.

While there are no official criteria concerning the relative proportions of specialists, the different disciplines themselves preempt undue competition in the respective specialties by controlling the number of recognized training establishments. It was the effective admission restrictions on specialists created by this policy that led the national government to make access to specialization compulsory for at least 40 percent of each year's class of new medical graduates. How that 40 percent is actually distributed among the various specialized fields is, in fact, dictated by the law of supply and demand which, despite certain shortcomings, tends to regulate the situation more or less adequately. However, at the national level, the demand for dermatologists, ophthalmologists, and especially anesthetists remains relatively unsatisfied.

Cross-Licensing of Physicians

The diploma of Doctor of Medicine awarded by Belgian universities is legally valid per se. Both Belgian citizens and nationals of other Common Market countries who are graduates of a Belgian Faculty of Medicine are therefore automatically licensed by the Ad Hoc Ministerial Committee and the Medical Council. EEC citizens who hold a general or specialist medical practitioner's diploma that is valid in their country of origin may practice in Belgium after fulfilling a few simple administrative formalities. This rule, although in operation for nearly ten years, has not, so far, greatly stimulated geographical mobility among doctors in Europe. There are various reasons for this, not least of which is the language difference. Belgium's high density of medical practitioners makes it a slight net "exporter" of medical skills. The average income of a Belgian doctor is also significantly lower than that of colleagues in neighboring countries.

With a few special statutory exceptions such as political refugees or foreign nationals who have acquired Belgian nationality, qualified doctors from outside the EEC and EEC citizens who hold qualifications gained outside the EEC cannot practice medicine in Belgium. In the case of persons covered by these statutory exceptions, a special Ministerial Committee is convened to assess the legal status of the application, while a different committee, appointed by the Academy of Medicine, evaluates the course of study followed and the value of the diploma awarded. On the basis of this evaluation, the committee may require the applicant to follow a further one to three-year course of study in a Belgian Faculty.

CONTINUING MEDICAL EDUCATION

The Faculties of Medicine organize continuing education for generalists in association with the Scientific Board of General Medical Practitioners. The Faculties have no statutory duty to organize such education, general practitioners are not required to participate, and continuing education entails substantial problems of financing. The Faculties, however, consider CME an obligation to their former students. The situation may change in the future, however, if proposals of the Belgian government and the EEC to make continuous education compulsory are adopted.

There is no organized continuing medical education for specialists, although practicing specialists are afforded the opportunity to attend some courses and seminars organized by the Faculties for aspiring specialists. Most specialties also have scientific societies that meet at regular intervals.

ROLE OF RESEARCH IN MEDICAL EDUCATION

Nearly all the public and semipublic funding for research in Belgium goes to the universities. Part of this is allocated to the Faculties of Medicine for research projects approved by panels set up by the National Fund for Scientific Research or equivalent organizations.

Professors of medicine are selected primarily on the basis of their research work. This is true for both the basic and the clinical sciences. The majority of basic science professors also head research laboratories, the administration of which, on average, occupies about half their time. The advantage of this system is to keep the content of their courses constantly at the forefront of knowledge.

In addition to their teaching and research duties, clinical professors normally spend a portion of their time as practitioners in the university hospital attached to each Faculty. The increasing demands placed on these hospitals to achieve profit targets detracts from the funds available for research. This leaves clinical practitioners increasingly dependent on clinical research and reduces their access to fundamental research, which, in turn, is increasingly left to biologists with no medical training. This is a disturbing development. Private industry (drug and appliance manufacturers) also helps finance research, although these funds are directed more toward applied than pure research.

The great advantage of this system is the extent to which research influences medical teaching in this country. It also affords medical students the opportunity to convert elective courses into a student research option at any time during their course. The drawback is that the strong emphasis on research work as a criterion for the selection and promotion of academic staff does little to encourage attention to the development of teaching and learning methods. Few Faculties undertake research into teaching methods, and the sources of both public and private finance take no interest in it. Educational matters are coordinated by committees that include both staff and students. Reforms are regularly introduced at the urging of these committees, but focus more on the volume and content of the courses than on teaching methods.

ISSUES AND TRENDS

Belgium is a small country whose geographic situation has laid it open to countless foreign influences throughout its history. An outward-looking tradition has developed that is reflected in the Faculties of Medicine. On the one hand, the nation attracts many foreign students; on the other, most academic staff have spent at least one year, and often more, of their training period abroad, frequently in the United States. This has served to strengthen the influence of international thinking in raising the level of medical teaching to high academic standards. Belgian Faculties attract many foreign students, and doctors trained in Belgium tend, on average, to obtain very high scores in accreditation examinations held in other countries, such as those administered in the United States by the Educational Commission for Foreign Medical Graduates (ECFMG).

The Belgian system of medical education remains strongly traditional, however, especially regarding its teaching methods. The various constraints described earlier are not conducive to stimulating interest in new teaching methods. The volume of coursework is great and yet is not geared toward self-learning. Practical training, while adequate, often remains less highly developed than in other countries.

Finally, the Faculties of Medicine have little direct involvement in the country's health policy, for a variety of historical and political reasons. Belgium's public health institutes are more involved with issues in the wider world, such as in the developing countries. Belgian Faculties still take too little interest in health education, prevention, the economic organization of health care in this country, and similar issues, but their considerable international linkages enable them to implement developments in medicine rapidly.

All this gives Belgium's Faculties of Medicine a partly positive, partly negative image. On the whole, they produce doctors who are highly qualified in terms of knowledge, scientific, and clinical aptitudes, but they do so by very traditional methods. Developments in medicine are continually, and swiftly, passed on into teaching, but Faculties lack the political and economic capacity to guide or control those developments.

This situation is rapidly changing, however. The Faculties will probably find themselves faced, before much longer, with admission restrictions that will cut their student enrollment by at least 30 percent. Most of all, the next century will find them in direct competition with the rest of Europe's Faculties of Medicine. Where the quality of their research and teaching puts Belgium's Faculties in a relatively strong position at present; in order to face that challenge with Belgium's limited financial resources, they must modernize their teaching methods and, most of all, obtain a greater say in policymaking.

REFERENCES

Blanpain, J., and L. Delesie. 1976. *Community health investment: Health services research in Belgium, France, Federal German Republic, and the Netherlands.* London: Oxford University Press for the Nuffield Provincial Hospitals Trust.

Deliège, D. 1988. Belgium. In H. Viefhues, ed., *Medical manpower in the European Community.* New York, Berlin and Heidelberg: Springer-Verlag.

Table 4.1
First Medical Enrollment 1990, Belgium

	Belgians			Foreign Students			Total First Enroll-ment	All Medical Students		
	M	F	Total	M	F	Total		M	F	Total
WALLONIA										
UC Louvain	82	126	208	35	55	90	298	1,782	1,650	3,432
FNDP Namur*	89	127	216	20	17	37	253	294	348	642
U.L. Bruxelles	91	130	221	74	71	145	366	1,513	1,247	2,760
U. Mons*	51	41	92	17	19	36	128	136	135	271
U. Liege	74	101	175	36	25	61	236	970	818	1,788
Wal-lonia Totals	387	525	912	162	167	369	1,281	4,693	4,198	8,893
FLANDERS										
K.U. Leuven	191	250	441	25	13	38	479	1,631	1,884	3,515
U.C. Limburg*	69	100	169	0	4	4	173	191	250	441

Table 4.1
First Medical Enrollment 1990, Belgium

	Belgians			Foreign Students			Total First Enrollment	All Medical Students		
	M	F	Total	M	F	Total		M	F	Total
U.I. Antwerpen								170	154	324
R.U. Antwerpen	36	46	82	12	6	18	100	155	160	315
R.U. Gent	83	110	193	9	7	16	209	603	580	1,183
V.U. Brussel	27	37	64	26	20	46	110	654	580	1,183
Totals Flanders	406	543	949	72	50	122	1,071	3,404	3,536	6,940
TOTAL Belgium	793	1,068	1,861	254	237	491	2,352			** 15,833

*Faculties offering only undergraduate medical education.
**Including 3,417 (21.5 percent) from other countries.

50

Table 4.2
New Med DOCT. Diplom. 1990--Belgium

Graduate Education (Enrollment 1991) Interns/Residents**

	M	F	Total	M	F	Total
WALLONIA						
UC Louvain	119	119	238	529	314	843
FNDP Namur*						
U.L. Bruxelles	89	88	177	393	234	627
U. Mons*						
U. Liege	52	52	104	232	138	370
Totals-Wallonia	260	259	519	1154	686	1,840
FLANDERS						
KU Leuven	116	115	231	513	305	818
U.C. Limburg*						
U.I. Antwerpen	10	9	19	42	25	67
R.U. Antwerpen	9	10	19	41	24	65
R.U. Gent	35	34	69	153	91	244
V.U. Brussel	34	34	68	151	90	241

Table 4.2
New Med DOCT. Diplom. 1990--Belgium

Graduate Education (Enrollment 1991) Interns/Residents**

	M	F	Total	M	F	Total
Totals-Flanders	204	202	406	900	535	1,435
TOTAL Belgium			925			3,275

* Faculties offering only undergraduate medical eduation.

**MDs who are training for a specialty, which involves an average of five years.

5

Brazil

ELIANA CLAUDIA RIBEIRO
LUIZ ANTONIO SANTINI

The largest country in Latin America and fourth in territorial area in the world, Brazil has an estimated population of 147.5 million. It consists of 26 states and a federal district and is divided into five macro-regions (North, Northeast, Midwest, Southeast, and South) that vary in social, economic, cultural and climatic features.

With diversified industrial production and, until recently, one of the major economies in the world, the country faces the contradictions of an economic development model that generates and perpetuates social inequalities. An increased concentration of income in the 1980s was associated with a higher poverty rate. Marked differences also persist among the country's different macro-regions with respect to standards of development.

A significant increase in the urban population, primarily because of migration, has occurred during the last three decades. Urbanization, along with modernization and industrialization, intensified during this period and was associated with a rapid drop in birthrate, a reduction in population growth (today estimated at less than 2 percent), and an increase in the percentage of elderly in the general population. Brazil's health status reflects the heterogeneity of the country's epidemiological profile, with disease and death rates (e.g., heart disease, cancer, and diabetes) typical of developed countries coexisting with a high incidence of infectious and parasitic diseases typical of developing countries. This complex situation reveals the diversity and dimension of the problems faced by the health care system.

OVERVIEW OF THE HEALTH CARE DELIVERY SYSTEM

The organization of the Brazilian health care system could be described, until the mid-1980s, as too centralized, having too many uncoordinated service institutions at federal, state and county levels, with priority placed on hospital care and an unequal provision of, and access to, care for different social groups. The

Ministry of Health was responsible for standards and control of preventive care and other public health measures developed by the basic state and county service network, while the Ministry of Social Security and Welfare was responsible for implementing curative care at an individual level. Gradually, Social Welfare became consolidated as the largest financing agent and, in practice, as the leader in establishing public health policy. Hospital and other health care services were delivered by private providers under service contracts with the Social Welfare agencies. The contradictions arising from this model, which is generally acknowledged as addressing the interests of service providers rather than the population's health care needs, caused widespread debate, particularly after the revival of democracy in the country. This debate culminated in a set of proposed guidelines to restructure the system and set up a new institutional framework.

The new 1988 Brazilian Constitution included some of these proposals and declared health care to be a right of every citizen and a duty of the state. Its provisions include a single health care system, with only one command in each sphere of government, universally accessible, organized under decentralizing guidelines, with comprehensive care and community participation. It further ensures the complementary involvement of free enterprise. The public health network has approximately fifteen thousand basic health care units and seven hundred hospitals distributed throughout the different macro-regions. The decentralizing process spreads the management of basic units and small hospitals over four thousand counties in the country, redefining the requirements and responsibilities within the system.

However, those charged with setting up this single system faced serious challenges. Economic recession led to an obvious withdrawal of public investment in health care, reflected in the scrapping of the service network, decreased operating capacity, and inferior quality of care. This decrease in public support was paralleled by an increase in private health care insurance and for-profit prepaid plans, which today cover an estimated thirty-five million persons and progressively include segments of the urban middle class. Silver (1992) described the state of health care in the country today as follows:

The general perception of the state of quality of care is that, while there exist islands of excellence in both the public and private sectors, the bulk of care provided to the population is of poor quality. This may be particularly so in the sector of private hospitals operating under agreements with the Social Security system. Grave structural problems exist in many health care facilities with respect to physical plant, staffing, norms and procedures, administrative and financial stability and, at times, probity. In spite of recent reforms and significant progress in primary care delivery, serious problems continue to exist in access to care, particularly secondary and tertiary care, in continuity of care [and] in the integration and technical quality of both preventive and curative services.

The job market reflects the trends in the organization of health care services in the country. Public policy responded to the dynamics of the job market mainly by increasing the supply and promoting specialization. The policy to extend social security medical care in the 1970s generated increased demand for health professionals, particularly in the private sector, where more than 50 percent of all health care jobs were then concentrated. In the 1980s, the policy of enlarging public capacity, especially for ambulatory care, brought the public sector to the forefront as a principal employer at the federal, state and country levels. By 1987, 55.1 percent of the health care jobs were in the public sector (Nogueira 1991). However, in spite of the lack of more recent data, we believe that the growing private sector in recent years has already altered health care professional employment patterns.

HISTORICAL BACKGROUND

According to Schwartzman (1979), Brazilian medical education dates from 1808, when two medicosurgical courses were created: one in Salvador, capital of Bahia State, and the other in Rio de Janeiro. The title of "doctor" was awarded in Brazil by the examination board itself, but officially recognized by Coimbra University in Portugal. Before 1808, medicine was practiced by doctors who studied through apprenticeship with more experienced physicians. Not until 1898, when Brazil became a republic, was another new medical school founded, in the state of Rio Grande do Sul.

The twentieth century saw considerable disorganization in Brazilian medical education in answer to various motivations and political, economic, and techno-scientific interests. During the first stage, from 1912 to 1950, ten medical Faculties were founded, seven at the initiative of the public authorities and three through private enterprise; these were later incorporated into the public system. During the second stage, from 1950 to 1965, another 23 schools were founded, mostly by the federal government, in an effort to create a medical school in every Brazilian state. During that period, the first privately funded, nonprofit medical school linked to Catholic universities emerged.

The third stage, from 1965 to date, can be divided into two periods. In the first period, from 1965 to 1971, a total of 37 medical schools were founded, most as profit-making business enterprises with low social commitment. These were situated predominantly in the Southern and Southeastern regions of the country, where most of the population, as well as the most modern and productive sectors of the economy, are concentrated. The rapid increase in the number of schools is reflected in a tenfold increase in the number of graduating physicians between the years 1941 and 1985 (Conclaves 1984).

The expansion in medical school capacity paralleled the boom in advanced education generally, representing the country's response to the demands of a growing urban middle class for university education. However, by 1971 a strong reaction against mass medical education had begun to set in among several sectors of society. Between 1971 and 1992, only seven new medical schools were created. Most of the public medical schools in Brazil were originally created as independent units and only later incorporated into a university framework by combining independent Faculties of medicine, law, or engineering. Of the 80 Brazilian schools in operation today, 45 are public and 35 private. Most of the public schools today are connected to the 29 federal universities. There are also ten state Faculties, one county Faculty and five independent institutions. They are distributed throughout almost all states with at least one federal school in each, except for the recently formed states of Acre, Amapa, Rondonia, Roraima, and

Tocantins in the North region. In 1988, a total of 8,188 undergraduate students were enrolled in Brazil's 80 medical schools. Of that number, 3,853 were women.

The funds for investment and costs of the public Faculties come almost exclusively from government sources. In the case of federal Faculties, the Ministry of Education is responsible for financing academic activities and staff remuneration equally in all national territory, with remuneration based on the criteria of title, full or part-time status, and exclusive dedication. In state Faculties, the funds come from the state's own treasury.

Almost all university hospitals belonging to both private and public Faculties are financed by the public sector from the social security funds. Private medical schools also receive government support through educational credit for fees to support poor students and for remuneration of services provided by their teaching hospitals. Many also obtained public subsidies for their installation from the Social Development Fund. Government agencies for scientific and technological development also contribute to a few medical schools that undertake research through direct research support and postgraduate human resources training programs. Until the 1940s, the prevailing pattern of Brazilian medical education was inspired by the European, particularly the French, model. From World War II on, closer contact with American medicine led to its strong influence. Medical education in Brazil still maintains close links with the French tradition in that medical schools have not incorporated experimentation and research as fundamental activities. Exceptions to this rule were the São Paulo Medical Faculty and Ribeirao Preto, both part of São Paulo University. Close contact with North American medicine led to creation of the medical residency, university hospitals, and, finally, university reform in 1968 . This reform featured an academic model inspired by the Flexner Report, including division of the course into basic and professional cycles, and the addition of departments of preventive and social medicine (Andrade 1974). These reforms, however, failed to alter the prevailing educational model.

In the mid-1970s, some innovative programs based on an integration of medical education and health care services were introduced. Some (limited to preventive and social medicine departments), were relatively successful; others, such as that at Minas Gerais Federal University, achieved deeper curricular changes. Most, however, did not succeed in breaking the politico-ideological barriers separating the academic orientation from the realities of health care. The need to define learning methods and processes (a basic presupposition of integrative programs) was not well developed by the teaching faculty members involved in the programs. Such a fact contributed, without question, to the failure of some programs that used the health services merely as extensions of practical training.

ROLE OF NATIONAL POLICY IN SHAPING MEDICAL EDUCATION

The funding policy adopted during the 1970s by the Social Security system for paying providers on a fee-for-service basis exacerbated the trend toward increased specialization and contributed to the exaggerated use of sophisticated technologies and higher costs of medical care. Without control on the quality of health service, such a policy encouraged the use of diagnostic and therapeutic technologies more valued for their remuneration than for their contribution to health care. Most medical schools, in focusing on hospital practice and early specialization, contributed to reproducing the prevailing model of professional specialization. The dichotomy in this model between public health and individual and curative care is clearly expressed in the medical curriculum. The limited attention to public health disciplines corresponds to the low priority given to endemic and epidemic diseases and to disease control policies. Environmental issues, new challenges from AIDS, and changes in the demographic status of the country, while subjects of widespread discussion in society, have had only limited influence on discipline-based medical curricula in most medical schools. These curricula have remained constant, almost unaffected by the demographic and epidemiological changes.

ADMISSION

Access to medical school is through the university entrance examination for students who have completed their secondary education. Each institution defines its criteria for admission and establishes the type of examination and minimum marks necessary for qualification. Strictly speaking, there is no direct interference from the government on admission to licensed medical schools. However, government incentives during the 1970s to expand educational capacity did greatly affect the number of admissions to medical courses. However, an evaluation of the effects of the policy (such as larger classes) on the quality of medical education led the Medical Education Committee of the Ministry of Education in 1981 to stop licensing new medical schools, thereby introducing an indirect measure of control. Admission has also been influenced indirectly by reduced governmental investment in social sectors. This has had an adverse affect on the quality of public primary and secondary education, leaving low-income groups, who do not have access to private education, unable to qualify for public university education. The university entrance examination has, therefore, resulted in selection based on socioeconomic criteria. Paradoxically, government subsidy of low-income students contributes to the maintenance of private medical schools. Last, government policy, which has encouraged the accelerating trend toward salaried employment of physicians, has led to a reduction in the ratio of applications to admissions, especially in the Southeast region.

CURRICULAR STRUCTURE AND INNOVATION

In accord with the 1969 resolution, the Federal Education Council (Conselho Federal de Educacao) prescribes the basic curricular framework and minimum length of medical programs in Brazil. The required subjects include biology, morphology, physiology, and pathology at the basic science level, and semiology, pathology, obstetrics and gynecology, pediatrics, surgery, anesthesiology, psychiatry, legal medicine and professional ethics and public health at the clinical level. The basic sciences phase lasts for approximately five semesters; it is essentially theoretical and is taught by nonclinicians (basic scientists). The clinical phase consists of medical and surgical specialties in the four basic areas (internal medicine, pediatrics, surgery, and obstetrics and gynecology), including both theoretical and practical experience in ambulatory settings and hospitals. Beyond theory, the curriculum includes at least 4,500 hours of practical experience in health care centers, ambulatory clinics, and teaching hospitals; however, students are not allowed to work directly with patients until they start their internship, whereupon they often find themselves unprepared for handling clinical problems. An internship under staff supervision for a minimum period of two semesters is also required; the requirement may be met by a rotating internship in the four basic areas or by a straight internship in the specialty of choice. The school program can be completed in a minimum of five years, and must be completed within nine years. Each institution is free to develop its own program within the general framework. However, despite the flexibility, the curriculum of most medical schools is quite uniform and can be generally characterized as follows:

- Inflexible structure with few electives;
- Disciplinary organization of the curriculum;
- Primary reliance on lectures for transmission of knowledge;
- Assessment by examinations that stress memorization of information;
- Reliance on lecture notes and little emphasis on actively consulting textbooks and scientific articles;
- Limited practical experience; laboratories, ambulatory settings and hospitals used primarily for demonstration purposes, with students functioning merely as passive observers;
- Late introduction to health care services, with a clear separation between the basic science and clinical curricula;
- Hospital-based instruction, in which the clinical phase is more directed to individual and curative care, early specialization, and sophisticated diagnostic and therapeutic procedures;
- Weak scientific orientation resulting from the clear split between teaching and research;
- Little emphasis on the epidemiological methods required for a critical assessment of scientific literature, and failure to prepare students to deal with uncertainties and probabilities;
- Emphasis on the biomedical model, where disease is reduced to its anatomicopathological expression in a body conceived of as a machine consisting of organs and systems and as an object of medical intervention; and
- A weakened ethical and humane approach in patient clinical services given the impact of technology on medical care.

It is worth mentioning that this profile has many exceptions with respect to both curricular structure and applied teaching methods. For example, there are medical schools in which the basic science curriculum is organized in terms of organ systems (e.g., locomotor, cardiorespiratory, etc.), thus promoting an interdisciplinary approach and early exposure to clinical practice. Other schools have redefined the student's role from the beginning of the course, placing the emphasis on problem solving and encouraging integration with health care services. Still other schools encourage their students' involvement in research, thereby motivating them to enter scientific careers. These examples reflect the diversity of institutions and illustrate the difficulties of defining a typical curricular profile.

For more than twenty years, the Ministry of Education, through the Medical Education Committee has urged that medical education programs be oriented to the country's health care requirements. The Brazilian Association of Medical Education, ABEM (Associacao Brasileira de Educacao Medica), and Brazilian Association of Postgraduate Collective Health Care, ABRASCO (Associacao Brasileira de PosGraduacao em Saude Coletiva), have undertaken many initiatives to stimulate change.

However, what Maria del Carmen Troncoso said about Argentina can also be said of Brazil:

Since 1950, it is assumed that the product should be a general practitioner. There is, however, a growing trend toward specialization. Greater emphasis on preventive and social medicine is recommended but there is a constant crisis in teaching this subject. The proposal is that a physician should be part of the community for primary care, while prevailing practice centers on individual hospital diagnosis with overuse of technology. The importance of research is always stressed but is limited and not part of the curriculum. Integrated care (the Americans' study-work or clerkship) is recommended but formal teaching prevails. Emphasis is on educating physicians according to the need of our people but most educators do not know what those needs are. (Silva 1983)

GRADUATE MEDICAL EDUCATION

The first medical residency programs in the country began in the 1940s in the states of Rio de Janeiro and São Paulo. Over the years, there has been a substantial expansion in the number of programs offered, particularly by public institutions. Increased demand for residency training during the 1970s was due primarily to accelerated growth in the private hospital sector which required new, special staff to meet the demands of the social security system. The need for cheap labor to fill the system's service requirements encouraged proliferation of programs without adequate regard for program effectiveness.

It is in this context that the National Medical Residency Committee was created in 1976 to establish standards, qualification criteria, candidate selection procedures, scholarships, and diploma requirements. Residency was thenceforth defined in Brazil as a "modality of graduate education for physicians at a specialty level, characterized by service training, exclusive dedication, working in health care institutions, universities or otherwise, under the guidance of medical professionals of high ethical and professional qualification" (Pierantoni 1989). Beginning in 1981, the law limited use of the expression, "medical residency" to programs licensed by the National Medical Residency Committee and set forth procedures for obtaining the title of specialist through registration in the Federal Education Council and Federal Medical Council. The specialist title is not required to practice medicine, and only some forty percent of medical graduates enter medical residency programs each year. The disproportionate selection of candidates from public universities reinforces the perception of unequal standards between public and the private schools.

According to data from the Executive Bureau of the National Resident Doctors Association in the Ministry of Education, there were, in 1991, a total of 11,281 residents training in 48 specialties offered in 237 hospitals in 1,550 medical residency programs.[1] Public institutions--federal, state, and county--offer the largest number of programs and training positions. There is, however, a remarkable inequality in the number of places and programs in the different regions of the country, with 65 percent of the trainees concentrated in the Southeast region. Clearly the number and distribution of medical residency programs is not related to the demand for specialists required to meet health care needs of the population in the different regions of the country. General pediatrics, general internal medicine, and general surgery are the most popular both as areas of specialization, and as required prerequisites for certain subspecialties. The average medical residency program is about two years in length; surgical specialties generally require a longer period.

LICENSURE

Brazilian legislation stipulates that a medical school must be authorized by the Federal Education Council, the agency of the Ministry of Education responsible for the standards and supervision of advanced education institutions. Once authorized, the Medical Faculty is qualified to award a diploma to its graduates who have complied with curriculum requirements. The graduate diploma must be registered at the Regional Medical Councils of the state where the individual expects to practice and can only be registered in two states simultaneously. There is no qualification examination to enter the profession, and graduates can practice as long as they have the diploma and are registered in the respective state Regional Council. These councils, under the Labor Ministry, are independent. They have the responsibility for enforcing ethical standards of the profession as well as punishing negligence, and they have the power to cancel the right to practice.

Recent discussions of professional quality and accusations of medical negligence in the press have led some Regional Councils to consider the

---

[1]This number of places corresponds to all residents in training and not to the number of vacancies offered to new entrants in that year's program.

possibility of initiating a qualifying examination. This is a controversial proposal, and no decision has yet been reached.

Board Certification for Specialists

The only specialist certificate recognized by Brazilian legislation is for medical residency in establishments certified by the National Medical Residency Committee. Specialty certification is awarded on the basis of examinations conducted by various professional associations such as the Brazilian Medical Association and the Brazilian College of Surgeons. Similarly, the Regional Councils and Federal Medical Council register professionals as specialists on the basis of qualifications granted for medical residency, and by the Brazilian Medical Association and Brazilian College of Surgeons. The title of specialist is recognized by professionals and by society for the intellectual and scientific prestige of those associations, but it has no legal value nor is it required to practice any medical specialty.

Cross-Licensing of Physicians

Legislation regarding licensing of foreign medical graduates, as published by the Federal Education Council in 1975, sets specific standards based on international agreements. Foreign medical graduates can request revalidation of their diplomas at an official university that offers a program equivalent to that of the candidate. When applying, foreign candidates must present documented proof of having completed the course satisfactorily and fulfilled all requirements. These documents are examined by the university and the competent department of the Ministry of Education. If the application is approved, candidates undergo examinations and tests to confirm that they meet standards equal to those required of local graduates. Once the diploma is validated, the professional is registered at the Regional Medical Council where he or she intends to practice

CONTINUING MEDICAL EDUCATION

There is no legal requirement for continuing education in Brazil, and the medical schools currently do not play any significant role in this matter. Professional updating is essentially by means of conferences and seminars organized by specialty associations. Most of these associations publish journals or newsletters for distribution to their members. Such a system, being voluntary and based on memberships, cannot guarantee widespread dissemination of information to all professionals. Furthermore, scientific events and publications often receive financial support from the pharmaceutical and medical equipment industry which may interfere in the choice of content, possibly biasing it toward the interests of the sponsors rather than the actual requirements of participants.

ROLE OF RESEARCH IN MEDICAL EDUCATION

It is estimated that between 1987 and 1989, federal and state financing agencies allocated approximately eighty million dollars to research training and research projects in the biological and health care areas. This represents approximately seventeen percent of all resources invested in science and technological areas during this period (Viacava, et al. 1991). Sixty-eight percent of all funds came from the National Fund for Scientific and Technological Development, FNDCT (Fundo Nacional de Desenvolvimento Cientifico Tecnologico), of the National Bureau for Science and Technology, which is the main source of financing health care research in the country. An analysis of the institutions considered in the projects financed by FNDCT between 1987 and 1988 reveals a high concentration of research activities in federal and state public universities, where 80 percent of the projects are conducted, with 86 percent of all institutions receiving federal training and research funds located in the Southeast region of Brazil. Thus, as a consequence of government policy during the last twenty years, the advanced education institutions have become the principal research centers.

Health research, particularly in the clinical area, is a recent development in Brazil. Traditionally, it has been a concentrated area in universities and related institutes. However, progress achieved in basic science areas has not reached the clinical research field, due to the lack of association between the two. Nor has much consideration been given to the academic relevance of medical research, indeed, its contribution to improved clinical care has been negligible. Further, interest in research on medical education itself is slight. Consequently, there is not enough information to evaluate the educational process. However, the Brazilian Association of Medical Education, ABEM (Associacao Brasileira de Educacao Medica), a nonacademic institution, is now coordinating a project to assess the program in all medical schools in the country; it is expected that this will help direct and consolidate changes

GOVERNMENT/PUBLIC SECTOR INVOLVEMENT

Government and university policies encourage faculty to obtain advanced degrees to promote their university career. Stimulated by the 1968 postgraduate regulations, the number of master's and PhD programs in the area of health care sciences had increased by 1986 to around two hundred and one hundred, respectively. More recently, the Ministry of Education's policy, formulated by the Coordination for Further University Graduate Education, CAPES (Coordenadoria de Aperfeicoamento de Pessoal de Nivel Superior), has favored the PhD level. However, the more highly qualified teachers, involved in their own specialty research, tend to undervalue teaching. Faculty at that level devote most of their time to work in subspecialty clinics and the teaching of postgraduate courses.

For universities that are succeeding in maintaining a wide-based pyramid of less qualified teachers for undergraduate education, in the context of the national economic crisis and restriction on the number of teachers contracted, there is certainly a less adverse effect of career advancement on medical education. It is worth emphasizing that the macroeconomic adjustment policies toward the state's foreign and fiscal crises tend to reduce public investment in university institutions. In this situation, fund-raising for research and postgraduate work will tend to be a major source of revenue for medical schools with a recognized academic production.

INTERNATIONAL LINKAGES AND COLLABORATION

Transnational influences on medical education must be examined in light of the country's scientific and technological dependence. The reform movements in medical education in Brazil (e.g., the Flexnerian model, the introduction of preventive and community medicine, and integration of this science with clinical study) tended merely to follow the changes made in developed countries. Medical education leans strongly toward specialist training, which implies proficiency in the use of technology. Such an approach encourages health care practices that may not correspond to the country's needs. This trend is exacerbated by students' necessary reliance on foreign textbooks, without adequate guidance about how knowledge from other countries can be applied and adapted, not merely copied, in the context of health care needs in Brazil.

Proposals by international organizations, such as WHO's goal of "Health for All by the Year 2000," have had little influence on the medical school program. Such proposals are identified as belonging only to the public health sphere, which limits their influence to preventive medicine, community medicine, and public health departments traditionally on the periphery of most medical school curricula. On the other hand, Faculties that have become more integrated with the service network have tended to include in the curriculum subjects relating to care recommended by international organizations and given priority by the Brazilian government. This is the case of the basic child health care package supported by the Pan American Health Organization (PAHO) and United Nations International Children's Emergency Fund (UNICEF).

ISSUES AND TRENDS

The Brazilian medical school's inflexibility and remoteness from the more pressing problems of society are more noticeable than its readiness to change. Questions raised by social groups and health care professionals, from different analytical viewpoints, on the limits and efficiency of medical practice and distortions in teaching are still uncoordinated. These groups have, as yet, been unable to define a new paradigm to overcome the polarities between cure/prevention, individual/collective, organic/psychological, biological/social, education/work, and health/disease. On the other hand, technological progress and the rapid expansion of new knowledge in the various health science fields offer major challenges to our present conception of professional competence and will require us to reformulate our objectives, programs and methods to better meet the country's needs. Success will depend on the political ability and desire to address development based on criteria of equality and social justice.

Teachers, students, and researchers are all part of this process.

REFERENCES

Andrade, J. M. 1974. *Conceptual de la Educacion Medica en la America Latina* (Conceptual view of medical education in Latin America). Washington, DC: OPS.

Brazil. *Diario Oficial da Uniao*, Decree 80.281, Section 1, Part 1, 6 September 1977. Quoted by C.R.Pierantoni. *Especializacao medica: Formacao e insercao no mercado de trabalho* (Medical specialization: education and entry to the job market). Paper given at the First International Human Resources Course ENSP/RJ, 1989. Mimeo, p. 5.

Nogueira, R.P. 1991. *Emprego em saude por natureza juridico-administrativa dos estabelecimentos, 1981-1987* (Employment in health care according to legal - administrative nature of units, 1981-1987). Mimeo.

Paim, J.S. 1991. *Educacion medica en la decada de 1990: el optimismo no basta* (Medical education in the nineties: Optimism is not enough). *Educacion Medica y Salud* 25:1.

Schwartzman, S. 1979. *Formacao da Comunidade Cientifica no Brasil-São Paulo* (Education of the scientific community in Brazil-São Paulo). Ed. Nacional Rio de Janeiro. Study and Project Financing Agency (*Financiadora de Estudos e Projetos*).

Silva, G.R. 1987. (quoted in) *Uma retrospectiva da educacao medica no Brasil* (Retrospective of medical education in Brazil). *Revista Brasileira de Educacao Medica* (September/December) 11 (3):83.

Silver, L. 1992. Quality assurance in health care: Issues in health care delivery and finance in Brazil. Preliminary version for the World Bank (December).

Viacava, F., et al. 1991. *A investigacao em saude no Brasil* (Health research in Brazil). Paper presented at the Science and Technology in Health Care seminar, Brasilia. Mimeo, p. 7.

6

Canada

EVA RYTEN

Canada stretches from the Atlantic Ocean in the east to the Pacific Ocean in the west, occupying an area just under 10 million square kilometers. In mid-1991, the population reached 27 million persons. Canada is a federal state, and its vast geographic area is divided into ten provinces and two territories, each of which has its own government. Both health and education come under the jurisdiction of provincial governments.

OVERVIEW OF THE HEALTH CARE DELIVERY SYSTEM

Each of Canada's provinces and territories administers its own health care system. To obtain partial financial support from the federal government, provincial health plans must meet the following five criteria. (1) Universality: all residents of a province must be covered under the same conditions. Waiting periods for coverage for new residents of a province or territory cannot exceed three months. (2) Portability: residents of a province cannot lose coverage while they are temporarily absent from their province of residence. (3) Comprehensiveness: all medically necessary hospital and physician expenses must be covered. Services not deemed medically necessary may be covered on an optional basis. (4) Accessibility: the provincial health care plan must provide all residents with reasonable access to care without financial barriers--very important in a country the size of Canada. (5) Public administration: the health care plan must be operated and administered by a public nonprofit body. Although physician services are publicly funded, most physicians in Canada are self-employed and are paid on a fee-for-service basis. Only 25 percent of health care expenditures are *not* paid through the public health care plans.

The chief problem facing Canada's largely publicly funded health care systems today is rapidly escalating costs. The health care policy agenda is

dominated by the need to deal with costs that are rising at a rate faster than can
be absorbed by the taxing powers of governments.

HISTORICAL BACKGROUND

In 1901 Canada's population was 5.4 million and there were 11 medical
schools, of which eight still exist today (two were absorbed by the University of
Toronto, and one by McGill University). During this century eight new medical
schools commenced operations, all as Faculties of universities. For further details,
refer to Table 6.1, p. 76.

Canada's system of higher education developed in the nineteenth century,
originally under the influence of Scottish and English models in English-speaking
Canada and French models in Québec. During the twentieth century, the influence
of the United States has been predominant. In medical education this influence has
been particularly strong through the joint accreditation standards applied to
undergraduate medical programs in both countries.

ROLE OF NATIONAL POLICY IN SHAPING MEDICAL EDUCATION

Both health and education are responsibilities of provincial governments in
Canada. However, the federal government makes major fiscal contributions to
provinces in order to assist them in meeting the costs of health and higher
education. The different levels of government arrive at national policies through
the working of interprovincial committees.

Policy decisions in recent years have been dominated by the need to bring
deficits under control at both the national and provincial levels. In the field of
medical education, this has been reflected in provincial governments
recommending policies that they believe can solve various problems that arise in
the health care system. The list of some issues involving medical education in
which governments currently play a determining or shaping role includes:

- Admissions quotas to medical schools. In a belief that increases in
  health care costs are driven by the number of physicians in
  practice, governments have recommended and ensured that the
  number of medical school places has been reduced by
  approximately 12.5 percent in the last ten years.
- Provincial governments are now heavily involved in the number
  and specialty mix of post-MD residency positions in an attempt to
  relate the size of the post-MD system to the output of
  undergraduate programs and to have graduating physicians enter
  those fields of medicine for which societal needs exist.
- Governments would like to see the chronic shortage of physicians
  in remote and climatically inhospitable regions solved (at least
  partially) through educational initiatives. These initiatives include
  student scholarships for physicians willing to locate in shortage
  areas; funding some undergraduate and post-MD training in remote

community and ambulatory settings; encouraging selection policies that favor categories of individuals whom governments believe are more likely to eventually locate in underserviced areas, and so forth.

The actions of government are quite directive, and it is fair to say that educational institutions have far less room for maneuver than was customary 15 or more years ago.

ADMISSION

The number of places for the study of medicine in each Faculty of Medicine is fixed by provincial governments in discussion with the universities. Quotas are firm and cannot be exceeded. Originally, the number of places offered for the study of medicine was determined by available educational resources, including the patient load for clinical teaching. Physician manpower considerations have been the overriding determinant of the number of places offered during the past forty years. In the early 1960s, a major study of medical education in Canada led to considerable expansion in capacity. Four new Faculties of medicine were created, and the number of places in the other 12 was increased. This expansion resulted in an approximate doubling of the output of Canadian Faculties of Medicine. During the decade of the 1980s, the sentiment grew that Canada had too many, not too few, doctors, and pressure was exerted on Faculties of Medicine to cut enrollment. Faculties of Medicine now graduate approximately 7.5 percent fewer MDs than in the peak year of 1985, and a new round of enrollment cuts is expected, starting with students commencing medical studies in 1993.

Starting in the late 1960s, there was a tremendous surge in the number of applicants for admission to Canadian medical schools. Strict quotas have meant that no more than one in four applicants can be admitted each year. Because the competition for admission is so severe, dropout rates tend to be very low. In recent years 96.5 percent of all students admitted to study medicine at a Canadian university have succeeded in earning the MD degree. Whereas provincial governments, the medical profession and the public are, to some extent, involved in discussions related to the number of medical school places, until recently, admissions policies were strictly left to the universities themselves.

Although universities are largely government-funded in Canada, with respect to academic matters, including admissions policies, they are autonomous institutions. The admission of medical students is handled at the faculty level. Each Faculty of Medicine has its own admissions committee. These committees set their own policies (which are approved by the senate of the university) and handle the administrative side of student selection.

Just as there is considerable diversity with respect to medical curricula in Canadian medical schools, so is there considerable diversity with respect to admission requirements and selection policies. Consequently, only a very general outline is given here. Those interested in greater detail should consult the current edition of *Admission Requirements to Canadian Faculties of Medicine and Their Selection Policies*, published biennially by the Association of Canadian Medical Colleges.

Medical schools consider not only the academic records of applicants in making admission decisions but also try to assess the applicants' suitability for a career in medicine. Prospective medical students must meet the educational prerequisites specified by the Faculties of Medicine to which they apply. In general, these range from a minimum of two years of postsecondary education to a completed undergraduate degree. Most medical schools also have specific course requirements for entry. The most commonly required courses are chemistry, organic chemistry, biology, and physics. A number of medical schools require students to have completed some courses in English and/or the social sciences, and most require applicants to take the Medical College Admission Test (MCAT) administered by the American College Testing Program.

Applicants' academic records, MCAT scores, and completion of entry requirements provide the basis for judging academic suitability. Other means used to judge suitability for a career in medicine include references, interviews, and autobiographical sketches. An excellent academic record is, by itself, not sufficient to guarantee acceptance into medicine. Age, sex, ethnic origin, and religious background are not used as criteria in admissions decisions; however, as universities are provincial institutions, place (province) of residence may be an important factor.

The applicant pool has changed dramatically in the last two to three decades and today the proportion of women and older candidates is far higher than it used to be. In recent years, 45 percent of admitted students are women and the median age of newly admitted students is rising. Demographic changes in the applicant pool are mirrored in the demographic characteristics of enrolled medical students and in recent graduating classes (see Tables 6.2, p. 77 and 6.5, p. 80).

CURRICULAR STRUCTURE AND INNOVATION

The first professional degree (undergraduate) in medicine awarded by Canadian universities is the MD, following a three- to five-year program of professional study. Over the years, the requirements for gaining admission into a program of study leading to the MD, the content, and duration of the course of study, have all changed. Principal factors driving curricular change have been: (1) exponential growth in knowledge, leading to the realization that medical students cannot possibly acquire all relevant information during a few years in medical school; (2) the need to foster attitudes and behaviors leading to life-long learning in fields related to the practice of medicine; (3) the need to foster appropriate behavior toward patients and other health care workers; and (4) the need for all medical students to acquire a common fund of knowledge enabling them to progress into any one of dozens of different medical or surgical specialties or into a career in research.

Canadian educational institutions have been at the forefront of medical education reform in postwar years. As of 1992, nearly all Faculties of Medicine were engaged in curricular reform, with most on the way to introducing problem-based learning. Another recent widely adopted change is the introduction of medical students to the clinical setting very early in the curriculum rather than only in the last year or two, as was previously the case.

Curriculum revision is in the hands of a curriculum committee in each of the Faculties of Medicine. These committees must deal with the twin problems of curriculum overload and constant pressures to include new disciplines and topics in an already crowded program.

A specific example of an MD curriculum of a Canadian Faculty of Medicine will convey more accurately the current situation than a general description covering the curricula of all medical schools. The curriculum given here is that introduced in 1990 at the University of Western Ontario (UWO). The UWO undergraduate medical curriculum is a four year program divided into five phases of variable length. It is designed to provide each student with an opportunity to acquire the knowledge, skills and attitudes required to advance to graduate and postgraduate studies leading to clinical practice, research, or other medical careers. The educational format is a blend of lectures, laboratory exercises, small group problem-based learning, and supervised clinical experience.

Phase	Curriculum
Intro-duction	In the week preceding Phase I, students are offered an orientation program, "Introduction to Medicine." Students are welcomed into medicine, see health care facilities, explore problems and issues in health care, and spend a complete day alongside a practicing physician.
Phase I and II	Phases I and II span the first two years of the curriculum and are divided into six 12-week trimesters, each including an examination period. This phase is designed to provide the student with a solid grounding in the basic and clinical sciences. These phases are structured around a Problem-Based Learning Day in each week. Students meet in small groups with a faculty tutor who acts as a facilitator. Each session starts with the discussion of a particular problem or situation, designed to provide a stimulus for students to identify their individual learning needs and to develop skills in information retrieval and critical appraisal. The problem-based learning approach gives students an opportunity to identify the areas about which they still need to learn in order to understand the problem. With this approach, students take responsibility for their own learning with the tutor assisting but not leading. Problem-based learning serves as a stimulus and focuses the student on broader concepts, around which the knowledge gained from the lectures, labs, and tutorials can be better organized. The problem-based sessions also allow students to develop skills in communication and in independent, self-directed learning. In addition to Problem-Based Learning Days, students participate in early patient contact and clinical skills tutorials, laboratories, and lectures. Electives are entirely at the students' discretion and do not count in the

academic record. The compulsory courses provided in Phase I include Anatomy, Biochemistry, Clinical Methods 1, General Pathology, Genetics and Early Post-Natal Development, Histology, Medicine and Society, Microbiology 1, Physiology, and Problem-Based Learning 1. The compulsory courses provided in Phase II include: Clinical Methods 2, Introduction to Clinical Clerkship 1, Medical Biophysics, Microbiology 2, Neurosciences, Pharmacology, Problem-Based Learning 2 and Systemic Pathology.

Phase III   Phase III is a single, 10 week trimester at the beginning of the third year. In this period the Problem-Based Learning Days continue, using more sophisticated clinical problems. Increased emphasis is placed on tutorials in clinical skills, clinical sciences and therapeutics. This phase is designed to integrate basic and clinical knowledge and skills in preparation for clerkship. Courses in Phase III include Clinical Methods 3, Problem-Based Learning 3, Therapeutics, Introduction to Clinical Clerkship 2, and the Pre-Clerkship Comprehensive Examination.

Phase IV   Phase IV, the clinical clerkship, is a 52-week integrated learning experience. The student becomes a member of a clinical care team, taking major rotations in Family Medicine, Medicine, Obstetrics and Gynecology, Pediatrics, Psychiatry, and Surgery. The clerkship provides students with an opportunity to participate in patient care in the hospital, clinic, and office settings. Under the supervision of faculty and more senior house staff, clinical clerks are given graded responsibility in the diagnosis, investigation and management of patients. At the end of Phase IV, students sit a comprehensive examination, which they must pass to begin Phase V.

Phase V   Phase V spans the final 22 weeks of the curriculum. Courses include Selected Topics, Clinical Selectives, and Electives 1, 2, and 3. During this phase students return to the classroom for six weeks' instruction on selected topics. During the remaining time, clinical selective and electives are available. Selectives are completed locally from choices available to students.

Electives are arranged entirely by the individual student, and may be in any area (basic or clinical), at UWO or in other centers. Students must have approval from their assigned faculty advisor and the Undergraduate Medical Education Office.

Medical Electives Overseas is a special program of study in a third world country, available as an elective in Phase V.

Calendar of the Faculty of Medicine, University of Western Ontario, 1991-92. London: Ontario.

GRADUATE MEDICAL EDUCATION

Canadian Faculties of Medicine are responsible for two types of postgraduate education: programs leading to university degrees at the master's and PhD levels and programs of post-MD clinical training leading to specialty certification and licensure.

In Canada, earning an MD degree is a necessary but not sufficient, qualification for the practice of medicine. Medical graduates must qualify for licensure, and one of the additional conditions for gaining a license to practice is the satisfactory completion of a period of post-MD clinical training. Until very recently, the minimum period of post-MD training required was one year, although only 25 to 30 percent of each year's graduates entered practice following a single year of training. At the present time, those provinces that have not already done so are in the process of changing their policy to require a minimum of two years' post-MD training for licensure.

All post-MD training has been under the jurisdiction of Faculties of Medicine since 1970. There are no freestanding hospital-based programs. Training programs exist in general medicine, family medicine, and over 50 recognized specialties and subspecialties.

The College of Family Physicians of Canada (CFPC) accredits programs in family medicine and training in emergency medicine, as well as care for the elderly for certificated family physicians. Family medicine certification programs are available at all 16 Canadian Faculties of Medicine. All other specialty programs must be accredited by the Royal College of Physicians and Surgeons of Canada (RCPSC).

It is rare for graduates of Canadian medical schools not to go on to seek post-MD clinical training and licensure upon graduation. In the recent decades, only one percent of new medical graduates each year have not gone on to training in Canada or the United States; approximately 96 percent enter post-MD clinical training in Canada each year.

The most notable trend with respect to the field of training sought by graduates has been the steady increase in the proportion of each graduating class choosing to enter family medicine training programs. At least half the physicians starting out in practice each year are general or family physicians. Some specialties do have difficulty filling the available number of training slots. These include neonatology, radiation oncology, geriatrics, psychiatry and various pediatric subspecialties. At present the concern is that the stock of surgeons is considerably older, on average, than the stock of general practitioners and that the current choices of graduating medical students may soon lead to a shortage of Canadian surgeons.

LICENSURE

Each province and territory of the Canadian federation has a licensing authority. The licensing authority has the responsibility for determining the conditions that must be met by those who wish to practice medicine in that particular geographic jurisdiction. The provincial licensing authority also has the right to determine who meets the prescribed conditions for the issuance of a license to practice. Licensure requirements differ among the twelve provinces; however, all licensing bodies are members of a voluntary organization, the

Federation of Medical Licensing Authorities of Canada, which has as one of its goals national discussions leading to uniformity in conditions for licensure. For example, physicians who wish to register in Saskatchewan to practice medicine must meet the following requirements: (1) an acceptable medical degree from a university approved by the Council; (2) acceptable performance on a licensing examination--either the Licentiate Medical Council of Canada (LMCC) Qualifying Examination, the US Federation Licensing Examination (FLEX), or the United States National Board of Medical Examiners (NBME) Part II exam [since replaced by USMLE Step II]; (3) satisfactory completion of an approved program of postgraduate training; (4) evidence of good character as documented by recent references; and (5) payment of the registration and annual license fees.

Satisfactory Postgraduate Training. For the purpose of registration, the following constitutes evidence of "satisfactory postgraduate training." (1) Applicants who wish to practice as a consultant specialist and to restrict practice to one of the disciplines recognized by the RCPSC must be certified in that specialty by the RCPSC. (2) Applicants who wish to practice primary care medicine must satisfy the following: certification by the CFPC; satisfactory completion of a CFPC-accredited residency in family medicine; eligibility to sit for the CFPC certification examination; and satisfactory completion of 24 months of postgraduate training in programs affiliated with a medical school accredited by both the Liaison Committee on Medical Education (LCME)/Committee of Canadian Medical Schools (CACMS) and either the RCPSC or the Committee on Accreditation of Pre-registration Physician Training Programs.[1] Increasingly, licensure is being linked to certification in either family medicine or a specialty. In the province of Québec, certification is already a requirement for licensure.

Board Certification

The Royal College of Physicians and Surgeons of Canada was established in 1929 for the purpose of ensuring quality training for medical and surgical specialists. It is responsible for accrediting training programs and running the certification examinations for each of the recognized specialties and subspecialties. During most of its existence, post-MD clinical training took place in teaching hospitals that were not answerable to Faculties of Medicine.

The RCPSC operates through specialty committees. However since all such committees report to a single, national organization, it is possible to adopt uniform policies. This is especially important with respect to establishing criteria for the recognition of new specialties, the evaluation and assessment of previous

---

[1] Excerpted from College of Physicians and Surgeons of Saskatchewan. 1992. "Requirements and Procedures for Registration."

post-MD training taken in Canada or another country, and programs for maintaining the competence of practicing specialists.

Cross-Licensing of Physicians

Canada relied on immigration to build up the general population, and approximately 25 percent of Canada's practicing physicians are graduates of foreign medical schools. Until the mid-1970s, physician immigration was actively encouraged, but the prospect of an oversupply of physicians led to the withdrawal of specific incentives to the immigration of physicians. In recent years, the number of physicians from abroad entering the country with the intention of practicing in Canada has far exceeded the rate at which they can be absorbed. Substantial numbers of physicians who earned the MD degree outside Canada, however, do manage to meet its licensure requirements each year.

In order to be eligible for post-MD training in Canada, graduates of medical schools outside Canada or the United States must pass the Evaluating Examination of the Medical Council of Canada. Prior to earning a license, graduates of foreign medical schools must also pass Parts I and II of the new Qualifying Examination of the Medical Council of Canada. This leads to enrollment on the Canadian Medical Register as a Licentiate of the Medical Council of Canada, as is the case for graduates of Canadian medical schools when they pass the Qualifying Examination. Approximately thirty percent of those passing the Qualifying Examination each year earned their undergraduate medical degree outside Canada. Once graduates of foreign medical schools have succeeded in passing the Qualifying Examination they are eligible for licensure on the same terms as graduates of Canadian medical schools. Provincial licensing authorities may temporarily waive some conditions of licensure when recruiting physicians from abroad to serve in difficult-to-staff medical positions.

CONTINUING MEDICAL EDUCATION

All Canadian Faculties of Medicine offer a wide variety of continuing medical education courses. At this time, participation in CME is not a condition for maintaining licensure. Medical audit and maintenance of competence programs are actively encouraged, and the terms under which they are pursued are under discussion between the provincial licensing authorities, the Faculties of Medicine, and the certifying bodies (RCPSC and CFPC).

ROLE OF RESEARCH IN MEDICAL EDUCATION

Research has an extremely high priority in Canadian Faculties of Medicine. Full-time faculty members are expected to participate in research, which, in addition to teaching and service, is one of the principal missions of Faculties of Medicine. The research interests of Faculties of Medicine cover the entire spectrum, including research in the basic biological sciences, as well as clinical, health services, pedagogical, and epidemiological research.

Most research is funded on a competitive basis from extramural funds provided from public research councils, not-for-profit foundations and agencies, government departments and private companies. Most research grants are awarded following peer review of research proposals. The principal funding council for biomedical research in Canada is the Medical Research Council, an arm of the federal government. In recent years the share of total funding provided by provincial governments, not-for-profit agencies and the private sector has increased compared to funding from the Medical Research Council (MRC) and other federal granting councils.

With respect to research in medical education, Canada has been a leader for many years. Canadian research in medical education has been particularly productive in the fields of measurement and evaluation of clinical competence and innovations in medical curricula, notably in problem-based and small group learning. The Canadian Association for Medical Education (CAME), a voluntary organization of medical school faculty members, plays a crucial role in fostering research in medical education and faculty development.

GOVERNMENT/PRIVATE SECTOR INVOLVEMENT

As described earlier, governments are playing a larger and larger role in many facets of medical education. The only area of medical education in which the private sector has any major involvement is in the funding of biomedical research. In recent years the proportion of research conducted by Canadian faculties of medicine that has been funded by private for-profit organizations, particularly pharmaceutical companies, has grown substantially.

INTERNATIONAL LINKAGES AND COLLABORATION

Canadian medical schools have a particularly close relation to medical schools in the United States, especially as regards cooperative research in medical education and the joint establishment and implementation of accreditation standards.

Canada is a member of the Pan American Federation of Associations of Medical Schools (PAFAMS) and participates in PAFAMS activities. Individual medical schools are engaged in an extensive variety of programs of cooperation with medical schools in countries all over the world. Additionally, many post-MD trainees are accepted into Canadian training programs on a contractual basis between their home government and the medical school of training.

ISSUES AND TRENDS

Looking toward the future, medical education will be affected by movements within the educational system and by broader social trends. Within the educational system, curriculum renewal is likely to be the dominant theme. Already, for students commencing medical studies in Canada in 1993-1994, more than half will be enrolled in curricula that are either entirely or partially organized around problem-based learning. Increased emphasis on attitudes and skills, the behavioral sciences, and nonbiological determinants of health seems to be the wave of the future.

On the broader social front, fiscal constraints are likely to continue to lead to downsizing of institutions within the health care system. Resources for expansion and/or change of both educational programs and health care facilities will not be as easily forthcoming in the future as they have been in the past. Educational institutions will be forced to adjust their activities accordingly.

REFERENCES

Association of Canadian Medical Colleges (ACMC). *Canadian medical education statistics*. Annual publication. Cited as ACMC.
---------. FORUM. Bimonthly publication of the ACMC.
University calendars of the 16 Canadian universities with Faculties of medicine. Annual publications.

Table 6.1
Canadian Faculties of Medicine

Name of Institution	Province	First Organized	Year First MD Awarded
McGill University	Québec	1829	1833
Université de Montréal	Québec	1843	1843
University of Toronto	Ontario	1843	1845
Université Laval	Québec	1848	1854
Queen's University at Kingston	Ontario	1854	1855
Dalhousie University	Nova Scotia	1867	1871
University of Western Ontario	Ontario	1881	1883
University of Manitoba	Manitoba	1883	1886
University of Alberta	Alberta	1913	1925
University of Ottawa	Ontario	1945	1951
University of British Columbia	Br. Columbia	1950	1954
University of Saskatchewan	Saskatchewan	1926	1957
Université de Sherbrooke	Québec	1961	1970
McMaster University	Ontario	1965	1972
University of Calgary	Alberta	1965	1973
Memorial University of Newfoundland	Newfoundland	1967	1973

Association of Canadian Medical Colleges.

Table 6.2
Percent Distribution of Age at Admission of Successful Applicants to Canadian Faculties of Medicine 1991-1992

| FACULTY OF MEDICINE | % OF SUCCESSFUL APPLICANTS AGED*: | | | | | NUMBER OF SUCCESSFUL APPLICANTS** |
	<20	20-22	23-26	>26	TOTAL	
Memorial University	0.0	57.1	32.1	10.8	100.0	56
Dalhousie University	0.0	53.0	27.7	19.3	100.0	83
Laval, Université	46.5	23.9	21.1	8.5	100.0	142
Sherbrooke, Université de	70.6	21.6	5.9	1.9	100.0	102
Montréal, Université de	34.1	22.0	30.0	13.9	100.0	173
McGill Univ. 4 yr. program	5.0	70.5	20.2	4.3	100.0	139
pre-med program	91.4	6.9	1.7	0.0	100.0	58
Ottawa, University of	2.5	70.0	21.3	6.2	100.0	80
Queen's University	8.6	62.8	15.7	12.9	100.0	70
Toronto, University of	7.0	63.9	19.1	10.0	100.0	230
McMaster University	0.0	26.8	36.1	37.1	100.0	97
Western Ontario, Univ. of	4.3	69.9	22.6	3.2	100.0	93
Manitoba, University of	1.3	63.5	23.0	12.2	100.0	74
Saskatchewan, University of	10.2	49.2	22.0	18.6	100.0	59
Alberta, University of	5.2	56.9	25.0	12.9	100.0	116
Calgary, University of	2.8	37.5	34.7	25.0	100.0	72
British Columbia, Univ. of	0.0	47.0	37.0	16.0	100.0	119
CANADA 1991-92	17.0	47.4	23.5	12.1	100.0	1,763

* Age calculated as of September 1991

** Number of successful applicants includes McGill premeds, first year entrants, and advanced-standing admissions.

Association of Canadian Medical Colleges

77

Table 6.3
Faculty Members in Each Canadian Faculty of Medicine by Rank 1991-1992

FACULTY OF MEDICINE FACULTÉ DE MÉDECINE	FULL-TIME FACULTY MEMBERS					Part-Time Staff		
	Professor	Associate Professor	Assistant Professor	Instructor/ Other	Total	Paid	Vol.	Total
Memorial University	57	49	59	6	171	68	204	272
Dalhousie University	108	81	95	9	293	635		635
Laval, Université	86	67	21	65	239	206	908	1,114
Sherbrooke, Université de	82	55	49	42	228	388		388
Montréal, Université de	158	132	78	-	368	589	794	1,383
McGill University	195	304	468	25	992	108	789	897
Ottawa, University of	91	105	180	4	380	21	660	681
Queen's University	108	90	131	8	337	22	216	238
Toronto, University of	284	299	358	99	1040	405	2,530	2,935
McMaster University	148	109	111	1	369	2	644	646
Western Ontario, Univ. of	163	155	174	11	503	144	414	558
Manitoba, University of	130	140	134	3	407	75	844	919
Saskatchewan, Univ. of	84	65	56	3	208	379		379
Alberta, University of	169	77	87	41	374	224	661	885
Calgary, University of	100	101	83	5	289	39	563	602
British Columbia, Univ. of	139	116	104	7	366	169	1,110	1,269
TOTAL	2,102	1,945	2,188	329	6,564	3,474	10,327	13,801

Association of Canadian Medical Colleges

Table 6.4

Enrollment in Canadian Faculties of Medicine by Year of Study, Sex and Faculty of Medicine 1991-1992

FACULTY OF MEDICINE FACULTÉ DE MÉDECINE	DURATION OF PROGRAM	FIRST YEAR			INTERMEDIATE YEARS			FINAL YEAR			TOTAL		
		M/H	W/F	T	M/H	W/F	T	M/H	W/F	T	M/H	W/F	T
Memorial University, Nfld.	4 yrs./ans	30	26	56	58	54	112	32	27	59	120	107	227
Dalhousie University, N.S.	4 yrs./ans	48	37	85	106	69	175	48	33	81	202	139	341
Laval, Université	4 yrs./ans	67	75	142	141	187	328	70	81	151	278	343	621
Sherbrooke, Université de	4 yrs./ans	37	65	102	80	119	199	43	48	91	160	232	392
Montréal, Université de	5 yrs./ans	70	108	178	206	289	495	74	95	169	350	492	842
McGill University	4 yrs./ans	83	62	145	170	127	297	93	61	154	346	250	596
Subtotal, Qué.		*257*	*310*	*567*	*597*	*722*	*1319*	*280*	*285*	*565*	*1,134*	*1,317*	*2,451*
Ottawa, University of	4 yrs./ans	49	35	84	101	67	168	49	29	78	199	131	330
Queen's University	4 yrs./ans	48	27	75	96	54	150	45	27	72	189	108	297
Toronto, University of	4 yrs./ans	158	95	253	345	160	505	160	86	246	663	341	1004
McMaster University	3 yrs./ans	40	59	99	27	75	102	35	65	100	102	199	301
Western Ontario, Univ. of	4 yrs./ans	61	36	97	136	73	209	63	41	104	260	150	410
Subtotal, Ont.		*356*	*252*	*608*	*705*	*429*	*1134*	*352*	*248*	*600*	*1,413*	*929*	*2,342*
Manitoba, University of, Man.	4 yrs./ans	54	27	81	102	64	166	48	34	82	204	125	329
Saskatchewan, Univ. of, Sask.	4 yrs./ans	37	24	61	75	51	126	41	16	57	153	91	244
Alberta, University of	4 yrs./ans	75	47	122	166	81	247	75	48	123	316	176	492
Calgary, University of	3 yrs./ans	45	28	73	47	25	72	40	34	74	132	87	219
Subtotal, Alta.		*120*	*75*	*195*	*213*	*106*	*319*	*115*	*82*	*197*	*448*	*263*	*711*
British Columbia, Univ. of, B.C.	4 yrs./ans	67	55	122	144	96	240	74	47	121	285	198	483
TOTAL, CANADA		969	806	1,775	2,000	1,591	3,591	990	772	1,762	3,959	3,169	7,128
% DISTRIBUTION BY SEX		*54.6*	*45.4*	*100.0*	*55.7*	*44.3*	*100.0*	*56.2*	*43.8*	*100.0*	*55.5*	*44.5*	*100.0*

SOURCE: Association of Canadian Medical Colleges

M = Men   W = Women   T = Total

Table 6.5

MD Degrees awarded by Canadian Universities by University Awarding Degree and Sex of Recipients, 1991 Calendar Year

UNIVERSITY AWARDING MD DEGREE		NUMBER OF GRADUATES			% WOMEN
		MEN	WOMEN	TOTAL	
Memorial University	Nfld.	32	26	58	44.8 %
Dalhousie University	N.S.	58	33	91	36.3 %
Laval, Université		51	69	120	57.5 %
Sherbrooke, Université de		30	56	86	65.1 %
Montréal, Université de		57	101	158	63.9 %
McGill University		92	60	152	39.5 %
	Qué.	*230*	*286*	*516*	*55.4 %*
Ottawa, University of		40	43	83	51.8 %
Queen's University		44	29	73	39.7 %
Toronto, University of		166	85	251	33.9 %
McMaster University		41	57	98	58.2 %
Western Ontario, Univ. of		62	37	99	37.4 %
	Ont.	*353*	*251*	*604*	*41.6 %*
Manitoba, University of	Man.	48	28	76	36.8 %
Saskatchewan, Univ. of	Sask.	39	15	54	27.8 %
Alberta, University of		75	40	115	34.8 %
Calgary, University of		38	30	68	44.1 %
	Alta.	*113*	*70*	*183*	*38.3 %*
British Columbia, Univ. of	B.C.	68	55	123	44.7 %
TOTAL, CANADA		941	764	1705	44.8 %
English language universities		803	538	1341	40.1 %
French language universities		138	226	364	62.1 %

SOURCE: Association of Canadian Medical Colleges

7

The Commonwealth (English-Speaking) Caribbean

HAROLD A. DRAYTON

Our concern in this chapter is the education and training of physicians for eighteen Caribbean countries, all of which, before the early 1960s, were colonies of the former British Empire. They are conveniently grouped together as the Commonwealth Caribbean. Today, this subregion, with a total land area of about one hundred five thousand square miles and a total population of about six million, includes 12 independent nations and six dependent territories.

Mention will be made of United States offshore medical schools in some Commonwealth Caribbean countries since the 1970s, but this chapter will deal almost exclusively with medical education programs of The University of the West Indies (UWI) in Jamaica, Barbados and Trinidad-Tobago. It will also examine the Medical Practitioner training program of the Faculty of Health Sciences of The University of Guyana (UG).

OVERVIEW OF THE HEALTH CARE DELIVERY SYSTEM

The Commonwealth Caribbean inherited at independence a government financed public assistance system, with major responsibility for both inpatient and outpatient services in public hospitals; some health centers/clinics offering first-level medical care and programs for health promotion and disease prevention, especially in rural communities; and sanitation services for refuse disposal and vector control. Although a private health sector with private physicians offering services for a fee always coexisted with the state system, medical care was generally available either free or at nominal cost. This is the foundation on which health care systems in the Commonwealth Caribbean have been developed.

Post-independence: who is really "in charge"? Independence, with a politically appointed Minister responsible for health, split the persona of the old-style Director of Medical Services. A senior administrative civil servant, the Permanent Secretary (PS), was delegated authority for day-to-day management and financial control of the Ministry and all its departments. A Chief Medical

Officer (CMO) became responsible for technical guidance and advice to both the Minister and the PS, and also for supervision of all technical units. This dichotomy between administrative and technical responsibility has been a source of continuing friction, especially with increasing demands during the 1970s and 1980s for efficient and effective management of technical information in order to cope with economic crises.

Beyond the dichotomy between administrative and technical leadership of the Ministry, many other elements in the structural pattern of Commonwealth Caribbean national health systems are quite similar. This is only to be expected given the common foundation on which they have been developed. The provider mix varies considerably, however, from country to country (see Table 7.1, below).

Table 7.1
Health Care in Commonwealth Caribbean Countries

	Number of Physicians (Circa 1988)	Physician: Population Ratio	Hospital Beds (1987)	Beds per 1,000 (1987)
Antigua & Barbuda	32	1:2468	373	4.5
Bahamas	187	1:1353	1,050	4.2
Barbados	225	1:1129	2,111	8.2
Belize	85	1:2115	186	1.1
British Virgin Islands	12	1:1232	50	3.8
Cayman Islands	35	1:737	64	3
Dominica	25	1:3120	322	4.1
Grenada	51	1:2157	676	6.9
Jamaica	330	1:7272	5,745	2.4
Montserrat	7	1:1750	67	5.6
St. Christopher - Nevis	25	1:1880	266	5.5
St. Lucia	68	1:2088	539	4.1
St. Vincent & the Grenadines	40	1:2825	524	4.9
Trinidad & Tobago	1213	1:989	4,613	3.8

Table 7.1

Health Care in Commonwealth Caribbean Countries

	Number of Physicians (Circa 1988)	Physician: Population Ratio	Hospital Beds (1987)	Beds per 1,000 (1987)
TOTAL	2335	1:2103		
Anguilla	6	1:1167	26	3.7
Turks & Caicos	5	1:2470	36	4.5
Bermuda	57	1:1063	490	8.6
TOTAL	2,403	1:2076		
Guyana	125	1:6000	2,204	2.2

PAHO/WHO 1992.

Financing Mechanisms. In all the countries, with the possible exception of Bermuda, by far the major share of health care costs (at the primary, secondary, and, often, tertiary levels) are met by the government from general taxation. Conceived of originally as "public assistance" for the poor, "free" medical care has been extended, in fact, to all but a privileged few who can afford to consult private physicians and use private hospitals or private wards. The degree of "freedom" of access to public health services is even further extended in some countries, such as Montserrat.

Extent and impact of the AIDS epidemic in the Caribbean. AIDS has compounded the problems of the subregion. Since the first report by Jamaica in 1982, all countries have recorded at least one case. Five countries--Barbados, the Bahamas, Guyana, Jamaica, and Trinidad & Tobago--account for more than 80 percent of the more than two thousand cases reported thus far. One report notes:

Data from a few countries suggest that AIDS has become a leading cause of death among young adults, having surpassed traffic injuries. Additionally, in some instances, the health care delivery systems are beginning to feel the impact of the epidemic. . . . To meet the challenge of AIDS and HIV infection a sustained and increased prevention and mobilization of resources should become a priority at national and regional levels. (CAREC/PAHO 1991, 1-2, 8-9).

The primary health care approach and local health systems development. Given the impact of structural adjustment policies on the population's health status, continuing financial stringencies with hardly an end in sight, the impact of new problems such as AIDS, and the resurgence of old ailments such as malaria in Belize and Guyana, what seems to be called into question is the viability of current systemic models for health care delivery. Ever since Alma Ata in 1978, formal commitment to primary health care as the "key" to achievement of Health for All has been universal among Commonwealth Caribbean governments, health ministries, most physicians, and other health professionals. Often, however, it has been limited in concept to "first-level" care, with less-than-significant shift of resources away from the secondary level in any of the countries. This has often been justified by the "role of the hospital" in the provision of "primary care" at outpatient and casualty departments.

HISTORICAL BACKGROUND

Medical education within the context of the University College of the West Indies is a British legacy in the Commonwealth Caribbean. Public administration and health care systems serve as further examples of British influence. Many basic features of form and function of this colonial inheritance endure, as do value systems and patterns of thought and behavior. Even after three decades of independence in the larger states, there are unresolved problems of how best to adapt or radically change models of political, administrative, and social organization inherited from colonial days. In these systems, the Director of Medical Services was a professional specialist, a physician who contributed to policy and program formulation and exercised managerial authority for all public hospitals and health services.

University education in the subregion. University education in the English-speaking Caribbean is of respectable antiquity and is primarily a legacy of Empire. A college for the training of clerics and classicists was set up in Barbados under the tutelage of Durham University in 1715, with resources made available under the will of a man named Codrington, a benefactor of All Souls College, Oxford. Up to the outbreak of World War II, Caribbean aspirants to a university education in subject areas other than theology, the classics, and agriculture took advantage of the "external degree" system of London University, using courses offered at a premium by correspondence colleges in the United Kingdom.

One unsuccessful attempt to create a university in the Caribbean was made in Jamaica in 1929-1930, but it was not until the early 1940s that the idea surfaced again, doing so in at least three of the West Indian colonies. During 1943, the Legislative Council of Jamaica passed a resolution in favor of a university. In Barbados, a committee was appointed to consider broadening the curriculum of Codrington College. In British Guiana (now Guyana), the "University of London British Guiana Association" dispatched a memorandum to the Colonial Office advocating establishment of a facility for higher education in the West Indies. This was also the recommendation of the Asquith Commission, appointed by the British government in the same year.

Teaching began on the Mona campus of the University College of the West Indies (UWI) in Jamaica in October 1948, with the admission of 33 students (including 10 women) to the UCWI Faculty of Medicine. The UCWI was to remain in a special relationship with the University of London until 1962, when its independence was acknowledged in a new Royal Charter.

ROLE OF NATIONAL POLICY IN SHAPING MEDICAL EDUCATION

There is no explicit policy articulated either nationally by any of the Commonwealth (English-speaking) Caribbean governments which contribute to the Faculty of Medical Sciences of the University of the West Indies, or subregionally, by the Caribbean Community Secretariat (CARIBSEC).

Nevertheless, statements have been made from time to time by government ministers and by CARIBSEC expressing the need for medical education to be "relevant" to the priority needs of the health services. This is perhaps most frequently stated by the government of Guyana in relation to its relatively recent (1985) medical education program, which is allegedly "community-oriented" and "problem-based."

ADMISSION

Candidates who wish to begin the degree course must fulfill the university's general requirements for matriculation and, in addition, the specific requirements of the Faculty of Medicine. These requirements may be satisfied by an acceptable standard of performance in chemistry, biology/zoology, and physics in the General Certificate of Education (GCE) Advanced (A) level examination. Students take the GCE after at least seven years of secondary schooling, the last two of which are spent studying a group of three or four subjects in sciences, languages, and/or arts (This is roughly equivalent to two years of U.S. higher education.) Alternatively, applicants may substitute acceptable performance in preliminary and introductory examinations in the Faculty of Natural Sciences, UWI; or in alternative university examinations recognized by the UWI matriculation board.

Because of the special relationship between UCWI and London University, UCWI employed the latter's admission policies and requirements until 1962. After independence in that year, UCWI became more liberal in its admissions policy, which now provides an option for those matriculating at a lower level than either the GCE (Advanced) or its Caribbean equivalent (the Caribbean Examinations Council, CEC, grades I and II General Proficiency). Students can still pursue a degree program but must spend at least four years (one year longer) at UWI (University of the West Indies 1989-90).

Between 1948 and 1953, on average, no more than a third of qualified applicants were admitted to universities each year. Enrollment growth continued to be relatively slow, so that by 1960 more than 3,000 students overflowed into overseas universities. In 1988, the total student body on all three campuses: Jamaica, Trinidad, and Barbados, was about twelve thousand (Parker 1971; Lewis 1960; Mcintyre 1988).

Applicants are accepted more or less in relation to demand which, especially during the early years of the UCWI, came much less from the small islands of the Eastern Caribbean (the Leewards and Windwards). Deficiencies in secondary schooling in those countries were reflected in much smaller numbers of applicants who could satisfy the stringent matriculation requirements of London, especially for admission to the Faculties of Medicine and Natural Sciences. Over more than forty years since the University's inception, the situation has improved considerably, so that by academic year 1988-1989, about five percent of the newly admitted students were from noncampus territories. Of this number, 13 percent gained admission to medical school.

Since admission to medical schools is very competitive, the majority of medical students are high achievers, at least academically. Therefore, the dropout rate is minuscule (not more than 5 percent) and the majority of all admitted students complete the program and obtain their degrees. Dropout cases usually take place after Stage I (preclinical), and virtually all students who make it through the clinical rotations eventually graduate. Tables 7.2 (p. 99) and 7.3 (p. 100) present UCWI student and faculty demographic information.

CURRICULAR STRUCTURE AND INNOVATION

From its inception, and throughout its 14-year period of tutelage, the curriculum of the London medical schools was replicated by the UCWI Faculty of Medicine. With very minor modifications, it included a solid and discrete preclinical foundation in the basic medical sciences over an 18-month period, as a preparation for three clinical years in which bedside teaching in a hospital was emphasized through a series of clinical clerkships. Students were evaluated at intermediate and final stages, not only by their teachers at the University College, but also by "external" examiners appointed by the University of London, who recommended the award of London Bachelor of Medicine, Bachelor of Surgery (MBBS) degrees to successful candidates. In so doing, the University of London could assure the British General Medical Council (GMC) that medical graduates of the UCWI had attained a standard equivalent to that of London graduates and could safely be accorded GMC recognition for practice in the United Kingdom, as well as in the West Indies. Periodic visitations were made by GMC representatives to verify that "standards" were being maintained and to approve hospitals in which graduates could intern prior to registration. Reciprocal arrangements for automatic registration in the Caribbean of graduates of UK medical schools were also assured.

The teaching of preventive medicine. Coincidentally, the UCWI Faculty of Medicine was established during the very period in which the reorganization of medical education was enjoying much attention in Europe, the USA and some Latin American countries. Conferences in Colorado Springs, USA; in Nancy, France (1952); the World Conference on Medical Education in London (1953); and seminars in Chile (1955) and Mexico (1956) all advocated the introduction of preventive medicine into the medical curriculum.

These discussions were echoed in the Caribbean and in the very year (1954) in which the first graduates emerged, the dean of the UCWI Faculty of Medicine sought support from the Rockefeller Foundation for the creation of a subdepartment of Social and Preventive Medicine. The Rockefeller Foundation responded with a five-year grant for the subdepartment Social and Preventive

Medicine (S&PM) which subsequently achieved full departmental status. Starting initially with a five-week clerkship in the second clinical year, the department currently offers an introductory preclinical course in addition to courses and seminars in every clinical year.

Students' performance in these courses counts in the final assessment for the degree. In many Commonwealth Caribbean countries, new medical graduates must complete a community health internship of at least six-months' duration, in addition to the 18 months spent in the traditional medical, surgical, obstetrics/gynecology, and pediatrics specialties, to be registered as a licensed physician. Community health internships may include, in addition to supervised attachments to health centers, supervised primary care responsibilities in casualty/emergency care and outpatient/ambulatory care departments. The Department of Social and Preventive Medicine is also acknowledged for the development of multidisciplinary graduate diploma programs in health education, health management and public health.

During the 1960s and 1970s, community clinics were established in selected localities in Jamaica (Hermitage, August Town and, Ellerslie) to provide medical students with a taste of health problems in real-life community situations away from the hospital, in which problems could be addressed by promotive and preventive measures and first-level primary care. The Department of Social and Preventive Medicine undertook a number of projects in the Eastern Caribbean islands to collect data on community health status, monitor infectious diseases and conduct epidemiological studies. The department's continuing and, as yet, unresolved problems are how to diffuse its very special concerns about epidemiology, health promotion, disease prevention, and primary health care throughout the faculty, and how to significantly influence teaching and research.

The Eastern Caribbean Medical Scheme (ECMS). After 1962, more use began to be made of government hospitals throughout Jamaica for medical teaching. This had been foreshadowed to a limited extent in the years prior to the opening of the 210-bed University (College) Hospital (UWIH) in 1952, when training in the specialties of ophthalmology, ENT, hematology, and radiology was based at the Kingston Public Hospital, some five miles away from Mona. At that time, however, the use for teaching purposes of any but the university hospital was considered both wearisome and undesirable, since the "proper separation" between "mere practitioners" and academic medical staff could not be rigorously maintained.

Pressure from regional governments to increase the annual medical student intake from 30 to 100 made it essential, however, to not only seriously consider government hospitals in Jamaica for clinical teaching, but to consider as well the newly built Queen Elizabeth Hospital (QEH) in Barbados and the Port-of-Spain General Hospital (POS) in Trinidad. In 1967, an innovative but controversial scheme was introduced under which final-year medical students could transfer to the QEH or POS to undertake 12 "senior clerkships" in medicine, surgery, and obstetrics/gynecology as well as a 12-week elective. Students who opted for either alternative returned to Mona some six weeks before their final examinations.

Introduction of the ECMS required some minor modifications to the original London curriculum: introductory courses in psychology, statistics and sociology during the last term of the five-term preclinical phase, compression of most of pathology and microbiology in the first clinical year, and a series of five- and ten-week clerkships during the second clinical year as an "introduction" to "senior" rotations in the final year--completed either at Mona, QEH or POS.

The truly innovative aspect of ECMS, however, was that despite overall university and faculty governance from Mona, a community of clinical teachers and practitioners was constituted. They included four university-appointed staff (an internist, a surgeon, an obstetrician/gynecologist, and a pathologist), complemented by a far larger number of government-appointed consultant specialists (as "associate lecturers") in all the other disciplines including pediatrics, radiology, ophthalmology, ENT, anesthesia, and psychiatry. Not only did this arrangement have a positive affect on the quality and standards of patient care, it also contributed to continuous upgrading of the skills and knowledge of physicians, nurses, and other health personnel, and above all, provided class learning experiences for senior medical students. Its results were even more extensive, forging, as it did, very strong linkages between faculty and ministry and providing the latter with high-quality, additional human resources both for advice on services organization and in the actual delivery of medical services. For the small Eastern Caribbean islands, it also meant that new referral centers had been initiated, which were located closer than the Mona facility.

The ECMS also called into serious question what had hitherto been considered essential: the exclusive reliance on full-time university faculty for clinical teaching/learning in a teaching hospital built for that purpose at a single location in the Caribbean.

Nine years after the start of the ECMS, in 1976, the faculty agreed to extend clinical teaching in both Barbados and Trinidad to the last two clinical years of the MBBS program (only the first clinical year having to be done at Mona). By the end of 1978, the first graduates completed their training under this new arrangement. In Barbados, there was a quite unexpected outcome: students' objective evaluations of the clerkships and lecturers offered . . . during academic year 1976-77

. . . .included comments on each clerkship and an assessment of each lecturer based on a four-dimensional profile - punctuality, content, organization and delivery of lectures. Although some staff were rated "poor" on one or more dimension, there was clearly a high regard for overall staff competence. On the other hand, there was less satisfaction in the way in which clerkships had been organized. (Walrond and Drayton 1984, pp. 3-7)

Concerns about relevance: medical education for what and for whom? As early as 1969 (some seven years after the UWI achieved its independence), the former dean of the Medical Faculty, Ken (later Sir Kenneth) Stuart, wrote of the "challenge . . . . to develop a medical school to meet broad regional needs and simultaneously to assist individual territories whose health needs may vary from those of a small village in Montserrat to a large modern city like Kingston or Port-of-Spain" (Stewart 1970a). In 1971, a committee appointed by the Inter-American Development Bank to study the feasibility of expanding or duplicating the UWI medical school was even more forthright:

The present curriculum of the Medical Faculty is "classical"--It is too detailed, intensive, rigid with little room for electives . . . Bearing in mind the health needs of the community in which it is hoped they will practice medicine, there is perhaps less need for medical undergraduates at UWI to understand the detailed scientific basis of medicine, whereas there is a greater need for them to appreciate the problems of the community . . . . More time should be allotted to the teaching of Pediatrics, Social & Preventive medicine, the study of normal and abnormal human behavior, and Community medicine. There is a need to place more emphasis on problems of health and disease that are of particular importance to the West Indies. (University of the West Indies 1971, pp. 12-20)

It was, however, in the mid-1970s that concerns about the relevance of the UWI medical curriculum began to be voiced at the level of the Caribbean Health Ministers Conference and its Secretariat.

The "new" UWI medical curriculum (October 1978). To ensure greater relevance of the curriculum to the health and medical problems of the Caribbean, it was thought desirable to introduce a number of changes: (1) the total duration of the program was reduced from four and a half to four years; (2) the postgraduate internship was increased from one to two years; (3) instead of the customary separation of preclinical and clinical instruction, the two were to be integrated; (4) community health was added to the traditional preclinical subjects of anatomy, physiology, and biochemistry, and students were required to complete all four subjects satisfactorily, in addition to "Stage 1" examinations, after only four terms (15 months) of study instead of five; (5) Community health/community medicine would be taught and examined in every year of the curriculum; and (6) a much greater emphasis was placed on self-instructional techniques.

Medical education at Mount Hope, Trinidad. In 1976, the UWI council agreed to the establishment of a second facility for medical education at Mount Hope, Trinidad, which was completed in 1985 and is now known as the Eric Williams Medical Sciences Complex. The educational objectives of this medical school are: (1) to produce graduates whose professional and academic standards will be of a level comparable to that of colleagues in the more developed countries and who can function efficiently in any environment in which they may work; (2) to provide the graduate with a strong grounding in the field of community health so the physician may play an active part in the control and prevention of disease and the promotion of health. The duration of the medical program is four and a-half years in addition to an internship of one and a-half years.

The curriculum strategy for all three programs (medical, dental and veterinary medicine) emphasizes integration of preclinical and clinical information. Although during Phase 1, the basic sciences of anatomy, physiology, biochemistry and pharmacology are emphasized, some clinical exposure does occur. Phase 2, the two-year second phase on the other hand, gives increasing emphasis to clinical training through a series of rotating clerkships. The program also emphasizes problem-based learning (PBL); self-directed learning using staff-prepared teaching materials, audiovisual aids, and similar tools; small-group teaching/learning experiences; and a triprofessional approach to classroom and laboratory teaching/learning. Thus, basic (preclinical) science training is the same in year one for medical, dental and veterinary students and is identical for medicine and dentistry during year two.

By the time the complex was eventually completed in 1985, petrodollar surpluses had disappeared and it was necessary to phase in the programs over an extended period. The 110-bed maternity hospital had been receiving patients for five years and more, but as of April 1992, the adult and children's hospitals had not been commissioned. The teaching program was initiated in October 1989, with an initial intake of 99 preclinical students, 71 of whom were admitted to the medical program. In 1990, the intake was 76 and in 1991, a total of 93. When fully operational, the proposed annual pre-clinical student intake will be 150 (80 medical, 35 dental, and 35 veterinary), about two-thirds of whom will come from Trinidad and other contributing territories of the Caribbean.

In his National Health Insurance study published prior to the start of the Mount Hope medical education program, Nicholls alluded to the potential of a "doctor explosion" in Trinidad and Tobago:

In 1984 a PAHO Health situation analysis of the country suggested that there would be a deficiency of 175 new physicians for the country as a whole in 1985. Since that time, 115 new doctors have been admitted to practice. With a minimum of six years for training a general practitioner (and an average of ten years for most of the specialties), it could be that by the time the [Mt. Hope] medical school produces its first practicing physician, the country would already be flooded with doctors. (Nicholls 1986, 45-46)

An equally cogent critique was offered by James-Bryan in an "Overview of the Health Manpower Situation in Trinidad and Tobago," presented in August 1989 to a Health Manpower Development Workshop organized by the Ministry of Health. The paper identified the issue of "preventive health care vs. curative health care" as one of five "core challenges for both the health care system and health manpower development":

While Trinidad and Tobago is theoretically committed to the primary health care approach as the key to achieving the goal of health for all by the year 2000, its practical applications say otherwise . . . Linked directly to the absence of a National Health policy is the failure or neglect to implement the stated commitment to PHC. This failure is currently being highlighted by the opening of the Eric Williams Mt. Hope Medical Complex (James-Bryan 1990, 4, 16).

Here it is relevant to note that one year earlier, in August 1988, the Trinidad and Tobago dollar (TT$) had been devalued by 15 percent; and government announced a reduction of the public service wage bill for the remainder of 1988 of about 70 million TT$. The health budget for that year was nearly 300 million TT$ less than in 1987, 74 percent of which was allocated toward personal compensations, salaries, and wages.

From 1954 to 1989, the UWI Faculty of Medical Sciences produced about twenty-five hundred physicians, even though some 40 percent of them (at a conservative estimate) emigrated to the "greener pastures" of the developed world, chiefly the US and Canada.

University of Guyana. The University of Guyana was established in 1963 with 164 students. Prior to that date, Guyana had been a contributing territory in the regional University of The West Indies. Initially, only undergraduate programs in the arts and sciences were offered, but in 1981, a full-fledged Faculty of Health Sciences was established, which by 1990 was offering four basic diploma programs, two postbasic multidisciplinary certificate programs for the preparation of teachers of the health sciences and health services managers; and an innovative community-oriented medical education program in which problem-based learning is employed.

The UG Medical Education Program. At the initiative of the Ministry of Health, the Medical Education Program of the Faculty of Health Sciences was established in October 1985. It is part of an international collaborative "network" of about one hundred seventy medical schools and other institutions that seek to make health sciences education much more relevant to the health needs of populations and that emphasize the primary health care approach to health development.

The curriculum was developed in Guyana with strong international support during a series of planning workshops, and after visits by a national team to institutions in the "network" in Canada, the US, and Mexico. What is intended is that medical students will learn through a process of understanding and resolving problems in a balanced diversity of settings, including community agencies, health centers, and clinics, as well as in hospitals.

Thirteen students had completed all academic requirements including the internship, of the six-year program in April 1992 and were eligible for registration by the Medical Council of Guyana. Given the deliberate focus on community medicine, it is interesting that only two of this first group of graduates indicated a real preference for community medicine, while all the others expressed a desire to go on to residency training in a clinical specialty.

From a preliminary analysis, it would appear that students with a strong academic background (most of whom were under age 24) performed better, but not markedly so, than those with previous health professional training (most of whom were aged 25 to 39). Students with a nursing or "medex" background performed slightly better than health sciences diploma graduates.

Through a number of small collaborative projects with the University of Texas Medical Branch (UTMB), and with support from the Health Foundation of New York, efforts are being made to refurbish at least two health centers to make them adequate for both service and training, to promote dialogue among medical teachers and practitioners through seminars and workshops about the meaning of community-oriented training and PBL methodology, and to ensure access to medical information utilizing advanced computer technology and databases.

The Offshore Medical School Phenomenon

During the 1970s, groups of United States entrepreneurs established "offshore" medical schools in a number of Caribbean island nations (in Dominica, Grenada, St. Lucia, St. Vincent, Montserrat, and Antigua) to cater primarily to those US students who could not secure admission to US medical schools. At that time and perhaps to a lesser extent today, there were far more applicants (some of them with high MCAT scores) than available places.

The oldest of these institutions is the St. George's University School of Medicine, established in 1976 by an Act of the Grenada House of Representatives; its affiliate, the Kingston Medical College in St. Vincent, was started in 1978. The first entering class, in January 1977, completed the nine-semester curriculum and was awarded the MD degree; by May 1981, a total of 127 graduates had started residency programs in the US. By 1992, more than seventeen hundred students had graduated, more than one-thousand had transferred to 93 US schools, and St. George's could boast that 99.6 percent of eligible graduates obtain ACGME -approved residencies. Affiliations have also been approved for St. George's students in New York, New Jersey, Connecticut, and Michigan, and also in Great Britain.

Of particular interest to this study were the discussions held in 1975 between some representatives of the government of Barbados and the International Medical Foundation (IMF) of Chicago, which proposed the establishment of a medical school in that island on the site of Codrington College. The IMF suggested the Codrington site because "it already possesses the mandate for such a facility and is willing to donate the land necessary for construction of a teaching hospital with 500 beds." In its preliminary report, the IMF stressed that "during the second [clinical year], the student's experience would differ dramatically from [the first]. In a system of clinical outposts . . . . the student would be introduced to the administering of health care under the more realistic conditions he would be likely to encounter in rural, underdeveloped and economically disadvantaged areas" (International Medical Foundation. 1975a, 1975b).

Despite strong reservations from both the UWI and PAHO, the IMF proposal did find favor for a while with the then Minister of Health, and it was only with the defeat of his party in the 1976 elections that it was finally aborted.

Most governments in the subregion were susceptible, nevertheless, to the entreaties of "offshore operators," and at one time St. Lucia was host to three such schools. This was only to be expected, given the financial compensation that was offered, as well as the small number of scholarships made available by the schools to Caribbean nationals. Some physicians, including UWI graduates, were by no means critical of these commercial ventures and accepted part-time faculty appointments. What the establishment of offshore medical schools also did was to kindle a deep awareness among governments and nationals of Eastern Caribbean island states of the national potential for medical training that existed in their hospitals and health clinics. Although constantly used, not only by the offshore schools but also by medical students from the UK, US, and Canada for elective externships, these resources still had not been tapped by the UWI. Such an awareness was but one aspect of a more general concern among Eastern Caribbean countries that they were being deprived of a fair measure of services and resources from the regional university. Under new arrangements agreed to in 1983, Offices of University Services (OUS) have been created at Mona and Cave Hill, Barbados, to ensure an adequate outreach to noncampus territories. In

1992, the OUS at Barbados was directed by a professor of the UWI Medical Faculty, himself a national of Dominica.

Degree Requirements

The course for the MBBS degree lasts a minimum of four and a half years and consists of two stages. The degree is awarded at the pass level or with honors following the satisfactory completion of the course. A student who has completed a course and passed an examination from either the local or another recognized university in a subject that forms a part or the whole of an analogous subject in the MBBS degree course may apply for exemption through the head of the department. The department head examines the syllabus, nature, and duration of the course, the student's grades in examinations in the course, the time that has elapsed since it was completed, and, in particular, whether it is a comparable subject, in whole or in part, to that offered in the university.

GRADUATE MEDICAL EDUCATION

Since the early 1970s, residency training in the major specialties for UWI postgraduate qualifications has been an alternative to self-preparation for higher diplomas of the Royal Colleges of London and Edinburgh. This did little to reduce the flow, and with the onset of the economic crisis, the brain drain of physicians with highly marketable and costly skills has persisted at an ever-increasing rate.

On a more positive note, mention must be made of the postgraduate training programs in Family Medicine inaugurated in Barbados through the establishment of a joint UWI-government general practice unit in a major public sector polyclinic. Trainees hold Ministry of Health appointments, and a staff member of the Medical Sciences Faculty directs training and offers service. A training program in Emergency Medicine has been similarly organized. There have also been other forays from time to time in the direction of Faculty-Ministry cooperation, such as the initiation in 1981 of a training program in Jamaica for ambulance personnel.

LICENSURE

All UWI medical graduates, after completion of a one-or two-year internship, are automatically entitled to full registration and licensure in all Commonwealth Caribbean countries. Because of the historical relationship between the Caribbean countries and Great Britain, similar privileges are accorded to all British-qualified medical graduates. Other foreign medical graduates may seek registration but must satisfy the local medical council of each of the Caribbean countries by passing certain tests and/or examinations to demonstrate competency and ensure safe practice.

Cross Licensing of Physicians

Under a reciprocal agreement, a license is valid throughout the British Commonwealth countries. Graduates of the UWI are eligible for automatic registration by the United Kingdom General Medical Council. The same holds true for all medical schools established under the British tutelage prior to and during the 1940s and 1950s. Exceptions apply to graduates from some medical schools in India. However, with the impending final agreement on establishment of the European Economic Community (EEC), the UK General Medical Council will no longer accord automatic registration to medical graduates of the UWI nor of any other Commonwealth medical school. Each case will be judged on its own merit.

Graduates of the offshore medical schools are not automatically eligible to practice within the Commonwealth Caribbean, except in Grenada. However, they may apply for registration as other foreign medical graduates.

CONTINUING MEDICAL EDUCATION

Since there is no process of annual or periodic re-registration, continuing medical education (CME) is not mandatory. Nevertheless, some of the leaders of Caribbean Medical Associations are intensely interested and organize substantial episodic courses on a variety of themes and topics. Much of this effort is supported by the PAHO/WHO, pharmaceutical companies, and the UWI Faculty of Medical Sciences.

Guyana and several other Caribbean countries are planning to start some organized continuing medical education programs.

ROLE OF RESEARCH IN MEDICAL EDUCATION

Until quite recently, "medical" research was almost exclusively biomedical/clinical. To the extent that much of it has been conducted under the aegis of the Commonwealth Caribbean Medical Research Council (CCMRC), led by the UWI Medical Faculty, it has been "fed back" in the medical education process and has influenced medical teaching and learning.

There is currently a deliberate attempt to promote health services research under CCMRC leadership, linked with day-to-day operational problems experienced in Ministries of Health of UWI-contributing territories.

GOVERNMENT/PRIVATE SECTOR INVOLVEMENT

The private sector is only marginally involved with medical education in the English-speaking Caribbean. Its role has been limited to sponsorship by pharmaceutical companies or agencies of continuing education seminars and workshops and to faculty travel across the sub-region.

INTERNATIONAL LINKAGES AND COLLABORATION

Both bilateral and multilateral linkages have been forged between the Faculty of Medical Sciences of the University of the West Indies and agencies in the US, Canada and the UK. Similarly, the Faculty of Health Sciences of the University of Guyana has entered into formal collaborative agreements with universities and other educational institutions in Brazil, the US, Canada, and the UK.

Of prime importance is international cooperation with PAHO/WHO and its specific program Caribbean Cooperation of Health (CCH), in the priority area of human resources development.

ISSUES AND TRENDS

Increasing economic pressures will almost certainly accelerate demands for policy reviews of both the dominant public assistance model for health care systems in the Caribbean and the existing arrangements for the development of human resources for health. In Jamaica, US private health insurance companies are making some headway; in the Bahamas, alternative financing mechanisms have been proposed; and in Trinidad and Tobago, the feasibility of national health insurance and cost-recovery mechanisms have been proposed and the government has, from time to time, been urged to divest itself of responsibility for all secondary care services and to adopt the Bermuda system: a hospital subsidized by government, operated as a private facility but managed by a government appointed board, with the Ministry of Health responsible only for health promotion and disease prevention programs.

The problem which will confront the political directorate is how to ensure that any changes that are introduced are in harmony with the increasingly popular demands for social justice and equity.

Economic and cost considerations will also dictate the resolution of at least three fundamental problems of human resources development for health: (1) determining, within available national and regional resources the most economical combination of skills that can, efficiently, effectively, and with safety, provide for the delivery of services in health systems based on the primary health care approach; (2) selecting the most appropriate strategies and mechanisms for relevant preparation, within each country and regionally, of the required manpower mix; and (3) ascertaining how trained health staff can be most effectively and efficiently utilized in the delivery of services and in the promotion of the primary health care approach.

Despite its splendid isolation, these past forty years, from the multiplicity of problems with which ministries of health have been confronted, we would like to hope that the UWI Faculty of Medical Sciences is either already prepared technically and socially or will seek to prepare itself, as will its much younger Guyanese counterpart, to assist the Caribbean Community Secretariat and the

Caribbean and Guyanese governments in resolving at least those three issues. Indeed, the Faculty's survival and its harmonious growth and development in the twenty-first century will depend on the extent to which tensions within its own internal environment can be reduced and the Faculty's external relationships improved, so as to permit: (1) the curriculum content of medical and other health sciences programs to reflect national and regional health priorities and the availability of affordable resources; (2) cooperation among the university and all relevant government and private sectors agencies in policy and program planning, implementation, and evaluation; (3) coordination of the education and training of all health workers, including physicians; increased opportunities for multidisciplinary approaches to teaching and learning, research, and service, and the development of health teams through team project work.

Over and above such considerations, other prospects for change in the twenty-first century will almost certainly include a further decentralization of health services and of the medical and health sciences education process, both regionally and within each of the larger national units. This would ensure concomitant increases in the number and range of settings and situations from which learning experiences might be derived, and perhaps ultimately, the preparation of generations of personnel with a judicious blend of capabilities for health promotion, disease prevention, and curative service.

REFERENCES

Bourne, C. 1989. Economic crisis in the Commonwealth Caribbean and its implications for the social services. In PAHO, ed., *Primary health care and local health systems in the Caribbean*, pp. 91-96. Proceedings of the workshop on primary health care and local health systems. Tobago November 7-11, 1988.

Bowers, J.Z. 1970. *Medical schools for the modern world: Report of a Macy Conference.* Josiah Macy, Jr. Foundation. Baltimore: Johns Hopkins University Press.

Boyd, P. 1975. The medical profession and the health of the people of the Caribbean. Paper presented at the International Medical Convention of the Trinidad & Tobago Medical Association, Tobago.

CAREC/Pan American Health Organization. 1991. *Statistical overview of HIV/AIDS in English-speaking Caribbean countries and Suriname, 1982-1990.* November. Cited as CAREC/PAHO.

Drayton, H.A. 1977. Problems of medical education in a changing Caribbean. Paper prepared for First Meeting of the UWI -CARICOM Joint Committee on Medical Education, February 4-5, Jamaica.

---------. 1969. The University of Guyana: A people's act of faith. *Guyana Graphic*, 24 April.

James-Bryan, M. 1990. Overview of the health manpower situation in Trinidad & Tobago. Paper prepared for the Health Manpower Development Workshop, August 4-5 at the Eric Williams Medical Sciences Complex, Mt. Hope, Trinidad.

Kessel, W.I.N., H.L. Duthie, and A.D.M. Greenfield. 1984. *Report on a visitation to the Medical School of the University of West Indies, 14 to 25 Nov 1983.* Washington, DC: PAHO, p. 84.

Khan, J. 1982. *Public management: The Eastern Caribbean experience.* Leiden, Netherlands: Royal Institute of Linguistics and Anthropology, Dept. of Caribbean Studies.

Le Franc, E.R.M. 1989. *Structural adjustment and the health care systems in the Caribbean region: An overview.* PAHO/WHO/CARICOM Secretariat (April).

Lewis, W.A. 1960. Merger of the Imperial College of Tropical Agriculture with the University College of the West Indies. An address in Port-of-Spain, Trinidad, 12 October. Mimeo.

Mcintyre, A. 1988. The West Indian university revisited. Sixth Eric Williams Memorial Lecture, 18 June. Central Bank of Trinidad & Tobago. Mimeo.

Nicholls, K.H. 1986. To probe the feasibility of a national health insurance scheme for Trinidad & Tobago. Report to PAHO on Project AM/ICP/O1O/P1/86-87/040. August-November, pp. 45-46.

Pan American Health Organization/World Health Organization. 1992. *Strengthening the implementation of local health systems: The English-speaking Caribbean countries, assessment for change.* Ed. by J. M. Paganini, M. Kisil, H. Dyer, and H.M. Novaes. HSD/SILOS-16:84. Washington, DC: PAHO/WHO. Cited as PAHO/WHO.

----------. 1990. *Health conditions in the Americas.* vols. 1 and 2. Sci. Pub. 524. Washington, DC: PAHO/WHO.

----------. 1984. *Integration of services and education,* p. 84. IRMD/07/AMRO. Washington, DC.

Parker, P.C. 1971. Change and challenge in Caribbean higher education: The development of the University of the West Indies and the University of Puerto Rico. Ph.D. diss., Florida State University.

Proceedings of the 34th Scientific Meeting of the Commonwealth Caribbean Medical Research Council. 1989. Plymouth, Montserrat, April 19-22. In *WI Med. J* 38 (Suppl 1):1-84.

International Medical Foundation. 1975a. Report on the establishment of a medical school in Barbados: Submitted to the Government of Barbados. Mimeo, p. 6. Preliminary report: February 2, 1975.

----------. 1975b. Report on the establishment of a medical school in Barbados: Submitted to the Government of Barbados. Mimeo, p. 2. Second Report: August 25, 1975.

Sherlock, P.M. and Nettleford, R.M. 1990. *The University of The West Indies: A Caribbean response to the challenge of change.* London and Basingstoke: MacMillan Caribbean.

Standard, K.L. 1979. The role of the University of The West Indies in promoting regional health services. In PAHO, ed. *Four decades of advances in health in the Commonwealth Caribbean,* pp. 133-143 .Sci. Pub No. 383. Washington, DC: PAHO/WHO.

Stewart, D.B. 1970. Faculty of Medicine, University of The West Indies, Jamaica. In Bowers (1970), pp. 31-47.

Tyler, R.L. 1971. The founding of The University of Guyana: A history of motives and reality in development planning. *Ball State University Forum* 12, (3):68-68. Muncie, IN: Ball State University.

University of The West Indies. Statistics 1988/89.

----------. Calendar, Volume 2, Academic Year 1989-90, pp. 148-160.

----------. 1970. St. Augustine Campus Development Plan 1990-2000 A.D. UPEC.P.70:89/90. 27 June.

----------. Faculty of Medical Sciences St. Augustine, Trinidad. 1988. Mimeo, undated.

University of the West Indies. Faculty of Medicine. 1992. Summary of recommendations. Medical Education Workshop, February 13 -16. Tobago.

---------. 1977. Report of the Faculty of Medicine Steering Committee on the Expansion of Medicine based at Mount Hope, Trinidad & Tobago. FMP86:76/77. June.

---------. 1971. Report of the Special Committee on the Feasibility of Expansion and/or Duplication of the Faculty of Medicine, pp. 12-20.

Walrond, E.R. 1988. The University of The West Indies at the Queen Elizabeth Hospital: The impact of the Faculty of Medical Sciences on health care in Barbados and the Eastern Caribbean. The Charles Duncan O'Neal Lecture. University of the West Indies.

Walrond, E.R., and K.B. Drayton. 1984. A pilot program in education theory and instructional techniques for medical teachers of The University of The West Indies (ECMS). *WI Med J* 33:3.

Table 7.2
Medical School Student Demographics, University of the West Indies, Faculty of Medical Sciences, Mona, Jamaica

Academic Year	Male Undergraduate Enrollment	Female Undergraduate Enrollment	Male Graduates	Female Graduates	Graduate Education: Male Residents	Graduate Education: Female Residents
1987-88	All campuses 71–1992 Class	All campuses* 47–1992 Class	30–Mona	20–Mona	N/A	N/A
1988-89	All campuses 81–1993 Class	All campuses 41–1993 class	38–Mona	24–Mona	72	58
1989-90	All campuses 59–1994 Class	All campuses 53–1994 Class	41–Mona	28–Mona	80	49
1990-91	All campuses 44–1995 Class	All campuses 69–1995 Class	58–Mona	42–Mona	71	15
1991-92	59	54	To sit * June 1992	To sit MBBS June 92	79	62

Residents not including DPH, MPH or Nutrition

1. At the end of the third year (first clinical year), students from Trinidad and Barbados return to their respective territories to complete the course, as for the years 1987-94. Therefore the figures for graduates represents those of students who complete the course at Mona.

2. The numbers that enroll for a particular year graduate five years layer.

Table 7.3

Faculty Demographics University of the West Indies, Faculty of Medical Sciences, Mona, Jamaica

Academic Year	Total Full-Time Male Faculty	Total Full-Time Female Faculty	Percent of Faculty with Degree from Foreign Medical Schools
1987-88	78	29	54* 53
1988-89	77	30	61* 46
1989-90	79	31	64* 46
1990-91	74	32	65* 41
1991-92	70	31	62* 39

* Staff with foreign and UWI degrees

8

Chile

PEDRO ROSSO
EUGENIO ARTEAGA

Over the last two decades, Chile's main health indicators--infant mortality, maternal mortality rate, and life expectancy--have improved to the extent that currently they are the best in South America and are comparable to those of Cuba and Costa Rica. The causes of these changes have not been clearly identified, but they are generally attributed to major societal events during the 1970s and 1980s and in the previous decade. These changes include a steep increase in basic education coverage, consistency in the government's health policies despite dramatic political changes, a steady yet modest increase in family income, and a significant improvement in the quality of housing and sanitation in low-income areas.

The improvements in Chilean health indicators and resulting demographic shifts have conferred on the country a mortality profile characteristic of the so-called epidemiological transition. Currently, cardiovascular diseases constitute the leading cause of death, followed by cancer--a profile similar to that of the industrialized countries. In contrast with the industrialized countries, however, morbidity caused by infectious diseases such as typhoid fever, hepatitis, tuberculosis and others, remains high.

OVERVIEW OF THE HEALTH CARE DELIVERY SYSTEM

Chilean interest in public health has a long tradition. It began during the 1920s as a component of government action on social problems. At that time, a progressive government passed some of the world's most advanced labor and social laws, including various health benefits for workers and their families. In the 1950s the organization of a national health service, inspired by the British and Israeli models, helped create a vast network of ambulatory clinics and small hospitals (less than 100 beds) in small towns. The national health service developed several preventive medicine programs designed to protect the health of mothers and infants.

The firm conviction that emphasis on preventive and ambulatory care was a better strategy than building new hospitals has been the guiding force of every national government during the last decades, whatever its political views. This intelligent use of the country's limited health budget deserves credit for some of its remarkable improvements in health indicators.

Chile has been slow to react to new health realities and resulting changes in medical care, especially the demand for more sophisticated hospital care. The situation climaxed in the mid-1980s when, despite press censorship, the disastrous conditions of the public hospitals became a national issue. The military government's policies in this area were strongly criticized, even by its own supporters. At that time the public hospital system operated only one computerized axial tomography (CAT) scanner for the entire country, while private hospitals had eight CAT scanners for a considerably smaller population. The situation has improved since but is still far from adequate.

Medical schools have been rather slow in adapting to the new situation. Specifically, their undergraduate programs have undergone relatively few changes over the last five decades. Outwardly, this conservative attitude seems to reflect a great respect for tradition, which is part of the national character. A closer look, however, reveals that Chilean medical education suffers from a lack of academic vitality (reflected in the lack of long-term planning), a meager, low-impact, scientific output; and a reluctance to change. Despite current and past limitations, Chilean medical schools have made a decisive contribution to the progress of Chilean health, and their medical graduates are considered among the best in Latin America.

HISTORICAL BACKGROUND

The first Chilean medical school was organized in 1833 at the Instituto Nacional in Santiago, the capital city. The Instituto was a state-owned school for higher education fashioned after the European models of the time. In 1842, when the Chilean government founded the Universidad de Chile as the first national public university, the preclinical and clinical chairs were moved from the Instituto Nacional to the university. Except for anatomy, however, the basic sciences chairs, including physiology and hygiene, remained at the Instituto; this separation lasted for more than five decades. Dr. Lorenzo Sazie, a Frenchman, trained in France and residing in Chile, was appointed dean. The new faculty included several French and German professors hired by the Chilean government.

In 1874, the government established a fellowship program to support the postdoctoral training of several promising young physicians, who at the time were in Europe at their own expense. After their return to Chile they were appointed chairpersons of key basic sciences and clinical departments, including histology, pathology, surgery, and ophthalmology. The government's fellowship program marked the beginning of a tradition, which remains active in all Chilean medical schools, of sending abroad (first to France and Germany and later to the US) the brightest young faculty members for training.

The 1920s was an important decade for Chilean medical education, since in 1924 and 1929 respectively, the Medical Schools of the Universidad de Concepción, in the Southern city of Concepción, and Universidad Católica, in Santiago, were created. The new medical schools shared the philosophy that scientific research and a full-time faculty, at least for the basic sciences, were essential for a high quality medical education. With the Universidad de Chile, they helped create the country's first generation of basic sciences researchers.

In the following decades, these young investigators benefited from the presence in Chile of a few distinguished European scientists, some of whom were hired by the universities, while others came to escape political or ethnic persecutions. They were attracted by the country's geographical remoteness and its reputation of stable institutions, including the universities. Immigrants from Italy, Spain, and Germany helped Chile become the first malaria-free country in South America, created the first strong university department of physiology, and were highly influential in the fields of neurology and pediatrics.

At present, the country has seven medical schools. The most recent has been in existence less than two years and belongs to a small private university (Universidad de Los Andes). The rest, except for the Universidad Católica, are primarily funded by the government.

Until 1981, the Medical School of the Universidad de Chile was the only school in the country legally authorized to grant the MD degree. Students from other medical schools had to pass a final examination given by the faculty of the Universidad de Chile to practice medicine. This policy compelled the rest of the medical schools to maintain programs of studies very similar to those of their *"primum inter pares"* colleague. Now, however, curricula have important differences in terms of content and organization.

The goal of Chilean undergraduate medical studies is to provide graduates with the knowledge and skills necessary to handle the most prevalent medical problems, including non-referable medical, surgical, and obstetric emergencies. This is particularly important in a few areas where quick referral to tertiary care hospitals is hampered by either distance or geographic isolation.

ADMISSION

Students enter medical school immediately after high school graduation. Selection is based on high school grades and the score obtained in a national Academic Aptitude Test. None of the medical schools use special entrance examinations such as MCAT or interviews, to select students. The lack of a more discriminating selection process helps to explain why 20 to 30 percent of those admitted to Chilean medical schools drop out during the first five years of the program, despite excellent high school records.

The number of medical school applicants greatly exceeds the vacancies offered. In 1992, medical schools (excluding the Universidad de Los Andes) received 5,158 applications for 502 openings, approximately a 10-to-1 ratio of applicants to places. Although the Association of Faculties of Medicine of Chile (ASOFAMECH) does not have a record of annual trends in the total number of medical school applicants, the separate records kept by the different institutions suggest that the demand is not declining.

A total of 540 students enrolls annually in Chilean medical schools. Despite a progressive deterioration of medical income over the last 20 years, medicine continues to be one of the most socially prestigious and, thus, more favored careers. However, some estimates suggest that the current output of Chilean medical graduates is exceeding the country's need for medical services. The experience of neighboring countries, such as Argentina, where an open-door policy of medical school admissions has increased the number of physicians to 2.9 per 1,000 people, is worrisome. In developing countries, an excess of physicians leads to medical unemployment and related problems, including substandard income, unethical medical practices, and the employment of physicians as nurses or paramedics. However, the Chilean medical schools have decided to maintain their present levels of enrollment because the estimates of a moderate "overproduction" of physicians are not conclusive. In addition, if the country maintains its present rate of economic growth (nearly 5 percent, on average, for the last eight years), new jobs should become available in both public and private hospitals. The progressive increase in life expectancy and the greater demand for medical services generated by the growing percentage of older people in the population will create a greater need for physicians in the future.

CURRICULAR STRUCTURE AND INNOVATION

Medical studies include an initial basic sciences and preclinical cycle which, on average, lasts five semesters, followed by a clinical cycle, which also lasts five semesters. This is followed by two years of a supervised clinical clerkship, called an internship, which includes rotations in internal medicine, surgery, pediatrics, and obstetrics and gynecology.

Teaching during the preclinical years includes the traditional lectures and laboratory activities given by various departments. During the clinical years, tutorial teaching is preferred and lectures are limited to the main integrated medicosurgical courses. Seminars are also organized to discuss specific problems from a basic, clinical, and epidemiological perspective. Problem-based tutorial teaching and seminars serve the same purposes as some of the most recent innovative programs adopted by US schools, the main difference being in the more passive student participation. Most of the clinical training occurs in public hospitals affiliated with medical schools, two of which have their own teaching hospitals that are used in conjunction with public hospitals.

The tutorial system employed during the clinical years requires a low student/faculty ratio; the Medical School of the Catholic University, for example, has a staff of 250 faculty for a total of 480 students and 160 residents.

Chilean medical school curricula can be criticized for their rigidity, unnecessarily high density of topics, emphasis on hospital care, and lack of stimuli for a more active participation of the students in the learning process.

GRADUATE MEDICAL EDUCATION

Most available residency programs are offered by the medical schools. Though they differ in length and characteristics according to specialty, they are fairly similar from one medical school to another. Accreditation of the residency programs is provided by an independent ad hoc commission whose chair is appointed by the deans.

Residents who have successfully completed their programs must pass a final examination given by the faculty of the same medical school to receive a specialty title. Residents in nonaccredited programs can also receive a specialty title if they pass an examination given by the National Commission.

Medical specialists are not required to be periodically recertified. For these reasons, the universities lack a formal continuing medical education program. However, many courses on various medical specialties are offered each year by the medical schools. Participation in these courses is certified by the organizers and is taken into consideration for jobs and academic appointments. Consequently, attendance at postgraduate medical courses is generally very good.

LICENSURE

The license to practice medicine is legally granted by the state,which has, in turn, delegated the right to the individual medical schools. Candidates for the MD degree must pass a final oral examination given by faculty of the same school. The possibility of establishing a national licensure examination has been a recurring topic for the last couple of decades, but the idea has never been implemented for a variety of funding and bureaucratic reasons.

Foreign-trained physicians who want to practice in Chile must have their certificates and diplomas legalized in their country of origin and accepted as valid by the University of Chile. The Medical School of this university may determine additional requirements (i.e., one year of clinical clerkship) depending on the type of medical studies.

Despite some of the institutional weaknesses described above, the average Chilean medical graduate performs surprisingly well when tested in the "real-life" situations of small rural hospitals or the crowded wards of urban hospitals. This favorable perception is supported by the excellent results obtained by Chileans in the ECFMG examination with respect to other countries. Although ECFMG applicants are a self-selected, highly motivated group, and, thus, a nonrepresentative one, they serve as a broad indicator of the quality of medical education in various countries. Another indicator of the quality of medical education is the performance of Chilean medical graduates in various training programs in both North America and Western Europe. With very few exceptions, these trainees are highly praised by their mentors and are often offered academic appointments. At present, the Chileans holding academic appointments in US and Canadian medical schools include associate deans, department and institute chairpersons, scores of full professors, and even more junior faculty. Despite its emphasis on tertiary care as a training model, another strength of Chilean medical education relative to US medical schools is its concern for public health issues and ambulatory care.

The fact that Chilean medical schools can graduate competent physicians despite their many limitations may appear a paradox. Furthermore, some critics may even be tempted to argue that perhaps US medical schools are unnecessarily costly and that they should do less research. Clearly, the comparison between Chilean and US schools suggests that it is possible, with relatively modest means, in terms of both faculty depth and facilities, to have a reasonably good medical undergraduate program. Apparently, the main ingredients to achieve that goal are to have bright students and dedicated teachers. Most of the clinical professors are professionally successful, and they devote to the medical school time and efforts that could be more profitably used in their own medical practice. In return, they receive a meager salary and the aura of prestige of their university affiliation. The dedication of these professors comes from a tradition dating from the turn of the century, when most of the teaching hospitals belonged to charitable institutions and the professors served as unpaid attendings. However, that type of medical school cannot support first-rate residency programs or postdoctoral programs, and little, if any, can be expected in terms of contributions to medical progress. Unfortunately, this is the sad reality of Chilean medical education; it also explains the constant exodus of junior faculty to the United States and other countries for training that is crucial for a successful academic career.

In all Chilean medical schools, only the basic sciences departments are staffed by full-time faculty. In the clinical departments, most of the staff members (and in some schools, the entire staff) have part-time appointments. Because there is no private practice in the teaching hospitals, geographic full-time is essentially nonexistent, with the exception of the faculty of the Catholic University Medical School, whose 600-bed medical center also supports a large private clinic. The lack of full-time faculty in the clinical departments is probably the single greatest weakness of Chilean medical education. It is, to a large extent, responsible for the present need of the Chilean medical schools to send its own faculty abroad for postdoctoral training, and it also explains their modest scientific output.

The situation is blamed on the chronic budgetary constraints suffered by the universities. Unquestionably, this is a key factor, but it is not the only reason. None of the medical schools has made a serious attempt to establish a full-time policy for the clinical faculty. This may be interpreted as misunderstanding the implications of having full-time faculty in the clinical departments, but it also reflects the difficulties of offering adequate salaries to the clinical faculty in a country with chronic two-digit inflation.

All medical schools have well-established procedures for faculty recruitment and promotion. The academic career starts at the instructor level, and continues, successively, to assistant, associate, and full professor. Universities do not have the equivalent of tenure and nontenure tracks; instead, the first contract offered to a young faculty usually represents a tenure appointment. This assumed job stability, and a minimal demand for publication, permits academic promotions that in US medical schools would be unthinkable.

CONTINUING MEDICAL EDUCATION

Continuing Medical Education is not required in Chile. See discussion of "Graduate Medical Education."

ISSUES AND TRENDS

During the last few years there have been some efforts to change the medical school curricula. An Ad Hoc National Commission, appointed by the medical schools to study curricular reform, recently proposed that: (1) tutorial teaching be expanded and self-education stimulated; (2) content related to ethical and humanistic values be increased; (3) basic and clinical subjects be integrated; and (4) undergraduate and postgraduate training in ambulatory medicine be increased.

Many of these ideas come from international recommendations and the positive results of established innovative programs in US and Canadian medical schools. Some of the medical schools are seriously attempting to implement these ideas. A drastic change in the curriculum may provide a more stimulating atmosphere for the students, but unfortunately it will leave untouched the underlying weakness of a system based on part-time faculty.

REFERENCES

Chile, Republic of. Ministry of Health. 1992. *Health situation and health care in Chile.* pp. 1-35.

Medina, E., and A. Kaempffer. 1988. Necisidad de Médicos en Chile. *Rev. Med Chile* 116:389-394.

Oficina Panamericana de la Salud. 1990. *Las condiciones de salud en las Américas.* Publición Cientifica no. 524. Washington, DC. 2:117-124.

9

The People's Republic of China

MA XU

The present Chinese educational system of health sciences is a complex continuum. Unlike that in many developed countries, it consists of schools of health sciences with three levels: primary, secondary, and higher. This arrangement has evolved from the emerging health needs of the people and the human resources required to address them. Over the last five decades, China has nurtured two branches of medicine: traditional and Western, for which there are separate schools. The two kinds of medical schools are neither competitive with, nor alternatives to, but rather learn from each other. This policy has guided the development of medicine and medical education in China.

Western medicine became popular for the Chinese population only in the past several decades, while traditional medicine has a long history, a large influence, and an enormous following, and is deeply rooted in the population. Although initially there was considerable resistance from Western-oriented professional groups to traditional medicine, this eventually waned. The policymakers in the Chinese Ministry of Health prevailed and carried out a program for maintaining both kinds of medicine and offering two kinds of education in the health sciences. The success and failure of this policy must be viewed in the context of actual improvement in the health of the people.

Education for Traditional Chinese Medicine

Chinese traditional medicine has several thousand years of history. According to the record in the ancient document *Rituals of Zhou Dynasty: Heavenly Officialdom* (1,000 B.C.), medical men in the court were of four different kinds: the diet doctor (dietitian), disease doctor (physician), ulcer doctor (surgeon), and animal doctor (veterinarian), whose knowledge and skill was transmitted at the beginning, mainly by a long period of apprenticeship. In the year A.D. 443, Emperor Wen of Liu Song Kingdom appointed medical doctors to conduct medical education, and in A.D. 624, the Imperial Medical Academy was founded.

The Academy was the first medical care and medical education institution run by the government. Under its leadership, five kinds of medical persons (physician, acupuncturist, masseur, religious healer, and pharmaceutist) were trained and worked either together or separately. In A.D. 1368, the Ming Dynasty ordered recruitment of first year medical students for the Imperial Medical College, by national examination once every three years. By that time, the college had ten departments, and medical education had become specialized.

There were two main tracks for cultivating medical personnel. Apprenticeship, the main track, was prevalent throughout the rural areas and served the common people. The other track was study in the Imperial Medical College, whose graduates were ordered to serve the feudal officials. This tradition lasted until the beginning of the twentieth century. In the 1930s, seven colleges of traditional medicine were established, and in 1990, there were 31 such colleges.

The Coming of Western Medicine

In the nineteenth century, doctors of Western medicine and missionaries came from Western capitalist countries into China and set up clinics and medical classes. These were the first outposts of Western medicine. At the beginning of the twentieth century, these classes joined to form several Union Medical Schools, backed by allied partners in their home countries. These were the so-called foreigner-run medical schools. Meanwhile, many young Chinese went abroad to study Western medicine, and returned to establish modern medical schools. Beijing Great Medical School, the predecessor of Beijing Medical University and the first medical school of Western medicine run by Chinese, was established in 1912. In 1990, there were 122 medical colleges and 563 secondary medical schools, 3,925 professional schools for nursing and midwifery, and 2,961 schools for medical technicians.

OVERVIEW OF THE HEALTH CARE DELIVERY SYSTEM

Chinese health policy has been shaped by her own traditions but influenced, to some degree, by foreign health policies. The introduction of Western medicine to China and the development of western medical schools, the longstanding use of traditional medicine and the development of traditional medical schools, the urgent health needs of the Chinese peoples, and the current health status and economy of the country all provide the basis for shaping health policy and for developing human resources for health. The educational system of health sciences has also been affected by many other factors, including the vast size of the population, the quantity and quality of present health care providers, the two kinds of medicine and medical schools, the characteristics of the health care delivery system, and the cultural status of the people.

China is a developing country, with 1.2 billion people, 80 percent of whom live in rural areas. Its health facilities and health providers are not easily compared with those of the developed countries. Policymakers are eager to change the health care situation, which explains why Chinese primary and secondary education for health sciences are well developed.

Before 1949, health care facilities were quite scarce. Health personnel stayed entirely in the cities. The country counted 80,000 beds in 3,670 health care institutions of all kinds; these were staffed by 36,000 health professionals and 505,000 technicians. After 1949, health care facilities grew rapidly. By 1985, the number of hospitals had grown to 60,000, clinics to 127,000, epidemic prevention stations to 3,410, maternal and child health centers to 2,724, hospital beds to 2.2 per thousand population, health personnel to 2.229 million, health workers to 4.313 million, and medical doctors (higher or middle-level) to 1.413 million.

Rural health services have three tiers. The county hospital, epidemic prevention station, and maternal and child health centers form the first tier, and are staffed with college graduates. Township health centers, usually with several beds, form the second tier, and are staffed with graduates from state-run secondary medical schools. The village health unit is the most basic. It is staffed with graduates from county-run primary medical schools. By 1986, there were only 643,000 village doctors. The secondary and tertiary health care units are all located in large cities and large enterprises. The educational system for health sciences has been built to serve the Chinese health care delivery system, which is structured on three-levels of four varieties.

State Ownership. Health care organizations controlled by the local authority of the county, of provincial governments, and of the ministries belong to this category. Examples include county hospitals, county anti-epidemic stations, provincial hospitals and provincial anti-epidemic stations, municipal hospitals and municipal anti-epidemic stations, and the affiliated hospital of medical colleges. The services provided by these organizations are high in quality academically, professionally, and technologically.

Collective ownership. This kind of health care organization is sponsored, controlled and owned by collective enterprises. The government gives some support if necessary. The financial resources come from the cumulative wealth of the collective enterprise. All health care organizations below county hospital (such as central township hospitals or production brigade hospitals) are of this category. Central township hospitals are small--usually with 20 to 40 beds, 15 midlevel health care personnel, and simple instruments. There are sixty-five thousand central township hospitals and six million production brigade clinics in China. The latter are staffed with primary health workers.

Individual practitioners. The shortage of health care personnel in China is so serious that the existence of individual practitioners is not only allowable, but also reasonable, especially in the case of physicians of Chinese traditional medicine, physicians of minorities, and persons with special treatment techniques. All these individual practitioners must be certified by the Bureau of Public Health at different levels in order to guarantee the patient's safety.

Free Medical Services. State employees, soldiers, and undergraduate students enjoy free medical care and pay a registration fee only if hospitalized. They also pay food costs, but no other payments are required. All workers and officers of state-owned or collective enterprises (labor-protection medical care) enjoy free medical services like those of government employees, and their families also enjoy partially free medical services, paying half the costs. Hospital expenses for the delivery of free medical care are submitted to the government for reimbursement, but the expenditures of labor-protection medical care must be reimbursed from the income of the enterprises.

Administrative system. The administration of health care organizations of different levels is twofold; vertical and horizontal. Governments of different levels have their own departments of public health. Each health care organization must be controlled by the departments of public health of governments from the upper and the same levels. Therefore, the administrative system is overly complicated, the regulations and guidelines are often not uniform, and administrative offices are duplicated, reducing efficiency.

Forces of Change

Government policy takes the decisive role in shaping medical education to meet the health needs of the people. Its implementation requires the cooperation not only of health services administrators, but also of health science educators. To formulate health policy, a series of nationwide conferences was held during the last decades. "The Four Guidelines for Health Care Services," adopted in 1952 at the First National Conference on Health Service and Education, were (1) putting prevention first; (2) serving workers, peasants, and soldiers; (3) uniting doctors of traditional medicine and doctors of modern medicine; and (4) joining health promotion with mass movement.

Under these guidelines, a network of community health services was established rapidly, and health work force resources had to be developed to meet the needs of the network. With the support of local government, several hundred secondary medical schools were set up within a couple of years. In the late 1950s, under the guidance of the "Great Leap Forward," "barefoot doctors" were trained to meet the urgent need for health services in rural areas. Meanwhile, the number of hospitals, whether in counties or large cities, increased rapidly, and the urgent need for additional doctors forced the medical colleges to enlarge their enrollments, usually to 400 students per class. In each province, several medical colleges were usually constructed simultaneously. The shortage of instructors and teaching assistants to teach basic medical sciences in the medical colleges became quite serious, so schools of basic medical sciences were set up in six top-level medical universities to meet this need. The rapid expansion of medical colleges and the reform of higher medical education, however, in combination with production and mass movement in health care services, seriously threatened the quality of the education provided to graduates.

A national conference held by the Ministry of Education in 1960 summarized the experiences of universities and colleges in the expansion years. The conference was led by the minister of higher education and lasted for half a year. Chancellors, college presidents, deans, and some eminent professors were among the approximately five hundred participants. This conference developed a guideline called "Sixty Items of Regulations Concerning Higher Education." The purpose of the "Sixty Items" was to limit the rapid expansion in the number of schools and in the number of student admissions that had been occurring without regard to the country's gross national product; to guarantee the quality of graduates; to run the universities and colleges, not by the personal experiences of some authorities (chancellors or deans)--that is, not on idealism--but on democratism; and to separate the authorities of chancellors and college presidents over administration from that of the dominant political party, with the former having the right to make decisions to guarantee requirements emphasizing solely academic quality rather than the politics of the students. Following this conference, the medical colleges recovered authority to implement their standards.

The basic medical sciences were emphasized, course hours were increased, laboratory training continued, clinical courses recovered, learning by doing was abandoned, and the number of days formerly used to go to the countryside to learn from the peasants was greatly reduced. However, these reforms lasted only about three years.

In the year 1965, the so-called Cultural Revolution occurred, causing many schools to close for several years. Medical schools reopened in 1970, but under the influence of the extreme leftists, the curriculum was reduced from five to three years. Time devoted to courses in the basic medical sciences was reduced to four months. All the clinical courses promoted learning by doing. Entry examinations were omitted, and no academic requirements for admissions were necessary. First-year students were recommended by new Communist party ruling authorities, and often the students were their relatives. This program of medical education predominated throughout the nation for the next five to seven years, until in 1977, the changes mandated by the Cultural Revolution were abandoned. With China's new open-door policy and modernization begun, medical education changed significantly.

Recent Progress

During the Cultural Revolution, a variety of diverse medical programs, without any control, emerged in all medical schools throughout the country. The Ministry of Higher Education made a decision to examine all these programs, and a series of national conferences was held within three years to finalize the necessary specialties in higher education for health sciences. A document was published calling for three- and seven-year health sciences schools. The Ministry of Public Health also held a series of nationwide conferences to enhance the quality of the graduates and emphasize the prevention strategy in health education. The most important decision made in 1985 by the Ministry of Public Health was the review and revision of the four guidelines published in 1952 into five guidelines to direct health care services and education. Realizing the following five targets is the responsibility of the health care education and delivery systems: (1) putting prevention first; (2) putting the advancement of people's health care upon the advancement of science and technology; (3) emphasizing two kinds of medicine (Chinese traditional and Western) equally; (4) mobilizing the whole society to participate in health care improvement; and (5) serving the people's health needs.

HISTORICAL BACKGROUND

Before 1949, control of medical education in China was quite diffuse. In addition to Chinese-run medical schools, foreign-run institutions from countries such as Japan, Germany, and America coexisted in the monopolized areas of the foreign suzerain state. All the professors of these foreign medical schools used their own language, textbooks, and regulations. Classes were small, and the school year the same as in the home country. The foreign-run schools seemed intended merely as showpieces for the culture and strength of the respective countries. China could not produce sufficient numbers of health professionals based on these models to serve the needs of its people.

After 1949, because of the political situation, China sought help from the Soviet Union. Medical education and the health care delivery system were copied from that of the USSR, and all foreign-run medical schools were reformed. For the sake of consistency between medical schools and the health care system and to meet the needs of the people, further modifications have since been made. The present organizational system of medical schools includes the graduate college to which graduates from a medical university or college, with two years work experience, can apply for advanced study. There are 82 graduate subspecialties, but few slots are available in any subspecialty. After completing the three or five-year training program, the master's or MD degree is awarded, respectively.

ROLE OF NATIONAL POLICY IN SHAPING MEDICAL EDUCATION

See "Overview of the Health Care Delivery System," p. 110.

ADMISSION

Except in the period of the Cultural Revolution, entrance into university or medical college has been exclusively by national examination. Prospective students must declare their choice of up to three specialties and three colleges before sitting for the examination. The criteria for admission include examination scores on Chinese language, a foreign language, mathematics, chemistry, physics, and politics. For some specialties, other supplementary courses may be examined. Before a candidate can take the admission exam, physical exams must also be passed.

The entry requirements for all categories of specialties are the same. Persons entering university or college must first graduate from high school, and those entering graduate college must have completed university or college training. No recommendation letters are required. For degree students, an interview is required. For minority students, no foreign language is necessary.

Graduates of high school must pass a preliminary test held by local educational authorities before taking the national examination. Those who fail to pass the preliminary test may enter various kinds of technical schools and may apply to retake the preliminary test in the next year for entry to the national examination.

College-level medical education. Eligible high school graduates may enter one of four curricula: a three-, five-, seven-, or eight-year program. The three-year curriculum prepares health personnel for community health care services, and no degree is awarded. The five-year curriculum prepares health personnel for health units at the county level and above, and the bachelor's degree is awarded. The seven-year curriculum educates higher health personnel with research abilities, and the master's degree is awarded to graduates. The MD is awarded to graduates in the eight-year curriculum. At present there are 57 specialties of higher education in the health sciences. The dropout rate is not more than 5 percent.

Primary and Secondary Education for Health Sciences. Due to the huge demand for health care services in rural areas, the limited number of graduates from colleges of health sciences could not meet all the needs of the people. Consequently, primary and secondary medical schools with three-year curricula developed rapidly to prepare health professionals for rural areas. Graduates from regular secondary schools are admitted to three-year medical primary or secondary school by local examination. Graduates from primary medical school serve as medical aids; those from secondary medical school serve as physician assistants.

There are 25 categories of midlevel health personnel, including doctors of modern and traditional medicine, public health, maternal and child health, dentistry, technician for dispensary, radiology department, clinical laboratory, nurse, midwife, and so forth. Doctors from the three-year secondary medical schools are appointed to work in community clinics within the provincial district.

Primary health schools employing a two or three year curriculum, turn out village doctors/medical aides. The schools are run by the county government, some attached to county hospitals . China has more than two thousand counties, and most have set up a primary health school. The graduates must serve their home village in clinics or in private practice.

CURRICULAR STRUCTURE AND INNOVATION

Under the five guidelines for the educational system for health sciences, a series of innovations occurred, such as the cooperative program between the US University of New Mexico School of Medicine and Xian Medical University. Although only two schools joined this program, it serves as a model for the reform of the three-year higher medical education curriculum based on community-oriented primary care (COPC) and the problem-based learning (PBL) method of instruction. Experience with this program will encourage many schools to reform their curricula in the coming years. The perspective of COPC in China is very promising.

The organ system approach and the problem-based method of organizing instruction have been tried in only a few schools. The PBL method of teaching of basic medical sciences is well developed in a few medical schools but is not accepted among most of the faculties in established institutions. The didactic teaching format is prevalent in most of the schools. Traditional curricula and teaching methods have been, and continue to, control medical education into the foreseeable future. The short essay evaluation format of student performance has been used exclusively for some time in all the medical schools. In the period of emulating the USSR system, the oral examination was introduced to evaluate college students' performance, but no sooner had it been used than it was opposed by the students and professors, and then abandoned. The Multiple Choice Question (MCQ) was introduced into China in the 1980s and is used universally in each kind of evaluation, whatever its purpose.

The main challenges for the reform of Chinese medical education for the health sciences include:

1. The introduction of innovations in medical education based on the experiences of advanced medical colleges in other parts of the world.

2. Training leaders in medical schools in the new concepts of education. The first cooperative Master of Health Professions Education (MHPE) was undertaken in 1991-92 at Beijing Medical University in cooperation with the University of Illinois at Chicago Department of Medical Education. China has also held many seminars on medical education with international colleagues in recent years to share their experiences. The reform of medical education to meet the needs of the people confronts many barriers, chief of which is the leaders' lack of information about what is going on in advanced medical colleges. They lack experience in innovation of medical education in advanced countries. There is no model to emulate in China and no experiences with scientific research methods in medical education, such as measurement and evaluation. The MHPE program may give some answers on these issues.

3. Setting up pilot experiments in medical education. A role model of a program is worth hundreds of words. Several pilot programs have been set up in recent years. Some use the PBL method in courses of basic medical science. Some emphasize primary health care, and others emphasize community medicine and rural clinics. In short, the COPC model of practice and education has not been well developed in China, and innovation in teaching methodology is limited in health sciences education.

The majority of curricula in medical universities, colleges, and secondary medical schools are discipline-based and employ didactic teaching. The curricular structure is composed of four parts (See Tables 9.1, pp. 117-120, and 9.2, p. 120). Basic natural sciences including general, organic, analytical, physical chemistry, physics, and calculus are taught in year one. Basic medical sciences are taught in year two and the first half of year three. The second half of years three and four are devoted to clinical courses, with the fifth year an internship.

Table 9.1
Comparison of Curricula in Chinese Health Sciences Education

SCHOOL OF:	Medicine	Public Health	Pediatrics	Oral Medicine	Traditional Medicine
Course	Hrs.	Hrs.	Hrs.	Hrs.	Hrs.
Politics	216	216	216	216	216
Athletics	144	144	144	144	144
Foreign Language	306	306	306	306	190
Medical Biology	72	72	72	72	54
Calculus	54	72	54	54	470
Medical Physics	126	108	126	126	
Basic Chemistry	234	216	234	234	
Human Anatomy	216	144	216	162	72
Histology Embryology	108	90	108	108	36
Biochemistry	162	162	162	144	90
Physiology	162	162	162	162	68
Parasitology	72	90	72	36	
Microbiology	126	162	126	108	36
Pathological Anatomy	144	126	144	144	56
Pathological Physiology	72	54	72	54	
Pharmacology	126	90	126	90	
Diagnostics	162	126	162	90	
Radiology	54	54	54		
Traditional Medicine	144	72	108	90	

Table 9.1

Comparison of Curricula in Chinese Health Sciences Education

SCHOOL OF:	Medicine	Public Health	Pediatrics	Oral Medicine	Traditional Medicine
Course	Hrs.	Hrs.	Hrs.	Hrs.	Hrs.
Internal Medicine	216	152	162	180	114
Surgery	225	90	180	198	34
Neurology	36	54	54		
Psychiatry	36				
OB/Gyn	108	54	72		
Pediatrics	90	54		36	
Infectious Diseases	54	60			
Epidem-iology	36				
Ophthal-mology	54	54	54	36	
Otolaryn-gology	54	54	54	90	
Derma-tology	54	40	54		
Oral Medicine	27	20	27		
Hygiene	108		90	108	
Nuclear Medicine	36	36	36	36	
Hygienic Chemistry		100			
Hygienic Statistics		100			
Hygienic Toxicology		60			
Community Medicine		30			
Environ-mental Hygiene		110			

Table 9.1

Comparison of Curricula in Chinese Health Sciences Education

SCHOOL OF:	Medicine	Public Health	Pediatrics	Oral Medicine	Traditional Medicine
Course	Hrs.	Hrs.	Hrs.	Hrs.	Hrs.
Laboring Hygiene		130			
Epidem- iology		140			
Nutritional Food Hygiene		110			
Children and Adolescent Health		50			
Basic Pediatrics			90		
Pediatric Medicine			189		
Pediatric Surgery				72	
Pediatric Infectious Disease and Epidem- iology				90	Traditional Medicine (18 courses, total hrs. 2,563)
Oral Histology Pathology				90	
Oral Anatomy Physiology				90	
Oral Internal Medicine				198	
Oral Maxillary Surgery				198	
Oral Orthopedics				238	

Table 9.1

Comparison of Curricula in Chinese Health Sciences Education

SCHOOL OF:	Medicine	Public Health	Pediatrics	Oral Medicine	Traditional Medicine
Course	Hrs.	Hrs.	Hrs.	Hrs.	Hrs.
TOTAL	3,834	3,964	3,726		3,920
Internship	48 Weeks	48 Weeks	48 Weeks	48 Weeks	48 Weeks

Only one college, Union Medical College, has three years of premedical courses taught at a separate university. Nearly one-third to one-half of the curricular time is used in laboratory training in the preclinical period. In clinical education, clerkship rotations in internal medicine, surgery, pediatrics, OB-Gyn, psychiatry, and neurology have been the norm for many years. The fifth year is an internship. All college graduates have the experience of one to two years of internship before taking up their career. Internships usually take place in large hospitals. Some interns rotate in clinical departments, while others major in one clinical specialty. In some provinces or large cities, the assignment of the graduate's job is after the internship, and some are just the reverse. There are no strict regulations.

Table 9.2

China--Curricular Structure

Year	Curriculum		Number of Weeks
1	General, Organic, Analytical, Physical Chemistry, Physics, Calculus, Physical Exercise		36 weeks
2	Basic Medical Sciences, Laboratory Training		45 Weeks
3	Laboratory Training	Clerkships	5 Small Groups rotate 45 weeks
4	Clinical Courses. Clerkship		
5	Internship		52 weeks

GRADUATE MEDICAL EDUCATION

Graduate medical education began in the 1950s. Enrollment was small and the specialties quite few. By the 1980s, however, graduate medical education had become well developed (see table 9.6, p. 126). At present, there are 86 subspecialties, but the enrollment is not more than one-tenth of college graduates, most of whom have no chance to enter graduate college (only 10% in 1985). The master's degree requires two to three years at the graduate level. For the doctor's degree, another two to three years must be added according to the categories of specialties. The plan is similar to that of the American residency program. Combined MD/PhD programs, cooperative MHPE programs, and cooperative master's degrees in health administration programs have been developed with the United States in recent years.

Postgraduate medical education was split into two varieties in 1985. One is research-oriented, while the other is patient-care oriented. The future career of the persons entering these tracks is quite different. Institutions and departments offering postgraduate medical education must be approved by the National Committee of Academic Degree. This differentiation marks an advancement in acknowledging that one cannot deny the differentiation of expertise, but board certification for specialists is not established nationally.

Staffs of medical colleges, secondary medical schools, and research units who have five years of work experience, have graduated from medical college, with two recommendation letters from experts, and have passed the relevant examinations can join the master's degree training program while retaining their positions and full salary during training.

LICENSURE

Licensure is not applicable.

CONTINUING MEDICAL EDUCATION

Since the 1950s and the rapid development of medical colleges and secondary medical schools, a large number of faculty was needed to teach basic medical sciences. Some of the graduates from medical colleges became teaching assistants and instructors, although they were not competent to undertake instruction in medical sciences. This was the background from which continuing medical education emerged in most of the eminent medical colleges. The Department of Continuing Medical Education of the Ministry of Health asked the medical universities and colleges to solve the problem. Professional organizations currently have little influence in this area. Refresher courses were offered for large classes of students and recognized as urgently needed to meet the requirements for expansion of medical colleges and secondary medical schools. This large-class teaching format was preferred by trainees and has a strong influence on present-day continuing medical education. Materials for individual study and self-study, therefore, are not well developed. Continuing education is one of the most pressing issues facing administrators of education for health sciences.

Another peculiarity of Chinese continuing medical education is the complex mix of trainees, who include graduates from college and secondary schools of health sciences, as well as learners by doing or by self-study, for qualification by national exam. All need the same opportunities to advance their knowledge and skills, so continuing education for health sciences is varied. In addition to continuing education classes in medical colleges, China has developed more than twenty-four special colleges of continuing education. There are many different kinds of classes in these colleges, designed to meet the needs of the students who have no chance to enter formal medical school, but rather learned- by-doing, by self-study, or by short-term courses. As soon as a student graduates from one of these colleges, a formal certification is awarded. Television broadcasts, and various short-term seminars are also offered to meet the needs of these trainees.

There are millions of village doctors and graduates from secondary schools of health sciences who need to upgrade their knowledge and skill for promotion, so the future of continuing education is optimistic and will guarantee the quality of health care service.

In the future, continuing education will include: (1) popularizing education in various fields, not only limited to technical people but also to fulfill the needs of administrators and other business people; (2) formalizing the curricula, the quality standards, and the student requirements in order to fit the participants to the corresponding level of the formal school; and (3) promoting the academic status of continuing education. The desire for academic knowledge and sophisticated skill is intense among young people and the number of people entering formal school continues to grow.

ROLE OF RESEARCH IN MEDICAL EDUCATION

Faculty in colleges of health sciences, whether in basic or clinical departments, must do research. Of their three major tasks (teaching, research, and patient care) research is considered the most important. Funds for research come from university budgets as well as grants from governmental enterprises and foreign foundations, Prominent among them are the China Board, W. K. Kellogg Foundation, and Project Hope. A university may give seed money to junior faculty to promote research, and similarly, the government may commission research in certain areas for which faculty can compete. The apportionment of grants, whether coming from abroad or at home, varies in accord with the individual policy of each college. Generally speaking, 60 percent of the grant may be allocated to the research project itself, while the administration of the university, college, and department may take the remainder as reimbursement for the use of facilities. China currently has no influential private foundations. Eminent researchers with extraordinary contributions may be rewarded by the national provincial universities or committees of research and technology. Of course, research contribution is one of the most important factors for promotion. Thus, we can say the majority of faculty are research-oriented voluntarily. The kinds of research vary quite widely according to each individual. Generally speaking, eminent professors of top medical universities do a lot of bench research, while younger faculty may do some applied research. Research on teaching or educational innovation is not as well appreciated.

The organizational systems for planning and arranging research projects, evaluating the results of the research, and promoting faculty are well developed in the central government, universities, and colleges. All committees at every level are staffed with experts in the respective areas and chaired by corresponding authorities. No private organization administers research projects.

ISSUES AND TRENDS

Health sciences must keep up with the rapid development of natural sciences, as must education for health sciences. The advanced health sciences and technology are the basis of education for health sciences. Subspecialization is the trend of medicine and education, so higher education of health sciences, residency, and PhD programs will inevitably be developed to meet the need of medicine and of high-quality health care. On the other hand, for the health care needs of 1.2 billion people and the promotion of community health status, China needs vast numbers of various health personnel. The educational system for health sciences must cope with this complicated situation. Among the many mechanisms adopted in recent years, the following were especially recommended:

1. Raising the academic level of five- and seven-year programs to meet the needs of hospitals at the county level and above;
2. Expanding and consolidating the three-year program to meet the needs of township hospitals and clinics;
3. Formalizing the curriculum for training village doctors in order to create uniform standards;
4. Reforming the admission policies and teaching methods in the training of community health personnel;
5. Reorganizing the curricula of three-year medical schools in terms of competencies, not disciplines; i.e., not as a condensed version of the five-year curriculum. The teaching methods must be PBL for cultivating ability. The policy of admission for students must guarantee the graduates work in the community.

To reform education for the health sciences, experiences of advanced schools in the world must be considered. The approaches of a number of American and Canadian medical schools have been introduced into China in recent years. Certain aspects of these experiences were adopted and are still in use in some medical schools. Scholar exchanges and other academic linkages with most of the advanced countries are very popular, and such forms of international cooperation should be continued. All these activities have produced encouraging results and are appreciated by faculty and students.

REFERENCES

Carlson, C., C. Martini, and M.R. Schwarz. 1990. Medical Education: A global perspective. Results of the International Survey of Medical Education. Informational paper distributed by the American Medical Association at the Fifth World Conference on Medical Education, October 24-28, 1990.

World Federation for Medical Education. 1988. Conference document. World Conference on Medical Education, August 7-12, 1988. Edinburgh, Scotland.

Yizhong, D. 1990. Development of medical education in China. *Acad Med* 65 (August).

Table 9.3
China--Medical School Demographics

Medical School	Type of School, Fall 1990	Undergraduate Enrollment Fall 1990	Graduates 1990	Graduate Education (Interns /Residents Fall 1990)
122	Medicine and Pharmacy	46,772	42,881	4,583
31	Chinese Traditional Medicine	7,893	7,427	
TOTAL # Medical Schools		Total Undergraduate Students	Total Graduates 1990	Total Interns/ Residents
153		54,665	50,308	4,583

Table 9.4
General Scheme of Chinese Medical Education

Level and Type	Total Years Required	Specialties
Graduate College	3-5	Subspecialties: 82
Medical University College	3, 5, 7, 8	Specialties: 57
Secondary Medical School	3	Traditional Medicine, Dentistry, Modern Medicine, Public Health, Pharmacy
Primary Medical School	3	Village Doctor

Table 9.5
China--Specialties in Secondary Medical School

Specialty	Years	Notes
Medicine	3	6 branches. Western and Chinese Medicine
Public Health	3	
Nurse	3	
Midwifery	2	Various curricula
Nursery Aide	2	
Pharmacist	3	2 Branches, Western and Chinese drugs

Table 9.6

Specialties for Chinese Graduate Education

Basic Medical Sciences (18 Categories):

Human anatomy, Histology and Embryology, Immunology, Pathology, Parasitology, Forensic medicine, Biomedical engineering, Physiopathology, Radiology, Aviation medicine, History of medicine, Physiology, Microbiology, Genetics

Clinical Medicine (23 Categories):

Internal medicine, Pediatrics, Neurology, Psychiatry and Mental health, Dermatology and Venereology, Infectious disease, Nuclear medicine, Clinical laboratory diagnosis, Geriatrics, Nursing, surgery, OB/GYN, Ophthalmology, ENT, Oral medicine, Imagery medicine, Radiotherapy, Rehabilitation and Physical therapy, Sports medicine, Anesthesia, War surgery, Ontology, Emergency medicine

Public Health and Preventive Medicine (13 Categories):

Epidemiology, Environmental hygiene, Nutrition and Good hygiene, Children and Maternal health, Biostatistics, Labor health and Occupational disease, Sanitary inspection, Social medicine and Health Care Management, Hygiene and Army hygiene, medicine related to antichemical/antinuclear war

Chinese Traditional Medicine (21 categories):

Basic theory of Chinese Traditional Medicine, Dispensing, Discussion on cold-induced diseases, Acupuncture and Moxibustion, etc.

Pharmacy (9 Categories):

Pharmaceutical chemistry, Pharmaceutics, Chinese materia medica, Pharmacology, Pharmacognosy, Pharmaceutical engineering, etc.

Table 9.7
Faculty Distribution--China

	Total Full-Time Faculty Fall 1990 Professor	Total Full Time Faculty Fall 1990 Associate Professor	Instructor	Teacher	Teaching Assistant
Number	15,052	84,150	148,428	12,207	134,730
Average Salary (US $)	$100-120	$80-90	$60-70	$60-80	$40-50

Table 9.8

Varieties of Specialties in Chinese Health Sciences Education

Basic Medical Sciences	IV Stomatology
Basic Medical Sciences	Oral Medicine
II Preventive Medicine	Oral Prosthetics
Preventive Medicine	V Traditional Chinese Medicine
Environmental Medicine	Traditional Chinese Medicine
Sanitary Inspection	Nourishing and Rehabilitating in
Nutrition and Food Hygiene	traditional Chinese
III Clinical Medicine	Medicine
Clinical Medicine	Ophthalmology and
Pediatrics	Otorhinolaryngology in
Gynecology and Obstetrics	Traditional Chinese Medicine
Ophthalmology and	Acupuncture and Moxibustion
Otorhinolaryngology	Massage
Psychiatry and Mental Health	Orthopedics and Traumatology in
Radiological Medicine	traditional Chinese medicine
Medical Imaging	Mongolian Medicine
Medical Laboratory tests	Tibetan Medicine
Medical Nutrition	
Anesthesiology	
Nursing	

Table 9.8
Varieties of Specialties in Chinese Health Sciences Education

VI Forensic Medicine
    Forensic Medicine
    Material evidence in Forensic
    Medicine
VII Pharmacy
    Pharmacy
    Pharmaceutical Chemistry
    Pharmaceutical Analysis
    Chemical Pharmaceutics
    Biological Pharmaceutics
    Microbial Pharmaceutics
    Pharmaceutics Preparation
    Pharmacology
    Traditional Chinese Pharmacy
    Pharmaceutics of Traditional
    Chinese Materia Medica
    Analysis and Assay of
        Traditional Chinese Materia
        Medica
VII Management
    Management of Health Science
    Management of Medical and
    Pharmaceutical Enterprises
	IX Applied Humanities, Sciences and
	Technology
	    Foreign Languages for Sciences
	        and Technology in
	        medicine and pharmacy
	    Library and Information Science
	        (in medicine and pharmacy)
	    Applied Mathematics (in
	    medicine and pharmacy)
	    Applied Physics (in medicine)
	    Applied Chemistry (in medicine)
	    Biomedical Engineering
	X Pilot Specialties
	    Basic Medical Sciences in
	        Traditional Chinese
	        Medicine
	    Literature in Traditional Chinese
	    Medicine
	    Surgery in Traditional Chinese
	    Medicine
	    Oral and Maxillofacial Surgery
	    Maternal and Child Health
	    Clinical Pharmacy
	    Pharmacology in Traditional
	        Chinese Materia Medica
	    Resources of Traditional Chinese
	        Materia Medica
	    Health Economics
	    Health Statistics

Table 9.9

China--Health Professions Education (non-Medical School)

Number of Schools	Type of School	Enrollment Fall 1990	Graduates 1990	Level of Training
3,935	Professional School	730,097	661,262	Nurse, Midwife
2,961	Technical School Medicine	502,802	427,573	Various Technicians
563	Secondary Medical School	93,261	93,175	Midlevel Doctor
TOTAL Health Professional Schools		Total Students	Total Graduates 1990	
7,459		1,326,160	1,182,010	

10

Czech and Slovak Federative Republic

JOSEF VYŠOHLÍD
VÁCLAV JANOUŠEK

The "gentle" revolution in November 1989 was a moving force for the creation of the Czech and Slovak Federative Republic (CSFR) in 1990[1] (previously known as Czechoslovakia). Within this general context, a gradual transformation of the former monopolistic state system of national economy toward the democratic and liberal market economy is occurring. Health care and the education of health personnel are also affected. Transformation of the existing system of medical education had already begun by 1990.

OVERVIEW OF THE HEALTH CARE DELIVERY SYSTEM

In 1991, the highest national authorities of the Czech and Slovak Federative Republic approved the basic and, thus far, general, policy documents, describing the main targets, processes, and structures of necessary changes in both the health and education systems. Transformation from a monopolized state to a democratic, pluralistic, and liberal system will not be easy. The steadily deteriorating situation in the health status of the population and existing shortcomings of the health system must be taken into account. The area once known as Czechoslovakia is in the heart of Europe, and the tendency is to be an active and recognized partner in the "European house." This is why endeavors in transforming the health system and the system of education and training of health personnel in general and medical education in particular, are oriented toward the general European trends in these fields. Both the health care system and the medical education system, which develops human resources for health, are organized with a recognition that the former Czechoslovakia contains two separate republics. Each had an

---

[1] On January 1, 1993, the CSFR became two separate countries, the Czech Republic (CR) and the Slovak Republic (SR).

essentially autonomous medical education system already in place, as described in this chapter.

As a founding and active member of WHO, Czechoslovakia was also committed to the European targets for attaining the global strategy of Health for All by the Year 2000, as approved by the WHO Regional Committee in 1984. The same also applies to nongovernmental organizations: the Association of Medical Education in Europe (AMEE); the Association of Medical Deans in Europe (AMDE[2]), where both the Czech and Slovak republics are represented. In addition, the recommendations of the Advisory Committee on Medical Training (a body of the Commission of the European Communities) are essential for the future.

Czechoslovakia has one of the world's highest ratios of doctors to population. At the end of 1989, there were 31.6 medical doctors per 10,000 population in the whole CSFR; 32.2 in the CR and 30.3 in the SR (Institutes of Health Statistics 1990). With the current restricted financial and material resources, tight controls (and possibly a quota system) on the numbers of graduates from medical schools may be required to avoid potential unemployment of doctors.

One notable aspect of health care in CSFR is a high and steadily increasing percentage of women doctors. As of December 31, 1989, a total of 50.9 percent of the medical population in the CSFR was female: 51.4 percent in the Czech Republic (CR) and 49.9 percent in the Slovak Republic (SR). In the CR, women doctors are now in the majority in all age groups. The proportion of female physicians is highest in pediatrics, dermatology, and ophthalmology and lowest in urology, orthopedics, and surgery. Concerns about the increasing percentage of female physicians arise, not from doubts about their competence, but rather from the perception that competing demands may lead to a higher rate of absenteeism, and thus lower productivity.

HISTORICAL BACKGROUND

The Higher Education Act, passed by the Federal Assembly in 1990, covered three forms of educational activities: (1) higher education studies, (2) postgraduate studies, and (3) continuing education. The new autonomy provided to higher education institutions requires a fundamental change in thinking, and a shift from the passive fulfillment of instructions toward active, creative, independent work. For example, medical schools now determine their own admission requirements and curriculum. Each medical school dean is now responsible for the curriculum in his or her institution, and all changes must be approved by the academic senate. The Higher Education Act also specified a wide range of student rights and duties and provided for students to become active participants in academic life

---

[2] AMDE was renamed in April 1993 to the Association of Medical Schools in Europe (AMSE).

and decision making, including participation in the academic senate. Table 10.1 describes the country's medical schools.

Table 10.1
Medical Schools in the Czech and Slovak Federative Republic

Parent University	Location	Number	Year Established	
Charles University	Prague	3		
			1st Med. School	1348
			2nd Med. School	1951
			3rd Med. School	1952
	Plzeň	1		1945
	Hradec Králové	1		1945
Masaryk University	Brno	1		1919
Palacký University	Olomouc	1		1946
Comenius University	Bratislava	1		1919
	Martin	1		1969
J.P. Šafárik University	Košice	1		1948

ROLE OF NATIONAL POLICY IN SHAPING MEDICAL EDUCATION

The priority in medical education is given to making the educational system pluralistic and liberal (nondependent on the government).

ADMISSION

Every student who successfully passes the General Certification of Education (maturity examination) at the end of secondary school is eligible to apply to medical school. There are various types of secondary schools in Czechoslovakia. According to the Higher Education Act of 1990, eight-year grammar schools, as a basic preparation for studies at the university, have been reconfirmed. The basic school is followed by secondary grammar school which has returned to purely general education, and by the system of vocational schools with a traditional combination of general and vocational education; this diploma confers the right to enter a higher education institution.

There are reasons for the introduction of a new, comprehensive, general secondary school for students from 15 to 18 years of age to promote general education in secondary schools. The tenets of secondary education mentioned above are under discussion, and a new system of education is being prepared at present. See Table 10.2 and Table 10.3 for enrollment figures in 1989-90.

Admission procedures vary from school to school, but the main features are as follows: applicants who pass multiple choice and oral exams in physics, chemistry and biology are then interviewed. The goal is to choose the students best suited for the study of medicine. Considering that the ratio between applicants and those who are admitted is four to one, the percentage of admitted students who actually complete their studies and receive their degrees is low, and differs among schools.

CURRICULAR STRUCTURE AND INNOVATION

The six-year curriculum is divided into four phases. The first phase, the theoretical phase, is devoted to the basic sciences: i.e., physiology, anatomy, histology, embryology, biophysics, biology, and biochemistry. This phase is two years in length, with the curriculum subject-oriented along traditional lines.

The second, preclinical phase, consists of microbiology, pathology, pathological physiology, and pharmacology. This phase lasts for one year and is the bridge to clinical study.

Table 10.2

Czech and Slovak Federative Republic--Medical Students 1989-1990

	Total	Men	(%)	Women	(%)
CSFR	12,843	5,109	(39.8)	7,734	(60.2)
CR	9,483	3,778	(39.8)	5,705	(60.2)
SR	3,360	1,331	(39.6)	2,029	(60.4)

Table 10.3

Czech and Slovak Federative Republic--Medical Students (excluding dental) 1989-1990

	Total	Men	(%)	Women	(%)
CSFR	11,748	4,769	(40.6)	6,979	(59.4)
CR	8,668	3,536	(40.8)	5,132	(59.2)
SR	3,080	1,233	(40.0)	1,847	(60.0)

The clinical study (phase three) lasts for two years, and is devoted mainly to surgery, medicine, ENT, ophthalmology, pediatrics, dermatology, obstetrics

/gynecology, anesthesiology, infectious diseases, epidemiology, hygiene, neurology, psychiatry, and social medicine. The sixth year of study (phase four) is reserved for clerkships in medicine, obstetrics/gynecology, surgery, and hygiene and social medicine. Students participate under supervision in the care of patients and also spend some time in outpatient departments and community clinics.

Faculty

Anybody who is properly qualified can be appointed as a teacher at the medical school through a competitive appointment process. In the future, teachers will be considered for reappointment every four years. All teachers are expected to engage in both teaching and research and are expected to take an active part in faculty life, such as by serving on various committees; teachers in clinical subjects also participate in patient care.

Faculty are appointed at three ranks: (1) Assistants, (2), Readers (Associate Professors), and (3) Professors. Assistants have, in the past, generally been appointed by the dean of the school. In the future, only those who have successfully passed the competition will be appointed to the assistant post. The assistants take an active part in teaching medical students in practical exercises, in preparing instructional materials, and in supervising students in their clinical work. Senior assistants act as tutors of a group of students. They also participate in research and as committee members. Associate professors deliver the lectures, are active as tutors and moderators of seminars, and are expected to write the teaching/learning texts and to be active in a chosen field of research. They also act as committee members or chairpersons. They participate in various functions, not only at the school but also at the university level. They are expected to hold both an MD and a PhD. Full professors are the most experienced teachers. They are active in all fields of teaching, prepare and write various teaching/learning texts and textbooks, and usually are the leading members of a group of research workers. From among them, the dean and the vice-deans are elected and members of the Scientific Council of the school are appointed. The full-time faculty/student ratio in the CSFR is one to 13.7; in CR one to 14.7; and in SR one to 11.5.

Teaching Methods

The whole class (numbering from 150 to 350, depending on the institution) is divided into study groups consisting usually of 18 to 20 students. One teacher in each subject is appointed for each group. Every teacher appointed for a group is responsible for teaching and supervision of that group. At present, the student/teacher ratio is not considered satisfactory, especially if the active methods of instruction and tutorials become more widely used.

Though employment of more active forms of learning is increasing, a substantial part of instruction is in the classical lecture format. This format is supplemented by laboratory, seminars, clinical rounds, and so forth. In some instances, programmed instruction (video and other forms of audiovisual presentation) is used. Student research is encouraged as a motivating device.

Innovative curricula, based on a problem-solving, integrative approach with emphasis on student participation, is being considered and introduced to a limited extent. The experience of foreign medical schools, such as Harvard and Cornell in the United States, has proved to be of great importance in preparation of the new curricula and bringing them into the practice. The Czech and Slovak medical schools, however, are autonomous and quite independent, which sometimes causes problems with regard to sharing mutual information on curricula. There is, at present, no overall body to ensure a coordinated approach in this respect.

Student Assessment

Oral examination is used in every subject, and is often supplemented with MCQ and/or essay tests. The results are expressed in four categories: (1) excellent, (2) very good, (3) good (satisfactory), (4) and fail (unsatisfactory). Students who fail an examination may repeat it twice. After a third failure, however, the student must repeat the entire year. (Such repetition is allowed only twice in the whole course of the study.)

The course of study is completed by a graduation ceremony at which the degree MUDr. (Medicinae Universae Doctor) is conferred; a graduate is eligible to practice within the health service under the supervision of a doctor with a specialty degree and longer experience (see Table 10.4 below).

Table 10.4
Czech and Slovak Federative Republic--Graduates of all medical schools, including dental graduates, 1989

	Total	Men	Women
CSFR	1,550 (100%)	636 (41.0%)	914 (59.0%)
CR	1,120 (100%)	451 (40.3%)	669 (59.7%)
SR	430 (100%)	185 (43.0%)	275 (57.0%)

GRADUATE MEDICAL EDUCATION

To date (1991) there is a single national Institute for Postgraduate Education in Medicine and Pharmacy in each of the Republics: Czech and Slovak. The Institutes were created in 1953 in Prague, and between 1953 and 1957 in Bratislava. They are in charge of specialty training and examinations, as well as continuing medical education activities (including teaching/learning and evaluation/assessment methods). Most vocational residency training, however, takes place in hospitals and polyclinics throughout the country. A network of local training centers, together with the Institutes, offer selected teaching/learning opportunities for residents, and especially for continuing education of practicing doctors.

Every doctor, after successful completion of undergraduate medical studies, is obliged to choose one medical specialty and to undertake specialty training in an adequate health facility in the field (usually a hospital). The Ministries of Health approve the list and the contents of medical specialties, as suggested by the Postgraduate Institutes. Prior to approval, the list is subject to thorough discussion and deliberation among medical associations, medical schools, and health care providers. A revision of the list takes place every eight to ten years. The recent list consists of 20 "basic" specialties (including general medicine), each with two grades. The first grade (lower) is compulsory for every doctor and is a requirement for any kind of independent practice. Residency training for this grade takes a minimum of two and one-half years and is terminated by a specialty exam before a commission, which is usually presided over by the respective head of the relevant department of the Institute. The second grade, with a specialty exam after a minimum of three to five years of residency training, is intended only for those wishing to occupy higher posts within the health care system (e.g., head of a department in a hospital).

In addition to the "basic" specialties, there are two rather extensive lists of advanced subspecialties (more than fifty in number). To enter such residency training, the doctor must be in possession of a required first (and eventually a second) grade in one of the "basic" specialties. Training programs at this level are generally three to five years. Some very narrow branches can be awarded only with a specific permission by the Ministry of Health.

At present, graduate medical education is essentially under the control of the Institutes for Postgraduate Education; however, proposed reforms include a provision for the establishment of a pluralistic Council for Education of Health Personnel with a wide participation of institutes, medical schools, health care providers (state, insurance, private, and charitable), chambers of doctors, and leading professional associations. This Council will deal with other professional categories of health personnel as well as medicine and, in close cooperation with the health care system, will take the responsibility for the numbers and types of specialties, and the contents, methods of teaching/learning, and assessment of training programs. Other reforms currently being advocated include a reduction in the number of specialties, elimination of the present two-grade system of specialty certification, and establishment of a system for accrediting health facilities that offer residency programs.

The process of residency training needs to be improved, especially the assessment of clinical competence. In this context, the residency training for general practitioners (in the future probably "family doctors") may be completely changed in order to be more relevant and more attractive. The numbers of specialists in this field have diminished each year over the past decade, due, among other factors, to the very limited attention given to primary care, both in basic and in graduate studies and to the predominantly unfavorable conditions in general medical practice (e.g., lack of material resources, equipment, extensive paperwork).

LICENSURE

License to practice in a supervised position is based on the successful graduation at a medical Faculty and obtaining the title MUDr. The right to begin independent practice is granted after successful examination in a chosen specialty.

CONTINUING MEDICAL EDUCATION

Continuing medical education (CME) is now considered a priority in the lifelong learning of physicians for two main reasons: (1) the newly transformed system of health care cannot be applied rationally in practice unless the entire practicing medical population is prepared, and (2) with increasingly restricted resources it will be necessary to improve the quality, efficiency, and effectiveness of health and medical care. Such an enormous task can be accomplished only by a solid network of training facilities, at the central, and especially at the local level. With some of the already mentioned changes in creating a two-level structure of the health care system, it would be necessary to enlarge and to improve CME activities, particularly for doctors and health personnel in primary health care and ambulatory facilities.

CME activities must be relevant to the needs and conditions in which the doctors work with their team members. Programs should be developed with the active cooperation of the future participants. Attractive and widely advertised activities with some possibility for compensation are already available. There is, however, no support for making CME compulsory. On the contrary, it is argued, CME should be based on an understood and accepted moral and ethical professional commitment. Increasingly, an accreditation system, such as the systems existing in the US, is being discussed in this connection.

It is felt that CME must be offered primarily locally, though active, self-learning, problem-based and problem-solving oriented activities might be enhanced by distant-learning methods. So far, however, no provisions for interactive teleconferencing are at hand. Nevertheless, thanks to the efforts of the organizers of the satellite transmission (EuroTransMed System), the national network of university and postgraduate centers and large health facilities is already in existence to provide continuing education for large sectors of doctors and other health professionals. The CSFR is also actively involved in a European CME project organized jointly by the WFME, AMEE, and WHO, and aimed at the promotion and improvement of CME systems and programs.

It is understood that CME will be a joint undertaking of the Postgraduate Institutes, medical schools, and professional associations, as well as social and health insurance, trade unions, and various health care providers. The most important objective is to ensure that CME brings about not only enhanced theoretical knowledge, skills, and attitudes in the participants, but also causes a measurable improvement in the quality of the care provided. Clearly, that would be a long-term and continuous endeavor. Relevant studies and research, as well as active international cooperation and collaboration, therefore, seem to be indispensable.

ROLE OF RESEARCH IN MEDICAL EDUCATION

Until 1990, research in medical education was carried out within the Research Plan individually or jointly organized by the Scientific Councils of the Czech Ministry of Health and Ministry of Education.

GOVERNMENT/PRIVATE SECTOR INVOLVEMENT

There are currently no private medical schools, but such a possibility is under discussion. The bill of the new Higher Education Act is being prepared and should be dealt with by the Czech Parliament soon.

INTERNATIONAL LINKAGES AND COLLABORATION.

The Czech Association for Health Manpower Education is a member of the Association for Medical Education in Europe and the Association of Medical Schools in Europe. Very close contact and collaboration exists with the WHO regional office in Copenhagen and with the World Federation for Medical Education.

ISSUES AND TRENDS

Given the uncertainties in the political and economic situation in our country, it is impossible to predict the direction of change in medical education. Of fundamental significance is the creation of an atmosphere for democratic dialogue and consensus among all involved--teachers, students, politicians, professional bodies, health care providers, and the public. Though there are conflicting priorities, good will, optimism and commitment are not missing.

We are happy that we can profit from the European experiences as well as from the prospective tendencies thoughtfully being initiated by the respective governmental and nongovernmental bodies and associations. The assistance and support coming from other parts of the world are especially appreciated. All that gives us confidence that changes in the system of medical education will contribute to a continuous improvement of the quality of health care and health status of our citizens.

REFERENCES

Czech and Slovak Federative Republic, Federal Assembly. 1990. Higher Education Act.
Institute of Health Statistics, Prague, and Institute for health statistics, Bratislava. 1990. *Health services in Czechoslovakia.* Cited as Institutes.

Czech Republic, Ministry of Health. 1990. *Reform of health care in the Czech Republic*.

Slovak Republic, Ministry of Health, 1990. *Reform of health care in the Slovak Republic*.

World Health Organization. 1985. Targets for Health for All. Targets in support of the European strategy for Health for All. Copenhagen: Regional Office for Europe.

11

Egypt

NABILA HIDAYET

Medical education in Egypt can be traced back to the time of the Pharaohs, when healers, magicians, and physicians received different types of training, each according to their disease realm, whether natural or supernatural. Priest-physicians ranked highest among all categories of healers, followed by lay physicians. From the strict hierarchy of their titles, it is surmised that some control was exerted on their activities, whether from their peers or the state. According to the Greek historian Diodorus, physicians were severely treated if their management of diseases deviated from the books, which implies the existence of formal teaching and recognized texts. There is no doubt that in their search for knowledge and wisdom, candidates frequently visited the "Houses of Life" attached to temples that functioned as documentation centers. In his book, Ghalioungi gave, with good justification, an important place to the influences exerted by Egyptian medical science on the beginnings of Greek medicine.

The Egyptians also developed medical knowledge, although most of their medical texts treat illness as supernatural in cause and cure, some show an understanding of the body probably gained from the practice of embalming the dead. A document called the Edwin Smith surgical papyrus . . . contains the idea that the heart is the source of the body's life and influences the rest of the body, . . . describes various kinds of bone fractures and suggests rest, diet, surgery, and various medications. Other texts show that there were Egyptian specialists in ailments of the eye, teeth and internal organs. A number of popular therapeutics actually practiced in Egypt today are no doubt directly inherited from ancestors and treatments prescribed in hieroglyphic documents (Ghalioungi 1973).

In contemporary Egypt, Mohamed Ali opened the first medical school at Abou Zaabal, Cairo, in 1827 (Mahfouz 1935). The curriculum of the school was based on the Western biomedical paradigm and modeled on the British system. The school was placed under the direction of a European and was intended to train medical specialists. In 1919, this medical school became the Faculty of Medicine in Cairo University. Medical and health services gradually developed, and in the late 1930s the Egyptian Health Department became the Ministry of Health. To meet the increasing demands for medical personnel, two more Faculties of Medicine were opened in 1942, one in Alexandria and the other in Ein Shams, Cairo (World Health Organization 1964).

OVERVIEW OF THE HEALTH DELIVERY CARE SYSTEM

Abdul Naser's revolution in 1952 had a radical affect on education, putting it as a number one national priority and offering free education for everyone. Primary education became compulsory, while preparatory and secondary education offered academic and vocational programs that tended to push students into definite career tracks starting at age 15. Rote learning and memorization were reinforced by standard, nationwide written examinations that students were required to pass to enter the next higher level of schooling (US Agency for International Development 1979).

The rapid industrialization of the country changed much of the community from agrarian to industrial life. This prompted a revision of the whole system of health services in 1960. At the same time, the system of medical education was reexamined and changed (in 1959) to respond to the new developments in the country. The medical research needs of the country were also planned for by increasing the number and types of postgraduate students, both at home and abroad, and establishing special institutes for the study of nutrition, cancer, and bilharziasis (World Health Organization 1964).

The current health care delivery system in Egypt is well structured, covering a very wide area of the country through comprehensive health care units. Health policies are ideologically influenced by the government's general policies. In the period that followed the 1952 revolution, socialist planners promoted health and sanitation programs with great intensity. Since the revolution, the right of every citizen to free health care and education has been a national commitment. Consequently, work in government service for at least two years after graduation from medical school became mandatory. However, by the end of the 1960s, a heavily indebted economy and a more flexible political atmosphere led to a reduced commitment to former ideologies. Although access to free medical care remained the right of all Egyptian citizens, the controls imposed on physicians gradually abated. While technically they are still obliged to serve in remote areas of the country, alternatives are now available.

The Ministry of Health (MOH) is currently the only organized provider of free health care for the population and the only authority responsible for preventive services. The MOH operates through a network of 4,500 rural and urban health units, each staffed by one or two junior physicians and one or two nurses who provide primary care. Secondary care is provided by a district hospital of approximately 120 beds in each town of 50,000 to 100,000 population and by larger government hospitals of approximately 300 to 500 beds in the capital of each governorate. Some of these large hospitals deliver tertiary care; however, most of this type of health care is provided by university hospitals. Administratively, university hospitals fall under the authority of the Ministry of Education and the respective university.

The total national health expenditure in Egypt in 1985 was 2 percent of the GNP. By 1987, this figure had fallen to 1 percent, barely enough to cover the salaries of the Ministry of Health employees and the physicians and nurses it employed, and leaving little for investments, maintenance and repair of buildings and equipment. This resulted in a very unsatisfactory standard of free public health service.

In spite of the reduction in government financing for health during the past few years, five large tertiary-care hospitals have been built in Cairo alone: Ein Shams University Hospital, the New Cairo University Hospital, and three other hospitals administered by the Organization of Curative Services of the Ministry of Health. A large sum of money was also spent by the Ministry of Health to establish a renal dialysis unit in every general hospital in the country and in some district hospitals as well (Khallaf 1990).

The health care delivery system is multidimensional, with the quantity and quality of benefits varying along a continuum based primarily on the employer. A government-operated health insurance plan for governmental employees covers 2.5 million workers. Other large-scale employers, including government-owned banks and oil companies, as well as privately owned businesses and joint government-private sector ventures, contract directly with specialists and private hospitals to provide health services for their employees. Both employees and employers contribute to these insurance plans; uninsured persons receive free health care at governmental hospitals and clinics. More than 80 percent of government-employed physicians also participate in the insurance plans and other private, fee-for-service practice, and are thus essentially part-time employees who derive their major income from private practice.

HISTORICAL BACKGROUND

In 1970, the aim of the government was to reach the ratio of 1 physician to each 1,600 of the population. This was achieved by increasing the number of students in the existing medical schools (World Health Organization 1964). In 1978, medical schools were graduating between four and five thousand physicians yearly. There were also four dental schools, graduating 1,000 dentists; six schools of pharmacy, graduating 1,700 pharmacists; two high institutes of nursing, graduating 120 nurses; 150 secondary technical nursing schools, graduating 5,000 nurses; and six health technical institutes, graduating 1,000 technicians (laboratory technicians, X-ray technicians, medical records clerks, dental technicians, and medical equipment maintenance technicians). In 1988, the total population was 50,273,000 with an urban-rural ratio (1986) of 44 percent urban: 56 percent rural. The number of physicians in 1984 was 73,300 (one physician per 635 persons). In 1990, the Minister of Health estimated the ratio at 1:467. Table 11.1 presents basic health information for 1978 and 1987.

Table 11.1
Basic health information: Egypt

	1978	1987
Population (millions)	39.8	49.6
Urban (%)	44.5	43.9
Birth rate (per 1000)	37.4	39.3
Death rate (per 1000)	10.5	8.7
Rate of natural increase (per 1000)	26.9	30.6
Infant mortality rate (per 1000)	85.0	44.2
Physicians/10,000 population	3.8	7.3
Dentists/10,000 population	0.6	1.1
Pharmacists/10,000 population	0.6	0.7
Nurses/10,000 population	6.7	8.4
Beds/10,000 population	2.1	2.0

Life expectancy at birth			
	1960	1980	1984
Male	51.6	54.1	56.4
Female	52.8	56.8	58.2

Source: Khallaf (1990)

Egypt has thirteen (13) national medical schools, each affiliated with a university and operating within the context of an academic medical center, responsible for teaching, research, training, and patient care. Students are admitted after successfully completing 12 years of basic education. The duration of the medical degree program is six years, and the language of instruction is English. Bachelor of Medicine and Surgery is the title of the degree awarded.

The National Supreme University Council Medical Sector declared in 1980 that the main objective of medical education is to graduate physicians capable of continuing their independent study of medicine in the way that best conforms to the needs of their community. The second main objective is to graduate physicians who have attained a clear conception of the health problems of the country, as well as an adequate level of scientific knowledge and technical training. The third objective is to enable physicians to expand their knowledge and thinking beyond the professional fields, and to provide them with a deep insight into human nature and a good knowledge of their environment. The fourth objective is that graduates be aware of their responsibilities toward the community and the role they can play in improving the living standards and working conditions of their fellow citizens through the preservation of health, prevention of disease, treatment of ailments, and relief of human suffering. The fifth is that the future doctors attain a high degree of technical and scientific efficiency. The sixth objective is that they attain a high degree of insight into the community that will make them capable of meeting its changing needs, and the seventh is to ensure that they are capable of fulfilling the responsibility of leadership in health and social concerns of their community (National Supreme University Council 1980).

ROLE OF NATIONAL POLICY IN SHAPING MEDICAL EDUCATION

See "Overview of the Health Care Delivery System," p. 142 and "Historical Background," p. 143.

ADMISSION

It has been estimated that there are approximately three candidates for every available place in the medical school. In the early decades of this century, the selection was based on the results of (1) interviews, (2) school records and reports, (3) examinations, and (4) intelligence and aptitude tests (World Health Organization 1964). Currently admission to higher education is governed by the National Coordination Committee and is based solely on grades and percentages achieved on exams with no regard to the student's aptitude for a specific profession, as indicated in the application submitted to the Committee. Those earning the highest grades usually choose the Faculties of Medicine (National Supreme University Council 1980).

School admission is based on the number suggested by the individual schools in consultation with the Ministry of Health and is ultimately determined by the National Supreme Council of the Egyptian Universities. Students compete fiercely to obtain the highest grades in their final secondary school certificate examination--science section, as this grade is the main criterion for admission. Which applicant is admitted to a specific institution and program of study is determined through a central computer. Recently, geographic boundaries were added to the criteria with which students are distributed to various medical schools. Approximately 85 percent of all admitted students complete the medical program and receive their degree.

CURRICULAR STRUCTURE AND INNOVATION

The core curricula for medical schools is uniform throughout the country. However, each Faculty is free to introduce the major subjects according to the needs of the local community. The curriculum is spread over a period of six years; clinical training is carried out mainly in university hospitals and partly in the educational hospitals of the Ministry of Health. Faculty members are all tenured, and all possess a doctorate degree (MD or PhD). They start their academic profession as lecturers and are promoted based on published research. However, all universities are governmental institutions; hence, faculty members are government employees appointed to the professional university cadre which, along with the judicial corps, is the highest in the country. There is a separate Civil Service scale for the administrative staff in the universities which is applied equally to men and women. Fringe benefits include time off, as well as time for research. Regulations allow university staff to engage in private practice.

The National Supreme Council/Medical Sector recognizes that medicine is a dynamic subject with continuous new developments that require frequent revision, evaluation, and monitoring of curricular content as well as learning methodologies. At present, two curricular models predominate in Egyptian medical schools: the traditional and the innovative, with a third model beginning to emerge that contains elements of both.

Traditional curriculum

In the traditional medical schools, the study of medicine is divided into three main phases: the basic, or preparatory premed phase (years one and two); the preclinical phase (year three); and the clinical phase (years four, five and six), as outlined in Table 11.2

Table 11.2

Traditional Medical Curriculum in Egypt

Year	Subject	Minimum Number of Hours
1	Chemistry and biochemistry	75
	Physiology, biophysics, and biostatistics	120 , 25 for biophysics and biostatistics
	Histology	60
	Anatomy and embryology	145
	English language	30
2	Physiology	140
	Histology	100
	Anatomy and embryology	140
	Biochemistry	100
	Behavioral and human sciences	30
	English language	30
3	Pathology	200
	Pharmacology	150
	Parasitology	60
	Community medicine	30
	Internal medicine	clinical 2 hours, 3 times/week, 2 months
	Surgery	clinical 2 hours, 3 times/week, 2 months
4	Internal medicine	30, 2 months
	Surgery	20, 2 months
	Obstetrics & Gynecology	40, 2 months
	Ophthalmology	40, 2 months
	Community medicine	30 open
	Forensic medicine and toxicology	30 open

Table 11.2

Traditional Medical Curriculum in Egypt

Year	Subject	Minimum Number of Hours
5	Internal medicine	60, 2 months
	Surgery	60, 2 months
	Obstetrics and gynecology	50, 2 months
	Pediatrics	30, 1 month
	Community medicine	30, 1 month
6	Internal medicine	80, 4 months
	Surgery[1]	80, 4 months

It is the role of each department, through its curriculum committee, to develop and/or monitor its specific curriculum and syllabi (lectures, practicals, and clinical rounds), set the timetable, designate the staff members responsible for teaching each topic on a yearly basis, and report to the faculty board for approval.

Student assessment in the traditional curriculum. Student progress is assessed through examinations. Twenty percent of the total grade in each subject is devoted to periodic student assessment during the academic year. The minimum pass level is 60 percent.

Integrated medical education. Medical educators realized during the 1960s that clinicopathological conferences are a good example of integration in medical education and an important feature in the educational methodology of graduate medical programs. Since then, attempts have been underway to correlate courses that could gradually replace a number of hours reserved for traditional departmental lectures. If half the hours were devoted to correlated courses, the other half would need a new type of lecture, since no duplication of textbooks would be possible and no "compartmented" courses would need to be covered. This would have a dual effect on medical education: integration, on one hand, and a more applied problem-solving approach, on the other.

Innovative Medical Curricula

---

[1] Branches of Internal Medicine include chest diseases, neurology, physiatry, tropical diseases, skin diseases, venereal diseases, physical medicine, cardiovascular diseases, clinical pathology, cardiology, neurology & psychiatry, "urgent" medicine and emergencies. Branches of surgery are orthopaedics, neurosurgery, chest and heart surgery, urogenital surgery, plastic surgery and burns, cancer surgery, paediatric surgery, anesthesia and intensive care. (National Supreme University Council, *University Rules and Regulations for Medical Education in Egypt.* Cairo: University Press.)

In March 1978, a conference on medical education in El Fayoum, Egypt, was attended by representatives of the Medical Syndicate, the Egyptian Medical Association, the Ministry of Health, all the medical schools in Egypt, and the Army Medical Corps. The conference's main theme was producing physicians relevant to the community's health service needs (Khallaf 1990). The conference theme was endorsed by a presidential decree supporting the establishment of two community-based medical schools, one in the Suez Canal region, at Ismailia, and the other in the Delta region, at El-Monoufia.

The program at the Faculty of Medicine, Suez Canal University, Ismailia, was initiated in 1981, with 49 students pursuing a community-oriented, problem-based track, a number well below the more usual five to seven hundred student medical school class. The program emphasizes problem-based tutorials and is governed by three strategies: (1) close collaboration with the Ministry of Health; (2) using the regional health services facilities for teaching and training; and (3) covering the health services needs of the whole Suez Canal and Sinai area (see table 11.3, p. 150).

The Suez Canal program is also a six-year curriculum divided into three phases, but the phases are slightly different from those of the traditional schools. Phase one (year one) deals primarily with prepathogenesis, emphasizing the phases of human life and their interactions with the environment in the broadest sense. Phase two (years two and three) deals with the major portion of the basic medical sciences through organ system blocks. Finally, phase three (years four, five, and six) is devoted entirely to clerkships. Each phase is composed of a series of five to six week blocks, and learning within the blocks is centered on individual or community health problems and/or needs. Students are assigned to groups of six to eight and meet regularly with their tutor, usually covering one problem a week. Two days each week are devoted entirely to field training, which includes clinical and community activities in rural or urban settings. Student evaluation takes many forms, including self-assessment, peer assessment, and tutor assessment. At the end of each block, students take written and skills examinations and submit a report on their community health activities. In addition, twice a year, students take a problem-solving test and receive feedback. Forty percent of the total grade for each phase is allocated for the end-of-phase comprehensive examination (Nooman, Schmidt, and Ezzat 1990).

Table 11.3

Innovative Medical School Curricula: Suez Canal, Monoufia--Egypt

Phase	Curricular Structure
Phase 1 (Year 2) Pre-pathogenesis	A series of blocks organized along the phases of the human life cycle stressing means of growth and development from conception to old age. The normal structural, functional and psychosocial characteristics of man are dealt with together with societal and environmental factors and their interactions relevant to health promotion or illness induction. Professional training includes as basic clinical skills the ability of communication. In addition, basic skills in field surveys and research methodology are practiced as well as simple clinical examination procedures (General examination procedures, body build and vital signs).
Phase II (Years 2 and 3) Pathogenesis	The bulk of biomedical sciences are integrated around individual and community health problems incorporating the behavioral and sociomedical aspects. The natural history of disease constitutes the organizing principle of learning. Problem design, selection and sequencing consider priority and common health problems as well as educational objectives of the phase. Student learning involves further training in clinical and community work-related skills.
Phase III (Years 4-6) Clerkships	In year four, clerkships take place in ambulatory care settings: primary care centres, hospital outpatient and occupational sites. In years five and six, clerkships are predominantly hospital-based: Out- and inpatient training, except for the primary care clerkships. Apart from periodic formative examinations that address the cognitive skills and attitude domains, each phase ends with a summative examination. Learning is self directed and problem-based in small groups throughout the curriculum.

This program and the similar curriculum of the new school in Monoufia, being extremely different from the traditional programs, faced great opposition, distrust, and skepticism on the local level. They were also considered very expensive, given the limited resources of the country and the small class size. However, on the international level they were highly regarded for their success in carrying out a problem-oriented, community-based approach and for dealing with all three domains of the learning process: cognitive, affective, and psychomotor.

In 1985, the Department of Community Medicine at the Faculty of Medicine, University of Alexandria, initiated a moderately innovative, horizontally and vertically integrated, community oriented educational training program designed to be implemented within ongoing programs and in affiliation with the MOH as represented by the local Health Directorate. Clinical departments, including pediatrics, obstetrics and gynecology, ophthalmology, pharmacology, parasitology, and forensic medicine, are all enthusiastic partners in this integrated medical curriculum. This program was partially sponsored by WHO.

In 1990 the Faculty of Medicine, Assuit University, feeling the need to upgrade the quality of their medical graduates, held a workshop on "How to Promote Community-Oriented Medical Education." They plan to launch an innovative parallel track adopting the community-oriented, problem-based initiative, into which they will direct 20 percent of their students.

GRADUATE MEDICAL EDUCATION

Graduate medical education follows licensure and is geared toward specialty/residency training programs. It is divided into two categories according to the type of training needed and the functions performed. The length of training for a specialist varies between different specialties and subspecialties, ranging from two to three years, and is linked to the type of degree the candidate will receive (a diploma or master's degree) upon fulfillment of the requirements. An advanced level of graduate education is also available for obtaining a doctorate degree, but this program is offered almost exclusively to medical school academic staff in special research-oriented institutions.

Three initiatives are being undertaken to expand graduate medical education in Egypt: (1) more candidates are being sent abroad for further training in doctoral programs; (2) the number of graduate study programs within the country is being increased; and (3) new institutions for graduate studies and training are being established.

LICENSURE

Before applying for licensure, all medical graduates must complete 12 months of internship distributed in two-month phases among four compulsory specialties (internal medicine, surgery, OB/Gyn, pediatrics) and two elective specialties. The Medical License Department of the Ministry of Health issues the license to practice medicine in Egypt. There is no specific national examination required. Applicants for licensure must be members of the Egyptian Medical Syndicate. All graduates, after obtaining the license, usually complete two years in government service as general practitioners. In addition to patient care, their duties include managing the health care units. The management skills needed for this additional responsibility are learned on the job, with preservice training for three months followed by continuous in-service training programs. These training courses are run by the Ministry of Health and shared by loans from the University staff. They are based on lectures, practical classes, and workshops. The Ministry of Health also offers its staff opportunities and financial support to join programs leading to diploma, master's, and doctorate degrees, announced twice yearly by the universities. Egyptian physicians with foreign qualifications must have their degree validated by the Supreme Council of the Universities/Medical Sector before they are permitted to practice in the country.

Cross-Licensing of Physicians

Foreign medical graduates are not allowed to practice in Egypt. However, invitations may be extended to experts or consultants in rare specialties for whom a temporary license is issued by the Medical Syndicate for a maximum period of three months in a given year. This temporary license is granted after a review of the applicant's qualifications, curriculum vitae, official documents of previous experiences and competency level.

CONTINUING MEDICAL EDUCATION

Continuing medical education has either formal structure, through enrollment in diploma, master's, or doctorate courses, or it takes the form of workshops, conferences, and training fellowships inside the country or abroad. These are usually sponsored locally by the Ministry of Health, the universities, drug companies, the medical technology industry, and/or international agencies and organizations.

ROLE OF RESEARCH IN MEDICAL EDUCATION

Research in medical education is localized at the institution level and, in general, is inadequate, nonsystematic, and not well organized. Generically, the purpose of research in medical education in Egypt can be summarized in four broad categories: (1) research to earn master's and doctoral degrees, (2) problem-driven and action-oriented research, (3) research in support of large scale intervention programs, and (4) research for policy and program development. It is envisioned that the recently established nucleus for the national network of information, ENSTINET (Egyptian National Scientific and Technical Information Network), will have a major impact on the development of research in Egyptian universities. This network will facilitate the exchange of information among universities in the different branches of science, and ultimately, the development of more sound research in Egypt as well as neighboring countries.

GOVERNMENT/PUBLIC SECTOR INVOLVEMENT

Like all other university education in Egypt, medical education is completely nationalized, with no contribution whatsoever from the private sector. The government is responsible for its financing and administration through the Ministry of Higher Education. The Egyptian Medical Association and the

Egyptian Medical Syndicate are the two formal bodies that represent the members of the medical profession. (The syndicate is the politically more powerful.)

INTERNATIONAL LINKAGES AND COLLABORATION

International collaboration takes various forms, either with an international organization such as the WHO Regional Office for the Eastern Mediterranean, United Nations Educational, Scientific, and Cultural Organization (UNESCO), the United Nations International Children's Emergency Fund (UNICEF), the UN Food and Agriculture Organization (FAO), the US Agency for International Development (USAID), and the World Bank, or through direct agreements with a number of countries, such as the US Peace Fellowships. Exchange of students and scholars for postgraduate and postdoctoral education is also common. In some instances, a joint faculty advisory committee is developed through the channel system between an Egyptian and a foreign school for the supervision of fellows' education and training in line with national needs. It is administered and financed by the Ministry of Higher Education, Directorate of Scholarships.

ISSUES AND TRENDS

Community-oriented medical education and problem based learning are gaining more recognition. At least three medical schools train their students in the community, where students study community health science at a health center or clinic or by conducting home visits. The programs include community, social, and preventive medicine, management of health services, and primary health care. Students also receive practical training in how to work as a team with members of other health professions. Given their success and recognition, it is expected that similar types of programs with the same visions will be launched in other medical schools.

Strong efforts will continue to be exerted to reduce the class size in medical schools for a more satisfying learning environment and to control the surplus of physicians. Simultaneously, other health professionals educational programs should be encouraged and supported to address the country's needs for primary health care and community well-being.

Both the government and the people are beginning to recognize the need for community participation and involvement in health care as a remedy for the deficiencies of the health system. Although fees are much lower than in private hospitals, 25 percent of governmental hospital beds are already being financed on a fee-for-service basis. It is expected that over the next few years, publicly funded primary health care facilities will offer some afternoon and evening hours on a fee-for-service basis. Dialogue continues between health personnel and the people to identify priorities and generate enthusiasm.

The Ministry of Health, acknowledging that management is probably the weakest point in the health delivery system, is increasing its grants for graduate studies in community medicine and public health, both locally and abroad. The government is also studying the wage structure for full-time physicians who opt for managerial roles.

With the recently developed ENSTINET, it is expected that more systematic and organized research will be conducted, especially in such long overlooked fields as health manpower development, current data regarding health status of the population, and real assessment of needs.

Also of importance is evaluation of the different, multiple, and versatile cooperative projects conducted in collaboration with international agencies and organizations to determine whether all these human and material resources are going in the right direction toward achieving the goal of health for all by the year 2000.

NOTE

Thanks are due to Miss Farida I. Youssef, former Librarian, WHO-EMRO, Alexandria, for her continuous assistance and valuable consultations from the early beginning.

REFERENCES

Ghalioungi, P. 1973. The house of life: Magic and medical science in ancient Egypt. Amsterdam.

Khallaf, A.G. 1990. Egypt: Winning in spite of economic problems. In E. Tarimo and A. Creese, eds., *Achieving Health For All by the Year 2000: Midway reports of country experiences*, pp. 64-79. Geneva: World Health Organization.

Mahfouz, N. 1935. The history of medical education in Egypt: The Egyptian university. The Faculty of Medicine, Cairo University Publication no. 8. Cairo: Government Press.

National Supreme University Council: Medical Sector. 1980. *University rules and regulations for medical education in Egypt.* Cairo: University Press.

Nooman, Z., H.G. Schmidt, and E.S. Ezzat, eds. 1990. *Innovation in medical education: An evaluation of its present status.* New York: Springer Publishing.

US Agency for International Development. 1979. *Health in Egypt: Recommendations for U.S. assistance.* Washington, D.C: Agency for International Development.

World Health Organization. 1964. *Proceedings: First Eastern Mediterranean Regional Conference on Medical Education, Teheran, 1962.* Regional Office for Eastern Mediterranean. Alexandria, Egypt: WHO-EMRO.

12

France

FRANÇOIS BONNAUD
A. VERGNENEGRE
J.M. CHABOT

The French Republic is one of the largest countries in Europe in land mass, with a population of approximately 56 million, a heavily industrialized economy, and a 1986 per capita GNP of $10,740. Birth and death rates are about average for Europe as a whole, and general health conditions compare favorably with other developed nations. Elementary and secondary education is publicly funded; a baccalaureate is the minimum qualification for entry to higher education.

OVERVIEW OF THE HEALTH CARE DELIVERY SYSTEM

The French health care delivery system is insurance-based, with central and local government controls. The social security system created in 1945 is a single nationwide service with a National Fund (Caisse d'Assurance Maladie) that oversees the regional and local funds. Fund representatives are elected by the contributors. The social security system provides three main services: health care coverage, old-age pensions, and family allowances. The money for the funds is drawn directly from the contributors' salaries. Health care insurance is based on gross salary, and the coverage provided ranges from 55 to 90 percent depending on the services rendered.

The health and social services administration is organized in four levels: national (Ministry of Health under the Ministry of Social Security); regional (Regional Prefect, Regional Department of Health and Social Security, and Regional Council); department (Prefect, Departmental Health and Social Security Administration, and General Council); and committee (councilors and local Departments of Health and Hygiene).

Ambulatory health care is based on a free-market system for physicians and paramedical personnel. Negotiations between the administrative authorities and health care professionals, under the guidance of the National Insurance Fund, determine agreements (conventions) on fees. The patient pays the health care professional directly after receiving care and is subsequently reimbursed from the various funds as a percentage of the total, according to the previously determined reimbursement rate. Health care expenditure under this system is increasing steadily at a rate of 14 percent per year.

Hospital services represent 50 percent of the overall medical expenditures; payments were initially based on a per diem rate. In 1984, the inflationary nature of the per diem system led to creation of an overall maximum operating budget for public hospitals in the health service. Since 1989, there is a trend to focus on diagnosis-related groups in an effort to contain hospital expenses and costs.

Health care expenditure represents 9 percent of the gross national product, that is, about 9,000 French francs per capita in 1990. About three quarters of the funds are provided by the Social Security System. (This percentage has fallen from 77 percent in 1980 to 74 percent in 1990.) The state and local authorities provide 1.5 percent, private health funds and insurance plans provide 6 percent, and the rest (around 20 percent) is borne by the patients. Rationalization of hospital expenditure was started ten years ago in the form of budget capping. The central government is now putting pressure on the health agreements reached under the guidance of the Health Insurance Funds by negotiating directly with each professional group separately. Without restricting rights to health care, the purpose of these negotiations is to progressively try to stem the slow but inexorable increase in expenditures. The Social Security system is a pillar of the French health care service and provides patients with a fourfold freedom of choice: freedom to choose their health provider, freedom to consult a specialist or general practitioner, freedom to consult several health providers, and free choice of hospital or clinic.

HISTORICAL BACKGROUND

The era of "modern" medical education began in 1804 under the direction of Antoine Fourcroy. As director of public education, and himself a physician, he established, in collaboration with the Minister of Home Affairs, a national code of medical education within the university system. Fourcroy's plan was not without political finesse. From then to the present day, there have been two main avenues for higher education in France: (1) universities with their various faculties, conferring degrees and diplomas with varying standards, but providing a decentralized system of education with the inherent risks and benefits of independence, and (2) Grandes Écoles, essentially Paris-dominated, for training an elite class of senior administrators and bureaucrats. The independence of the universities is thus counterbalanced by the control exercised from the centralized Grandes Écoles.

This rather odd, and apparently conflicting, duality in the education system is also found in medicine and can also be traced to Fourcroy's original plan. Unable to restrict medical education to a single medical school in Paris, he allowed the establishment in 1794 of three centers: Paris, Montpellier, and Strasbourg. They became medical schools in 1796 and by 1808 were Faculties of Medicine in their own right. However, the fundamental structures of the French medical education system had been laid down by 1802: (1) *Externat* (clerkships); (2) *Internat* (internships); (3) and *Doctorat*.

Entry into clerkships and internships is determined by selection exams. Hence, a more practical and socially-oriented course (*Officiat Santo*) was added, based on the equivalence of three training years or five years' practical experience in public or military hospitals.

This system, for which the Internship entrance examination is the mainstay, is akin to the elitist system of the *Grandes Écoles*. Medical education is thus decentralized, with the risks and advantages of independence, but nevertheless adheres to a well-defined curricular structure, based essentially on the centralized hospital system and modeled mainly on the Paris internship entrance exam. This system led to a considerable expansion of the French hospital system over the following century.

Between 1813 and World War II, the following changes occurred: creation of the position of *Chef de Clinique* (hospital consultant) as assistant professor in 1913; competitive examination for *Agrégation* in Medicine in 1923; creation of 20 premedical schools controlled by the universities in 1841; abolition of the Health Officer Corps and creation of PCN (certificate of aptitude in physics, chemistry and natural sciences) as a requirement for entry to medical school in 1893, a change stemming from the need for a systematic scientific training of future doctors. The medical curriculum was extended from four to five years in 1909, and by 1919, a total of 32 medical specialties were taught. In 1935, the PCN became PCB (B for biology instead of natural sciences), and, in 1945, the *Ordre National des Médecins* (General Medical Council) was created. The Social Security System was created in 1947. In 1958, Hospital and University Centres (CHU, CHR) were created.

From 1893 to 1958, medical education was a two-tier structure: schools of medicine that housed most of the senior staff (*Agrégations*) from the basic sciences, and hospitals that housed the consultants and other clinical faculty who, although participating in some general teaching activities, functioned mainly in an apprenticeship system. At that time, the internship was run exclusively by the hospitals, with a longstanding conflict between the basic science staff and the hospital clinicians.

At the turn of the century, the Flexner Report (1910) in North America underscored the value of a firm grounding in the basic sciences for the development of medical knowledge and skills. A system that integrated clinical training in hospitals, experimental research, histomorphological microscopic studies, active teaching, and partial private funding was established in North American medical schools. Under the instigation of R. Debre, French hospital and university centers were set up to emulate the American system. The centers grouped together senior staff (university hospital, medical faculty, regional hospital, and research) creating a better balance between basic science research in the Faculties of Medicine and clinical research in the hospitals. However, the scope of the reform was less than in the US, being hampered to some extent by the traditional Faculty-hospital conflict of interest. Within the regional and university hospital centers, clinical considerations were clearly more important, although basic science staff were increasingly preparing students for more advanced degrees (license, master's, doctorates in both human biology [BH] and biological and medical sciences [SBM]). This provided a framework for high-quality clinical research.

Fundamental and clinical research quickly sought recognition from the national research bodies: CNRS (Centre National de la Recherche Scientifique created in 1939), INSERM (Institut National de la Santé et de la Recherche Médicale, created in 1964), and CEA (Commissariat á l'Energie Atomique) and INRA (Institut National de la Recherche Agronomique). These organizations, although independent from medical schools, collaborate with them scientifically, technically, and financially. University staff work in the research units, and full-time research staff from the research bodies work in university laboratories.

Within this framework, clinical work and research flourished. Unfortunately, medical education and modern educational methods have been stifled by the presence of a parallel Internship curriculum, and little has been achieved in educational research. In 1960, the PCB was replaced by the CPEM (*Certificat Préparatoire aux Études Médicales*). As a result, all preclinical education is now in the Faculties of Medicine and under the control of the basic medical scientists.

A major movement began in 1968 with passage of the Edgar Faure Higher Education Orientation Act. The act gave all universities, whatever their discipline, a common legal status with increased autonomy. Nevertheless, the spirit of the 1958 act that joined regional hospital centers and medical schools has tended to confer a certain specificity to the health sciences within the university system. These differences, however, tend to have more impact on the career structure of the staff than on the actual training of the medical students.

The application of the concept of selective primary health care as defined by WHO varies considerably between countries and brings a fundamental new idea to the medical curriculum, i.e., the obligatory cost of services in their socioeconomic context. This idea was not taken up wholeheartedly in France. Currently, it is being taught in medical schools, but only in those departments that are specifically involved such as health care economics, evaluation and public health.

In 1984 a new higher education act, referred to as the Savary Act, maintained the specific relationship of medical schools with hospitals. The medical schools (UFR, for Unité de Formation et Recherche) lost their status as public bodies which they had possessed since 1971. The medical UFR now have overall control over the clinical stages of the medical course (second and third cycles, general medicine, specialties and public health). The preclinical course (first cycle) is controlled by the universities. In 1992, the initiative for a reform in the preclinical course was launched.

ROLE OF NATIONAL POLICY IN SHAPING MEDICAL EDUCATION

The preclinical course (first cycle) has always been controlled by the universities under the authority of the Ministry of Education. The clinical course, however, depends more directly on the teaching programs of the individual medical schools, albeit within national guidelines. Several policy making bodies are involved in a supervisory capacity. There is currently no nationwide coordination of these local commissions. It is likely that bodies such as the CNEM (Commission Nationale des Etudes Médicales) or ANDEM (Agence Nationale pour le Développement de l'Evaluation Médicale) will have at least a consultative role in the supervision of medical education.

ADMISSION

French universities have always been opposed to the principle of selection of intake to different programs, and the medical schools have gone along with this principle. (For medical school demographics, see Table 12.1, p. 171.) However, in view of the recognized physicians' surplus, the Ministry of Education in 1972 began to limit intake into the second year of the medical course by enforcing a required score for the exams taken at the end of the first year. In 1972, a fixed intake of medical students was established after the first year of preclinical studies (*numerous clausus*). The number was initially set at about 15,000 nationwide, was progressively reduced to 3,750, and will probably go down to 3,500 by 1993.

In 1992, for a population of more than 58 million, France had 170,000 physicians, (i.e., approximately 1 physician per 350 persons). The threshold of 1 physician per 300 population is widely regarded as a critical limit. Each school of medicine is allotted a number of places depending on its past status and the catchment area it serves. These thresholds are a source of concern to the deans of French medical schools who are worried about potential operating difficulties in hospitals due to the reduced number of junior staff.

The other concern is the potential influx, within seven to ten years, of large numbers of physicians from EEC countries such as Italy, Spain, Belgium, and others that do not adopt an intake ceiling strategy, simultaneously producing large numbers of physicians in excess of their needs. These intake ceilings are the subject of ongoing discussions among the Ministries of Education and Health, the deans of medical schools, and the medical unions.

Medical Student Demographics

Students apply to medical school after 12 years of general education. In 1992, slightly more than half of French medical students were female. The number of female medical students increased from 36.4 percent in 1984 to 52 percent in 1991. Women physicians in the age range of 65 to 69 account for only 10 percent of the physician work force, with the percentage increasing as the age range decreases: 26 percent in the age range of 40 to 44; 44 percent in the age range of 30 to 34; and 52 percent in the under-30 age cohort. Fifty-three percent of the female students possess a biology-based baccalaureate (Bac D).

This student profile will tend to please those who were critical of the bias toward enrollment of students with a Bac C (fundamental sciences) with good grades in mathematics, physics, and chemistry. In fact, medical demographics has considerably affected the financial prospects of the medical profession, and the hard sciences students now tend to choose other options. In line with this trend, the recent decisions of the Ministry of Education are designed to emphasize the teaching of human and social sciences in the preclinical course, with subjects including epistemology, history of medicine, psychology, languages, medical ethics, and moral philosophy.

CURRICULAR STRUCTURE AND INNOVATION

Several modifications of the preclinical and clinical curricula took place over the last decade. Until 1983, the medical course lasted seven years: two preclinical years (first cycle) devoted to basic science and normal human biology; four years of clinical studies (second cycle), with hospital clinical work in the mornings and the afternoons devoted to pathology (human pathology and semiology, signs and classification of disease being introduced in the first clinical year), and one year in a hospital clinical training post (third cycle). Specialization could take place via the internship in the fifth year or via a CES (*Certificat d'Études Spéciales*), the duration of which depended on the particular specialty. Teaching was essentially theoretical in nature.

As shown in Figure 12.1, since 1983 the preclinical years have become increasingly medical, with semiology included in the second year (PC2). Certain basic sciences are now taught at a later stage. The preclinical stage still lasts two years. The clinical (second cycle) still takes four years, and culminates in the *Certificat de Synthèse Clinique et Thérapeutique*, a pass/fail nongraded proficiency test designed by each of the 43 medical schools in France. The final stage (third cycle) comprises two main categories: general medicine and specialties. The new DES (*Diplômes d'Études Spécialisées*) replaced the traditional *Internat* and CES diplomas, thus ending the dual training routes for French medical specialists. All medical students must pass a nationwide medical examination (with multiple choice questions and written clinical problems) designed by a new organization: the Centre National des Concours d'Internat (CNCI). Following this national exam, the students take the DES and an *Internat* (internship) with either four/five-year tracks for specialization (*Internat de Specialtés*) after success, or a two-year track for general practice (*Internat de Médecine Générale*).

Preclinical Cycle

The current preclinical first cycle concentrates on basic sciences, although semiology in the second year has not yet been introduced in all Faculties. The following disciplines are taught: physics-biophysics, mathematics, chemistry-biochemistry, embryology, cell biology, psychology, physiology, and anatomy.

In the second year, anatomy, biochemistry, physiology, social science, biophysics and computer science, radiological semiology, gerontology, hospital administration and hygiene, and nursing services are covered.

Exposure to clinical work in the second year takes the form of a few weeks of nursing training. Some schools have introduced more clinical material in the form of full-time presence in a hospital department guided by a tutor who is a full-time hospital physician. The student assists at all the routine professional activities, including ward rounds, outpatient consultations, procedures and clinical teaching.

Clinical (Second Cycle)

Clinical pathology is taken throughout the second, third, and fourth years of the clinical cycle. There are considerable differences in the teaching of pathology between the Faculties. The first clinical year includes bacteriology, virology, immunology, general pathology, surgical semiology, medical semiology, and anatomy as applied to semiology. The clinical work includes a six-week course in medical semiology, a six-week course in surgical semiology, a two-week course in psychiatric semiology, and a one-week course in radiological semiology. Therapeutics, forensic medicine, industrial medicine, and public health are commonly taught in the fourth clinical year. This clinical course consists of a set of fundamental modules which are considered basic requirements in the training of any physician whatever the future specialization.

The clinical program in France differs markedly from what is taught elsewhere. First, clinical material is introduced early (second preclinical year). In the first year of the clinical course, students attend hospital departments every morning from 9:00 a.m. till noon. Students have normal university holidays (Christmas, Easter, and summer). In the third and fourth clinical years, students have hospital status (trainee grade), a reincarnation of the previously abolished *Externat* grade. Students attend hospital departments every morning and receive a stipend (around $200 per month). They are allowed a one-month holiday.

The pedagogic methods used throughout the clinical course are centered on the formal lecture. However, with the encouragement of local faculty work groups, teaching in small groups and problem-solving exercises have been introduced in some medical schools. No medical school has yet adopted these techniques exclusively. Efforts have been made to replace the formal lecture, leaving the choice of methods to those in charge of the particular course (matching the teaching method to the objective).

Significant changes have been proposed in the preclinical course for 1992-1993. The main disciplines will be taught and evaluated as 60-90 hour modules. For the first two or three years, students will take six modules--up to a maximum of 500 hours per year. Increased emphasis on the human sciences has led to a proposal for one module to concentrate on epistemology, history of medicine, languages, psychology, medical ethics, and moral philosophy. A student who does not pass the first year examination but obtains a specified grade is considered to have completed the equivalent of the first year grade in the natural sciences program and may enter the second year of the College of Science.

Within the clinical course, some medical schools favor the *Internat* system, where their academic reputation is based on success rates, while others integrate faculty-based teaching with the *Internat* system. The latter more complex system provides a more comprehensive theoretical and practical grounding for all students in the clinical course, including those who have either failed or not taken the specialist examinations.

GRADUATE MEDICAL EDUCATION

It should be noted that during the clinical course, any student aiming for a career in research or a university hospital or hospital appointment must either follow a parallel curriculum in the biological and medical sciences (SBM) to obtain a master's degree (300 hour certificate) followed by a DEA (*Diplôme d'Études Approfondies*), or perform one year of fundamental or clinical research. The DEA is the prerequisite for entry to the doctoral program, which generally requires two to four years of further research.

Third Stage: Residency (Third Cycle) in General Medicine

Students enter this residency either as a personal choice or due to failure in the *Internat* national examination. Residents spend two years in full-time hospital posts (three semesters in a general hospital and one semester in a university hospital). There is no additional theoretical teaching, but practical seminars are given in the medical schools one afternoon per fortnight. These are taught by university hospital physicians and general practitioners. The general practitioners are members of a regional college led by a professor of general practice with a part-time appointment in a medical school, who spends the remainder of his or her time in private practice in the community. Representatives from continuing medical education programs also participate. During these two years, students must also complete 20 half-days of practice with an accredited clinician or clinical tutor. In some medical schools, this commences in the fourth year of the clinical course. The residency training (third cycle) is supervised and evaluated by a commission of representatives of all relevant teaching faculty.

Third Stage: Specialties Training

For students passing the *Internat* national examination, choice of specialties depends largely on the score obtained. The DES in medicine, surgery, psychiatry, occupational medicine (with a specific examination for doctors qualified for more than three years, including those from other EEC countries), public health, and medical biology includes 27 subspecialties. The DES lasts from four to five years, and each includes a requirement for practical training. A further series of complementary DES (or DESC) is available, each lasting two years. The DES and DESC training programs are both theoretical and practical. Evaluation is based on a written report and an oral presentation (*Mémoire*) adjudicated by a panel of university hospital specialists drawn from different regions. Although this rather complex system was initially designed to control the output and regional distribution of specialists and maintain a balance between general practitioners and specialists, it has fallen far short of these objectives. Nevertheless, its main merit is that it has favored the mobility (often involuntary and forced) of many students.

The output of general practitioners and specialists has been a major concern of the Direction Generale de la Sante (Health Services Directorate), the Ministries of Health and Education, the Confederation of Medical School Deans, and the medical unions. Over the last few years, the number of posts available for those passing the specialist *Internat* examination (2,340 in 1991) has corresponded with the reduced intake ceilings (3,750 in 1991). This has led to a marked change in the general practitioner/specialist ratio: 60 percent to 40 percent in 1982, 49 percent to 51 percent in 1991; and, given current trends, 35 percent to 70 percent by 1998, giving rise to a significant alteration in the structure of the medical profession. It should be pointed out that polls of clinical students in 1991 showed that 60 to 69 percent wished to become specialists, while only 11 to 19 percent wished to become general practitioners. The regulation of output proposed in 1983 has thus been of the free-market type and has affected groups of disciplines such as medicine, surgery, and psychiatry rather than the DES themselves. Thus, between 1980 and 1989 there have been abrupt changes in choices as a function of fashion or perceived financial incentives. For example, Neurology increased 282 percent, Child Psychiatry increased 449 percent, and Orthopedic Surgery increased 4,900 percent. Other disciplines have followed a more rational progress: Cardiology up 81 percent, Rheumatology up 71 percent, Pulmonary Medicine up 44 percent. Apart from obtaining a DES, students may also register for the *Capacité*, with 11 national diplomas (accident and emergency medicine, angiology, gerontology, medical hydrology and climatology, aerospace medicine, sports medicine and biology, catastrophe medicine, prison medicine, tropical medicine, and drug and alcohol abuse) that may take from one to three years, or the University Diploma (DU), a regional diploma delivered by the relevant medical school. These may be in a highly specialized field or in any specialty not leading to a DES. They are open to most students and are designed to enhance training, but exclusive practice of the specialty is not officially recognized.

LICENSURE

The Commission of the Third Cycle of Medical Studies or the Department of General Practice have overall responsibility for overseeing participation in the requisite hospital scholarships and attendance at seminars. The student submits a thesis in General Practice in the fourth semester after completion of the third cycle course. The qualified doctor then registers with the Ordre des Médecins (Departmental and Regional Council), which delivers an authorization to practice. Simultaneously, he or she registers with the DRASS (Direction Régionale des Affaires Sanitaires et Sociales).

Specialist Licensure

To obtain a specialist qualification, the candidate must submit a thesis (in the 4th semester) and present a written and oral report (*Mémoire*) before a Commission of Specialists drawn from the various regions. This commission delivers the DES qualification after ensuring that the student has attended the requisite hospital scholarships and after consideration of the candidate's report and recommendations from the relevant department heads. There is no direct or official involvement of a Board of Certification, although the interregional

Specialist Commission in fact acts in this capacity at a more local level. Some specialties, especially in surgery (e.g., orthopedics), have set up Colleges that have the right to oversee decisions of the interregional Specialist Commission with their agreement. Registration with the Ordre des Médecins and the DRASS is the same as that for general practitioners.

Cross-licensing of Physicians

Licensure requirements differ for physicians from countries in the European Common Market and nationals from non-EEC countries.

Free circulation of doctors is included in the EEC directives drawn up in 1975 and adopted in France in 1976. An accurate list of foreign medical diplomas that are valid in France, lists of specialist qualifications, and medical registration details in the various EEC countries have been established. Since the inception of the EEC directives, 9,000 doctors have migrated within Europe, 850 of whom have come to France. This movement has considerably increased over the last few years, tending to confirm the worries of the medical school deans with respect to intake ceilings.

Medical studies--toward standardization. The educational requirements of the French general practitioner comply with the directives of the EEC, namely, 5,000 hours of training spread over six years, ending with two years' hospital experience (*Résidanat*). Standardization is harder to achieve within the medical specialties: EEC directives stipulate an *Internat* with both practical and theoretical training at a certain level of responsibility with a minimum duration of five years for surgery, internal medicine, urology, and orthopedics, and four years for all other disciplines, except for endocrinology, clinical hematology, dermatology, anesthesiology, allergology, ophthalmology, ENT, stomatology, and rehabilitation and physical therapy, which require three years. These EEC requirements with respect to duration of training, responsibilities in regional or university hospitals, theoretical training in Medical Faculties, and granting of the authorization to practice after submission of a report (*Mémoire*) to the Interregional Specialist Commission were accepted in France in 1982 and officially adopted in 1984.

Any foreign doctor from outside the EEC who wishes to practice in France must follow one of two routes: (1) The student may pass the PCEM1 examination after registration in the first year course at a medical school. A student who passes, may be eligible to waive courses and enter the DCEM3 or DCEM4 years directly. The student then follows the normal progression of French medical students. (2) A student may obtain authorization from the Ministry of Health to take the *Certificat de Synthèse Clinique et Thérapeutique* (at the end of DCEM4). If granted permission, she or he may be allowed to practice by the Ministry of Health after a review of the applicant's file. In fact, however, very few individuals have taken this route.

A foreign doctor generally acquires a specialist qualification by taking a DIS (*Diplôme Universitaire de Spécialité*) identical to the corresponding DES. The number of posts available is regulated (around two thousand salaried appointments per year). Candidates sit an examination on the same day in France or in French embassies in other countries under the supervision of the cultural attachés. This arrangement tends to address candidates from countries without third cycle specialist courses. In addition, the students may also take a DISC (*Diplôme Universitaire de Spécialité Complémentaire*).

The AFS (*Attestation de Formation Spécialisée*) and AFSA (*Attestation de Formation Spécialisée Approfondie*) are partial training certificates designed as supplements to the third cycle training of foreign doctors. They involve both theoretical and practical training of a specialized or advanced nature. The AFS is four semesters long, and the AFSA, one or two semesters.

In addition, foreign students (except those from Andorra and EEC countries) may be authorized to take the *Internat* examination under special conditions (external route). These students must possess a medical qualification authorizing them to practice in their own country and posses an adequate proficiency of the French language. They may then be eligible for a French qualification.

Foreign students who have undertaken and/or completed their medical studies in France also take the *Internat* examination at the end of the clinical course (second cycle). They are granted the right to practice medicine in France if they comply with the immigration laws and regulations.

General practitioners of EEC countries with three years professional experience, may, like French general practitioners, take the specialist *Internat* examinations (in line with quotas), and then take the DES courses. They are not eligible for the DIS.

CONTINUING MEDICAL EDUCATION

Continuing medical education in France takes two forms. The first is the free system open to all physicians and consisting of short meetings on specific topics held in the evenings either in a medical school or private institutions. Much of the funding for these activities is provided by the pharmaceutical industry, and the participants are not remunerated. The second form is the medical convention. The second form was created in 1990, when an agreement was reached between professional unions and the National Health Insurance Fund. This scheme is optional in principle and was organized by universities, medical unions, the Ordre des Médecins and continuing medical education working groups. In order to qualify under this scheme, the themes of the medical conventions must be selected from a list of subjects published every year. The system operates at both the national and regional levels and is based on a 48-hour unit of continuing medical education. Each participating physician is remunerated on the basis of an equivalent of 15 consultations per day, with the costs financed from a 0.135 percent deduction from gross national medical fees agreed upon under the medical convention.

ROLE OF RESEARCH IN MEDICAL EDUCATION

Those wishing to pursue a career in the university hospital system with a view to clinical research (DEA is required), or within the hospital system (DEA is an advantage), or pure scientific research must also take a master's course in biological and medical sciences (SBM). The SBM master's degree consists of three certificates that may be taken any time during and after the PCEM2 (second clinical year). The specialist *Internat* is regarded as equivalent to one of these certificates. The master's degree leads to the DEA program in the other scientific disciplines such as pharmacy, veterinary medicine, dentistry and science. Those in charge of supervising the DEA programs include rather few doctors and are generally Paris-based.

While acquiring the DES, under certain conditions (e.g., obtaining good grades), students may be exempted from one year of research leading to the DEA. The two- to four-year DEA leads to a doctoral program equivalent to an American PhD.

The final official category in this research course, taken in conjunction with the medical school course, is that of a research supervisor or demonstrator (HDR, for *Habilitation à Diriger les Recherches*). These one- to three-year fellowship programs (*postes d'accueil*) in national research institutions, such as INSERM, are also open to specialists and senior interns. Finally, other not-for-profit organizations such as the Fondation pour la Recherche Médicale, the ARC (Association pour la Recherche en Cancérologie), and the LNC (Ligue Nationale contre le Cancer) may give grants and finance scholarships.

GOVERNMENT/PUBLIC SECTOR INVOLVEMENT

All medical education in France is under the direct authority of the Ministry of Education. There is, thus, no participation from the private sector, except for the part played by private practitioners during the third cycle of the General Practice course and occasional conferences or seminars sponsored by drug companies and banks.

INTERNATIONAL LINKAGES AND COLLABORATION

Outside the EEC, these linkages are exclusively limited to direct interuniversity cooperation. However, special privileges are granted to French-speaking African countries via the AUPELF (Association des Universités Partiellement ou Entièrement de Langue Française), the UREF (Université des Réseaux d'Expression Française), and the DAGIC (Direction des Affaires Générales, Internationales et de la Coopération). There are also strong links with the CAMES (Conseil Africain et Malgache de I'Enseignement Supérieur) and with those in charge of international exchanges in Maghreb countries (Tunisia, Algeria, and Morocco).

The *Revue d'Éducation Médicale* is the only pedagogic journal in French and covers the following geographic areas: Quebec, Switzerland, Belgium, Maghreb, French-speaking Africa, some countries in Eastern Europe, Haiti, Lebanon, and some countries in Southeast Asia.

The French organizations involved in international exchanges of professors and scholars are: Commission des Relations Extérieurs de la Conférence des

Présidents d'Université (COREX); the International Conference of Deans of French-speaking Medical Schools, with its major goals and objectives of standardizing medical training, continuing medical education, initiating new forms of cooperation, documentation and research among French-speaking countries; UREF-AUPELF; CIME (Cursus Intégré pour la Mobilité des Étudiants), designed to provide funding for student mobility, external courses and their recognition (scholarships for travel, accommodations and tuition); ERASMUS, an EEC program for student mobility in operation since 1987 and designed to favor mobility of students within the EEC. ERASMUS also involves faculty exchange, development of common teaching programs, intensive courses, and study visits, as well as interuniversity collaboration. In addition, the TEMPUS program is designed to facilitate transfer of teachers and students in higher education toward Eastern Europe. Links are established between various institutions in EEC countries and eligible countries in Eastern Europe. The CAMPUS program is centered on Africa and Madagascar; CSTD (Coopération Scientifique, Technique et du Développement) provides scholarships for visits to foreign countries under the authority of the Ministry of Foreign Affairs. DAGIC, under the Ministry of Education, encourages activities stemming from agreements reached between Ministries of Education in different countries with respect to specific projects or specific periods. French faculty are active in AMDE (Association of Medical School Deans of Europe)[1], ASME (Association for the Study of Medical School Education), AMEE (Association for Medical Education in Europe), WFME (World Federation for Medical Education), and IFMA (International Federation of Medical Students Associations). Finally, DARC Med (Développement, Approche et Reconnaissance des Différents Curriculum de Médecine) is designed to standardize the curriculum of medical studies in EEC countries in order to establish equivalent qualifications that are valid throughout the EEC.

ISSUES AND TRENDS

A working group from the National Conference of Deans of French Medical Schools was set up in 1990 to study modifications to the medical course to adapt it to the needs of the next century. From now until 2010, the French health system will face various economic difficulties and must succeed in managing an increasing number of physicians. The place and role of physicians will need to be redefined in a country in which health expenditure is increasing and where everyone believes that health care should be free. General practice has lost prestige and is not as attractive to medical students as formerly. The current attractiveness of high-tech specialties may well diminish if they become exclusively technical and neglect the holistic approach to the patient.

Issues for the next century include the following:

---

[1] AMDE was renamed in April 1993 to the Association of Medical Schools in Europe (AMSE).

Medical practice. The freedom of physicians to prescribe diagnostic and therapeutic measures will be preserved, although it will be subject to negotiations. Some complementary investigations and treatments will require a second opinion. The status of general practitioners and specialists will be contingent on the degrees obtained, length of study and respective levels of responsibility. Each physician will sign a contract with the paying party, subject to frequent review. This contract will take account of qualifications and will fix fees in a two-tier system: one at fixed rate for everybody and the other on a sliding scale; it will be adjusted from time to time depending on attendance at continuing medical education programs, and on individual conditions of practice. Remuneration will not be based on the technique used but rather on the value-added service provided by the physician on a unit consultation basis.

Health care structures. External consultation, outpatient and emergency services are now essential elements of medical practice. In certain cases, patients may be accommodated in hostel-type facilities outside the care-giving unit. Those in charge of care-providing units will act in collaboration with managers who will supervise the financial aspects of the service. It is desirable that these managers also be physicians. General practitioners will have access to these care-providing units via an expansion of part-time positions.

Pedagogic perspectives. It is predicted that in the future, 75 percent of the time spent in the first preclinical year (PCEM-1) course will deal with the scientific basis of normal human function, 15 percent with human and social sciences, and the last 10 percent with human pathology. This will entail a reduction in the present levels of basic science content. The second preclinical year (PCEM-2) will include continuing instruction in sciences, in addition to semiology and pathophysiology. It is anticipated that a reduction in the number of students will facilitate the use of more interactive teaching methods, including problem solving, small group teaching, and the practicum. The year will be initiated with practical instruction in semiology in hospital settings under direct supervision and will be goal-oriented.

DCEM-3 to DCEM-4. This is the most critical period in the training of medical students. Teaching focuses on organ systems, the assessment and evaluation of functional performance (the patient's general condition and chief complaints), deductive thinking required to determine management strategies, and understanding and prescribing available therapeutic measures. In general, this curricular structure attempts to adhere to a pedagogical continuum rather than the traditional split into arbitrary sections.

Entry to third cycle course. A general practice option in the *Internat* course is desirable, and the two-year residency requirement could be replaced by an increase of two to four years in the general practice third cycle. In this arrangement, all DCEM-4 students would take the CSCT test, and be evaluated via the *Internat* examination. Their future course would depend on the score obtained at this stage. It is yet to be decided whether replacing the *Internat* examination and CSCT test by a single examination for further course assessment is desirable. It seems clear that each course option will have to be more rigorously reviewed to preserve the equilibrium between the practice of general and specialized medicine as well as among the individual specialties. An extension of the third cycle course to nonmedical disciplines such as management, communication, marketing, and law may also be envisaged.

NOTE

The authors wish to acknowledge the following individuals for their assistance: Dr. Charles Boelen, Chief, Educational Development of Human Resources for Health, Division of Development of Human Resources for Health, World Health Organization, Geneva, Switzerland; Mr. J.P. Pittoors, Head of the Division of Health Personnel Management, Ministry of Education; Mrs. G. Canceill, Head of Statistical Department, DEPS 5, Ministry of Education; Mrs. C. Viatte, Head of Health Training Bureau, Ministry of Education; Mr. P. Chiristmann, Head of Organization and Study Bureau, DEPS 5, Ministry of Education; Mr. G. Vicente, General Secretary, Faculté de Médecine de Strasbourg (AUFEMO); Mr. J.C. Passounaud, Administration Service, Faculté de Médecine de Limoges; and Mrs. S.M. Authier, Dean's secretary.

REFERENCES

Administration universitaire francophone ou européen en médecine et odontologie (AUFEMO).

Argellies, J.L. 1988. La formation des médecins, systèmes institutions et acteurs, Archéologie du pouvoir en médecine. Thèse de doctorat, Paris, p. 687.

Associations des secrétaires généraux des facultés de médecine et d'odontologie francophone (ASGFMOF). 1988. *Systèmes de formation et de gestion des facultés de médecine et d'odontologie dans 7 pays de la CEE*, p. 138. Imprimerie de la faculté de médecine de Strasbourg.

Bandelier R., P. Bonamour and P.J. Jean. 1984. Le budget global. *Journal d'économie médicale* 2:77-93.

Centre de recherches, d'études et de documentation en économie de la santé (CREDES). 1991. *Le système de santé en France*. Paris: presses de la CNAM, p. 28.

Durin F. 1990. Les Dépenses De Santé en Europe. *Solidarité et santé* 2:9-15.

Ferland J. J. 1987. *Les grandes questions de la pédagogie médicale*, p. 476. Québec: presses de l'Université Laval.

Flexner, A. 1910. *Medical education in the United States and Canada: A report to the Carnegie Foundation for the Advancement of Teaching*. Bulletin no. 4. Boston: Updyke.

Heran J., et al. 1982. Guide pratique des études médicales, pp. 378, 478. Tome 1: le 1er cycle. Tome 2: le 2éme cycle et l'internat. Paris: Flammarion médecine sciences.

Mizrahi, A., and A. Mizrahi. 1991. Les tendances à long terme de la consommation médicale. *Problèmes économiques* 2:1-8.

O.M.S. Bureau régional de I'Europe. *La spécialisation en médecine dans la région Européenne*, p. 151.. Copenhagen: WHO.

Ordre national des médecins. 1991. *La démographie médicale française, 10 ans d'évolution: 1980-1990*, p. 65. Paris: Herissey imprimeur.

Strasbourg. Imprimerie de la faculté de médecine. 1989. 7èmes journées d'études, p. 277.

Verbist, J.P., and C. Velliet. 1991. Les étudiants en médecine face à leur avenir professionnel in 1990, p. 100. Thèse de doctorat en médecine, Lille.

Table 12.1
Medical School Demographics-France

Medical School	Undergraduate Enrollment Fall PCEM 1	Undergraduate Enrollment Fall DCEM 4	Graduates 1990– Medical Doctor	3rd Medical Cycle 1991 Residents = G.P. Internes = specialities (DES) + (D.U>) + capacities + (D.I.S>) + (A.E.P.S.)
PARIS (Total)	4,498	1716	1159	14,101
BICHAT	512	182		
BOBIGNY	259	96		
BROUSSAIS	383	130		
COCHIN	388	149		
CRETEIL	399	159		
KREMLIN-B	290	144		
LARIBOISIERE	492	189		
NECKER	382	169		
PARIS-OUEST	344	122		
SALPETRIERE	502	176		
ST ANTOINE	547	200		
AMIENS	351	114	130	773
ANGERS	330	133	125	796

Table 12.1
Medical School Demographics-France

Medical School	Undergraduate Enrollment Fall PCEM 1	Undergraduate Enrollment Fall DCEM 4	Graduates 1990— Medical Doctor	
BESANCON	327	103	83	796
BORDEAUX	1,177	316	277	3,041
BREST	336	106	79	548
CAEN	379	101	126	524
CLERMONT-F	435	120	86	657
DIJON	575	100	131	665
GRENOBLE	498	157	180	1,369
LILLE	1,329	504		
LILLE (LIBRE)	174	64	287	2,018
LIMOGES	302	147	98	580
LYON	1,264	424	371	3,138
MARSEILLE	1,080	377	320	3,424
MONTPELLIER	908	256	298	3,263
NANCY	810	239	306	3,058

Table 12.1
Medical School Demographics-France

Medical School	Undergraduate Enrollment Fall PCEM 1	Undergraduate Enrollment Fall DCEM 4	Graduates 1990— Medical Doctor	
NANTES	537	151	167	1,126
NICE	436	105	86	853
POITIERS	311	114	103	630
REIMS	437	144	145	579
RENNES	550	214	189	1,151
ROUEN	451	140	112	1,201
ST ETIENNE	345	93	56	578
STRASBOURG	740	288	247	2,039
TOULOUSE	1,095	292	375	2,186
TOURS	506	196	145	1,404
TOTAL	20,181	8,430	5,681	50,498

Figure 12.1: France--Curricular Structure by Year

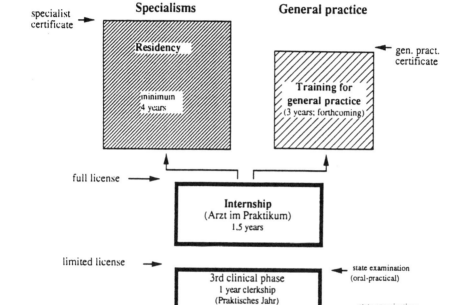

specialist certificate →

Specialisms

General practice

Residency

minimum 4 years

Training for general practice (3 years; forthcoming)

← gen. pract. certificate

full license →

Internship
(Arzt im Praktikum)
1.5 years

limited license →

3rd clinical phase
1 year clerkship
(Praktisches Jahr)

← state examination (oral-practical)

← state examinations (mcq and oral)

2nd clinical phase
2 years
17 compulsory courses (516 hours)

1st clinical phase
1 year
8 compulsory courses (300 hours)

← state examinations (mcq)

preclinical phase
2 years
14 compulsory courses (624 hours)

← state examinations (mcq and oral)

13

Germany

Hendrik van den Bussche

Since the unification of Germany in 1990, the educational system, research policy, and administration of health care in the former German Democratic Republic (GDR) have been undergoing dramatic transitions. Most probably, this process will consist of a progressive adaptation to the standards of the former West Germany (*Wissenschaftsrat* 1991). As this process is still underway, the data and the analysis in this chapter refer to West Germany only.

OVERVIEW OF THE HEALTH CARE DELIVERY SYSTEM

Health services in the German Federal Republic (FRG) are delivered within a comprehensive and highly bureaucratic social security system that covers more than 90 percent of the population and provides for direct reimbursement to health care providers. The health services system employs approximately two million people (3.3 percent of the population), consumes more than 10 percent of the GNP, and is still growing, both in budget and work force, in spite of the expenditure containment laws of the last 15 years (Sass and Massey 1988; Deneke 1988). The FRG is a leader among Western European countries with regard to the accessibility of services and the freedom of their use, acute hospital bed density (72 beds per 10,000 inhabitants), the number of hospital care days/population (*Sachverständigenrat* 1987), the availability of sophisticated equipment (*Sachverständigenrat* 1988*)* and the physician:population ratio. For example, the ratio of hospital care days to population is 100 percent higher than in the US and 200 percent higher than in the UK.

The German health care system is a loose aggregation of subsystems. The degree of coordination and cooperation among and within the subsystems (ambulatory care, hospital care, public health care, and rehabilitation) is low and competition is intense, including that among the sick funds (health insurance funds) for new members (Light et al. 1986). The health care system is dominated by the providers, is disease and cure-oriented, and excels with regard to the amount of technology-based services and drug prescriptions. On the other hand, preventive approaches and quality assurance measures are negligible and a comprehensive human resources planning system is lacking. Planning and decision making in such a system are extremely complex processes, in which the governments, both the federal government and the governments of the states *(Länder)*, do not necessarily play the decisive role. Cost containment measures have succeeded in stabilizing the percentage of the GNP spent on health between 1975 and the present *(Sachverständigenrat)*.

The implementation of the health care cost reduction policy is the responsibility of a coalition called Concentrated Action in Health Care (Konzertierte Aktion), in which the major interest groups (i.e., the federal, state, and local governments, the associations of physicians, dentists, and pharmacists; the pharmaceutical industry; hospital owners; health insurance funds; employers; trade unions; and private health insurance) are given responsibility for developing annual budget guidelines for the different sectors of the health care system.

The system is highly physician-oriented, with a low participation of other health professionals. The availability of nursing services, for example, is problematic for ambulatory as well as hospital and geriatric care *(Sachverständigenrat* 1987, 1988, 1990, 1991). The number of active physicians grew by 150 percent during the last thirty years, resulting in a physician/population ratio of 1:330. Whereas a similar growth rate is found in several other European countries, the FRG shows a singular development with regard to the number of specialists. The growth of the profession is, in fact, almost entirely due to the increased numbers of specialists and residents. The increase in the number of general practitioners has been negligible, and specialists exceed the numbers of primary care physicians, even in ambulatory care settings by a ratio of 1.4:1 (van den Bussche 1986; *Sachverständigenrat* 1990).

Due to the growing number of students entering medical school, there is a widespread consensus that the health care system is experiencing a growing physician surplus (see Figure 13.1). Very probably, this surplus will increase the number of general practitioners and, of course, that of non-clinically active or unemployed physicians.

With regard to the gender distribution of positions in the medical profession, women account for 45 percent of all medical students, 32 percent of all medical licenses, 31 percent of all practicing physicians, 18 percent of all specialists licenses, and 3.5 percent of all chief physicians (Marburger Bund 1985; Sieverding 1990). With the current competition in the medical labor market, these figures will very probably not improve for women during the next decades.

HISTORICAL BACKGROUND

At the beginning of this century Germany was a world leader in medical education. Abraham Flexner's recommendations for medical education in the US (Flexner 1912) were heavily influenced by the science-based concepts of German medical education. This type of education, however, underwent a series of transitions and cutbacks, which makes it difficult to consider the current state of affairs as typical for a "German" model of medical education.

Between 1918 and the takeover of power by the National Socialists in 1933, medical education in Germany suffered from equipment shortages and budgetary problems. During the Nazi period, the expulsion of 15 percent of the professors because of their Jewish origin, the dedication to eugenics ("racial hygiene") as the so-called "new German medical science," the early orientation towards military medicine for warfare, and the subsequent isolation of German scientists during World War II contributed to an almost total breakdown of medical education in 1945 (van den Bussche 1990a). After the War, the major preoccupation of medical educators was to eliminate the gap in research and clinical work between Germany and the Western world, especially the US. Simultaneously, the largely deteriorated and destroyed classroom facilities, hospitals, and laboratories required reconstruction, a process lasting until the 1970s.

The first national legislation on undergraduate medical education, the Bestallungsordnung of 1953, was basically a restoration of the pre-Nazi system. It again placed high value on the scientific basis of medicine and on lectures by the head of the department as the main educational methodology. This idea, which valued academic (*Bildung*) over professional training, postponed the clinical education of medical students until a 24-month internship (*Medizinal-Assistentenzeit*), which began only after completion of the academic program.

The Bestallungsordnung did not describe general aims and objectives of medical education. It was merely an assemblage of all the recognized scientific disciplines, sharply divided into preclinical and clinical periods of almost equal length leading to a license for general practice. Beginning in 1959, general practitioners began to ask for specific postgraduate training leading to a specialist certificate in general practice. Undergraduate medical education, they argued, should become basic, both for future general practitioners and future specialists. The specialists opposed this proposal, arguing that the license should allow every physician to practice medicine under "independent" and "self-responsible" conditions; in other words, to open a general practice. This intraprofessional debate has dominated the discussions on medical education for the last thirty years without final clarification (van den Bussche 1990b).

Seven new medical schools were opened between 1960 and 1984. The total medical faculty grew by 250 percent and the number of professors grew by 500 percent. As a result, the student-professor ratio was significantly reduced. Following the "oil crisis," however, this trend was reversed (Wissenschaftsrat 1988a).

The period 1960-1984 constituted an expansive phase in university and medical school development. This development was largely due to the belief that the academic layer of the population should be developed in order to remain competitive on the international market (similar to the "after-Sputnik" development in the US). In medicine, there was a general belief at that time that a shortage of physicians was likely. Most of the schools began to implement some new ideas on medical education; after a short time, however, they joined the traditional educational philosophies.

The curriculum of 1953 underwent growing criticism from the physicians' associations and, during the "revolutionary" 1960s, from students. The explosion of medical knowledge, the lack of practical training, the "medieval" teaching methods, and the supposed irrelevance of the curriculum with regard to societal needs were central in this widespread dissatisfaction.

In reaction, the government issued a new decree (*Approbationsordnung*) in 1970, which explicitly sought to modernize medical education. Major features of the reform included: (1) the introduction of bedside teaching as the key element of the clinical phase and the reintegration of the internship into the six-year curriculum in the form of a 12-month clerkship (*Praktisches Jahr*) in university or affiliated hospitals under the supervision of the Medical Faculties; (2) the introduction of new subjects (e.g., medical psychology, medical sociology, social medicine, occupational medicine, psychosomatics) as a counterbalance to the biomedical approach; (3) national multiple-choice examinations replacing oral examinations to guarantee the objectivity and reliability of the grading procedure.

Several problems, however, remained unsolved. Because of the intraprofessional contradictions described earlier, a definition of the overall objectives of undergraduate medical education was deliberately omitted. The number of biomedical disciplines was increased and the total number of examination subjects was approximately doubled. The decree of 1970, like its predecessor, was subjected to severe criticism from different sources. In light of the debate on physician oversupply and cost containment needs that emerged shortly after the "oil crisis" of 1974, the increase in the number of students admitted, and the worsening student/professor ratio, a dramatic decrease in the qualification of the graduates and a corresponding danger for the quality of health care was predicted. It should be noted that substantial empirical evidence for this "diagnosis" was never put forward. Nevertheless, the continuous debate led to a series of further modifications, which progressively reduced the decree from an educational reform project to an instrument of manpower supply containment.

Within the last twenty years, no fewer than 16 governmental proposals for a revision of undergraduate medical education and access to the health care insurance scheme were proposed, and ten were enacted. The decree itself was altered seven times, and three further legislative steps concerned the access of physicians to the health care insurance scheme.

The major aspects of these "reforms" were: (1) the introduction in 1986 of oral examinations by the faculty after years two and five, complementary to the nationwide multiple choice examinations. Each student is also examined in two subjects selected at random from the disciplines represented in the national examination. (2) In 1988, limitations were placed on the size of groups in seminars, courses and bedside teaching, thereby allowing a reduction of admissions by 20 percent. (3) In 1988, an 18-month internship (*Arzt im Praktikum*) was reintroduced as a requirement for full licensure; successful examination after the sixth year leading only to a limited license to work as a physician under supervision. The content of this internship is unspecified and it can be performed in whatever medical setting the student chooses.

The number of proposals and regulations shows the intensity, even the feverish character of the debate and corresponding governmental action. But it also demonstrates the difficulty of compromising the interests of the different parties involved with regard to the questions of the intake of medical students, the status of the medical license, and access to the medical market (van den Bussche 1990b). One need not be a prophet to predict the continuation of this debate and of curriculum reform for noneducational reasons in the future.

ROLE OF NATIONAL POLICY IN SHAPING MEDICAL EDUCATION

The national decree on medical education is issued by the federal Ministry of Health within the framework of the federal law on the medical profession (Bundesärzteordnung), but each change of this decree requires the consent of the governments of the *Länder*. Furthermore, the ministry is responsible for the law of 1987 on the distribution of physicians working within the health insurance system, which prohibits the opening of new practices for three years in any discipline or region with a supply of physicians that is 50 percent higher than the federal average.

During these legislative procedures, the ministry will consult a long list of interest groups. Its role is more to mediate between these lobbies and to find an acceptable compromise than to push through its own positions. Important interest groups pursue the following agendas.

The associations of physicians. Physicians are organized in countless associations, each with its unique interests to be integrated by the federal Chamber of Physicians, the umbrella organization of all physician associations. The federal chamber favors concepts of undergraduate medical education that secure the physicians' monopoly over the delivery of health services and the "unity" of the medical profession. Furthermore the profession advocates a reduction in the number of students. With regard to postgraduate and continuing medical education, the Chamber has opposed curricular regulations and quality assurance methods.

The scientific and professional associations. The teaching staff may see its interests better represented by the medico-scientific societies (e.g., German Society of Surgery) or the professional associations of specialist disciplines (e.g., Professional Association of German Surgeons). There are approximately 150 of these associations and the number is growing steadily. The representation and influence of faculty members within these associations varies, as does the relation of political to academic activities. With respect to undergraduate medical education, the major political aim of these associations is (1) to maintain and strengthen the relative status of their respective disciplines by increasing the scope of compulsory knowledge of that discipline, the number of teaching hours and positions it controls, and the importance of the subject in the examination; and (2) to prevent subdisciplines from acquiring independence within the curriculum.

The health insurance funds. In the former FRG there were approximately 1,200 governmental health insurance funds operating within the complex judicial regulations of the federal laws on social security. Basically, the health insurance funds are in favor of any measure that limits or reduces the number of physicians in any sector of the health care system. They also bargain directly with the hospital owners on hospital costs and on the number of physician positions in hospitals, including the teaching and university hospitals.

The medical schools. In the course of this century, the lobbying power of the schools has decreased. This is due to their inability to react adequately to changing societal demands. In discussions of reform proposals, the professorate generally favored the status quo. Faculty proposals tended to recycle previous models and to avoid new ones. Professorial influence also declined because of sometimes strident individualism within the teaching staff. Finally, as compared to research and clinical work, teaching is less valued and thus considered largely irrelevant for the professors' well-being and the career aspirations of younger researchers.

Staffing and equipping the schools of medicine is regulated at the level of the Ministries of Science of the *Länder*. In theory, these ministries are responsible only for providing an infrastructure sufficient for the teaching duties of the professorate. In practice, however, they also support up to 30 percent of its costs for clinical care. The remaining equipment and staff for hospital care is negotiated with the health insurance funds, numbers of positions in the outpatient departments with the associations of physicians working for the health insurance scheme, and the budgets for research with private and governmental funding agents. Thus, the total number of staff in a clinical department is the result of negotiation processes with at least four institutions. This leads to a situation in which both the sources and the use of the budgets are largely a mystery.

ADMISSION

Applicants are admitted to medical school by the Central Bureau for the Administration of Admissions (Zentralstelle für die Vergabe von Studienplätzen [ZVS]), a national bureaucracy for the selection and distribution of university applicants for overcrowded disciplines, including medicine. Applicants are selected for the available openings according to the following formula: (1) 10 percent of the places are distributed based on the results of a nationwide aptitude test; (2) 45 percent are based on a combination of the results in the test (weighted 55 percent) and secondary school grades (school grades weighted 45 percent); (3) 20 percent are based on a combination of the secondary school grades and time on the waiting list; and (4) 15 percent are based on an interview by the school from a randomly selected pool (three times larger than the number of places) of applicants who were not accepted through the channels described above (Hinrichsen and Lohölter 1986). Ten percent of admissions are reserved for foreign or stateless applicants and hardship cases.

In the interview, which is conducted by two professors of the school and lasts thirty minutes, the interviewers check personality and motivation and study the aptitude of the applicants. The development of the criteria and procedures for the interview is largely left to the individual schools. Research findings on the interview procedure itself or on the performance of this group of first year students compared to other entrants have not yet been published.

In 1987, the relationship between applicants and places in medicine was 2.4:1, an average figure for all university curricula under the national numerus clausus. This ratio was much higher during previous years (e.g., 5.3:1 in 1977), the decrease probably being due to the decreasing attractiveness of the medical profession.

The number of places is fixed by the governments of the *Länder*, which are in turn bound by judicial considerations rather than criteria of qualified teaching or learning opportunities. In the FRG, the right of free choice of an occupation and of the corresponding educational opportunities is guaranteed by the constitution. As a result, the Supreme Court in 1972 required the medical schools to take in as many applicants as a complete use of the teaching resources would allow. Both forecasts on future work force needs and educational standards were explicitly rejected as acceptable criteria for a limitation of the number of entrants. The ministries of science of the *Länder* decided to link the number of admitted students to the faculty numbers in the medical schools and affiliated hospitals. As these numbers grew in the course of medico-scientific progress, enrollment doubled from 1975 to 1985. By 1990, approximately eleven thousand five hundred applicants were admitted per year. As the dropout rate is low, up to eleven-thousand licenses are issued per year.

In 1991, the administration of the states managed to reduce the number of entrants by 20 percent. This measure, however, may be in contradiction with the jurisdiction of the Supreme Court, and its impact for the future is therefore still uncertain.

Students enter university at an average age of twenty or twenty-one. The final examination in medicine is at the age of twenty-eight or twenty-nine (the difference between years in medicine and university is due to students who took a nonmedical course before entering medicine), and candidates obtain the license at the average age of thirty. The percentage of female students has grown steadily during the last decades to approximately 42.7 percent in 1986, a figure that corresponds to the average female participation in German universities in general (*Wissenschaftsrat* 1988c).

CURRICULAR STRUCTURE AND INNOVATION

Undergraduate medical education in reunified Germany takes place in 37 medical schools (36 state institutions and 1 private school). As the decree on undergraduate education stipulates the curriculum and the examination system in detail, (see figure 13.2, p. 189) the variance of the programs among the 29 institutions in the former FRG is low. The impact of reunification on the curricula and examination processes in the nine schools of the former GDR is yet to be seen.

The mandated curriculum is divided into 2-year preclinical, 4-year clinical, and 18-month internship periods. The curriculum is further subdivided by four state examinations administered after years two, three, five, and six.

The preclinical section contains the natural sciences, anatomy, physiology, biochemistry, sociology, and psychology. A preparatory course in clinical medicine and clinically oriented seminars in anatomy, biochemistry, and physiology and an "introductory course on medical work settings" have been introduced recently to bridge the gap between the preclinical and clinical curriculum. The first year of clinical training is largely devoted to pathology, pharmacology, radiology, clinical chemistry, and microbiology, with student clinical work limited to a course in history taking and physical examination. Clinical disciplines are offered during the fourth and fifth years, with lectures and bedside teaching in 12 medical and surgical disciplines: internal medicine, surgery, pediatrics, obstetrics and gynecology, dermatology, urology, emergency medicine, orthopedics, ophthalmology, ENT, psychiatry, psychosomatics, and psychotherapy. Courses in general practice and medical ecology (hygiene, occupational medicine, social medicine, and forensic medicine) are also required.

Student Assessment

At the end of these courses, the departments administer an examination, the passing of which is a prerequisite for admission to the state examinations. These state examinations are national multiple-choice examinations administered by the Institut für Medizinische Prüfungsfragen, situated at Mainz. After years two and four, the student must also pass additional oral examinations in selected disciplines administered by faculty members. The final sixth year (*Prakisches Jahr*) is a full-time clerkship in a university or affiliated hospital, with four months each of internal medicine, surgery, and an elective. At the end of the sixth year, a comprehensive oral and practical examination is required for a limited license and admission to an 18-month internship (*Arzt im Praktikum*) in a clinical setting that leads to full medical licensure. During the 1980s, more than half the students also presented the thesis required to obtain the Dr. med. degree. A significantly lower proportion of women applied for the Doctoral degree (*Wissenschaftsrat* 1986, 1988c).

Curricular Innovations

During the last 20 years, almost all responsible institutions and concerned lobbies have published memoranda demanding fundamental reform in medical education. (Gewerkschaft 1982; Sachverständigenrat 1991; Stiftung 1989; *Wissenschaftsrat* 1988a). Apart from the curricular reforms at the level of the governmental decree, several local initiatives were undertaken by interested professors, student groups, or the small number of research projects in medical education (Göbel and Remstedt 1991; Habeck et al. 1993; Habeck and Schwartz-Flesch 1991). Most of these projects concentrate on a better orientation and tutoring of students, instruction in clinical and communicative skills and improved bedside training. There are few schools that are reform-oriented at the institutional level. A private medical school was opened at Witten/Herdecke, in 1983, which admits only 25 entrants per year. It is devoted to patient-centered medical education and to a broad philosophical orientation of medical students. Students must, however, take the same examinations as their fellow students from the state universities. Since 1989, the Free University of Berlin has developed an experimental curriculum which aims at introducing problem orientation and integrated learning into medical education. This curriculum will probably be tested in the academic year 1993-1994.

Role of Faculty

The concept of part-time faculty does not exist in the FRG; all professors are full-time and most are tenured. The teaching load of the assistant staff, i.e., individuals preparing for a specialist certificate and/or an academic career, varies according to the different categories within this academic group but is generally lower than that of the professorate. Access to a professorship depends on the acquisition of the *"Habilitation"* degree at the PhD level. Together with this degree, the *"venia legendi"* (the license for university teaching) is awarded without an assessment of educational abilities. Today, women account for 21 percent of the total scientific staff but only 3.5 percent of the professorate and 1.4 percent of department heads. It is estimated that annual gross faculty income ranges from $60,000 US (salary of the lowest category of basic sciences professor) to more than $1,000,000 US (salary and private practice income of the highest category of clinician in certain disciplines).

GRADUATE MEDICAL EDUCATION

Postgraduate training of physicians is controlled by the Chambers of Physicians; the influence of the state, the scientific associations, and the universities being marginal. Requirements are set by the Chambers of Physicians of the *Länder*, in accord with the central directives of the Federal Chamber of Physicians, which provide for certification in 46 medical specialty or subspecialist categories, following minimum training periods of four to seven years, and 20 additional related subspecialties such as physical therapy and psychotherapy (Parkhouse and Menu 1989; World Health Organization 1985). These subspecialties cover smaller and/or less professionalized fields of study and require a shorter period of postgraduate training.

In spite of the growing importance of the specialists in the health care system, postgraduate training is still not considered an educational process leading to a distinct profession but as a special setting of medical work after the completion of undergraduate education. Specialty certification is, in this view, more a by-product of daily medical work than the result of a structured educational experience (van den Bussche 1990b). Consequently, the scientific quality of postgraduate training is not sufficiently assured. The criteria for the accreditation of training hospitals are based on the size (number of beds) and the level of equipment of the department. As educational criteria (e.g., rotation schedules, scientific activities) are not applied, accreditation for postgraduate training is quasi-automatic for all medium and large-sized hospitals. The number of training positions is based on the number of available beds rather than human resource needs in the specialty. The more hospital beds for a discipline and the more they are concentrated in larger departments, the more trainee positions will be available and the more specialists the discipline will produce, resulting in a self-induced pattern of perpetual growth. The reports of the heads of the departments in which the candidate completed postgraduate training are the major basis for the certification procedure, whereas the 30-minutes oral examination (officially called *Fachgespräch* or "professional colloquium") conducted by a specialty board of the local Chamber of Physicians, plays a minor role. Although postgraduate training is exclusively hospital-based, permanent hospital-based positions are limited. Nearly all graduates of postgraduate training must leave the hospital to open a private, usually solo, practice.

Further growth in the number of specialists could theoretically be retarded by a reduction of the number of hospital beds and assistant physician positions in hospitals. This possibility is primarily dependent on the effectiveness of health resource planning and cost control policies of the government and the sick-funds; however, previous efforts have been unsuccessful. Between 1970 and 1990, the number of beds for acute hospital care was constant, while the number of hospital physicians grew by almost 100 percent (*Sachverständigenrat* 1990). Despite the manifest oversupply of specialists, postgraduate training has remained largely outside the scope of public debate and reform proposals, both of which have focused primarily on undergraduate education.

LICENSURE

See "Student Assessment", p. 182, under "Curricular Structure and Innovation."

Cross-Licensing of Physicians

In 1989, approximately 5 percent of the physicians working in the FRG were of foreign origin. Approximately 30 percent of these foreign physicians come from countries of the European Economic Community (EEC). For them, automatic cross-licensing and cross-recognition of specialist certificates take place according to the EEC rules of 1975 (Komission der Europäischen Gemeinschaften. 1987; Walton and Binns 1984). For physicians of non-EEC countries, the recognition of the diploma is conditioned on proof of equivalence by the Ministry of Health of one of the *Länder*. Usually, a special permit good for a limited number of years of medical practice is issued for postgraduate training or for research; however, physicians from these countries are virtually excluded from ambulatory care under the health insurance scheme.

CONTINUING MEDICAL EDUCATION

There is no mandatory continuing medical education in the FRG. A debate on the need for quality assurance and control of continuing medical education has recently begun. At present, the field is dominated by the biomedical (especially pharmaceutical) industry, although the number of independent offerings of the

Chambers of Physicians is increasing. There has been no formal evaluation of the effectiveness and efficiency of existing programs, and statistical data on continuing education activities of physicians do not exist.

ROLE OF RESEARCH IN MEDICAL EDUCATION

Personnel and material resources allocated to the departments by the Ministry of Science are insufficient for research. Therefore, the competitive search for research grants plays an important role in the life of the medical school. The volume of grants for clinical research supported by the state can be estimated at only DM 200 million per year (*Wissenschaftsrat* 1988c). Comprehensive statistical data on the amount of grants given by the large number of foundations and private companies are not available.

There is a wide consensus among both staff and students that individual career opportunities depend primarily on research and publication, to which individuals efforts are therefore predominantly devoted, to the detriment of teaching. In the clinical area, this condition is exacerbated by the demand of a high work load on the ward and the clinical requirements that must be met to obtain the specialist certificate or other accreditation. Furthermore, the concentration of university hospitals on tertiary care and the corresponding selection of patients, as well as the growing number of subspecialties, tend to make university hospitals increasingly unsuitable for undergraduate training.

As a result, a growing dissatisfaction with the dedication to teaching is observed among students and administrators. Programs aiming at a revitalization of teaching, in medical schools as well as in other university departments, are under development; however, they are unlikely to have significant impact, unless they are accompanied by relevant changes in the funding of the departments and the requirements for individual career advancement.

GOVERNMENT/PRIVATE SECTOR INVOLVEMENT

The description of both the health care delivery system and the national policy in medical education have shown that the administration of health care and medical education in the FRG are complex processes involving multiple institutions and interest groups. The debates on--and the changes of the decree on--medical education are always compromises between the positions of these groups. Currently, the influence of the academic community on the major parameters of medical education (the number of entrants, curriculum content, examination procedures, and dropout level) is relatively low (van den Bussche 1990b).

On the other hand, private influence on medical education is restricted to the funding of research (as described earlier). The domain of influence of the private sector is the field of continuing medical education, which is largely sponsored by the biomedical (and especially the pharmaceutical industry), without governmental influence.

INTERNATIONAL LINKAGES AND COLLABORATION

The debate on medical education in Europe, largely promoted by international associations and organizations for medical education such as WHO, the Association for Medical Education in Europe (AMEE), and the World Federation for Medical Education (WFME) has had little influence on medical education in the FRG. Whereas WHO's concepts of Health for All and the Edinburgh Declaration of the WFME are beginning to influence the thinking of leaders and institutions in the field as well as the educational policy of the government, these ideas are still unfamiliar to, or strongly opposed by, most of the professorate.

The most important foreign influence may well be the guidelines for compulsory postgraduate training for panel general practice issued by the EEC in 1986 (European Economic Community 1986). According to these guidelines, member states must introduce (before 1995) a specific postgraduate training period of two years minimum for general practitioners working within the health insurance scheme. In the FRG, there is an inclination to extend this phase to three years. Because of this external decree, the national debate on this issue, which lasted for more than 30 years, may now come to a productive end.

ISSUES AND TRENDS

For the coming decades, undergraduate medical education in the FRG will continue to be controlled by the complex interaction of government and special interest groups described above. On the political level, concern for integrating the education and health care systems of the former GDR with those of the former FRG, as well as the search for measures to control growth in the number of physicians and the costs of health care, will dominate policy. These occupations, together with the strong preference of the professorate for traditional, discipline-oriented, hospital-based programs, make major innovations of curricular content, organization, or instructional methodology unlikely in the foreseeable future.

REFERENCES

Deneke, J.F.V. 1988. Federal Republic of Germany. In H. Viefhues., ed. *Medical manpower in the European community*. New York: Springer-Verlag.

European Economic Community. 1986. Guideline 86/457. In *Amtsblatt für die Europäische Gemeinschaft*. L 267/26. Brussels 19.9.

Flexner, A. 1912. *Medical education in Europe*. Carnegie Foundation for the Advancement of Teaching. Bulletin no. 6. New York.

Gewerkschaft, Ö.T.V., ed. 1982. *Vorschläge und Forderungen der Gewerkschaft ÖTV zur ärztlichen Aus--und Weiterbildung in der Bundesrepublik Deutschland*. Stuttgart.

Göbel, E., and S. Remstedt. 1991. *Leitfaden zur Studienreform für Medizinstudierende*. Frankfurt a. M.

Habeck, D., et al., eds. 1993 (reprint). *Neue Wege der ärztlichen Ausbildung.* Jena.

Habeck, D., and P. Schwarz-Flesch. 1991. Innovationen der ärzlichen Ausbildung in der Bundesrepublik Deutschland im Überblick. In *Medizinische Ausbildung.* 8:39-41, 65-75.

Hinrichsen, K., and R. Lohölter, eds. 1986. *Das Interview bei der Zulassung zum Medizinstudium.* Stuttgart.

Kommission der Europäischen Gemeinschaften. 1987. *Die ärzliche Ausbildung in der europäischen Gemeinschaft.* Berlin. (Available in English as Document Nr. EUR 10780, EEC, Brussels.)

Light, D., et al. 1986. Social medicine vs professional dominance--The German experience. *American Journal of Public Health* 76:78-83.

Marburger Bund, ed. 1985. *Ärztinnen - ins berufliche Abseits gedrängt?* Cologne.

Parkhouse, J.P., and J.P. Menu, eds. 1989. *Specialized medical education in the European region.* Copenhagen: WHO-Regional Office for Europe.

Sachverständigenrat für die Konzertierte Aktion im Gesundheitswesen. 1991. Das Gesundheitswesen im vereinten Deutschland (Jahresgutachten 1991). Baden-Baden.

---------. 1990. Herausforderungen und Perspektiven der Gesundheitsversorgung (Jahresgutachten 1990). Baden-Baden.

---------. 1988. Medizinische und ökonomische Orientierung (Jahresgutachten 1988). Baden-Baden-Baden.

---------. 1987. Medizinische und ökonomische Orientierung (Jahresgutachten 1987). Baden-Baden.

Sass, H.M., and R.U. Massey, eds. 1988. *Health care systems - moral conflicts in European and American public policy.* Boston and London: Dortrecht.

Sieverding, M. 1990. *Psychologische Barrieren in der beruflichen Entwicklung von Frauen - Das Beispiel der Medizinerinnen.* Stuttgart.

Stiftung, R. B., ed. 1989. *Das Arzbild der Zukunft.* Gerlingen.

van den Bussche, H. 1990a. *Im Dienste der "Volksgemeinschaft"--Studienreform in Nationalsozialismus am Beispiel der ärztlichen Ausbildung.* Berlin.

---------. 1990b. The history and future of physician manpower development in the Federal Republic of Germany. *Health Policy* 15:215-231.

---------. 1986. The growth of medical specialization in Europe since World War II. Draft Report to WHO, Regional Office for Europe. Mimeo, Hamburg.

Walton, J., and T.B. Binns, eds. 1984. *Medical education and manpower in the EEC.* London.

World Health Organization Regional Office for Europe. 1985. *Medical specialization in relation to health needs.* Copenhagen: WHO.

Wissenschaftsrat: Empfehlungen zur klinischen Forschung in den Hochschulen. 1986. Cologne.

Wissenschaftsrat: Grunddaten zum Personalbestand der Hochschulen. 1988a. Cologne.

Wissenschaftsrat: Empfehlungen zur Verbesserung der Ausbildungsqualität in der Medizin. 1988b. Cologne.

Wissenschaftsrat: Empfehlungen des Wissenschaftsrates zu den Perspektiven der Hochschulen in den 90er Jahren. 1988c. Cologne.

Wissenschaftsrat: Empfehlungen zur Hochschulmedizin in den neuen Ländern und in Berlin. 1991. (Drs. 406/91). Mimeo. Cologne. 27.9.

Figure 13.1: Physicians:Population, Germany

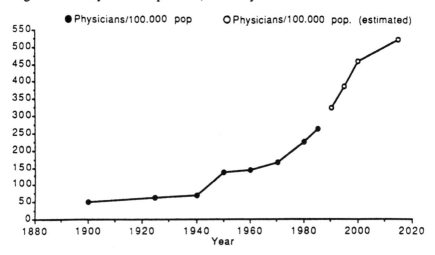

Figure 13.2: German Curriculum and Licensure Requirements

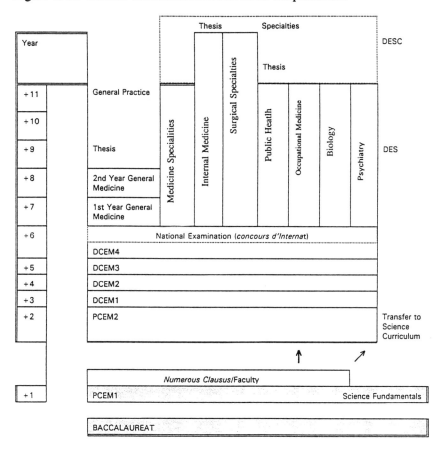

14

Hungary

GÁBOR SZABÓ
FERENC BOJÁN

Hungary is a landlocked country in Central Europe. It covers approximately thirty-six thousand square miles and has a relatively homogeneous population of 10.3 million (as of 1990). The population is increasingly urban (60 percent), with more than 2 million people living in the capital, Budapest. The Hungarian economy was almost exclusively agricultural until after World War II, when great emphasis was placed on industrial development. Traditionally, all sectors of Hungarian life were influenced heavily by Germany.

OVERVIEW OF THE HEALTH CARE DELIVERY SYSTEM

Hungarian medicine was also rooted in the West, with strong ties to Austria and Germany before World War II. Medical doctors were well trained and concentrated in the large cities. They were usually in private practice and often associated with insurance companies. The number of hospital beds was comparable to that in other European countries. However, access to health service was very selective, dependent primarily on the socioeconomic status of each individual, and unavailable to many. Only 31 percent of the population was covered by health insurance in the 1930s. Agricultural and poor urban workers had no insurance. Consequently, Hungary was chronically far behind the West in terms of health status. After World War II, Hungary was occupied by the Soviet Union. The Communist party took power in 1948, and Hungary became a socialist state along Soviet lines, with a planned economy and centralized society, including the organization of health services and education, though these were never as centralized in Hungary as in other Soviet satellites.

After World War II, a new strategy was adopted to reconstruct and develop the health care infrastructure and to establish the socialist health services system. The major elements of the health policy included the right to free health services, universal accessibility to health services, equality of access to services for the entire population, entitlement to the highest level health care required by each individual's needs, and priority in preventive and rehabilitative services. It was believed that these requirements could be fulfilled only if all health care institutions belonged to a single homogeneous, centralized system financed from the state budget and reflecting the socialist state's responsibility for the health of the population

Socialist medicine required a kind of planning. The number of students was predetermined, and there were always open positions for all graduates. The provision of the countryside with physicians was always difficult, and the central government tried to solve this problem by appointing the graduates to specific positions. For example, between 1954 and 1958, 18 percent of all graduates were forced to accept positions in the countryside as general practitioners. The centralized assignment of MDs had many drawbacks and was soon changed into a competition in which all vacancies were publicly advertised. "Distribution" by competition gave MDs the feeling of more freedom, while by controlling the announcement of vacancies, the authorities still had the means to influence a more balanced policy of health work force development.

Beginning in the 1950s, the government substantially increased the number of medical doctors and hospital beds. By the late 1980s, the ratio of working physicians to population was among the highest in the world (29.0 per 10,000 population) and the ratio of hospital beds exceeded that of many Western countries (98.2 per 10,000). These results were achieved at minimal cost, the former because of the low salaries and the latter through placing additional beds in existing wards.

A "New Economic Mechanism" launched in the late 1960s introduced some market modalities and substituted profit for output targets in some sectors. Some private businesses were permitted and encouraged, especially in agriculture. These and other steps toward further decentralization of the society brought about significant changes in the Soviet model and affected almost every sector of society.

The postwar Hungarian health care system was organized along the lines of the Soviet model. It had three levels: (1) primary medical care provided by district general practitioners, district pediatricians, dentists and industrial doctors; (2) polyclinics providing consultations by specialists; and (3) hospitals (municipal and county hospitals, regional and national institutions) with well-defined catchment areas.

These efforts to develop a more equitable health services system were reflected in improvements in the health status of the population. From the late 1940s, infant mortality, mortality from many diseases and conditions, especially from infectious diseases such as tuberculosis, permanently decreased and, consequently, life expectancy at birth steadily grew. By the mid to late 1960s, the gap in health status between Hungary and the West seemed to close. But this did not continue: the ensuing twenty years saw a dramatic worsening in the country's health status.

The overall mortality rate rose primarily due to increases in cardiovascular diseases, cancers, injuries, chronic liver diseases, and suicides; the greatest increase was observed in middle-aged men. Both Hungarian men and women died at nearly twice the age-adjusted rate of Americans from circulatory diseases and more than three times the US rate from cerebrovascular disease. The infant mortality rate decreased but is still twice that of many Western nations (15.8 per 1,000). As a consequence, the gap in life expectancy reemerged. By the late 1980s, Hungarians were living approximately five to seven fewer years than the Western average, and due to the high mortality rate and low birth rate, Hungary's population decreased throughout the 1980s.

The health of Hungarians was a cause of considerable concern by late 1980s. It became obvious that the health care system, with its major impressive dimensions, had been based on a number of unintegrated vertical programs, leading to fragmentation and duplication of services, with consequent poor quality and waste of resources. There was a total imbalance between primary and secondary care, and substantial geographical inequity. The health care system was poorly managed, nor were finances and wages oriented toward performance and quality. In addition, the Hungarian national health services system was severely underfinanced. Its share of the low gross domestic product (GDP), about $2,500 US per capita in late 1980s, was always under 4 percent, much less than in any Western country. Major elements of the "socialist" health policy seemed to have proven a fiasco.

In addition to shortcomings in health care delivery, the quality of the environment, and the life-style of the population (characterized by smoking, alcohol consumption, drug abuse, poor eating habits, physical inactivity, and obesity) currently leave much to be desired. There is little interest in health promotion. Disease prevention and health promotion activities have low prestige among professionals as well as laymen.

A new pattern of morbidity can be foreseen. The unemployment rate and the number of persons with incomes insufficient for a decent living standard are increasing rapidly, as are the number of refugees and homeless persons, broad strata of the population are threatened by pauperization, and more and more individuals are overworked. Consequently, tuberculosis and nutritional deficiencies are of public health importance again, new infectious diseases and sexually transmitted diseases, including AIDS are spreading, and new life-style risks (such as drug abuse and teenage pregnancy), as well as environmental and occupational risks are increasing.

The recent political changes in Hungary have provided a stimulating environment for reorganizing the whole health care and medical education systems. Now Hungary is undertaking a review of its health care system, and its future shape has just been decided. The principal ruling parties favor a move to a market system based on health insurance. However, in a reorganized system, responsibility for preventive services' priority will be given to the state. The new model for the health care system has two levels: primary care, including outpatient care, and inpatient hospitals. The reforms are threefold, covering structure, finance, and education.

Structure

Provision of health care is moving toward a pluralistic system with several forms of ownership. Much emphasis will be placed on the development of efficient primary care. District practitioners will be replaced by family doctors, the majority of whom are expected to be independent contractors. An underlying tenet of the new system is that individuals should have a free choice of their family physician. Prior to 1991, a total of 90 percent of health care facilities were owned by the municipalities. Under the new system, however, municipalities will be permitted to obtain health care from their own facilities, from charitable foundations, or from private sources. The number of hospital beds is adequate, but the ratio of acute to chronic care facilities is inappropriate. Within the next three to four years the pattern of hospital beds is to change to give a 60:40 ratio of acute to chronic beds.

Finance

Prior to 1989, health care was financed from the state budget. At present, it is financed through the National Social Security Fund. The fund is also responsible for pensions, but a new fund dedicated solely to health care is to be established. To be known as the National Health Insurance Fund, it will be able to contract with privately owned and charitable hospitals, as well as state-run facilities to purchase health services for all entitled. Contributions to the National Health Insurance Fund will be paid by both employers and employees. Contributions will be paid from the state budget for those who are not able to pay (e.g., the unemployed and handicapped). Until 1984, hospitals were paid on the basis of inpatient days. Since then, budgets have been largely historical, with an element of negotiation. Currently (1993), the introduction of a prospective payment system based on Diagnostic Related Groups (DRGs) is proposed. It is recognized that a considerable investment in information technology is required. Moreover, the system for paying hospital doctors remains undecided. In 1992 an age-adjusted capitation system was introduced for primary care doctors. The capitation will be higher for both children and the elderly than for the intermediate age groups.

HISTORICAL BACKGROUND

The universities in Central-East Europe were founded in the second half of the fourteenth century (Prague, 1348; Cracow, 1361; Vienna, 1365; and Pécs, 1367). The first Hungarian Medical Faculty was founded at Nagyszombat (1783) by the order of Maria Theresia and was modeled after the first medical school of Vienna. The University of Kolozsvár was founded in 1872. In 1912, the Universities of Debrecen and Pozsony were founded, but the Medical Faculties were opened only several years later (in 1918 and 1921). Because of the territorial truncation of Hungary by the treaty ending World War I, the Faculty of Kolozsvár moved to Szeged and the Faculty from Pozsony went to Pécs. There are currently four medical schools in Hungary: Semmelweis Medical School, located in the capital (Budapest); University Medical School of Debrecen, in the northeast; Albert Szent-Györgyi Medical School, in the south at Szeged; and University Medical School of Pécs, in the west. There is one postgraduate medical university, located in Budapest.

Until 1951, these schools were Faculties of the traditional universities in the same town working under the Ministry of Religion and Public Education. After 1951, however, the Medical Faculties were separated from the universities, subsumed under the Ministry of Health, and renamed University Medical Schools. In Budapest and Szeged, the university medical school Faculties are joined by schools of pharmacy and dentistry and common courses such as anatomy and physiology are taught by the same staff. In Debrecen and Pécs, dentists are trained without having a formal separate Faculty.

ROLE OF NATIONAL POLICY IN SHAPING MEDICAL EDUCATION

See "Overview of the Health Care Delivery System," p. 191.

ADMISSION

An admission examination was introduced in 1947. The purpose was twofold: to select students with better qualities for the limited number of places and to increase the number of students from working class families. (After World War I, the number of students from working class families did not exceed 6 percent; there was also a quota system enforced for Jewish students.) With political pressure exerted by the communist system, the number of working class students rose to 50 percent, but in the 1960s and 1970s it sank back to 30-35 percent and even lower.

The number of applicants exceeded the number of places three- or fourfold. Selection was based partly on the results achieved in high school, and there were written and oral admission examinations for biology and physics. The fact that the authorities wanted to influence admissions to achieve a higher percentage of students from working class families (even if their scores did not match those of other applicants) resulted in a situation in which, until the last decade, family background (origin) and/or religious affiliation sometimes excluded applicants or placed them at serious disadvantage. The admission examination in other respects was useful. The "worst," unprepared students were not admitted and the most "talented," the outstanding few, were recognized and, if members of disadvantaged groups, were often somehow helped to gain admission. The subjects of the admission examination, biology and physics, cover the contents of the relevant textbooks used in the four years of high school studies. In many respects the level of these books does not differ essentially from those used in the Anglo-Saxon colleges. In physics, special emphasis is placed on the applicants' problem solving abilities.

General intelligence and personality characteristics are judged by a personal interview of thirty to forty-five minutes by an experienced clinician. Except in special cases, the examination marks and high school results are decisive. Several attempts to use psychological tests to evaluate personality traits were introduced, but these remain at an experimental stage. A good knowledge of a foreign language is considered favorably. More than 20 percent of the first year students are fluent in one foreign language (mainly English). In 1964, the dropout rate of the admitted students over the six-year curriculum was 15 to 20 percent. This number has not changed substantially (15 percent in 1981).

CURRICULAR STRUCTURE AND INNOVATION

In 1769-1770, the first class in medicine started with five teaching chairs and a five-year study period. Admission required three years of previous studies at other Faculties of the university. Five professors taught the following subjects: pathology and medical praxis, physiology and materia medica, chemistry and botany, anatomy, "chirurgy" and obstetrics. For graduation two examinations were mandatory: (1) anatomy, chemistry, botany, pathology, and pharmacology, and (2) clinical practice.

Specialization of the departments and, accordingly, the courses developed gradually: surgery, ophthalmology, a distinct department of chemistry, practical obstetrics, pathology (1851), histopathology (1870), pharmacology (1872), internal medicine (1872), pediatrics (1872), forensic medicine (1873), public health (1873), embryology (1874), psychiatry (1882), dentistry (1889), and dermatology and venereal diseases (1891).

In 1901, an additional required year of hospital training was added to the five years of studies. In 1922 the undergraduate program was increased to six years, of which the sixth was a kind of clinical practice in the ward. The duration of studies has remained constant.

The problems of Hungarian medical education after World War II stem from conditions that existed throughout Europe as well as some that were unique in the so-called socialist countries. For example, the development of biological and clinical sciences provoked worldwide debate and controversy about which existing knowledge to keep or discard and what new knowledge to include as essential in the curriculum. However, the tripling in enrollment without expansion of facilities and the "planned," centralized, and often bureaucratic administration of these institutions is specific to the particular country.

In the nineteenth and the first half of the twentieth century, the student was free to choose the manner of learning. For five years (ten semesters) there was no compulsory examination. The student attended lectures and practicals and participated in clinical activities in the ward. It was left to each individual and his or her supervisor to choose the textbooks and select the chapters for study in order to be able to understand what was seen and done in the ward. With a small number of students, this method of learning probably functioned quite well. It was an apprenticeship in the traditional sense, and the quality of the preparation depended on the personality of both teacher and student. New problems arose when, after World War II, the number of medical students tripled. The personal relationship between supervisor and student was lost. The idea of the "planned" society demanded centralized leadership and control.

In 1951 the medical schools were separated from the universities and came under the supervision of the Ministry of Health. Society's requirements of the health care system and the curriculum and training provided by medical education were supposed to be coordinated by the new organization. The Ministry of Health, however, never had the professional authority to guide the medical schools toward the needs of patients, or of the needs for health for all, although various reforms and regulations since 1951 tried to achieve such aims. Since the fragmentation of the traditional universities, the higher educational institutions are financed from the state budget through the supervising Ministry. The private sector has not yet been involved.

In 1957 (Budapest) and in 1958 (Cracow), the Ministers of Health of the socialist countries accepted common guidelines that determined the policy of the Ministry of Health, namely that most of the MDs in practice would work as specialists. Behind this reasoning was the fact that only 20 percent of all MDs were involved in primary health care, and half were employed in the larger cities where outpatient services and hospitals were available. Undergraduate training, therefore, was expected to prepare students for subsequent specialty training.

With improving communication between Hungary and the western countries, and with the help of study trips sponsored by WHO, reform ideas on medical education such as those emanating from the University of Illinois at Chicago in the United States had an impact. The most characteristic slogans were: "The aim of the medical school is to educate general practitioners," "integrated teaching," "the needs of the society," "preventive medicine and rehabilitation." The need for family doctors as well as specialists became apparent with the perception that certain psychological and social needs of patients are not satisfied by even the best specialists and that there are preventive and rehabilitation activities that can be provided only with continuity in follow-up consultations, visits, counseling, and care taking, all welfare activities of family doctors.

Curricular Reform

Countrywide curricular reforms aimed at integration of knowledge were introduced in 1951, 1954, and 1963. Course content of the different subjects was set, and student presence at lectures and practicals became compulsory. Because of the large number of students, ward practicals were turned into group demonstrations and discussions. New subjects were introduced (e.g., genetics, molecular genetics, biophysics, biometrics, oxyology, medical psychology, and biochemistry as a separate subject to be taught for two semesters). Participation of students in the work of county hospitals, at outpatient services, various preventive health care centers and services, and in health care units of factories broadened their scope of experience.

The methods of teaching, learning, and evaluation have improved by defining the objectives of a given medical subject, including both the cognitive knowledge and the skills. Innovation in teaching methods was supported by establishing special groups to help disseminate technical knowledge and instrumentation. Teaching aids, films, videotapes, and handouts were produced and provided to the teaching staff.

Student assessment. New methods of examination were introduced. Written tests or short essays became routine practice, although the oral examination is still dominant. The preparation of test questions had positive effects on the definition of the contents of discussions and reform plans of the Ministry of Health. In the 1970s, radical experimentation took place in the structure of teaching in the Medical School of Pécs, and to a lesser degree, in Debrecen and Szeged. Integrated lectures were introduced in Pécs. In Debrecen the coordination of the lectures by different departments around the same subject was called synchronization. Since 1984 the national curriculum has aimed specifically at the education of general practitioners. Nonetheless, in spite of these struggles to improve medical education, the effect has been limited.

Because of the large number of students, practicals in the wards very often remained group demonstrations and discussions. Clinical instruction in the county hospitals was poor because of the low quality of work by the teachers, who were not attached by moral or economic forces to the medical school. The curriculum, and the whole structure, remained essentially unchanged.

The teachers at the medical schools and clinics have no economic motivation for teaching. Promotion does not depend on the quality of instruction. Financial reward comes from the patients and professional appreciation follows scientific achievements. Consequently, without the sincere support of teachers, the balance swung back toward the traditional structure and methods.

Clinical experience. Students participate in three weeks of nursing care after the first and second year, four weeks of internal medicine after the third year, two weeks of obstetrics and two weeks of traumatology after the seventh semester, four weeks of internal medicine after the eighth semester, three weeks internal medicine and one week of public health after the ninth semester, and finally, two weeks pediatrics and two weeks of neurology and psychiatry after the tenth semester. In addition to the ward practicals, students in the sixth year work on the wards and then face the examiners. They participate in eight weeks of pediatrics, six weeks of surgery and two weeks with the first aid ambulance, eight weeks of neurology and psychiatry, ten weeks of internal medicine, two weeks of general practice, six weeks of obstetrics and gynecology, and two weeks of district maternity care.

Since 1987 an English language curriculum has been available for foreign students in all medical schools. There were 66 such students in the first year at Debrecen in 1992. This development resulted from the financial crisis in Hungary in the 1980s, which deeply afflicted the medical schools. Hungarian students do not pay tuition or fees at all, and the budget allocated to medical schools from the state budget is not adequate to keep the standard of research facilities and to compensate for the inflation of salaries of the teaching staff. The tuition and fees paid by the foreign students in US dollars have provided the opportunity for the medical schools to earn money to upgrade their research facilities, pay for participation in conferences in the West, and to give some compensation to the teaching staff for the extra lessons. It is true that English courses have several beneficial consequences, but as a whole they are a burden that should be discontinued as soon as the economic conditions provide the necessary means to the medical schools. As far as we can see, there is little hope of raising medical education to a qualitatively new, higher level if the number of admitted students does not decrease substantially.

According to questionnaires and a survey of "consumers" (directors, leading teachers, and heads of personnel departments in hospitals hiring our graduates, etc.), 79 percent found that the preparation of Hungarian graduates was satisfactory, their theoretical foundations were good, and they were able to quickly overcome any shortcomings in skills. After graduation (obtaining the MD), the student is entitled to work independently as a general practitioner, although there was a period for a few years when everybody had to spend two years in hospitals before starting a private practice.

GRADUATE MEDICAL EDUCATION

In principle, all physicians in the socialist system were required to participate in postgraduate education, one form of which enables physicians to become specialists. Specialty training, regulated by law, has been available in Hungary since 1924, but mandatory examinations were introduced only in 1936. These programs generally require three to four years post-MD. The president of a centralized National Board of Examination and the Rector of the Postgraduate Medical University grant the degree of specialist in more than thirty-five specialties. In 1938, about 50 percent of all doctors were specialists; today, the number is more than 70 percent.

Postgraduate training in Hungary has almost one hundred years of tradition. In 1883 summer courses were initiated, a Central Committee for Postgraduate Education was officially founded in 1912, and foreign scholars as well as clinic and hospital staff delivered lectures at the courses. The committee developed into a central, countrywide organization in 1956 when the Postgraduate Medical University (PMU) was established and gradually expanded to include 33 departments. It became the center of a postgraduate and continuing training system including the National Institutes, the four Hungarian Medical Schools, and the county hospitals.

The PMU identifies the important new fields of knowledge for medical practice in medical teaching, administration, research, and medical technology. It establishes the program and courses of the would-be specialists by defining what they should learn, and offers training in many forms: individual, small group, and conference instruction.

LICENSURE

Following the successful fulfillment of six years of study and the preparation and defense of a written diploma-thesis, students are required to pass a national examination as a condition of licensure. In principle, this examination serves as a means of quality control. The examination consists of a written and an oral section. The comprehensive written test is prepared jointly by the departments of all Hungarian medical schools and representatives of the Ministry of Health. Though centrally approved, its content and level are essentially determined by the medical schools. It may develop later to serve as a control by the "consumer." At the oral examination the candidate is required to examine and establish the differential diagnosis of a patient. The examination board includes five members drawn from among professors, head physicians of different hospitals or departments, and health care specialists.

After the successful state examination, the graduate submits a request to the School Council, the supreme body of the medical school, to be granted the MD. Then, according to the Health Act of 1972, which is still in effect, the new MDs apply for licensure to the Ministry of Health which is authorized by law to issue the license. A new Health Act is under preparation which may change the present licensing procedure.

CONTINUING MEDICAL EDUCATION

According to the Health Act of 1972, every MD must take part in some kind of continuing education at least once every five years. The PMU organizes required courses which are differentiated according to the needs of MDs working at different levels of the health care system, that are relevant to medical practice, and that provide new information. Altogether, about 10 percent of active MDs take part annually in the different forms of postgraduate training. In addition, there are more than fifty journals providing information in Hungarian, and hundreds are available in foreign languages.

For the general practitioners, refresher training consists of two months spent in hospital wards. Postgraduate (refresher) training is decentralized in the sense that the general practitioners go to the hospitals to participate in the work of the wards where they are familiar both with the personnel and the institution. The length, frequency and locations of the "refresher" study has changed during the last forty years to come to the present form. The medical schools have recently established new departments for general practice. In the near future these departments will organize the "refresher" courses to be held in accredited teaching hospitals to better meet local needs for training.

Centralization of responsibility for postgraduate and continuing education in a single postgraduate institute that has the full authority and support of the state has certain advantages. It permits a complete overview of the health care system and encourages an organized, coherent response to fulfill these requirements. However, the drawbacks that accompany the bureaucratic nature of the central organization, including the lack of initiative by the participants and the loss of responsibility for one's own development, have led to the conclusion that with increasing the autonomy of the medical schools, the right and responsibility for postgraduate training should be restored to them. Although the departments of the medical schools are often closer to the practice than any central organization, there remains the problem of providing programs of continuing education and stimulating individual initiatives that will be appropriate at different levels and in different sections of the health care system (e.g., general practitioners, public health services).

ROLE OF RESEARCH IN MEDICAL EDUCATION

Hungarian medical schools have traditionally placed high value on outstanding research. This was self-evident when the medical faculty still was a part of the university, but this spirit has also survived in the time of separation. Hungarian medical schools consist of strong departments of basic sciences. In the University Medical School of Debrecen, for example, there are about three hundred basic science faculty and about four hundred sixty-five clinical faculty (in an eighteen hundred-bed hospital) actively engaged in research.

A small, but very important and valued, segment of the student body (about 20 percent) joins the so-called "scientific circle of students." They carry out experimental research, read foreign journals, learn how to use the library and prepare themselves for continuing self-education. These students engage in research during their undergraduate years with the tacit understanding of the teachers. Since mandatory attendance at lectures is rarely enforced, students often take advantage of being able to spend extra time with research. Sometimes excellent scientific studies are produced by these students.

Between 1950 and 1963, a total of 123 university textbooks were published of which 57 were first editions. Textbooks were officially approved and were available in practically all subjects. The students bought them and used them. The prices of these books were kept low by state subsidy. Monographs in Hungarian are also frequently used by students.

However, many students are not deeply motivated. Participation at lectures is, in principle, mandatory, but in practice it is rare to find even half the class present. Students rarely attend conferences to gather new information. However, the *Hungarian Medical Weekly,* established in 1857, is widely known and read regularly.

GOVERNMENT/PRIVATE SECTOR INVOLVEMENT

The private sector has not been involved in medical education in Hungary since World War II. All Hungarian medical schools have been government-supported institutions.

INTERNATIONAL LINKAGES AND COLLABORATION

Traditionally, international linkages of Hungarian medical schools have been substantial, and the recent political changes have broadened the spectrum of these international collaborations.

ISSUES AND TRENDS

The present political and social revolutions in Hungary will change medical education, but it is too early to predict what will happen. We do not see how the economy will recover, and when, or what financial sources will open up, how the international environment will influence the system, how fast the reforms of health care will take place, or how quickly the changes in the health care system will feed back into medical education. There are many unknown basic factors; therefore, the future is far from certain.

Despite the uncertainties, however, there are challenges arising from the national health priorities and health care reforms that can be met by the Hungarian medical schools. Therefore, all medical schools are reviewing their curricula with the aim to restructure. In this process, the schools and their departments are studying the trends in medical education of the Western countries and seeking collaboration with partners from the European Community's medical schools.

In the future, the curriculum will place more emphasis on the role of lifestyle, focusing on psychosocial and environmental factors in disease prevention and health promotion. Because of the increasing importance of primary care among the health reform issues, improvements in training for primary care are needed. We would expect that in developing the new curricula, recent health and educational policy issues and initiatives, as elaborated by international experts' bodies in documents such as the Edinburgh Declaration, the Statement on Medical Education in Europe, and WHO's Health for All by 2000, will be given much greater consideration.

In the near term, four factors will play a major role in influencing the structure and quality of medical education. First, because of the previous overproduction of medical doctors, there is likely to be a reduction in the number of medical students which, by increasing the teacher/student ratio may lead to more personalized education. Second, all medical schools are strongly committed to the decentralization of postgraduate education and to developing broad-scale postgraduate programs. Third, there is a strong commitment to developing the structure and content of undergraduate programs in such a way that the degrees and diplomas issued by the Hungarian schools will be equivalent to those issued in the European Community. Finally, the recent reform process has embraced moves to reestablish the classic university system. In Debrecen the existing separate Faculties have already decided to merge in order to reestablish the "old" university structure, and similar steps are expected in the other cities. Considering, however, the experiences and the history of medical education in

Hungary, it would be difficult to overestimate the power of tradition in both directions. Tradition helped to avoid frivolous innovations, however, it was also an obstacle to badly needed improvement.

REFERENCES

Boján, F. 1990. Facts and thoughts on health care (in Hungarian). *Nepegeszsegugy* 71:280-284.

Boján, F., P. Hajdu, and E. Belicza. 1991. Avoidable mortality: Is it an indicator of quality of medical care in Eastern European countries? *Quality Assurance in Health Care* 3:199-203.

Forgacs, J. 1991. Postgraduate and continuing education in Hungary. *Cah. Socio. Demo. Med* 31:5-14.

Fülöp, T., and M.I. Roemer. 1987. *Reviewing health manpower development. A method of improving national health system.* Public Health Papers, no. 831. Geneva: WHO.

Gellhorn, A., T. Fülöp, and Z. Bankowski. 1977. *Health needs of society: A challenge for medical education.* CIOMS. Geneva: WHO.

Guilbert, J.J. 1987. *Educational handbook for health personal.* 6th ed. Offset Publication no. 35. Geneva: WHO.

Hungary. Ministry of Welfare. 1991. *Program for reform of health care system in Hungary* (in Hungarian). Budapest.

Raffel, N.K., and M.W. Raffel. 1988. The medical care system of Hungary. *J. Med. Pract. Manag* 4:142-149.

Szabó, G. 1987. Unsolved problems of medical school admission system (in Hungarian). *Magyar Tudomány* 3:190-194.

Vargáne Hajdu, P., and F. Boján. 1991. Medical demography. In: F. Boján, ed. Lecture - notes on social medicine. Debrecen: University Medical School of Debrecen (in Hungarian).

Table 14.1
Medical School Student Demographics—Hungary

Medical School	Male Undergraduate Enrollment Fall 1991	Female Undergraduate Enrollment Fall 1991	Male Postgraduates 1991	Female Postgraduates 1991	Male Interns/ Residents Fall 1991*	Female Interns/ Residents Fall 1991
Budapest Semmelweiss Medical School	1,480	1,354	197	211	303	290
Budapest Postgraduate Medical University					2,196**	2,713**
Debrecen	666	549	100	123	176	154
Pécs	819	629	97	105	220	114
Szeged	764	598	79	95	174	147
Total	3,729	3,130	473	534	873	705
GRAND TOTAL	6,859		1,007		1615	

*Includes all types of postgraduate and continuing education, as well as certificate and diploma courses.
**Not counted in totals.

204

Table 14.2
Medical School Faculty Demographics--Hungary

Medical School	Total Male Full-Time Faculty, Fall 1991	Total Female Full-Time Faculty, Fall 1991	Percent of Faculty with Degrees from Foreign Medical Schools	Average Salary (in U.S. $)— Male Full-Time Faculty	Average Salary (in U.S. $)— Female Full-Time Faculty	Average Age— Full-Time Faculty
Budapest Semmelweiss Medical School	752	537	.03%	4,824 /year	4,568 /year	48.1
Budapest Postgraduate Medical University	223	161	.03%	4,867 /year	3,997 /year	43.1
Debrecen	494	313	.02%	4,474 /year	3,512 /year	38.1
Pécs	420	110	.02%	5,120 /year	3,840 /year	44.9
Szeged	419	349	.001%	5,294 /year	4,146 /year	36.0
TOTAL	2,308	1,470				

15

India

SHRIDHAR SHARMA
SANTOSH S. KACKER
B. V. ADKOLI

India's Constitution envisages the establishment of a new social order, and it directs the individual states to bring about improvement in the public health as one of their primary duties. Health is a national objective, but items like population control, medical education, and drug control are under both the central and state governments. As such, constitutionally, the responsibility for health care is at the state level, while national health policy formulation and overall coordination of the work of the state health departments is overseen by the central union government.

OVERVIEW OF THE HEALTH CARE DELIVERY SYSTEM

The health structure in India has three main levels: central, state, and local. At the central level is the Ministry of Health and Family Welfare (MHFW). The Directorate General of Health Services is the technical wing of this ministry. The MHFW is headed by a cabinet minister and has two departments: Health and Family Welfare. The Department of Health is headed by a Secretary to the Government of India, and the Director General of Health Services acts as advisor to the government on both medical and public health matters. At the national level, a Central Council of Health and Family Welfare was set up in 1952 as an advisory body to consider and recommend broad guidelines of policy health in all its aspects.

India includes 25 states and 7 union territories. At each state and union territory level, a Ministry of Health headed by a minister looks after health and family welfare. All the states have established Directorates of Health, and some states also have separate Directorates of Medical Education. Each state is divided into districts, of which there are approximately 460. The district is the principal unit of administration in India. These districts vary widely in size and population. In each district there is a district hospital and a district health officer who is in overall charge of all elements of district health administration. The district is divided into subdistricts (*Talukas*), each having a community health center or upgraded primary health center. There were 1932 community health centers, 22,065 primary health centers, and 130,983 sub-centers at the end of September 1991. These primary health centers provide universally comprehensive health care services relevant to the actual needs and priorities of the communities, at a cost people can afford. Their services include preventive (vaccination and public health training), promotive (healthy life-style practices), and curative (medical-surgical) services. Each primary health center caters to 29,000 to 30,000 people and is headed by a physician. Under the primary health center are subcenters, each subcenter covering a population of 3,000 to 5,000.

HISTORICAL BACKGROUND

Medical education in India dates from ancient times. The philosophy of the Ayurveda, which took into account the holistic nature of health, was predominant between 800 B.C. and 600 A.D. and traveled in all directions to Asian countries, including Thailand, Indonesia, Mongolia, and North Siberia. The Siddha system of medicine, practiced in some parts of south India, is another early development. The Unani system, brought to India by Muslim rulers, flourished during the thirteenth century. The blending of the Ayurveda and Unani systems resulted in Tibbi medicine. The system of homeopathy gained a foothold during the early part of the last century. However, the allopathic system introduced with the advent of British rulers made a major impact. Nevertheless, the indigenous Indian systems of medicine, including herbal medicine and homeopathy, are still popular, especially in rural India. See A Note on Ayurveda at the end of this chapter.

The pattern of medical education is modeled after the British system, for obvious reasons of colonial influence. The early medical schools were established at Calcutta (1822), Bombay (1826), and Madras (1827) with the limited objective of training apprentices with minimum qualifications to help the army personnel. The first full-fledged medical college was established at Calcutta in 1838 under the supervision of the General Medical Council of Britain. The period between 1838 and 1916 witnessed the establishment of approximately nineteen medical colleges with an annual intake of 1,000 students. Following the passage of the Indian Medical Council Act of 1933, the Medical Council of India (MCI) came into existence in 1934. Along with the establishment of Medical Colleges, another category of institution, offering three to four years of training, was established by the provincial governments, missions and private organizations. These institutions trained students for the degree of Licentiate Medical Practitioner (LMP). Though LMPs helped in overcoming the acute shortage of trained medical manpower in India, they were subject to criticism as imperfectly trained health workers, and therefore the system was discontinued.

The appointment of the Health Survey and Development Committee, popularly called the Bhore Committee (1946) was the first attempt to lay down a comprehensive blueprint of health service in India, in the quest for Indianization of modern medical education. The Committee laid foundations for the development of a national system of health care based on primary health centers. It recommended expansion of medical colleges, abolition of Licentiate courses, upgrading medical schools into Medical Colleges, measures to improve the quality of training, and the establishment of an All India Institute of Medical Sciences (AIIMS).

Following independence in 1947, and in pursuance of the recommendations of the Bhore Committee, India witnessed a phenomenal increase in the production of medical personnel. In spite of this increase in the medical work force, the actual health needs of the people could not be satisfied, as the distribution of doctors was erratic and irrational. For instance, the doctor:population ratio varied from state to state (from 1:820 to 1:14,015), with grossly unequal distribution between rural and urban areas within each state. The concentration of doctors in a few urban areas, the inadequacy and short supply of nurses and other health personnel, the lack of relevance of the training program to the actual health problems and needs of the population was a disturbing trend, resulting from the absence of a well-planned health information system for regulating human resource development. The two major challenges for undergraduate medical education, therefore, were: (1) maintaining standards and responding positively to modern concepts and methods in medical education, and (2) promoting among graduates a sense of social outlook and a spirit of dedicated service to the people, especially in the rural areas. (See table 15.1).

Table 15.1
India--Growth of Medical Education in Independent India (Allopathic System only)

Period	Increase in Number of Medical Institutes	Increase in Enrollment
1947-65	17-87	1,400-5,387
1965-75	87-105	5,387-11,911
1975-85	105-106	11,911-12,278
1985-91	106-129	12,278-13,714

Note: The figures are for the 129 medical colleges reported on by the MCI. In addition, there are approximately 20 other unrecognized medical colleges. The total enrollment is estimated to be 15,000 per year. (See Table 15.3., p. 220)

The government of India appointed a number of committees and working groups to respond to these needs. The Health Survey and Planning Committee (Mudaliar Committee--1961), Committee on Multipurpose Workers under the Health and Family Planning Program (Kartar Singh Committee--1974), Group on Medical Education and Support Manpower (Prof. J.B. Srivastav Committee--1975), Report of the ICSSR-ICMR (Indian Council for Social Science Research-Indian Council for Medical Research) Study Group (led by Prof. V. Ramalingaswami--1981), Adoption of National Health Policy (1983), Medical Education Review Committee (Mehta Committee--1983), Working Group on

Medical Education, Training and Manpower Training, Planning Commission, National Policy on Education (1986), and the Expert Committee on Health Manpower-Planning Production and Management (Chairman Prof. J.S. Bajaj-- 1987) were among the efforts to support or streamline the Indian medical education system.

The Re-orientation of Medical Education, popularly called the ROME Scheme, is a significant experiment that was tried in India with partial success. It was introduced in 1977 by the Group on Medical Education and Support Manpower headed by Prof. Srivatsav. Objectives of the ROME Scheme were (1) to orient medical faculty, residents, interns and medical students to the conditions existing in the rural communities and provide training in the management of health problems encountered there; and (2) to render comprehensive health care to the villages in collaboration with the concerned primary health centers. Accordingly each medical college was to assume the total responsibility for comprehensive health care in three community blocks (primary health centers) and gradually extend its sphere of activity to cover the entire district. For this purpose, each medical college was to establish a well-knit rural referral system. Outreach activities, the posting of medical students in the community, provision of mobile clinics, and the involvement of the entire faculty of the medical college all combined to achieve the purpose of community based training.

The ROME Scheme met with only partial success due to such factors as lack of necessary infrastructure, poor logistics, the lukewarm attitude of medical faculty to participate in community based training, and the lack of concerted effort and institutional mechanisms for implementation. Moreover, there was neither a reward structure nor a system of accountability and evaluation of these activities built in as part of the program. On the positive side, some medical schools with effective leadership and faculty motivation made significant progress toward community-oriented training.

Table 15.2
India--Total Number of Doctors, 1990

Type of Registered Doctors	Number
Modern Medicine	365,000
Ayurveda	272,800
Unani	28,711
Siddha	11,581

ROLE OF NATIONAL POLICY IN SHAPING MEDICAL EDUCATION

The Indian government instituted a National Health Policy in 1983 which emphasized that the effective delivery of health care services depended largely on the nature of education, training, and appropriate orientation toward community health of all categories of medical and health personnel, as well as their capacity to function as an integrated team, each member performing given tasks within a coordinated action program. The National Health Policy reiterated that the entire basis and approach toward medical and health education, at all levels, must be reviewed in terms of national needs and priorities. Curricular and training programs must be restructured to produce personnel of various grades of skill and competence who are professionally equipped and socially motivated to deal effectively with day-to-day problems within the existing constraints.

Toward this end, legislators believed it necessary to formulate a separate National Medical and Health Education Policy that (1) sets out the changes required in the curricular contents and training programs of medical and health personnel at various levels of functioning; (2) takes into account the need for establishing the essential interrelations between functionaries of various grades; (3) provides guidelines for the production of health personnel based on realistically assessed manpower requirements; (4) seeks to resolve the existing sharp regional imbalances in availability of manpower; and (5) ensures that personnel at all levels are socially motivated toward rendering community health services.

The need for a national education policy in the health sciences was also expressed in the reports of the Medical Education Review Committee in 1983 and the Expert Committee on Health Manpower, Planning, Production and Management in 1986. The National Policy on Education in 1986 brought into sharp focus essential interlinkages between health and education policies. It emphasized that health planning and health services management should optimally interlock with the education and training of appropriate categories of health manpower through health-related vocational courses.

ADMISSION

Regulations of the Medical Council of India require that candidates for admission to medical college should be at least 17 years old and have passed the Higher Secondary qualifying examination or equivalent held after 12 years of schooling. Most states have adopted a "10 plus 2" pattern of education, which means 10 years of secondary and 2 years of higher secondary courses. The last two years of study should consist of physics, chemistry, biology and mathematics or any other elective with English as the core subject. A candidate seeking admission to the Bachelor of Medicine, Bachelor of Surgery (MBBS) course must have passed the qualifying examinations with a minimum of 50 percent aggregate marks in English, physics, chemistry, and biology.

Selection of students to medical college is based solely on the merit of the candidate. In states having only one medical college, the marks obtained at the qualifying examination are considered in deciding merit. In states with more than one university/examining body conducting the qualifying examination, an additional competitive entrance examination is held. The All India Institute of Medical Sciences has its own multiple-choice entrance examination. Most states have a residency requirement for admission to 75 percent of seats. In institutions like AIIMS, all seats are open to candidates from all states and union territories.

The government recently introduced All India entrance examinations for selecting 15 percent of the seats to be allocated to each medical college based on merit. Each medical school must reserve 15 percent of its seats for students from the national merit exam list. Thus, 15 percent of students usually belong to other states and 85 percent live in the state in which they will study. The Council has also established a minimum requirement of 50 percent aggregate marks in English, physics, chemistry, and biology for admission to medical college. The requirement is under review. For candidates belonging to the Scheduled Castes/Scheduled Tribes[1], the minimum marks required are 40 percent instead of the 50 percent required for general candidates.

Certain self-financing colleges admit students on merit as well as donation, in such proportions as are agreed by the government. These institutions are run by a private trust or a society and are not entitled to receive any government grants. It is estimated that there are approximately 40 private medical colleges in the country. Until recently, they could adopt their own fee structure and charge capitation fees ranging from Rs 200,000 to Rs 1,000,000 (US $ = Rs 30). Recently, the Indian government, banned capitation fees and made the fee structure subject to control by the government.

Demographic Profile of Medical Students and Faculty

A demographic profile of medical students and medical faculty is not available. However, the general trend is that medical school admission is most coveted in the career market as evidenced by a large number of applicants every year. Increasing numbers of candidates belonging to the upper middle class, whose parents are educated and employed in urban settings find places in medical school.

CURRICULAR STRUCTURE AND INNOVATION

The Indian medical curriculum, except for AIIMS, is under the purview of the Medical Council of India which prescribes curriculum, lays down procedures for admission and patterns of examination, and regulates subjects such as minimum requirements for physical space, equipment, and staffing patterns. While the Council sets broad principles and minimum requirements, the details are left to the universities.

The medical course consists of four and a half years of undergraduate study followed by a one-year compulsory rotating internship. The curriculum is discipline based. The first 18 months (known as Phase 1), include preclinical subjects: anatomy, human physiology and biochemistry (15 months), followed by an introduction to a broad understanding of the perspectives of medical education

---

[1] The Indian Constitution guarantees that educational institutions will reserve seats for applicants from specific Scheduled Castes (SC) and Scheduled Tribes (ST) that have traditionally lacked such opportunities.

(3 months). Phase II covers paraclinical subjects, and is taught over a period of 18 months. This course consists of pathology, microbiology, pharmacology, forensic medicine, and community medicine. Phase III consists of medicine, surgery (including orthopedic), OB-Gyn, pediatrics (including social pediatrics), Eye and ENT, and a Community Medicine posting.

Clinical postings begin with the first clinical year (i.e., after one and a half years of preclinical), and students are posted for not less than three hours per day. University examinations are usually held at the end of preclinical and paraclinical phases. The examination in the clinical phase is held in two parts: the first consisting of Community Medicine, ophthalmology, and ear-nose-throat; the second of medicine, surgery, and OB-Gyn. The examination consists of theory, practical and an assessment conducted by the student's medical college teachers which counts for approximately 10 percent.

The Medical Council has emphasized the objective of producing a medical graduate capable of functioning independently and effectively in both rural and urban settings. It has highlighted the importance of social factors in relation to the problem of health and disease, the teaching of health education, the need for stressing population control and family planning, and provision of teaching opportunities in outpatient departments, emergency departments, and community settings.

Though a subject-based (discipline-based) curriculum has been suggested, the council has recognized the need to reduce artificial compartmentalization of the curriculum into preclinical, paraclinical and clinical disciplines by a system of integrated teaching. For this purpose, the Council has recommended one hour per week for conducting interdepartmental activities. The MCI has recommended that mechanisms be established to promote both horizontal and vertical integration among the preclinical, paraclinical and clinical disciplines, but this recommendation has not yet been instituted in most medical colleges. Regarding the method of instruction, the Medical Council favors reducing the amount of didactic teaching and increasing participation in small group discussions and seminars. Traditionally, however, instruction in medical schools has been teacher-oriented rather than learner-oriented. Attempts to reverse this trend are limited to a handful of medical schools. The paucity of innovative approaches is attributed mainly to inadequate opportunities for teacher training and orientation, lack of incentive structures to recognize and reward the teaching effort, and preoccupation with patient care or research as a preferred activity.

Other deficiencies also need to be addressed in launching curricular innovations. Teaching is not currently aligned with the morbidity pattern prevalent in the primary health care setting. It is alleged that the topics of rare diseases and complicated cases take precedence over the topics of common interest that have great relevance to the public health situation. Community health problems prevalent in India are covered. However, the curriculum of undergraduate education does not adequately emphasize the instruction and evaluation of these aspects. The activities and skills expected of the primary care physician, such as communication and managerial skills, working with health teams, rational drug utilization, and cost-effective interventions are not addressed. Sites of training, being predominantly hospital based, are also not congenial for training in primary care.

While the level of knowledge of facts in medical sciences is highly satisfactory, medical graduates are often found lacking skills in patient management and especially in the management of common emergencies. Development of communications skills and attitudes, including ethical and humanistic attitudes, is yet another area of concern. The need for the introduction of psychological and social aspects of health and disease, possibly through courses in behavioral sciences, is keenly felt. The assessment system in vogue is held as a main culprit as it tests the students' recall of information rather than the ability to analyze facts, interpret data, and arrive at conclusions for a meaningful application of the knowledge gained in solving the real problems of the individual and the community. The greatest challenge to medical education in India, therefore, is to design a system that is deeply rooted in the scientific method and yet is profoundly influenced by the local health problems and by the social, cultural and economic settings in which they arise.

Attempts to innovate the curriculum are isolated to the institutions, sometimes even to individual departments of an institution. Nevertheless, they reflect modest attempts to swim against the current with perseverance. The following changes have been introduced, with the approximate number of institutions involved indicated in parentheses.

- Community based training activities and support to national health programs (six);
- Teacher training activities and establishment of Medical Education Units (eight);
- Objective assessment strategies, including the use of objective structured clinical/practical exams (one);
- Selection methods encompassing attitudes, motivation, and related factors (two);
- Consortium of Health Institutions for Reorienting Medical Education (four);
- Introduction of rational therapeutics (four);
- Recognizing the social paradigm (one);
- Practice of social or community pediatrics (three);
- Establishment of University of Health Sciences (two); and
- Contribution to the dissemination and promotion of educational development and research in medical education (one).

GRADUATE MEDICAL EDUCATION

After passing MBBS examinations, candidates are granted provisional registration for one year, during which time they undergo compulsory rotating internships. The internship should be done in teaching and non-teaching approved hospitals such as district hospitals and Rural Health Training Centers/Upgraded Primary Health centers attached to the training institutions. The internship includes hospital training in medicine, surgery, and OB-Gyn for six months and training in community health work provided in an appropriate health center for an additional six months. This also includes in-service training in family planning clinics for one month. The Council provides for training in any elective clinical subject such as pediatrics, ophthalmology, otorhinolaryngology, dermatology, and psychiatry.

LICENSURE

There is no structured curriculum for the training and evaluation of interns. However, broad guidelines have been provided by the Medical Council. The intern maintains a record of work that is verified and certified by the medical officer under whom he or she works. Based on the record of work, the dean will issue a certificate of satisfactory completion of training, after which the university awards the MBBS degree. Full registration is given by the state medical council on the award of the MBBS degree by the university. The medical colleges are affiliated with different universities which are responsible only for conducting examinations and awarding degrees.

Board Certification of Specialists

Specialist training in India consists of a postgraduate degree comprising three years of study in a specialty after full registration, including one year of junior residency. The Council emphasizes that thorough and systematic training in a planned program should be given to the student during all stages of the course, and such a program should be available for the inspection and scrutiny of the Council during its accreditation visits. Since 1992, all postgraduate degrees are of three years duration and are broadly based on a residency system in specialties. Each university gives its own postgraduate degree called MD (for medical subjects) or MS (for surgical subjects). Either degree requires three years after the MBBS. For the "super-specialties" such as neurology, cardiology, and others, another three years leading to the DM or MCH are required (for a total of six years beyond the MBBS). To work out a unified pattern for the whole of India, the specialty boards are patterned on the United States or the Royal College of the United Kingdom. These specialty boards are optional, however, and do not affect licensure.

During the last few decades India has witnessed increased specialization--and super-specialization--due to the rapid growth in medical knowledge and technology, unchecked by efforts to consider the effective demand for the employability of the specialist. There are fifty broad specialties and super-specialties recognized by the MCI. On one hand, these developments have provided certain positive benefits to the patients. On the other hand, this overspecialization has resulted in excess reliance on sophisticated gadgets and diagnostic aids that dehumanize medicine, has created new ethical issues and problems, and has stimulated the out-migration of medical personnel leading to a significant "brain drain."

Cross-Licensing of Physicians

The Medical Council of India maintains a list (Schedule II) of the degrees awarded by foreign universities that are considered equivalent on a reciprocal basis. In addition, Part II of the MCI's Schedule III has been added to facilitate the Indian national who migrates back to India after training abroad. The consideration of equivalence is based on international agreements irrespective of political alliances.

CONTINUING MEDICAL EDUCATION

Continuing education is not mandatory for Indian health professionals. However, the need for developing a well-coordinated system of continuing education for health workers of different grades to ensure their effective performance and participation in the health team has been emphasized by various committees. At present, various professional bodies are independently involved in this activity. The National Academy of Medical Sciences created the National Board of Examination as an independent examining body under the control of the Ministry of Health. It conducts examinations to award Diplomat of National Board (DNB) and Member of National Academy of Medical Sciences (MNAMS), degrees that are yet to become popular in comparison with the MD and MS degrees awarded by the universities. The Medical Council of India has also set up a CME cell to organize CME activities with support from nonresident Indian doctors who have settled abroad but whose expertise is used by MCI when these doctors visit India. Various professional bodies and associations hold CME sessions in their forums. Recently private hospitals and medical establishments have also shown interest in this field. Various medical colleges are involved in activities related to the training and continuing education of other health professionals. The Christian Medical College in Vellore has made a modest beginning in introducing CME activities for general physicians, using a distance learning technique.

ROLE OF RESEARCH IN MEDICAL EDUCATION

One of the serious deficiencies noticed in Indian medical education, analogous to the situation prevailing in many other countries, is the lack of adequate motivation and opportunities for faculty development, with the resultant indifference to research efforts in teaching and education. While medical teachers may be highly efficient professionals in their respective branches of specialization, they display a kind of amateurism in playing the role of effective educators. This might be because of the fact that teaching efforts are not rewarded and not even considered as a desirable criterion for selection or promotion as compared with clinical skills or contribution to research in medical sciences. It is for this reason that innovative approaches to curriculum planning, instructional design and application of educational technology have not received much stimulus in past decades. However, there are reasons to believe that the trend is shifting. Recent emphasis on faculty development by the Education Policy on Health Sciences and a fresh look at faculty development by the MCI are likely to have significant impact on promoting faculty development and research in medical education.

At present, there are three National Teacher Training Centers (NTTCs) at Pondicherry, Varanasi and Chandigarh; a Center for Medical Education and Technology (CMET) at AIIMS, New Delhi, and approximately a dozen medical education units as part of medical schools actively engaged in medical education activities. With the establishment of two Universities of Health Sciences, a few more regional centers are expected in the near future.

GOVERNMENT/PRIVATE SECTOR INVOLVEMENT

Traditionally, the Indian medical education system has been scarcely influenced by the private sector, as 100 out of 129 medical schools are fully financed and controlled by the government. However, of late there has been fresh thinking to encourage private initiative and investment, particularly in view of the resource constraint, provided they satisfy minimum standards. While this has reduced financial pressure on the government, it has also promoted high technology culture with excessive reliance on diagnostic tools and techniques.

INTERNATIONAL LINKAGES AND COLLABORATION

India is a signatory to the goal of Health for All by the Year 2000, and as such, the production of physicians able to play their roles effectively as leaders of the health team in providing comprehensive primary health care is considered in the foreground of medical training. The points of view raised in the Edinburgh Declaration have been fully endorsed at the national level, thanks to the initiative taken by the Indian Association for the Advancement of Medical Education (IAAME).

ISSUES AND TRENDS

Some major initiatives that have taken place recently are the planned constitution of a Medical Education Commission, an attempt by the MCI to design a need-based curriculum, and the establishment of a Consortium of Health Institutions, including the All India Institute of Medical Sciences, New Delhi; Institute of Medical Sciences, BHU, Varanasi; Jawaharlal Institute of Postgraduate Medical Education and Research, Pondicherry; and Christian Medical College, Vellore, in collaboration with the Department of Medical Education, University of Illinois, Chicago, US, to spearhead the reorientation of medical education. Thus, medical education in India is at a significant point of transition. With the initiatives coming from both external and internal influences, and the political will to attain the goal of Health for All, India hopes to be in a better position to meet the needs of physicians entering the twenty-first century. Although the Medical Education Commission is yet to be constituted, it is expected to assume a threefold function of analyzing the needs of education in the health sciences, deciding a pattern of financing the same, and establishing mechanisms of coordination among different professional councils and other bodies.

Well-defined and broad-based revisions of rules and regulations governing undergraduate and postgraduate education are currently being undertaken by the Medical Council of India. This will help every Indian medical school improve its training and teaching.

NOTE

A note on Ayurveda:

Ayurveda is a traditional Indian system of medicine whose name literally means "Life" (Ayuh) "Knowledge" (Veda); in other words, knowledge of life. The origin of Ayurveda dates back to the later part of the Vedic period (1000-500 B.C.). There are two well-known Ayurvedic treatises, one by Charaka Samhita (compendiums), a physician, and the other by Sushruta Samhita, a surgeon who lived near the first millennium B.C. (8th-7th century B.C.). Out of the four Vedas which are supposed to be the oldest books known to the library of mankind, the Atharvaveda contains descriptions about the various medical problems and the concept of health. The most fascinating contribution in Ayurveda relates to understanding the phenomenology of disease. A systematic attempt was made to classify diseases into eight broad disciplines. It was also thought that diseases are the result of imbalance of the "humors." Each disease was supposed to be influenced by a specific type of humor. Another interesting contribution of the Ayurveda was its knowledge regarding the relationship of diet and disease.

The approach to training in Ayurveda was holistic and integrated. The state of health and disease is explained in this system based on the interplay of the constituent elements of the body: the general and alimentary regimen, and the influences of time and the season.

In the field of materia medica and pharmacy, the properties of drugs and foods were investigated. Diagnosis was to be made by the five senses, supplemented by interrogation. Diagnosis was based on cause (*nidana*), prenomitary indications (*purva-rupa*), symptoms (*rupa*), therapeutic tests (*apace*) and natural history of the development of the disease (*samprapti*).

According to Shusruta, the physician (*chishak*), the drug (*dravya*), the attendants or the nursing personnel (*upasthata*), and the patient (*rogi*) are the four pillars on which rests the success of the therapy.

The science of Ayurveda received its highest patronage from Buddhist kings (400-200 B.C.). With the spread of Buddhism to Asian countries, Ayurveda also spread to those countries and was adapted to the local needs.

Siddha System. The Siddha system of medicine is quite akin to the Ayurvedic, but is practiced more in southern India. It gives greater importance to the preparation of potions, syrups, and the like, from herbs with medicinal value.

Unani Medicine. Unani medicine is Greek in origin and was brought to India by Muslim rulers. It is still practiced in certain parts of northern India.

Tibbia Medicine. The *Hakeems* or royal physicians of the Muslim rulers followed a hybrid system resulting from the blending of Ayurveda and the Greek Unani medicine which was called Tibbi. Each well-known *Hakeem* had a few students under his preceptorship to be trained in the Tibbi system. This system flourished during the period of Emperor Akbar (1555-1605 A.D.) (Keswani 1968).

REFERENCES

All India Institute of Medical Sciences. 1991. Inquiry driven strategies for innovations in medical education in India, p. 3. All India Institute of Medical Science on behalf of the Consortium of Health Institutions under SEARO Project IND HMD 017.1.

Atharva Veda Samhita. 1962. *The hymns of the Atharva Veda*. Trans. with commentary by Ralph T.H. Griffith and ed. by M.L. Abhimanyu. 2 vols. Rpt. Varanasi: Master Khelari Lal and Sons.

Bajaj, J.S. 1989. Draft national education policy for health sciences. *Indian Journal for Medical Education* 29 (1 and 2). New Delhi: Indian Association for Advancement of Medical Education.

Charaka Samhita. trans., Shri Gulabkunverba Ayurvedic Society. 1949. *The Charaka Samhita*. 6, vols. Sanskrit text with introduction and translations, into Hindi, Gujarati, and English. Jamnagar, Gujarat: Gulabkunverba Ayurvedic Society.

Dahanukar, S. A., and S.M. Karandikar. 1987. Tridosha concept in Ayurveda and scientific correlates in modern medicine. *J Health Sci* 13:102-109.

India, Government of. Ministry of Health and Family Welfare. Central Bureau of Health Intelligence (CBHI):DGHS. 1990. Health Information of India.

———. 1982. Compendium of recommendations of various committees on health manpower development 1943-1975.

———. 1988. Medical education in India. New Delhi.

———. 1983. The national health policy. Government of India.

Keswani, N.H. 1968. Medical education in India since ancient times. Talk presented at the International Symposium on the History of Medical Education. Los Angeles.

Medical Council of India. 1987. Report of Expert Committee on Health Manpower Planning Production and Management. Government of India.

———. 1981. *Recommendations on graduate medical education*. New Delhi: Aiwan-e-galib Marg.

———. 1988. Recommendations on postgraduate medical education. New Delhi: Aiwan-e-galib Marg.

———. 1992. Draft paper on revised curriculum for undergraduate medical education. New Delhi: Aiwan-e-galib Marg.

Medico Friends Circle. 1991. Medical education re-examined. *MFC Anthology*. Bombay: Medico Friends Circle.

National Academy of Medical Sciences. 1981. *Continuing medical education programs: A compilation 1968-1981*. New Delhi: NAMS.

Sharma, S.D. 1990a. Medical education and medical manpower development. Inaugural address at the meeting of the expert group. Feb. 1990. New Delhi.

———. 1990b. *National policy of education in health sciences*. Regional seminar on Higher Medical Education. Bhubanaswar: National Board of Examination.

———. 1989. National policy of education in health sciences. Regional Seminar on Higher Medical Education. Bhopal, India: N.B.F.

———. 1972. Problems and perspectives in medical education. *Ind. J. Med. Edu.* 11(2-3):1-3.

———. 1962. Medical education in India. *Intermedica* (London) 4(1):11.

Sharma, P.V. 1972. *Indian medicine in the classical age.* vol. 85 of *The Chowkhamba Sanskrit Studies.* Varanasi: Chowkhamba.

Susruta. *The Susrutasamhita of Susruta.* 1945. With various readings, notes and appendix etc. Ed by Narayan Ram Acarya with cooperation of Jadavji Trikamji Acharya. Bombay: Nirnaya Sagar.

World Health Organization. 1988. *Reorientation of medical education.* WHO SEARO Publication no. 18. New Delhi: WHO.

Table 15.3

Total Number of Medical Colleges--India

Govt. of India/State Government	Recognized	100
	Unrecognized	4
	Total	104
Private/Trusts	Recognized	16
	Unrecognized	9
	Total	25
Total		129
Students Admitted	1989-90	13,714

Figures provided by MCI in 1991.

Table 15.4
India--National Health Indicators

Health Indicator	1947	1992
Infant Mortality	134/1000 (1946-1951)	90/1000
Doctor:Patient Ratio	1:6000	Varies between 1:820 in Chandigarh to 1:14,015 in Gujarat
# of Hospital Beds/Population	.24/1000	.73/1000
Average Age + expectancy Life expectancy at birth	1941 = 32.09 Male; 31.37 Female 1951 = 32.35 Male; 31.66 Female	59 Male; 59.2 Female
Maternal Mortality	10-14/1000	5-8/1000
Smallpox		Eradicated April, 1977
GNP expenditure on health	3.3% on Health-1st plan; nothing on family welfare	1.9% on Health; 1.8% on Family Welfare (VII Plan)
Primary health care utilization	Practically non-existent	20,532 (September 1990)

Table 15.5
Medical School Demographics--India 1989-90

Medical School	Founded	Total Admitted	Graduates 1989
ANDHRA PRADESH Andhra University Andhra Medical College	1923	122	142
Rangaraya Medical College	1958	100	82
Nagarjuna University Guntur Medical College	1946	123	121
Siddhartha Medical College	1981	98	62

Table 15.5
Medical School Demographics--India 1989-90

Medical School	Founded	Total Admitted	Graduates 1989
Osmania University			
Osmania Medical College	1926	152	150
Gandhi Medical College	1954	97	116
Deccan College of Medical	1985	100	52
Kakitiya University			
Kakatiya Medical College	1959	99	165
S.V. University			
Kurnool Medical College	1957	120	179
S.V. Medical College	1960	100	193
ASSAM			
Gauhati University			
Gauhati Medical College	1961	136	118
Silchar Medical College	1968	65	89
Dibrugarh University			
Assam Medical College	1947	156	147
BIHAR			
L.N. Mithila University			
Darbhanga Medical College	1946	90	94
Bihar University			
Sri Krishan Medical College	1970	50	44
Patna University			
Patna Medical College	1925	100	120
Ranchi University			
Rajendra Medical College	1956	90	113
M.G.M. Medical College	1961	50	
Patliputra Medical College	1979	50	-
Bhagalpur University			
Medical College	1971	50	61

Table 15.5
Medical School Demographics--India 1989-90

Medical School	Founded	Total Admitted	Graduates 1989
Magadh University			
Magah Medical College	1970	47	49
Nalanda Medical College	1956	54	
DELHI (U.T.)			
All India Institute of Medical Science	1956	50	42
Delhi University			
Lady Hardinge Medical College	1916	129	117
Maulana Azad Medical College	1958	175	165
University College of Medical Sciences	1971	100	-
GOA			
Goa University			
Goa Medical College	1963	70	60
GUJARAT			
Gujarat University			
B.J. Medical College	1946	210	257
Municipal Medical College	1963	100	118
M.S. University of Baroda			
Medical College	1949	140	278
Saurashtra University			
M.P. Shah Medical College	1955	175	222
South Gujarat University			
Govt. Medical College	1964	100	99
Sardar Patel University			
Pramukh Swami Medical College	1987	155	-
HARYANA			
Maharshi Dayanand University			
Govt. Medical College	1960	115	117

Table 15.5

Medical School Demographics--India 1989-90

Medical School	Founded	Total Admitted	Graduates 1989
HIMACHAL PRADESH			
Himachal Pradesh University			
Indira Gandhi Medical College	1966	65	82
Kashmir University			
Govt. Medical College	1959	122	
Jammu University			
Govt. Medical College	1972	90	
KARNATAKA			
Mysore University			
Mysore Medical College	1924	159	234
J.J. M. Medical College	1966	250	85
J.S.S. Medical College	1984	200	-
Sri Adichunchanegri Medical College	1985	182	-
Mangalore University			
Kasturba Medical College	1953	250	
Manipal/Mangalore	1953	300	139
Bangalore University			
Bangalore Medical College	1955	169	335
St. John's Medical College	1963	59	54
M.S. Ramiah Medical College	1970	100	165
Dr. Ambedkar Medical College	1980	165	260
Kampegowda Institute of Medical Science	1980	54	136
Sri. Devraj Urs Medical College	1986	145	-
Siddartha Medical College	1988	150	-
Karnataka University			
Karnataka Medical College	1957	115	127
J.L.N. Medical College	1963	185	239

Table 15.5
Medical School Demographics--India 1989-90

Medical School	Founded	Total Admitted	Graduates 1989
Al-Ameen Medical College	1984	116	
B.L.D.Medical College	1986	100	
Gulbarga University M.R.Medical College	1963	185	102
Medical College, Bellary	1961	104	128
KERALA Kerala University Medical College, Trivandrum	1961	199	196
T.D. Medical College	1973	105	91
Gandhiji University Medical College	1960	99	143
Calicut University Medical College, Calicut	1957	200	183
Medical College, Trichur	1981	154	79
MADHYA PRADESH Rani Durgawati Vishwavidyalaya Medical College	1955	136	220
Jiwaji University G.R.Medical College	1946	134	132
Devi Ahilya Vishwavidhyalaya M.G.M. Medical College	1948	154	345
Bhopal University Gandhi Medical College	1955	146	127
A.P. Singh University S.S. Medical College	1963	55	41

Table 15.5
Medical School Demographics--India 1989-90

Medical School	Founded	Total Admitted	Graduates 1989
Ravishankar University Pt. J.N.M. Medical College	1963	95	
Bombay University Grant Medical College	1945	209	435
Seth G.S. Medical College	1925	188	195
T.N. Medical College	1964	123	182
L.T.M. Medical College	1964	102	107
Poona University B.J. Medical College	1946	201	221
Armed Forces Medical	1962	128	145
Rural Medical College	1984	100	
Shivaji University Miraj Medical College	1961	100	72
Dr. V.M. Medical College	1963	99	91
Krishna Institute of Medical Sciences	1984	112	37
Marathwada University Govt. Medical College	1956	100	216
S.R.T.R. Medical College	1975	49	48
Medical College, Nanded	1988	50	-
Nagpur University Medical College, Nagpur	1947	208	188
Indira Gandhi Corporation Medical College	1968	61	
Mahatma Gandhi College of Medical Sciences	1969	62	66
Amarvati University Dr. Panjabrao Alias Bhausaheb Deshmukh Memorial Medical College	1984	107	93

Table 15.5

Medical School Demographics--India 1989-90

Medical School	Founded	Total Admitted	Graduates 1989
MANIPUR			
Manipur University			
Regional Medical College	1972	74	
ORISSA			
Utkal University			
S.C.B. Medical College	1944	125	117
Sambalpur University			
V.S.S. Medical College	1954	113	105
Behrampur University			
M.K.C.G. Medical College	1961	107	101
PONDICHERRY			
Pondicherry University			
Jawaharlal Institute of Postgraduate Medical Education and Research	1956	63	62
PUNJAB			
Punjabi University, Patiala			
Govt. Medical College	1953	152	182
Guru Gobind Singh Medical College	1973	40	49
Panjab University			
Christian Medical College	1963	50	109
Dayanand Medical College	1963	51	56
Guru Nanak Dev University			
Medical College	1943	153	166
RAJASTHAN			
Rajasthan University			
S.M.S. Medical College	1947	180	166
S.P. Medical College	1956	112	93
R.N.T. Medical College	1961	98	100
Dr. S.N. Medical College	1965	72	83

Table 15.5
Medical School Demographics--India 1989-90

Medical School	Founded	Total Admitted	Graduates 1989
J.L.N. Medical College	1965	86	109
TAMINLADU			
Madras University			
Madras Medical College	1835	164	155
Stanley Medical College	1838	175	
Kilpauk Medical College	1960	132	
Christian Medical College	1942	60	60
Medical College, Chingleput	1965	66	60
Sri Ramchandra Medical College	1985	101	71
Salem Medical College	1985		-
Institute of Road Transport Taramani	1987		
Bharathidasan University			
Thanjavour Medical College	1959	143	163
Medical College, Coimbatore	1967	101	78
P.S.G. Institute of Medical Sciences	1985	100	-
Annamalai University			
Medical College Chidambaram	1985	131	-
Madurai University			
Madurai Medical College	1954	174	
Tirunelveli Medical College	1965	93	153
UTTAR PRADESH			
Agra University			
S.N. Medical College	1939	121	116
Allahabad University			
M.L.N. Medical College	1961	102	199
Aligarh Muslim University			
J.N. Medical College	1961	97	40

Table 15.5
Medical School Demographics--India 1989-90

Medical School	Founded	Total Admitted	Graduates 1989
Banaras Hindu University Institute of Medical Sciences, BHU	1960	61	47
Kanpur University G.S.V.M. Medical College	1955	193	
Bundelkhand University M.L.B. Medical College	1968	83	49
Lucknow University K.G. Medical College	1911	150	182
Meerut University L.L.R.M.Medical College	1966	179	83
Gorakhpur University B.R.D. Medical College	1972	117	
WEST BENGAL Calcutta University Medical College, Calcutta	1836	180	306
R.G. Kar Medical College	1916	150	144
N.R.S. Medical College	1948	152	285
Calcutta National Medical College	1948	150	
B.S. Medical College	1956	50	48
North Bengal University North Bengal Medical College	1969	49	90
Burdwan University Burdwan Medical College	1970	49	45
TOTAL:		15,110	

*The figures were provided by the MCI in respect to 1989-90. Figures in respect to "graduates" are incomplete. In many cases the figures are higher because they include the candidates who pass in the supplementary examination. In some cases, no convocation was held in that year. Hence, figures must be considered as approximate only.

16

Israel

MOSHE PRYWES
DAVID M. MIRVIS

The professional training of physicians is one of the most challenging educational tasks a nation can undertake. The educational institutions are highly elaborate and sophisticated, the Faculties are highly specialized, and the sheer volume of material to be taught is prodigious. Responses to these challenges vary widely from country to country. This variability reflects not only differences in fiscal and personnel resources, but also distinctive national educational philosophies, cultural values and health care systems. In this chapter, we describe key elements of the medical education system in Israel and consider several important challenges currently facing the Israeli medical educational establishment.

OVERVIEW OF THE HEALTH CARE DELIVERY SYSTEM

Health care is provided to virtually the entire population of Israel through a complex matrix of governmental and nongovernmental organizations. Over 95 percent of the population is enrolled in one of four national sick funds. These function as health maintenance organizations, providing or funding comprehensive services in return for prepaid membership fees. The largest of these, the General Sick Fund or Kupat Holim Clalit of the national labor federation, the Histadrut, serves over 75 percent of the population. The small segment of the population not covered by one of the sick funds is protected by various governmental, charitable, or private health care programs.

These sick funds either provide care directly in facilities they own and operate, or they fund such care through contractual arrangements with independent physicians or facilities owned either by the Ministry of Health, by another sick fund, or by a private agency. Kupat Holim Clalit, for example, delivers care directly to its members through over sixteen hundred neighborhood primary-care clinics, eight acute-care hospitals (30 percent of all acute-care beds in the nation), three psychiatric hospitals, three long-term-care hospitals and numerous other types of facilities, all of which it owns and operates. Other hospital facilities are owned by the Ministry of Health or municipalities (46 percent of acute-care beds), by several not-for-profit health care organizations (20 percent of acute-care beds), or by for-profit corporations (only 4 percent of acute-care beds). Over 90 percent of all physicians are salaried employees. Most are employed by either the government or by one of the sick funds, and a smaller number are employed by private institutions such as Hadassah Medical Center in Jerusalem.

Health care funds are derived from membership fees paid to sick funds (estimated at 42 percent in 1990-1991), direct government funds (22 percent), not-for-profit institutions (13 percent), and out-of-pocket payments by patients (23 percent) (Central Bureau of Statistics 1992). In 1990-1991, health care expenses consumed 7.9 percent of the gross national product. Important measures of national health care status include an infant mortality rate of 8.2 deaths per 1,000 live births for the Jewish population and 9.9 for the entire population, and an expected longevity of 74.6 years for men and 78.1 years for women in 1990 (Israel 1991). Infant mortality rates for the United States and Sweden were 11.0 and 6.7 infant deaths per 1000 live births, respectively (World Health Organization 1991).

HISTORICAL BACKGROUND

Israel has four medical schools. The oldest school was founded in 1949, only one year after the formation of the independent nation, as a joint venture between Hebrew University and Hadassah Medical Organization, the American Women's Zionist Organization. This initial school in Jerusalem was viewed as accomplishing part of the national mission of developing a self-sustaining Jewish society that has traditionally valued health care and respected medicine as a career, and as an effort to meet the projected human resource needs of the new nation. From the outset, it implemented a medical curriculum similar to that of most American medical schools with emphasis on scientific approaches to medical care and on research, and established a very high standard of academic achievement for the nation.

Subsequently, other schools were established in Tel Aviv as a unit of Tel Aviv University, in Haifa as a Faculty of the Technion--Israel Institute of Technology, and in Beer Sheva as part of Ben Gurion University of the Negev.[1] These were opened after considerable debate to help meet various national, regional, or local needs. It was already apparent by the early 1960s that additional medical schools were not needed to meet the nation's health care work force requirements. By 1962, Israel had one of the highest ratios of physicians to

---

[1] In addition to these four universities, two other universities with extensive undergraduate and graduate programs but without a medical school exist in Israel. These are Bar Ilan University, located in Ramat Gan near Tel Aviv, and Haifa University in Haifa. In addition, the Weizmann Institute has extensive graduate programs in the physical and biologic sciences but no undergraduate curricula.

population (1:405) of all countries in the world, a trend that has continued to this date (Shuval 1990). The second school, opened in Tel Aviv in 1964, was justified as advancing the regional health care needs of the coastal area, as providing an additional training facility for Israelis not admitted by Hebrew University-Hadassah Medical School (who were therefore forced to travel abroad for medical education), and for students from the Tel Aviv area who wished to remain at home for school, and as providing a valuable competitor for the Hebrew University-Hadassah Medical School. Enhancing the prestige of the university by having a medical school was also a significant factor. This school followed the lead of Hebrew University-Hadassah in implementing a traditional curriculum based upon the biomedical sciences.

Specific programmatic missions were proposed for the third and fourth schools, the Technion and Ben Gurion University, respectively. The Technion is an internationally respected technical and scientific institute, and its medical school opened in 1971. It was proposed that this medical school would emphasize disciplines such as bioengineering and biotechnology, although factors such as enhancing the prestige of the sponsoring institution and local hospitals were also important.

Ben Gurion University opened its medical school in 1974. This school is located in the largely desert area of southern Israel, the Negev, with major manpower needs for primary medical care for a widely dispersed, rural population. The medical school undertook, as an intrinsic part of its mission, intensive curricular development and training in primary-care medicine and in the application of social sciences to medicine, as well as the coordination of all health care services in the region (Rotem, Barnoon, and Prywes 1985; Prywes 1987). As part of this unique mission of the Medical Faculty, the dean of the school also serves as the regional director of all health care services in the Negev.

This new school has implemented many novel approaches to medical education. These include (1) integration of the clinical and basic science portions of the curriculum with each other and with relevant aspects of social science, (2) promotion of education in outpatient settings and coordination of inpatient and ambulatory care medicine in both education and practice, (3) advancement of the credibility of primary care and community medicine practitioners in the academic arena, and (4) establishment of a close relation between medical education and health care delivery. These innovations, widely called the "Beer Sheva experiment," have been emulated in education reforms of many countries around the world.

ROLE OF NATIONAL POLICY IN SHAPING MEDICAL EDUCATION

Until recently, national health care policy concerns have had only minimal, indirect impact on medical education. With the exception of the Ben Gurion University school in which the regional health care delivery and educational systems are fused, medical schools have remained largely outside the health care delivery process. As a result, many national health care responsibilities have been undertaken without the involvement of the universities.

This dichotomy may reflect the fact that the first three most prestigious schools were organized by European scholars who came from a strong tradition of separation between university and state. This tradition was followed in Israel until recent times. Another possible reason for this limited involvement is the organizational structure of the clinical faculty. As will be described, clinical faculty members are employees of the affiliated hospitals, not of the universities, and universities do not own teaching hospitals. Medical school management thus has little direct responsibility for or involvement in health care delivery.

However, in 1988, the government established the State Commission of Inquiry into the Operation and Efficiency of the Healthcare System in Israel to examine deficiencies in the national health care system (Israel 1990). Among many other recommendations, the commission made several specific proposals for additions to the curricula of medical education programs, including expanded instruction in ambulatory medicine, health care policy and economics, and biomedical ethics. These were proposed as responses to perceived deficiencies in the ability of physicians to function appropriately within the current and future health care systems. Thus, the medical education process may come under closer scrutiny by policy makers and planners.

Organizational Structure

Deans of three schools are elected by the faculty for three- to five-year terms. At the fourth, the dean is selected for a defined term by a committee representing the University, the major teaching hospital, and Kupat Holim Clalit, which owns the hospital facility. That choice must then be ratified by the faculty. The deanship may be a part-time position and the dean may simultaneously be the chief of a service in an affiliated hospital. It may occur that the dean holds a PhD or even a dental degree rather than a medical degree. At Hebrew University-Hadassah Medical School, for example, it is an established practice that the deanship alternates between members of the clinical and the basic science faculty.

Basic science faculty. Preclinical courses are taught mostly by the staff of the medical schools, although some introductory science classes are taught by faculty from the natural or physical science divisions of the university. Faculty salaries are provided from government funds received through the University Grants Committee of the Council on Higher Education of the Ministry of Education or from private sources. They are not dependent upon grant sources.

Clinical faculty. Clinical training of medical students occurs in teaching hospitals that are owned either by the government Ministry of Health, the sick funds, or by nonprofit organizations such as Hadassah. Teaching hospitals are not owned by the medical schools.

Clinical instruction takes place in virtually all the hospitals in Israel. The Hadassah Medical Center in Jerusalem has a comprehensive relationship with Hebrew University-Hadassah Medical School in which all services are intrinsic components of the medical school. Other hospitals have affiliations with medical schools that are department specific, i.e., certain departments in a hospital may be affiliated whereas others are not. For example, Hebrew University-Hadassah

Medical School has affiliations with numerous departments at Kaplan Hospital of Kupat Holim Clalit in Rehovot, but only with the departments of internal medicine and pediatrics at Shaare Zedek Hospital, an independent nonprofit hospital in Jerusalem. In addition, larger hospitals commonly contain several departments of the same specialty; each of these may be affiliated with the medical school or some may not be affiliated.

The clinical faculty in the affiliated services have university appointments but are the employees of the hospital, not of the medical school. This status of teaching faculty as employees is not unique; over 90 percent of all physicians in Israel are employed by the government, one of the sick funds or by private organizations such as Hebrew University-Hadassah Medical Center. In return for their teaching activities, faculty receive benefits including paid sabbatical leaves and funds for various professional activities. These benefits are usually, but not universally, provided by the university; in selected cases, individual hospitals or the sick funds pay for these benefits.

Thus, medical schools in Israel do not have clinical departments as intrinsic components of the schools of medicine. Rather, clinical training is highly decentralized, located in any number of different hospitals. Furthermore, hospitals commonly have more than one affiliated department in a given specialty and each affiliated department has a chief who enjoys considerable programmatic autonomy. At the Ben Gurion University medical school, a single departmental chair provides overall coordination; in the other schools, a loosely formed council of all departmental chiefs in a given specialty seeks to coordinate education functions, but single departmental chairs with line authority do not exist. A national trend to establish rotating chairs for each of the major specialties including internal medicine, surgery, obstetrics and gynecology, pediatrics, and psychiatry is currently developing.

Clinical faculty may or may not have the same status as basic science faculty within the university. In certain schools, some clinical staff are given titles as "clinical" faculty, and are not eligible for academic tenure (although they do receive employment tenure from the affiliated hospital); others do not distinguish between clinical and nonclinical faculty by title. Faculty members with clinical appointments generally receive reduced sabbatical and professional expense reimbursement rights, and may not have voting privileges in the faculty councils.

Faculty appointments are considered an important source of prestige. Senior faculty members are called "professor" rather than "doctor." The public gives great respect to academic titles and functions, as a correlate or predictor of superior quality medical care and as a manifestation of a general cultural respect for knowledge. This deference is then translated into significant prestige for the affiliated service, for the hospital with affiliated services, and for the individual practitioner holding a faculty appointment. In addition to prestige, faculty appointment is an important factor in attracting private patients; private practice by hospital staff physicians is allowed by some institutions after normal working hours and is an important source of supplemental income.

Medical School Finances

Medical school budgets are allocated from government funds by the Grants Committee of the National Council on Higher Education of the Ministry of the Education. Funds are distributed based upon a capitation system. Currently, a school is granted 80,000 NIS per student in the clinical years and less for each preclinical student.[2] These funds, granted directly to the universities for their medical schools, pay the salaries of preclinical faculty and may be used in various ways to support clinical training programs. These include hiring additional hospital staff or subsidizing the expenses of existing faculty at affiliated hospitals. Additional funds may be derived from direct donations or from grants. However, funds generated by clinical practice are not directly available to the medical school to support basic science programs.

Tuition, currently approximately 4,200 NIS (approximately $1,700 US) per year, provides only a small portion of school finances. Although this tuition is low by American standards, it is considered quite expensive by most Israelis, especially when considering the prolonged duration of study and the relatively low salaries that new graduates will earn as physicians.

ADMISSION

Medical schools admit students after graduation from secondary schools and, generally, after completion of compulsory military duty (three years for men and two years for women). This military duty provides students entering Israeli medical schools with extensive real-life experiences in leadership and responsibility that are uncommon in other countries. A select minority of high school students is chosen by the military to complete medical school before beginning active duty; after graduation they are obligated for five years of military service as a medical officer.

The number of students admitted annually is determined on a national level by the Council on Higher Education. A total of 306 students were enrolled in the first-year programs of the four schools for the 1989-1990 academic year. The small size of the medical school classes was established to permit closer student-teacher interaction than in larger classes common in other countries. Enrollment quotas may be adjusted to meet national goals. For example, the number of students in the clinical years was recently increased to accommodate the influx of immigrants from the former Soviet Union who had only partially completed medical school training before moving to Israel.

Admission requirements and priorities vary somewhat from school to school. Hebrew University-Hadassah medical school and those of Tel Aviv University and

---

[2] NIS = new Israeli Shekel, equal to approximately US $0.41 in August 1992.

the Technion emphasize academic performance. Criteria include scores on high school matriculation examinations and standardized university entrance examinations as well as general academic performance. Other requirements include a high level of English language proficiency. The schools in Jerusalem, Haifa, and Beer Sheva also require personal interviews. Virtually all students who enter complete the curriculum and graduate.

The Ben Gurion University program, in contrast, emphasizes personal qualities as determined by an extensive, multistage interview process (Antonovsky 1987). Examination scores are used only as minimal thresholds for entry into the interview process and not as competitive criteria for admission. At the interviews, candidates are rated on characteristics such as personal integrity, empathy, self-identity, decisiveness, tolerance of ambiguity and sense of social responsibility. A score of one to five (in nine half-point steps) is given for each of the eight categories as well as for overall response. This process preselects students with personal qualities that match the goal of the school to develop socially conscious physicians with interests in community medicine.

Medicine is one of the most difficult Faculties into which to be accepted. For example, Tel Aviv University Medical Faculty requires an average matriculation examination score of 85 and an admission examination score of 666 (maximum is 800). In contrast, admissions to the Faculties of electrical engineering, physics and law require admission examination scores of 630, 540 and 634, respectively.

For the academic year 1990-1991, a total of 1,151 students applied for admission to medical school, representing an applicant to position ratio of 3.8:1. This ratio is higher for medicine than for almost any other subject area; only law school has as high a ratio. By comparison, ratios for engineering and architecture, mathematics, and physical and biological sciences range from 1.1 to 1.6 (Israel 1992a).

Thus, entry into medical school is highly competitive. Demand, as measured by the ratio of applicants to positions, has also remained relatively stable (3.8-3.9) over the past several years (Israel 1992a) despite the relatively low salaries, poor working conditions, and increasing difficulty of finding prestigious hospital-based jobs. The Israeli experience is thought to reflect the persistently high status of the medical profession in the society that is independent of income, as well as similar problems in most other academic professions.

Significant numbers of Israeli students not accepted into Israeli schools leave the country to attend medical schools in other countries, such as Italy, Spain, and various Eastern European countries. Many of these return to Israel after graduation; an average of 150 Israelis studying abroad apply for Israeli licenses annually (Shuval 1990).

CURRICULAR STRUCTURE AND INNOVATION

The medical curriculum is a six-year program, plus a mandatory seventh, rotating internship year. Upon completion of the full program, students receive an MD degree. Students may receive the bachelors or "first" degree (B.Med.Sc.) at the end of the preclinical years.

Basic Science Curriculum

The first three to three and one-half years are largely devoted to basic and biomedical sciences. Courses include those taught in the United States as part of premedical undergraduate curricula (e.g., physics, mathematics, inorganic and organic chemistry, and computer science). Biomedical science courses are typical of those taught in the first two years of American medical schools (e.g., anatomy, histology, biochemistry, pharmacology, etc.). Students may, in addition, take elective courses taught in other Faculties of the parent university. The Technion also requires more extensive courses in mathematics, physical sciences and in computer sciences than do the other schools.

The program at Ben Gurion University differs from the others. The preclinical curriculum has a heavy emphasis on organ systems with numerous clinical demonstrations and a continuous concentration on social sciences as related to medical practice. A "spiral curriculum" was introduced that "is based on the premise that learning and its retention occur more effectively when reinforced concurrently across diverse components of the curriculum and longitudinally over its successive phases" (Segall, Benor, and Susskind 1987). It includes a horizontally integrated program of basic science, clinical sciences and community health during each year, beginning with the first, and continuing through the sixth year. Subjects are repeated in sequential years, with increasing depth and complexity.

Clinical Curriculum

The remaining years are dedicated to rotating clinical clerkships at one or more of the teaching hospitals. The clinical program at Hebrew University-Hadassah medical school, for example, includes a twelve-week rotation in general internal medicine, twelve weeks in medical subspecialties, seven weeks in general surgery, twenty-one weeks in surgical specialties, thirteen weeks in pediatrics, eight weeks in obstetrics and gynecology, and five weeks in psychiatry. There are shorter rotations in neurology, family practice, and geriatrics. Clinical training relies heavily upon direct, supervised patient contact.

An "Early Clinical Program" at Ben Gurion University introduces students to clinical medicine beginning with the first week of medical school. The program consists of one-day sessions as well as short (one-week) mini-clerkships in selected clinical areas (Benor 1987).

All students are also required to complete a thesis project under the supervision of a faculty mentor. The project may present a literature review or results of individual research.

Student Assessment

In 1992, students in all four schools began to take identical final examinations. The first examination was in internal medicine, with additional examinations in clinical subjects to be introduced in subsequent years. There is no process for accreditation of Israeli medical schools.

Israeli students also commonly take the Foreign Medical Graduate Examination in the Medical Sciences (FMGEMS) for licensure in the United States. Between 1984 and 1991, over 50 percent of graduates took the examination (unpublished data), representing one of the largest percentages of any country (Mick and Mou 1991). Of graduates of Israeli medical schools taking the examination for the first time, 51.6 percent passed the basic science sections and 90.9 percent passed the clinical portions (unpublished data). Success varied from school to school, particularly on the basic science examination; the highest percent passing the examination were from Hebrew University-Hadassah medical school (68 percent on basic science and 96.8 percent on clinical portions).

GRADUATE MEDICAL EDUCATION

All internships are rotating programs. A typical program includes three months of internal medicine, two months of general surgery, two months of pediatrics, one month of trauma/emergency medicine, and three months of elective rotations. A final month is for vacation. Internships are viewed as part of medical school education and are programmatically supervised by a committee composed of the deans of the four medical schools. Hospitals wishing to train interns must receive the approval of the Ministry of Health and the committee of medical school deans.

Students applying for internships are assigned positions by a national lottery program in which students request positions in specific hospitals in order of preference; hospitals do not rank the applicants they prefer. Assignment to rural hospitals is encouraged within the system; students agreeing to serve in an outlying facility are offered elective rotations in the hospital of their choice.

Residency programs in medical and surgical specialties are hospital-based with no direct connection to a medical school. Programs must be approved by the Scientific Council of the Israeli Medical Association based upon staff qualifications, workload levels and availability of appropriate clinical and educational facilities. Approval, once granted, is subject to review every five years, and whenever a new service chief is appointed or complaints about the quality of the training are received.

The durations of some residency programs are longer in Israel than in the United States. For example, general surgery, internal medicine and pathology programs are each one year longer in Israel than in the United States. This has been attributed to extended mandatory military leave during training that reduces actual experience, as well as the difficulty in finding employment in many specialties once training is completed. It may also be considered an attempt to deal with the national shortage of primary care physicians (see below) by inhibiting the desire to pursue specialties with prolonged training periods (Anderson and Antebi 1990).

Specialty choices of graduates from 1980 through 1984 indicated a strong preference for internal medicine (20 percent), pediatrics (18.1 percent), surgical specialties (13.1 percent), and obstetrics and gynecology (12 percent) (Prywes and Biton 1986). Only 7 percent planned training in family practice, 5 percent in psychiatry, and 1.5 percent in radiology. More recent data are not available but trends appear to suggest increased interest in surgical subspecialties and gynecology as well as in primary care fields. The former reflects the higher earning capability of surgical fields, while the latter results from the increasing difficulty in obtaining hospital-based specialty positions as well as greater educational emphasis on generalist practice.

Men and women chose specialization in internal medicine and pediatrics with equal frequency. On the other hand, whereas women more often selected psychiatry (17 percent vs. 9 percent; 46 percent of all psychiatry residents were women in 1989) and family practice (15 percent vs. 8 percent) than did men, men chose surgery (19 percent vs. 7 percent) and gynecology (13 percent vs. 7 percent) more often than did women (Notzer and Levi 1991). Shortages of specialists in family practice, radiology, psychiatry, anesthesiology and geriatrics are currently felt to exist within the country (Israel 1990). Patterns of specialty choice are similar. Schools generally choose the same specialties; Ben Gurion University medical graduates do, however, choose family medicine more often than do graduates of other schools (Prywes and Friedman 1987).

LICENSURE

Graduates of Israeli medical schools are automatically licensed to practice medicine upon completion of internship without passing a specific licensing examination. The introduction of such an examination has been a high priority of the Ministry of Health for several years but has been blocked by national political forces. There is also currently no recurrent registration or recertification process required of physicians.

Board Certification for Specialists

The Scientific Council of the Israel Medical Association approves certification of physicians as specialists once residency training is complete. This is dependent upon passing both a written and an oral examination. The written examination may be taken during the residency training period; the oral one is given after completion. Failure rates for all specialties are in the range of 30 percent, and candidates are given three opportunities to pass.

Cross-Licensing of Physicians

Since 1987, graduates of foreign medical schools, whether immigrants or Israelis who trained abroad, must take a licensing examination that tests only clinical knowledge. Those who have not completed an internship similar to that offered in Israel and who have practiced medicine less than two years in their native country are also required to take an internship (Nirel et al. 1992). In addition, non-Israelis must demonstrate competence in the Hebrew language. Once these requirements are completed, the candidate is granted a one-year provisional license; upon the satisfactory conclusion of this year and submission of a letter of recommendation from a licensed colleague, the applicants are granted a full license.

However, some foreign graduates may receive exemptions from these requirements (Nirel et al. 1992). Exemptions are granted, for example, to immigrants with outstanding personal credentials, those who have practiced more than twenty years who will work for at least six months in a supervised setting, and for those graduating from medical schools in countries recognized by the Scientific Council of the Israel Medical Association, for example, from the United States, United Kingdom, Canada and South Africa.

CONTINUING MEDICAL EDUCATION

There is currently no requirement for continuing medical education. However, the national Commission of Inquiry has recommended that plans for such a requirement be developed as part of a national recertification program (Israel 1990).

ROLE OF RESEARCH IN MEDICAL EDUCATION

Research is an intrinsic component of medical education systems in Israel. Expenditures for biomedical research in the four Israeli universities with medical schools totaled 31.9 million NIS in 1986-1987, down from the 39.1 million NIS spent in 1984-1985 but significantly greater than the 20.6 million NIS expended in 1970-1971 (all in 1986-1987 prices) (Israel 1991). In 1986-1987, biomedical research accounted for approximately 13 percent of all university research and development expenditures. Government funds include those from the offices of Chief Scientists of the Ministry of Health, Ministry of Labor and Welfare, and Ministry of Industry and Trade. Considerable additional funds for clinical research are derived from the operating budgets of teaching hospitals and from foundations abroad, especially those in the United States and Germany.

GOVERNMENT/PRIVATE SECTOR INVOLVEMENT

Government involvement in medical education is significant, as it is in most facets of Israeli life. The vast majority of the budget of medical schools is, as described above, derived from the government. In addition, 13 acute-care hospitals (46 percent of acute-care beds in the nation), including many of the largest teaching hospitals, are owned by the government and are operated by the Ministry of Health. In these hospitals, the medical staff who serve as clinical faculty are government employees.

An additional 30 percent of acute-care hospital beds are in hospitals owned and operated by Kupat Holim Clalit, the largest national sick fund. This sick fund is operated by the National Labor Federation, the Histadrut, which has close alliances with the Labor party, the majority party in the coalition government formed in June 1992. Therefore, government involvement in these facilities, while less direct than in the government-owned facilities, does exist.

Private practice medicine represents only a small portion of the medical care delivery system in Israel and is generally used to supplement rather than to replace the national health care systems. Many physicians employed by the government or one of the sick funds engage in private practice in their own homes or private clinics after their normal work day. This represents an important source of personal income to supplement the relatively low salaries prevalent in the country at this time. Such private practice is not, at this time, included in medical education programs.

For-profit acute care hospitals do exist in the country. Currently such facilities provide only 4 percent of the nation's acute-care beds. They most often specialize in elective surgical procedures that are available in public facilities but only after significant waiting periods. These private facilities are not, at this time, affiliated with medical schools although clinical faculty members commonly practice within them.

INTERNATIONAL LINKAGES AND COLLABORATION

Two schools have comprehensive teaching affiliations with universities in the United States. The medical school of Tel Aviv University has, in addition to its Israeli model school, a four-year program designed exclusively for American college graduates. This program is accredited by the State of New York; however, its graduates must take the FMGEMS examination to obtain a license to practice medicine in the United States.

The Technion school has an affiliation with Touro College (New York, NY). Students from Touro complete basic science courses and receive all their clinical training in Haifa. They then receive an MD degree from the Technion. Other schools such as that of Ben Gurion University and Hebrew University-Hadassah have more limited affiliations with overseas schools, mainly involving periodic exchanges of small numbers of students for short periods of time.

ISSUES AND TRENDS

Several issues currently face Israeli undergraduate medical education. These include national concerns over health care delivery systems and manpower as well as key curricular issues.

National Physician Surplus

The ratio of physicians to population is higher in Israel than in virtually any other country. In 1986, the ratio was 330 physicians per 100,000 citizens, compared to 230 in the United States (Anderson and Antebi 1990.) This ratio is likely considerably higher now because of the recent immigration from the former Soviet Union described below.

A physician surplus has resulted mainly from the extensive immigration of physicians to Israel from other countries. More than eight thousand physicians immigrated to Israel between September 1989 and December 1991, mostly from the states of the former Soviet Union. Currently approximately 2.5 percent of all new immigrants are physicians (Nirel et al. 1992). This persistent immigration pattern results from the national goal of being a Jewish homeland, and a policy of actively encouraging immigration of all Jews without concern for national economic or labor market issues. The results of the surplus include underemployment of medical personnel, reduction in earning capacity, and difficulty in securing high-quality, prestigious, hospital-based positions.

Primary Care Training

A second concern is the ongoing inability to recruit skilled primary care physicians. Only 7.1 percent of Israeli graduates from 1980 through 1984 were trained in or practiced family medicine (Prywes and Biton 1986). This number has increased recently due, at least in part, to the shortage of prestigious hospital-based positions. The need for primary care physicians is compounded by the nature of the Israeli health care system. More than sixteen hundred neighborhood primary care clinics staffed by primary care physicians and allied health personnel form the backbone of this system. Thus, a large and continuing supply of primary care physicians is needed to maintain the integrity of the health delivery system. Furthermore, inpatient medicine is separate from outpatient practice in most regions of the country so that clinic staffing must be addressed independent of the needs of hospitals.

The notable exception to this observation is in the Negev. Department chiefs in Soroka Hospital, the largest hospital in this part of the country and the major teaching hospital of Ben Gurion University School of Medicine, are responsible for regional outpatient as well as inpatient health care in their specialty and the regular hospital staff work in clinics several days per week (Prywes 1987).

Hospital trained residents also tend to view clinic-based primary care practice as of lower quality with less prestige. Thus, most Israeli graduates prefer hospital based specialty practice, and a disproportionate percent of clinic slots are then filled by immigrants. Over 80 percent of all physicians working in outpatient clinics are immigrants (Shye 1991; Rosen et al. 1992) with highly variable training and competence. Finally, few clinic physicians have training in a primary care specialty. Fewer than 12 percent have had residencies in either family medicine or internal medicine (Rosen et al. 1992). Hence, there is an ongoing, major need for skilled primary care staff.

As noted above, part of the rationale for establishing the Ben Gurion University medical school was to promote primary care and community medicine. From 1980 through 1984, over 21 percent of Ben Gurion University medical school graduates were training or engaging in family practice; percentages from the three other schools ranged from 2.5 percent for Hebrew University-Hadassah to 7.6 percent for Technion (Prywes and Biton 1986).

Efforts to address this problem include curricular changes and expansion of training programs in primary care or family medicine. Expansion of primary care curricula will be complicated by the separation of inpatient and outpatient practices in Israel. Because of this separation and the existing predominance of inpatient teaching, very few outpatient clinics are affiliated with universities and very few clinic staff have faculty appointments. Thus, to develop training programs in ambulatory care settings will require not only development of new curricula, but also recruitment of new faculties and identification of new teaching facilities.

Family practice programs are also expanding, with a small but increasing interest of Israeli graduates. This effort is facilitated by the funding of these programs by Kupat Holim Clalit, which requires a significant payback period of employment after completion of training.

Limited Outpatient Training

Virtually all undergraduate and most graduate clinical training is provided in hospital-based programs. This approach to medical education is based upon the common (but highly suspect) assumption that management of the most complex cases occurs in the hospital setting and that the knowledge gained in that arena can be easily transferred to the outpatient setting. Expanded outpatient training is now required to reflect the emerging nature of the health care system and for students to appreciate the true spectrum of health care problems present in the population which they will encounter in practice. Diseases encountered in ambulatory care practices differ considerably from those seen in the hospital and are not just less severe examples of the same abnormalities. Moreover, as outpatient practice becomes more sophisticated, additional diagnostic procedures and treatments will be completed solely in clinics so that inpatient experience will become even more limited.

This is a problem not only for primary care training but also for specialty practice where outpatient evaluations and treatments are becoming the preferred mode of operation. Outpatient clinics that are part of hospitals could serve this need but inclusion of ambulatory care rotations in clerkships is sporadic. In addition, in at least some cases, the sick funds do not permit patients to remain in the hospital-based clinics. Free-standing diagnostic clinics operated by sick funds or independent physicians are growing, diverting patients from hospital facilities. Sick funds may also require patients to return to neighborhood primary care or local sick fund-operated secondary clinics in which financial control is tighter than in the hospital-based clinics.

Curricular Reform

Preclinical training in Israel generally parallels that in the United States. Hence, the preclinical years are heavily loaded with lectures and little attention is given to independent learning and to subjects such as decision theory, preventive medicine, and health care policy and economics. Changes that are needed include reduced numbers of lecture hours, expanded time for self learning (Ben Bassat 1990), and, as recommended by the health care reform commission, increased instruction in such disciplines as decision making, policy, and public health.

Limited Involvement in Health Care Delivery

Medical schools, with the noted exception of Ben Gurion University, have little involvement in or influence over the health care delivery system and in formulating health care policy within Israel. Medical school curricula contain little or no instruction in health policy, health economics, and related subjects. While the need is recognized, little has been done to implement change.

This, in turn, limits the influence of the schools in shaping health care policy. In particular, they have a limited ability to promote the values of teaching and research, and they are less able to promote their own interests in the face of health care finance reform.

Health Care Reform

The medical educational process also faces challenges from the proposed plan for extensive reform of the nation's health care delivery system. As noted above, the Cabinet of the State of Israel established in June 1988, a State Commission of Inquiry to diagnose the root causes of the public's rising dissatisfaction with the nation's health care system and to recommend corrective actions (Israel 1990). Areas of concern included inadequacies in the services provided to the public (including the long waiting times for elective surgery), limited budgeting and finance procedures, and low levels of employee satisfaction and motivation.

Beyond the specific changes in medical school curricula referred to previously, this Commission's report contained many recommendations, including the institution of procedures to introduce competition between hospitals, proposals to make hospitals financially independent entities with fixed budgets, and plans to expand private practice opportunities within the hospital system.

These proposed health care reforms may present major challenges to the medical education process in Israel. Tight budget controls and emphasis on competition may result in serious questions about the high costs of health care in teaching hospitals, constraints on clinical research, and controls over patient testing for educational or research purposes. Expanded opportunities for private practice may also increase the commitments to clinical practice, reducing the time available for clinical teaching and for research, and may alter the relationships between patients, trainees, and staff physicians.

Israeli medical education represents a highly sophisticated and well-differentiated national effort that has achieved considerable successes but which is faced with significant challenges. Within the relatively short lifetime of the nation and during periods of significant financial instability and necessary emphasis on security, four highly effective medical schools with productive education and research programs have been created. In particular, the Beer Sheva program has become an acknowledged model for international reform in medical education.

REFERENCES

Anderson, G.F., and S. Antebi. 1990. A surplus of physicians in Israel: Any lessons for the United States and other industrialized countries? *Health Policy* 17:77-86.

Antonovsky, A. 1987. Medical student selection at the Ben-Gurion University of the Negev. *Israel Journal of Medical Sciences* 23:969-975.

Ben Bassat, J. 1990. Trends in undergraduate medical education (Hebrew). *Harefuah* 118:99-102.

Benor, D.E. 1987. Early clinical program for novice medical students: 13 years experience at Ben-Gurion University of the Negev. *Israel Journal of Medical Sciences* 23:1013-1021.

Israel. 1992a. *Monthly bulletin of statistics supplement, March, 1992.* Jerusalem, Israel.

----------. 1992b. *Monthly bulletin of statistics supplement, May, 1992.* Jerusalem, Israel.

----------. 1991. *Statistical abstract of Israel, 1991.* Jerusalem, Israel.

----------. 1990. *Report of the Commission of Inquiry into the Israeli Health-Care System.* Jerusalem: Government Printer.

Mick, S.S., and T.W. Mou. 1991. The foreign medical graduate examination in medical studies (FMGEMS). *Medical Care* 29:229-242.

Nirel, N., B. Rosen, G. Ben Nun, A. Shemesh, and P. Vardi. 1992. *The process of recognition and licensing of immigrant physicians--A status report.* Jerusalem: JDC-Brookdale Institute.

Notzer, N., and O. Levi. 1991. Women entering medicine: Implications for health in Israel (in Hebrew). *Harefuah* 120:639-641.

Prywes, M. 1987. Coexistence: The rationale of the Beersheva experiment. *Israel Journal of Medical Sciences* 23:945-952.

Prywes, M., and Y. Biton. 1986. Survey of graduates of Israeli medical schools from 1980-1984 (in Hebrew). *Harefuah* 110:197-199.

Prywes, M., and M. Friedman. 1987. The Ben-Gurion University profile: An evaluation study. *Israel Journal of Medical Sciences* 23:1093-1101.

Rosen, B., D. Yuval, U. Gabbay, and C. Braude. 1992. *Independent physicians and clinic physicians in Kupat Holim Clalit: The impact on health care expenditures.* Research Report RR-29-92. Jerusalem: JDC-Brookdale Institute.

Rotem, A., S. Barnoon, and M. Prywes. 1985. Is integration of health services and manpower development possible? The Beer Sheva case study. *Health Policy* 5:223-239.

Segall, A., D.E. Benor, and O. Susskind. 1987. The curriculum: A 13 year perspective. *Israel Journal of Medical Sciences* 23:955-963.

Shuval, J.T. 1990. Medical manpower in Israel: Political processes and constraints. *Health Policy* 15:189-214.

----------. 1980. *Entering medicine. The dynamics of transition.* New York: Pergamon Press.

Shye, D. 1991. Gender differences in Israeli physicians' career patterns, productivity and family structure. *Social Science and Medicine* 32:1169-1181.

World Health Organization. 1991. *WHO statistical annual, 1991.* Geneva: WHO.

17

Italy

Vittorio Ghetti
Alessandro Martin

OVERVIEW OF THE HEALTH CARE DELIVERY SYSTEM

Italian health care is delivered by the National Health Services (NHS), which provides free medical care for all citizens and residents. Patients pay a small contribution to the cost of medical tests and prescriptions, but nothing for hospital admissions or operations. The NHS is financed through taxes at a cost estimated at $72 billion US in 1991, or 5.8 percent of GNP.

A limited proportion of the medical care is delivered outside the NHS, as private practice. Private medical centers with inpatient departments or outpatient clinics may be authorized to deliver health care on behalf of the NHS: this sector involves 700 clinics in the country, with a cost of $4.8 billion US. Twelve percent of these private institutions belong to religious orders.

Physicians are required to register after graduation with the section of the National Order of Physicians of the province where they practice. The professional Order has a role in controlling professional ethics and also functions as a union, although physicians may also belong to one of the other larger unions operating in the country.

The major issue currently affecting the NHS is its cost, which is widely considered too high, especially considering the quality of its performance, which is considered poor, particularly in southern Italy. Although the number of general practitioners is high (63,000 out of over 200,000 registered practitioners), the health care system is generally oriented toward specialist care.

HISTORICAL BACKGROUND

In this century, the Italian educational system has been based on the German model, with the "Master" and his "*ex cathedra*" lectures at the center. Before 1987, there was no selection for access to medical schools, which caused overcrowding at most universities. In the last fifteen years, there has been a trend to experiment with more modern approaches to teaching, and this led to the introduction, in 1986, of a new curriculum of medical studies.

ROLE OF NATIONAL POLICY IN SHAPING MEDICAL EDUCATION

The curriculum of Italian medical schools is mandated by national legislation (Bompiani, Carinci, and Ghetti 1992; Ghetti 1988). There is no official liaison between the NHS and the Ministry of Universities aimed at responding to changing health care realities and corresponding changes needed in medical education. The new curriculum of medical studies, introduced in late 1986, placed emphasis on the problems of the aging of the population, degenerative diseases, and "new" diseases.

ADMISSION

Entry requirements are by law the same in all Italian medical schools: the candidates need to possess a secondary school diploma. Until 1969, only two secondary school diplomas (*liceo classico* and *liceo scientifico*) were valid for entering a university. In the 1960s this condition came to be considered too elitist, since students possessing these diplomas usually came from the more affluent families. With the aim of expanding access to higher levels of education to students from less privileged environments, entry to all university Faculties was opened to all diplomas. This change caused an explosion in the number of university students, with an especially high increase in the number of medical students (from ten thousand to more than thirty thousand per year). This expansion tended to come from lower socioeconomic strata, with an increased number of female students. Selection of medical students is now controlled by each medical school, which determines the number to be admitted each year and the admission tests. The cost to the student for a medical school education remains quite low: equivalent to approximately $1,000 US per year. Tables 17.1 (p. 255) and 17.2 (p. 257) present demographics for medical school students and faculty, respectively.

As of 1992, about 30 percent of students who entered the new curriculum have not yet finished. They will graduate in 1994. At present, only about 25 percent of students entering their fourth year have regularly completed their exams.

CURRICULAR STRUCTURE AND INNOVATION

The 1986 law (described above) defined the new curriculum of medical studies which was basically the same for all 31 Italian medical schools. As of 1992, the first four years of new curriculum have been implemented in most Italian medical schools. The need for a change was apparent for two reasons: (1) students were receiving theoretical instruction almost exclusively and were allowed to sit for exams without attending classes or medical rounds; and (2) an excessive number of new disciplines (such as parentology, experimental surgery, gynecological oncology, surgical semiotics, and clinical and experimental oncology) were introduced to accommodate the six thousand new associate professors who were upgraded from tutors to the professorate in 1981.

The current curriculum is based on 18 "areas" which comprise several "integrated courses." Objectives for each curricular area are specified in the legislation, along with the integrated course, the disciplines included and the required number of hours. The total teaching time in the six-year course is 5,500 hours, of which one-third and two-thirds must be devoted to practical learning in the first and second triennium, respectively.

The new law attempted a definition of the learning objectives and teaching methods (especially in their practical aspects), provided for integration of teaching among the various disciplines, and made student attendance obligatory. On the other hand, the separation between the preclinical and clinical portions of the curriculum still exists, the assessment of students is still based primarily on traditional oral examinations, and the goal of a student-centered approach has not yet been reached.

GRADUATE MEDICAL EDUCATION

There is no national board certification for Italian medical specialists, since certification of specialists is given locally. After graduation from medical school, doctors who successfully pass the admission examination can enter a postgraduate school of specialization, which is located in the university. After the prescribed number of years (four to five), and having passed examinations and the discussion of a thesis, the doctor receives the title of Specialist in the chosen branch. There is no specific definition of the levels of professional competence that the specialist must have achieved before completion of training.

The period 1970-1990 saw a great increase in the proportion of graduates who took postgraduate courses for specialization, because such courses were mostly based on theory, with the only obligation being attendance at a limited number of lectures per year. These courses were, therefore, compatible with other occupations, but a diploma of specialization was not in itself a guarantee of adequate professional competence. In 1988, new curricula for the postgraduate courses of specialization were introduced in compliance with the recommendations of the European Economic Community (EEC). Before that time, approximately ninety percent of physicians sought this training. In 1991, however, national law defined the total number of places for each specialty (approximately ninety for gastroenterology, for example). Now, although the number of training places is limited, criteria for admissions, exams, and similar policies are decided at the local medical school level. Individual specialties within the university decide their own criteria for admission and graduation.

The new curricula prescribed a four-year, full-time training program, with 400 hours per year of clinical training and 400 hours of theory, concluding with discussion of a written thesis that results in the title "specialist in" the field (e.g., "Dr. X, Specialist in Cardiac Surgery"). In 1992, a new law stipulated that postgraduate students should receive a salary for their full-time training period, with a corresponding dramatic reduction in the number of positions available (about 2,500 for all specialties in Italy). Despite these attempts at rationalizing postgraduate training programs, the positions available and their distribution are not based on objective assessments of needs. However, regional governments financed, according to local needs, a limited number of residency programs in order to integrate those decided at the national level.

LICENSURE

Each medical school has the power to graduate the medical student, after completion of all prescribed examinations and discussion of a written thesis prepared in collaboration with one of the faculty members. The thesis requirement is similar to that of other professions. In order to be allowed to practice medicine after graduation, the new doctor in medicine must also pass a licensing examination. This is, however, administered by a commission of professors from the same medical school, and failures are exceedingly rare.

Cross-Licensing of Physicians

Admission into medical practice for graduates from the EEC is straightforward, with few bureaucratic requirements. Graduates from non-EEC countries must obtain an Italian graduation: their curriculum is assessed by a commission appointed by the local medical school, which decides which examinations are required for the candidate to be awarded an Italian diploma. In many cases, some integrative exams are required (e.g., for graduates from Eastern European countries), or the discipline can be recognized as valid. In this case the foreign graduate can sit directly in the state licensure examination and, if successful, can enter practice. A language proficiency examination is also required. Some countries (e.g., Syria) have special agreements that allow the foreign graduate to practice in Italy without having to pass integrative examinations.

CONTINUING MEDICAL EDUCATION

No requirements for continuing education are specified, although regional governments organize update courses that are obligatory for physicians working in certain fields (e.g., drug abuse, AIDS, etc.). Hospitals must, by law, allow physicians a defined number of days per year of study leave in order to attend such update courses. They also provide financial support to attend such courses or to subscribe to journals and purchase items such as books. However, although a variety of activities are regularly organized by universities, professional orders, and similar organization, and although there are notable exceptions in some regions, continuing medical education is largely left to the responsibility of the individual doctor. As a result, CME is often based on pharmaceutical industry-originated activities and materials, such as symposia, journals, and handouts.

ROLE OF RESEARCH IN MEDICAL EDUCATION

In all Italian medical schools, both part-time and full-time faculty members are required to conduct research in their own chosen fields. Research is funded by national institutions, such as the Ministry of Universities and Research (MURST), and the National Research Council (CNR), or by private sources, such as pharmaceutical companies (the latter, in some cases, may be the prevalent source, especially for departments likely to be involved in drug trials).

Research grants for educational purposes are extremely rare and have no impact on the quality of teaching in the medical schools. The time devoted to actual teaching by faculty members, although stipulated by law (200 hours per year for full-time and 120 for part-time professors), is variable and not verified.

Research or experimentation in medical education is conducted in several medical schools, often promoted by teachers who are members of the Italian Society for Medical Education, who took advantage of the opportunity presented by the introduction of the new curriculum to initiate research and implement experimentation.

GOVERNMENT/PRIVATE SECTOR INVOLVEMENT

The governmental agency responsible for medical education, as for all other university fields, is the MURST. The 31 medical school deans, together with the deans for educational affairs, belong to a national conference that analyzes problems and makes recommendations. Rules and norms concerning medical schools are given by the MURST to the deans, who are mainly concerned with the general and administrative management of their schools. Problems concerning education are mainly dealt with by the deans for educational affairs, often assisted by an education committee made up of professors, research fellows and students.

In the private sector, the Smith Kline Foundation has organized, since 1979, many basic and in-depth seminars for training medical teachers on the principles of medical education. A total of 84 workshops have been arranged, involving all Italian medical schools, with at total of 3,250 teachers attending some of these activities. The Smith Kline Foundation, a WHO Health Manpower Development Collaborating Center since 1987, also organizes conferences and meetings and has published 65 books on medical education-related subjects (Fondazione Smith Kline 1983, 1984; Ghetti 1991). In 1985, the foundation fostered the creation of the Italian Society for Medical Education, now 500 members strong, which holds an annual meeting and publishes the quarterly journal *La Formazione del Medica*.

INTERNATIONAL LINKAGES AND COLLABORATION

Most faculty members spend some part of their training period in other countries and have, therefore, experienced different educational systems, which often affect their approach to teaching. A recent stimulus toward crossnational linkages has come with the introduction of the European Community Action Scheme for the Mobility of University Students (ERASMUS) and Trans European

Mobility Programme for University Studies (TEMPUS), which have promoted exchanges of experiences and a more homogeneous approach to medical education, even if on a still limited scale. Both programs encourage circulation of students and teachers in various European universities participating in Interuniversity Cooperative Programmes (ICP). ERASMUS and TEMPUS provide travel and accommodation expenses for participants. The WHO policy of "Health for All" and the Edinburgh Declaration are not incorporated in the criteria for training programs, because they are not widely known and because their impact on the teachers' approach has not been significant (Menu and Garcia-Barbero 1991; Ghetti 1991).

ISSUES AND TRENDS

Competencies of graduates for the next century are still debated and have not been yet defined at the national level, but it is thought that with the increasing unification of the European countries, progressive educational policy will be discussed and agreed upon at a multinational level. Up to now, educational technology has played a limited role, although a national research program on computer-aided learning in medical education has now involved 14 medical schools. (Ghetti 1988a; Lucchelli 1991; Fondazione Smith Kline 1981)

A new health paradigm is not yet apparent and health care is still very much focused on high-technology, and extremely specialized, medical care. However, economic constraints are rapidly emerging and regional governments are already taking steps to reduce costs of medical care. A reorientation of health care, with more emphasis on prevention and primary care, is therefore to be expected in the near future.

REFERENCES

Bompiani, A., P. Carinci, and V. Ghetti, eds. 1992. *Facoltà di medicina e Servizio Sanitario Nazionale (II)* (Faculty of Medicine and national health service ([II]; in Italian). Fondazione Smith Kline.

Fondazione Smith Kline. 1984. *Introduzione alla Pedagogia Medica (*Introduction to medical education. (in Italian.) Fondazione Smith Kline.

----------. 1983. *La sperimentazione didattica nella Facoltà di Medicina (I)* (Didactic experimentation in medical schools ([I] in Italian.) Fondazione Smith Kline.

----------. 1981. *La Facoltà di Medicina verso il futuro* (The medical school facing the future, in Italian.) Fondazione Smith Kline.

Ghetti, V., ed. 1991a. *La prevenzione: un problema da governare.* (Disease prevention: a problem to be faced; in Italian). Fondazione Smith Kline, Franco Angeli Series.

----------. 1991b. *Il sistema sanitario europeo senza frontiere* (The European health care system without barriers, in Italian). Fondazione Smith Kline, Franco Angeli Series.

----------. 1988a. *Bisogno di salute e risposta della Medicina: ruolo dei servizi* (The relevance of medicine to present health needs: The role of health services and medical education; in Italian). Franco Angeli Series: Fondazione Smith Kline.

----------. 1988b. *Nuove tendenze nella formazione del medico (*New trends in medical education; in Italian). Franco Angeli Series: Fondazione Smith Kline.

Lucchelli, S., ed. 1991. *Il computer nella formazione del medico* (The computer in medical education, in Italian). Franco Angeli Series: Fondazione Smith Kline.

Menu, J.P., and M. Garcia-Barbero, eds. 1991. *Health manpower education for Health for All: Issues to be considered.* Franco Angeli Series: Fondazione Smith Kline.

Table 17.1

Medical School Demographics--Italy

Medical School	Undergraduate Enrollment Male/Female Fall 1991	Graduates Male/Female 1989
Torino	333	507
Genova	215	368
Milano	619	1,069
Brescia	260	113
Pavia	378	566
Verona	169	210
Padova	368	570
Udine	61	0
Trieste	76	122
Parma	192	106
Modena	112	161
Bologna	283	713
Ferrara	96	90
Ancona	153	108
Firenze	226	320
Pisa	178	325
Siena	119	151
Perugia	160	260

Table 17.1
Medical School Demographics--Italy

Medical School	Undergraduate Enrollment Male/Female Fall 1991	Graduates Male/Female 1989
Roma(La Sapienza)	572	1,318
Roma(Tor Vergata)	120	36
Roma (Cattolica)	199	372
Napoli	620	1,629
L'Aquila	126	59
Chieti	211	267
Bari	615	550
Catanzaro	80	64
Palermo	255	620
Messina	265	650
Catania	317	500
Sassari	133	165
Cagliari	206	189
Total no. Medical Schools	Total Male/Female Undergraduate Students	Total Male/Female Graduates
31	7,393	11,676

Table 17.2
Medical School Faculty Demographics--Italy

Medical School	Total Full-Time Male/Female 1989	Average Salary (in US $) Full-Time Male/Female
Torino	272	$70,000
Genova	281	
Malino	686	
Brescia	63	
Pavia	201	
Verona	127	
Padova	297	
Udine	15	
Trieste	90	
Parma	160	
Modena	176	
Bologna	318	
Ferrara	122	
Ancona	71	
Firenze	298	
Pisa	186	
Siena	165	
Perugia	138	
Roma (La Sapienza)	807	
Roma (Tor Vergata)	127	
Roma (Cattolica)	173	
Napoli	513	

Table 17.2
Medical School Faculty Demographics—Italy

Medical School	Total Full-Time Male/Female 1989	Average Salary (in US $) Full-Time Male/Female
L'Aquila	96	
Chieti	101	
Bari	225	
Catanzaro	61	
Palermo	237	
Messina	262	
Catania	258	
Sassari	90	
Cagliari	162	
TOTAL # Medical Schools	Total Full-Time Male/Female Faculty 1989	Average Salary (in US $) Full-Time Male/Female
31	6,536	$70,000

18

Japan

DAIZO USHIBA

OVERVIEW OF THE HEALTH CARE DELIVERY SYSTEM

Japan enjoys one of the highest standards of health in the world. Life expectancy was 75.9 years for males and 81.8 years for females in 1989. To sustain this level of health, approximately seven percent of the general national product and three percent of the labor force are devoted to health. Health care and medical services are supplied both by public and private sectors. While curative services are financed on a fee-for-service basis by national health insurance that covers the entire population, public health services are provided by the public sector and financed by general taxation. The health insurance system covers the unemployed and is financed either by the government or by the health insurance unions of the organizations in which the individual is employed.

The public sector facilities and services include hospitals and clinics established by the national or local government, and public groups designated by the Ministry of Health and Welfare, such as the Japanese Red Cross Society. Public facilities are eligible for a subsidy from the government when necessary. The government may exercise control over the establishment of public medical facilities, the utilization of buildings and equipment, and some other matters engaged in by doctors outside hospitals. It is also responsible for furnishing the necessary conditions and facilities for the clinical training of doctors. Public hospitals were expected to deal with those medical services that are difficult, from the technical and economic points of view, for private hospitals to handle. With the recent improvement of private sector health care, however, almost the same quality of service is now being supplied both groups.

While the present trend in health and medical care in Japan is still oriented toward specialties, particularly in large hospitals, there is increasing national interest in primary health care. Large hospitals can be overcrowded, and there is a growing general preference for the old tradition of having a family physician to whom access is easier and more available. At the same time, changes in national health demographics, resulting from the increase in chronic diseases associated with the aging of the population, require adaptations in the current system. A comprehensive, continuous, and rational health care system including extensive health education, disease prevention, and rehabilitation is needed.

HISTORICAL BACKGROUND

After a long period under the influence of Chinese medicine, Japan officially introduced the German system of medical education in 1870. The existing feudalistic atmosphere exemplified by the old family system at that time was congenial to the German system in which the head of a department had ultimate authority in the management of research and education. This general pattern remains unchanged in some Japanese medical schools.

The first revolutionary change in undergraduate medical education followed soon after World War II, under American influence. It was represented by two important events: the introduction of the one-year internship for clinical training following graduation, and a national examination for physicians' licensure to be taken by medical school graduates. In addition, a new course in public health (along with the preexisting course in hygiene), and an emphasis on practical learning methods instead of didactic teaching methods were introduced.

The internship system created many problems that led to student dissatisfaction. In consequence, the internship was finally abandoned in 1968 after a period of some twenty years, due to the lack of appropriate action by both the government and medical teachers at that time in providing amenities and financial support for the interns. Since the abolition of the internship, students take the national examination immediately after graduation and, after passing it, are urged by the Ministry of Health and Welfare to obtain at least two years of general clinical training, although this is not mandatory.

ROLE OF NATIONAL POLICY IN SHAPING MEDICAL EDUCATION

Undergraduate medical education in all medical schools in Japan, regardless of their status--national (governmental), public (municipal and prefectural), or private--is under the jurisdiction of the Ministry of Education, Science and Culture, while the two years of postgraduate clinical training is controlled mainly by the Ministry of Health and Welfare, except in hospitals attached to national universities. The Ministry of Health and Welfare has the authority to designate hospitals qualified for the two-year postgraduate clinical training.

In the 1960s and early 1970s there was a growing demand for medical care, particularly after 1961, when a national health insurance system was instituted to cover the entire population. At the same time, a maldistribution of physicians leading to the existence of "non-physician villages" strengthened the demand for increased production of physicians. Consequently, in 1970-1971 the government declared that the nation would need approximately 150 doctors per 100,000 population in the future, and a committee from the leading political party (Liberal/Democratic) recommended that at least one medical school should be located in each prefecture to correct the maldistribution of physicians. This strategy was known at that time as the "one medical school in one prefecture" plan.

Between 1950 and 1969, the number of medical schools in Japan remained constant at 46; following the government actions of 1970-1971 the number increased rapidly and reached a total of 80. Of these eighty schools, forty-three are national, eight are public, and twenty-nine are private. They are evenly distributed so that every prefecture has at least one medical school. The total enrollment of medical students in the 80 schools in 1991 reached 50,352, and the average class size was 104.9. The ratio of male to female students was 3.29:1.

However, since the target of producing more physicians was achieved much earlier than expected, anxiety about potential oversupply of physicians became evident during the 1980s, and the government decided to investigate ways of reducing the number of entrants by around ten percent. In 1990 Japan had 164.9 physicians per 100,000 population, ranging from 224.5 per 100,000 to 99.7 per 100,000. Many large cities throughout the country have more than 200 physicians per 100,000 population, with progressively declining ratios in suburban and rural areas.

ADMISSION

Graduation from high school, following 12 years of general education, is required for admission to medical schools. Admission is generally based on a series of entrance examinations conducted by each medical school; the final decision is made by a committee consisting of school faculty members. Traditionally, admission to medical schools has been highly competitive, and the number and geographic distribution of applicants have not substantially changed in recent years. Since 1978, the first nationwide screening test has been conducted, mostly at national and public schools, the second test being given by each medical school for the final decision. It was recommended that the second test should assess applicants' personal qualities that are adaptable to each school's particular character. Recently, some new types of admissions screening such as interviews, short essays, and group discussions have been introduced in several national and public medical schools. At private schools, on the other hand, entrance examinations traditionally consist of interviews, short essays, and an evaluation of the high school record, in addition to paper and pencil tests. In most medical schools, relatively more weight in the final admissions decision is given to natural science over liberal art subjects. In the final decision tests and records other than paper and pencil tests are generally given less weight, thus making it necessary to investigate a more reliable way of judging the results of various tests. Recently, some medical schools have arranged with selected high schools to provide personal recommendations that are considered along with traditional tests scores and other evidence. Very few students drop out during the undergraduate course; though some require an extra year or two, most obtain the MD degree after the regular six-year course. Table 18.1, p. 268, presents medical school demographics.

CURRICULAR STRUCTURE AND INNOVATION

Japan has a so-called 6-3-3 school year system: that is, six years for primary, three years for middle, and three years for high school education. After these 12 years, general university courses are offered for four years, and medical and dental courses for six years. At one time, the medical education course was clearly divided by law into two stages, a two-year premedical and a four-year medical stage (the 2-4 system), but the law has recently been revised to allow continuous education throughout the six years. Medical schools can now adopt either a continuous six-year program or the 2-4 system. Formerly, the premedical course of 64 units included the humanities, physics, chemistry, biology, mathematics, foreign languages, and physical education, and that for the medical course included all basic science and clinical medicine disciplines. Prior to 1992, 20-25 percent of the required medical course, totaling 4,200-4,800 hours, was officially allotted to basic medical sciences; 15-20 percent to clinical basic medicine; 40-50 percent to clinical medicine; 5-10 percent to social medicine; and 5-10 percent to other. However, the detailed classification of teaching requirements was abandoned by the Ministry of Education, Science and Culture in 1992, so that each medical school can construct a rather free program of teaching units throughout the undergraduate six-year curriculum.

Various degrees of integration between basic science and clinical medicine or among subjects in either course now characterize curricula in the majority of medical schools. Parallel teaching of the premedical course with general medicine subjects and structural or functional integration among clinical disciplines is occurring at many schools. Special subjects such as introduction to medicine, behavioral science, emergency medicine, medical engineering, community medicine, primary care medicine, or rehabilitation medicine are now included in the regular curriculum. "Introduction to Medicine," including such topics as medical ethics, history of medicine, and medical humanities, is now a regular part of the curriculum in more than two-thirds of the schools. These newer courses are taught either in the premedical course or integrated with the medical course throughout the six years. While some of them are electives, the majority are required.

Under the influence of the old German system, undergraduate medical education in Japan was mainly didactic. In response to strong pressure following World War II, instructional methods have gradually changed to encompass laboratory practice and bedside teaching. Though, at present, there is no extensive use of "high technology" in medical education in Japan, self-study using computerized learning tools is becoming more popular.

Examples of Curricular Innovation

The curriculum of the University of Tsukuba School of Medicine, a national school established in 1974, is a complete departure from the classic type, being extensively integrated, with emphasis placed on problem solving, self-learning, and small group instruction. There is no departmental section of disciplines, and student evaluation is done by a special central committee. The school is now an associate member of the Network of Community Oriented Educational Institutions for Health Sciences. Two other schools have special missions in primary health care and community medicine. Kawasaki Medical College, a private school, has opened a new department of general clinical medicine for the purpose of promoting primary care and comprehensive medicine in the community. Jichi Medical School, established by local self-governing bodies, is designed to train doctors to practice in rural areas. Applicants are selected from each prefecture; admitted students receive a full scholarship during the six-year course and are exempted from reimbursement if they agree to work for nine years at local institutions designated by the prefecture from which they were selected. The school has an attached center for community medicine where teaching and research on community medicine are systematically conducted. Curricular integration and small-group learning are also particularly emphasized in several medical schools such as Saga Medical School (national), Kitasato University School of Medicine (private) and others. Quite recently two private schools, Tokyo Women's Medical College and Tokai University School of Medicine, introduced the tutorial system in small-group teaching and are studying its future improvement.

Japan has two other medical schools with unique characteristics, the University of Occupational and Environmental Health, School of Medicine (Industrial Medical School) and the National Defence Medical College (NDMC). The Industrial Medical School was established by a private foundation connected with the Ministry of Labor for training medical students who are expected to work in industry-related fields after graduation. Its curriculum includes many hours with a wide range of subjects in which extramural lecturers, including those from social sciences, participate. The NDMC has the special mission of training doctors for the Defence Force under the control of the Defence Force Agency. Although these are the only medical schools outside the jurisdiction of the Ministry of Education, Science and Culture, their graduates are qualified to take the national examination for licensure.

Clinical Training

Clinical training of undergraduate medical students in Japan is unsatisfactory; although bedside teaching and clerkship are strongly emphasized in the third and fourth year of the medical course, student participation in patient care is strictly limited by the Medical Practitioners Law. In order to obtain a general consensus, the role of unlicensed students has been debated. A special committee was formed by the Ministry of Health and Welfare to investigate this problem. In April 1992, this committee concluded that basic clinical care which undergraduate students can experience with patients should be classified into three categories: (1) care that can be performed by students under the guidance and supervision of teaching physicians, (2) care that can be performed by students under the guidance and supervision of teaching physicians, but under special circumstances, and (3) care for which the student role is limited to observation and/or assistance. Thus, medical students can now, for example, perform physical examinations, clinical tests, some emergency treatments, and others according to the above classification. As a part of the clinical training many schools now offer a course in the premedical curriculum called "early exposure" in which students are introduced to the medical care environment by "shadowing" nurses in the ward or watching various procedures in ambulatory settings in hospitals.

GRADUATE MEDICAL EDUCATION

There are two types of postgraduate medical education in the present system: One, as mentioned earlier, the two years of clinical training recommended immediately after graduation and the other, the usual residency training in a specialty. Although medical school graduates may legally enter individual practice immediately after passing the national examination for licensure, postgraduate clinical training is strongly recommended, and almost all graduates now undertake it.

The two-year general postgraduate clinical training is available in all university hospitals and in other teaching hospitals designated by the Ministry of Health and Welfare. On the average, during the past several years, 80 percent of medical graduates have chosen to take their training at university hospitals. The training programs are designed by the individual institutions, however, the Ministry recommends the general type of clinical practice and some specific rotations that provide experience with clinical skills basic to all disciplines and that are of special value in primary health care. Some standardization of the content and various improvements in those training programs is now widely discussed by various organizations.

The residency system in Japan is not yet well organized among academic societies. The board of each academic society has its own program for the certification of specialists and other doctors registered in its discipline, but there is no national body with the authority to accredit the content of a program. The relationship between the two-year postgraduate clinical training and the residency also varies according to the specialty. In response to this undesirable situation, a council has been set up among academic societies to try to solve these problems, and to encourage negotiations among academic societies concerning methods of certification and recertification of specialists.

LICENSURE

The Ministry of Health and Welfare is responsible for issuing the medical license to medical school graduates who pass the national medical examination. The examination is offered once a year and there is no limitation on the number of times candidates may repeat it; the rate of success was 84 percent in 1992. Once this examination consisted of essay tests and an oral exam, but in 1975 it was changed exclusively to a multiple choice format. The quality of the multiple choice questions has been constantly studied by a standing committee of the Ministry of Health and Welfare, and the inclusion of problem-solving questions relevant to clinical practice is being tried every year. The guidelines for making questions are also distributed to members of the committee that writes the exam.

Cross-Licensing of Physicians

Cross-licensing of foreign medical doctors is not permitted. Foreign medical school graduates can take the national examination after passing a preliminary examination.

CONTINUING MEDICAL EDUCATION

Continuing medical education (CME) for practicing physicians is voluntary. Applicants attend various meetings for study organized by special groups of enthusiastic practitioners, or scientific congresses held by branches of the Japan Medical Association or academic societies. Medical schools and academic societies are also becoming more and more interested in participating in the planning of CME in cooperation with regional teaching hospitals.

The Japan Medical Association established a new system in 1987 in which members are requested to report annually their record of self-learning, including attendance at academic meetings, case studies, reading, group conferences, and other efforts. The record is evaluated based on the number of hours spent in learning, but has no relation to recertification or relicensure.

ROLE OF RESEARCH IN MEDICAL EDUCATION

The majority of Japanese medical schools have the department system called "Koza" in the Japanese language. Funds for research and education are secured every year for each department, which seems to be an advantageous feature of the system. However, since the budget is never enough, faculty search for outside research grants, to the detriment of the status of education. In addition, the academic reward system usually favors research activities, as shown by published papers, over teaching ability, and no system of rewards or promotion for educational activities prevails.

In order to change this unfavorable condition and improve medical education, many schools are now making efforts such as setting up a vice deanship for education, forming a centralized curriculum committee, holding a special meeting for teacher-training, and so forth. Medical school faculty concern for medical education itself is now progressing nationwide. The percentage of teaching hours is gradually increasing at the expense of research or clinical service. The emphasis on teaching should be encouraged by organizational arrangement of educational activities and institution of a reward system for effective teaching in every medical school and teaching hospital.

GOVERNMENT/PRIVATE SECTOR INVOLVEMENT

The Japan Society for Medical Education was established in 1969 by a group of medical educators with the objective of creating opportunities for open discussions about teaching and learning in medicine and for scientific study of medical education itself. The Society holds an annual scientific congress at the time of the general assembly and publishes a bimonthly official journal, *Medical Education* (Japan). As routine activities, the Society has formed standing committees on student selection, undergraduate education, the national examination, postgraduate education, continuing education, teaching methods, and international affairs, as well as working groups on behavioral science, and evaluation of clinical performance. All these study groups hold several meetings or workshops every year, proposing many recommendations that have become useful bases for reform and improvement of medical education in Japan. The Society has also published monographs including medical education manuals, and white papers on medical education and evaluation technology.

A nationwide medical teacher-training workshop has been held once a year since 1974, first under the auspices of voluntary research group members and now sponsored by both the Ministry of Health and Welfare and the Ministry of Education, Science and Culture. The workshop has the objective of training medical teachers in new teaching skills so that they can carry out more effective medical education. Key persons of the Japan Society for Medical Education always participate in the meetings as task force members. Echoing this nationwide workshop, many small scale workshops with similar objectives have been held in individual medical schools and teaching hospitals throughout the country.

The Japan Medical Education Foundation was established in 1979 with the assistance of all medical schools. It holds annual international symposia inviting medical educators from abroad, and makes grants for research on medical education to individuals and groups. It also conducts inspection tours and holds conferences on medical education every year in different regional medical schools. A study group on the Medical College Admission Test (MCAT) in the US has been organized under the auspices of the Foundation, supported by the Ministry of Education, Science and Culture.

The Association of Japanese Medical Colleges has formed a committee to survey the curriculum of all medical schools, publishing *The Present State of Medical Education Curriculum* every other year.

INTERNATIONAL LINKAGES AND COLLABORATION

The General Professional Education of the Physician (GPEP) report of the American Association of Medical Colleges (1984) has been given attention and discussed among Japanese medical educators. In response to that report, the Ministry of Education, Science and Culture of Japan convened a conference for medical educators on "conducting research on reform in medical education" and published the proceedings, findings, conclusions and recommendations of the conference in a report in 1987. The Edinburgh Declaration (1988) of the World Federation for Medical Education also stimulated reform of medical education in Japan. Different models of reform in medical education have been voluntarily started in almost all medical schools in Japan.

The basic principles and methods of reform mentioned in the above reports have been noticed and strengthened by recommendations and activities sponsored by the private sector connected with medical education. Innovative teaching and learning methods, problem-oriented education, self-learning, and the introduction of educational technology are now being considered in medical schools throughout the country.

ISSUES AND TRENDS

Japan was once concerned about the potential oversupply of physicians. On the other hand, inasmuch as the increasing demand for physicians for administrative fields, international cooperation, and participation in new health systems is gradually becoming apparent, the national policy is now being reexamined.

The public demand for health care of an ever expanding aging population, for a universal health care system and for a reexamination of medical ethics and other social problems will stimulate the reform of Japanese medical education in the 1990s.

REFERENCES

Clinical Training Research Conference and Ministry of Health and Welfare, eds. 1993. *Guidebook of clinical training hospitals* (in Japanese). Tokyo: Nihon Iji Shimpo.

Japan Medical Association. 1991. *Annual report of national health services 1991* (in Japanese). Tokyo: Japan Medical Association, 2-18-16, Honkomagome, Bunkyoku. (In Japanese.)

Promoting medical education research (A Proposal, in Japanese). 1990. *Igaku Kyoiku* (Medical Education, Japan) 21 (2):130-131.

Teacher training in Japan (International News). *1992. Teaching and Learning in Medicine* 4 (4):247-248.

Ushiba, D. 1985. Trends of medical education in Japan. *Medical Education* 19:258-265.

Table 18.1
Medical School Demographics--Japan

	Medical School	Enrollment Fall 1991-- Male	Undergraduate Enrollment Fall 1991--Female	Graduates 1991+	Total Full-time Faculty Fall 1991++
1.	Hokkaido University School of Medicine	612	86	111	39
2.	Sapporo Medical College	511	117	101	44
3.	Hirosaki University School of Medicine	561	118	125	36
4.	Asahikawa Medical College	534	148	121	36
5.	Iwate Medical University School of Medicine	423	102	74	46
6.	Tohoku University School of Medicine	603	80	125	45
7.	Akita University School of Medicine	494	157	88	31
8.	Yamagata University School of Medicine	460	179	132	32
9.	Fukushima Medical College	399	112	95	39
10.	University of Tsukuba School of Medicine	435	197	95	51
11.	Jichi Medical School	557	66	104	67
12.	Dokkyo University School of Medicine	529	172	107	68
13.	Gunma University School of Medicine	441	173	96	34
14.	Saitama Medical School	585	170	91	72

Table 18.1
Medical School Demographics—Japan

Medical School	Enrollment Fall 1991—Male	Undergraduate Enrollment Fall 1991—Female	Graduates 1991 +	Total Full-time Faculty Fall 1991 ++
15. School of Medicine, Chiba University	500	144	113	44
16. Faculty of Medicine, University of Tokyo+++	384	35	106	74
17 Tokyo Medical and Dental University Faculty of Medicine	412	90	76	36
18. School of Medicine Nihon University	510	231	110	43
19. Nippon Medical School	473	137	104	72
20. Toho University School of Medicine	444	205	87	85
21. Tokyo Medical College	593	126	122	59
22. Tokyo Women's Medical College	0	615	102	108
23. The Jikei University School of Medicine	592	104	118	80
24. Keio University School of Medicine	556	65	95	50
25. Showa University School of Medicine	600	123	122	69
26. Juntendo University School of Medicine	440	115	102	59
27. Kyorin University School of Medicine	424	227	81	58
28. Teikyo University School of Medicine	621	240	143	86

Table 18.1
Medical School Demographics--Japan

Medical School	Enrollment Fall 1991-- Male	Undergraduate Enrollment Fall 1991--Female	Graduates 1991 +	Total Full-time Faculty Fall 1991 + +
29. Yokahama City University School of Medicine	292	100	63	27
30. School of Medicine, Kitasato University	513	262	131	55
31. St. Marianna University School of Medicine	478	179	96	63
32. School of Medicine, Tokai University	526	171	85	61
33. Yamanashi Medical College	477	124	98	35
34. Niigata University School of Medicine	552	142	116	36
35. Shinshu University School of Medicine	468	156	108	37
36. Faculty of Medicine Toyama Medical and Pharmaceutical University	460	170	99	36
37. School of Medicine Kanazawa University	581	86	121	34
38. Kanazawa Medical University	541	137	66	60
39. Fukui Medical School	477	161	79	35
40. Gifu University School of Medicine	388	132	79	34
41. Hamamatsu University School of Medicine	496	149	96	43
42. Nagoya University School of Medicine	499	109	100	42

Table 18.1
Medical School Demographics--Japan

Medical School	Enrollment Fall 1991--Male	Undergraduate Enrollment Fall 1991--Female	Graduates 1991 +	Total Full-time Faculty Fall 1991 + +
43. Nagoya City University Medical School	395	89	77	32
44. Fujita Health University School of Medicine	476	201	85	70
45. Aichi Medical University	505	207	92	46
46. Mie University School of Medicine	485	151	93	32
47. Shiga University of Medical Science	472	151	95	39
48. Kyoto University Faculty of Medicine	633	61	117	40
49. Kyoto Prefectural University of Medicine	500	132	100	40
50. Osaka University Medical School	588	66	106	53
51. Osaka City University Medical School	421	89	79	32
52. Osaka Medical College	472	157	109	36
53. Kansai Medical University	453	160	100	39
54. Kinki University School of Medicine	551	140	88	38
55. Kobe University School of Medicine	537	147	110	34
56. Hyogo College of Medicine	447	209	106	45

Table 18.1
Medical School Demographics--Japan

	Medical School	Enrollment Fall 1991-- Male	Undergraduate Enrollment Fall 1991--Female	Graduates 1991 +	Total Full-time Faculty Fall 1991 + +
57.	Nara Medical University	494	146	89	42
58.	Wakayama Medical College	281	94	54	43
59.	Tottori University School of Medicine	416	174	115	41
60.	Shimane Medical University	444	186	101	37
61.	Okayama University Medical School	587	97	113	42
62.	Kawasaki Medical School	572	238	98	61
63.	Hiroshima University School of Medicine	585	92	116	33
64.	Yamaguchi University School of Medicine	503	146	122	33
65.	The University of Tokushima School of Medicine	444	112	122	34
66.	Kagawa Medical School	440	178	106	38
67.	Ehime University School of Medicine	520	127	103	32
68.	Kochi Medical School	478	136	99	39
69.	Faculty of Medicine, Kyushu University	619	77	136	42
70.	University of Occupational and Environmental Health, Japan	491	126	111	45

Table 18.1
Medical School Demographics--Japan

Medical School	Enrollment Fall 1991--Male	Undergraduate Enrollment Fall 1991--Female	Graduates 1991+	Total Full-time Faculty Fall 1991++
71. Saga Medical School	392	220	99	39
72. Fukuoka University, School of Medicine	486	180	98	42
73. Kurume University School of Medicine	558	183	133	47
74. Nagasaki University School of Medicine	540	152	120	37
75. Kumamoto University Medical School	538	121	117	45
76. Medical College of Oita	433	175	101	39
77. Miyazaki Medical College	483	145	108	34
78. Faculty of Medicine Kagoshima University	575	104	128	33
79. University of Ryukyus, Faculty of Medicine	478	141	96	41
80. National Defence Medical College	352	40	64	41
TOTAL	38,626	11,726	8,189	3,688

+ The number of graduates who took the national examination for licensure in 1991

++ The number of professors only

+++ The first- and second-year students belong to the Faculty of Culture

19

Malaysia

Sharifah H. Shahabudin

Malaysia lies at the heart of Southeast Asia. It is the only country to share a common border with its ASEAN neighbors. ASEAN, an acronym for the Association of Southeast Asian Nations, is comprised of Thailand, Singapore, Brunei, Indonesia, the Philippines, and Malaysia, and is the fastest growing economic region of the world today. Malaysia occupies a land area of 129,000 square miles with two distinct regions: West Malaysia, which is the more densely populated peninsular area, and East Malaysia, consisting of the states of Sarawak and Sabah with the mystic Kinabalu, the highest peak in the region located on the island of Borneo, separated from the mainland by 400 miles of the South China Sea.

The population numbers 18 million, with 65 percent below the age of 30 years. The majority are of ethnic Malay stock while the other one-third are of Chinese and Indian descent. Malaysia is proud of its multicultural and multireligious heritage. The official religion is Islam, but people are free to practice their respective faiths, and the official language is Malay, but English, Mandarin, Tamil, and the indigenous languages are also taught and freely spoken. Free education is provided up to pre-university level, and extensive funds are allocated for university scholarships and loans. There are approximately 60,000 Malaysian students in various foreign universities and an equal number in the seven local universities.

The system of government is a constitutional monarchy under a parliamentary democracy where representatives are elected to the legislature every five years by universal adult suffrage. The other two arms of the government are the executive and the judiciary. The national development policy has as its goal for Malaysia to be a fully developed nation by the year 2020. Embodied in this goal is the vision of an industrialized nation, with a confident and united Malaysian people infused by strong moral and ethical values, living in a society that is democratic, liberal and tolerant, caring, economically just and equitable, progressive and prosperous, and with an economy that is competitive, dynamic, robust, and resilient.

The nation's health status is reflected by a life expectancy of 74 years for women and 69 years for men; a crude death rate of 4.7 per 1,000; an infant mortality rate of 13.5 per 1,000 live births; a toddler mortality rate of 1.3 per 1,000 children aged one to four years; and a maternal mortality rate of 0.3 per 1,000 live births. Health status has improved tremendously since independence in 1957. The doctor-population ratio varies from 1:700 in the cities to 1:5,000 in East Malaysia. The overall ratio is 1:2,560. There are 1.5 acute hospital beds per 1,000 population and 6.05 health centers per 100,000 rural population (Malaysia 1991). Development allocation for the Health sector under the Sixth Malaysia Plan (1990-1995) is 4.1 percent of the total federal budget, but the majority (60 percent) goes into curative care. Since the 1970s, infectious diseases, while not eradicated, have diminished in relative importance as more and more people suffer and die of diseases of modernization, industrialization, and urbanization, with heart disease, cancer, and motor vehicle accidents topping the list. See Table 19.1.

Table 19.1
Malaysia--Improvement in Health Indices

Indicators	1957	1991
Life Expectancy (years)	57.0	72.0*
Crude Death Rate (per 1000)	12.4	4.7
Infant Mortality Rate (per 1000 live births)	102.0	13.5
Toddler Mortality Rate (per 1000 children 1-4 years)	11.0	1.3
Maternal Mortality Rate (per 1000 live births)	7.0	0.3
Note: *as reflected by the life expectancy of 74 years for women and 69 years for men, crude.		

OVERVIEW OF THE HEALTH CARE DELIVERY SYSTEM

The government, through its various ministries, plays a dominant role in the provision of preventive and promotive public health programs as well as the curative, rehabilitative and regulatory concerns. In addition to the Ministry of Health, the Ministry of Environment, Science and Technology and the Ministry of Agriculture are involved in environmental health through the regulation and monitoring of waste disposal, use of pesticides, and control of zoonotic diseases. The Ministry of Labor ensures that employers provide adequate health care and occupational safety for workers. It also maintains the Social Security Funds for medical and rehabilitative care for victims of occupational accidents. The Ministry of Unity and Community Development provides rehabilitative and institutional care for the aged, mentally retarded, and various groups of persons with disabilities. The Ministry of Home Affairs extends treatment and rehabilitation for drug addicts (the problem of drug addiction and trafficking is an internal security matter in Malaysia), as well as providing health care for the indigenous natives (called Orang Asli). Health care for pilgrims to Mecca is given by the Pilgrims Management Board. The Ministry of Education is involved in medical training and provides health care through its teaching hospitals and clinics. It also runs the school health program that encompasses immunization and vaccination, nutrition, and dental care.

Although many governmental bodies are involved in health care, the Ministry of Health remains the primary provider, planner and organizer of health and medical services for the entire country. The highly subsidized government health system covers a wide range of preventive and curative services. With a registration fee of one Malaysian ringgit, a patient seen in primary care services can have access right up to specialist services in a tertiary center. A network of rural health centers and mobile clinics forms the base for a range of public health programs (family health, control of communicable and vector-borne diseases, environmental sanitation) and primary care services with referral to relevant district and general hospitals, with university medical centers and national referral centers at the pinnacle of the system. Each health center serves a population of 50,000. The rural health system relies to an overwhelming degree on paramedics, particularly medical assistants and community nurses. Doctors often act more in a supervisory than operational capacity. This extensive rural network accounts for 60 percent of all primary (as opposed to specialized) outpatient visits to government clinics, and it has been largely responsible for the declining maternal and infant mortality rates.

Private Health Care

A striking feature of the Malaysian health care system is the rigid separation of government health services from those rendered by the private sector. The private sector, where 55 percent of the doctors currently serve, is the faster growing and more lucrative. Before 1980 most doctors in the private sector were general practitioners, but in recent years the improvement in income, rising expectations, and demand for services has led to the mushrooming of private hospitals, and maternity and nursing homes. These, however, are predominantly urban and curative-based, with a tendency to high-technology hospital care. Costs of private sector services are either borne directly by the patients themselves or paid through medical insurance or by the patients' employers as part of the employment contract. Private hospital growth, with its concomitant increase in cost of inpatient care, is largely responsible for the steep rise in the consumer price index for medical care and health expenses compared to the rise in the general index (Leng 1988). Cost escalation cannot be checked because at the moment there are no controls on private health care charges, nor are there mechanisms to control and coordinate private sector purchase of high technology equipment. Consequent to the public and private sector competition, Malaysia still suffers from the rural-urban disparity in health status due to inequitable distribution of health personnel, facilities, and services, despite the priority for the extensive expansion and development of rural health services. To meet this shortage, all doctors are required to complete a compulsory three-year service with the government. The introduction of compulsory service leads only to a temporary retention of young doctors while the older, more experienced physicians move into private practice. There is also an acute shortage of nurses because of the rapid private sector growth and foreign demand.

Voluntary Organizations

Voluntary agencies provide health care that includes a substantial portion of social and rehabilitative services. They include international agencies, such as the Red Crescent, International Planned Parenthood Federation, and St. John Ambulance Service, as well as national or local associations dealing with specific problems, such as the National Cancer Society, Association for the Blind, Association for the Deaf, Association for Mentally Retarded Children and the Women's Aid Organization. Professional organizations such as the Malaysian Medical Association and specialty bodies also provide free clinics and consultation. Most, though not all, of these organizations receive financial support from the government.

Traditional Medicine

For personal health care, the dominant system is modern western medicine. However people do use and practice numerous alternative health systems-- Chinese, Ayurvedic and Malay--alongside the western system. Very little information is available about the distribution and number of traditional practitioners because a register is not maintained. Most practice their skills on a part-time basis. In the Malay system, there is the traditional medicine man (*bomoh*) and the traditional midwife (*bidan*, designated "traditional birth attendant" [TBA] by the government). In many villages, these traditional midwives are well respected, much sought after, and given training by the government. The Chinese system can perhaps be considered the most formally organized. These hospitals provide western medical care; some still maintain a branch or a separate block that provides traditional Chinese medical care. The Chinese traditional medical practitioners are of a wide range, including those who practice herbal medicine (the *sinseh*), the acupuncturists, and those who specialize in bone setting. In addition, there is also the Chinese "medicine man," who practices a mixture of magic and medicine. Indian medical practitioners are also of a wide range, and many are herbalists and lay practitioners.

HISTORICAL BACKGROUND

The history of medical education in this region is usually associated with the British colonial government's establishment of the King Edward VII College of Medicine in Singapore in 1905 as a response to public petition for local medical training (Danaraj 1988). The curriculum of the school was strictly discipline oriented with no semblance of integration. British influence was very strong, and even today recognition by the General Medical Council of Britain is thought to be an important yardstick of "standards." The college became part of the University of Malaya in Singapore, but with independence from British colonial rule it became the Faculty of Medicine, University of Singapore.

The Federation of Malaya, formed in 1957 before Sabah and Sarawak joined the union to form Malaysia in 1973, soon felt the need to establish its own medical school. In 1963, headed by Dean T. J. Danaraj and staffed by several senior faculty mainly from the King Edward College, the first medical school in Malaysia was established at the University of Malaya (UM) in the capital city of Kuala Lumpur. Established primarily to meet the needs of the rapidly expanding health services of the new nation, the UM medical school was equally dedicated to excellence in scholarship and to the practice of medicine-- "to promoting health and preventing disease, to healing and rehabilitating the patient, and to lengthening the span of man's productive years" (University of Malaya 1963). The medical school has remained as the premier school in the country, producing graduates who now staff and help to establish the newer medical schools.

The second school was established in 1972 at the National University of Malaysia (UKM), following the massive economic and social restructuring of 1970 which called for the establishment of a national university to provide tertiary education for students who were now being taught in Malay rather than English as the medium of instruction. Even these two schools were not producing enough doctors for the country, and a third school was established in 1979 at the Science University (USM) in Penang. This medical school is in the rural state of Kelantan, on the east coast of west Malaysia. Together they produce about 400 doctors annually.

ROLE OF NATIONAL POLICY IN SHAPING MEDICAL EDUCATION

The government has targeted a ratio of one doctor for every 1,500 population by year 2000. This means that 16,000 doctors would be required for the projected population. The total number of doctors currently is approximately 8,000. The 4,500 new graduates expected from the three medical schools, plus those returning from foreign training (mainly in India, Pakistan, Bangladesh, Britain, Australia, New Zealand, and Egypt) for the same period, are clearly insufficient to meet the needs. Two more schools are being planned for 1994, one at the International Islamic University (IIU), and the other to be based at the newly established University of Malaysia Sarawak in East Malaysia. The development of the latter two schools is a challenging venture. The proposed school in Sarawak marks an exciting departure from university-based medical education, toward greater integration between medical education and the health care system. It calls for the active contribution of the school to improving the quality and coverage of health care to this relatively underserved region of the country. The school at IIU aims to integrate religious and spiritual components with the bio/psychosocial aspects of patient and health care. This approach reflects the concern for integrated care and the increased humanization of care. Except for the

International Islamic Medical University, which is a corporate body, all universities in Malaysia are government funded.

ADMISSION

The national policy for student admission to university reflects the political climate and the social aspiration of national integration. Student admission is based on ethnic representation in society. For medicine, the proportion is further modified to correct existing gross imbalances in favor of the ethnic Malays and natives of Sabah and Sarawak. Admission into universities is processed by the University Processing Unit, a central agency under the Ministry of Education. Prior to 1970, students entered Medicine after completing advanced secondary education; they were mainly from urban schools, because rural schools rarely had facilities for advanced level education. To ensure equal access and quality of students, all three universities now conduct two-year matriculation programs for premedical students. Academic criteria are used in selecting students who choose to study medicine, and an interview is sometimes conducted. The decision to accept or reject a candidate is usually left up to the medical school indicated as the student's first choice. Students enter medical school at the average age of twenty. In the early 1960s the enrollment of female medical students was about 20 percent, but by the mid-1980s, it had soared to about 70 percent. The female enrollment now varies between 50 and 65 percent.

A study of six cohorts (1977-1987) of UKM students revealed an attrition rate of about ten percent every year. However, the medical school allows students to repeat an academic session once if they do not fail too badly; overall, about 20 percent fail to complete the course. The study also showed a significantly higher proportion of female students who completed the course within the five years. See Table 19.2, p. 289.

CURRICULAR STRUCTURE AND INNOVATION

All three of our present schools share the common goal of producing doctors "made in Malaysia, for Malaysia," who have the relevant knowledge, skills, attitudes, and ability to make reasoned decisions and who are competent to critically apply the latest technologies in their practice of medicine. These doctors will also be able to respond to the needs of their community by initiating, adapting to and participating in change; obtain the community's involvement in health; be capable of continuing work with others, even outside the health sector, and of making better use of information and managerial techniques in planning and performing their duties. The period of training is five years, with English and Malay as the language of instruction. Strategies to achieve these goals, however, differ slightly from school to school.

The UM curriculum maintains its traditional discipline-based approach, but recently incorporated early introduction of clinical sciences. The UKM school started with a traditional curriculum but made a major change in 1987, using strategies that were evolved for what appeared to be a monumental and difficult process of change (Shahabudin 1991a). This change consisted of the introduction of an integrated organ-system approach in the preclinical phase and the adoption of the comprehensive examination (not discipline-based) in the clinical phase. Problem-based learning is used as one of the learning strategies, but the approach on the whole remains mainly didactic. The momentum of change lost some impetus in 1990, and the preclinical phase reverted to a more discipline-oriented format though still maintaining the organ-system approach. A more integrated problem-based and student-centered approach is a feature of the innovative USM curriculum, which has employed this strategy since its inception.

Electives and community-based programs are major features in all schools. Students spend varying periods of time in the community, usually in remote rural areas, to learn about the community and to participate in community based health programs. In USM, students adopt villages, families or individuals as early as the second year, and work with them to improve their health status throughout the medical course. In UKM, theoretical aspects of community medicine are studied in the first two years. Students then spend eight weeks in a rural community conducting a public health survey and, using the problem-solving cycle, they then carry out interventions, which may be in the form of public health education or projects such as deparasitization and immunization.

Students also spend another eight weeks in a rural hospital where the emphasis is on learning patient management at the primary care level. Back in the teaching hospital, students concurrently study the problems of the urban community and the health services provided for them. While undergoing the clerkship in both the urban and rural centers, students learn to appreciate the real work of the doctor and have hands-on experience of the health team concept where the doctor is more often than not the team leader. A similar program is conducted in UM. The interaction and participation in patient and health care management, particularly in the community settings, are important for the future doctor to appreciate the work of the other members of the health care team. With the exception of dentistry and pharmacy which are university programs, all other allied health training programs are conducted by the Training Division of the Ministry of Health. Hence, there is very little interaction between students of medicine and students of the other health professions. Electives are usually taken in other institutions, either locally or abroad.

All schools require at least three years of clinical clerkship, during which students are expected to follow their cases from admission to discharge, taking notes; examining sputum, blood, urine, and feces, and assisting in post mortems, if necessary. However, this type of clerkship is regrettably declining because of the trend toward specialization and fragmentation of medical care. Excluded from the clinical clerkship in varying degrees are ambulatory medicine, rehabilitation, care of the elderly, chronically sick, the disabled and the terminally ill. University hospitals have become tertiary care hospitals at the apex of the health delivery system, with specialists-academicians concentrating on complex patient care problems requiring sophisticated investigations, and with less emphasis on prevention and promotion of a healthy life style. The practice of medicine is fragmented into specialties and thus, the ambition of students is to become specialists. Those who do not (the majority), become ill-equipped general practitioners. The extent of specialty training in relation to the primary objectives of undergraduate medical education and issues regarding undergraduates' adequate exposure in the "ward without walls" (namely, the community) is under review.

Realizing that medical education for primary health care cannot take place in a vacuum, and that it needs models and demonstrations of primary health care practice based on methods not less scientific or stringent than those for tertiary medical care, important steps are therefore being taken to ensure that primary health care in its true sense is really being practiced. Both UKM and UM have established departments of primary care (now Family Medicine). An innovative postgraduate program in Family Medicine using distance learning strategies has been developed that will be jointly implemented by the universities, the Ministry of Health, and the College of General Practitioners. The development of the program has also induced structural changes within the Ministry of Health which will be reorganized to provide family medicine services (Shahabudin 1991b).

Efforts are being made to apportion more curricular time to primary and ambulatory care, particularly in the rural setting, with de-emphasis on the highly disease-centered, technology-biased, over-investigation and over-treatment style of practice. This is to reduce the likelihood that the urban-based ethos of university medical practice will be followed in a rural setting with its relatively less developed community. There is now a greater tendency to integrate medical education with the health care system, making it more relevant. Currently, the universities utilize the government health institutions as learning environments, but teaching remains largely by faculty and hospital based. The efforts for greater integration are reflected in the approach recommended for the Sarawak medical school that has more direct and extensive exposure to real life situations, with the health service staff participating in teaching. Another alternative is proposed for the Islamic Medical University, where the medical faculty, apart from owning a teaching hospital through an arrangement with the health care system, also runs all subsidiary medical and health services in the catchment area of the teaching hospital, and uses them for teaching. This is to enable the faculty to have direct access to all the resources in the area and to demonstrate new or innovative approaches.

There have been many attempts to introduce learning methods that encourage the habits of reading and learning, use of the library, and application of information to computer technology, particularly in the two older schools, but these efforts are often thwarted by a faculty steeped in traditional didactic teaching. The failure of innovations to be sustained is often traced to lack of continuity in faculty leadership, poor support from policymakers, faculty resistance due to unfounded fears, and lack of skills in newer teaching-learning approaches. Too often curricular change involves merely shuffling of timetables rather than true improvement. All schools have curriculum committees, and the UKM and USM Faculties have medical education departments to assist in curricular development and teacher training. However, the efforts of these departments are strictly defined by directions from the top.

All schools utilize continuous assessment, but the degree to which it contributes to the summative assessment varies from school to school. In all schools the final examination is fully integrated (not discipline-based), with participation of external examiners. In the UKM medical school for example, the summative examination consists of two parts, the theory and clinicals. The continuous assessment contributes 30 percent to the theory marks. The other 70 percent consists of marks obtained from 4 patient management problems (28 percent), 180 multiple-true false questions (28 percent) and 20 data interpretation stations (14 percent). In the clinical examination, each student is given a patient to interview and examine. He or she is then orally tested on the ability to formulate a diagnosis and to discuss a rational plan of management that reflects integrated care for the patient. In addition, the student is observed performing specific clinical skills on three other patients. There is no national board for undergraduate medical examination, and each school is autonomous with regard to the certification of competence.

GRADUATE MEDICAL EDUCATION

Formal specialty training within Malaysia was essentially nonexistent until the early 1970s when UM introduced three courses at the Master's level in disciplines identified as acutely short of human resources (Psychological Medicine, Public Health, and Pathology). In the clinical specialties, most doctors seek fellowship in the various Royal Colleges of Britain by taking the relevant examinations. In 1980, following a governmental decision to base postgraduate medical education in the universities, UKM embarked on two four-year structured clinical mastership training programs in General and Orthopedic Surgery. Within a period of six years, UKM aggressively expanded its postgraduate programs to include all clinical specialties, the latest being Family Medicine. Apart from clinical training, conducting a research project is an important component of the program. Upon graduation, depending on the specialty chosen, either a Master of Medicine (specialty), a Master of Surgery (specialty) or Master of Obstetrics and Gynecology is awarded. The doctors are registered as specialists within six months of practice in the public service.

All three medical schools now conduct postgraduate courses. In total, about six hundred postgraduate students are currently enrolled in the various specialties. The Ministry of Health also participates in the training program through approved training posts either for the local postgraduate courses or foreign certification, e.g., Fellow of the Royal College of Surgeons (FRCS), Member of the Royal College of Physicians (MRCP), or member of the Royal College of OB-Gyn (MRCOG). All disciplines are filled, indicative of the shortage of training posts and great number of applicants. The specialties most acutely short of doctors are anesthesiology, otorhinolaryngology, ophthalmology, pathology, and radiology.

The proliferation of postgraduate courses requires a coordinating mechanism. On the initiative of the then Dean of UKM, Professor Dato Dr Mahmud Mohd Nor, a National Coordinating Committee for Postgraduate Studies in Medicine was established by the Ministry of Education. The committee consisted of representatives from the medical schools, the Ministry of Health, and the profession (Academy of Medicine). Under the main coordinating committee are specialty subcommittees with similar representation for each of the disciplines.

LICENSURE

The Malaysian Medical Council (MMC) is the legally constituted body to approve licensing for practice. Chaired by the Director General of Health, it includes elected as well as appointed representatives from the medical profession and medical schools. Following licensing, all doctors must apply for an annual Practicing Certificate to continue practicing, but the relicensure is issued automatically upon payment of a small fee. The MMC approves licensing to any doctor who obtains the basic degree from an accredited medical school. All three local schools are recognized by the MMC and 258 foreign schools are on the approved list. Another 55 foreign schools are on a special list. Graduates of schools on the special list have to pass an examination equivalent to the final professional examination of any of the local schools before being allowed to practice. At the moment, there is no licensing body for specialist practice, but a specialist register will soon be established by an Act of Parliament.

CONTINUING MEDICAL EDUCATION

There is no mandatory requirement for CME. Currently in Malaysia, organized CME is conducted by various specialty bodies mainly in weekend courses, workshops, talks, seminars and scientific meetings. These are usually held in the larger towns. Hospital programs are usually confined to local staff. Hence CME activities are not generally accessible to the majority of primary care practitioners, who often work in geographical isolation (Shahabudin and Edariah 1991). With an increasing awareness of the importance of CME in enabling doctors to participate in change, steps are being taken to develop systematic CME programs that will be accessible to most doctors. A needs assessment survey conducted in 1989 revealed that doctors preferred practice-linked CME with built-in self evaluation and opportunities for consultation (Shahabudin 1990). A national seminar in 1990 recommended the establishment of a CME Board, an idea that is currently being actively pursued by the Malaysian Medical Association and the Ministry of Health (Shahabudin 1991; Shahabudin and Edariah 1989).

ROLE OF RESEARCH IN MEDICAL EDUCATION

All faculty are expected to do research because their promotion largely depends on research publications. Research grants are obtained through the University Research Grant program or the very substantial National Research and Development Grant called Intensified Research in Priority Areas (IRPA). Medicine, along with Agriculture and Industry, is identified as a priority area. Research and Development in medical education is carried out as part of the curricular development process in all schools. However, research in CME, and in particular, practice-linked CME, is assuming importance. As in most medical schools, the premium placed on research has discouraged or reduced efforts toward innovation in teaching and learning. Faculty are more willing to invest time in interdisciplinary research than on interdisciplinary discussions about the curriculum, an activity so essential in an integrated curriculum. Faculty are unhappy with the system of reward and promotion which places more stress on research and publications than on teaching skills, educational development and provision of quality health care services. Those who are attracted by private sector rewards generally do not stay long with the faculty, usually leaving after two or three years. The reward system affects those who have for years ignored the lure of the lucrative private sector. They are given the final push when they feel that their contributions to other equally important areas of medical school development are not given due recognition in promotion exercises. These are usually faculty who are known to be dedicated and excellent doctors who would not have otherwise left the university. As a result, many leave for the private sector or go to other countries, leaving the school with relatively young and inexperienced faculty (average age, 39 years).

INTERNATIONAL LINKAGES AND COLLABORATION

The Malaysian Association for Education in the Medical and Health Sciences (MAEMHS) brings together teachers of health personnel who are keen on developing innovative methods in the education of health personnel. Formed in 1981, MAEMHS conducts workshops in teaching and learning as well as seminars for the further development of medical and allied health personnel education. The association has been instrumental in pressing for the upgrading of allied health personnel education to university level. The UKM has just established its Faculty of Allied Health Sciences. The association is a founding member of the Western Pacific Association for Medical Education, (AMEWPR) established in 1988 with its secretariat at the UKM in Kuala Lumpur. This regional association, comprising national associations for medical education and medical schools in the Western Pacific area, is affiliated with the World Federation for Medical Education (WFME). It prepared the regional proposals to the World Conference on Medical Education in Edinburgh in 1988. The UKM and USM medical schools belong to the Network of Community Oriented Educational Institutions for Health Sciences, and currently a UKM faculty member sits on the Executive Board of the Network. UKM is a cosponsor of the international Symposium on Student Assessment organized by the Network in Penang in January 1993. UKM, being a board member, is also responsible for implementing some of the other Network projects at a regional level.

ISSUES AND TRENDS

In 34 years as an independent nation, Malaysian health services, both private and public have shown vast improvement, concomitant with the rapid economic development that raised the standard of living. The governmental network of rural health services helped to reduce urban: rural inequalities, thus hospital and specialized care were strengthened. The improvement in health status was rapid and significant; diseases characteristic of underdeveloped areas are giving way to diseases associated with modernization and industrialization. However there is still disparity in health status with the more advanced areas enjoying better facilities and more health personnel than the rural areas. The influx of migrant labor has brought back malaria and tuberculosis that had previously been well controlled. Infectious diseases, malnutrition and conditions associated with poverty still take their toll. In the more urban areas, less acute diseases of modernization are making their presence felt through escalating health care costs attributed to sophisticated and expensive forms of investigation and treatment. AIDS is appearing in the region, although it has not yet reached alarming levels. The impact of HIV/AIDS is beginning to be felt, not only in terms of the gravity of the problem, but also, increasingly, in terms of its socioeconomic consequences. Hospital beds are not yet full of AIDS patients, but diagnostic awareness can be expected to increase.

Urban-rural discrepancies are due to the inequitable distribution of basic amenities such as safe water, sanitation and health services, which in the rural and peri-urban slum areas are exacerbated by limited education and poverty. Professional isolation, geographical inaccessibility, lack of social amenities, and inadequate facilities in which to practice discourage many doctors from serving in rural areas (Malaysian Medical Association 1980). While the maldistribution may be due to imbalance in political and economic power, bureaucratization (overregulation and monopolistic practices) and commercialization of the health sector are equally at fault. The unplanned growth of a highly lucrative private medical sector over which there is very little government control further accentuates imbalances that may already exist. Doctors concentrate in cities and practice fee-for-service medicine. They avidly adopt expensive technological advances and sophisticated investigations and downgrade financially what the masses of people really require: a safe water supply and sanitary sewage disposal. The salary is not reasonable enough to keep doctors in public service. A "critical service" allowance amounting to 10 percent of the recently revised basic salary has just been introduced for doctors and other health personnel. Whether this will work as an incentive remains to be seen. Compared to others in the civil service, the system of reward and promotion does not seem commensurate with the tasks.

Gross mismatch between problems and solutions is another reason. Where preventable health problems predominate, there is often inadequate attention to their prevention. Huge institutions are often built and run at high cost to treat the aftereffects of preventable diseases.

The Malaysian health care system seems to be at a critical juncture. The formulation of the National Development Policy for the next 30 years has given a clear guide to policy planners and for budget allocation. The vision of a developed nation by year 2020 sees Malaysia a united nation, with a confident people infused by strong moral and ethical values, living in a democratic society, and with a robust economy. The goals are to have sufficient food and shelter, with easy access to health facilities and basic amenities, to eradicate poverty, and to achieve a fair distribution, ownership, control, and management of the economy with balanced growth in all sectors. The population growth rate is also to be maintained at 2.5 percent per annum with a doubling of the GDP every 10 years (Malaysian Business Council 1991). In the health sector, the budget allocation has been increased tremendously. The government is improving health services management for resource mobilization and utilization through greater efforts at intersectoral coordination. A National Health Plan has been formulated and is under review, while a feasibility study for a National Health Security Fund is underway. Actions already initiated to relieve physician shortage include recruitment of foreign doctors, reemploying retired personnel and improving the terms and conditions of service and salaries of doctors (Malaysia 1990).

What is the responsibility of medical schools? What has all this to do with university education? In a keynote address on the reorientation of medical education, presented to participants of the Western Pacific Association for Medical Education in 1988, the then Director General of Health for Malaysia emphatically said that medical education has a definite role in dealing with the relative ineffectiveness of current health care systems. However, medical education must be reoriented, and the reorientation must be focused on the education of doctors (Khalid 1988). This is because doctors, now and more so in the next century, directly provide services and thus are in a position to determine what type and quality of care to provide. They are also the leaders in the health team, providing guidance and supervision to other members. They have a high credibility rating within the community, and thus can influence others. They also plan and manage health services, and so decide the distribution and use of resources, as well as the strategy and content of programs. What is most important, however, is that the decisions of doctors also determine the bulk of health care costs. It is obvious that doctors, individually and collectively, have a big influence on the development and operation of health care systems. How appropriate and effectively doctors are being prepared for these roles should be a matter of great concern.

Knowledge, skills, and attitudes can only be acquired through properly planned practical learning experiences in a representative range of health problems encountered in the real setting. The teaching hospital is but one setting. A few weeks posting to a rural hospital or a day visit to a health center cannot provide that essential practical learning experience. The purpose of the medical school is to provide models of patient care for student emulation. There need to be varied settings and role models other than tertiary care specialist academicians. Complex patient care problems requiring sophisticated investigations must be accompanied by emphasis on prevention and promotion of a healthy lifestyle.

There is an increasing interest among medical schools to revise the curriculum so as to reflect the health needs of the country and the new paradigm in health care: concern for greater humanization of care, integrated care, more consumer participation, technology assessment, cost containment, environmental protection and promotion of healthy lifestyle. There is also a growing tendency to integrate medical education with the health care system in varying degrees, in order to make it more relevant. The emphasis on primary and ambulatory care and the establishment of academic departments of Family Medicine to demonstrate models of primary health care practice provide the scientific basis of primary health care. Of more importance is the demonstration of the university's responsiveness to health needs and the reciprocal ability of the health care system to induce structural changes to accommodate Family Medicine services (Shahabudin 1991b). Not only will the contribution of Family Medicine be crucial to maintaining health but the trend toward partnership that is being forged augurs well for medical education and the health care system for the next century. Of special importance is the increasing emphasis on humanization of care and interpersonal skills. However, reforms can only progress with commitment from teachers, administrators and policy makers.

NOTE

I wish to thank Professor S.T Teoh, Dean of the Faculty of Medicine, UM, for providing the necessary data and for reading the manuscript; Dr Rogayah Jaafar for providing and checking data on USM and Dr. Edariah Abu Bakar for her useful comments.

REFERENCES

Danaraj, T.J. 1988. *Medical education: Problems and challenges.* Kuala Lumpur: Pelanduk Publications.

Khalid, S. 1988. The integration of medical education with the health care system: Reorientation of medical education. Report of the Western Pacific Regional Conference on Medical Education (March).

Leng, C.H. 1988. The development of the health care system in Malaysia: Achievements and pitfalls. Paper presented at the ISIS-Ministry of Health; MMA Forum on the Health Plan for Malaysia (December).

Malaysia. 1991. Annual Report of the Ministry of Health.

─────. 1990. The Sixth Malaysian Plan, 1990-1995. Government document.

Malaysian Business Council. Center for Economic Research and Services. 1991. *Malaysia as a fully developed nation.*

Malaysian Medical Association. 1980. *Report on the future of the health services.*

Shahabudin, S.H. 1991a. Managing the initial period of implementation of education change. *Medical Teacher* 13:205-211.

─────. 1991b. *The curriculum for the postgraduate course in family medicine and report of the implications for implementation. A national report.* University of Kebangsaan, Malaysia (November).

─────. 1990. Designing a CME programme based on practitioners' needs in Malaysia. *Medical Education* 24:264-370.

─────. 1988. Changing a conventional curriculum in an established medical school. *Medical Teacher* 10:149-157.

Shahabudin, S.H. and A.B. Edariah. 1991. Profile of doctors who participate in CME in Malaysia. *Medical Education.* 25:430-437.

─────. 1989. Better health care through CME. Report of the CME seminar. University of Kebangsaan, Malaysia (November).

University of Malaya. Faculty of Medicine. 1963. [Brochure]

Table 19.2
Malaysia--Medical School Demographics

Medical School	Undergraduate Enrollment Fall 1991-Male	Undergraduate Enrollment Fall 1991-Female	Graduates 1991-Male	Graduates 1991-Female	Graduate Education (Interns/ Residents Fall 1991)-Male	Graduate Education (Interns/ Residents Fall 1991)-Female
UKM	446 (INTAKE 112)	348 (INTAKE 78)	64	97	205	87
USM	227 (INTAKE 57)	274 (INTAKE 55)	35	63	30 MMed: 28 PhD: 2	6 MMed: 3 PHD: 3

20

Mexico

JOSÉ LAGUNA
OCTAVIO CASTILLO Y LÓPEZ
JOSÉ DE JESÚS VILLALPANDO-CASAS

OVERVIEW OF THE HEALTH CARE DELIVERY SYSTEM

The National Health System of Mexico contains three main components: (1) the social security subsystem covering workers and employees, their families, and retired personnel; (2) the public welfare subsystem (i.e., federal and state institutions providing health services to people not covered by a social security institution--mainly rural and marginal urban populations); and (3) entities of the social and private sectors, which usually have the financial means to provide medical care of good quality.

Persons affiliated with the social security subsystem enjoy a stable labor situation, reside in urban localities, and have access to other basic needs such as education, housing, and transportation. People in the public welfare subsystem lack steady employment: they are frequently peasants who work only part of the year and have limited access to other health resources, medical or non medical (clean water, nutrition, etc.); moreover, they live in marginal socioeconomic and cultural conditions. In any of the subsystems it is possible to identify two schemes for health care delivery: one oriented to individual-based medicine and the other to the provision of "community-oriented primary care." The first model prevails in all subsystems.

The Ministry of Health plays a most important role in the national health system, as it is responsible for the definition and operation of national policy in matters of medical care, social welfare, and public health. Specific activities include the sanitary control of goods and services (pharmaceuticals, cosmetics, etc.), as well as the coordination of health care service programs in the states and the Federal District. The Ministry of Health also coordinates the subsystem derived from the National Institutes of Health, which provide tertiary level medical care, advanced education, and training, and a setting for basic, applied, and clinical research in medical specialties, including cardiology, nutrition, endocrinology, pediatrics, perinatology, neurology and neurosurgery, oncology, respiratory diseases, and psychiatry.

In the social security subsystem the most important institutions are the Instituto Mexicano del Seguro Social (IMSS) which by law provides coverage to all employed workers in any business or industry, the Instituto de Seguridad y Servicios Sociales para los Trabajadores del Estado (ISSSTE), supplying services to government employees, the national oil company Petroleos Mexicanos (PEMEX), and the Ministries of Defense and of the Navy, which also provide coverage to their employees. IMSS covers almost forty million people; ISSSTE nearly eight million; PEMEX, one and a half million, and the armed forces nearly a half million. The Social Security subsystem thus provides care to almost 60 percent of the population. Another 25-30 percent of the population receives care through the Ministry of Health facilities, and the remaining 10 percent to 15 percent, through the private sector.

All these services reinforce "individual-based medicine," devoting relatively less attention to disease prevention or risk control activities. However, in the last several years important progress has been made in public health matters not related directly to medical intervention, as for example in the universal vaccination program which has successfully eradicated poliovirus in Mexico (Soberón and Laguna 1988).

HISTORICAL BACKGROUND

Early in the twentieth century, the main influence in medical education came from the French model. After World War II, a great number of Mexican physicians were trained in specialty residencies in the United States. As a result, medical school curricula were gradually modified and adapted to the Flexnerian model, emphasizing individual-based, curative and hospital-oriented medicine. Before World War II most of the medical schools and health facilities were concentrated in Mexico City. After the war, however, a number of medical schools were founded throughout the Mexican states. Today, there are 59 medical schools, with 11 located in or near the capital city.

According to governmental policy, great support was given to building new medical schools during the 1970s at a time when several so-called "innovative" curricula were being launched. The curricula were called innovative because anatomy, physiology, biochemistry, nutrition, and so forth were not taught as different subjects but rather were integrated and inter-related. The amount and type of innovation ranged from modest curricular additions and/or reorganization, including multidisciplinary approaches to some subjects, to attempts at fully implemented, problem-based, community-oriented tutorial instruction. For example, the "General Integral Medicine Plan A-36" of the Medical School of the National Autonomous University of Mexico (UNAM) linked medical and social aspects of general practice with an emphasis on preventive medicine and community oriented care (Laguna et al. 1974). Another innovative curriculum was developed at the Metropolitan Autonomous University (UAM) with the modular plan structured around the social factors influencing health and disease. Multidisciplinary plans were also implemented by UNAM'S Zaragoza and Iztacala campuses. Other medical schools, such as those of the National Polytechnic Institute (IPN) and of the states of Guanajuato and Nuevo Leon, modified their curricula to achieve greater emphasis on family practice and public health. At the same time, a new residency of Family Medicine incorporating social and preventive activities was established and thereafter accepted by the three main health institutions: the Ministry of Health, IMSS, and ISSSTE (Hernández 1982).

Mexico offers two main medical education models, the traditional and the "innovative," the former being more common. The traditional model has a classic Flexnerian structure. The "innovative" or comprehensive model focuses on primary care, prevention and control of risk factors, looking for a balance between the biomedical and psychosocial components of the health/disease binomial. This model is intended to qualify the physician for a type of medical practice different from the classic specialties; however, it has relatively little influence, either on the vast majority of medical schools or on the pattern of medical practice in Mexico. Social expectations, the individual struggle for a better economic position, and the challenge of mastering new technologies along with other factors have moved doctors' interests toward the practice of "scientific" (curative) medicine and away from providing comprehensive health care through service. It has been argued that sociomedical aspects can be handled--and at an advantage--by other professionals such as nurses, educators, psychologists, and health promoters.

Medical centers themselves seem more appreciative of the efforts and achievements of specialized medical practice, while they value support professionals who deal with comprehensive or primary care, community participation, and risk prevention only to a limited extent. These institutions have made few efforts to involve their units in these activities or to promote the training, hiring, professional development, and stimulation of such personnel, a factor that has affected the employment of graduates of the innovative medical school programs.

The prevailing model in the health services sector influences the educational model and, as result, medical students and residents focus on medical specialties in most of the schools. Innovative curricula appear to have had negligible impact on student activities and career preferences; the most important factor seems to be the role model of clinical professors (especially in the hospital settings), which reflects the prevailing medical care model that has many deep socioeconomic and cultural roots.

ROLE OF NATIONAL POLICY IN SHAPING MEDICAL EDUCATION

In 1936 a program of "social medical service" was introduced for rural communities without doctors. This social service was staffed by medical students who had completed their five-year medical program. Later, this program was expanded, with little variation to all careers in Mexico. (In most careers, however, social service is not carried out in rural areas.) This program had no impact at all on the medical curriculum which remains deeply attached to hospital services in the traditional schools. In spite of the compulsory nature of this community service program, medical students are not given specific training related to the epidemiological and socioeconomic conditions to be faced in the small rural town where they practice for one year.

When the rate of industrialization accelerated sharply in the 1940s, government actions in health matters first focused on urban populations. Thus, in 1943, the social security institutions--IMSS for workers and ISSSTE for government employees--were founded. At that time most Mexican universities, influenced by international conferences in Colorado Springs, US; Viña del Mar, Chile; and Tehuacan, Mexico, urged their medical schools to include preventive medicine as a key curricular subject, thereby accepting the importance of the public health model both for the training of physicians and for the organization of health care units. However, neither students, clinical faculty, nor the health services implemented this curricular modification, and no changes in educational and health care activities were observed (FAPAFEM 1990).

Finally, at the end of the 1960s, two important programs were implemented: (1) comprehensive health services and (2) coordination between health and educational institutions, mainly through the IMSS Family Medicine Residency Program and the "General Integral Medicine" curriculum of the Medical School at UNAM. Both programs were committed to the development of a sound practice of comprehensive medicine including as key components: disease prevention, risk control, community health and all the other primary health care actions as defined in the Alma Ata Declaration of 1978 (World Health Organization 1978). Unfortunately, due to the lack of interest of practicing health personnel, practice models again failed to follow suit, and limited impact on the type or quality of services was observed. The response of graduate medical students was also unfavorable. During the last several years the number of applicants to Family Medicine residency has significantly diminished, and most of the recently graduated physicians apply for the traditional specialty courses.

In spite of the introduction of thousands of family doctors into the health services, it has been very difficult to secure a firm and respected place for them. This results partly from the medical establishment's attitudes and partly to some degree of dissatisfaction among the consumers themselves who have not recognized the benefits of the comprehensive medicine with its preventive, curative, public health, environment, family planning, nutrition, and other components.

ADMISSION

There is no national policy concerning admission requirements to medical school. Each school or university establishes its own rules based on its resources, available academic personnel, and pressure from applicants to medical careers. Some schools admit as few as 20 to 30 students per year, while others accept more than 1,000. In 1991, 59 Mexican medical schools admitted a total of 11,929 students; only about 5 percent of the total (653) was admitted to the country's 12 private schools, whose admissions have recently diminished. In contrast, in 1991 the private schools graduated 717 physicians, about 11 percent of the total number (6,279) of graduates in the country. At least 80 percent complete their medical studies and receive their degrees. See table 20.1, p. 301.

Some institutions accept students with passing marks in the previous academic phase (the baccalaureate or high school diploma); other institutions also require applicants to pass admission exams, which are used to restrict the class size to school capacity as measured by available physical plant and human resources. In a few medical schools, student selection is based on the results of psychological tests and performance in a preparatory course of several months duration.

In 1986, the Council for International Organization of Medical Sciences (CIOMS) recommended that medical school admissions be determined by a joint decision of authorities from health services and educational institutions, and be based on actual physician needs and available educational resources. Accordingly, the Interinstitutional Commission for Human Resources Development, made up of high level officers from the Ministry of Health and the Ministry of Education, was established with the mission of studying the problem of excessive supply and inadequate distribution of physicians in Mexico. So far, due in part to its own restricted function, this commission has acted merely as an advisory board to regional medical schools, urging the local bodies to carry out their own studies.

In recent years the applicant profile has changed, with a higher number of women entering medical school (women comprise more than 50 percent of the admission cohorts). Increasing numbers of students from lower socioeconomic levels are being admitted to public institutions and more students from higher socioeconomic levels are entering private medical schools.

CURRICULAR STRUCTURE AND INNOVATION

Two main types of medical curricula are seen at present. The most common is patterned after the Flexnerian model, with a strong emphasis on basic sciences (the first two years of the course) and hospital-based clinical teaching (two additional years). Students are required to spend a fifth and final year in a pregraduate internship, plus one year following graduation in a public service assignment (the Medical Social Service requirement). The other curriculum is oriented toward integrated, comprehensive clinical medicine, with an emphasis on preventive care and community based instruction. This plan was often piloted as an innovative program. However, traditional and innovative curricula, though differing in course content and strategies, appear very similar when clinical teaching and learning activities are considered. In both programs, students examine hospital patients and review clinical records which they discuss with house officers or residents.

Unfortunately, clinical personnel with teaching duties in outpatient departments or health centers often lack the specific training to perform successfully as instructors of clinical medicine, within an operational health service model not corresponding to a comprehensive health care approach. These inadequacies indirectly reinforce the students' tendency to model their careers after those of the prestigious clinical specialists working in tertiary-level hospitals using the latest technological innovations.

Some efforts have been made to promote educational theory, methods, and technology in medical education, but it has been difficult to involve clinicians who often consider professional competence equivalent to good teaching and disregard pedagogic training. For instance, little progress has been achieved in promoting humanistic aspects of medicine, when current practice concentrates on most recent medical technologies.

GRADUATE MEDICAL EDUCATION

It is difficult for a physician to qualify for a position in a health institution, public or private, and to be accepted by the society at large, without residency training in one of the medical specialties. The residency program constitutes the hallmark of competence and the source of confidence for both doctors and institutions alike. Accordingly, special efforts have been made by medical schools and health institutions to develop graduate education programs of high quality. Admission to a residency program requires that all applicants competing for the available positions pass a National Examination of Medical Knowledge. Selections are made according to examination grades. Applicants indicate their choice of specialty and preferred training institution at the time of admission. The acceptance rate depends on the institutional needs for certain specialists and the educational capacity of the specific area. In the last year approximately 40 percent of all applicants were admitted (i.e., 3,730 individuals from nearly 10,000 applications). There are no specific labor plans for physicians who do not achieve graduate training.

Most residency programs are from two to five years in length. The majority of surgical subspecialties require one or two prior years of general surgery, and basic training in internal medicine or general pediatrics is required for most medical subspecialties. The most popular specialties are general surgery, gynecology and obstetrics, internal medicine, and pediatrics, which together account for more than half of all the admissions. Anesthesiology accounts for 10 percent of admissions, orthopedics for 5 percent, and radiology for 25 percent, followed by the other specialties. Pathology has few applicants, and the interest in family practice has decreased considerably in the last several years; in other branches of medicine, including otolaryngology, ophthalmology, and genetics there are more applicants than positions, and thus, admission is highly selective.

LICENSURE

Licenses to practice medicine are issued by the Director of Professional Activities of the Ministry of Education upon the presentation of the diploma issued by a university or medical school. The diploma is delivered upon satisfactory completion of all the curricular activities and the submission of the report of Medical Social Service or, in some schools, of an individual research report. Individual schools administer a mandatory multiple choice, general comprehensive examination. To evaluate the professional competence of graduates, most schools have implemented a practical type of clinical examination based on the study of selected patients.

Board Certification for Specialists

Specialists are eligible for certification by any of 39 existing specialty boards in Mexico. The certifying tests cover basic and applied knowledge and include practical examinations using selected patients. Specialty boards do have an impact on curricula and training in relation to the orientation of residency programs but do not influence undergraduate teaching activities

Cross-Licensing of Physicians

Generally, it is difficult for foreign doctors to revalidate university studies, but either through testing or administrative action, some individuals are allowed to practice medicine in Mexico. This is the case for those physicians who, for political reasons, have received asylum in Mexico (according to historic Mexican policies) and are able to obtain the permit to practice medicine once they have produced evidence of past university studies.

CONTINUING MEDICAL EDUCATION

Continuing medical education is available both to physicians employed by an institution and to those devoted exclusively to private practice. The former have access to structured institution-based activities--mainly refresher courses--on diagnostic or therapeutic aspects in any of the specialty fields, including family practice. Some courses are compulsory for certain physicians, but the majority are freely selected. Professionals have the opportunity to take in-service training courses in specific subjects. They also can work closely with colleagues in the same field of interest or in other type of medical activities. There are no compulsory courses.

When doctors in private practice are located in large urban settings, they can choose from a variety of courses offered by educational or health service institutions, or local medical societies. Generally, courses consist only of lectures and are of a few hours' or days' duration. Both institutional and private physicians join in continuing education to secure the credits needed either for job promotion or to comply with specific specialty board requirements.

There is an increasing acceptance by doctors of the need to participate in continuing medical education activities, probably because of the orientation toward independent study and self-learning skills at the undergraduate level.

ROLE OF RESEARCH IN MEDICAL EDUCATION

Some medical schools located in the largest cities and organized under a departmental structure carry out basic biomedical research. Researchers have both lecture and clinical teaching responsibilities at the undergraduate level. In recent years, the promotion of academic tutorials has been useful in recruiting bright young people into science. However, most researchers have no pedagogic background and do not feel committed to teaching, so they are motivated to restrict their best efforts to graduate students. Furthermore, heavy pressure on scientists and difficulties in obtaining the necessary funding for research projects has discouraged many promising young professionals from joining the scientific ranks. Instead, they prefer to devote themselves to highly remunerative and socially satisfying medical practice. The emphasis on research varies significantly from school to school (De la Fuente, Martuscelli, and Alarcón 1990).

Student interest in research, stimulated by basic science teachers in the first years of medical school, is frequently lost when students begin clinical training in hospitals where there is less interest in research. However, in the large hospitals, the national institutes, and medical centers of the social security subsystem, clinical investigators influence graduate medical students and the residents being trained as specialists. Frequently, the clinical investigator is productive as a researcher in a particular biomedical branch as well as a successful practitioner, thus becoming an attractive role model for young residents working in the area.

Financial support for research comes primarily from the university budget and from different government agencies. In addition, it is often possible to secure economic support for clinical research from national and international foundations. In recent years a keen interest has developed in educational research--especially that focused on topics such as valuation, teaching and learning strategies, motivational studies, curriculum development. Researchers in this area are highly motivated teachers with solid background in education, psychology, and other related disciplines.

GOVERNMENT/PRIVATE SECTOR INVOLVEMENT

Private enterprises have founded medical schools within universities or as autonomous entities. Fees and tuition are much higher than those of public institutions, and frequently, stricter requirements are set for both students and faculty. Curricula in these schools do not differ from those of the official schools. They tend to emphasize traditional aspects of education and health care--those typical of individual-based medicine, curative approach, and the use of latest medical technology.

In private schools the basic sciences are taught in their own facilities; very seldom do they engage in any type of research activity. In the clinical phase of the educational process, some private schools have access to their own university hospitals but most depend primarily on public facilities, such as government hospitals and health centers. Accordingly, both the type of practice and the instructional activities are very similar in private and public medical schools.

INTERNATIONAL LINKAGES AND COLLABORATION

In 1957 the Mexican Association of Medical Schools (AMFEM) was created and launched a national academic-administrative program to promote medical education. As a consequence, a close relation was established between AMFEM and other international organizations such as the Panamerican Federation of Associations of Medical Schools (PAFAMS), the World Federation of Medical Education, and the Latin American Union of Universities. With a higher level awareness, some commitment has been made to views expressed in the Alma Ata Declaration of 1978 (including its primary care strategy), and the Edinburgh Declaration of 1988 (World Federation of Medical Education 1988). However, since some of these linkages arise from personal relationships, their implied commitments often do not filter down into the operational ranks and even less so into clinical practice. Though they represent sound concepts, which are invaluable as reference marks and goals for the future endeavors of medical education, ideas originating in the international community have, as yet, had only a modest impact on the educational process or clinical practice in Mexico.

ISSUES AND TRENDS

In considering trends of medical education in Mexico it is necessary to be aware of the future national and regional epidemiological situation, its transitional characteristics, and the type of socioeconomic factors present, including the response of society itself through the type and amount of services provided (Bankowsky and Mejía 1987).

Today (1993), Mexico faces a profound socioeconomic crisis that has affected both the efficacy and the quality of health care services. The excessive urban concentration, followed by an inordinate proportion of doctors in the largest cities, has accentuated regional differences and the marginality of rural populations, who often fall under the care of poorly qualified auxiliaries. Under these conditions the challenge of medical education is to provide new tools and/or perspectives in looking for better training and the development of more helpful attitudes among future physicians.

At present, the 40 percent of graduates who enter specialty training can look forward to probable employment in some type of medical institution, whether public or private. The remaining 60 percent, work as private general practitioners in any city or town, using whatever knowledge and skills they achieved during their medical studies.

To obtain a balance between the needs of the population, the operation of health services, and the fulfillment of educational objectives, all medical students should acquire the following: (1) the knowledge and abilities to perform as good general or family doctors, mastering the principles of primary health and comprehensive medical care of individuals, families, and social groups, and (2) the training and capacity to successfully pursue further levels of graduate medical studies including sophisticated and highly technical subspecialties. During specialty training, the health service system, supported by the universities, must assure, through adequate supervision and evaluation, that educational goals and objectives are reached. On the other hand, when doctors do practice without residency training, the full responsibility for their performance will fall upon the medical schools, where they should obtain the knowledge and skills to provide the best care to individuals, families, and social groups.

From a formal standpoint, the recommendations in 1988 from AMFEM and the Ministry of Health to the World Conference on Medical Education in Edinburgh, and as stated in the project titled Medical Education in the Americas (EMA), and carried out by PAFAMS under the auspices of the Kellogg Foundation, point to the following critical issues for the future of medical education: (1) to adapt the professional profile of physicians to the actual needs of the society, securing a sound general professional education; (2) to reach a balance among the knowledge, skills, values, and attitudes that students require in order to deliver effective health care and to continue learning through independent study; and (3) to promote the highest cooperation and coordination between the health services and the educational institutions.

REFERENCES

Bankowsky, Z., and A. Mejía. 1987. *Health manpower out of balance: Conflicts and prospects*. Geneva: CIOMS.

Consejo Asesor en Epidemiología. 1990. México: Información Prioritaria en Salud, SSA. México.

De la Fuente, J.R., J. Martuscelli, y D. Alarcón, eds. 1990. La investigación en salud: balance y transición. México: Fondo de Cultura Económica.

FEPAFEM. 1990. *Educación Médica en las Américas. El Reto de los Años 90*. Federación Panamericana de Facultades (Escuelas) de Medicina. vol. 17. Caracas: Fondo Editorial FEPAFEM.(Cited as FEPAFEM.)

Hernández, A. 1982. *Estado Actual de la Educación Médica en México*. México: AMFEM.

Laguna, J., et al. 1974. Plan de Estudios Experimental de Medicina General (Plan A-36). *Educación Médica y Salud* 2:205-225.

Narro Robles, J., et al. 1990. Challenges in medical education in Mexico (Los desafíos de la Educación Médica en México). México, D.F.: UNAM.

Soberón, G., J. Kumate, and J. Laguna. 1988. La Salud en México: Testimonios 1988. México: Fondo de Cultura Económica.

Villalpando-Casas, J., et al. 1988. Los estudios de Especialización en Medicina. (Specializing studies in medicine). Ciencia y Desarrollo 110. CONACYT 79:113.

World Federation for Medical Education. 1988. Edinburgh Declaration. World Conference on Medical Education. Edinburgh, Scotland: World Federation for Medical Education.

World Health Organization. 1978. Alma Ata Declaration. *Report of the Conference on Primary Health Care at Alma Ata, USSR, 6-12 September*. Geneva: WHO.

Table 20.1
Mexico--Medical School Demographics

Medical School	Undergraduate Admissions Fall 1991--Male	Undergraduate Admissions Fall 1991--Female	Under-graduates Graduating 1991	Interns Fall 1990
1. Aguascalientes, AGS	41	31	61	25
2. Mexicali, BAJA CALIF.	37	39	54	21
3. Tijuana, BAJA CALIF.	48	52	65	46
4. Xochicalco, BAJA CALIF.	22	11	7	0
5. Campeche, CAMP.	40	18	16	20
6. Saltillo, COAH.	27	40	29	25
7. Torreón, COAH.	42	39	62	36
8. Colima, COL.	26	30	47	3
9. Ciudad Juárez, CHIH.	31	16	112	12
10. Chihuahua, CHIH.	55	41	55	32
11. Chiapas, CHIS	33	20	35	18
12. Durango, DGO.	19	14	29	44
13. Gómez Palacio, DGO.	21	12	15	3
14. Guerrero, GRO.	*320		177	84
15. León, GTO.	46	30	51	32
16. Hidalgo, HGO.	70	87	116	38
17. U. Aut. Guadalajara, JAL.	76	50	396	205
18. U. de Guadalajara, JAL.	164	171	305	319
19. Anáhuac, Mexico City	90	43	45	27
20. IPN, Mexico City	153	207	207	154
21. CICS, IPN, Mexico City	--	--	--	24

Table 20.1
Mexico--Medical School Demographics

Medical School	Undergraduate Admissions Fall 1991--Male	Undergraduate Admissions Fall 1991--Female	Under-graduates Graduating 1991	Interns Fall 1990
22. Homeopatía IPN, Mexico City	27	43	41	6
23. Homeopatía Libre, Mexico City	14	8	12	--
24. Médico Militar, Mexico City	78	46	30	1
25. La Salle, Mexico City	*80		116	52
26. UAM Xochimilco, Mexico City	*110		61	32
27. UNAM, C.U., Mexico City	530	674	945	709
28. UNAM, Iztacala, Mexico City	251	330	399	173
29. UNAM Zaragoza, Mexico City	92	101	140	66
30. Toluca, MEX.	98	110	92	78
31. Michoacán, MICH.	577	513	358	207
32. Cuernavaca, MOR.	38	37	45	34
33. Nayarit, NAY.	327	372	48	13
34. Montemorelos, N.L.	29	13	15	4
35. Tec. Monterrey, N.L.	16	10	21	10
36. U. de Monterrey, N.L.	*60		55	10
37. U. de Neuvo Leon, N.L.	426	364	368	0
38. Oaxaca, Oax	259	199	110	59
39. Sureste, Oax	29	20	7	14
40. Popular de Puebla, PUE.	60	60	41	38

Table 20.1
Mexico--Medical School Demographics

Medical School	Undergraduate Admissions Fall 1991--Male	Undergraduate Admissions Fall 1991--Female	Under-graduates Graduating 1991	Interns Fall 1990
41. U. de Puebla, PUE.	*1,678		435	131
42. Querétaro, QRO.	28	27	35	29
43. San Luis Potosí, S.L.P.	72	60	69	64
44. Sinaloa, SIN.	*289		168	54
45. Tabasco, TAB.	*151		57	35
46. Matamoros, TAMPS.	38	50	57	12
47. Mexico Americano, TAMPS.	5	5	10	0
48. Noroeste, TAMPS.	42	40	47	24
49. Tampico, TAMPS.	46	55	98	60
50. Valle del Bravo, TAMPS.	3	4	18	1
51. Ciudad Mendoza, TAMPS.	45	44	74	38
52. Jalapa, VER.	*129		147	89
53. Poza Rica, VER.	*126		86	28
54. Minatitlán, VER.	42	36	67	30
55. Veracruz, VER.	96	104	148	78
56. Yucatan, YUC.	83	67	171	94
57. Zacatecas. ZAC.	120	102	121	33
Total no. Medical Schools	Total Students		Total Graduates	Total Interns
57	11,792		6,616	3,494

*includes male and female

21

The Netherlands

PETER A.J. BOUHUIJS

The Netherlands is a small country in Western Europe of approximately forty thousand square kilometers. Many areas of the country have been reclaimed from the sea. Twenty-seven percent of the country lies below sea level, and about 60 percent of the population lives in this area. The country is densely populated, increasing from about four million in 1880 to about 15.1 million in 1991 (442 people per square kilometer). About two-thirds of the population lives in urban or suburban areas. For many years the birthrate was higher in the Netherlands than in neighboring countries. This factor, combined with a low infant mortality and a favorable life expectancy, produced a considerable annual population growth until 1970. Since 1970, however, the situation has changed. In a few years the birthrate declined sharply, from 16 per thousand inhabitants in 1970 to 12.9 per thousand inhabitants in 1976, as a reflection of the changes in attitude toward birth control and of other changes in life-style. Population forecasts proved to be dramatically wrong; the current population is about 15 percent less than expected twenty years ago. Due to increased immigration and a slight increase in the birthrate over the past few years (13.2 per thousand in 1990), the population will increase with a growth rate of about 0.5 percent during this decade.

Industrial and trade activities are the most important income sources for the national economy. According to generally accepted indices of national health conditions, the Netherlands is in a rather good position in comparison with many other countries. Perinatal death is 9.6 per thousand live births (1990), among the lowest rates in the world. According to the *Statistisch Jaarboek,* average life expectancy at birth was 73.8 years for men and 80.1 for women in 1991 (1992). The sex difference in life expectancy is mainly due to the higher risks of lung cancer, heart failure and traffic accidents among men. A generous social system has resulted in a society in which almost everybody lives in housing which has a safe water supply, sanitary facilities, and electricity. Irrespective of their income situation, the population has access to a sophisticated network of health services.

OVERVIEW OF THE HEALTH CARE DELIVERY SYSTEM

The Netherlands does not have an integrated national health service and public health care system, but rather a mixture of services developed largely through private enterprise. The role of the government has been traditionally to stimulate these services by direct subsidies, by social and health legislation, and by establishing additional services. The government's role in health care is administered through the Ministry of Welfare, Health, and Cultural Affairs (Ministerie van Welzijn, Volksgezondheid en Cultuur). Health care is heavily regulated by national laws and procedures, but the implementation of the system is left to private organizations, rather than government agencies. Advisory councils and boards play an important role in policy-making. Their major function is to assure the cooperation of providers, insurance agencies, and consumers in policy-making.

Historically, general practitioners have held a strong position in the health care system of the Netherlands. This position is reinforced by social insurance and private health insurance regulations, which require in most cases that specialist care and hospital treatment can be refunded only if prescribed by a general practitioner (GP). Most general practitioners are in private practice. They do not have hospital privileges, and work in offices outside the hospitals. In order to be registered as a GP, a physician must finish a two-year postgraduate training program in general practice. There are about 6,400 general practitioners in the Netherlands. They provide an easily accessible network of services. More than eighty percent of the population lives within one mile of the nearest GP office (De leefsituatie 1989). About fifty percent of general practitioners still work in solo practices. The proportion of GPs working in group practices or primary care centers is increasing, reflecting a different view of younger physicians on primary care delivery.

In clinical health care, the government sees its role in the creation of appropriate conditions for responsible private actions. The basic policy framework consists of several laws regulating the health sector. The Hospital Provisions Act (Wet Ziekenhuisvoorzieningen) of 1971 regulates the construction and renovation of institutions. Based on this law the government formulated a national norm of 3.7 hospital beds per one thousand population. During the last ten years, some hospitals closed, others reduced their number of beds, and some mergers have been effected. Total number of hospitals decreased from 231 in 1980 to 169 in 1990. Overall, the number of beds decreased from 73,150 in 1980 to 64,580 in 1990. In 1983, a new Health Care Provisions Law (Wet Voorzieningen Gezondheidszorg) gave the government additional powers to control health care facilities, including non-hospitals.

The Health Care Charges Law (Wet Tarieven Gezondheidszorg) came into effect in 1982. Under its provisions, all charges and fees in the health care sector are regulated. The Central Health Care Charges Agency (Centraal Orgaan Tarieven Gezondheidszorg), made up of representatives of employers, employees, institutions, doctors' organizations, funding bodies, and independent experts has the responsibility of drawing up guidelines for the setting of charges and fees. Each general hospital is now under a global budget, a form of prospective payment. Medical equipment is included in the budget. Potential investment in equipment is based on a formula including number of beds and number of specialists in the hospital. However, the actual amount is determined in negotiation. The government has the authority to reduce fees to standardize incomes for the professions. However, this is seldom done. Although these laws do not provide the government direct power in health manpower planning in the medical specialties, clearly the control over budgets and facilities places the Minister of Health in a strong position in negotiations with the specialty boards. Specialist care is provided by about twelve thousand two hundred registered specialists. Their number increased considerably until 1989, but has been stable since as a consequence of a sharp reduction of residency slots. Residency places were reduced in the early 1980s when it became clear that future manpower needs would be considerably lower in view of the slower growth of the population.

Mental health and long-term care services are provided by a mix of private and public institutions. However, the government has followed a policy of reducing the size and number of institutions and effectuating alternatives to institutionalization through ambulatory and home care services. About one thousand physicians work in these institutions. The number of physicians working in nursing homes for the elderly is rapidly increasing, reflecting the increased needs of geriatric care for a growing number of elderly in the population.

The government has the primary responsibility for providing preventive care services. Since the early 1970s, the Dutch government has set itself the specific goal of encouraging preventive and primary care and reducing institutionalization. A system for providing preventive care to the entire population was developed through *Basisgezondheidszorgdiensten* (basic health care services). Public and private institutions are a part of this system. The system provides preventive care such as baby and toddlers' clinics, school health services, immunization, infectious disease control, and health education. About twenty-two hundred physicians are registered as public health physicians.

The quality of health care delivery is controlled by a system of national and regional inspectorates. There are seven state inspectorates, including one on health, one on mental health, one on drugs, and so forth. The inspectorates can evaluate health care activities, have the authority to inspect institutions, and have a prosecuting function in case of complaints or negligence. The inspectorates are related to the Ministry of Health, but are independent agencies. The National Organization for Quality Assurance in Hospitals, CBO, is an independent foundation financed by the hospitals, which plays a leading role in the development and implementation of quality assurance systems in Dutch hospitals.

Financing of Health Care

Health care costs rose 11 to 18 percent per year between 1973 and 1977. By 1980, health care expenditures accounted for 8.4 percent of gross national product. Cost reduction policies, some of which were mentioned before, were reflected in lower growth rates of about 6 percent per year between 1985 and 1990. In 1990, the total expenditure on health care was 8 percent of the gross national product. Analyses of the increase in diagnostic and therapeutic services have highlighted the issue of the use of health care technology. It will, nonetheless, be particularly hard to restrain costs in the future because of expected technological advances, consumer pressure, and the aging of the population.

The insurance system can be divided into three parts. The first is sick fund insurance, which is a compulsory insurance scheme dating from 1941. Sick fund insurance (Ziekenfondsverzekering) covers about 60 percent of the population. Members of the scheme include employees whose total wages fall below a certain level, people living on welfare payments, and those over the age of 65 with incomes below a certain level. The scheme covers almost completely the lower and middle income groups. The benefit package is comprehensive, including so-called "closed" benefits, such as specialist care, which are paid for under a philosophy of accepted medical practice. The sick fund insurance is administered by independent sick funds. Usually their boards include representatives of health professionals, employers, and clients. The sick funds are supervised by the Sick Funds Council (*Ziekenfondsraad*), representing government, employers, unions, sick funds, institutions, and professionals. The Council approves agreements between sick funds and providers and advises the Minister of Health concerning the premiums of the insurance schemes. The Council also develops the package of health care benefits included in the insurance.

The second part is voluntary private insurance, which is utilized by most of the remaining 40 percent of the population. Though similar to sick fund insurance, provisions may vary somewhat from company to company. Hospital and specialist care are ordinarily included, but general practitioner care may not be fully covered. Deductibles and coinsurance are common.

The third part is the General Insurance Against Special Sickness Costs (Algemene Wet Bijzondere Ziektekosten, AWBZ), established in 1968 legislation. Every resident of the Netherlands is compulsorily insured by this fund, and the employers of all those over a certain income level must pay premiums. This insurance finances the most expensive forms of care, including long-term care, nursing homes, and mental health services. Although expensive technological services such as those for end-stage renal disease, including renal transplant, are sometimes covered for the entire population by this insurance plan, it is not analogous to catastrophic insurance, which might primarily involve high-technology services. Since 1980 home care services have been provided by AWBZ. Currently, the government is trying to use this law to convert the various health insurance schemes into one national insurance system. One of the main reasons is that older people (a rapidly increasing proportion of the population) are covered automatically by the sick funds scheme. The effect is that private insurance companies have a more limited risk than the sick funds. Consequently, they can set a lower insurance than the sick funds. This results in the paradoxical situation in which higher-income groups pay less for their insurance than middle-income groups. By including more health services under the AWBZ, this effect would disappear. It is feared however, that without strong additional changes in the coverage of such a national insurance, the costs of health care will increase rapidly.

Specialists are paid fee-for-service for all patients, both those with sick fund insurance and private patients. Fees are set in negotiations between the organizations of physicians (Landelijke Specialisten Vereniging and Landelijke Huisartsen Vereniging) and the sick funds. Fees for private patients can be much higher. Technical specialties of medicine such as radiology have the highest incomes among physicians. The relatively high fees for specialists services have been heavily criticized in recent years. General practitioners are paid on a capitation basis for sick fund patients and on a fee-for-service basis for private patients. Fees for private patients are comparable to payment from sick fund patients.

There is great concern about the considerable increase in the cost of health care. In spite of the changes in policies introduced over the past ten years, the system of health services displays insufficient cohesion. There is a lack of coordination between services at different levels as well as between those at the same level, thus causing a duplication of care in some instances. The present structure for the financing of health care is fragmented and obscure; in certain cases it does not foster the necessary collaboration between the services. Because financing adapts passively to existing organizational situations, it does not exert sufficient corrective influence on the coordination of the various services. As one of the means of arriving at an effective and efficient health care system, the government tried for a long time to implement a regionalization policy, which was still based on nationally set standards. In recent years, there has been a tendency to allow market forces to play a role in fighting the inefficiencies. As a first step, sick funds and private insurance companies are allowed to merge, and to negotiate individually with care providers. This more active role for insurers could lead to development of health maintenance organizations with more direct influence on health care delivery. It remains to be seen whether these innovations can be effective in a country with a strong tradition of policy making based on societal consensus.

HISTORICAL BACKGROUND

The three oldest medical schools in the country, Leiden, Groningen, and Utrecht, were established between 1575 and 1636, as parts of newly founded universities. At that time, the Netherlands had only recently become an independent state, one hospitable to the new ideas of the Renaissance. Leiden in particular developed itself rapidly as a center of excellence among the West-European universities. Initially the study of medicine was merely a specialization following a general study of philosophy, classical grammar, arts, mathematics, science, and astronomy, and the emphasis was largely theoretical. Hermann Boerhaave (1668-1738), a famous physician, chemist, and botanist, is acknowledged as a teacher emphasizing an empirical approach to medicine; he was the first teacher who tried to integrate the newly discovered basic science concepts in clinical medicine. Bedside teaching became an important part of the study of medicine in Leiden. The first national law on medical education and licensure was passed in 1865. At that time Amsterdam was added as the fourth medical school. Since the last quarter of the nineteenth century, several new universities have been founded, reflecting the increasing importance of science and technology for the national economy. The expansion of medical education in this century was generally in line with the rapid growth of the population and the increasing role of medicine. The Calvinist Free University in Amsterdam (1907), the Catholic University of Nijmegen (1951), the Erasmus University in Rotterdam (1966), and the University of Limburg in Maastricht (1974) all developed medical schools.

ROLE OF NATIONAL POLICY IN SHAPING MEDICAL EDUCATION

See "Overview of the Health Care Delivery System" and "Curricular Structure."

ADMISSION

The Netherlands has eight Faculties of Medicine with a total annual student intake of 1,485. The government controls both the total numbers of admissions and that of each school. Most students start their studies immediately following six years in secondary school. Secondary education in the Netherlands is tracked according to abilities. Selection for one of the tracks takes place after finishing primary school or after one year of secondary education. The pre-university track, called VWO, is concluded with a final exam in seven subjects, including at least Dutch, English, science, and chemistry. Fifty percent of the exam consists of national tests, the other 50 percent of local school tests. By law, this exam grants the right of access to any university course. However, since 1974 admission to medical school has been restricted, and students are submitted to a national admission procedure. Small numbers of places are reserved for applicants without a regular Dutch diploma, and for specific exceptional cases. All other students are placed in various categories based on their national secondary school exam results in the seven subjects. Within each category of students, a lottery determines which receive the right to start their studies in medicine; however, higher school exam marks will improve an individual's chances in the lottery. Applicants have the right to apply for admission in consecutive years. Although this procedure initially met with national and international skepticism, it has been used since 1974. The number of applicants did not increase over the years, and is generally about 2.5 times the number of places available (1991: 3,143 applicants; 1992: 3,255 applicants). After the general admission, the accepted candidates are divided over the available places in the medical schools. Each school has a fixed number of places, which has not changed since 1984. An administrative committee of the joint medical schools reviews the admission requests of the candidates, which contain a first and second choice for a medical school and a short personal statement explaining the motivation for the choice indicated. Candidates are placed as much as possible according to their expressed first preference. There are no personal interviews at any point in the admission procedure. Since some schools consistently are more popular among students, the committee ranks candidates according to their motivation for the most popular schools. The proportion of women in the applicants pool has increased over the last 20 years. For the past few years, about sixty percent of the first-year students have been women.

Financial Aspects of Medical Education

All medical schools are completely funded by the Ministry of Education for their basic teaching and research efforts. The ministry also provides funds for the extra infrastructure in the academic health centers needed for teaching and research. The budgets for teaching, research and services are clearly separated, but the university has the right to redistribute the total budget according to its needs. In teaching, a national budget system for all university studies was developed about ten years ago. Roughly, this results in about one full-time teacher for every ten medical students. Clinical education is included in this system, which means that hospitals are paid by the medical school for their teaching efforts.

All Dutch students receive a student grant, which includes free public transportation throughout the country. The grant covers about 50 percent of the total costs for education, housing, food and health insurance for an average student. Students from lower income groups receive additional financial support, usually a mixture of a grant and a loan. Most of the research funds are now dependent upon five-year, peer-reviewed research programs involving at least five full-time equivalents of researchers. Since this system is not linked to student numbers, there is some variety in the number of research places among Faculties. Funding from other sources, such as national research funds, foundations, and industry plays an increasingly important role.

CURRICULAR STRUCTURE AND INNOVATION

Until the mid-1960s, curricula were shaped according to the continental tradition of the nineteenth century. The program lasted seven years, but it usually took students much longer to graduate. There was a strict distinction between the preclinical and the clinical phase. Zoology, botany, inorganic chemistry and physics were part of the first-year curriculum. The typical timetable for students was lectures in the morning and lab work in the afternoon. The final years consisted of clerkships in a large hospital. The Academic Statute, the legal framework for all university studies in the Netherlands, prescribed which subjects should be examined after each phase. A change in curriculum therefore required a change in national legislation. As in the area of health, the Netherlands has a tradition of central decision making in the area of higher education. Appointments of full professors had to be approved by the Queen. The procedure included the stipulation that the other medical schools would second the faculty's recommendation to the Minister of Education to appoint a candidate. Within the medical schools, full professors had the power in all academic affairs. It is easy to conclude that this state of affairs did not stimulate innovations.

According to a recently completed national review of medical schools (VSNU 1992), three factors were responsible for fundamental changes since the mid-1960s: (1) The rapid development of medicine and other sciences. Since these developments could not easily be introduced because of the structure of the Academic Statute, parliament accepted a new Statute in which for all university studies a more comprehensive statement of the objectives was accepted, now permitting a faster response to changes without a revision in the law. (2) The rapidly rising costs of university education stimulated the universities to review their educational practices. Following the example of the University of Technology in Eindhoven in 1963, all universities established centers for higher education research and development. Most medical schools founded their own departments of medical education. (3) Student revolts at the end of the 1960s resulted in changes in the governance of the universities. New legislation provided that associate and assistant professors, non-academic staff, and students have representation on decision-making and advisory bodies.

In 1965, the undergraduate curriculum was reduced to six years, as a result of the introduction of mandatory postgraduate training for general practitioners. By law, there are exams after years one, four, and six. The new graduates are called "basic physicians." Most Faculties reduced their curriculum by cutting back on zoology, science, and botany. Since new topics were introduced, in particular social sciences, the curriculum remained overcrowded. The new legislation allowed the Faculties more flexibility. Small scale innovations, aimed at bridging the gap between the preclinical and the clinical part of the curriculum were tried out in various programs.

In 1974, the Faculty of Medicine of the University of Limburg (Maastricht) accepted its first cadre of students. Since the need to produce more physicians vanished during the planning stage of this new Faculty, its founders decided for political reasons to promote a different approach to medical education in order to gain approval for the new school to open. The basic philosophy of the new school stressed a primary care orientation and the use of effective teaching approaches as the mission of the school. Following the model of McMaster University in Canada, Maastricht became the second medical school in the world to implement a problem-based curriculum, and the first one applying this educational strategy in a six-year curriculum.

Barrows (1984), one of the founders of this method, explains that in problem-based learning, three important goals of professional education are advanced. These are acquiring knowledge that can be remembered and applied, learning to learn (self-directed learning) and learning to analyze and solve problems. Problem-based learning is an educational method that can be characterized as follows: to start the learning sequence, a problem is presented to the student, i.e., prior to studying the problem-relevant subject matter. It is the student's task to analyze the problem (which is usually done in a small group). The group initially tries to make a provisional analysis of the problem on the basis of available prior knowledge. In the course of that analysis, there will be questions about a number of things that have not been understood, clarified or explained. This creates the basis for formulating learning objectives for self-directed study. After the self-study phase, students verify in a next session to what extent they now have a better understanding of the problem.

At the start, there was widespread skepticism whether problem-based learning could be implemented for students, who are considerably younger than McMaster students and who are not specifically selected for such a program. Like the University of Newcastle, Australia, the Maastricht school chose a more structured approach to problem-based learning. Specific introductory courses were developed to orient the students to this approach, and problems were selected so that their level of complexity would match the sophistication of the learner. Other innovative aspects included early exposure to patient care in the first year, clinical skills training, involving a wide range of simulation techniques such as manikins and simulated patients, a three-month clerkship in general practice, annual objective structured clinical exams (OSCE) for each student, and the development of a comprehensive knowledge test.

Economic recession forced the government to change its long-term policy of expansion of higher education in the early 1980s. Since universities receive most of their income from direct government grants, they were hit hard by these changes occurring over a period of a few years. New budget systems were introduced for undergraduate education resulting in a lower appropriation; research grants were no longer dependent on student numbers, but awarded on a competitive basis; Faculties were forced to cooperate in certain areas; the number of senior staff positions was cut nationally; and all teachers had to take a salary cut of about 5 percent. The government showed great determination in forcing these cuts by setting examples. In dentistry, three out of six schools were closed, including the oldest school which had just moved into a new building. Medical schools were forced to reduce their student intake by about 20 percent, a sensible reduction in view of the rising unemployment of physicians. As a result of these measures, public expenditure on higher education declined between 1983 and 1987. Since the new budget regulations were more dependent upon faculty performance, medical schools needed to introduce real changes. With the exception of Maastricht, which fit well in the new system, most Faculties had to introduce new curricula that were less overloaded to allow students to finish their studies without great delay. Modular courses, integrated teaching, small group learning, skills training in the early years, better assessment methods, and improved student counseling facilities were introduced in several Faculties. As a result, the curricula are more student-centered than a decade ago, and the revised legislation provided opportunities to pay more attention to topics such as epidemiology, health economics, AIDS, and geriatric problems.

Clinical education in the undergraduate curriculum still takes place largely during the last two years. Each medical school is linked to one medical center, called the academic hospital. The responsibilities and budgets are separate, with the Faculty of Medicine being responsible for teaching and research, the hospital for medical services. The Dean of the medical school has no seat on the hospital board. Originally, these hospitals were developed as training facilities, and only indigent patients would go there for treatment. The academic medical center also was the place where clinical faculty could practice medicine. After World War II, academic hospitals increasingly became centers of excellence, having a referral function for general hospitals. Postgraduate training functions also became more prominent, and, the increasing research base for clinical staff gained more prominence. As a result, the academic hospital is less suited for its original use, the training of undergraduates. All medical schools also have contracts with a limited number of general hospitals. Originally, these contracts were made because of inadequate training facilities in academic hospitals. Today, these so-called affiliated hospitals are still needed because students may have a chance to see "ordinary" hospital patients. About 50 percent of the places needed for clinical training are provided by affiliated hospitals. However, most exams must be taken at the Faculty of Medicine. A recent national survey (Metz, Bulte, and van Paridon 1990) reported considerable variety in clinical training. The clinical phase averages 85 weeks; most Faculties have long lists of required clerkships and provide little opportunity for electives; most schools require students to have their clerkships in several hospitals; all schools have a required clerkship in general practice, but it varies in length from two to 12 weeks. As a follow-up of the survey, a national working group has been set up by the medical schools to develop national objectives and recommendations for the clinical part of the curriculum, which could be used to reduce the current variety in models.

GRADUATE MEDICAL EDUCATION

Legally, the final medical school exam is the licensing exam allowing the graduate to practice medicine. However, in reality this right is restricted because insurance organizations will reimburse only those physicians registered as general practitioners or medical specialists. Postgraduate training is a requirement for such registration. Graduate education is divided in three areas: general practice, clinical specialties, and public health. (See table 21.1, p. 315).

General practice.   Rules and regulations for the two-year program are formulated by the College of Family Medicine, set up by the Royal Dutch Medical Association. The College consists of representatives of the general practitioners' association, the government, departments of general practice of the medical schools, health insurance organizations, and trainees. The departments of general practice of the various medical schools are the program providers. Training consists of supervised work in a general practice and hospital rotations. In line with other European countries, the training period will soon be increased to three years.

Clinical specialties.   The Central Committee, set up by the Royal Dutch Medical Association, determines which medical disciplines are recognized as a clinical specialty and stipulates the training requirements for each. It has an advisory board, the Specialist Registration Committee which is responsible for supervision of approved training programs and registers specialists who follow the required training programs.

Public health.   A Central Committee and a Specialist Registration Committee have been set up in this field with responsibilities similar to those of analogous bodies responsible governing the clinical specialties.

Most specialties have national admissions procedures and a required program. Programs are peer-reviewed regularly. In view of the reduced need for new physicians, most specialties cut the number of training places considerably in the early 1980s. Small programs were concentrated in the academic health centers and the affiliated hospitals. The medical schools have no direct influence on these programs, since the financing comes from the health budget and is given to the hospitals.

Since the number of first-year medical students was decreased after the reduction in the number of postgraduate places, and since there was a six year lead time for the limitation on medical school admissions to affect the numbers of graduates, a general shortage of graduate training places resulted. Over one thousand young physicians are still working on short-term contracts in hospitals hoping to find a training place. Many others had to give up their ambition to find a clinical training place in their chosen field, and switched to less popular branches of medicine.

Table 21.1
The Netherlands--Graduate Medical Education Overview

Specialty	Required Training Years
General Practice	3 (effective 1994)
Anesthetics	4.5
Dermatology	4
Geriatrics	5
Internal Medicine	5
Cardiology	5
Chest Medicine	5
Neurology	4
Obstetrics & Gynecology	5
Ophthalmology	4
Paediatrics	4
Pathology	4
Clinical Chemistry	4
Microbiology	4
Histopathology	5
Psychiatry	4.5
Radiodiagnosis	4

Table 21.1

The Netherlands--Graduate Medical Education Overview

Specialty	Required Training Years
Radiotherapy	4
General Surgery	6
Neurosurgery	6
Orthopaedics	6
ENT	4
Cardiac Surgery	6
Urology	6
Occupational Health	2

LICENSURE

See "Graduate Medical Education."

CONTINUING MEDICAL EDUCATION

There are no legal requirements for continuing medical education. Professional bodies, hospitals, medical schools, private foundations, and industry organize activities. In 1992 an advisory council, representing physicians, medical schools, the health inspectorate, consumers and industry advised the Minister of Health unanimously to develop an accrediting system for CME providers to assure quality. Since CME issues are part of a larger debate on relicensing requirements, no decision yet has been taken.

ROLE OF RESEARCH IN MEDICAL EDUCATION

The Dutch university system for research training traditionally consisted of a supervised research project and the writing of a thesis; no formal educational programs were provided. Since 1986, a more structured system has been introduced in all universities. Under this new scheme, graduate research students are offered four-year contracts as junior researchers. In most areas, special courses are offered during the first two years. These are developed locally and sometimes nationally. The junior researchers are supposed to spend maximally 20 percent of their working hours on teaching undergraduates. In the medical field, junior researchers consist mostly of graduates with a Master's degree in biology or health sciences and medical school graduates. Some residency programs offer residents an opportunity to undertake a research project and write a PhD thesis as part of their residency training.

ISSUES AND TRENDS

The Dutch Ministry of Health funded several scenario studies over the past ten years that provide interesting visions on possible future developments, ranging from the use of home-care technology to the future treatment of coronary artery disease. Unfortunately, no attempts have so far been made to link these studies with health manpower training. The studies do not provide a straightforward answer to the question of how the physician of the twenty-first century must work, but at least they show that the health sector is well aware of the changes in technology, delivery systems, and requirements of an aging population. Two contrary trends are visible already: the need for both the high-tech, cure-oriented specialized physician, on the one hand, and for the generalist, care-oriented physician on the other.

The European dimension will increasingly become important. Each year over two hundred Dutch physicians move permanently to another EEC country and about one hundred physicians from other EEC countries move to the Netherlands. The EEC has a generous student exchange scheme, called the ERASMUS program, which allows students to do parts of their training in another EEC-country. An increased mobility within Europe will at some point activate discussion of a European training standard for physicians. Strong national traditions must change in view of the development of a European policy in this area.

REFERENCES

Barrows, H.S. 1984. A specific, problem-based, self-directed learning method designed to teach medical problem-solving skills, self-learning skills and enhance knowledge retention and recall. In H.G. Schmidt and M.L. De Volder, eds. *Tutorials in problem-based learning*. Maastricht: Van Gorcum.

De leefsituatie van de nederlandse bevolking. 1989. The Hague: CBS.

Metz, G.C.M., J.A. Bulte, and H.I.M. van Paridon. 1990. Basisarts: bevoegd en bekwaam. Report. The Hague: Ministerie van Onderwijs en Betwnshappen.

Parkhouse, J.P., and J.P. Menu, eds. 1989. Specialized medical education in the European region. *Euro Reports and Studies* 112. Copenhagen: WHO.

Statistisch Jaarboek 1992. 1992. SDU/Ultgeverij. The Hague: CBS Publikaties.

VSNU. 1992. Onderwijsvisitatie Geneeskunde en Gezondheidswetenschappen. Utrecht. (Cited as VSNU.)

Table 21.2
Medical School Demographics--The Netherlands

University	Undergraduates 1991--M	Undergraduates 1991--F
Erasmus Universiteit Rotterdam	92	113
Katholieke Universiteit Nijmegen	75	91
Rijksuniversiteit Limburg	61	92
Rijksuniversiteit Groningen	82	127
Rijksuniversteit Leiden	73	92
Rijksuniversiteit Utrecht	58	113
Universiteit van Amsterdam	92	116
Vrije Universiteit Amsterdam	106	107
TOTAL	639	851

Table 21.3

Medical School Faculty Demographics--The Netherlands

University	Full Prof.	Assoc.	Assist.	Junior	% Women
Erasmus Universiteit Rotterdam	62	47	105	80	24%
Katholieke Universeit Nijmegen	66	61	77	59	17%
Rijksuniversiteit Limburg	48	46	130	56	19%
Rijksuniversiteit Groningen	57	73	205	28	22%
Rijksuniversteit Leiden*	61	84	138	15	18%
Rijksuniversiteit Utrecht*	64	74	192	55	29%
Universiteit van Amsterdam	65	69	158	91	22%
Vrije Universiteit Amsterdam	59	42	157	40	27%

* Includes staff for other health science programs.

22

Nigeria

OLATOYE OGUNBODE

Nigeria is a Sub-Saharan African country with a 1988 population of 112 million, distributed 85 percent in rural areas and 15 percent in urban centers. The nation's birthrate of 50.4 per 1,000 (world average 29) is countered by an infant mortality rate of 114 per 1,000 live births and a death rate of 17.1 per 1,000 (compared with the world average of 11); projections made in 1988 were for a population of 119 million in 1990 and 166 million by the year 2000. Life expectancy for males is 46.9 and for females 50.0; with expenditure for health at 3.3 percent of the GDP (*World Almanac Supplement* 1988). Indigenous medical traditions were the basis of Nigerian health care before the introduction of Western medicine. Traditional medicine still plays a role, especially in the rural areas. English is the official national language. The Nigerian Minister of Health noted in 1990 that:

Although Nigeria has no accurate data, publications from Nigerian universities and surveys conducted by various government agencies provide a good picture of the state of people's health. These sources indicate that the major health problems in Nigeria are infectious diseases, especially diarrhoeal diseases and respiratory tract infection in children. Malaria is a major cause of death for children under five. Malnutrition and poor health practices are prevalent among the population. Pregnancy and childbirth continue to constitute a major threat to the lives of women between 15 and 45 years of age. It is also estimated that the country's high mortality rates for all ages are similar to those of other developing countries. (Alike-Catha 1990)

OVERVIEW OF THE HEALTH CARE DELIVERY SYSTEM

The health care delivery system in Nigeria evolved from the public health services originating in the British Army Medical Service (Makanjuola, Osuntokun, and Erihosho 1990). Following integration of the army with the colonial government, medical care was extended to local civil servants and their families and eventually to the local population living close to government stations. Further extension of Western medicine occurred following World War II under the guidance of English expatriates. Since independence in 1960, there has been a rapid expansion of the health care system, but it retains essential elements of the British model. The present health care delivery system is formed of three tiers: primary health care under the auspices of the local government; secondary health services rendered in general or district hospitals under the supervision of the state governments; and tertiary health services provided by teaching hospitals belonging to the Federal Ministry of Health. Not all health facilities are staffed by physicians. Some physicians, perhaps half, are government employees and are paid by the respective provincial government. However, many other physicians practice privately and/or in private hospitals.

In Nigeria, on average, there is approximately one physician per 10,000 population, but physicians are not evenly distributed throughout the country; they are often reluctant to practice in underserved communities because of the lack of many basic facilities such as drinking water, waste disposal, electricity, and elementary schools. In Lagos, the former capital city, there is one physician per 500 persons, while some rural communities have only one per 200,000 population. Nurses staff most of the rural health centers; however, they are seldom adequately trained to deliver primary health care. Recently, a new category of health care provider, the community health officer (CHO)/community health extension worker (CHEW), was created to provide primary health care in rural areas. Nineteen health technology schools were recently established, one in each state, to train CHO/CHEW. Graduates of these schools are the main providers of primary health care, and they constitute the link between the community and the clinic. They are also charged with mobilizing and motivating the community for preventive measures and health promotion. They encourage community participation and integration of services.

The purchase of sophisticated medical equipment consumes a significant part of the budgetary allocation for health services, but often such equipment cannot be adequately used due to the lack of necessary skills of both health service and maintenance personnel or deficiencies in essential facilities such as electricity.

Since 1986, a new strategy has been implemented according to which every college of medicine and every school of health technology is helping a nearby local government to set up its Primary Health Care (PHC) system, which, in turn, is used as a practice site to train students in community based settings. Nonetheless, traditional medicine still plays a significant role in health care delivery. For example, it is estimated that only around twenty percent of all deliveries are supervised by trained personnel. Traditional medicine is recognized by the government, and attempts to standardize practice have been encouraged. Traditional medicine, however, is not financed by the government and there is no formal training of traditional healers as in China.

Massive international assistance is being provided from UNICEF, WHO, the World Bank, USAID, EEC, UNDP and the Ford Foundation through grants and program development not only to promote immunization, antimalaria and antidiarrheal programs, but also to upgrade health workers' skills and administrators' expertise. The government recognizes that primary health care alone cannot be effective. A stronger infrastructure is needed, and emphasis is being placed on training of health professionals to care for the community, not only for individuals. Medical schools are beginning to respond to the call for a review of their curricula to meet these emerging needs.

HISTORICAL BACKGROUND

Before the twentieth century, Nigerian physicians were trained abroad. However, the first medical program started at the Yaba College in 1934. The University of Ibadan Faculty of Medicine was established in 1948 with the goal of producing hospital-based physicians. Shortly after the country's independence in 1960, additional medical schools were established in Enugu, Lagos, Zaria and Ife. These schools can, in this context, be called the second generation medical schools, and their curricula are similar to that of Ibadan Medical School. Nigeria now has 14 medical schools graduating about 1,000 physicians annually. Students may enter medical school following 11 or 13 years of primary and secondary education, depending on the admissions track chosen. Instruction is conducted in English and the basic medical degree, Bachelor of Medicine and Bachelor of Surgery (MBBS), requires five years plus one year of internship. Governmental service after graduation is mandatory for one year.

In 1978, however, following a report of the Medical Education Working Party, the National Universities Commission recommended a more relevant educational system that was to be community oriented. This report was a significant historical landmark in the evolution of medical education in Nigeria and formed the platform for the new curricular developments at Ilorin, Bayero, and Ogun State Universities. Two other medical schools, Calabar and Maiduguri, also provided community based programs in their curricula. These schools constitute the third generation of medical schools, sharing the common feature of providing community-oriented medical education.

Medical education in Nigeria can thus be classified into two types: the traditional curriculum, characteristic of first and second generation schools; and community-based programs, characteristic to varying degrees of the third generation medical schools. However, the same core content is offered in all medical schools. With the educational academic programs strengthened by minimum academic standards for all Nigerian universities (1989), greater political approval has been given to the educational system with respect to medicine. Traditional schools are now revising their curricula in response to the national policy adopted in 1986, that makes primary health care the philosophy of health programs, and the standards adopted in 1989, that require all medical schools to devote at least 25 percent of the curriculum to community-oriented instruction.

ROLE OF NATIONAL POLICY IN SHAPING MEDICAL EDUCATION

As noted above, the National Universities Commission expects a minimum of 25 percent community oriented programs in the medical school curricula. National policy therefore provides the enabling instrument, although not backed by financial support, for the implementation of community based educational systems. It is this lack of financial base more than anything else that has constrained the progressive development of appropriate curricula in many Nigerian medical schools.

ADMISSION

There are two routes to admission in Nigeria, and both must go through the Joint Admission Matriculation Board (JAMB). The first is the Joint Matriculation Examination (JME). Entrants take a national examination and must achieve a minimum of 50 percent pass marks to be eligible for University admission. However, since the number of applicants to medicine greatly exceeds the number of places, the cutoff entry point for admission to medical school may be as high as 70 percent. This score is combined with the applicant's performance on the General Certificate of Education (GCE) ordinary level (with credits, at minimum, required in the science subjects of physics, biology, chemistry, and mathematics). Entry is into year one of the medical school program.

There is also an admission route that takes into account G.C.E. ordinary level examination scores, results as for the JME entrants, and also a high point score in the G.C.E. advanced examinations. These candidates enter year two of Medical School. Generally, candidates for admission into the Medical School must also prove proficiency in English language.

Ten percent of admissions are reserved for foreign students who are free to go through the national entry examinations or an equivalent qualification recognized by the Joint Admissions Matriculation Board. Most of the foreign students come from other African countries, and a few come from some Asian countries. Eighty to eighty-five percent of the students who matriculate into medical schools actually complete their studies and receive their degrees.

CURRICULAR STRUCTURE AND INNOVATION

The Nigerian curricular structure is based on the traditional British system, consisting of a period of 18-24 months, mainly didactic instruction in the basic sciences, followed by three years of clinical clerkship, mainly hospital-based experience. Each medical school has a curriculum committee and reviews are conducted approximately every four years.

Clinical training of medical students is generally by rotation through the various clinical disciplines, which include: laboratory sciences, obstetrics and gynecology, pediatrics, pharmacology, medicine, surgery, and community medicine.

New methods of teaching such as community experience or problem-based learning are introduced into the medical curricula through a standard process that applies to all medical schools in Nigeria. Generally, the medical faculty leadership or a faculty core group suggests guidelines for reforms. These are taken up by the appropriate faculty committee, and then the faculty board. A faculty workshop including students, is then usually organized to explain proposed changes, discuss them, and come to a consensus acceptable to the faculty and students. If the changes are major, the recommendations are forwarded to the University Senate, after which they become statutory or regulatory.

Curricular Reform

In response to federal government directives to train physicians and other health personnel to be more sensitive to community needs and more able to deliver satisfactory primary health care, the Faculty of Health Sciences at the University of Ilorin and other new medical schools adopting the philosophy of community-oriented/community-based education implemented four innovative approaches in their curricula: integrated teaching, problem-based learning, student-centered learning (i.e., encouraging independent learning versus didactic lectures) and the provision of community experience and service. In Ilorin, students begin their community rotations eight weeks after entry into the medical school, with the experience repeated again in years two, four and five. Altogether, students spend 28 weeks (12 percent of their training) in the community (Hamilton and Ogunbode 1991). Students, in their first community rotation, assume minimal responsibility for patient care, which does not exceed observation and questionaire. The community-based programs are multidisciplinary in nature, giving the students intimate knowledge of the socioeconomic status of different rural communities as they undertake demographic and priority health studies, health promotion, and primary health care delivery. Faculty from all specialties contribute in the community rotations, thus encouraging faculty members to be actively engaged and committed to the program (Ogunbode 1991). During years four and five, the community-based programs are more practically-oriented.

The medical school is for undergraduate education. At the end of year five, successful students obtain a professional degree, MBBS (Bachelor of Medicine and Bachelor of Surgery).

GRADUATE MEDICAL EDUCATION

Following the establishment of a National Postgraduate Medical College in 1976, there has been an opportunity for medical graduates to obtain specialty training within the country. These opportunities were further enhanced when Nigeria became a member of the West African Postgraduate Medical College (1979). Generally, postgraduate training programs require a minimum of four to five years after full registration as medical officers. The most popular programs are obstetrics and gynecology, surgery and internal medicine. However, as yet, relatively few physicians have qualified for full fellowship status. Accurate data are not available, but it is clear that the health care burden is so heavy that the current production of specialists does not match the requirements for satisfactory health care delivery. See table 22.2, p. 329.

LICENSURE

The professional licensing body is the Nigerian Medical and Dental Council (NMDC) set up by the government according to the Medical and Dental Act of 1963. All graduates must register with NMDC, which automatically grants the license to practice to every applicant who holds the degree of Bachelor of Medicine or Bachelor of Surgery or the equivalent from a recognized medical school and who has satisfactorily completed one year as an intern.

Accreditation

The NMDC with the National Universities Commission (NUC) establishes minimum standards for academic programs, and training facilities for medical schools. Also, NUC facilitates academic and physical development of universities, and NUC sets the academic standards for graduation from medical schools. Accreditation goes on periodically and jointly by both NUC and NMDC. The NMDC concentrates on training facilities, while the NUC accredits academic contents of the curriculum and faculty development.

CONTINUING MEDICAL EDUCATION

There are no structured continuing education programs. However, medical graduates are encouraged to pursue postgraduate studies and attend conferences and workshops in addition to departmental or faculty seminars.

ROLE OF RESEARCH IN MEDICAL EDUCATION

Academic medical centers are responsible for conducting research as well as teaching and service. Research opportunities exist in the medical schools and are governed by individual university guidelines. Interested faculty members develop their research proposals and submit their requests to the Research and Ethics Committee of the medical school. Once approved, the application is forwarded to the University Senate Research Grant Committee where it is considered along with research proposals from other schools. Generally, funds are made available every two to three years to allow resources to circulate among all faculty members. The National Universities Commission ensures that research is supported by requesting the universities to set aside 10-15 percent of their annual budget for research. Research on medical education is conducted on a limited scale in a few schools.

GOVERNMENT/PRIVATE SECTOR INVOLVEMENT

Medical education in Nigeria is at the moment entirely governmental (federal and state).

INTERNATIONAL LINKAGES AND COLLABORATION

A number of medical schools have international linkages through associations like the Network of Community Oriented Educational Institutions for Health Sciences. There are also collaboration with the World Health Organization and a number of institutions/corporations overseas, particularly in the US, including Carnegie, Johns Hopkins, and the Ford Foundation.

ISSUES AND TRENDS

At the present stage of our development, there is general consensus that the following are urgent priorities:

1. Fostering community-based medical education while simultaneously maintaining a balanced production of qualified hospital-based physicians, (i.e., specialists).
2. Redirecting the training of community health workers and nurses toward the delivery of primary health care in order to meet the population's health needs.
3. Developing a comprehensive data base and information network to provide precise and accurate information regarding the health profile of the population and available resources and services.
4. Strengthening interinstitutional and multidisciplinary research to address the numerous and diverse societal concerns and needs.

However, given the limitations on our resources, clearly we will require considerable time to achieve our goals.

REFERENCES

Alike-Catha, A. 1990. Nigeria: Developing the primary health care system. In E. Tarimo, and A. Creese, eds. *Achieving Health for All by the Year 2000: Midway reports of country experiences*, pp. 202-212. Geneva: World Health Organization.

Medical Council of Nigeria. 1984. Guidelines on minimum standards of medical education in Nigeria [brochure].

Hamilton, J.D., and O. Ogunbode. 1991. Medical education in the community: A Nigerian experience. *Lancet* 338:99-102.

Joiner, K.T. 1990. Report of Secretary. West African College of Surgeons.

Makanjuola, J.D.A., B.O. Osuntokun, and O.A. Erihosho. 1990. Priorities and process for health research in Nigeria. A publication from the Department of Planning, Federal Ministry of Health (Lagos).

National Universities Commission. n.d. *Approved minimum academic standards in medicine, nursing, physiotherapy, physiology and anatomy for all Nigerian universities.*

National Universities Commission (NUC). 1978. Report of the Working Party on Medical Education [document].

Ogunbode, O. 1991. Development of the Faculty of Health Sciences at the University of Ilorin, Nigeria. *Teaching and Learning in Medicine* 3:200-202.

World Almanac Supplement. 1988.

Table 22.1

Nigeria--Medical School Demographics

Medical School	Undergraduate Enrollment Fall 1991-Male	Undergraduate Enrollment Fall 1991-Female
Ibadan	300	107
Lagos	178	84
Nigeria	214	88
Zaria	88	12
Ife	162	55
Benin	125	19
Jos	94	15
Bayero	60	11
Maiduguri	15	2
Dan Fodio	45	13
Ilorin	101	21
Port-Harcourt	89	17
Calabar	154	34
Totals		
13	1,625	478

Table 22.2

Nigeria—Fellowship Examination Results, 1979-1990 Totals

Faculty	Primary			Part I			Part II		
	S*	P*	% P	S	P	% P	S	P	% P
Obstetrics and Gynecology	1,705	361	18.5	383	138	36.0	91	41	38.9
Anaesthesia	207	52	25.1	80	19	23.8	4	2	50.0
Ophthalmology	159	69	43.4	58	32	55.2	12	8	66.7
Otorhinolaryngology	73	30	41.5	23	10	43.5	6	3	50.0
Dental Surgery	231	99	42.9	108	25	23.1	6	3	50.0
Radiology				64	37	57.8	31	22	71.0
Surgery	1,447	424	16.6	419	121	28.9	49	22	44.9
Laboratory Medicine				86	35	40.7	12	5	41.7
Paediatrics	675	186	27.6	337	97	28.8	58	32	55.2
Internal Medicine	650	213	32.3	342	121	35.4	53	27	50.9
Psychiatry	117	50	42.7	77	33	42.9	10	4	40.0
Community Health	133	74	55.6	84	49	58.3	4	4	100
1990 TOTALS	5,397	1,558	42.74	2,061	717	34.79	336	173	51.49

S = sat exam; P = passed

23

Pakistan

NAEEM A. JAFAREY

Located in southern Asia, Pakistan has a population estimated in 1990 at 122.6 million, of which about eighty million live in rural areas and forty million in urban areas (UNICEF 1992). The country has a wide range of geographic features, climates, and cultures. Starting with a cluster of very high mountains and glaciers in the north, the terrain gradually changes to green valleys, and then to flat alluvial lands fed by the Indus River and its tributaries. The southeastern region of the country, bordering India, is a desert, while the western part is formed of arid mountains. The southern boundary is the Arabian Sea. The country has a largely agricultural economy: wheat, rice, cotton, and sugar cane are the main crops.

OVERVIEW OF THE HEALTH CARE DELIVERY SYSTEM

Pakistan has a federal administrative structure with four provinces. Health and education are provincial responsibilities, but policies and directions are given by the federal government. With the exception of some nominal user charges in a few institutions, all services provided by government health agencies are free. However, many people use both traditional (*Hakim*, homeopath, etc.) and modern health providers in the private sector. Workers in large industrial units are covered by social security services, but otherwise, there is no health insurance scheme available for those who wish to use private facilities. The government health services start with a Basic Health Unit (BHU) for every 10,000-15,000 population. BHUs provide both curative and preventive services and are staffed by one physician and seven auxiliaries. The BHUs are supported by a tier of secondary and tertiary care services at the provincial and district levels, backed up by specialized services available at hospitals attached to medical colleges. The utilization and referral facilities of the BHUs, provincial- and district- level facilities have not been evaluated in recent years.

All the institutions training health personnel (paramedics, nurses, and physicians) are a part of the health departments. The expectation in such a situation would be that since both the production of health personnel and their utilization (service) are under the same administrative control, the number of different categories of health personnel and their quality (competencies) would be determined by the needs of the service. However, this has not happened, for reasons that have not yet been identified.

The number of physicians is greater than can be employed by the government services and absorbed by the private sector. According to one estimate, an additional 1,000 doctors are added to the surplus each year (Bankowski and Megia 1987), so that, at present, there are approximately ten thousand physicians who are un- or underemployed. On the other hand there is a shortage of nurses and other health auxiliaries, as is evident in the total number in each profession in 1990: physicians, 51,883; dentists, 2,007; nurses, 16,928; midwives, 15,029; Lady Health Visitors, 3,106. Graduates of medical colleges are generally unwilling to work in peripheral areas and those who do, having been totally trained in hospitals, find it difficult to work with the available facilities. Thus, there are imbalances both in the number of different categories required by the health services and the kind of training given to the health workers.

Health Profile

Life expectancy in Pakistan is 58 years (UNICEF 1992). The crude birthrate is 44 per thousand, while the crude death rate is 12 per thousand. Accurate data on the disease pattern is not available, but according to figures given in different official documents, infectious diseases continue to be the major cause of death (Pakistan 1991). With the introduction of the Extended Immunization Program (EPI) in the 1980s and the use of Oral Rehydration Salts (ORS), it is expected that child survival will greatly increase, changing the present age structure of the population. The EPI program, which covers 96 percent of children (UNICEF 1992), includes immunization against diphtheria, poliomyelitis, pertussis, tetanus, measles, and tuberculosis; the addition of hepatitis B vaccine is under consideration.

With an increased life expectancy, chronic diseases such as diabetes, coronary heart disease, stroke, and cancer are emerging as major health problems. Thus, the health picture is in transition, with problems of both acute infectious diseases and chronic diseases.

General Education

The literacy rate in Pakistan is 35 percent (UNICEF 1992). Primary education is not compulsory, although where it is available, education up to secondary school level is free. It is estimated that only 40 percent of children enter the education system and only 49 percent of these reach the final grade of primary school (UNICEF 1992). On completion of 10 years of schooling, students appear for the Secondary School Certificate (SSC) examination, often called the

High School Certificate. Those wishing to pursue higher studies join a two-year college and obtain a High Secondary Certificate (HSC) before going to professional colleges or university. Technical schools are also available for secondary school graduates.

HISTORICAL BACKGROUND

When Britain took control of the Indo-Pakistan subcontinent in the nineteenth century, two systems of medicine were in use. One was Tibb or Hikmat which, through famous Persian and Arabic physicians, could be traced to its origin with the Greeks. The other was the Ayurvedic system developed in ancient India by the Hindus. (For additional information on these systems, see "A note on Ayurveda," p. 218.) Training for both systems was by apprenticeship.

The British established a number of medical schools, the first of which was founded in 1822 at Calcutta. Some taught Tibb and Vedic systems in local languages, while others offered a license in allopathic medicine, using English as the medium of instruction. In 1860, a licentiate medical school was established at Lahore, and in 1886 a medical college leading to a Bachelor of Medicine (MB) degree was also started near the same hospital (now called Mayo Hospital). In 1910 the medical college was renamed King Edward Medical College, the name it still carries. In 1912 the name of the degree was also changed to the current MBBS. In 1920 the medical school was shifted to another city while the college remained in Lahore. During British rule of India, several medical colleges offering the Bachelor of Medicine and Bachelor of Surgery (MBBS) degrees as well as schools leading to a License of the State Medical Faculty (LSMF) were established in the public sector and a number of schools/colleges offering training in Tibb, Vedic medicine and homeopathy were established in the private sector (Hussain 1986).

When British rule ended in 1947, the territory that became Pakistan had only two medical colleges: the King Edward Medical College at Lahore and the Dow Medical College at Karachi, established in 1945. In addition, there was a school of hygiene at Lahore which offered a one year course leading to a Diploma in Public Health (DPH), and two LSMF medical schools. The LSMF program was abolished immediately after independence and the schools were upgraded to colleges for the MBBS program (Pakistan 1947).

Pakistan currently has 19 medical colleges offering a five-year MBBS degree, two of which are in the private sector, plus six dental colleges, one of which is private. The 19 medical colleges are affiliated with eight universities, one of which is private. In addition, there are some private colleges providing qualifications in Tibb and Homeopathy. Health Departments of the provincial governments control 14 institutions; two are supported by the provincial government but are semiautonomous; Defense Services administers one; and two are private.

Education in public sector medical colleges is heavily subsidized. The total fee for the entire five-year course is Rs.7,000 (equivalent to US 280$).

ROLE OF NATIONAL POLICY IN SHAPING MEDICAL EDUCATION

Medical and dental education is controlled by three different agencies: the Health Department of the government, the universities, and the Pakistan Medical and Dental Council (PMDC). The health departments of the provincial governments provide the total funding for public medical colleges, and the staff of the colleges and of the affiliated hospitals are employees of the government. Recruitment and appointments are the responsibilities of the health departments. The universities are responsible for the educational programs and for conducting the examinations (four in a five-year course) and granting the degree. The PMDC is a statutory body set up by an Act of the National Assembly (equivalent to the US Congress) whose functions include licensing of physicians and dentists and overseeing the standards of practice. It is as a part of the overall mandate of establishing standards, that the council lays down the required curriculum of medical and dental colleges: what subjects are to be taught and when, the minimum number of hours each subject is to be taught, and the format and timing of the examinations (Pakistan Medical and Dental Council 1988). It also determines the qualifications of teachers and examiners. In effect, the PMDC controls the entire educational process.

Council membership is drawn from the federal and provincial health departments, representatives of universities, and elected representatives of medical practitioners, and includes all the principals or deans of the various colleges. The Director General of Health of the federal government (counterpart of the US Surgeon General) is traditionally the chairperson of PMDC.

Of the three bodies concerned with medical education in Pakistan, the PMDC has the greatest impact on the academic program. Though a licensing body, the PMDC does not conduct a national licensing examination (as in the US and many other countries); rather, these functions have been delegated to the university and Faculties of Medicine. Instead, defining the educational process has been adopted by the Council as the major mechanism for standardizing the quality of graduates entering practice. Unfortunately, the rigid requirements of PMDC have stifled the ability of the medical college faculty to innovate and modify the educational process according to changing needs. This is the major reason the curricular model has not changed in the more than 45 years since Pakistan was founded.

Because most medical institutions are in the public sector and employment is regulated by government rules, staff members are required to have their primary residence in the province in which the institution is located; no expatriates are employed in public sector institutions. In contrast, Aga Khan

University, a private institution, employs a number of foreigners in key positions, including that of the dean of the Faculty of Health Sciences.

ADMISSION

Applicants to governmental medical schools must be at least 17 years old and must have obtained the Higher Secondary Certificate (HSC) after 12 years of schooling. In 16 of the 19 colleges under the administrative control of provincial governments, the major criterion for admission is the applicant's place of birth or residence. Only residents of that particular province are eligible for admission. In two of the four provinces (Sindh and Baluchistan), districts or groups of districts within the province each have their own quota. Within each quota group, admission is based on the scores obtained in the HSC examination. For this reason, these seats are classified as "Merit" seats in table 23.1 (p. 343) which reports the number of seats available in each school in 1992 and the number of staff positions. The district quota often produces distortion, so that applicants with high HSC marks from a district with high achievers may not be admitted while those from another district may be admitted with lower marks.

In summary, admission to government-administered medical colleges is based principally on place of birth or residence and then on marks obtained in the HSC. The exceptions to this practice are the two private medical colleges (Aga Khan and Baqai), the Army Medical College and the newly established Karachi Medical and Dental College. Aga Khan and Baqai have the same minimal qualifications as the others, but in addition require an admission test followed by an interview of potential candidates. Place of residence is not a condition for admission in these two private schools. The Army Medical College was the first to require an admission test, but there is no interview for selection; it offers admissions to all citizens of Pakistan without consideration of residence. The Karachi Medical and Dental College holds an admission test and interviews candidates, but offers admission only to those who live in Karachi.

In addition to merit seats, most of the government-administered medical colleges have some seats reserved for foreigners, children of physicians, children of defense personnel, and other special interest groups. The federal government usually nominates the candidates to be admitted on these reserved bases.

The number of seats for women in medical colleges has been changing over the years. Initially, the seats for women were very few, not more than 15 percent. Then, in 1949, an exclusive Women's College was established in Lahore, and for a few years the admission of women to other colleges was stopped in some and curtailed by others. In the late 1980s, women applicants won a lawsuit by virtue of which admission to all open seats (excluding special quota or reserved seats) is based on grades obtained in the HSC examination, without sex discrimination. As a result, in some colleges more women have been admitted than men, although the overall sex distribution is approximately equal.

As noted above, some seats are reserved for foreign students. In the early 1950s, most of the foreign students were East Africans of Pakistani origin. From the late 1950s to the mid 1970s, large numbers of students from the Middle East were admitted and the quotas for foreign students were raised. With the establishment of medical schools in the Middle East, and especially in Saudi Arabia, the number of foreign applicants has diminished and most of those now admitted as foreign students are children of Pakistanis settled outside Pakistan.

CURRICULAR STRUCTURE AND INNOVATION

The curriculum followed is the one followed in British India in 1947, which, in turn, was based on the curriculum followed in the United Kingdom before World War II. This is the traditional subject-based model, where the first two years are devoted largely to anatomy, physiology, and biochemistry. Recently, it has been recommended that introduction to community and clinical medicine be incorporated in the first two years. Hospital-based clinical teaching now begins in the third year, along with formal courses in pathology, pharmacology, and forensic medicine. Several minor modifications, (e.g., shifting the examination for a given subject from year three to four or increasing the number of hours of a subject) have been made, but the overall model remains subject-oriented and hospital-based. Officially, Community Health is included as a required subject, but except for Aga Khan University Hospital (Karachi), Ayub Medical College (Abbottabad), and the recently established Baqai Medical College (Karachi), it is mostly confined to classroom activities. Aga Khan University Hospital was the first to emphasize community health sciences by allocating up to 20 percent of its total curriculum time to this subject, which is scheduled from year one through year five. Students do fieldwork and are attached to communities during their clinical years. Ayub Medical College has also included some clinical training in settings outside the main hospital, while Baqai Medical College has designed its program using Aga Khan University Hospital as a model.

Lectures are the predominant form of instruction. According to PMDC regulations, the university holds examinations at the end of the second, third, fourth, and fifth years. Theoretical examinations are entirely essay, heavily based on recall of information. The *viva* (oral/interview) is also given great importance, but it is highly subjective and questions in this format are also at the recall level. The overall effect of the teaching methodology and the type of examinations has led to memorization of texts and lecture notes. Except at Aga Khan University, continuous assessment is not conducted.

GRADUATE MEDICAL EDUCATION

As noted, when Pakistan came into existence in 1947 there were two undergraduate medical colleges (one only two years old) and one school of public health in the new country. The school of public health offered a one-year diploma course, the only formally organized graduate program available at that time.

The older of the two medical colleges (King Edward Medical College) offered facilities for Master of Surgery (MS) and Doctor of Medicine (MD) degrees on the pattern of similar qualifications in the United Kingdom. Between 1947 and 1970, less than a dozen individuals obtained the MD/MS qualification.

The MD/MS program has no course requirement or structured training. The candidate applies to a professor to do research on a selected topic under his or her guidance. If accepted and approved by the university, the candidate then submits a thesis for which he or she has unlimited time. The acceptance of a thesis is followed by a written and clinical examination for the individual candidate. Therefore, the standards not only vary from university to university but also from one candidate to the next.

In the 1980s the number of candidates applying for the MD/MS qualification suddenly increased, but is again on the decline. This increased popularity was because additional universities had established programs, which were preferred by persons who found the Fellowship program of the College of Physicians and Surgeons Pakistan (CPSP) difficult. The recent decline in popularity is due to the controversy over whether this qualification should be considered equivalent to the Fellowship program for teaching and consultant appointments.

In the early years of Pakistan (1947-1966), individuals wishing to acquire postgraduate qualifications went to the UK, where they obtained either diplomas or Membership/Fellowship in one of the Royal Colleges. To meet the urgent need for specialists, the army initiated an Armed Forces Medical College in the early 1950s. The program was open only to Army officers; after a stipulated training, they were called "Graded Specialists."

Major development of specialty training began in the 1960s. To overcome the shortage of basic sciences teachers, an institution was established in 1959 in collaboration with Indiana University (United States) and the support of USAID. The program accepted junior teachers in each of six disciplines (anatomy, pathology, microbiology, biochemistry, physiology, and pharmacology) from different undergraduate medical colleges of Pakistan for a two-year course leading to the M.Sc. Later, this degree was renamed Master of Philosophy, since it required a thesis, and thus, had to be distinguished from other M.Sc. qualifications in the country that had no such requirement. In the 1970s, two more universities initiated the Master of Philosophy program for basic medical science subjects. Some three hundred teachers have now been trained by the initial institute and about one hundred or so have been trained by the other universities; these graduates now staff the different undergraduate colleges of the country. Some went on to obtain the PhD in Pakistan or abroad, and quite a few have found jobs in foreign countries.

The other notable development was the establishment of the College of Physicians and Surgeons Pakistan (CPSP) in 1962. This is an autonomous body established through an Act of the National Assembly with a charter entitling it to take all necessary steps to improve the standards of medical practice in Pakistan. CPSP is performing functions comparable to those of the various Royal Colleges in the UK and Specialty Boards in the US. In this respect CPSP is similar to the Canadian College, which also has all the different disciplines under one umbrella (Robinson 1992). Taking the Royal Colleges of the United Kingdom as a model, this College instituted two tiers of qualifications: Membership and Fellowship. Initially, CPSP offered examinations only in medicine, surgery, obstetrics and gynecology, anesthesia, and clinical pathology. Membership required at least one year of training, while Fellowship required a year of training in basic science and two years in the chosen specialty. All training had to be in institutions/programs approved by the College. After completing basic science training the candidates was required to pass a Part 1 examination covering anatomy, physiology and pathology. The first group of candidates began training for basic sciences in 1963 and the first Part-I examination was held in 1964. By July 1992, a total of 745 candidates had qualified for Fellowship in various disciplines, and 2,897 had passed the various Membership examinations. Over the years, many modifications have taken place. Fellowship is now offered in 25 different disciplines as varied as Dentistry, Community Medicine, and Family Medicine, as well as subspecialties such as nephrology and plastic surgery.

In the thirty years of its existence CPSP has also worked toward building a structured training program for different disciplines on a national basis. This has gone a long way in meeting the country's need for specialists. A faculty has been formed for each discipline, which lays down the objectives, competencies to be acquired, the minimum requirements a department/service must have for recognition as an approved program, and the examination format. The shorter Membership program has been phased out in medicine and surgery and will gradually be abolished for most of the other disciplines. Through exchange of examiners with the Royal Colleges of the UK, the Fellows of CPSP have been granted certain exemptions if they wish to appear in the Royal College examinations.

Another category of qualification available for specialization is the diploma offered by different universities. These are courses of one academic year conducted by medical colleges in different clinical subjects, followed by an examination administered by the respective university and the award of a diploma, for example, Diploma in Child Health (DCH). These diplomas are also patterned on the model of similar qualifications available in the United Kingdom. PMDC categorizes these diplomas as minor qualifications equivalent to the Membership qualification of CPSP. The FCPS and MD/MS are considered as major qualifications.

In summary, Pakistan has two groups of postgraduate qualifications. One is the Membership and Fellowship of CPSP, which has a structured, defined training program and a national level examination; while the other is the Diploma and the MD/MS awarded by universities, where the requirements and the standard of examinations may vary somewhat.

LICENSURE

On passing the final MBBS qualifying examinations, the graduate obtains a full license from the PMDC. A twelve-month internship is required prior to independent practice--either as two six-month hospital assignments in two different specialties or as one full year in any specialty. A move to make this requirement a one-year *rotating* internship has been deferred.

Cross-Licensing of Physicians

Recognition of Pakistani qualifications in other countries. Prior to 1947 the MBBS degree given by the Medical Colleges of British India had full recognition from the General Medical Council (GMC) of the UK. Thus, graduates from King Edward Medical College, Lahore, the only established Medical College in Pakistan after independence, were given full registration in the UK. Later the GMC requirements changed for overseas graduates, and now graduates are required to pass an examination, the Professional and Linguistic Ability Board (PLAB), before they are granted limited registration.

CPSP has a number of bilateral agreements with some of the Royal Colleges of the UK under which the Fellows of CPSP are given some exemptions for appearing in the examinations of the UK and for getting into postgraduate training programs. There is no other official licensing agreement with any other country although MBBS and postgraduate qualification holders from Pakistan are employed in many Middle East countries.

Recognition of foreign qualifications in Pakistan. Until recently, a license (registration with PMDC) to graduates from medical colleges outside Pakistan was granted on an individual case-to-case basis. However, graduates from India and other Commonwealth countries whose qualifications were recognized by the GMC or the UK were accepted. Since 1991, PMDC has introduced a registration examination for all graduates from outside Pakistan. Most of those taking these examinations are Pakistanis from private colleges in such areas as the former USSR, the West Indies, or the Philippines.

British qualifications, both undergraduate and postgraduate are given full registration in Pakistan. Those specializing are considered on an individual case-by-case-basis, but generally registration has been granted to applicants with Boards and Fellowships from Canada.

CONTINUING MEDICAL EDUCATION

There is no organized continuing education program in Pakistan, nor is continuing education a requirement of any licensing or certifying body. No system of audit or recertification so far exists. The only CME programs are those offered by about two dozen professional organizations at the time of their annual meetings, in the form of short workshops, state of the art lectures or seminars. Participation in these meetings is voluntary and no credits are awarded for participation.

ROLE OF RESEARCH IN MEDICAL EDUCATION

Research lacks the priority in Pakistan that it has in Europe and America. Nearly all medical institutes are in the public sector, the staff of these institutions (colleges, hospitals, dispensaries, etc.) are government employees, and their appointment and advancement are regulated by the rules applicable to other such employees. Thus, research is not a requirement for either initial appointment or promotion. Some individual physicians undertake research, but only as part of their personal desire and initiative.

The College of Physicians and Surgeons Pakistan has made an effort to remedy this situation by requiring the submission of a review or original work as a condition for admission for the final Fellowship examination, a requirement designed to stimulate research and professional writing. Initially, candidates found it difficult to meet the requirement, as their seniors/supervisors had not done research and could not guide them. Now, the situation is somewhat better and the quality of original work by the candidates is improving. The Department of Medical Education of the CPSP conducts regular workshops on research methodology and professional writing, both for supervisors and candidates.

Research relating to medical education. Three studies are available in published form, one on causes of failure among medical students, a second on a retrospective look at the medical curriculum, and the third on the socioeconomic background of medical students (Pakistan Medical Association 1969; Fazal, Siddique, and Jafarey 1985; Zaidi and Malik 1985); all three had significant findings, but none has been utilized for change.

In contrast, the Department of Medical Education of CPSP has undertaken several internal studies for the College, which have led to important changes in College policies. For example, training objectives have been defined, training programs have been designed in greater detail, logbooks (work records) have been introduced, and certifying examinations have become more valid and objective.

In 1974 the WHO Regional Teacher Training Center (RTTC) at Shiraz, Iran, conducted three Itinerant Workshops on Educational Planning in Pakistan. For the first time, medical teachers of Pakistan were introduced to current concepts of education. In the ensuing years WHO supported a number of similar workshops in which some of those who had shown interest in medical education were recruited as facilitators. Ultimately, these groups of local professionals started conducting workshops on their own and departments of medical education were set up in four medical institutions. In 1979, one such department was established at CPSP. This became the most active of all the departments, and was recognized by the Ministry of Health as the National Teacher Training Center (NTTC). WHO has continued to provide generous support to the teacher training program.

The Department of Medical Education of CPSP has held over one hundred workshops. The range of topics--and that of participants--has grown. At this time more than 1,000 physicians and approximately 200 nursing and paramedical teachers have completed the workshop on Educational Planning and Evaluation. This six-day workshop is based on the design originally prepared by the late Dr. Aziz-ur-Rehman Chowhan and Dr. Bahman Joorabchi of the RTTC at Shiraz. The other workshops on MCQ, Evaluation of Clinical Competence, Research Methodology, and Medical Writing have been designed by the staff of the department with the help of a number of foreign consultants provided by WHO. These workshops follow the same philosophy of experiential learning as used for the original educational planning and evaluation workshops.

In the initial years, the educational workshops were attended out of curiosity. Now, there is an increasing demand from different medical colleges, and the Department is finding it difficult to meet all the requests. In 1991, the department conducted 14 workshops in Karachi and one at Islamabad.

The workshops are basically designed to sensitize participants to basic concepts of education. The department hopes to begin offering a Master of Health Professions Education Program (MHPE) in Pakistan in which a number of medical and nursing teachers will be formally trained in education and will return to their institutions to provide leadership for change.

GOVERNMENT/PRIVATE SECTOR INVOLVEMENT

Pakistan has never had a health manpower policy, although starting within months of the nation's 1947 birth and continuing over the years, a number of conferences and commissions have made recommendations regarding this subject. A number of individuals have also submitted proposals for the formulation of health manpower policies (Khan 1965; Jafarey 1989). Some of the above-mentioned recommendations and proposals were accepted by the government but they never became a part of a long-term policy.

In 1990 a health manpower development (HMD) plan was prepared by a group of consultants with the assistance of the Asian Development Bank (Pakistan 1990b). The major recommendations of the plan, currently under review by the government, are: (1) to double the public sector health personnel and increase by 50 percent health personnel in the private sector, and (2) to achieve development of these human resources not by means of major expansion in the production capacity but rather by qualitative improvements.

INTERNATIONAL LINKAGES AND COLLABORATION

Aga Khan University (AKU) has some institutional agreements with Harvard University, US, and McMaster University, Canada. The McMaster program has largely been utilized by the AKU Nursing School.

ISSUES AND TRENDS

In 1989, the National Assembly approved a health policy, the medical education section of which included the establishment of several community-based medical colleges and reorientation of the existing medical curriculum toward the community (Pakistan 1990a). This policy is currently under review, but the expectation is that the medical education section will remain unchanged.

If the above mentioned decisions in the health policy and the HMD plan (Pakistan 1990b) are implemented, the medical education program in the first decade of the twenty-first century will produce physicians who will be better prepared to meet the health needs of the country.

The success of such programs will depend on faculty development activities, leadership development, and the ability of the new leaders to implement the changes. The proposed MHPE program will become a key factor if desirable change is to occur.

REFERENCES

Bankowski, Z., and A. Megia, eds. 1987. *Health manpower out of balance*. Geneva: CIOMS.

Fazal, E., M.G. Siddique, and N.A. Jafarey. 1985. A prospective look at the medical curriculum. *JPMA* 35:85-92.

Hussain, S.A. 1986. Evolution of medical education in the nineteenth century; Indo-Pakistan sub-continent. *Pakistan Journal of Ophthalmology* 2:85-97.

Jafarey, N.A. 1989. Some suggestions about improvement of medical education in Pakistan. *JPMA* 39:136-142.

Khan, N. 1965. *Manpower in the health program of Pakistan*. Lahore: Pakistan Association for the Advancement of Science.

Pakistan. 1991. *Annual report of the Director General Health (July 1990-June 1991)*. Islamabad: Government of Pakistan.

---------. Ministry of Food, Agriculture and Health. 1947. *Summary of the proceedings of the All Pakistan Health Conference*. Karachi: Government of Pakistan.

---------. Ministry of Health. 1972. *Report of the Committee to Review Medical Education*. Islamabad: Government of Pakistan

---------. Ministry of Health and Social Welfare. 1960. *Report of the medical reforms commission*. Karachi: Government of Pakistan.

---------. Ministry of Health, Special Education & Social Welfare. 1990a. *National health policy*. Islamabad: Government of Pakistan.

---------. Ministry of Health, Special Education & Social Welfare. 1990b. *Pakistan's health manpower and training plan project. Vols.1,2 and 3*. Islamabad: ACTS Inc.

Pakistan Association for the Advancement of Science. 1958. *Proceedings of the Symposium on Medical and Veterinary Education in Pakistan*. Lahore: Pakistan Association for the Advancement of Science.

Pakistan Medical Association. 1969. *A study on the causes of failure of undergraduate medical students in medical colleges of West Pakistan*, Karachi: Pakistan Medical Association.

Pakistan Medical Association (East Zone). 1969. *A study on the causes of failure of undergraduate medical students in medical colleges of East Pakistan*. Dacca: Pakistan Medical Association.

Pakistan Medical and Dental Council. 1988. *Regulations for the degree of Bachelor of Medicine and Bachelor of Surgery (MB., BS)* Islamabad: Pakistan Medical and Dental Council.

Robinson, S.C. 1992. The College of Physicians and Surgeons Pakistan as seen by a Canadian. *Annals RCPSC* 26:65-66.

United Nations International Children's Emergency Fund. 1992. The state of the world's children. Oxford: Oxford University Press. (Cited as UNICEF.)

Zaidi, S.A., and S. Malik. 1985. *Medical students: Their socio-economic background and urban choice*. Karachi: University of Karachi, Applied Economics Research Center.

Table 23.1
Pakistan--Medical School Demographics

Medical College	Year Est.	Available seats for 1st year admission in 1992			Teaching staff employed 1989			
		Merit	Reserved	Total	Professor	Assoc. Prof.	Assist. Prof.	Demonstrator
King Edward Medical College, Lahore	1860	214	13	227	40	37	60	106
Dow Medical College* Karachi	1945	431	64	495	39	23	27	103
Fatima Jinnah Medical College Lahore	1948	181	47	228	19	22	32	81
Liaquat Medical College* Jamshoro	1951	421	13	434	27	15	33	106
Khyber Medical College, Peshawar	1953	153	57	210	31	30	41	67
Nishter Medical College, Multan	1953	184	44	228	26	21	34	99
Allama Iqbal Medical College, Lahore	1973	213	14	227	16	18	25	69
Punjab Medical College, Faisalabad	1973	186	42	228	16	17	35	80

Table 23.1
Pakistan—Medical School Demographics

Medical College	Year Est.	Available seats for 1st year admission in 1992			Teaching staff employed 1989				
		Merit	Reserved	Total	Professor	Assoc. Prof.	Assist. Prof.	Demonstrator
Quaid-e-Azam Medical College, Bahawalpur	1973	186	42	228	17	19	29	106
Rawalpindi Medical College, Rawalpindi	1973	182	42	228	21	19	31	98
Sind Medical College* Karachi	1973	340	53	393	6	9	11	4
Chandka Medical College, Larkana*	1973	291	15	306	10	6	31	76
Nawabshah Medical College, Nawabshah*	1974	167	5	172	10	9	22	60
Bolan Medical College* Quetta	1974	110	39	149	19	10	48	89
Army Medical College, Rawalpindi	1975	70	30	100	11	9	26	-
Ayub Medical College, Abbottabad	1976	75	100	175	11	14	27	35

Table 23.1
Pakistan--Medical School Demographics

Medical College	Year Est.	Available seats for 1st year admission in 1992			Teaching staff employed 1989			
		Merit	Reserved	Total	Professor	Assoc. Prof.	Assist. Prof.	Demonstrator
Aga Khan Medical College, Karachi	1983	70	0	70	62	17	38	139
Baqai Medical College, Karachi	1988	70	0	70	-	-	-	-
Karachi Medical & Dental College, Karachi	1992	50	0	50	-	-	-	-

* The seats are distributed among different districts of the provinces. Admission for each district group is determined based on SSCmarks.

345

24

Poland

ANDRZEJ WOJTCZAK

At the end of 1990, the Republic of Poland comprised 312,683 square kilometers, and was inhabited by 38.5 million people, 29 percent of whom were below 18 years of age. There are 808 towns and 2,128 communes, with 40 percent of the population living in rural areas. Administratively, Poland is divided into 49 *voievodships* (provinces) varying in size from 250,000 to more than three million inhabitants, with communes as the second tier. A division of the country into 12-14 regions with counties as the second tier is currently contemplated.

OVERVIEW OF THE HEALTH CARE DELIVERY SYSTEM

The Constitution promulgated in 1952 guarantees all citizens free health care. Today, more than 99 percent of the population is covered by state health insurance. The legal, administrative and financial responsibility for health policy and the organization of public health and medical care is in the hands of the Ministry of Health and Social Welfare.

Health care services are integrated, with the health care district forming the basic structural unit for serving the residents of a given territory. Health care is provided at various levels: community, province, regional and national. At the community level, primary health care is integrated with the hospital in what is known as an Integrated Health Care Center (ZOZ). The typical ZOZ covers roughly the territory of the commune or district, but its function is not limited by the administrative division of the country. The ZOZ serves small towns, their surrounding villages, and neighborhoods or districts in cities with populations from 30,000 to 150,000 or more. These are subdivided into reyons of 3,000 to 5,000 inhabitants, who are served by a local primary health care clinic. In addition to ambulatory services, and general, specialized and emergency services, the ZOZ hospital contains at least four specialty wards: internal medicine, surgery, pediatrics, and obstetrics/gynecology. The director of the ZOZ has the authority to transfer physicians and other personnel between different organizational units according to changing needs.

At the provincial level, health care is provided by the hospitals and outpatient specialized clinics, which also function as a referral center for the ZOZ. At the regional level, which is not reflected in the administrative division of the country, medical care is delivered by the teaching hospital of local medical schools, which serve several provinces. At the national level, the 14 National Research Institutes and a few highly specialized National Medical Centers provide medical care to all patients referred to them. At the end of 1991, there were 82,925, or 21.5 physicians per 10,000 persons. Fifteen thousand physicians were employed in primary health care, of which 4,055 worked in rural areas. There were significant differences in the distribution of physicians among provinces, ranging from 9.6 to 39.9 per 10,000 of population. In total, there are 436 Integrated Health Care Centers (ZOZ), 6,477 polyclinics, and 3,283 rural health clinics. In the 664 general hospitals, 213,389 beds provide 56.8 beds per 10,000 of population and account for more than 4.6 million hospitalizations yearly. The average stay in hospital is 12.9 days. In psychiatric hospitals, the number of beds in 1990 was 35,310 (9.4 per 10,000 of population) with 160,000 hospitalized persons yearly. The hospitals, as a rule, are integrated with outpatient clinics, and the emergency services include first aid units and emergency care centers.

The health status of the population has declined during the last two decades, and is characterized by a high mortality rate due to diseases typical for industrialized societies. Deteriorating environmental conditions, unhealthy lifestyles, and growing dissatisfaction with health care have, in recent years, prompted the Ministry of Health and Social Welfare to prepare a program of reforms consisting of: (1) long-term plans to achieve the WHO goal of "Health for All," in part by increased emphasis on health promotion (The National Program of Health); and (2) the short-term plan, for improving the effectiveness of health care through better use of available personnel and facilities, increased and diversified financial resources, and privatization of some services. The health services development plan is a part of the national socioeconomic plan approved yearly by Parliament, and the level of financial support is the crucial element in the reform of the health care system.

HISTORICAL BACKGROUND

Until 1949, medical education was the direct responsibility of the Ministry of Education and the medical schools were parts of the universities. In 1950, the Faculties of Medicine and Faculties of Pharmacy were separated from universities and established as the Academies of Medicine under the aegis of the Ministry of

Health, making that organization directly responsible for education and management of all health personnel.

ROLE OF NATIONAL POLICY IN SHAPING MEDICAL EDUCATION

This move also enabled the functional integration of teaching hospitals with the overall health system to provide health care in the region. Since then, the education and training of medical personnel are planned, supervised and financed by the Ministry of Health and Social Welfare. It is carried out by 11 Academies of Medicine (medical schools) and the Medical Center of Postgraduate Education in Warszawa (MCPE). The eleven Academies of Medicine include Białystok, Bydgoszcz, Gdańsk, Katowice, Kraków[1], Łódź, Lublin, Poznań, Szczecin, Warszawa, and Wrocław. Most consist of a Faculty of Medicine, Faculty of Stomatology, and Faculty of Pharmacy, and some also include a Faculty of Nursing and Division of Medical Analysis. The teaching hospitals provide highly specialized medical care in the region. Thus, each of these 11 Academies of Medicine serves more than one province (i.e., populations from two to five million). The 12th Academy of Medicine is military and is supervised by the Ministry of Defence.

Personnel policy is developed by the Ministry of Health and Social Welfare in cooperation with the Physician Chamber, an independent physician's organization similar to Germany's Arzt Kamera. Membership in the Physician Chamber is required of all physicians, and its tasks are considered similar to those of the American Medical Association. As an independent professional body, the Chamber prepares opinions for the Ministry of Health and also the Parliament and Senate on all issues related to physicians' practice and health system organization. The Chamber is involved in planning of medical personnel, the scale of physicians' salaries, organization of the health care system, postgraduate education of physicians, and ethics. At the national level, the members of the Chamber are represented in the Main Council, and at the regional level by the Regional Council of Physician Chambers.

The health service and personnel development plans are prepared according to estimates of the needs and educational possibilities of medical schools. The plans are developed in consultation with the Ministry of National Education and coordinated with the Ministry of Finance that secures the necessary finances.

Medical education, both graduate and undergraduate, is free of charge to all health personnel employed in the national health service system. Scholarships,

---

[1] In May 1993 the Academy of Medicine in Krakow became part of Jaggielonian University as the College of Medicine.

lodging and food benefits, travel, and research grants are financed from general taxation.

ADMISSION

Pre-university education takes 12 years. Secondary school concludes in a final examination *(matura)*, the passing of which entitles candidates to apply to an Academy of Medicine. Academies of Medicine hold annual competitive entrance multiple-choice examinations that include biology, chemistry and physics plus additional written and oral examination of foreign language. On this basis, 3,000 medical, 900 stomatology, 900 pharmacy, and 300 nursing students have been admitted yearly; however, in 1991, admissions were reduced by about 20 percent. A special commission is currently working on a new exam, which is expected to be introduced sometime in the near future.

Demographic Profile of Medical students.

By 1972 when new regulations were introduced, the percentage of female students in the first year of the Medical Faculties had reached 65 to 70 percent; In the stomatology Faculties 85 percent, and in the pharmaceutical Faculties 95 percent. Because absenteeism due to family responsibilities seemed higher among female doctors and because they tended to avoid surgical specialties, policy was changed in 1972 to require that equal numbers of men and women be admitted, and that separate lists of examination results be prepared for male and female applicants. In 1988 this rule was questioned by the Constitutional Tribunal. In two years, the admission of women has again increased to more than 60 percent of the total enrollment. Currently admissions are based solely on the results of the competitive exams administered by the Academies, and there are no gender restrictions.

Demographic Profile of Medical School Faculty.

The demographic profile of medical school faculty differs according to academic position. On the level of assistants (instructors), the male to female ratio depends on the specialty--females predominate in pediatrics, ophthalmology, and psychiatry. In the higher ranks, the ratio of men to women steadily increases: whereas the Doctor of Medicine degree is obtained by a similar proportion, men predominate at the level of the Doctor of Medical Sciences degree, which is necessary to apply for the post of associate professor (docent) or full professor. Overall, women are predominant in the Faculties of Stomatology and Pharmacy;

however, the proportion of men and woman is approximately equal at the level of professor.

CURRICULAR STRUCTURE AND INNOVATION

The curricular framework is developed by ad hoc committees consisting of the academic teachers of different disciplines, representatives of medical societies, and the Ministry of Health. This curricular framework is reviewed and approved by the Council of Medical Education of the Advisory Council for Higher Education and Science before acceptance by the Minister of Health. The Council of Medical Education determines the percentage distribution of hours among basic, social, behavioral and clinical sciences and the so-called "educational minima" for blocks of different disciplines.

Details of the content of curriculum and educational process are left to the Medical Academies. They are periodically reviewed by the medical schools and Ministry of Health and Social Welfare. The yearly meetings of deans and rectors with the Minister of Health serve for discussion of new educational policy issues and changes in curriculum required by emerging new topics.

Undergraduate Medical Education

In the immediate postwar period, the length of medical studies was five years. In 1956, the undergraduate program was extended to six years, including one year of internship. Both the length and configuration of studies were modified in 1962, in an effort to accelerate the increase in the number of physicians. The current program takes seven years, including the one-year required internship.

The undergraduate curriculum can be described as a hybrid of British and Scandinavian models adapted to Polish needs and tradition. The first two years include basic sciences. The third year is preclinical, consisting of pathophysiology, pharmacology, pathology, immunology, introduction to internal medicine, clinical skills laboratory, hygiene, social medicine, and public health. The preclinical year is followed by three years of clinical subjects and bedside teaching inside and outside of academic teaching hospitals. Students are encouraged to take a "self-adjusted program of study" and perform research in "students' scientific circles."

These "scientific circles" have been informal activities for those who express an interest to learn more about a given discipline or specialty. The senior staff member of the given department is appointed as the supervisor and tutor for the circle. The students are "attached" to the staff members who do research. They help the faculty in performing investigations and, according to their effort and invention, become coauthors of publications or even proceed with their own investigation. Members of the circles organize seminars presenting review papers or their own research. Research papers have also been presented at National Conferences. Although once a very lively activity, the scientific circles could be currently described as "in hibernation," due to the state of the national economy.

The educational methods used in medical schools include lectures, case demonstrations, seminars, teaching hospital rounds, film displays and clinico-pathological discussions. Examinations are predominantly of the multiple choice type, supplemented in clinical disciplines by practical exams to evaluate diagnostic communication and skills. After six years of medical studies and passing of the final exams, students are granted the "Physician Diploma" at the age of approximately twenty-four to twenty-five years.

In the early 1960s, the Ministry of Health and Social Welfare initiated reforms in medical education to focus more directly on health needs. New subjects and disciplines were introduced such as clinical immunology, clinical pharmacology, genetics, medical sociology, and clinical psychology. Medical sociology and psychology were not taught before the reforms; however many of these subjects had been taught prior to the 1960s as part of other disciplines (i.e., genetics with biology; clinical pharmacology with pharmacology; or, during clinical work, immunology with pathology). The number of lectures was reduced and more time was devoted to small group instruction and to training in hospitals, laboratories and outpatient clinics. The total number of examinations was also reduced by combining tests in related subjects and improved methods of evaluation were introduced. By 1965, the new curriculum had been adopted by all Academies of Medicine.

Since high technology-oriented teaching hospitals are not optimal sites for training in general practice, the medical academies have entered cooperative agreements with Voievodship Health Care Departments to enable part of the practical medical training to take place outside the teaching hospitals.

As early as 1965, "affiliated clinical teaching centers" were organized in provincial hospitals and health centers. Teaching was done by the practitioners and members of the medical faculty. At present, many professors are also employed by the affiliated hospitals. They are responsible for both the organization of instruction and the delivery of health care. The medical school maintains supervision and assures proper conditions for educational activities. Students in the fourth, fifth, and sixth year are sent for periods of several weeks to such centers for clinical training in selected disciplines. In well organized and staffed centers, they may stay even longer. Students welcome such arrangements, but the faculty is not very enthusiastic since they consume both time and money.

Recently, the Ministry of Health and World Bank experts have urged better preparation of graduates for primary health care practice. In some medical schools, sixth-year students work for four weeks in the outpatient clinics. For example, sixth year students in the Gdańsk Academy of Medicine work for 144 hours in the district outpatient clinics, where two students are attached to one general practitioner in his or her normal working environment. The Department of General Practice provides overall supervision. Physicians participate in this program on a voluntary basis; however, they do receive special training and additional payment from the Academy of Medicine.

All these innovations demand constant attention of the medical school authority to prevent return to traditional forms of education. These innovations also require appropriate staffing patterns, additional funding and incentives for staff. Unfortunately, due to economic difficulties, the extent of educational reform has been limited.

GRADUATE MEDICAL EDUCATION

Two forms of postgraduate education and training can be distinguished: (1) studies in selected medical or pharmaceutical disciplines (specialty or graduate training) called--"specialization," and (2) systematic studies throughout a professional career--continuing medical education.

Postgraduate education as a uniform, countrywide system was established in Poland in 1951 and organized for physicians only by the Institute of Postgraduate Training as part of the Warsaw Medical Academy. By the end of 1970, by governmental decree, the Medical Center of Postgraduate Education was established. It is financed and supervised by the Ministry of Health and Social Welfare. The MCPE has responsibility for the overall organization and coordination of the national system of postgraduate education. The internal structure of the Center resembles that of the Academy of Medicine.

The system of postgraduate education consists of three levels: (1) the central level, conducted by the MCPE in cooperation with the National Research Institutes; (2) the regional level, conducted by the 11 Academies of Medicine; and (3) the local level, conducted by the 49 Voievodship Training Centers for Health Personnel (VTCHP) as a part of the Voievodship Department of Health and Social Welfare. The Voievodship Training Centers are assisted by staff from the academies and are responsible for training activities mainly for the primary health care personnel.

Actual training takes place in the clinical departments of the Medical Center of Postgraduate Education, in all Academies of Medicine, in National Research Institutes, and in selected Voievodship hospitals and outpatient clinics. In total, more than 400 different medical institutions are involved in those activities. All physicians are eligible for specialty training and for various CME courses. The regional health departments grant leaves of absence with full salaries for the duration of a course. About ninety percent of the medical personnel participate in various kinds of training programs.

Specialization

Specialization is chosen by almost eighty percent of graduating physicians, who usually begin their study immediately after completing the internship and receiving the practice license. The program consists of two to three year phases, each concluding in a state-board examination and acquisition of the title of a First or Second degree specialist, (i.e.,"junior" and "senior" specialist, respectively). There are 55 specialties and an additional 25 subspecialties on the official list.

Very recently, the National Committee for Medical Education was established as an independent body consisting of the representatives of the Main Council of the Physicians' Chamber, Ministry of Health and Social Welfare, the MCPE, the Academies of Medicine, and the Medical Societies. The Committee is charged to consider the full spectrum of issues related to both undergraduate and postgraduate medical education, and is now working on a new system of specialties. It is anticipated that approximately 25 main specialties will be approved, and that the system of First and Second Degree specialist will be replaced by a single designation based on the results of a state administered examination. The content of each specialty will be determined by a Specialty Commission consisting of the experts from that field and representatives of the National Committee. All subspecialties will be left to the discretion of the medical societies, which will decide on the programs and the requirements for subspecialty certification. The most popular specialties are pediatrics, internal medicine, gynecology/obstetrics and otolaryngology. The least popular are neurology, psychiatry, radiology, and the surgical specialties, especially orthopedics and neurosurgery. Recently the specialty of general practice or family medicine, as the focus of the reform of the health system, has attracted more recruits.

Specialty training takes place in Medical Academies, National Research Institutes, and approved hospitals. The training program must conform to the guidelines developed by the MCPE and must be approved by the Ministry of Health and Social Welfare programs. In each setting, a "tutor" or "patron" of specialization is nominated, who is obliged to plan the educational program and to assess periodically the knowledge and practical skills of the graduate student. Self-learning and on-the-job training are supported by formal courses, seminars, and workshops under supervision of a tutor.

LICENSURE

Before obtaining permission to practice independently, physicians must complete one year of internship in a community hospital under the supervision of a tutor. The internship consists of three months each of internal medicine, surgery, pediatrics, and obstetrics/gynecology, and concludes with a final assessment by tutors of the practical skills and competencies necessary to start medical practice. The training takes place both in hospital and outpatient clinics. On completion of the internship, the license to practice medicine is awarded by the Regional Chamber of Physicians and the physician is registered in the Voievodship (Provincial) Department of Health. Now he/she may begin to practice medicine or may enter specialty training. The majority begin work as "district" or "rural" physicians.

Recently, the Ministry of Health and Social Welfare established the State Examining Commission that has the responsibility of preparing a state final exam, to be introduced after internship as a basis for licensure. Results of the examination will also serve for determining the relevance of medical education to health care needs and as a basis for granting subsidies to Academies of Medicine. The current plan is to use these subsidies as incentives, with the additional funds rewarding those academies whose graduates score better than others. This plan has generated significant controversy.

Board Certification for Specialists

The examinations for junior specialists' certificate are organized and executed by the Voievodship departments of health in cooperation with the Medical Academy. The examinations for second-degree specialists are organized by the Medical Centre of Postgraduate Education, which also offers preparatory courses of one or two months' duration before examination. The examination consists of three parts: (1) a 180-question multiple-choice test, prepared centrally by the Specialty Board and administered at the MCPE; (2) a practical bedside examination (and, in surgical specialties, an exam at the surgical table), scored by the examiner on a specially developed assessment scale; and (3) an oral examination focused on problem-solving abilities. The title of junior specialist (first degree) is required for all posts in hospitals and specialist outpatient departments; heads and directors of such departments are recruited from senior (second degree) specialists.

Cross-Licensing of Physicians

There are still no specific regulations for cross-licensing physicians from foreign countries. A draft of the Parliamentary Bill is being prepared, but until it is approved it is necessary to apply to the Minister of Health and Social Welfare for such permission. Permission is granted in agreement with the Main Council of the Chamber of Physicians. In case of a negative decision there is the possibility to appeal to the Administrative Court.

CONTINUING MEDICAL EDUCATION

Continuing medical education (CME) programs are based on studies of the needs of the various medical specialties, an analysis of tasks of city district physicians and physicians employed in rural health centers, and on reports of national and regional consultants. The central plan of CME activities is prepared by the Programme Committee of the Medical Centre of Postgraduate Education and is implemented by all levels of the national system of postgraduate education. The main purpose of this plan is to ensure that the leading personnel of health services (mainly the heads of hospital wards (ordynator) and outpatient clinics of different medical specialties) maintain a high level of knowledge, skills, and competencies to ensure a similar level of quality of medical services in all areas of the health care system. These refresher courses are held at the MCPE, and take the form of short consultations, seminars, discussion sessions, lectures by eminent experts, a debating session on issues distributed earlier to participants, and a test comprised of 80 to 120 multiple-choice questions on a given theme.

The local plan of CME activities encompasses those postgraduate training activities that are related to the specific needs of regions supervised by an individual Medical Academy, and which are to be taken by health personnel of the Medical Academy and *Voievodship* Training Center for Health Personnel. It is within the local plan that the first-contact physicians and other health personnel can pursue continuing education activities. Typically, the programs are organized within the institutions where the participants are actually employed.

Widely varying forms of studies are used: three-hour-long meetings including case demonstrations held once a week, periodic seminars, teaching hospital rounds given by specialists from a medical school, presentation of papers by participants, consultations, film displays and other forms of training or applied consultations, case demonstrations, discussion on diagnostic and therapeutic problems, workshops, and one-day, single-topic conferences. Content of courses varies widely and their duration is from three days to (exceptionally) three months.

The heads of specialty hospital wards (*ordynator*) are responsible for the training of the doctors on his or her ward and also for those working in outpatient clinics, and district or rural health centers supervised by these physicians.The essential task for organizers of local training activities is to attain the objectives without taking health personnel away from their workplace.

The Polish Physicians Association and other medical societies traditionally play an important role in postgraduate education. They consider the improvement of physicians' and pharmacists' professional skills and competence as one of their most important tasks. They are regularly consulted on training programs and activities. An especially active role is played by local branches of associations in implementation of local plans of continuing medical education.

ROLE OF RESEARCH IN MEDICAL EDUCATION

Except for some in the affiliated teaching centers, all academic teachers, in principle, are employed full-time. Depending on the post occupied, they are responsible for teaching 160-220 hours in an academic year. The rest of their time is available for research and other activities. All medical schools have units or departments of medical education, which have both teaching and research functions. The financial support for research is partially included in the regular funding coming from the Ministries of National Education and Health and Social Welfare. Research is also supported by grants from the Governmental Committee for Research and the Commission of Medical Education of the Polish Academy of Science. The Ministry of Health and Social Welfare finances the journal *Problems of Medical Education and Research,* which publishes the more valuable works from this field. Unfortunately, interest in research on medical education is not great among academic teachers. Funding for research activities from private foundations is still marginal.

GOVERNMENT/PRIVATE SECTOR INVOLVEMENT

Economic difficulties have limited financial support for educational activities from the Ministry of National Education. Therefore, attempts are being made to organize private foundations to support educational research and innovation in medical education. One of the first is located in the Medical Center for Postgraduate Education.

INTERNATIONAL LINKAGES AND COLLABORATION

There is a long tradition of cooperation between Academies of Medicine and medical schools in other countries. Several hundred academic teachers have studied in medical schools of the United States and/or Europe. The working links with the World Health Organization in the field of medical education are also longstanding. The association of Poland with the European Economic Community (EEC) will have further impact on the content and process of medical education, and assistance from the World Bank is helping to change the focus of education from hospital-practice to primary care and family practice.

ISSUES AND TRENDS

Medical education should be viewed as a continuous process throughout the professional life of doctors. More attention therefore needs to be given to development of motivation and skills for problem-solving, self-learning, and self-evaluation. To support these skills throughout life, students will need more knowledge about where to find relevant information, and how to collect, store, and retrieve it.

The graduates should have more understanding of the influence of physical, social and psychic environment on health; to develop this understanding students will need more knowledge of sociology, psychology, behavioral sciences, and bioethics. We also need to put much more emphasis on health promotion and disease prevention. This means that physicians will need to know how to deal with the community and community problems as well as individual patients and episodes of acute illness. To accomplish these objectives, physicians will need to learn how to work in teams.

Development of such competencies, including new knowledge, skills, and attitudes is also important for health personnel already working in the health care system. This implies that health promotion, the teamwork approach at the primary health care level, ecological orientation, communication skills, and cost-conscious attitudes are important topics in programs of continuing education.

The strategy of "Health for All" and the Edinburgh Declaration will, to a greater extent, influence medical education, providing the conceptual frame for new curriculum development and the basis for the formulation of general and detailed objectives guiding the educational process. Finally, in Poland, the National Program of Health, the philosophy and principles of which are based on the "Health for All" strategy, and the reform of the health care system will play important roles in reshaping the education and training of health personnel.

REFERENCES

Kostrzewski, J. 1980. An integrated approach to health services and manpower development: The experience of Poland. *Health Policy and Education* 1:197-211.

Kryst, L., and A. Wojtczak. 1989. Kształcenie przeddyplomowe lekarzy w świetle potrzeb Polskiej strategii "Zdrowie dla Wszystkich" (Undergraduate medical education in view of Polish Strategy "Health for All"). *Probl.Szk. Nauk Med.* 14(1):1-12.

Lewartowski, B. 1973. Postgraduate medical education in Poland. *Polish-Swedish Symposium on Medical Education*, pp. 33-38. Warsaw: Publisher Pol.Med.

Missett, J.M., J. Karefa-Smart., F.C. Redlich, and D. Sencer. 1974. Undergraduate medical education in Poland: Variations on the Soviet theme. *J Med Educ* 49 (October):979-984.

Oszacki, J. 1973. Undergraduate medical education in Poland. In *Polish-Swedish Symposium on Medical Education*, pp. 25-33. Warsaw: Publisher Pol.Med.

Roemer, M.I., and R. Roemer. 1981. *The health care system of Poland.* In *Health care systems and comparative manpower policies,* pp. 217-280. New York and Basel: Marcel Dekker.

---------. 1977. Health manpower in the socialist health care system of Poland. US Department of Health, Education, and Welfare. Publ. (HRA) 78-85. pp. 1-81.

Rużyłło, E. 1989. Reflexions on the modes of medical education. *Materia Medica Polona* 4 (72):331-335.

---------. 1970. Postgraduate medical education in Poland. *Brit J Med Educ.* 4 (4):262-267.

Wojtczak, A. 1989a. Implementation of integrated health system and manpower development. Poland country case study. Geneva: WHO.

---------. 1989b. Zdrowie, praktyka i nauki medyczne w świetle strategii "Zdrowie dla Wszystkich" (Health, medical practice and sciences in the view of "Health for All" Strategy). Nowiny Lekarskie. Państw. Wydawn. Naukowe, Poznań, pp. 23-35.

---------. 1988. Aktualne problemy kształcenia medycznego (Actual problems of medical education). *Probl. Szkoln. Nauk Med.* 13 (1):11-21.

---------. 1987a. New direction in health policies and education of medical doctors. *Intern. Symp.* Poznań: Anestes.

---------. 1987b. *Polish system of postgraduate education with focus on continuing medical education for primary health care.* Geneva: WHO.

---------. 1982. The role of medical academies and their teaching hospitals in the regionalization of health care in Poland. In *The role of the university teaching hospital: An international perspective,* pp. 157-180. New York: Josiah Macy, Jr. Foundation.

---------. 1973. Development of the educational system of medical personnel in Poland. In *Polish-Swedish Symposium on Medical Education,* pp. 20-24. Warsaw: Pol. Med. Publisher.

25

Russia (Former USSR)

FELIX VARTANIAN

This chapter was prepared at a time of extraordinarily rapid changes and profound economic, political and social transformation, affecting the very foundation of Russian society. The outcomes for the system of health care and medical education are difficult to predict. The information presented here reflects the situation at the entire country level as of January 1992. Since the original submission of this chapter, the republics which formerly comprised the Union of Soviet Socialist Republics continue to evolve. The information presented in this chapter presents an overview of Russia as it was and the direction in which it is moving.

OVERVIEW OF THE HEALTH CARE DELIVERY SYSTEM

The organization of health services within territories of the former Soviet Union encompasses a broad complex of socioeconomic and medical measures. These are based on a system of national, public and individual contributions implemented to maintain and steadily improve the health of the population. The right of all citizens to free health care is embodied in the constitution[1] of the former USSR. Health care is guaranteed through free and qualified medical services, provided by the state health institutions. The Ministry of Health in each republic is responsible for the overall control and coordination of health system development, while these functions are performed by the health departments and their local branches in autonomous regions.

Preventive health services and medical care are provided by a total of more than seven million health workers of different categories, including 44.4 physicians per 10,000 population. Such a high physician/population ratio is not

---

[1] A new constitution was approved in November 1993.

an accurate indication of the real situation; nevertheless, it is a sign of an existing potential in the health care systems.

The extensive development of health systems over many years without the introduction of managerial changes and in the absence of new economic approaches in the health and related sectors, has created several problems. First, the economic conditions of the country made it impossible to provide the necessary financial and other resources for health. Second, a simple analysis showed that a quantitative increase in health sector resources, by itself, would not improve the quality of health care. Third, the country as a whole is in transition to a market economy, and the health sector, therefore, will function under new economic conditions that require a search for ways to minimize the adverse interim effects of this change.

The first measures to reform the health system were taken in 1987-1988 when decentralization of the management of the health system was implemented; this resulted in a significant expansion in the responsibilities of local health authorities and a change in their terms of reference. Second, at the same time (1987-1988) three regions of the country with a total population of about 11 million, launched a large-scale experiment to introduce new economic relations within the health sector. The majority of financial resources were allocated to ambulatory/polyclinic institutions, which were responsible for providing all medical services to the population within their geographical boundaries. A basic goal of this experiment was to determine, for the first time, the medical efficiency and actual costs for all kinds of health care. Third, early in 1991 health workers' salaries were increased and directly linked to qualifications and the quantity and quality of the work each performed. Fourth, in addition to state and municipal health sectors, there are also private physicians and a few private diagnostic and treatment institutions. Fifth, measures are being taken to eliminate state ownership of hospitals and outpatient facilities. The transfer of ownership of medical institutions to the professionals running them, on collective or rental basis, was chosen as the most appropriate form for the transitional period.

Before these reforms, the state had been essentially the only payer for medical care in this country, and it completely covered the financing of health institutions through its own budget. One of the most important tasks, therefore, was to transfer the partial responsibility for payment for medical services from the state to the actual consumers of medical care. This does not mean the introduction of a system of payment for all medical care directly by patients. In some cases, the payer may be the organization where a patient works; for members of certain groups it will be the local authorities. The most important element in the reform of health care delivery is the fundamental change of the whole system of allocating health resources in the country; i.e., the transition from pure budget financing to a budget/insurance approach. In addition to funding the main portion of biomedical research, the state budget will finance medical care for children, students, and members of non-working groups; several prevention activities. It will also fund parts of national sociomedical programs. Medical care for the working population will be paid from contributions to insurance companies for medical insurance of different institutions and enterprises. The introduction of such a system will not only more than double funds for health care, it will also provide the basis for the functioning of the system under market conditions.

Health Services

It is worthwhile to underscore that health care expenditures and socioeconomic indicators are not always directly related to the quality of health care and the health status of the population. Though the situation is not yet satisfactory, the data suggest considerable progress especially as compared with conditions before 1960.

The system of institutions for training middle-level staff consists of about six hundred nursing schools providing basic training and 17 postgraduate nursing schools distributed throughout the former USSR. These schools are considered institutions of specialized secondary training, and they train 12 types of specialists, including feldshers and midwives.

Primary health care and its further development remain the principal aim of the health strategy. First-contact care is based on the network of polyclinics that provide district doctors and specialist services. These polyclinics are subdivided into pediatric and adult units, which may share the same premises. There is also a separate system of emergency medical service.

Polyclinics are widely distributed in urban areas, providing easy accessibility for most people. In Moscow there are 230 adult and 150 child polyclinics. Although it is difficult to compare numbers across different systems, it is worth noting that Russia has a high number of doctors compared with other countries. It is our goal to have 50 doctors per 10,000 population by the year 2000. These figures may be misleading, however, because they do not account for the physicians who do not treat patients, pursuing instead careers in biomedical research or academic medicine.

In the Moscow region, with its responsibility for approximately 10 million people, 58,000 doctors are employed in the public health service. On average, polyclinics provides 25 doctors per 10,000 population, compared with a total of 16 per 10,000 population in the United Kingdom (5.5 of whom provide primary care) and a total of 22 per 10,000 in the more comparable Finnish system.

The health care system in rural areas differs in important respects. Small communities may be dependent on medical assistants/feldshers or nurses, while slightly larger communities will have doctors' services available to provide a range of care similar to the comprehensive care provided by general practitioners in other countries. There is accessibility to a wider range of services at regional polyclinics, but transportation difficulties can limit access. Doctors providing rural district services are often new graduates with limited qualifications and experience who spend a period of time in the rural medical services before going to postgraduate training.

Availability of hospital care depends on the population's needs for inpatient medical treatment, population demographics, density of population and composition by sex and age, state of communications, organization of ambulance services, and a number of other factors. In hospitals, diagnostics and specialized treatment are promptly performed. The development of large, multipurpose hospitals offers much promise. However, their effective utilization is yet to be realized. The structure, organization, and functioning of inpatient institutions must be improved to upgrade the curative-diagnostic process. More effective utilization of high technology is required to enhance the efficiency of hospital operations, and better integration of outpatient ambulatory care, continuity of the treatment process, and rational organization of the care of patients are of great importance. Optimization of specialized care for curative institutions and establishment of distinct interrelation among these institutions could become the main factor in improving secondary prevention.

HISTORICAL BACKGROUND

Medical education in this country dates back to the eleventh century, however regular training courses in medicine were initiated only in the second part of the seventeenth century. Real development in this field was linked with the founding of Moscow University in 1755 and with the medical Faculty created in 1764. Early medical training was similar to that adopted in Germany and the Netherlands. At the beginning of this century there were 16 Medical Faculties and by 1935 55 medical institutes (schools).

In 1930, Medical Faculties were separated from universities, renamed Medical Institutes, and given independent status under the supervision of the Health Ministries. This step was taken to bring medical education closer to governmental bodies of the same profile and for better integration with health services. Systems of Medical Institutes for both undergraduate and postgraduate levels were established.

Medical education in this country is under the auspices of institutes of education responsible to the Ministries of Health. Basic medical education requires six years training that usually starts at age 17. Training of doctors and pharmacists is provided in 91 higher medical and pharmaceutical institutions.

Before the current political/economic situation, medical education was subsidized by the state and planned to correspond to the country's needs for medical personnel. All funds for higher medical institutions were allocated from the state budget and given to the Republics' Ministries of Health for distribution among the Institutes. The ministries coordinated educational, methodological, and organizational work conducted at the medical establishments, planned the medical institution networks and determined the number of applicants admitted.

ROLE OF NATIONAL POLICY IN SHAPING MEDICAL EDUCATION

See "Overview of the Health Care Delivery System" and "Historical Background."

ADMISSION

Education in medical and pharmaceutical institutions is free of charge. Students are granted monthly stipends and, if necessary, accommodated in hostels. Medical and pharmaceutical institutions are open to applicants under 35 years old who have completed general secondary (equivalent to US high school) and/or nursing schools. The admissions examinations cover biology, physics, chemistry and language. Medical Institute admission was once highly competitive, when medicine was seen as a prestigious profession, with approximately eight students competing for each available opening. With the decline in physician income and prestige, the ratio of applicants to openings declined to two or three applicants per opening. Students generally complete 10 years of schooling prior to entry into medical school.

Approximately fifty-five percent of students are females. This male/female ratio has both advantages and disadvantages. Biological and cultural differences between men and women lead to the limitation of female activities and further career development in terms of qualification, but at the same time, it is known that women doctors are working very productively in health services, especially at the primary health care level. The problem of equality of opportunities for women still exists in all branches of human activities, including medicine.

CURRICULAR STRUCTURE AND INNOVATION

Higher medical institutions are organized in five separate Faculties: Faculty of Curative Medicine (a six-year course, specialty--general medicine); Faculty of Pediatrics (a six-year course, specialty--pediatrics); Faculty of Hygiene (a six-year course, specialty--sanitary hygiene); Faculty of Stomatology (a five-year course, specialty--stomatology); Institute or Faculty of Pharmacy (a four-five year course, specialty--pharmacist).

The curriculum for the first two years is the same at all Faculties. It includes preclinical and fundamental medical sciences that are the essential basis for any medical specialty. Medical specialization starts at the third year of studies; the curriculum includes propaedeutics, biochemistry and pathology (pathological anatomy and pathological physiology) clinical and special subjects, depending on the orientation. The principal feature of the curricula for both the Faculties of curative medicine and pediatrics is the introduction of a new approach to the training of internists and pediatricians that implies a two-year continuing primary specialization, one year while at the institution and the other year after graduation.

The curriculum at these Faculties is designed to cover all the general medical education within five years. During the third, fourth, and fifth years, students perform clinical work as nurses, feldshers, and clinical assistants. In the sixth year, medical students take their primary specialization in one of the following clinical subjects: Faculty of Curative Medicine (surgery, obstetrics, and gynecology) or Faculty of Pediatrics (pediatrics, including child infectious diseases, and pediatric surgery, including orthopedics). Subspecialization in clinical areas is not an option during the undergraduate program, as profound knowledge of the main clinical subjects is believed to be fundamental for adequate training of doctors.

After primary specialization in their sixth year, students pass a state examination according to the curriculum, obtain a Doctor's Diploma, and complete a one year internship in medical units under the supervision of specialists. Instruction in physiotherapy, ophthalmology, otolaryngology, dietology, climatotherapy, endocrinology, clinical biochemistry, and such aspects of surgery as oncology and neurosurgery is provided by the appropriate departments. The instructional methodology in higher medical institutions includes lectures by the leading specialists and regular practical classes throughout the course of studies.

Training programs at medical institutes both on undergraduate and postgraduate levels are adjusted to the needs of population in accordance with health priorities. Thus, when at the end of the 1950s the noncommunicable diseases became a real health problem, these subjects were strengthened and introduced more widely into curricula. In many institutes specialized departments for cardiology, oncology, endocrinology and other subspecialties were established. When the role of primary health care became more evident in the 1970s, the training programs were adapted to this target-problem. After the Chernobyl tragedy, aspects of radiobiology became an integral part of most programs within medical education curricula. The same approach was taken after AIDS became a major medical problem.

Following annual examinations at the end of the fourth and fifth years, senior students of all Faculties usually spend the breaks between semesters in professional training. Students are taught to use their knowledge, develop their professional skills, master up-to-date methods of diagnostics and treatment, and become familiar with all other work they will do in the future. It should be emphasized that at least 25 percent of the time within the training programme of all specialties is devoted to practice at the primary health care level.

Student assessment. On completing their practical training, students take credit tests before the term examination and at the end of each year, they take examinations on clinical skills and theoretical knowledge in subjects they have studied, with the five-point marking system being used for evaluation.

Finally, students must pass state examinations in general and special medical subjects (depending on the orientation of a particular Faculty) to receive a diploma as physician of general medicine at the Faculty of Curative Medicine (VRAC), as pediatrician at the Faculty of Pediatrics, as sanitary officer at the Faculty of Hygiene, as stomatologist at the Faculty of Stomatology, or as pharmacist at the pharmaceutical institution or faculty.

Every year more than 52,000 students graduate from medical institutions, nearly 50 percent of these from the Faculties of Curative Medicine. Pediatrics and Pharmacy graduate 20 percent each, and the remaining 10 percent graduate from the Faculty of Hygiene. During the last twenty years, biomedical faculty in the Second Moscow Medical Institute have been responsible for training research workers for scientific institutions. Almost two hundred students graduate from this faculty annually.

GRADUATE MEDICAL EDUCATION

Postgraduate medical education in the former Soviet Union is comprehensive and systematic, perhaps uniquely so. The first successful effort to establish a prototype of the postgraduate training system was the institute for postgraduate training of physicians in St. Petersburg, founded some one hundred years ago. However, it was not until the Soviet government came into power that government legislation on this subject was introduced. The Special Act on the Scientific Mission of Physicians of 1927 ensured that physicians undergoing postgraduate training continue to receive their salaries for the entire period of training. In 1934, the Government Act on Medical Training became the first state decree to establish a uniform system of postgraduate medical training and to create specialization facilities. Further legislation, the Act on Medical Training, required periodic postgraduate training once every three years for rural physicians and once every five years for urban physicians. Thus, postgraduate training is organized by the state and subject to central management and goal setting, while the planning process is decentralized and responds to priority educational needs to ensure relevance in training programs, continuity in professional development, and compliance with existing standards of professional performance.

Implementation of postgraduate programs is managed by Ministries of Health through their departments of medical education, and by regional and district health departments. Most of the work is undertaken by undergraduate and postgraduate educational institutions. These include 56 Faculties for advanced medical training attached to undergraduate institutions and 16 separate and specialized institutes for advanced medical training.

At the national level in the Central Institute for Advanced Medical Education every year some twenty-five thousand qualified medical physicians from more than 80 specialties take formal courses. This is done according to the planned quantitative targets specified by the Ministry of Health and based on health care needs. In the same manner, at the republic levels, including the Russian Federation, more than two hundred thousand medical personnel pursue courses in the republic's Institutes for Advanced Medical Education and in Faculties for advanced medical training at the undergraduate institutions.

At the regional level, a still larger proportion of health care personnel is regularly involved in postgraduate training at highly specialized regional hospitals, health care institutions, and services. In addition, at any given time, hundreds of thousands of medical personnel are engaged in different kinds of training in numerous central district hospitals and health care institutions and services at the district level and in their places of work. Formal educational programs in medical specialties are designed, periodically reviewed, and required for all 16 institutes for advanced medical training. The training programs offered at regional, district, and local levels are normally developed at the respective levels, to ensure relevance to local needs and problems. This can be done either independently or under the technical guidance of the institutes and Faculties for advanced medical training.

Options in postgraduate training are numerous. There are three main patterns of postgraduate training: self-education and learning at the individual's home, periodic education and learning experiences at the workplace, and formal courses and programs at institutes and Faculties for advanced medical training. At the national and local levels, thousands undergo regular formal courses and programs, while more than a million engage in postgraduate training at their workplaces in the form of organized seminars, conferences, and teamwork exercises, in addition to self-education and learning on an individual basis.

There is one additional level of postgraduate education: the two-year residency (*ordinature*) program designed to train clinicians to supervise departments or hospitals, and presided over by advisers of an academic and university level.

Motivation is a key factor, and it should be emphasized that promotion is significantly dependant on the successful completion of advanced training, a prerequisite for achieving second, first, and top professional qualification categories and substantial increases in salary. Each physician is awarded a standard certificate on graduating from a course, and the dates and duration of advanced medical training are recorded in the physician's personal file.

Increasing emphasis is being placed on systematic course design models and all forms of "learning by doing," while formal lecturing is gradually, but not without resistance, being reduced in favor of problem-solving and logical decision-making learning experiences. This kind of learning has proven to be more motivational and effective than didactic teaching. The importance of postgraduate education is recognized, but only a few people, if any, can admit to knowing how to measure success or the direct and tangible benefits of postgraduate training of health care personnel. Does postgraduate education genuinely upgrade capabilities and ensure quality of health care? Is it cost-effective?

LICENSURE

See "Curricular Structure."

CONTINUING MEDICAL EDUCATION

See "Graduate Medical Education."

INTERNATIONAL LINKAGES AND COLLABORATION

The history of cross-national collaboration in medical education on global and regional levels is rich and interesting. International cooperation has stimulated positive development of medical education for many years. Intergovernmental and nongovernmental organizations during the last decade have intensified collaboration in health personnel development.

The World Health Organization, World Federation for Medical Education, and other international organizations took some useful steps toward the creation of world contacts by organizing joint research and training programs, conferences, and meetings. The professional spectrum of those activities is very wide, ranging from different clinical disciplines to public health problems.

The usefulness of international collaboration could be recognized in many medical institutions in the country. The results of WHO's program activities in various fields are incorporated into the medical curricula, and especially in postgraduate programs. The main themes of the Edinburgh Declaration were extremely valuable in the course of the development of new curricula and its composition. Several institutions maintain bilateral and multilateral cooperation with medical schools abroad and esteem this activity very highly, especially exchange of students, teachers and research workers. Taking into account the present world situation and trends in population migration, including specialists, there is a need to promote internationally the process of cross-licensing of physicians between the countries. Exchange of information on training programs and requirements for certification and licensing facilitate a certain predisposition for such activity. This work itself will be very useful for promotion of medical education on the country level as well. It should be mentioned here that joint efforts in this respect must be linked with the idea of quality of care in medicine, which is a priority area in health at present. The problems of public health are becoming vital again around the world. Cooperation in this direction brings new promises and ideas for health development. The Public Health summit organized by WHO and the Declaration of the conference calling for new public health action is timely. A new situation in the former Soviet Union and ideas concerning reforms in the social sphere, including the health sector, require new optimal models of health care systems and innovative public health philosophy. Finally, it should be said that international collaboration in general, and in health personnel development in particular is focusing on the tendencies in medical education for the twenty-first century, when we can dream about a united world, at least in medicine.

ISSUES AND TRENDS

The trend toward disease prevention and health promotion constitutes the main approach within the health care services. Steps are being taken to use the potential of medical science and the results of basic and applied research in order to improve methods for prevention, diagnosis, and treatment, including rehabilitation. Within the health system, scientific research is being conducted at more than three hundred research institutions and their branches. The focal point in this system is the Academy of Medical Sciences, which has drawn up many scientific programs now being carried out at research centers and institutions.

Medical education and its development are a reflection of the health system and population requirements in health care. This is why directions within medical education will depend on the situation in the health field as a whole. If we can analyze and predict peculiarities of health system development and the influence of market psychology on it, we can visualize the perspectives of medical education.

A country of the size and complexity of Russia has diverse needs. It is likely that having provided an effective, easily accessible and comprehensive health care system, there is a need to provide greater flexibility so that individual areas can develop services for their own needs. Any particular health system cannot be transferred to another country. Moreover, some elements of the health care system may need to be specifically adapted to different regions within the country itself.

In developing this more flexible service, consideration must be given to holding down costs, maintaining equity, and constantly improving the quality of the service. There is an attempt to move toward a pluralistic approach operating in the conditions of a market economy. At the same time, market forces on their own, although they will make the service responsive to individually perceived needs, will not necessarily hold down costs, maintain equity or improve quality. This is partly because health cannot be a subject of the market in any real economic sense.

In these circumstances there is a need to revise the role of central authorities in monitoring standards, evaluating the services, and stimulate new developments. This will enable firm, validated suggestions on improvement to be made. It is essential to underline also the role of central authorities in monitoring and influencing changes in the undergraduate, postgraduate and continuing education of doctors that will ensure that they are in a position to provide a high quality service.

The future of the health system, biomedical research and medical education are inextricably linked with the economical situation in the country. If, for example, substantial additional funding were not forthcoming for the state health care system managed by the Ministries of Health, innovative financing and reorganization of resources alone would not substantially improve the quality of the system. Conversely, even if the Ministries of Health were infused with increased funding, if the ideological vision of high-quality free health care for all were diluted, there would remain the potential for the rise of a multitiered system of health care.

This leads to the conclusion that what we have today may not be perfect. In other words, in order to achieve the impossible, we have to see the invisible. This is the only real way toward the progress.

REFERENCES

Vartanian, F.E. 1993. Continuing medical education and its management. *Journal of Management in Medicine* 7(2):29-24.

———. 1988. Information technologies: Their inevitable impact on CME (Illusions, realities, perspectives). *Journal of Continuing Education in the Health Professions* 8:313-319.

———. 1987. Continuing medical education in the Union of the Soviet Socialist Republics. *JAMA* 258(11 September):1358-1360.

26

South Africa

JOSEPH H. LEVENSTEIN

The Republic of South Africa is situated at the southernmost portion of Africa and is bordered by the Atlantic and Indian Oceans. It has a population of more than 33 million people of black, white, Asian and "colored" ethnic groups. Approximately 50 percent of financing for health care comes from the government sector and a similar percentage from the private sector. About 80 percent of the population (mainly nonwhite people) receive health care from the public sector, which employs about 45 percent of the medical practitioners.

OVERVIEW OF THE HEALTH CARE DELIVERY SYSTEM

The health care delivery system is three-tiered: (1) the central government, (2) the provincial government, and (3) the local authorities. The central government is responsible for the overall policy for national health services, planning, health education, and communicable diseases, for example. The provincial government provides facilities such as public hospitals and ambulatory care clinics At least 70 percent of the health care budget is allocated to the provinces. Finally, the local or municipal authorities have responsibilities related to immunization, rehabilitation, sanitation, and other public health activities for their community, i.e., preventive and promotive activities. This already fragmented system was fragmented further by the apartheid policy, which sought to create black homelands within the confines of the South African border. There were ten such homelands, and all had separate health care systems. Private health care is mainly conducted through about two hundred medical insurance companies.

Both the private and the public sectors are under pressure from rising medical costs. South Africa spends 5.9 percent of its gross national product on health care, with most of this being allotted to secondary and tertiary care. Less than 5 percent of the total allocation is spent on primary and preventive medicine. In a country that represents both industrialized and developing countries, medicine is largely geared toward the standards of the industrialized world and reflects the traditional hospital-based, technological and specialist value system. Symbolic of this emphasis is South Africa's leadership role in heart transplantation. The traditional system has been the basis for medical education. The medical schools and their teaching hospitals are responsible for a large portion of the public health care delivery system. Therefore, these predominately specialized health services are mainly focused in the large cities where the teaching institutions are located, thereby creating a great void of care in the periurban and rural areas.

While most medical organizations, professional associations and institutions, to a lesser or greater extent, sought to oppose apartheid[1] policy and advocated equitable health care, the apartheid policy nevertheless affected health care delivery, exacerbating inherent inequities seen in similar third world countries and other situations in inner city or rural areas around the globe. Notwithstanding this situation, it was still argued that the standard of medical care both in public and private sectors was by far the best in all of Africa.

At present, there is consensus among the government, medical schools, and other medical bureaucracies, that there is a need for the delivery of comprehensive primary care to all South Africans and for a greater orientation of medical education to community-based care. The major difficulties still facing health care are the fragmentation of services, as outlined above, access to care (rural and periurban versus urban), and the increasing costs of health care. Further difficulties include the medical education system, which, in general, has not been able to change its direction and values to meet current societal needs.

HISTORICAL BACKGROUND

Medical education was initiated in South Africa at the University of Cape Town (UCT) in the year 1900. The first preclinical three years were conducted in Cape Town, and the latter three in medical schools in the United Kingdom. In 1920, UCT graduated its first locally educated class. Currently there are eight medical schools in Southern Africa, including the Medical School of the University of Transkei (UT), established in 1985[2].

The schools are modeled after the six-year British traditional medical school system, with the first half being devoted to preclinical activities (basic sciences), and the latter three years devoted to clinical and hospital-based training. This

---

[1] Apartheid literally means "separateness," but a more accurate translation would be segregation. Segregation existed in South Africa prior to 1948, the year the Nationalist party came to power. The latter, however, enshrined segregation and extended it legislatively to social, educational, and vocational arenas, and in so doing coined the term apartheid. In terms of the apartheid policy, an attempt was also made to create independent nation states (homelands) for various black tribes within the confines of South African borders.

[2] Transkei is an "independent" black homeland.

model was influenced by the international post-World War II trends which emphasized postgraduate education and research. This model still comprises the basis of medical education in South Africa. While all schools are making some attempts to become more community and primary-care oriented, only the UT has instituted a curriculum with as much as one third of the clinical teaching taking place in the community.

Most medical institutions cite financial constraints as being the reason not to make major changes. Without additional funds, it is correctly interpreted that some of their existing hospital-based activities would be sacrificed should changes be introduced. However, if the emphasis of medical education is to change to a more person-centered, primary care, and community, preventive orientation, it is obvious that fewer resources could be allotted to traditional technological hospital-based medicine. Many educators are apprehensive of this type of change, equating it with a "drop in scientific standards." The challenge will be to deal with society's medical needs with the same intellectual vigor as does hospital-based medicine, thus continuing with the scientific tradition, albeit in a different arena.

ROLE OF NATIONAL POLICY IN SHAPING MEDICAL EDUCATION

By and large, South Africa's medical schools have been autonomous in deciding how direction of their curricular, research and service activities should be focused. In implementing their service obligations, they have been involved predominantly with the provincial governments, whose main thrust has been toward tertiary-care hospitals, some of which are the medical schools' teaching hospitals. There has been no centralized planning with regard to health care. However, the central government issued a National Health Facilities Plan in 1985, emphasizing inter alia community, primary, and preventive care. This apparent difference in agendas between governmental medical priorities and the medical schools has resulted more recently in open conflict between the two groups.

The political parties, however, have offered no centralized, coherent plan with regard to health care in general, and no broad scale provisions have been made to cope with major public health problems such as AIDS, lack of immunization, dehydration from gastroenteritis, malnutrition, and lack of health care in rural and periurban areas.

ADMISSION

Determination of admissions criteria to medical schools is the prerogative of each institution. These criteria relate to the philosophy, both educational and general, that the school or its parent university may have. Generally speaking, a specific educational standard is required. This usually relates to the high school leaving examinations where a high academic standard must be attained. Only about 10 percent of those applying are admitted to medical school in South Africa. A concerted attempt appears evident to increase the number of black South Africans in medical school training by the following measures. First, some medical schools that did not admit black students in the apartheid era are now doing so; certain schools are increasing their number of black students; two medical schools exclusively for black South Africans have been opened in the past 15 years, making a total of three that admit only black students. Finally, certain medical schools have provided support instruction for those students who may have come from a deprived educational background, and one (Witwatersrand) has gone to imaginative lengths to broaden the entrance criteria and thereby increase the ethnic and gender diversity of the class. Up to 25 percent of medical students are now "black"; additionally, and in tandem with the worldwide trend, the percentage of female students is increasing at all medical schools. Approximately eleven hundred students per year graduate as medical doctors from the eight medical schools.

CURRICULAR STRUCTURE AND INNOVATION

While the curriculum is regularly reviewed in the institutions, the basic format of the British model (i.e., three years preclinical and three years clinical) is adhered to. In the preclinical years, chemistry, physics, mathematics, anatomy, physiology, biochemistry, pathology, pharmacology, and cellular biology and microbiology are the basis of the curriculum. However, all medical schools have introduced required courses such as sociology, psychology, human behavior, community health, family health, and ethics. The University of Transkei, a community-based medical school, has greater emphasis on communication skills, behavioral sciences, and community medicine.

The three clinical years cover predominantly surgery, internal medicine, pediatrics, obstetrics and gynecology, and the subspecialties of these disciplines. Medical schools usually have clinical departments of community health and family medicine/general practice. There is a strong emphasis on clinical instruction and medical tutorials. Obviously, in an environment where there is industrialized world medical expertise combined with developed and developing countries' illnesses and diseases, there is an enhanced opportunity to focus on physical examination, diagnosis, and other clinical skills. Attempts have been made, to a certain extent, to incorporate exposure to community and family medicine in the form of clerkships in the traditional medical schools. At the UT there are such clerkships in the fourth, fifth, and sixth years in the community.

Basic clerkship requirements are set by the educational committee of the South African Medical and Dental Council (SAMDC) which has representatives from all medical schools. While the basic curriculum is generally stable, all medical schools have curriculum and educational committees, as well as faculty, and other personnel to review the content and teaching strategies. However, the medical schools, other than UT, do not have any profound curricular changes taking place which would result in a shift in emphasis from hospital to community-based medicine.

GRADUATE MEDICAL EDUCATION

It is estimated that between 30 and 40 percent of students enter traditional specialist and subspecialist training, which may require up to five years. Technically, to practice general medicine (i.e., general practice/family medicine), only one year of internship is needed, but there are vocational training (residency) programs in general practice/family medicine. The College of Medicine of South Africa (COM-SA) is the body responsible for higher or licensing examinations for all the disciplines including general practice/family medicine. These higher degrees are registerable with the medical licensing body, the South African Medical and Dental Council. The COM-SA is thus comparative to all the specialty boards of North America or the Royal Colleges in the UK. It also undertakes other educational activity related to continuing medical education and health care in general. The number of residents in specialty training at each medical school and its hospitals is allocated by the SAMDC; however there is no formula available as to the type of residency positions to be filled and certainly no evidence that an attempt is made to regulate them in relation to societal need. The most popular residency programs appear to be radiology, anesthesiology, and orthopedics.

LICENSURE

After successfully completing six years of medical study, the medical student is awarded the MB ChB degree. The graduate is then licensed to practice only under supervision in a training situation.

Cross-Licensing of Physicians

England, Northern Ireland, the Republic of Ireland, and Belgium are the only four countries where cross-licensing for "basic" medical degrees is accepted. In order for graduates from other countries to be licensed, at least two years' hospital "practice" at a teaching or an approved hospital must take place, and the physician must pass an examination for full registration.

CONTINUING MEDICAL EDUCATION

Continued licensing is not contingent on attending continuing medical education courses. Professional associations, medical schools, and pharmaceutical companies provide extensive courses, programs, conferences, lectures, and meetings, but attendance is not compulsory.

ROLE OF RESEARCH IN MEDICAL EDUCATION

The conflicts of patient care, research, and teaching in medical education are subject to the usual stresses, with various schools having different resources, policies, and regulations. Some schools divide their mission between patient care and teaching/research. Faculty involvement can range from 50/50 percent to 60/40 percent patient care versus teaching/research. In the latter component, all or a portion of the time may be devoted to research.

GOVERNMENT/PRIVATE SECTOR INVOLVEMENT

Within the medical schools there are research funds, but the main source of research funding is the Medical Research Council which has approximately eleven million rand (the purchasing power of the rand is approximately equivalent to the US dollar) available for research. Most of this funding goes to the traditional subjects of research with only a small portion being allocated to community health. There are also other sources of funding available such as national and international foundations.

INTERNATIONAL LINKAGES AND COLLABORATION

South African medical schools have made no public commitment to declarations such as the Edinburgh Declaration. However, organizations such as the recently created South African Health and Social Service Organization, the Medical Association of South Africa (MASA), UCOM-SA, and professional discipline bodies such as the Academy of Family Practice, have all sponsored policy conferences and made statements in relation to adapting the health care system to the health care needs of South Africa and all South Africans.

Health systems research by the Medical Research Council and departments of health care research have gone a long way in defining the health care problems for South Africa in the twenty-first century. There is little doubt that with the new political climate there is a great opportunity to respond to this new challenge, but how the medical establishment will do so remains to be seen. Ideally, the resolution of the political problems will place industrialized South Africa in a position to be the organizing force for health in the region. A more equitable and democratic dispensation would also allow for more participation in World Health Organization initiatives, such as changing medical education. South Africa, with its vast inequalities, has even more of an imperative than other countries to ensure that it changes its medical education system from the traditional medical model to the needs of society in the twenty-first century.

ISSUES AND TRENDS

The future of health care financing and administration is in large part dependent on the future political dispensation of South Africa. However, the medical establishment, including its educational institutions and its supporting bureaucracies, have it within their power to gear their service, educational, and research thrusts to meet society's needs. To a certain extent, the shift from a traditional hospital-based focus to a community-based primary care orientation has begun. This trend must be vigorously pursued. The current funding of health care at 5.9 percent of the GNP must be increased and the percentage allocated to primary care (5 percent of health funding) dramatically increased.

REFERENCES

Benatar, S.R. 1991. Medicine and health care in South Africa. *N Engl J Med* 325:30-36.

DeBeer, C., and J. Broomberg. 1990. Financing health care for all: Is national health insurance the first step? *S Afr Med J* 78:144-147.

Medical Research Council of South Africa. 1991. *Changing health in South Africa.* California: Henry J. Kaiser Family Foundation.

Mitchell, G., and J. Haupt. 1990. Selection of medical students: A follow up study. *S. Afr Med J* 78:3116-3119.

Levenstein. J.H. 1990. Apartheid ends in government hospitals in South Africa: One struggle is over, another begins. *BMJ* 300:1419.

---------. 1988. Family medicine, medical bureaucracies and society. *S. Afr Fam Prac* 9:173-182.

Summit Meeting: The future of academic medicine in South Africa. 1990. *S. Afr Med J* 77 (12):vii-ix.

27

Thailand

TONGCHAN HONGLADAROM

Thailand is a country of 513,000 square kilometers situated in Southeast Asia, with Myanmar on the west, Laos and Kampuchea on the east, Malaysia to the South, and Myanmar and Laos to the north. According to the 1990 census it had a population of 56.4 million with an annual growth rate of 1.4 percent. More than 25 percent of the population live in urban areas. The country consists of seventy-three provinces; each is divided into eight to ten *amphurs* (districts) and each *amphur* into eight to ten *tambons* (groups of villages), with eight to twelve villages in each *tambon*.

OVERVIEW OF THE HEALTH CARE DELIVERY SYSTEM

The Ministry of Public Health has taken major responsibility for the delivery of health services. It operates the health centers in every *tambon*, the community hospitals (10-90 beds each) in every *amphur*, the 89 provincial hospitals (200-500 beds each) that provide specialized care in every province including Bangkok. In addition to the Ministry of Public Health, many other ministries, such as Defense, Interior and the Office of University Affairs also take part in providing health services. The government owns and operates 70 per cent of the hospitals; the remaining 30 percent are private sector, have fewer beds but more sophisticated equipment and are located in big cities (Thailand 1991).

In the past decade, the Thai economy has grown rapidly. The average annual rate of growth in the Fifth Five-Year National Economic and Social Development Plan (1982-1986) was 4.5 percent, in the Sixth Plan (1987-1991), it was 10.5 percent, and in the Seventh (1992-1996), it is estimated to be 8.2 percent (NESDB 1987-1991). However, the income gap between the rich and the poor is widening. Between 1976 and 1986 the share of total national income received by the upper 20 percent of the population increased from 49.5 percent in 1976 to 55.6 percent in 1986, while the share received by the lowest, 20 percent decreased from 6.1 percent to 4.6 percent.

The increase in the nation's gross domestic product has come mainly from the industrial sector which accounted for 16 percent of the GDP in 1970 and 34 percent in 1990; over the same period, the share from the agricultural sector declined from 27 percent to 15 percent.

It is predicted that by the year 2000, the Thai population will reach 64 million. Due to continuing migration from rural areas, urban populations will increase more rapidly then the overall population, which is expected to grow at 1.2 percent per year. The death rate is expected to decline to 4.4 per 1,000 population. Life expectancy, now 66 for females and 62 for males, will increase substantially; moreover, the number of children under five will decline while the number of active elderly increases. All these changes will alter family structures in ways that will reduce the importance of extended family.

With respect to disease patterns, malnutrition and some communicable diseases (e.g., malaria), have declined while others such as tuberculosis, pneumonia, dengue hemorrhagic fever, Japanese encephalitis, hepatitis, and rabies, still pose significant problems (National Epidemiology Board of Thailand, 1990). Due to the widening gap between the rich and poor, and increased tensions among the population, psychiatric problems and social disorders (e.g., injury, violence, drug dependence, and AIDS and other sexually transmitted diseases) are becoming more and more burdensome to society. Other unwanted behavioral choices affecting the health of the people include alcohol and food indulgence, reckless driving, heavy smoking, and unsafe sex. Non-communicable diseases, such as diabetes mellitus, coronary insufficiency, hypertension, cancers and especially those due to unhealthy life styles (e.g. overeating and lack of exercise) are also increasing.

Thailand also faces new issues in environmental health. People suffer from chemical pesticides used to protect their crops, and diseases due to toxic substances released from industrial factories are also appearing more frequently. Occupational health is also a growing problem as industrialization proceeds. Finding ways to clean up and protect the environment and to ensure occupational safety without hurting the economy has become a major issue, since businesses do not have the resources to initiate protective measures. To complicate the matter, these changing patterns are occurring in various regions of the country, making it imperative to focus policy, research and action at the most appropriate administrative levels. Since much of the change involves complex socioeconomic factors that affect health, minor supplements to the traditional approaches to public health are no longer adequate to deal with the dynamics of the health situation. Innovations in public health services and medical education are needed.

HISTORICAL BACKGROUND

Medical education in Thailand originated at the same time as medicine. It was based on the Ayurveda system of India, and was understood to have come to Thailand with Buddhism. (See "A Note on Ayurveda," p. 218.) Every old treatise in ancient Thai medicine refers to Shivok Komarabhaj, personal physician to the Lord Buddha, who wrote the medical treatise (Ouay 1978). In ancient times, knowledge was gained by apprenticeship, and transferred directly among relatives, from father to son or grandfather to grandchildren. Students memorized the texts and the practices of elders or teachers, often following teachers to their households.

At the time of the founding of Siriraj Hospital in 1888, training at Bhaedhayakorn Medical College included both traditional and modern medicine. However, there was no systematic education in traditional medicine and no provision for change or adaptation to new knowledge. Medical students, therefore, gradually lost interest in traditional medicine, and it disappeared from the curriculum (Sood 1978). Modern medical education began when Siriraj Hospital accepted its first class in 1889. Literacy was the only requirement for entry into the three-year program, which was extended to four years in 1903 and to five years in 1913. However, the full-fledged introduction of modern medical education to Thailand occurred in 1922 when Prince Mahidol of Songkla (the father of the present King) donated his personal funds to construct buildings and sent young instructors to study abroad. The Rockefeller Foundation responded to Prince Mahidol's request for assistance by funding a curriculum development project for the Siriraj Medical School and providing support for potential administrators and department heads to study in the United States. The resulting six-year program, which students were eligible to enter after obtaining a secondary school diploma, was similar to the American system in requiring two years of premedical science (plus English), two years of preclinical studies and two years of clinical subjects.

ROLE OF NATIONAL POLICY IN SHAPING MEDICAL EDUCATION

Since the Fifth Five-Year National Economic and Social Plan (1982 onward), Thailand has considered health development as an integral part of total social development. The so-called "Four Principle Ministries" (Education, Public Health, Agriculture and Cooperatives, and Interior), have been working together as a team to implement or plan for total social development of the people and lands. They adopted standard criteria for evaluating all village development, called "Basic Minimum Needs" of the villagers, against which the outcomes of the programs have been measured. Indicators of health status, educational progress and economic growth have been created by experts and are now being used extensively throughout the country. Concepts of Health for All, primary health care and basic minimum needs have been translated into concrete action, especially in the rural areas.

In the Seventh Five-year National Economic and Social Development Plan (1992-1996), the Ministry of Public Health adopted the following four principles as the basis for health development: (1) Coverage and Justice: public health service should be available in every area in such a way that each person can have access to it regardless of sex, age, social status, or culture. Fair and accessible service must be made available to low-income people, senior citizens, children, women, and socially disadvantaged minorities. (2) Integrated Development: public health development should be based on an integration of health promotion, disease prevention, rehabilitation, and curative services. Moreover, coordination and referral of patients should be done in such a way that the patients are cared for appropriately and completely. Referrals should be timely, people should have access without delay to more sophisticated service when needed, and the nearest public health center should be utilized most effectively. (3) Relevancy: the planning and implementation of public health service should be flexible and sensitive to the realities of the communities. Care must be taken regarding the different economic, social and cultural conditions of the people. Methods of implementing health services should be sufficiently adaptable so that improvements in health can occur in both urban and rural areas, congested slums and rich neighborhoods. Though flexible and sensitive, services should be standardized with regard to high quality. (4) Self-Reliance of the People and Community: public health development should take into consideration local participation and responsibility according to the existing potentials of the people. Reliance on local wisdom (such as folk medicine and use of herbs), will guarantee the success and the maintenance of health development; it will also significantly increase valuable resources in public health development.

Influenced by these concepts of health development, and with the encouragement of the World Health Organization (WHO), the Thai medical curricula since the Fourth National Conference on Medical Education in 1979 have been reoriented toward the concept of integrated health services and health manpower development (HSMD).

Cost of Medical Education

Cost of medical education is difficult to estimate because it involves cost of hospital services that students use in partial fulfillment of their study. However, the Division of Planning of the Office of University Affairs estimated that in 1986, 1987 and 1991, the average annual per capita operating expenses (without capital outlay) for medical education was 163,000, 177,000 and 214,000 Bahts (equivalent to US $ 6,392, 6,941 and 8,392, respectively) (Division of Planning, 1992). The public medical schools usually charge nominal tuition fees around 4,000 Bahts per year, or 1.8 percent of the operating expenses.

With this figure in mind and compounded by the fact that there was a shortage of doctors in rural areas, the government passed a regulation in 1972 under which medical graduates must serve the government for at least three years or pay a fine of 400,000 Bahts (equivalent to US$ 15,686), an amount reduced proportionately for time the doctors spend in government service. The regulation has temporarily relieved the shortage of doctors in remote areas, but most doctors continue to prefer specialist training when they are freed from the bond.

Physician Manpower Planning

Collecting data on the number of doctors in Thailand is, at present, difficult and the resultant figures are often misleading. The Thai Ministry of Public Health estimated the number of working doctors (excluding those retired and migrated) to be 12,660 by 1992, and some 800 to 850 new physicians are produced each year. At this current rate of production, it is predicted that by the year 2000 supply will be more or less equal to demand. (Thailand 1988).

However, the high rate of economic growth in the past five years has resulted in a tremendous increase in the demand for health care. The government has encouraged the private sector to share in meeting these needs. It is now estimated that by the year 2000, between 4,500 and 6,000 physicians will need to move from the public sector to the private sector to accommodate expected expansion in the number of private hospitals in Bangkok and other large cities. Thus the shortage of doctors in small cities and rural areas will become worse. For this reason, in November 1992, the government mandated an increase (beginning in the 1993 academic year) of 320 per year in the output of physicians from existing medical schools.

ADMISSION

In general, the academic qualification of students who enter Thai medical schools is a secondary education qualification or its equivalent. Only in a few innovative programs do the medical schools admit applicants with bachelor's degrees or students who have earned credits at the university level.

At present, there are three ways of gaining admission to government and private medical schools. These are the joint examination, the provincial medical school quota system, and admission to the innovative programs. In the 1993 academic year, eight government and one private medical school participated in the joint entrance examination. The Office of University Affairs is responsible for arranging and coordinating the examination.

In order to select medical students whose attitudes are favorable to serving the needs of the rural people in the appropriate region, the three provincial medical schools administer their own selection examination. Chiang Mai in the North, Khon Kaen in the North-East, and Songkla in the South each reserve a 50 percent quota of available seats for residents of the region.

The third admission route is through the innovative programs. Projects for students in rural areas conducted at Mahidol and Chulalongkorn universities admit rural secondary school graduates who pass attitude and aptitude screening in addition to the entrance examination of the schools. The Problem Based Learning (PBL) program at Chulalongkorn admits applicants with a bachelor's degree who have acquired at least 26 semester credits of science and mathematics. Applicants must pass the entrance examination conducted by the medical school. Thammasat's PBL course, following a similar pattern, admits medical students who have earned at least 80 semester credits at the university level, as well as applicants with bachelor's degrees.

CURRICULAR STRUCTURE AND INNOVATION

Since the modern medical curriculum was established at Siriraj in 1923, there have been few modifications in the structure and length of the course other than modest changes in the subjects taught and instructional techniques employed. The one-year compulsory internship added to the curriculum in 1960 was eliminated in 1985. Beginning in 1969, a BS degree was awarded to those completing the pre-medical and preclinical courses, but this was abolished in 1979.

In 1973, Khon Kaen, then the newest medical school, introduced an integrated curriculum in preclinical subjects; otherwise it was not until 1979 that there was a general change in the curriculum at which time the two year premedical requirement was reduced to one year, the clinical component increased to three years and the compulsory internship was abolished. These changes were possible because graduates of secondary schools had already acquired adequate basic knowledge for further study in the medical schools.

Innovations in Thai medical education have been significantly influenced by the recommendations of the National Medical Education Conferences which have been held periodically since 1956. The First National Conference in 1956 brought about clearer concepts on the roles of pediatrics, preventive medicine and psychiatry in medical education. As a result, greater emphasis was given to pediatrics in the curricula, and departments of preventive medicine and psychiatry were founded in the then two existing medical schools.

The Second National Conference in 1964 recommended integrated teaching within each discipline and among disciplines. It was suggested that teachers should encourage students to develop self-learning skills; thus, teacher training in the area of pedagogy and the establishment of a medical education unit in every medical school were recommended. With WHO support, in 1970, Chulalongkorn established the first medical education unit to fulfill the needs for teacher training. In 1971 this unit was designated as the WHO Regional Teacher Training Center (RTTC) for Southeast Asia.

In 1965, Ramathibodi was founded and with the assistance of the Rockefeller Foundation an outstanding community medicine program was established. By virtue of its affiliation with the Ministry of Public Health, the school was able to arrange for students and interns to work and study at Bang-Pa-In District Hospital, and for the staff of the District Hospital to serve as supervisors of the program.

In 1971, the Third National Conference recommended integration of the subjects in the curriculum and re-emphasized the importance of teacher training. The WHO concept of health services and manpower development was introduced and medical schools were encouraged to revise curricula to be more relevant to the needs of the society. Among the three schools established in 1972, Khon Kaen was the first to develop an integrated curriculum for preclinical subjects which permitted the clinical experience to be extended to three years.

In 1973, partially in response to student demonstration demanding more relevant instruction, a curriculum committee appointed by the Medical Council proposed three models. These stimulated widespread discussion about the relation of the curriculum to the needs of the community (New perspectives in education, 1974; Charn 1974; Adulya 1974).

In 1974, Mahidol University initiated a special program designed to serve rural needs. It entailed recruiting students from rural areas, establishing a selection committee composed of both university and Ministry of Public Health staff, and adopting broader admission criteria that included consideration of attitudes toward medicine and willingness to return to serve their villages. Chulalongkorn instituted a similar program (MESRAP) in 1975, in which rural students were sent to provincial hospitals for the entire period of their clinical training, and were required to work in district hospitals and health centers in the rural areas. These programs were established to encourage high school graduates from the provinces to return to give health care in their province of origin. A 1988 study reported that in comparison with graduates of other programs MESRAP doctors had demonstrated equal clinical competence, better attitudes and greater ability to work in the community (Hongladarom et al. 1989). Since 1979, some institutions (Chiang Mai, Khon Kaen, and Songkla) have introduced required courses in community medicine and mandatory clerkships in district hospitals and health centers in rural areas. Others (Siriraj and Ramathibodi) have extended their affiliation projects with the Ministry of Public Health to include district hospitals.

The Fourth National Conference, in 1979, introduced the WHO concept of Health for All through primary health care (PHC). This served to better emphasize the importance of relevancy in the curriculum, to encourage community health programs and to stimulate affiliation with the Ministry of Public Health.

At the Fifth National Conference in 1986, the concepts of problem-based learning and community-based education were introduced; these were fully implemented in 1987, in a new MD program developed jointly by Chulalongkorn and the Royal Thai Air Force Hospital and in the most recently established school at Thammsat.

In the 100-year history of Thai medical education, more than fifteen thousand doctors have graduated from Thai medical schools. The graduates have demonstrated their competence as physicians; many have been nationally and internationally renowned in their profession. But this excellence has been demonstrated primarily in highly specialized fields characteristic of tertiary care in large urban hospitals, not in solving the health problems characteristic of poor rural communities in a developing country. Even though the main objectives of the medical education programs described above have been achieved, it is generally accepted that other skills such as critical thinking, clinical reasoning, decision making, problem solving, leadership and the ability to work in a team required of all medical graduates are still in need of improvement. The Fifth National Medical Education Conference recommended that innovative medical curricula which promote the desired abilities must be sought.

Problem-based learning (PBL) has interested the faculty of Chulalongkorn as one method of achieving these objectives (Barrows and Tamblyn 1980). Consequently, groups of faculty members were sent to McMaster and Maastricht to collect information about the system. Eventually the successful experience of the innovative parallel track of the Faculty of Medicine, University of New Mexico at Albuquerque, suggested the way. In May 1988, with the admission of nineteen students, a problem-based program, called Community Targeted Problem-Based Medical Education Program (CTPB) was launched for the first time in Thailand, as the third parallel track at Chulalongkorn. It required two years in curriculum development and preparation and included teacher training in the form of seminars and workshops conducted periodically by groups of experts from Maastricht, McMaster, the Center for Educational Development (now Department of Medical Education) University of Illinois at Chicago, University of New Mexico, and Newcastle.

The CTPB program is a five-year curriculum, admitting bachelor's degree graduates of any disciplines except health sciences. Applicants must be not older than 25, have achieved at least a 2.5 grade point average and have completed at least 26 credits of basic sciences. The first two and a half years covers 10 blocks of instruction in basic medical sciences (preclinical), while the second phase of two and one-half years, is devoted to instruction in the clinical sciences at the Royal Air Force Hospital and other affiliated hospitals of the Ministry of Public Health and Bangkok Metropolitan Administration. Topics of study are arranged in blocks and selected on the basis of patterns of illness in Thailand (Table 27.1). Community activities and skills instruction are integrated into each block.

Table 27.1

Thailand--Overview of PBL Course Structure

Year 1	Introduction to Problem Based Learning	Trauma	Infection and Inflammation	Behavioral Science and Psychiatry	
	Clinical Experience				
Year 2	Oncology	Administra-tion	Reproductive Health	Growth and Nutri-tion	Envir-onmen-tal & Occupa-tion Health
	Clinical Experience				
Year 3	Degenerative Diseases and Diseases of Aging Clinical Experience	Clinical and Community Experience			
Year 4	Clinical and Community Experience				
Year 5	Professional Experience (Rotating Externship)				

The curriculum reflects consideration of primary health problems in Thailand, our standards for medical practitioners, and the medical school's educational objectives. With the assistance of faculty from Bangkok and other experts from Maastricht, Thammsat University implemented a similar curriculum in 1991. The PBL course is the newest innovation in medical education in Thailand. The success of the program is yet to be evaluated. However, Chulalongkorn experience of four years shows that the students are highly motivated in self-learning and new educational technologies are widely used.

GRADUATE MEDICAL EDUCATION

Between the inception of the first medical school at Siriraj in 1888 and 1927, a total of 560 diploma certified doctors were graduated. Most of them worked in the hospitals and relied on themselves to gain new knowledge and experiences by reading books and journals, some went abroad to continue their studies. In 1928, when the first group of MDs graduated, Siriraj offered a Doctor of Science Degree to those doctors who wrote an acceptable thesis. From 1928 to 1947, continuing education of doctors remained unchanged: some went abroad, a few worked in the specialized departments of Siriraj as house officers to prepare themselves for academic positions, but most worked in government services as general practitioners (GPs) both in Bangkok and in rural provinces. As years passed, the GPs who were interested in specialization undertook independent study of the discipline and through their own experiences became specialists in their own right; such persons were accepted by the public and by colleagues without any kind of formal certification.

Formal postgraduate education began in 1948 when the Faculty of Public Health was founded at the then University of Medical Sciences (Mahidol University), it has offered the MPH degree as the first postgraduate program ever since. In 1960, a Faculty of Tropical Medicine was established as the second postgraduate institution. These two institutions in collaboration with the Graduate School of the Mahidol University later developed several Master's and Doctoral programs in health sciences. Universities founded later have followed that pattern and there are now no less than fifty formal postgraduate programs in the country. Instruction is mostly in Thai, only a few courses are in English.

Specialist Training

Since the inception of the Medical Council in 1968, residency training programs and the specialty board certification examinations have been the responsibility of the Medical Council. In 1969, the Medical Council initiated formal residency training with 13 programs; there are now 34. As the number of training programs expanded, the number of licensed specialists with certificates from the Council has increased steadily. In 1987, there were 4,801 specialists, 52 percent of the total number of active doctors. In 1987, there were 388 first-year residents, 384 second-year residents, and 312 third-year residents. In that year, 54 percent of medical graduates entered specialty training; today (1992), that figure has reached 74 percent. Internal medicine, pediatrics, orthopedic surgery, general surgery, ophthalmology and otolaryngology are the most popular programs.

All programs require three years of training in approved institutions across the country. The curricula have been designed by the corresponding Colleges or associations of specialization. The accreditation of the hospitals involved in training and the specialty certified board examinations are conducted de facto by specialty of the colleges or associations, but the Medical Council remains the official body for issuing the certificates.

There have been many discussions about the issues of specialization. At the moment, the following are of special concern: (1) What is the optimum number of specialists in Thailand? (2) What is the government policy concerning specialists? Does the Ministry of Public Health want a specialist for every 10-bed district hospital? If so, then the total number of doctors must be substantially increased. (3) Finally, as the country becomes more industrialized, there will be more demand for specialists, since the people tend to prefer specialized services; however, too many specialists imply that the country will spend more on health care, because the use of expensive and sophisticated technologies will prevail.

LICENSURE

Graduates of accredited medical schools are automatically licensed by the Medical Council. The Medical Council accredits the curricula of all Thai medical schools. Accreditation is based on quality and relevancy of subject matter, facilities, library, laboratories, teaching rooms, teaching-learning methods and numbers of hours taught. Prior to the establishment of the Medical Council in 1968, accreditation was done by the Registration Office of the Ministry of Public Health. Graduates of foreign medical schools whose curriculum has been approved by a subcommittee of the Medical Council are eligible to sit for the licensing examination conducted every year by the Medical Council.

Cross-Licensing of Physicians

The cross-licensing of physicians does not exist in Thailand. Before practicing medicine in Thailand, foreign graduates must pass the licensing examination conducted every year by the Medical Council. In the case of those who work under supervision of UN agencies or foreign governments, the Medical Council issues temporary licenses without examination.

CONTINUING MEDICAL EDUCATION

There are now a number of informal training activities organized by universities, hospitals and various divisions of the Ministry of Public Health. These include short courses, on-site lectures and demonstrations. Programs of self-study, employing not only books and journals, but also audio tape, videotape and personal computer as well, are also popular. Medical schools often provide learning materials at no, or nominal, charge. Thailand has invested substantial effort and resources in continuing education since the inception of the first medical school, but so far there has been no systematic program evaluation. It has been proposed that an organizational structure is needed to plan, implement and evaluate continuing education programs (Subcommittee on Postgraduate and Continuing Education 1979).

ROLE OF RESEARCH IN MEDICAL EDUCATION

Health research implies the use of scientific methods to analyze health situations, identify problems and solve them. The universities and Ministry of Public Health have tried for several years to promote the research effort needed by the country to assess its major health problems and to develop the responses that are most appropriate to its own circumstance. Until recently, health research in Thailand has been predominately biomedical in focus. Since the National Epidemiology Board of Thailand was established in 1987, there is more emphasis on health policy and health development research that requires an intersectoral, multidisciplinary approach to health programming and delivery. Despite the full effort of universities and the Ministry of Public Health to promote health service research, the overall outcome is still unsatisfactory. This may be due to defects in current systems of research in Thailand, namely, (1) policy makers do not make use of research findings in decision making; (2) managers of health care programs do not always use research results, nor do they apply scientific methods in planning, monitoring, and evaluating services that they deliver; and (3) researchers often do not address the health problems that are perceived as top priorities by policymakers, public health care managers, and the general public.

The situation is primarily attributable to the fact that researchers, policy makers and health care providers tend to work in isolation without effectively interacting with each other, even though doctors who belong to these three groups are graduates of Thai medical schools. This suggests needed reorientation in the medical curriculum.

GOVERNMENT/PRIVATE SECTOR INVOLVEMENT

Due to the shortage of doctors (discussed under "physician manpower planning"), the Thai government has encouraged private universities to establish more new medical schools. Rangsit University is the first private university to respond to the government's need, and, in 1988, established a new medical school admitting 50 new medical students each year.

The Rangsit medical program is a six-year curriculum comprised of one year premedical, two years preclinical, and three years of clinical teaching. The government has permitted Rangsit to use public facilities and staff at Rajvithi and Children's hospitals for clinical teaching. The administrative problems arising from this type of affiliation are still being worked out.

INTERNATIONAL LINKAGES AND COLLABORATION

As described above, the Rockefeller Foundation has played a major role in assisting Thailand to develop high-quality medical education. Following World

War II and the severance of diplomatic relations between the United States and China, the China Medical Board of New York Inc. (CMB), a subsidiary of the Rockefeller Foundation, redirected its grants to fund health professions education programs in 14 South-East Asian Countries, including Thailand. The CMB provided very substantial support to research and medical education programs in the form of supplies and equipment, fellowships, library construction, visiting professors and purchasing books and journals. After the normalization of relations between the US and China, the CMB helped to establish permanent endowment funds to secure long-lasting support of Thai medical education programs. At present, new grant support from the CMB has been reduced to a minimum, and a great number of medical education programs are now being funded by the income of the endowment funds (Preecha 1979).

Medical Education in Thailand has also received support from other sources: the U.S. Agency for International Development (USAID), the UN special agencies (i.e., WHO, UNDP and UNICEF), the Colombo Plan countries, other countries and volunteer organizations.

There was a debate during the Fourth National Medical Education Conference as to the advantages and disadvantages of technical assistance from abroad. The argument was that Thai medical graduates trained through international aid received highly sophisticated training and adopted Western ideas and values which were not sensitive to the needs of the Thai people, especially in rural areas; medical curricula were then implemented following the Western concepts and ideas which were not relevant to the needs of the Thai community.

However, through the 70 years of international assistance it has become apparent that Thai medical education is well developed. Many medical schools have shown the capacity to carry out significant research in both the basic and clinical sciences, in health services and medical education at all levels. The problem of insensitivity of foreign-trained doctors can be solved by collaboration of both donors and recipients in planning the appropriate training programs. It was concluded in the Fourth National Conference on Medical Education that it is necessary to review the advantages and disadvantages of all international aid including the mechanisms for distribution of funds and the goals to be achieved.

ISSUES AND TRENDS

General Practice

In Thailand, there is currently no clear concept of general practice (GP) shared by policy makers, academicians and general practitioners themselves. The following have been formulated by a subcommittee of the Medical Council which is working on general practitioner issues. The subcommittee envisions two types of GP in Thailand: (1) the GP who provides first line care directly for a small number of patients (the usual type of GP found in Thailand), and (2) the district hospital GP, who is responsible for the larger population of a whole district, and who delegates first-line care to auxiliary or paramedical personnel in health centers but remains personally responsible for the quality of care. The latter necessarily devotes much attention to supporting and supervising the health center's staff and must also be prepared to act as a referral point for the health centers.

The residency training program of general practice is not popular. Of the approximately 550 applicants for residency training each year, only 12 to 14 apply for general practice training. The number of GPs relative to the number of specialists is now decreasing. If this trend continues, the cost of health care will rise sharply but the quality of care may not improve proportionately. The reasons for unpopularity of GP training programs are as follows: (1) There is no clear conceptual model for general practice. (2) General practice has low prestige as compared to other specialties. It is seen as a mix of low technology competencies rather than a distinct specialty. (3) The present working conditions for GPs are unfavorable; they work hard but receive low pay. (4) The training program is boring and not sensitive to the needs of the GP. The GP residents rotate among the specialty departments in a tertiary-care hospital, where they are sometimes treated like a second-rate specialist when they are learning and working together with the specialist residents in the same department. The Medical Council has appointed a subcommittee to study the issues of general practice and it is expected that the report of the committee may give directions in revising the undergraduate medical curriculum and the GP training program.

Consortium of Thai Medical Schools (1991)

On April 7, 1989, another important milestone of Thai medical education was reached when the deans of the eight medical schools in Thailand met and agreed to form a Consortium of Thai Medical Schools. The objectives of the Consortium are as follows: (1) to review, recommend, and help implement policy on medical and health science education; (2) to promote research and service in the health professions with the ultimate aim of improving the health of the population in line with government public policy; (3) to foster collaboration and academic exchange in medical education and related fields; (4) to develop leadership and management skills among senior administrators in medical and other health professional Faculties in Thailand; and (5) to create information networks between schools of medicine and others in public health and private institutions interested in medical education and its interface with public health and the health sciences.

The Consortium, a nongovernmental organization, has a governing board, a secretariat and project and ad hoc committees. The governing board, which consists of the deans of all member schools, the secretary-general, and appointed members, sets policy and administrative guidelines, approves budgets and reviews financial reports. The secretariat consists of the secretary-general, associate secretaries-general, and one representative from each of the member schools. The secretariat, initiates and carries out project activities of the Consortium in line with policy recommendations of the governing board, and prepares annual budgets and financial reports for review by the board. Project and ad hoc committees consist of the secretary general or other members of the secretariat, as well as special members appointed by the governing board. These committees, acting through the secretariat, carry out special tasks assigned to them by the governing board. In addition, the governing board may appoint special groups to advise the board on policy and activities of the Consortium. Financial support for the Consortium is provided by subventions from members and solicited donations from national and international organizations.

Consortium activities are diversified in all areas of medical education, and to date have included organizing seminars on such subjects as evaluation methods, national board examination for undergraduates, information technology in medicine and allied health sciences and conducting workshops on leadership and management skills for senior personnel and administrators of the member school. The Consortium has accepted the responsibilities to plan and organize the Sixth National Medical Education Conference scheduled in November 1993. It is expected that preparation of doctors in the next decade will be the central theme, and topics for discussion will include selection of medical students, holistic approach of the curriculum, community-based and problem based learning, self-study, evaluation of student performance, program evaluation, continuing education, health research, specialization versus general practice, demand and supply of the physicians, and health resource management.

REFERENCES

Adulya, V. 1974. Recommendation for physician production. *Siriraj Hospital Gaz.* 26 (4):735-764.

Barrows, H.S., and R. Tamblyn. 1980. *Problem-based learning: An approach to medical education.* New York: Springer.

Charn, S. 1974. Recommendation for physician production. *Siriraj Hospital Gaz.* 26 (3):439-447.

Consortium of Thai Medical Schools. 1991. Office of the Secretariat. Faculty of Medicine, Chiang Mai University, Chiang Mai, Thailand.

New perspectives in education. [editorial]. 1974. *Siriraj Hospital Gaz.* 26 (2):267-279.

Hongladarom, T., et al. 1989. Assessment of MESRAP graduates (a comparative study): An abstract. *J. Med. Assoc. Thail.* Vol. 72:S(1): 5-10.

Medical Council. 1992. Bangkok, Thailand: Medical Council.

National Epidemiology Board of Thailand. 1990. [summary]. *Report of the National Epidemiology Board of Thailand: The first four years 1987-1990.* Bangkok, Thailand.

NESDB. 1987. *The Sixth national economic and social development plan 1987-1991.* Bangkok, Thailand: NESDB. Cited as NESDB.

Ouay, K. 1978. Thai medicine and western medicine. *J Med. Soc. Sci.* 1 (1):10-18.

Preecha, V. 1979. China Medical Board and its changing concepts, pp. 347-349. In *Proceedings of the 4th National Medical Education Conference. October 29--November 2, 1979.* Bangkok, Thailand: Mahidol University.

Subcommittee on Postgraduate and Continuing Education. 1979. Report of Subcommittee on Postgraduate and Continuing Education. In *Proceedings of the 4th National Medical Education Conference October 29-November 2, 1979.* Bangkok, Thailand: Mahidol University, pp. 127-143.

Sood, S. 1978. End of Thai traditional medicine and beginning of Thai modern medicine. *J. Med. Soc. Sci.* 1(1):20-27.

Thailand. Division of Planning, Ministry of Public Health. 1991. Bangkok.

---------. Division of Planning, Office of the Permanent Secretary, Office of University Affairs. 1992. Bangkok.

---------. Ministry of Public Health. 1988. Report on Health Manpower Development, pp. 308-315. In *Proceedings of the First Thai Health Assembly*. September 12-15, Bangkok.

28

United Kingdom

LAURA R. AZIZ
MICHAEL S. CULLEN

The United Kingdom, which comprises Great Britain (England, Scotland, and Wales) and Northern Ireland, was once the center of a worldwide empire, on whose colonies "the sun never set." This island nation has had a global impact on medical education far greater than its size or numbers alone would predict. The United Kingdom also has been a pioneer in instituting a comprehensive health care delivery system and supporting the primary care general practitioner.

General Demographic Profile

In 1990, the United Kingdom had a population of 57.4 million (England, Wales, Scotland and Northern Ireland), with 91 percent in urban areas and 9 percent in rural districts. There was approximately one physician for every seven hundred persons, relatively equally distributed throughout the country; this included one general practitioner (ambulatory care) per 1,900 persons. Birthrate per 1000 population was 13.9, and death rate was 11.2 per 1,000; the infant mortality rate was 7.9 per 1000 live births (1990). In 1988, life expectancy at birth was 72.4 years for males and 78 years for females. The per capita GNP was $8,570 US (1988). Virtually 100 percent of the population is literate.

OVERVIEW OF THE HEALTH CARE DELIVERY SYSTEM

The British National Health Services (NHS) is both comprehensive and highly centralized. This comprehensiveness is dual: it provides universal coverage to the whole population and coverage includes the whole range of health services. The British NHS differs from other national systems in organizational structure and in financial mechanisms that avoid the complexity of multiple independent financial sources (Roemer 1991).

The first National Health Insurance Act, passed by the British Parliament in 1911, extended the limited insurance protection provided by trade unions, fraternal associations and "friendly societies" to cover low-income manual workers for the cost of ambulatory medical care and loss of wages due to sickness. Contributions were required from both workers and employers; governmental subsidies provided for the indigent and covered administrative costs. During World War II, a multidisciplinary committee headed by Sir William Beveridge recommended a comprehensive national health service that would assure for every citizen access to whatever medical services were required (Beveridge 1942). In 1946, the government passed the National Health Services Act to implement the Beveridge recommendations. By 1948 and after intensive negotiations between the Ministry of Health (MOH) and the British Medical Association (BMA), agreement was reached to enact universal coverage to be financed from general governmental revenues, with only a small fraction of the cost derived from insurance contributions. The system was initiated with the following features:

General practitioners (GP). GPs provided general medical services in ambulatory care settings and did not have hospital privileges. Their reimbursement was on a capitation basis, and patients were free to choose their GP and could change to another, at any time, if they so wished.

Hospital and specialist services. At the end of World War II, private hospitals were struggling with heavy financial pressure, large debts coupled with diminishing funds and rising costs. Therefore when nationalization was instituted in 1948, it was met with little resistance.

Since GPs had no hospital privileges, once a patient needed hospitalization, the GP referred the patient to a hospital outpatient clinic to be examined by a specialist and admitted to the hospital. This arrangement had the drawback of fragmenting patient care.

Specialists and consultants (highest rank) were appointed by the hospital board of governors, hospital management committee or regional hospital board (RHB). Once appointed, specialists received regular salary that was periodically raised and that increased with tenure and responsibilities. In the early days of the NHS, there was a significant difference between GPs' and specialists' incomes. However, by the mid-1970s GPs were awarded additional fees for preventive services, house calls and special procedures, which reduced the income disparity.

Public health services. These authorities were responsible for preventive services, ambulance transport, visiting nurse services (home care), care for chronically ill, elderly housing, maternal and child health, well baby clinics, immunizations, environmental sanitation, water supply, sewage disposal, and housing inspection.

The economic support of the NHS was built on the basic assumption that substantial financial support would be received from the government. This would change the health care services from a market commodity that could be purchased, to a basic right for everybody, financed by governmental resources. Over the years, these arrangements facilitated capping health care expenditure, and maintaining it at a level lower than many other developed countries. The 1974 reorganization of the NHS attempted to integrate the three differing aspects of the service.

Current trends in the health services. The 1970s and the early 1980s saw a change in the mode of practice of general practitioners. GPs moved from solo to "corporate" group practice, where a number of physicians ranging from three to six shared an office. In 1961 there were 5,337 single-handed general practitioners and 7,157 in practices with more than three physicians. This changed in 1991 to 2,990 in solo practice and 15,310 in practices with three or more physicians (NHS Handbook 1989). This provided an atmosphere of professional challenge and stimulation, facilitated consultation and sharing of knowledge and promoted a new model of GP with the opportunity to develop specific areas of interest (e.g., pediatrics, psychiatry, or OB-Gyn). The development of this model was encouraged by the rapid increase in the number of health centers which almost doubled in less than a decade. The local health authorities rented these health centers to GPs who had contracts with the NHS. These developments facilitated the creation of primary health care teams that included among other providers: district nurses, health visitors, allied health professionals, dietitians, etc., whose salaries were paid by the local health authorities, and social workers whose salaries were paid by the local government.

Better geographic distribution of physicians was achieved by, among other policies, a ban on the selling of medical practices by retiring physicians, and the prohibition against new graduates practicing in areas designated as over-served.

Although the British NHS was formally launched in its current format in 1948, it underwent radical restructuring in 1974, designed to achieve greater administrative/managerial efficiency. The changes, however, were criticized as adding an extra layer in the organizational hierarchy, and dissatisfaction, which has intensified with the apparently uncontrollable increase in the cost of health services, has since led to a small but growing private health insurance system available as an alternative to the NHS (Roemer 1991).

HISTORICAL BACKGROUND

Historically, medical education in the United Kingdom has focused more on clinical teaching than on scientific research and specialization, in contrast to the German model and later the medical schools in the United States. It concentrated on the study of bacteria, parasites, and viruses as causes of disease (i.e., the biological model), and adopted a curative approach with emphasis on practical training and bedside teaching. Little attention was paid to basic sciences, laboratory teaching, scientific innovations and biomedical research (Hollingsworth 1986, 32-33; McKeown 1975, 1976; Navarro 1976, 1980)

Currently there are 26 medical schools in UK, 9 of which are in London (different sources list different numbers of medical schools. The number of schools has decreased due to ongoing mergers between medical schools in London.) The teaching load within the schools is shared by full-time and part-time faculty, who now total approximately seven thousand faculty members.

ROLE OF NATIONAL POLICY IN SHAPING MEDICAL EDUCATION

The British Parliament since 1858 has assigned the General Medical Council (GMC) responsibility for supervising basic medical education. The GMC issues a set of recommendations every 10 years advising medical schools about recent curricular developments and educational innovation. In 1973, the Educational Committee of the GMC conducted a comprehensive survey of all medical schools to reach a better understanding of the different practices in curricular planning, teaching methods, student assessment, and the barriers and hurdles schools face in their endeavors. This survey was conducted by the Centre of Medical Education, University of Dundee, and the results were published in two volumes by the Nuffield Provincial Hospital Trust.

ADMISSION

Competition for medical school admission is very intense, although this had been expected to change after the institutionalization of the National Health Services. Tuition and fees, in the majority of cases, are provided by governmental scholarships and grants.

Students apply to medical schools after 12 years of general education and A level secondary school examinations. Admission requirements include a high school certificate with a science concentration (chemistry, physics, biology, and/or math). Few schools require students to take a special entrance examination.

In academic year 1983-1984, approximately 4,000 applicants were admitted to medical schools, with a class size ranging between 75 and 200. The total number of graduates for the same year (the class admitted in 1978-1979) was around thirty-five hundred. The overall enrolment in British medical schools in 1983/84 was around eighteen thousand, almost equally divided between men and women. The dropout rate is negligible, and almost 95 percent of all those admitted to medical schools are able to finish the program and graduate (World Health Organization 1988). It is important to note that these data are cross-sectional, collected at only one point in time.

CURRICULAR STRUCTURE AND INNOVATION

Programs of basic medical education in the UK vary in length. The majority are of five years' duration. The degree offered upon graduation is a Bachelor of Medicine and Bachelor of Surgery (MBBS or MBChB). There are, however, two variations. The first is for students without the appropriate science A level examinations; this will add a year to the beginning of the program. The second variation allows the student to take an additional year during the program to achieve an intercalated Bachelor of Medical Science degree in addition to the medical degree.

According to the GMC, the main goal of this basic medical education phase is to provide physicians with all that is necessary to the comprehension of medicine as an evolving science and art, and to provide a basis for future vocational training; it is not to train students to be scientists, surgeons, general practitioners or any other kind of specialist (General Medical Council 1977). Individual medical schools are free to plan their own curricular time, method, and content.

Course Requirements

The classical preclinical disciplines include anatomy, biochemistry and physiology. Psychology and sociology (behavioral sciences) are occasionally integrated with community, environmental and genetic studies. Due to the relative novelty of teaching behavioral sciences in the medical curricula, great variation exists in time allocation, content, and methods of teaching.

Statistics and biometrics methods are now taught in almost all schools in combination with preclinical laboratory subjects. Research methods are often included to familiarize students with data presentation and analysis, and to develop their critical skills when reading the literature.

Clinical pharmacology and therapeutics are presented later in the curriculum, in integration with other clinical disciplines to enable students to observe and assess effects of medication and medical decision making.

Medical physics (a preclinical science) is taught in association with radiology (a clinical diagnostic/investigative tool). The latter is taught informally in small group tutorials and clinical conferences. Social and Community Medicine is a relatively new science which gives more breadth to medical education by considering the social, cultural and family background of patients. It ties in with medical sociology and other behavioral sciences taught in earlier years. Students follow discharged hospital patients, work on community projects and other field work assessing the development and problems of the system. This course in many cases is taught in conjunction with general practice, focusing on medicine in the community and other social aspects of health care.

The major clinical disciplines include medicine, surgery, obstetrics/gynecology, child health (pediatrics) and psychiatry. They all have distinct locations and time allocations in the curriculum, and are usually offered in separate blocks known as clinical attachments or clerkships. Wide variation exists among different schools due to inclusion or exclusion of subspecialties. Teaching time is often calculated in weeks and months rather than hours, but the data available are not comparable between schools. Minor clinical specialties include anesthesiology, dermatology, infectious diseases, ophthalmology, orthopedics, otolaryngology, and venereology, again with wide variation among schools in teaching time ranging from a few hours to a few weeks.

The main objective of these courses is to teach students the basic skills of interviewing and examining patients and making a preliminary diagnosis in general and as specific to the discipline. Communication skills are also stressed during this period, as well as the signs and symptoms of common disorders, their pathology and preferred treatment. The hope is to teach the future physician to realize the scope of each specialty and the available services to refer patients and at the appropriate time and place (General Medical Council 1977).

On completion of the degree program the student receives provisional registration with the General Medical Council. Each student is then required to undertake a pre-registration year in an approved post in a recognized hospital. This will entail six-month rotations in the two major clinical disciplines of Medicine and Surgery. Successful completion of this year earns full registration with the General Medical Council. In the majority of the British medical schools, training at this level provides exposure to community, social, and preventive medicine.

Problems encountered include: (1) quality control of the educational experience of students during clinical rotations in affiliated teaching hospitals and clinics. Physical distance from the academic medical center creates difficulties in obtaining consensus on learning objectives and assessment of the educational experiences and outcomes. (2) The need to rely on non-academic staff in teaching some of the subjects. (3) An unfavorable staff to student ratio, resulting in heavy teaching loads and exhaustion of staff. (4) Conflict between patient care, teaching time, research and other responsibilities.

Curricular Innovations

Three major recent innovations were: (1) The establishment of a General Practice Department in all medical schools, with both formal teaching and clerkships; teaching in some instances is associated with the Community Medicine course as described earlier. (2) Geriatrics is receiving extra attention, particularly special techniques of interviewing and examining older people and the development of a better understanding of physical aging and its impact on pathology and response to treatment. Attention is also given to fostering a positive and sympathetic attitude toward the older population. (3) Ethics and law as they relate to medical practice, legal and ethical dilemmas are receiving additional emphasis.

Concerted attempts have been made to integrate preclinical with the clinical courses by using clinical illustrations that include patients and involving clinical staff (medically qualified teachers). In general, "vertical integration is more popular than horizontal integration with concurrent subjects" (General Medical Council 1977, p. 442).

Almost all medical schools offer elective opportunities to students, especially in the clinical portion of the curriculum. In most schools only one elective is allowed, two at most. Time allocation is usually eight weeks, continuous, full-time. Students may select a research project or clinical specialty; the latter is more common, and can be in a teaching hospital or a general practice clinic, away from their own school, in some instances abroad (i.e., Africa, Asia, South America, and North America).

Selectives, usually of one month duration, are also generally available in the final year of study; however these are restricted as to subject (only the major clinical specialties) and location (a recognized teaching hospital), and may be used to guide students who are weak in a particular field.

The *World Directory of Medical Schools* reports that in the mid 1980s, 30 percent of the medical schools in the United Kingdom reoriented their curricula toward the definition of the role and tasks of physicians in the community and used this as basis for curriculum planning. Eighty-three percent of medical schools offer students an opportunity to study community health services at a health center, community clinic and/or through home visits. Almost all schools offer courses in community medicine, social and preventive medicine and 45 percent train students in managerial skills for health services. Fifty-nine percent emphasize the primary health care approach, and 70 percent of the students receive practical training in how to work as members of a team with other health professionals (World Health Organization 1988).

Student Assessment

A wide assortment of techniques is used for student assessment. Almost all schools use periodic student assessment in addition to the final qualifying professional examinations. External examiners are used in almost all schools. This practice helps in maintaining the over-all standard of the examinations and equivalence among schools.

The GMC encourages every medical student to:

have as his objective the medical degree of his own University . . . . [and every] University to . . . . contribute to the education of the student. Since the educational process and the system of assessment and examinations are inseparable . . . The primary object should be to test the student's understanding of what he has learnt and his capacity for thinking for himself, and not simply his factual knowledge. (General Medical Council 1977, p. 853)

The last stage of basic medical education is a 12-month supervised clinical practice following graduation from the medical school, split equally between medicine and surgery. This preregistration period may be at the university hospital or in any other recognized general hospital. There is a general feeling of dissatisfaction among faculty and medical education leaders as to the educational outcome of this period. Interns are generally overworked and do not have enough time to read and reflect. The GMC recommends that interns be given at least six hours weekly, other than their free time, for educational purposes. Also, their educational program should be supervised and supplemented by clinical conferences, case presentations, and scientific contests.

Accreditation

Accreditation is exclusively the responsibility of the General Medical Council, which is made up of 46 members representing all medical schools, Royal Colleges, the medical profession and three laymen; some members are nominated by the Queen and the others are elected. The GMC's role is to inquire about different types of courses offered, number of hours devoted to theory and practice, and methods of assessment and examinations. The GMC also sends visitors to attend/take part in some of the activities and report the findings. The evaluation is then pronounced as "sufficient" or "insufficient." If a program is described as insufficient, it must try to improve, according to the GMC guidelines, until the GMC clears it and declares it sufficient. The guidelines set by the GMC are based on extensive discussions, deliberations and consultations with faculty and institutions.

GRADUATE MEDICAL EDUCATION

Vocational training and specialization, the third stage in a physician's preparation, is conducted under the auspices of the Royal Colleges. The Royal Postgraduate Medical School at Hammersmith Hospital, since its establishment in 1935, has been awarding several postgraduate degrees and diplomas. The Royal College of Physicians (RCP), which includes all areas of medicine and the Royal College of Surgeons (RCS), which covers all surgical specialties and anesthesiology, offer membership (MRCP) and fellowship (FRCS) by examination. However, it is important to note that:

The examinations of the colleges were designed not so much to test the training and performance of the applicant but to select the doctors best suited eventually to become consultants. Indeed, both colleges stressed that the passing of these examinations did not signify the completion of postgraduate training but only indicated that the candidate was prepared to continue his education. (Hollingsworth 1986, p. 40).

The Royal College of Obstetricians and Gynecologists, which was established in 1929, the Royal College of Pathologists, the Royal College of Psychiatrists and the Royal College of Radiologists are more specialized in nature. More recently the Royal College of General Practitioners described earlier has been established with the purpose of granting general practitioners higher status and greater prestige.

LICENSURE

Graduates, after successfully completing their internship (preregistration) year, are licensed by the GMC to practice independently. The GMC keeps a register listing all licensed physicians, an informative tool for hospitals, employers and the public at large, but the GMC does not exercise any direct control on practitioners.

Cross-Licensing of Physicians

Nationals and non-British physicians with foreign qualifications must either hold a primary qualification recognized by the GMC for full registration, or have qualified in a country to which the United Kingdom's legislation concerning the recognition of overseas qualifications applies. With the establishment of the European Economic Community, legislation has been introduced to allow for the mutual recognition of primary medical qualifications between the member countries. In general, non-British physicians may be allowed limited registration that enables them to practice in an approved hospital post for not more than five years, after which they must return to their home country.

CONTINUING MEDICAL EDUCATION

The GMC calls on all physicians to continue learning after the completion of vocational training until "retirement or death" (General Medical Council 1977, p. 864). However, it is expected that physicians will continue to do so out of their own sense of responsibility and commitment to their patients. CME is not a requirement for renewal of licensure nor for promotion.

ROLE OF RESEARCH IN MEDICAL EDUCATION

The Medical Research Council (MRC) was launched in 1911 as a central institute for medical research, spearheaded by Sir Walter Fletcher, who promptly developed a strong partnership with The Rockefeller Foundation, and later with the British Nuffield Endowment and Dunn Trust, which channeled grants to support medical education and research (Austoker and Bryder 1989). In 1920 the National Institute for Medical Research (NIMR) was established with a focus on basic sciences research (bacteriology, biochemistry, pharmacology, statistics, etc). Research moved slowly from the laboratory (scientific experimental research conducted by scientists) to the wards (clinical research conducted by physicians) which later led to the establishment of the Clinician Research Center (CRC) in 1970. These centers, together with the Postgraduate Medical Schools and other university research units throughout the country, developed research programs that were instrumental in reorienting medical education towards research. Usually the MRC provides initial funding for a "five year period with a guarantee by the University Grants Committee to provide funds for complete takeover . . . at the end of that time." (Austoker and Bryder 1989, p. 240). The *British Medical Journal* (*BMJ*) played a significant role in publishing leading articles that enthusiastically supported research initiatives.

GOVERNMENT/PRIVATE SECTOR INVOLVEMENT

The British Medical Association has a long-standing reputation of supporting general practitioners and defending their rights and benefits, which has inevitably fostered the role of universities in strengthening the teaching of general practice and encouraging its development as a specialty. The BMA also assisted the GMC in the extensive survey of all medical schools which was instrumental in compiling information on what was going on in the different schools and what constraints they were facing. The Educational Committee of the General Medical Council is the national statutory body responsible for establishing and maintaining standards. The Medical Research Council over the years was instrumental in orienting medical education toward research practices and supporting the status of research and researchers in medical schools.

INTERNATIONAL LINKAGES AND COLLABORATION

The World Federation for Medical Education (WFME) is housed at the University of Edinburgh. The WFME was instrumental in gathering leaders of medical education from all over the world around six themes to bring around change in medical education as announced in the Edinburgh Declaration in 1988. The WFME is a strong supporter of the Network of Community Oriented Educational Institutions for the Health Sciences. The United Kingdom is also the home for AMEE, the Association of Medical Education in Europe, and ASME, the Association for the Study of Medical Education. The role of both AMEE and ASME is becoming more crucial now that the EEC is allowing the free exchange of students and health professionals. The United Kingdom also participates in the Council of Deans of Medical Schools of Europe, renamed in April 1993 the Association of Medical Schools in Europe (AMSE).

A landmark in the history of medical education was the establishment of the Centre of Medical Education at the University of Dundee. This center, with an overall mission of making medical education more relevant, has been instrumental in training health professionals from all over the world in instructional methodologies, curriculum development and evaluation, and competency assessment.

The EEC agreement is developing new paradigms in the exchange of students, professionals and people among European countries. The nature and magnitude of the impact of EEC on individual countries and their health and educational infrastructure is yet to be assessed.

ISSUES AND TRENDS

Admission to medical schools continues to be highly competitive. The question remains, will the UK face a physician surplus like most of the other countries of the world?

Shortening the curriculum is a controversial issue, but continues to attract attention from faculty and medical education leaders. Faculty continue to be interested in devising new methods for curriculum planning, development and change. More attempts to integrate various subjects both vertically and horizontally and to make them more clinically oriented are anticipated.

There is substantial interest in developing more electives and providing more optional tracks, both to make the course of study more interesting to students and to foster an atmosphere conducive to creativity, initiative and resourcefulness.

Over the last decade, there have been significant changes and innovations in systems for assessing students' competency; more is expected in the coming years. This will include greater use of in-course progressive assessment and objective structured tests employing multiple choice questions (MCQ) and of objective structured clinical examination (OSCE).

All schools have a curriculum committee responsible for the overall coordination of the curriculum in cooperation with different departments through sub-groups and task forces, especially when it relates to multidisciplinary courses. Almost all schools undertake regular curricular reviews, defining and redefining their objectives, planning their courses and adapting their teaching methods.

A separate department and a chair position for general practice now exist in almost all medical schools, and the general practitioner continue to be the backbone of the National Health Services and the gatekeeper to all other forms of highly advanced-technologic medical care; hence, more attention will continue to be given to general practice and community medicine.

REFERENCES

Abel-Smith, B. 1976. *Value for money in health services.* London: Heinemann.

----------. 1965. The major pattern of financing and the organization of medical services that have emerged in other countries. *Medical Care,* 3:33-40.

----------. 1964. *The hospitals, 1800-1948.* London: Heinemann.

Abel-Smith, B., and R. Titmuss. 1956. *The cost of the national health service in England and Wales.* Cambridge: Cambridge University Press.

Austoker, J., and L. Bryder. 1989. *Historical perspectives on the role of the MRC.* New York: Oxford University Press.

Beveridge, W. 1942. *Social insurance and allied services.* New York: Macmillan Co.

Buckley, E.G. 1991. Editorial: Postgraduate medical examinations. *Medical Education* (25):455-456

Carlson, C., C. Martini, and M.R. Schwarz. 1990. Medical education: A global perspective. Results of the international survey of medical education. Informational paper distributed by the American Medical Association at the Fifth World Conference on Medical Education, 24-28 October 1990.

General Medical Council. 1977a. Basic medical education in the British Isles. The report of the General Medical Council Survey. *Vol. 1, General section and school profiles.* London: Nuffield Provincial Hospitals Trust.

----------.1977b. Basic medical education in the British Isles. The report of the General Medical Council Survey. *Vol. 2, The disciplines and specialties.* London: Nuffield Provincial Hospitals Trust.

Hargad, P. 1990. National conference at the Medical School, University College of Galway. *Medical Education* (24):470-471.

Hollingsworth, J. R. 1986. *A political economy of medicine: Great Britain and the United States.* Baltimore: Johns Hopkins University Press.

McKeown, T. 1976a. *The modern rise of population.* New York: Academic Press.

----------. 1976b *The role of medicine: Dream, mirage, or nemesis?* London: Nuffield Provincial Hospitals Trust.

----------. 1975. *Medicine in modern society.* London: George Allen and Unwin.

Montague W., and C.F Odds. 1990. Academic selection criteria and subsequent performance. *Med Educ* 24.

National Health Services. 1989. *National Health Services Handbook.* 4th edition. London: Macmillan Press, Ltd.

Navarro, V. 1980. Work, ideology and science: The case of medicine. *Social Science and Medicine*, 14:191-203.

----------. 1976. Social class, political power and the state and their implications in medicine. *Social Science and Medicine* 10:437-56.

Raffel, M.W. 1984. Health services in the United Kingdom. In M.W. Raffel, ed., *Comparative health systems: Descriptive analyses of fourteen national health systems.* University Park: Pennsylvania State University Press.

Roemer, M. 1991. *National Health systems of the world: Vol. 1, The countries.* New York: Oxford University Press.

Silver, G. 1972. The community-medicine specialist: Britain mandates health service reorganization. *New England Journal of Medicine* 287:1299-1301.

Torrens, P. 1982. Some potential hazards of unplanned expansion of private health insurance in Britain. *Lancet* 2:29-31.

White, K., and J. Connelly, eds., 1992. *The medical school's mission and the population's health.* New York: Springer-Verlag.

World Health Organization. 1988. *World directory of medical schools.* 6th Edition. Geneva, Switzerland: World Health Organization.

Yates, J. 1987. *Why are we waiting? An analysis of hospital waiting lists.* New York: Oxford University Press.

29

United States of America

ROBERT F. JONES
M. BROWNELL ANDERSON

OVERVIEW OF THE HEALTH CARE DELIVERY SYSTEM

The American health care system involves several major participants, each with a special role to play. Among these players are physicians in private or group practice and managed care settings, teaching hospitals, Veterans Administration (VA) hospitals, and the federal government.

Reform of the health care system has risen to the top of the American domestic policy agenda. Health care costs appear to be out of control. Between fifteen and twenty percent of the American population are uninsured, with many more under-insured, and there is increasing concern about quality and efficacy of care. Precursors to major reform have already appeared, in the form of incentives to curb utilization of services and changes in the payment system for hospital and physician services.

Teaching hospitals, which serve as sites for clinical education of medical students and residents, contribute uniquely to the nation's health care delivery system by the magnitude and types of services they offer and the patient populations they serve. They account for 18 percent of the beds, 20 percent of the admissions, 23 percent of the outpatient visits, 17 percent of the emergency room visits, and 23 percent of the births for all short-term, nonfederal hospitals in the United States. Over 60 percent of these teaching hospitals are located in urban areas with populations greater than one million; a third are in major metropolitan centers with populations of 2.5 million or greater. Many of these are located in poverty-stricken, inner-city areas. By default, urban teaching hospitals, through their emergency rooms and outpatient clinics, have become the primary providers for the poor and medically indigent and a safety net for their health care needs. Academic medical centers also care for a disproportionately large share of Medicaid patients. The patient populations of urban teaching hospitals present health problems embedded in the social ills that plague large cities, including drug abuse, violence, and homelessness.

Payment for health care changed dramatically in the United States during the past decade, in an attempt to curb the growing escalation of health care costs. In the private sector, the changes are seen in the growth of managed care systems, typified by health maintenance organizations (HMO) and preferred provider organizations (PPO). Large-scale corporate purchasers of care increasingly are using their buying power to contract directly with hospitals and other providers for health care services for their members or employees.

In the public sector, the federal government has shifted the payment system under Medicare, an insurance program for the elderly. Hospitals that formerly received reimbursement for costs now receive a prospectively-priced fixed payment according to patient diagnosis. Physician payment reform has followed changes in payment for hospital services. In 1989, Congress passed legislation to create a new fee schedule for the payment for physician services to Medicare beneficiaries. In January 1992, the Health Care Financing Administration (HFCA) implemented the schedule, which is derived from a resource-based relative value scale (RBRVS), covering more than seven thousand identifiable physician services. Payment is based on the sum of three components of cost: physician work (time and intensity), practice expense, and malpractice insurance premium expense. The relative values for each component are adjusted to reflect, in part, geographic variations in these costs. A dollar-conversion factor then "converts" the cost components to a payment amount. Congress sets the conversion factor each year. Through this system, the federal government hopes to slow the growth in Medicare expenditures, encourage evaluation and management services, reduce the payment for "overpriced" procedures, and maintain access to services by Medicare beneficiaries.

Payment reform springs from the need to control escalating health care costs and finance access to care by those with inadequate or no means to pay for it, but it represents but one component of the demand for major changes in the American health care system. Health care reform is needed to meet the changing needs of the population. Efforts to reduce teenage pregnancy, education in AIDS and drug abuse prevention, and the restructuring of services to focus greater attention on chronic medical conditions that are the consequence of an aging population are all required.

HISTORICAL BACKGROUND

American medical education is the product of important initiatives taken during the mid-and late nineteenth century by the University of Pennsylvania, the College of Physicians and Surgeons in New York, Lind (later Northwestern) University, Harvard University, and the University of Michigan. The vision and leadership of those associated with the founding of the John Hopkins Medical Schools in 1893 led to the creation of a university-based, graded, four-year educational program, combining laboratory instruction with supervised hospital experience. The Hopkins model eclipsed the many proprietary programs of marginal quality that existed at the time. In 1910, Abraham Flexner, supported by the Carnegie Foundation, published a thorough review and critique of medical schools in the United States and Canada, leading to further reforms and institutionalization of the current model of the scientifically trained physician.

Despite fidelity to this heritage, the complex of institutions and programs devoted to medical education near the end of the twentieth century bears little resemblance to that present at its beginning. Before World War II, medical schools were fewer in number and concerned primarily with education for the MD degree. Postwar investment in biomedical research transformed medical schools into large-scale research institutions. Medical capability expanded and with it the demand for health care services. By the 1960s, the nation mobilized for a substantial expansion of its capacity for training health professionals.

In the ensuing years, medical schools and teaching hospitals have evolved into large, complex academic medical centers, under university auspices or as affiliated institutions with varied inter-institutional agreements and arrangements. The historic mission of academic medical centers has remained constant throughout the century: to teach, conduct research, and provide patient care. However, the institutions and resources dedicated to this mission have undergone enormous growth and change.

As the nation prepares for the next century, it faces new challenges in advancing the health of its population: the escalation of health care costs, the persistent problems of access to services, and the variable quality of care. In the face of these problems, academic medical centers are being asked to reexamine and expand their missions, restructure their services, and review and revitalize their programs.

Patterns of mortality and morbidity have shifted dramatically in the latter part of the twentieth century. Vaccines, antibiotics, and improvements in public health and sanitation have largely eradicated the infectious diseases that earlier accounted for the major portion of premature deaths. Much of the focus of medical care, and thus medical education, has taken a decided turn from the young to the old and from acute to chronic conditions. Issues confronting the curriculum include the need for primary health care, the expansion of family medicine, and the problems of aging and senescence--cancer, emphysema, cirrhosis, atherosclerosis, and osteoarthritis.

Serious afflictions of the young and middle-aged remain, for example, infant mortality, drug abuse, and AIDS. Many of these health problems are embedded in culture and lifestyle and need to be understood in an overarching biopsychosocial context. Most observers believe that medical education must focus more on prevention of disease and health promotion, and on population-based approaches to health care.

Coupled with these concerns are the striking advances in areas such as molecular biology that raise the possibility of understanding the genetic basis of a host of degenerative and disabling diseases. Improved medical technology and capability is dual-edged, improving and extending life, but sometimes driving up health care costs and posing new ethical considerations. Medical educators today are attempting to introduce instruction in medical decision making into clinical training. Emphasis on medical ethics in the curriculum continues to increase as new technology introduces further moral quandaries for physicians, patients, and the families of patients.

ROLE OF NATIONAL POLICY IN SHAPING MEDICAL EDUCATION

Medical education in the United States is largely self-regulated. Colleges and universities that award medical degrees must conform to minimal accreditation standards that meet federal guidelines and graduates must meet the minimal licensure requirements imposed by state agencies. National policy indirectly shapes medical education in the various forms in which federal and state agencies provide funding for schools and faculty and in the way patient care services are reimbursed under Medicare and Medicaid, health care programs for the elderly and the poor. As pressures mount for changes in the "products" of the American medical education system, particularly an increase in generalist physicians, federal and state governments may play a more directive role in medical education.

ADMISSION

In contrast with the open enrollment policies of some other countries, admission to one of the 126 accredited medical schools in the United States is selective. The selection process allows medical schools to admit men and women who, in the faculty's opinion, have the academic abilities and personal qualities requisite for a profession that is based on high standards of competence and service to others. By retaining the prerogative to select their students, faculty also can ensure that the number of matriculants matches the resources available for an optimal education.

The criteria used by faculties in their selection process are broad-based. They include prior academic achievement, judgment by college faculty and advisors of the candidate's academic abilities and personal qualities, and evidence of values and attitudes commensurate with a career of service. Nearly all medical schools conduct personal interviews to assess personal qualities, values, and attitudes of applicants, a practice that is rarely followed in business, law, and other professional schools. The evaluation of academic abilities is assisted by the Medical College Admission Test (MCAT). This standardized examination now includes tests on the biological and physical sciences, a verbal reasoning component, and a writing sample. The examination is taken by students toward the end of their third year or beginning of their fourth (senior) year of college or university study. The science components require only information taught in introductory courses. The inclusion of a writing sample in the examination was motivated by the desire to reinforce the importance of a broad liberal undergraduate education for medical students.

The number of applicants to US medical schools reached its historical peak in 1974 when 42,624 applied for 15,066 first-year positions, a ratio of 2.8 to 1. The number then declined steadily to a low of 26,721 in 1988, but has since sharply rebounded, to an estimated 37,500 for the 1992 entering class. The doubling of the applicant pool from the mid-1960s to mid-1970s was an outgrowth of burgeoning college enrollments during that period. The baby-boom generation had come of age and Vietnam-era draft deferments encouraged college attendance. Subsequent declines in the pool during the 1980s represented a return to normalcy. Recent increases may relate in part to the recessionary economy of the late 1980s and early 1990s. Interest in graduate and professional education programs has tended to rise when jobs are less plentiful.

Medical school applicants and accepted students average approximately 24 years in age. The proportion of women in the applicant pool has increased every year since 1969, a trend that shows no sign of ending. In 1992 women constituted 42 percent of applicants and only a slightly smaller proportion of first-year entrants. Racial-ethnic minorities have not achieved the same success as women in entering the medical profession. Blacks constituted less than 8 percent of medical school applicants in 1992. American Indians, Mexican-Americans, and mainland Puerto Ricans raised the proportion of under-represented minorities to just under 11 percent. Both figures are only slightly higher than those observed a decade earlier. Through a special program, Project 3000 by 2000, medical schools have committed to raising the number of under-represented minorities admitted to medical school, now 1,700-1,800 nationally, to 3,000 by the end of the decade.

Medical schools vary in the size of classes they admit and enroll. Enrollment ranges from 32 at one school to 300 at the largest multicampus school; the average first-year class size is 127 students. Overall, nearly 16,000 students matriculated at US medical schools in 1992, with approximately 96 percent expected to graduate. See Table 29.1, p. 416.

CURRICULAR STRUCTURE AND INNOVATION

Medical school curricula, although quite varied, have as their goal the preparation of students to enter a period of graduate medical education. Students typically enroll following four years of baccalaureate education and completion of the BA or BS degree, although a few programs admit students directly from secondary school into accelerated six-year curricula that combine the baccalaureate and medical studies.

The four years of medical school preceding graduate medical education are divided into a preclinical phase and a clinical phase. Typically, the preclinical phase occupies the first two years after matriculation and the clinical phase the last two. Basic science departments are largely responsible for the content of the preclinical curriculum. The major preclinical courses are anatomy, biochemistry, physiology, microbiology, pharmacology, and pathology. A course introducing students to concepts of physical diagnosis and clinical medicine is commonly taught during the second academic year of the preclinical phase. The principal method of instruction is the lecture, with small group discussion, self-instruction, and laboratory experiences comprising the remainder of the scheduled time. Approximately eight schools have organized their preclinical curriculum into organ system units. In this approach the basic disciplines are taught in the context of their relevance to each organ system. Another 15 schools have adopted a small group tutorial curriculum taught around cases and emphasizing problem solving. This approach requires students to take responsibility for obtaining information to answer questions they raise. It encourages students to become active learners rather than memorizers of information.

The final two years of the curriculum are usually devoted to education in the clinical setting. The periods of instruction are called clerkships. The usual length of the clerkship is six to eight weeks. In the clerkship, students are assigned patients and expected to obtain the history of their illnesses and their personal situation. Clerkships are based primarily on experiential learning, with limited lectures and seminars to augment the "bedside" teaching. Several factors now conspire to make inpatient services less than ideal as educational sites, particularly for the training of medical students. Technological advances in various specialties and the financial incentives inherent in managed care systems have narrowed the range of medical conditions for which patients are now hospitalized. Those who do receive hospital care tend to stay for a shorter period, with much of the initial diagnostic workup and post-treatment follow-up occurring in the ambulatory setting. As a result, medical students have little time to get to know hospitalized patients, to study their medical conditions, and to follow the course of treatment and care. Nearly all schools include some training in ambulatory settings as part of the clinical program in the third or fourth years. This training takes place in hospital-related ambulatory clinics, physicians' offices, family medicine centers, geriatric centers, community-based centers, indigent care centers, and rural clinics. These settings provide a more representative patient population and may enable a stronger educational focus on physical examination and history taking, patient management, continuity of care, and understanding the social, psychological, and cultural aspects of disease and disability and their implications for care.

During the fourth and final year, students are permitted to elect their own courses. Elective courses in the basic, behavioral, and clinical sciences allow students to explore career options and augment aspects of their undergraduate program.

There has been little change in the past 60 years in the educational programs of medical students in the United States. Innovation has been introduced very slowly in US medical schools. Only about 15 schools have undertaken a comprehensive reform of their medical education program, and the majority of these efforts has taken place in the preclinical years. The innovations include the introduction of problem-based learning methods into the preclinical curriculum, an increase in the use of small-group learning, a modest reduction in lectures, and organization of the curriculum around organ systems, rather than disciplines.

GRADUATE MEDICAL EDUCATION

Graduate medical education, residency and fellowship training, varies in length from three to seven years and is essential for preparing physicians for independent practice. The complex and elaborate process by which medical school graduates secure residency positions is facilitated by the National Resident Matching Program (NRMP), a computerized process that links student choices for graduate training programs with available positions and preferences of program directors for candidates.

In 1992, a total of 14,030 fourth-year students at US medical schools sought graduate training through the NRMP, with 12,957 or 92 percent successfully matched to a program of their choice. The NRMP also facilitates the matching of foreign medical graduates and US graduates educated abroad, Canadian medical school graduates, osteopathic medical school graduates, and other physician candidates to graduate medical education programs. The number of residency positions offered each year exceeds the number of candidates. For example, in 1992, a total of 20,294 first-year residency positions was offered through the NRMP, but 1992 graduates of US medical schools filled only 64 percent of the positions. Other applicants filled another 16 percent of the positions, leaving approximately 20 percent of the positions unfilled. There is increasing sentiment for controlling the number of residency positions to approximate more closely workforce needs. Historically, the growth of residency positions has been driven largely by hospital service needs. In 1992, the specialties of orthopedic surgery and diagnostic radiology filled nearly all first-year residency positions offered, an indication of their popularity. Family medicine has been one of the specialties whose percentage of positions filled is the lowest. Interest in surgical specialties has remained fairly constant, while interest in medical subspecialties (i.e., internal medicine and pediatrics, allergy and immunology, psychiatry and neurology, and dermatology) and support specialties (i.e., anesthesiology, radiology, pathology, physical medicine and rehabilitation, emergency medicine, and preventive medicine and public health) has increased.

Specialty choices of graduates have come under scrutiny as consensus develops that the nation suffers from a shortage of generalist physicians. Generalist physicians--those practicing family medicine, general internal medicine, or general pediatrics--increasingly are viewed as critical to addressing the problems of access to health care and containment of costs. Yet little more than one-third of all active physicians can be classified as generalists. As the needs of the patient population change and the sites for delivery of health care move out of the hospital and into the ambulatory setting, the need for generalist physicians will increase. The inability of medical schools to produce more generalist physicians has understandably frustrated state and federal government policymakers. Work is underway nationally to identify and recruit more generalist physicians as faculty members, to expose medical students early and frequently to primary care experiences during their undergraduate years, to add more ambulatory care experiences in medical school, and to elevate the status of the generalist physician in academic medical centers.

LICENSURE

Throughout the course of this century an intricate network of accreditation bodies, licensing authorities, and specialty certification boards has developed to provide assurances that physicians in practice have acquired the requisite knowledge and skills to practice medicine safely and competently. For US medical school graduates, this evaluation process begins with the careful and selective process by which each student is admitted to medical school and continues with the ongoing assessment by medical school faculty of the student's satisfactory progress through the curriculum. Faculty observations and judgments regarding the clinical skills and competence of medical students are particularly important in the award of the M.D. degree, which indicates a readiness to enter graduate medical education. These same faculty are involved in assessing the clinical skills of residents during their graduate medical education program.

The Liaison Committee on Medical Education (LCME), jointly sponsored by the Association of American Medical Colleges (AAMC) and the American Medical Association (AMA), accredits programs of medical education leading to the MD degree. LCME accreditation means that medical schools in the US and Canada meet the standards for organization, function, and performance that assure that graduates are qualified to undertake the next phase (residency) of medical education. The LCME conducts regular surveys of US and Canadian schools for these purposes.

Similarly, the Accreditation Council on Graduate Medical Education (ACGME), of which the AAMC is a sponsor, is charged with determining the essential requirements of graduate medical education programs and ensuring their compliance by institutions in the conduct of their graduate programs. Discipline-based Residence Review Committees (RRC) complement these general requirements with a review of programs based on specific training requirements determined for each specialty. The involvement of specialty boards in the determination of residency program requirements is appropriate since these boards certify physicians as meeting certain standards based in part on satisfactory completion of an acceptable training program.

While the efforts of these voluntary agencies are invaluable to the process of ensuring physician competence for practice, the legal authority to grant a license to practice medicine rests with 54 different state and jurisdictional licensing authorities. The requirements to obtain a license to practice medicine are not uniform among these jurisdictions, but at a minimum they include the completion of an acceptable educational program, successful passage of an external examination, and, in all but three jurisdictions, at least one year of graduate medical education. Beginning in 1994, the United States Medical Licensing Examination (USMLE) will be required of all candidates for licensure, whether graduates of accredited US schools or of programs outside the US. It replaces the multiple examination system that imposed separate pathways to licensure for US and foreign medical graduates.

Uncertainty about the quality of education received by graduates of some programs has prompted many jurisdictions to impose additional requirements at the interface between medical school and residency. Foreign medical graduates (FMGs) seeking entry to accredited graduate medical education programs, participation in which is required for licensure, must first obtain a certificate awarded by the Educational Commission for Foreign Medical Graduates (ECFMG). This certificate is now based upon satisfactory completion of the first two parts of the USMLE, an English language proficiency requirement, and complete documentation of specified medical credentials. At the moment, the surrogate for accreditation of foreign medical schools is ECFMG certification.

While the array of agencies, associations, and authorities involved in these processes is confusing, their respective roles and interrelationships are based on several principles: the need for multiple agencies to provide checks and balances on assessment of the competence of individuals and the quality of programs, the desire to complement standardized paper-and-pencil evaluations of physician knowledge with judgments of clinical skills based on observation by experienced physician-educators, and the assurance provided by completion of a documented and accredited program of studies and supervised clinical experiences.

The most pressing challenge facing evaluators is developing a reliable and valid means to assess the clinical skills of medical students, residents, and practitioners seeking professional licensure or relicensure. Two promising directions for improved clinical assessment are computer-based examinations and performance-based examinations using standardized patients.

CONTINUING MEDICAL EDUCATION

Continuing medical education (CME) evolved because physicians must keep pace with developments in science and technology. By participating in specified levels of CME, physicians fulfill their professional needs while meeting requirements of some licensing and specialty boards for continued licensure or certification. Accreditation of institutions and organizations to provide approved CME programs is conferred by the Accreditation Council for Continuing Medical Education, the Association of American Medical Colleges, the American Hospital Association, and the American Board of Medical Specialties. There are also many venues of nonaccredited CME. Most US medical schools have a department or office for continuing medical education programs. The programs are developed both locally and nationally.

There has been considerable discussion among the leaders of American medical education about the need to involve offices of continuing medical education in the efforts to re-certify the competencies of practicing physicians. The discussion is in its beginning stages, but there is broad recognition that measures need to be taken to assure the public of the continued competence of its practicing physicians.

ROLE OF RESEARCH IN MEDICAL EDUCATION

In American medical education, the terms "research" and "medical education" are often perceived to be diametrically opposed concepts, their combination constituting an oxymoron. The institutional priorities of the academic medicine culture do not give students' education a high priority. The system of faculty rewards and recognition does not provide a clear incentive for faculty members to teach, whereas the demands on faculty members' time for research and patient care are clear. As a result, many faculty members must devote most of their time to their research (which brings funding to the institution), or to patient care (which brings funding to their departments) at the expense of time spent teaching medical students.

Recently, the use of animals in biomedical and behavioral research and concerns about the ethical conduct of researchers have become the focus of public scrutiny. Although different, these issues are examples of the obligation of the medical centers to earn public trust and support as they pursue their research missions. A related, but potentially more difficult, set of issues for institutions is the growth of academia-industry relationships and the real or perceived conflicts of commitment and interest for the academic researcher. The research accomplishments of the past four decades have not only expanded the frontiers of science, but have also created significant opportunities for translating basic research findings into commercially viable products. This development has expanded research relationships between industry and academia, the former drawing from the collective intellectual and creative talents of medical school faculty, the latter benefiting from an additional source of funding. As such relationships expand, faculty members find themselves with obligations and responsibilities that extend beyond the institution. Time available for teaching and other institutional responsibilities may be reduced as they attempt to live up to the expectations of the industrial sponsors.

GOVERNMENT/PRIVATE SECTOR INVOLVEMENT

The federal government's involvement in medical education has been indirect. Through the National Institutes for Health (NIH), the federal government provides the bulk of research money to medical schools. Through its Medicare program, it finances a proportional share of the cost of training medical residents. State governments contribute similarly by providing funds under Medicaid for resident training. State governments also contribute significant appropriations for public medical schools and some for private medical schools in their areas. Some state governments have been active in seeking to influence both the number and types of students admitted to medical schools, as a way to direct the output of those schools to meet state needs for physicians.

The involvement of the private sector in medical education has been far less significant, but it is growing. Private enterprises support an increasing amount of biomedical research in medical schools, although it is still a small component to most schools' research budgets. Proprietary medical schools, common in the last century, are non-existent among the universe of accredited schools.

INTERNATIONAL LINKAGES AND COLLABORATION

International linkages are mainly centered in medical school-to-medical school programs, although many medical schools and individual departments within universities in the US have been World Health Organization Collaborating Centers for many years, and several US institutions are active in the international Network of Community Oriented Educational Institutions for Health Sciences. Visiting teams of observers from medical schools in other countries are frequently seen on medical school campuses.

ISSUES AND TRENDS

Several issues dominate current debates in American medical education: 1) the need to produce more generalist physicians; 2) the need to modify the educational paradigm to include more emphasis on population-based medicine and preventive care; 3) the need to conduct more of clinical training in ambulatory and community sites, and less in tertiary care hospitals; 4) the need to develop more active methods for learning and to integrate advances in information technology into that process; and 5) the need to develop a stable and sensible approach to the financing of medical education.

REFERENCES

Bennett, C.T., ed. 1993. *1994-95 medical school admission requirements, United States and Canada*. 44th ed. Washington, DC: Association of American Medical Colleges.

----------. 1992. *AAMC directory of American medical education, 1992-93*. 39th ed. Washington, DC: Association of American Medical Colleges.

----------. *1991. 1991-92 AAMC curriculum directory*. 20th ed. Washington, DC: Association of American Medical Colleges.

Flexner, A. 1910. *Medical education in the United States and Canada*. A report to the Carnegie Foundation for the Advancement of Teaching. Bulletin no. 4. Boston, Massachusetts: Updyke.

Jolly, P., and D. Hudley, eds. 1993. *AAMC data book: Statistical information related to medical education*. Washington, DC: Association of American Medical Colleges.

Jones, R.F. 1993. *American medical education: Institutions, programs, and issues*. Washington, DC: Association of American Medical Colleges.

Ludmerer, K. 1985. *Learning to heal: The development of American medical education*. New York: Basic Books.

Muller, S. (Chair). 1984. Physicians for the twenty-first century: Report of the Project Panel on the General Professional Education of the Physician and College Preparation for Medicine. *J Med Educ* 59, Part 2 (November).

Swanson, A.G. (Principal Investigator), and M.B. Anderson (Project Director). 1993. Educating medical students: Assessing change in medical education--The road to implementation: The ACME-TRI Report with supplements. Prepared for the Association of American Medical Colleges and Charles E. Culpeper Foundation. *Acad Med* 68 (6) (supplement).

Table 29.1
United States--Medical School Demographics, 1991-1992

Allopathic Medical Schools	Undergraduate Students Enrolled	Degrees Awarded	Residents	Faculty
126	65,600	15, 969	86,217 59,812 M 25,923 F 17,279 International Medical Graduates	80,084 15,969 Basic Science 64,115 Clinical Science

30

Venezuela

PABLO PULIDO
ROBERTO RONDÓN

According to the 1991 census, the population of Venezuela was 18,105,265, with 80 percent of the population living in cities. It is estimated that by the year 2000, the urban population will have reached 93 percent of the total.

OVERVIEW OF THE HEALTH CARE DELIVERY SYSTEM

Article 76 of the national constitution guarantees the right to health for all citizens. Health services are organized into three levels of care: primary--general urban and rural ambulatory care; secondary--specialized ambulatory services and general hospitalization; and tertiary--subspecialized ambulatory clinics and specialty hospitals. Theoretically, roughly 85 percent of the population receives medical services, including medical consultations, laboratory examinations and medications from the following public institutions: (1) the Ministry of Health and Social Service (MSAS), provides 49 percent of the care for this 85 percent of the population through a network of 277 hospitals, 526 outpatient clinics, 646 rural ambulatory services, and 2,819 simple rural dispensaries; (2) the Venezuelan Institute of Social Security (IVSS) (to which the worker contributes 4 percent of his or her salary and the private or public employer contributes 8 percent) provides 31.5 percent; (3) the Institute of Social Security and Health Care of the Ministry of Education (IPASME) is responsible for 3 percent; (4) the Armed Forces Institute of Social Security (IPSFA) is responsible for 1.6 percent; (5) and the National Geriatric Institute (NAGER) is responsible for 0.28 percent.

The remaining 15 percent of the population is, theoretically, attended by the private sector through direct payment or commercial insurance. This is the sector of the most growth, increasing from seven hospitals in 1950 to 256 in 1982.

The health system is characterized by diffuseness, ineffectiveness, and high costs, and in reality 30 percent of the population is not adequately covered. For this reason, a National Health System law was passed in 1987 to put under one authority the approximately 150 institutions which receive their financing from the federal, state, or municipal government.

Venezuela has a rather young and increasing population which is primarily urban. Of the country's nearly twenty million inhabitants, one quarter are under ten years of age. Another 25 percent are in the 10-20 year age bracket. The birthrate in 1990 was estimated at 27.2 and the death rate at 4.4, while the average life expectancy is seventy years (see Table 30.1).

The health system assists the following age groups:

Table 30.1
Venezuela--Age Cohorts 1985 and 2000 (Projected)

Year	Age <15 years	Age 15-64 years	Age >64 years	Total
1985	6,839,000	9,889,000	591,000	17,319,000
2000	8,250,000	15,120,000	1,071,000	24,441,000

In 1988, a study of 90,525 health care workers showed that 23 percent were doctors, 15 percent were nurses, and 62 percent were technicians and other health care professionals; this demonstrates an inappropriate ratio of nurses to doctors. The overall ratio of doctors to the population is 1/743 but there is a very poor geographic distribution with the majority of the physicians in the urban areas, leaving the rural areas without adequate medical care.

HISTORICAL BACKGROUND

Prior to World War II, there were two university medical schools and the medical school curriculum was based on the French model of teaching and clinical practice. In the 1950s, the Flexnerian focus was introduced with three separate phases: basic sciences, preclinical, and clinical studies. Later innovations included both the Case Western Reserve model of horizontal and vertical integration of teaching and the University of Colorado model incorporating departments of social and preventive medicine. The joint academic and service conferences in Viña del Mar and Tehuacán sponsored by Latin American Medical Schools and PAHO during the 1950s played a determining role in these innovations. The Association of American Medical Colleges (AAMC, 1953) and the American Medical Association (AMA, 1951) stimulated the establishment of objectives for medical education and minimum requirements for accreditation of medical schools.

Particularly important were the trends generated in the first Colombian Seminar on Medical Education (1955) that advocated a careful selection of students, the creation of medical school departments, horizontal and vertical teaching coordination, full time teaching staff, and a rotating undergraduate internship encompassing internal medicine, pediatrics, OB/Gyn, and urban and rural general surgery. These important discussions and meetings led to the creation in 1962 of the Pan American Federation of Associations of Medical Schools (PAFAMS), an academic nongovernmental organization dedicated to the development of medical education in relation to community and health services needs. It was sponsored by 12 national associations, (including AAMC and ACMC), as well as individual medical schools. Another important milestone was the first Pan American Conference on Medical Education (1966), the theme of which was "The Physician That the Country Needs."

Venezuela's population and economic growth during the 1970s brought new medical schools and the exaggerated expansion of others, promoting the graduation of more doctors than either the public or private sector could absorb (a condition which is especially true of the present situation.) The current economic and social crises and the commitment to primary health care, have caused a polarization in medical education between those who are concentrating on the technical, scientific aspects and those who desire a high social focus. The reconciliation of these two points of view has proven difficult.

From the epidemiological point of view, there is an overlap of the three pathological phases described by J. Evans: infectious, contagious and deficiency diseases; degenerative illnesses; and those caused by the environment. There are epidemiological transitions from one to the other phase such as the reappearance of once eradicated diseases for which the medical schools and the health system do not have adequate answers. From the demographic point of view, the health system and the medical schools are also unable to provide adequate answers to the phenomenon of urbanization. There are also no plans for the future health care of the ever increasing population, especially the aged, whose numbers will double by the year 2024.

ROLE OF NATIONAL POLICY IN SHAPING MEDICAL EDUCATION

See "Overview of the Health Care Delivery System."

ADMISSION

In Venezuela any student wishing to take any undergraduate course, including medicine, must register in a national admission system. This national pre-inscription mechanism instituted in 1973 considers the high school grade point average as well as the score on a national aptitude test. All students who participate in the national pre-inscription admissions system are classified by an academic index. The index takes into account the high school grade point average (60 percent) and the academic aptitude test (40 percent: 20 percent verbal, 20 percent mathematics). This index is the main factor used for assigning students although other variables such as the year of graduation from high school, the region in which the student lives and socioeconomic status are also considered. The universities petition the national system for a number of students with a certain grade point average. Medical schools are usually allocated students with the highest grade point average.

There are also less formal ways to enter undergraduate medical school. Children of professors and employees of the university are admitted without the requirement of complying with the required grade point average. Others enter medical school by transferring from other universities. These practices are beginning to disappear. Some medical schools also require that a student be from the region where the school is located. A revision of this admission process is presently being considered which will include other factors such as the student's knowledge, attitude and aptitude to study and practice medicine.

There has been heavy criticism of the use of the grade point average for admission. It seems that students with the highest grades usually study in private secondary schools which better prepare them for the aptitude test. Thus, it is believed that admissions are slanted toward a higher social and economic class, to the detriment of other less fortunate groups. This process also favors a greater number of female admissions because women tend to have a higher grade point average. It appears to some that control over student admission to medical school is determined by the parents' economic status.

The percent of admitted students who complete the six years of medical school has been gradually increasing from 46 percent in 1979 to a maximum of 95 percent in 1985 (average 75 percent). Maintaining an annual production of 2,000 doctors for the rest of the century means that Venezuela will have more than 50,000 doctors by the year 2000. In 1990, there were 26,543 Venezuelan physicians, already considered an oversupply.

Since all the medical schools are located in public universities, the cost of a medical education to the individual is minimal.

CURRICULAR STRUCTURE AND INNOVATION

The Flexnerian curriculum is divided into three stages: (1) basic--the study of normal human structure and function, morphology and physiology; (2) preclinical--the study of the factors that alter the normal structure and function, epidemiology, pathology, pathophysiology, and symptomatology; and (3) clinical-- the study of treatment and recuperation, medical/surgical clinics.

The most important changes in the medical education process that have occurred in the last thirty years include the following: (1) the introduction of epidemiology, behavioral sciences and demographics. However, this has not resulted in real change because teaching in these areas continues to remain theoretical and there has been no way to tie the subjects into actual health practice. (2) The introduction of community medicine, with a focus toward the prevalent rural and urban pathologies, especially in ambulatory care centers. This change was accomplished by incorporating a year of social service internship in a rural or semi-urban setting at the end of medical school education as a requirement before beginning medical practice. This program provides the students with an awareness of social and community problems and broadens their views on the need for clearly defined health policies as well as preparing them for the initial years of medical practice. Unfortunately, the lack of political and technical importance accorded to this approach, the lack of resources, and the lack of participation of prestigious clinics has lessened the actual impact of community medicine on medical education. (3) The commitment to primary care which has recently stimulated such changes as the following: an attempt to link basic sciences with clinical and social sciences, increased attention to the prevalent pathologies, greater emphasis on problem solving, an enhanced importance accorded ambulatory training, and its gradual incorporation early in the undergraduate program.

Some of these curricular reforms have coincided with the country's social and economic changes. The first changes occurred during the period of prosperity when new medical schools appeared and existing schools expanded. The last changes came during the economic and social crisis of the early 1990s.

Clinical Education

While students spend time in hospitals for training in interviewing, physical examination and other diagnostic modalities during the preclinical stage (3rd and 4th year), their major clinical training takes place in the last two years of a six year course. Though the sequence and duration vary from school to school, traditionally this hospital training includes internal medicine, pediatrics, OB/Gyn and general surgery. Urban and rural outpatient clinics are utilized for the teaching of community medicine. Table 30.2, p. 430, shows variations of curricula among schools.

All the medical schools have been established and are supported by the federal government. The universities have agreements with the Ministry of Health for student clinical training. Other schools complement this clinical experience by utilizing IVSS hospitals, while in the Federal District students are also sent to the municipal hospitals.

In all areas, the students are responsible for the admission, continuing care and discharge of the patient. They also train in consulting offices, emergency rooms, and eventually in the operating room. All student activities are under direct supervision of their professors. The experiences in both rural and urban outpatient services where the students participate in community development (including visits to water treatment plants, waste disposal sites, and food outlets) are not as closely supervised and very much depend on the student's own interest and initiative rather than the orientation of the faculty.

Teaching Methods

Teaching/learning methods are traditional: lecture halls, cadaver dissection, laboratory practice, clinical case study, social and epidemiological studies of small towns, visits to health institutions, immunization campaigns, and so forth. During the 1960s, learning and evaluation by objectives, audiovisual technologies, and self-learning were introduced. A few attempts at problem solving instruction and case studies were initiated, such as the examination of a particular geopolitical area (local health areas) in which health problems, solutions and participation of the community have been delineated. The majority of these experiences have come from participation in the so-called rural internship, occurring at the end of the medical school course. Several communities in the states of Lara, Miranda, and Mérida, as well as the Federal District, participate in these activities.

In addition, in the past two years, considerable interest has been generated in the use of modern computer techniques which enhance learning and education through specific data bases pertinent to epidemiological, managerial, and continuing medical education topics. Initially these attempts are being catalyzed by PAFAMS and carried out with the participation of the Venezuelan Association of Medical Schools (AVEFAM).

GRADUATE MEDICAL EDUCATION

In Venezuela, a student who successfully completes the undergraduate medical requirements, including an internship, receives an academic title from the university. The Medical Practice Law obligates all medical school graduates to practice during their first year in towns with less than 5,000 inhabitants, after which the Ministry of Health and Social Security grants them authorization to practice freely. There are two ways to complete this requirement: (1) to live and practice medicine in a rural ambulatory setting for one year; or (2) to work in a hospital for two years, one of which must be in a rural or suburban environment. In both cases the doctor works as a general practitioner.

The tremendous surge in urbanization and the fact that the rural areas cannot absorb all the recent graduates has led to a revision of this law. Once the student has complied with the previously mentioned obligation, he or she can choose a postgraduate residency which will lead to specialization. There are two types of medical residencies: (1) training in a non-teaching qualified hospital for at least two years or (2) completion of an academic program which could include a research project, and training in certified services of a qualified hospital for at least two years. About 50 percent of the Venezuelan doctors choose one of the two types of residency.

Before 1980 a significant number of doctors completed their residency in the United States, United Kingdom, Europe, USSR, or Mexico (pediatrics or cardiology), but now there are economic constraints and US immigration barriers against this practice.

A year after graduation from medical school, doctors are permitted to practice freely as general practitioners. Those who have completed a residency are allowed to practice as specialists. There appears to be no relationship between the need for specific specialties and the number of residencies available. No studies have been done to determine the need for specialists.

Board Certification for Specialists

The Medical Practice Law authorizes the professional organization of each state to grant permission for specialist practice after reviewing the physician's credentials. In addition, the Venezuelan university system called the National Board of Universities has established a national accreditation program for residencies which has important academic requisites and which is directed by the medical schools. This idea has not been readily accepted because at present the professional association recognizes residencies without academic components and based on only two years work in a supposedly prestigious health service institution. There is no recertification of specialists, although the subject has been discussed.

Venezuelan Medical Federation. All of the state professional associations are affiliated with a central body called the Venezuelan Medical Federation, under which forty recognized medical specialties are registered. Each specialty has formed a scientific society that carries out special activities such as continuing education.

LICENSURE

The requirements to practice medicine are: to be a graduate of a national or foreign school (there is a revalidation process for foreigners); completion of the rural service requirement; registration in the professional association; and the authorization of the respective ministry. Practice can be as a general practitioner or as a specialist if a residency has been completed. This authorization to practice is permanent, except for grave charges which would require the association to suspend the offender's license.

Cross-Licensing of Physicians

Both Venezuelan citizens and foreigners who obtain their medical training and credentials abroad are required to undergo a process of revalidation or endorsement of their diploma before practicing in Venezuela. The first process is utilized when the physician has finished studies in a country that does not have cultural agreements with Venezuela, the second when the country does have cultural agreements. The difference is solely a matter of form.

In the first case, the physician applies directly for revalidation to a university with a medical school. An ad hoc committee compares their curriculum with the applicant's course of study. Generally the candidate must take some courses and examinations in national subjects such as tropical medicine, public health, epidemiology, and other essential subjects such as care of the mother, child, and adult. When these requirements are fulfilled the university issues a new medical diploma.

For endorsement, the candidate introduces a petition, along with the notarized medical diploma from the Venezuelan consulate in the foreign city where he or she studied, to the Ministry of Education, which in turn submits it to a university with a medical school. After that the requirements are the same as previously outlined except that when completed the candidate's foreign diploma is endorsed with an authorization to practice in Venezuela. Once the diploma is revalidated or endorsed the physician is obligated to fulfill a rural medical social service, as was outlined previously.

Before 1970, due to the scarcity of physicians in the rural environment, the federal government authorized the practice of foreign graduates without revalidation or endorsement. Now, however, due to the excess of physicians, the requirement for revalidation or endorsement is obligatory.

In 1985, the president of Venezuela signed contracts with some countries of the Caribbean, Andean Region, and northern Europe which state that professional graduates of those countries, among them physicians, do not need revalidation or endorsement to practice their profession in Venezuela. This move was taken without enough serious consideration to the consequences and naturally has generated much discussion in the professional associations, the specialties, health service management and the universities.

Before 1980, due to a booming economy, there was considerable immigration of doctors, especially from the Andean countries and the South Cone. This flow has diminished due to the economic depression and the oversupply of Venezuelan doctors. The immigration of foreign graduates was due to the need for manpower in a growing economy, and there does not seem to be any pattern of foreign immigration as a result of international accords. Agreements with Spain, Brazil, and the Andean countries seem to have little influence on the immigration of foreign physicians. Certainly there is an economic factor.

CONTINUING MEDICAL EDUCATION

It is accepted that continuing education is the ideal instrument to guarantee actualization of professional competencies. Since there is no required specialization recertification, continuing education is completely voluntary.

Numerous organizations offer continuing education programs. Medical schools offer pedagogical courses as well as technical and scientific programs. The Ministry of Health, the IVSS, and other health institutions which employ doctors offer courses in clinical practice, epidemiology, health service management, specialty topics, and special public health problems. Private institutions have assumed the important role of educators in clinical, technical, and management areas. Independent efforts such as those of the Federación Médica Venezolana, (the Venezuelan Medical Association comparable to the American Medical Association), the specialty scientific societies and nonprofit teaching and health care centers such as La Trinidad Teaching Medical Center and the Children's Orthopedic Foundation, among others, are providing new leadership in this area. The professional associations and scientific specialty societies usually offer activities in their own fields of interest. There are also other nonacademic nonmedical institutions involved in continuing education activities connected with medicine, such as pharmaceutical companies and medical equipment businesses.

The Venezuelan Medical Federation, made up of all the state associations, has established an accreditation system. This system is more than just registration and authorization of the continuing education courses sponsored by the previously mentioned institutions. This accreditation is useful for entrance into medical service or teaching and also for promotion within an institution. It is hoped that it will also serve in the future for recertification of specialists.

ROLE OF RESEARCH IN MEDICAL EDUCATION

According to the final report of the project, "Profile and Tendencies of Scientific Production in Health in Venezuela," by J. Díaz Polanco, L. Yero, and N. Prado B. (1988-1989), three-quarters of the 1,776 health research projects, were conducted in public universities (Universidad Central de Venezuela, Los Andes, and Zulia). Government institutions such as the Ministry of Health and the Venezuelan Institute for Scientific Research, as well as private institutions accounted for the rest of the projects in more or less equal proportions. About 68 percent of the institutions with projects in the health area are located in the capital region.

CONICIT, the National Council for Scientific and Technological Research is the federal organization in charge of promoting and developing research. Between 1981 and 1986, CONICIT dedicated 20-30 percent of its budget to medical science and technology. The Central University and Venezuelan Institute for Scientific Research (IVIC) are the most prominent recipients of CONICIT.

The percentage of the gross national product assigned to science and technology has fluctuated between 0.28 percent to 0.42 percent in the last eight or nine years. The amount recommended for a country of Venezuela's development and infrastructure is 1 to 2 percent while the present figure for developed countries is greater than 3 percent.

The subjects most frequently addressed are illnesses and biological sciences with approximately 30 percent, while 70 percent is directed to applied research. The classifications according to disciplines are (in descending order) medical sciences, life sciences, pathology, internal medicine and clinical sciences. The ten leading causes of death and their share of research dollars are:

1. Cardiovascular disease (5.0 percent);
2. Traffic accidents (0);
3. Cancer (4.5 percent);
4. Prenatal illnesses (1.8 percent);
5. Cerebral vascular accidents (0.3 percent);
6. Enteritis and other diarrheal illnesses (3.4 percent);
7. Pneumonias (0);
8. Suicide and homicide (.3 percent);
9. Congenital anomalies (2.0 percent); and
10. Diabetes mellitus (1.2 percent).

The remaining funds--up to 30 percent of the CONICIT budget allocated for health--goes to social health and biology oriented projects not related directly with the 10 leading causes of death.

Venezuelan researchers have found it difficult to apply research results to practical health services and educational activities for the following reasons: (1) the wide gap between research subjects and actual community problems; (2) the lack of a tradition of solving health problems with results emanating from research as is common in more developed countries; and (3) the absence of a management infrastructure capable of converting results into practice. Little research is conducted on medical education itself, and what there is refers to the demographic and social characteristics of the students and the results of physiological evaluation for admission to medical school.

GOVERNMENT/PRIVATE SECTOR INVOLVEMENT

In the government sector, various institutions have an influence on medical education and medical schools. The National Council of Universities (CNU) to which all the Venezuelan universities are affiliated, is the body through which the government analyzes the university budgets and then disburses the necessary funds. This body also directs the National Preinscription System which assigns students to medical schools based on the number and qualifications of the applicants. It is the organization that authorizes the creation of new universities and professional schools, including medical schools. The National Advisory Council on Postgraduate Studies is involved in these activities and is also working on creating an accreditation mechanism.

The second governmental organization is the Ministry of Health and Social Service, which is the principal political and financial health provider in the country. Other institutions with less influence are the Venezuelan Institute of Social Security, as well as the principal employers of Venezuelan doctors. The relationships are established through agreements that attempt to iron out the political, technical, legal, and financial differences that are evident between the training institutions and the employers of human resources.

CONICIT influences medical schools through the financing of research projects and the establishment of priorities within the schools. Another public organization, although not governmental, is the Venezuelan Medical Federation, with obligatory membership of all practicing physicians. All of the aforementioned organizations indirectly influence medical education. Occasionally there are meetings of the various organizations to exchange information of common interest.

The leading private organization involved with medical education is the Venezuelan Association of Medical Schools (AVEFAM), which is made up of the ten existing medical schools located within seven universities: two in the Central Venezuelan University in Caracas, two in the University of Carabobo (one in Valencia and another in Maracay), two in the Eastern University in Ciudad Bolivar and Barcelona, one in the Central Western University Lisandro Alvarado in Barquisimeto, one each in the University of Los Andes in Merida and the University of Zulia in Maracaibo, and one in the National Experimental University Francisco de Miranda in Coro. Representatives from MSAS, IVSS, and the Venezuelan Medical Federation work closely with AVEFAM. The Association plans for the improvement of medical education, especially in the area of information, methodology and human resources training, but has the disadvantage of not having enough funding for its important projects.

Private foundations finance small research projects or health related activities, participating in the acquisition of equipment and/or completing library and informational resources.

An additional emerging positive factor has been the creation in 1976 of La Trinidad Teaching Medical Center, located in Caracas, which is a nonprofit foundation effort. It runs an ambulatory health care facility, continuing medical education courses and a small research unit dedicated to the study of the biology of parasites (*Trypanosomiasis cruzi*) as well as cytogenetics and other projects. A hospital facility is currently under construction, and a proposal to create a new health technology institute has been submitted to the Consejo Nacional de Universidades (CNU), at the Ministry of Education.

INTERNATIONAL LINKAGES AND COLLABORATION

The medical schools affiliated with AVEFAM are automatically part of, the Panamerican Federation of Associations of Medical Schools (PAFAMS), and they also maintain close contact with the local PAHO office. Through these two international organizations and other informational mechanisms, the medical schools keep abreast of the trends in world medical education.

The incorporation of international commitments within the academic affairs and management of the medical schools is not easy. The inclusion of the political and social declaration "Health for All by the Year 2000" and the Primary Health Care Strategy have not been easy either. These subjects create an ardent discussion between those who believe they represent an oversimplification of medical education and health services that conspires against quality and excellence and those who affirm that the declarations call for a greater social commitment from education and health services for the general population and particularly for the underserved.

The current economic and social crisis, which has affected the whole country, and particularly the education and health sector, has necessitated a reformulation of the curriculum, which had been concentrating on primary care, the influence of the prevalent pathologies, larger amounts of training in outpatient clinics, and community integration. The control of the resources to carry out these proposals has been affected as well.

The Edinburgh Declaration by the World Federation for Medical Education (WFME) has helped to strengthen this process. There are other initiatives, such as subregional meetings of Health Ministries, in which the presidents of the Social Security Institutes have been included for the purpose of integrating health programs for the community.

There is little real appreciation of the changes in medical education that are occurring to meet social and/or community needs. It is not clear whether the changes are due to a real commitment to social health as expressed in the Declarations of Alma Ata and Edinburgh, or are simply a reflection of the economic crisis which has caused a cutback in the number of medical school admissions, the annualization of the academic organization and control of the curriculum. The establishment of programs aimed at ambulatory care and the community is mainly due to the hospital crisis. A follow-up study is needed to determine if these are just temporary reforms or if they will lead to real change.

ISSUES AND TRENDS

Medical education in Venezuela has its main challenge in responding to a series of political issues. Decentralization of health services at the federal level gives added responsibility to the states and counties and requires integrating the country's multiple levels of services: systems operating under the Ministry of Health and Social Welfare (free services), Social Security (prepaid services), and private enterprises (fully paid services). This national system would be oriented by criteria of extensive coverage, rational costs, quality, and efficiency.

Medical education should respond to the needs of both public and private institutions. It should also orient its educational services to prepare future health professionals to fully understand the new challenges of financing the increasing cost of health services and cost-containment efforts through national insurance practices, private insurance endeavors, and functional improvement of profit or nonprofit health care organizations.

Populational health (community and environmental), with emphasis on health promotion and prevention of disease, will be a social requirement that will substitute in the future for the current emphasis on healing and rehabilitation.

REFERENCES

Asociación Venezolana de Facultades de Medicina (AVEFAM). 1992. VIII Seminario Nacional de Educación Médica. Notas. Tucacas, Venezuela: AVEFAM.

---------. 1987a. VII Seminario Nacional de Educación Médica. Memorias. Maracaibo.

---------. 1987b. Aspectos Cuantitativos y Cualitativos de la Formación de los Médicos en Venezuela. Ed. T. Garrido. Caracas.

---------. 1978. Seminario Utilización y Formación del Médica General. Memorias. Publicación 7. Caracas: AVEFAM.

---------. 1967. Tercer Seminario de Educación Médica. Primaera Conferencia de la Asociación Venezolana de Facultades de Medicina. Publicación 2. Caracas.

AVEFAM-FEPAFEM. 1974. Quinta Conferencia Panamericana de Educació Médica. Memorias. Caraballeda, Venezuela.

Ministerio de Sanidad y Asistencia Social. 1986. VII Congreso Venezolano de Salud Pública. Memorias. Caracas: Ministerio de Sanidad y Asistencia Social.

Oficina de Planificación del Sector Universitario. 1987. Boletín Estadístico no. 12. Tomos I y II. Caracas: Oficina de Planificación del Sector Universitario.

Universidad Central de Venezuela. 1961. Bases y doctrina para una reforma de la educación médica en Venezuela. Memorias. Ed. C.G. Yépez. Caracas: Universidad Central de Venezuela.

---------. 1991. Facultadad de Medicina Informe de gestión, 1987-1990. Tomos I y II. Caracas: Universidad Central de Venezuela.

Table 30.2

Venezuela--Variations of Curricula among Venezuelan Medical Schools. Time allotted to each specialty also varies.

	UNEFM	UDO	UCLA	LUZ	UC	UCV (LR)	UCV(JMV)	ULA
I*	Community Work I Anatomy I Methods of Research English I							Biology I Microbiology I Anatomy I Embryology I Histology I
II	Community Work II Anatomy II English II							Biochemistry I Behavior Science Parasitology Physiology I
III	Community Work III Anatomy III English III Microbiology I		General Anatomy General Microscopic Anatomy Biochemistry Physiology Statistics	Anatomy I Histology Embryology	Anatomy I Histology & Embryology	Anatomy I Histology I Preventive & Social Medicine I Biochemistry	Anatomy I Histology I Preventive Social Medicine I (Statistics)	Anatomy III Histology II Embryology II Statistics I

Table 30.2

Venezuela--Variations of Curricula among Venezuelan Medical Schools. Time allotted to each specialty also varies.

	UNEFM	UDO	UCLA	LUZ	UC	UCV (LR)	UCV(JMV)	ULA
IV	Community Work IV Pathophysiology IV English IV Microbiology II Intro. to Medical Practice		Cardio-Pulmonary System Basic Neurology Medical Psychology Ecology Epidemiology	Anatomy II Neuro-anatomy Biophysics	Anatomy II Physiology & Biophysics Biochemistry I	Anatomy II Histology II Physiology Psychiatry I	Anatomy II Histology II Biochemistry II Physiology I	Microbiology II Physiology II Biochemistry II
V	Community Work V Pathophysiology II Medical Practice I Pharmacology I	Anatomy Histology Psychology/Psychiatry Preventive & Social Medicine I	Digestive-Renal System Endocrinology Reproductive System Microbiology	Biochemistry Microbiology Statistics	Biochemistry II Physiology & Biophysics II Medical Psychology	Anatomy III Preventive & Social Medicine II Physiology II Physiopathology I Psychiatry II	Anatomy III Physiology II Preventive Social Medicine II (Medical Sociology) Parasitology	Pathological Anatomy Preparatory Clinic Epidemiology Pharmacology I Genetic Medicine

430

Table 30.2
Venezuela--Variations of Curricula among Venezuelan Medical Schools. Time allotted to each specialty also varies.

	UNEFM	UDO	UCLA	LUZ	UC	UCV (LR)	UCV(JMV)	ULA
VI	Community Work VI Pathophysiology III Medical Practice II Pharmacology II Professional Training	Physiology Biochemistry Orientation to Medicine I Psychology/Psychiatry II Preventive & Social Medicine II	Parasitology/Epidemiology II Pharmacology I Pathophysiology	Physiology Pharmacology Parasitology	General Pathology Physiopathology I Microbiology Psychopathology Preventive & Social Medicine I	Preventive & Social Medicine III General Epidemiology Psychological Medicine Psychiatric Medicine I Surgery I	Physiopathology I Medicine IA Pediatrics IA	Preparatory Clinic Pathological Anatomy Pharmacology II Medical Demography
VII	Medical Practice III OB/Gyn Clinic Medical Practice III Medical Clinical	Cytology-Zoology Microbiology-Immunology Orientation to Medicine II Psychology/Psychiatry III Preventive & Social Medicine III	Pharmacology II Physiopathology General Pathology Preparatory Course	Pathological Anatomy Medical Psychology Tropical Pathology	Pharmacology Medicine I General Pathology & Physiopathology II	Special Epidemiology Pharmacology Physiopathology II Microbiology Pediatrics I Parasitology Pathological Anatomy	Physiopathology II Microbiology I Medicine IA Medicine IB Preventive Social Medicine (Epidemiology)	Medical/Surgical I Medical/Surgical II Pediatrics I Legal Medicine

431

Table 30.2
Venezuela--Variations of Curricula among Venezuelan Medical Schools. Time allotted to each specialty also varies.

	UNEFM	UDO	UCLA	LUZ	UC	UCV (LR)	UCV(JMV)	ULA
VIII	Medical Practice IV Medical Clinic Medical Practice V Surgical Clinic	Pharmacology Pathology Medicine I Psychology/ Psychiatry IV Preventive & Social Medicine IV	Maternal/ Child Health Pathology	Pediatric Medical Sur- gery Psychiatry Epidemiology & Statistics	Medicine II Parasitology Pharma- cology II Surgery	Tropical Medicine Preventive & Social Medicine V Psychiatry IV Radiology Patho- logical Anatomy	Pharma- cology I Microbiology II Pathological Anatomy I Medicine IIA Pediatrics IIA & IIB	Medical/ Surgery III Surgical Techniques Obstetrics I Public Health

432

Table 30.2
Venezuela–Variations of Curricula among Venezuelan Medical Schools. Time allotted to each specialty also varies.

	UNEFM	UDO	UCLA	LUZ	UC	UCV (LR)	UCV(JMV)	ULA
Specialty and Clinical Curriculum 1986								
IX	Medical Practice V OB/GYN Medical Practice Pediatric Clinic	Medicine II Surgery I-II OB/Gyn I Preventive Social Medicine V	Medical/ Surgical Pathology II Health Administration Medical & Health Care	Pediatric Clinic Genetic Clinic	Obstetrics & Pediatrics I Pathological Anatomy	Pediatrics II Surgery II OB/Gyn I	Pharmacology II Pathological Anatomy II Preventive & Social Medicine IV (Health Administration) Surgery I OB-I Medicine IIA Pediatrics IIA & IIB	Clinical Cycle Maternal Child Health Program Subprograms OB clinic Pediatric Clinic

433

Table 30.2
Venezuela--Variations of Curricula among Venezuelan Medical Schools. Time allotted to each specialty also varies.

	UNEFM	UDO	UCLA	LUZ	UC	UCV (LR)	UCV(JMV)	ULA
X	Medical Practice VI	OB/Gyn II-III IV Pediatrics Medicine III Preventive & Social Medicine VI	Medical Clinic OB/Gyn Clinic Pediatric Clinic Surgical Clinic	Medical Clinic History of Medicine	Medicine III Surgery II Psychiatric Clinic Legal Medicine	Preventive & Social Medicine V Psychiatry IV Legal Medicine Medicine III Pediatrics III	Preventive & Social Medicine (Integrated Medicine) Surgery II Medicine III Pediatrics III History of Medicine Tropical Medicine OB-II Legal Medicine	Medical Surgical Program Sub-programs Medical Clinic Surgical Clinic

Table 30.2

Venezuela–Variations of Curricula among Venezuelan Medical Schools. Time alloted to each specialty also varies.

	UNEFM	UDO	UCLA	LUZ	UC	UCV (LR)	UCV(JMV)	ULA
XI	Integral Medical Practice	Pediatrics III-IV Medicine IV Surgery III Preventive & Social Medicine VII	History of Medicine Legal Medicine	Surgical Clinic Health Administration I Legal Medicine Industrial Medicine	Obstetrics II Pediatrics II Preventive & Social Medicine II History of Medicine	Surgery III OB/Gyn II Occupa- tional Medi- cine Surgical Tech- niques History of Medicine	Surgery II OB-II Legal Medi- cine Preventive & Social Medicine (Internal Medicine) Tropical Medicine Medicine III Pediatrics III History of Medicine	Medical Surgical Program Sub-programs Community Medicine Emergencies
XII		Surgery IV Medicine V Psychology & Psychiatry V-VIII Preventive & Social Medicine VIII Legal Medicine	Internships outside hospital Rural Internships Social Anthro- pology	OB Clinic Health Ad- ministration II Medical Ethics Rural Medicine	Rotating Internship XI	Medicine IV Surgery III Pediatrics IV Integrated Medicine OB III- (Rotating Internship)		

*Semester. Note: Time alloted to each specialty also varies.

435

Table 30.3 Venezuela—Medical School Demographics

Medical School/ Universities	Undergraduate Enrollment Fall 1991-Male	Undergraduate Enrollment Fall 1991-Female	Graduates 1991-Male	Graduates 1991-Female	Graduate Education (Interns/ Residents Fall 1991)
UCV*	256	317	210	151	518
ULA	176	264	375		285
LUZ	316	361	529	362	
UC*	145	206	344		
UDO*	65	35			15
UCLA	80	96	74	66	74
UNEFM	11	20	24		
UNIV. R. URDANETA					4
CENT. INV. PSIQ. PSIC.					12
TOTAL # Medical Schools 10	Total Male Undergrad. Students 1,049	Total Female Undergrad. Students 1,299	Total Male Graduates 813	Total Female Graduates 579	Total Interns/ Residents 908

* There are 2 medical schools in these universities

Appendix A: General Country Demographics, 1989

Country	Size (sq. km) 1 km = 1,600 ml	Population	Density: Persons per square mile	Urban/Rural Ratio	Physician/ Population Ratio
Australia	7,682,300	16,470,000	5.6	85.7% / 14.3%	1 per 552 persons
Belgium	30,521	9,865,000	837.2	72.4% / 27.6%	1 per 331 persons
Brazil	8,511,965	147,562,000	43.9	74.2% / 25.8%	1 per 1,200 persons
Canada	9,970,610	27,000,000	7.3	75.9% / 24.1%	1 per 516 persons
Chile	736,905	12,750,000	43.6	80.8% / 19.2%	1 per 983 persons
China	9,572,900	1,088,200,000	294.4	46.6% / 53.4%	1 per 724 persons
Czechoslovakia	127,896	15,604,000	316.0	74.1% / 25.9%	1 per 321 persons
Egypt	997,739	50,273,000	127.6	43.9% / 56.1%	1 per 635 persons
France	543,965	55,860,000	266.0	73.4% / 26.6%	1 per 350 persons
Germany (former FRG)	248,667	60,782,000	633.0	85.5% / 14.5%	1 per 370 persons
Germany (former GDR)	108,333	16,588,000	396.6	76.6% / 23.4%	1 per 424 persons
Hungary	93,036	10,591,000	294.8	59.2% / 40.8%	1 per 343 persons
India	3,166,414	801,806,000	655.8	25.5% / 74.5%	1 per 2,522 persons

Country	Size (sq. km) 1 km = 1,600 ml	Population	Density: Persons per square mile	Urban/Rural Ratio	Physician/ Population Ratio
Israel	20,700	4,512,000	564.6	89.4% / 10.6%	1 per 345 persons
Italy	301,263	57,401,000	492.6	67.0% / 33.0%	1 per 250 persons
Jamaica	10,991	2,407,000	567.2	49.1% / 50.9%	1 per 7,186 persons
Japan	377,801	122,620,000	840.6	76.7% / 23.3%	1 per 668 persons
Malaysia	329,747	16,965,000	133.3	38.2% / 61.8%	1 per 2,986 persons
Mexico	1,958,201	82,721,000	109.4	69.7% / 30.3%	1 per 1,100 persons
Netherlands, The	41,508	14,741,000	1,125.0	88.4% / 11.6%	1 per 438 persons
Nigeria	923,800	112,258,000	314.7	16.1% / 83.9%	1 per 8,059 persons
Pakistan	796,095	109,434,000	356.0	29.8% / 70.2%	1 per 2,086 persons
Poland	312,683	38,864,000	313.6	60.5% / 39.5%	1 per 498 persons
Russia (former USSR)	22,402,200	285,796,000	33.0	66.4% / 33.6%	1 per 229 persons

Country	Size (sq. km) 1 km = 1,600 ml	Population	Density: Persons per square mile	Urban/Rural Ratio	Physician/ Population Ratio
South Africa	Exact figure not available	29,628,000	68.3	55.9% / 44.1%	1 per 1,510 per- sons
Thailand	513,115	54,862,000	276.9	19.8% / 80.2%	1 per 5,988 per- sons
United Kingdom	244,100	57,400,000	604.8	91.0% / 9.0%	1 per 700 persons
United States	9,372,571	245,800,000	66.8	73.9% / 26.1%	1 per 419 persons
Venezuela	912,050	18,757,000	53.3	83.2% / 16.8%	1 per 722 persons

Source: Britannica World Data 1989.

Appendix B: Medical School Demographics, by Country

	Number of medical schools	Yrs. education required before admission	Duration of medical degree course	Language of instruction	Title of degree awarded	Government service after graduation?
Australia	10	12	5 or 6 years	English	Bachelor of Medicine, Bachelor of Surgery	Not obligatory
Belgium	11	12	7 years	Dutch or French	Doctor of Medicine, Surgery, and Midwifery	Not obligatory
Brazil	76	11	6 years	Portuguese	(Physician)	Not obligatory
Canada	16	13-15	3-5 years	French at the Universities of Laval, Montreal, and Sherbrooke; English at the other institutions.	Doctor of Medicine (MD)	Not obligatory
Chile	6	12-13	7 years	Spanish	Physician and Surgeon	Not obligatory
China	114	12	4-8 years	Chinese	Bachelor	All physicians work in government service.

	Number of medical schools	Yrs. education required before admission	Duration of medical degree course	Language of instruction	Title of degree awarded	Government service after graduation?
Czech and Slovak Federative Republic	10	12	6 years	Czech or Slovak	Doctor of Medicine (MU Dr)	All physicians work in government service.
Egypt	13	12	6 years	English	Bachelor of Medicine and Surgery	Obligatory for 2 years.
France	37	13	7 years (8 years from 1984)	French	Doctor of Medicine	Not obligatory
Germany	37	13	6 years	German	(Graduate physician)	Not obligatory.
Hungary	5	12	6 years	Hungarian	(Doctor of Medicine)	All physicians worked in government service. Recently not obligatory.
India	129	12	5 1/2 years	English	Bachelor of Medicine and Bachelor of Surgery	Not obligatory

	Number of medical schools	Yrs. education required before admission	Duration of medical degree course	Language of instruction	Title of degree awarded	Government service after graduation?
Israel	4	12	7 years	Hebrew	Doctor of Medicine	Not obligatory
Italy	31	13	6 years	Italian	Diploma in Medicine and Surgery	Not obligatory
Japan	80	12	6 years	Japanese	Doctor of Medicine (MD)	Not obligatory
Malaysia	3	13	5 years	Bahasa Malaysia and English	Bachelor of Medicine and Bachelor of Surgery	Obligatory for 3 years.
Mexico	57	12	6 years	Spanish	Physician and Surgeon	Obligatory for 1 year
Netherlands, The	8	12	6 years	Dutch	Arts (Physician)	Not obligatory
Nigeria	14	11-13	5 years	English	Bachelor of Medicine and Surgery	Not obligatory
Pakistan	17	12 or 14	5 years	English	Bachelor of Medicine and Surgery	Not obligatory

	Number of medical schools	Yrs. education required before admission	Duration of medical degree course	Language of instruction	Title of degree awarded	Government service after graduation?
Poland	11	12	6 years	Polish	Lekarz (Physician)	Most physicians work in government service.
Russia (former USSR)	87	10	6 years	Russian	Physician, therapeutician, pediatrician, stomatologist, sanitary engineer with a medical degree: Doctor's Diploma	All physicians work in government service.
South Africa	8	12*	6 years	English	Bachelor of Medicine and Surgery (MB ChB)	Not obligatory
Sweden	6	12	5 1/2 years	Swedish	MD (Physician's examination)	Not obligatory
Thailand	10	12	6 years	Thai	Doctor of Medicine	Obligatory if no tuition was paid

	Number of medical schools	Yrs. education required before admission	Duration of medical degree course	Language of instruction	Title of degree awarded	Government service after graduation?
United Kingdom	26	12-14	5 or 6 years	English	Bachelor of Medicine and Bachelor of Surgery (MBBS/MBChB)	Not obligatory
United States	126 allopathic	15 or 16	4 years	English	Doctor of Medicine (MD) or Doctor of Osteopathy (DO)	Not obligatory
Venezuela	10	11	6 years	Spanish	Physician /Surgeon	1 year obligatory

*Slight variation exists among different medical schools.

Appendix C: Admission Policies and Requirements, by Country

Country	Education required prior to entry into medical school	Exam(s) required prior to entry into medical school	Body that makes medical school admissions decisions	Factors which determine medical school admissions	Average age of applicants
Australia	Generally, Higher School Certificate Top 2% aggregate	Very few have exam or interview prior to selection	Faculty boards, university	Oversupply, competition for places	18
Belgium	Upper secondary school leaving certificate or university entrance certificate	General university entrance exam	Medical school admission committee	Statute and competition	18-19
Brazil	Completed high school	Medical school/ university entrance examination	Medical school or university	Examination grades; relationship between number of applicants and number of places	18
Canada	Range from two years of postsecondary education to a complete undergraduate degree	(MCAT) Medical College Admission Test (most medical schools)	Admission Committee of each institution	Academic records, MCAT scores; references, interviews and autobiographical sketches; place of residence	21-23

Country	Education required prior to entry into medical school	Exam(s) required prior to entry into medical school	Body that makes medical school admissions decisions	Factors which determine medical school admissions	Average age of applicants
Chile	High school degree	National Academic Aptitude Test Entrance Test in one medical school	University board	Academic achievements	18
China	High school	National exam	Ministry of Higher Education	By Ministries	18-19
Commonwealth Caribbean	Completion of at least seven years secondary school	Advanced-level passes in a GCE exam in three sciences subjects	Admissions Committee of the University of the West Indies Faculty of Medical Sciences	Merit; A-level grades	18-19
Czech and Slovak Federative Republic	High/secondary or vocational school	Multiple choice exam in physics, chemistry and biology and an oral exam in the three subjects	Medical school admission committee	Academic Senate in achievement; personal interview	18-19

Country	Education required prior to entry into medical school	Exam(s) required prior to entry into medical school	Body that makes medical school admissions decisions	Factors which determine medical school admissions	Average age of applicants
Egypt	12 years	Final Secondary School Certifying Examination	National Coordination Committee	Student's choice; final secondary school percent score; place of student's residence; Ministry of Health needs; National Supreme Council of the Universities	18
France	High school		General Medical Council	Academic achievement and competition for limited places	18-19
Germany	13 Years	Final secondary school examination (*abitur*)	Central Bureau for the Administration of Admissions	Admission test results; *abitur* grade; interview	20-21

Country	Education required prior to entry into medical school	Exam(s) required prior to entry into medical school	Body that makes medical school admissions decisions	Factors which determine medical school admissions	Average age of applicants
Guyana (See Commonwealth Caribbean)	High school (five to seven years)	Either: GCE O "A" levels in specified subjects; or a certificate /diploma in a health science discipline	Admissions committee of the Faculty of Health Sciences of the University of Guyana	Merit as evidenced by grades; competition	19+
Hungary	High school graduation	biology and physics (both oral and written); oral interview	School's admissions committee	Total number of scores collected is decisive. Performance in major subjects in high school (up to 50% of total) and entrance examinations (up to 50%) of total are scored. Recently, for command of foreign languages, extra scores are given.	19.5

Country	Education required prior to entry into medical school	Exam(s) required prior to entry into medical school	Body that makes medical school admissions decisions	Factors which determine medical school admissions	Average age of applicants
India	Pass 12th class under 10+2 scheme with physics, chemistry, biology (botany and zoology) and English; or pass first year examination of three year B.Sc. degree course with physics, chemistry, and biology	1. Senior School Certificate of Central Board of Secondary Education or equivalent; or first year of three year B.Sc. degree course in Science with Biology. 2. In most of the state/university-funded medical colleges, candidates are required to pass a separate entrance examination.	Basic rules and guidelines are provided by Medical Council of India and various university/state govt., and institutional bodies take the final decision to implement them.	1. Merit. 2. Age—minimum 17 years. 3. 15% of seats open for All India competition by national examination. 4. 22.5% of seats reserved for Scheduled Castes and Scheduled Tribes candidates in govt.-funded medical colleges. 5. Medical fitness.	18 (approximate)
Israel	Secondary school graduation	Matriculation and psychometric examination	Medical School admissions committees	Academic credentials; personal qualities (Ben Gurion Univ.)	21-24

Country	Education required prior to entry into medical school	Exam(s) required prior to entry into medical school	Body that makes medical school admissions decisions	Factors which determine medical school admissions	Average age of applicants
Italy	Secondary school	Multiple choice questions; personal interview	Medical Faculty	High school performance; answers to multiples choice questions; assessment of motives through personal interviews	
Japan	12 years	Entrance exams at each school	A special committee of each school	Vary according to the characteristics of each school	About 19
Malaysia	1. 11 years of school followed by two years university matriculation classes or 2. 11 years of school followed by two years "A" level.	1. Matriculation 2. "A"-level exams	University Processing Unit, Ministry of Education	1. Academic achievement 2. Ethnic quota	20

Country	Education required prior to entry into medical school	Exam(s) required prior to entry into medical school	Body that makes medical school admissions decisions	Factors which determine medical school admissions	Average age of applicants
Mexico	Baccalaureate, high school diploma	Basic knowledge exam in natural sciences and humanities	Department of Academic Affairs; Medical school admission committee	Grades of high school; grades of admission exam; capacity of the school	18
Netherlands, The	Pre-university secondary school (VWO)	National secondary school diploma	Administrative government agency	secondary school exam results; lottery to reduce candidates to fixed number of places	18
Nigeria	1. Senior Secondary School Certificate with credits in physics, chemistry, biology, mathematics, and English 2. physics, chemistry and biology (or zoology) at "a" level with a minimum of credit in English at "O" level (Direct entry)	Joint Matriculation Examination (JME)	Joint Matriculation Examination (JAMB)	Merit Catchment areas	1. 18 2. 20

Country	Education required prior to entry into medical school	Exam(s) required prior to entry into medical school	Body that makes medical school admissions decisions	Factors which determine medical school admissions	Average age of applicants
Pakistan	Higher Secondary Certificate (H.S.C.) with physics, chemistry, and biology	Four medical colleges hold written tests	Depends on type of medical college: provincial health departments, defense authorities, Karachi Metropolitan Authority, Faculty	For 15 medical colleges which do not hold examinations, the H.S.C. marks and place of domicile; for others, H.S.C. marks and performance on test/interview	18
Poland	12 years of secondary education	"Matura" final secondary school exam and an MCQ in biology, chemistry, physics, and a foreign language	Each school makes its own	Academic achievement	
Russia (former USSR)	General secondary (high school) certificate; graduates of nursing schools	Examination in biology, physics, chemistry, and language	Systems of medical institutions	Academic achievement and competition	17
South Africa	Higher school certificate	High school leaving exam	Each school makes it own decision based on its philosophy	High academic achievement Racial/ethnic mix and gender	18-20

Country	Education required prior to entry into medical school	Exam(s) required prior to entry into medical school	Body that makes medical school admissions decisions	Factors which determine medical school admissions	Average age of applicants
Thailand	High (secondary) school diploma; in some programs, a bachelor's degree	Central entrance exam by Office of the University Affairs, except for a few innovative programs	Admission Committees of each school	Academic achievement and national need	17-22
United Kingdom	High school certificate with science concentration	Science "A" level examinations or special entrance examination in few schools	Admissions Committees of individual schools	Academic achievement and competition	17-18
United States of America	Baccalaureate degree (generally BA or BS)	Medical College Admission Test (MCAT)	Individual medical schools	Academic Achievement (MCAT, GPA); values and attitudes consistent with a service profession	24

Country	Education required prior to entry into medical school	Exam(s) required prior to entry into medical school	Body that makes medical school admissions decisions	Factors which determine medical school admissions	Average age of applicants
Venezuela	High school degree	National general aptitude examination for all students who wish to enter university (not specific to medicine)	The National University Council oversees all admissions	The capacity of the medical schools; academic index; geographic location	17-18

Appendix D: Policy Making Bodies with a Role in Medical Education

Country	Policy Making Bodies with Role in Medical Education
Australia	University Medical Faculties Governments Registration Boards Specialist Colleges
Belgium	Council of Deans Scientific Board of General Medical Practitioners National Fund for Scientific Research
Brazil	Boards of Medical Faculties Ministry of Health Ministry of Education Federal Education Council (Conselho Federal de Educação--CFE) National Medical Education Committee (Comissão Nacional de Ensino Médico--CFE consultancy department National Medical Education Committee--Comissão Nacional de Ensino Medico (CFE consultancy department
Canada	Committee on Accreditation of Canadian Medical Schools (CACMS/ACMC) Liaison Committee on Medical Education (LCME/AAMC and AMA)

Country	Policy Making Bodies with Role in Medical Education
Chile	Ministry of Health Ministry of Education National Council of Rectors National Association of Faculties of Medicine (ASOFAMECH) National Commission for Medical Accreditation (CONACEM)
China	Ministry of Higher Education Ministry of Public Health
Commonwealth (English-Speaking) Caribbean	Board of the Faculty of Medical Sciences, University of the West Indies (UWI)
Czech and Slovak Federative Republic	Scientific Council Council for Education of Health Personnel Academic Senate of the Medical Faculty Institute of Post-Graduate Education
Egypt	National Supreme Council of the Universities Ministry of Health Egyptian Medical Association Physicians' Syndicate
France	Special Advisors for the Medical Sector within the Ministry of Education National Council of Deans of Medical Faculties National Council of Higher Education and Research (CNESER) National Conference of University Presidents National Committee of Evaluation National Internat Examination Board National Commission of Medical Studies (which is to be replaced by the Pedagogic Commission of Medical Studies)
Germany	Governments of the Federation and of the *Lander* Associations of Physicians Association of Medical Faculties National Scientific Council (*Wissenschaftsrat*) Scientific Associations Sick Funds (Health Insurers) Trade Unions

Country	Policy Making Bodies with Role in Medical Education
Guyana (see Commonwealth Caribbean)	Faculty of Health Sciences, University of Guyana Guyana Agency for Health Sciences Education, Environment and Food Policy (GAHEF)
Hungary	National Accreditation Committee (new 1992) Rectors' Conference National Council of Higher Education Advisory Committee on Medical Education Scientific Health Council National Students' Association National colleges of specialists Local committees of medical education
India	Medical Council of India
Israel	Council on Higher Education (Ministry of Education) Scientific Council of Israel Medical Association University Faculty Councils
Italy	Ministero Dell 'Universita' E Della Ricerca Scientifica E Tecnologica (Ministry of University and Research) Ministero Della Sanita' (Ministry of Health) Assessorati Regionali Alla Sanita' (Regional Branches of the Ministry of Health) Consiglio Superior Di Sanita' (National Advisory Board for Health) Consiglio Sanitatrio Nazionale (Council for National Health Service)
Japan	National government Standing committee in the Diet on Education, Science and Culture
Malaysia	Faculty Board University Senate University Council Coordinating Committee for Postgraduate Medicine, Ministry of Education Higher Education Committee of the Ministry of Education Malaysian Medical Council Postgraduate Training Committee, Ministry of Health

Country	Policy Making Bodies with Role in Medical Education
Mexico	Each university, and very often each medical school, establishes its own policies on academic and administrative matters, usually within the University laws. Proposals originated in the Dean's office go through approval motions in the Technical-Academic Council of the School, representative of the faculty, and then finally to the University Council
Netherlands, The	Ministry of Education Joint Committee of the medical schools Medical Schools Specialist Registration Committee Ministry of Health Specialist Colleges
Nigeria	Federal Ministry of Education through the National Universities Commission Nigerian Medical and Dental Council Federal Ministry of Health, responsible for teaching hospital facilities and health policies
Pakistan	Ministry of Health Pakistan Medical and Dental Council College of Physicians and Surgeons Pakistan
Poland	Ministry of National Education Ministry of Health and Social Welfare Physician's Chamber Council of Medical Education (Branch of National Advisory Council for Higher Education and Science) National Advisory Council for Higher Education and Science Committee of Postgraduate Education (representatives of Ministry of Health, Chamber of Physicians, Medical Centre for Postgraduate Education, Medical Academies, Medical Societies Committee for Scientific Investigation) Rectors of Medical Academies Conference
South Africa	Medical Research Council South African Medical and Dental Council (SAMDC) College of Medicine of South Africa (COM-SA)
Thailand	The Medical Council National Board of Epidemiology Office of the University Affairs Ministry of Public Health National Economic and Social Development Board

Country	Policy Making Bodies with Role in Medical Education
United Kingdom	Educational Committee of the General Medical Council (GMC) Ministry of Health The British Medical Association
United States of America	Liaison Committee on Medical Education (LCME) Accreditation Council for Graduate Medical Education (ACGME) Accreditation Council for Continuing Medical Education (ACCME) National Board of Medical Examiners (NBME) Educational Commission for Foreign Medical Graduates (ECFMG) American Hospital Association (AHA)
Venezuela	The Ministry of Education through the National Council of Universities, CNU The National Congress votes laws and makes budget appropriations that influence health policies The Public Health Ministry, the political body of the Venezuelan government for the health sector The Ministry of Labor, responsible for the workers, and for some segments of the public through the Venezuelan Social Security system The Planning Ministry, which prepares drafts for the general governmental policies and budget The Venezuelan Association of Medical Schools, AVEFAM The National Council of Scientific and Technologic Research, CONICIT National Association of Private Hospitals and Clinics, which intends to coordinate activities of this growing sector

Appendix E: Professional Organizations with a Role in Medical Education, by Country

Country	Professional Organizations
Australia	Australian Medical Council State Postgraduate Committees Australian Postgraduate Federation in Medicine Specialist Colleges Australian Medical Association Australian and New Zealand Association of Medical Education
Belgium	Belgium Medical Associations
Brazil	Brazilian Medical Association and affiliate specialist associations Brazilian College of Surgeons Federal Medical Council and Regional Medical Councils Brazilian Association of Medical Education (ABEM (Associação Médica) Brazilian Postgraduate Collective Health Care Association -ABRASCO (Associação Brasileira de Educação em Saude Coletiva) National Council for Medical Schools Assessment - CINAEM (Commissão Nacional de Avaliação das Escolas Médi-Andes Union of Physicians

Country	Professional Organizations
Canada	The Association of Canadian Medical Colleges (ACMC) The Royal College of Physicians and Surgeons of Canada (RCPSC) The College of Family Physicians of Canada (CFPC) The Canadian Medical Association
Chile	National Association of Faculties of Medicine National Commission for Accreditation Chilean Medical Association Santiago Medical Society Societies of various medical specialties Academy of Medicine
China	Chinese Medical Association Chinese Medical Education Association Chinese Educational Association Chinese Teacher's Union
Commonwealth Caribbean	Medical Association of Jamaica Medical Association of Trinidad and Tobago
Czech and Slovak Federative Republic	Professional Associations Chambers of Doctors
Egypt	The Egyptian Medical Association Physicians' Syndicate
France	French Medical Association Regional councils Specialties boards and commissions
Guyana	Guyana Medical Association (GOYA)
Hungary	Advisory Committees for Ministry of Welfare, by every major specialty National Societies for every major specialty and subspecialty Hungarian Medical Chamber Medical Division of Hungarian Academy of Sciences Joint Commissions of Hungarian Academy of Sciences and Ministry of Health by major fields of medical sciences

Country	Professional Organizations
India	Many professional organizations. (Indian Medical Association is the largest.) Specialty organizations National Academy of Medical Sciences
Israel	Israel Medical Association
Italy	Federazione Nazionale Degli Ordini Dei Medici Chirurgei E Degli Odontolatri (National Federation of Professional Orders)
Japan	The Japan Society for Medical Education The Association of Japanese Medical Colleges (Medical School Deans and Hospital Directors Association) The Japan Medical Association The Japan Medical Education Foundation
Malaysia	Malaysian Association for Education in the Medical and Health Sciences Academy of Medicine Malaysian Medical Association Specialty bodies (approximately 20)
Mexico	National specialty boards Medical societies of different specialties National Academy of Medicine Mexican Academy of Surgery Mexican Association of Medical Schools (AMFEM)
Netherlands	The Dutch Medical Association Specialty boards and professional bodies
Nigeria	Nigerian Medical and Dental Council, whose main responsibility is to indicate the general requirements and the standards which, in contemporary conditions, ought to be achieved and maintained in the public interest.
Pakistan	Pakistan Medical Association and over 20 other societies and associations of different specialties
Russia (former USSR)	Central Institute for Advanced Medical Education

Country	Professional Organizations
Poland	Physicians Chambers (Main and Regional Councils) Committee of Postgraduate Education Polish Physician Association Polish Academy of Science
South Africa	Medical Association of South Africa (MASA) South African Health and Social Service Organization Academy of Family Practice and other Professional Associations and discipline bodies
Thailand	The Medical Council Consortium of Thai Medical Schools Colleges or Associations of the Specialists
United Kingdom	The British Medical Association Royal Colleges Council of Deans of Medical Schools

United States of America	Association of American Medical Colleges (AAMC)
	American Board of Medical Specialties and its specialty
	    Colleges
	American Medical Association Council on Medical
	    Education

Venezuela	Venezuelan Medical Federation, which by law affiliates
	    all physicians practicing in the country;
	National Academy of Medicine, which by law is a
	    government advisory board on health issues. It is made
	    up of a fixed number of outstanding physicians select-
	    ed by the votes of the Academy's members;
	Societies, that represent physicians practicing any of the
	    34 specialties approved by the Venezuelan Medical
	    Federation;
	State Medical Colleges, whose enrollment represents all
	    physicians participating in each of the geopolitical
	    divisions of Venezuela.

Appendix F: Governmental Agencies with a Role in Medical Education, by Country

Country	Governmental Agencies
Australia	Australian Medical Council Federal and State Health Departments State Medical Boards
Belgium	Ministry of Education Ministry of Health
Brazil	Ministry of Social Security and Welfare National Medical Residency Committee (Comissão Nacional de Residência Méca) National Scientific and Technological Research Council (CNPq--(Conselho Nacional de Desenvolvimento Científico e Tecnologico) Coordination for Further University Graduate Education-- CAPES (Coordinadoria de Aperfeiçoamento de Pessoal de Nível Superior)

Country	Governmental Agencies
Canada	Provincial Departments (Ministries of Health) Provincial Departments of Higher Education Provincial Licensing Authorities The Newfoundland Medical Board, College of Physicians and Surgeons of P.E.I. College of Physicians and Surgeons of New Brunswick Provincial Medical Board of Nova Scotia Corporation professionnelle des médecins du Québec College of Physicians and Surgeons of Ontario College of Physicians and Surgeons of Manitoba College of Physicians and Surgeons of Saskatchewan College of Physicians and Surgeons of Alberta College of Physicians and Surgeons of British Columbia The Newfoundland Medical Board, Professional Licensing Department of Safety and Public Services, Government of the NorthWest Territories Yukon Medical Council
Chile	None
China	Ministry of Health Ministry of Education
Commonwealth Caribbean	Medical Councils of Barbados, Jamaica, etc. Caribbean Community Secretariat (CARICOM) Ministries of Health
Czech and Slovak Federative Republic	Ministry of Health Ministry of Education
Egypt	Ministry of Health Ministry of Education
France	Ministry of Education Ministry of Health
Germany	Ministry of Health of the Federation Ministry of Education and Science of the Federation Ministries of Health of the *Länder* Ministries of Education of the *Länder*

Country	Governmental Agencies
Guyana	Guyana Medical Council Ministry of Health Guyana Agency for Health Sciences Education, Environment and Food Policy
Hungary	Ministry of Welfare Ministry of Education
India	Union Government State Health Departments
Israel	Ministry of Education Ministry of Health Ministry of Finance
Italy	Commissione Affari Sociali Della Camera Dei Deputati (Social Affairs Commission of the Parliament) Commissione Igiene E Sanita' Del Semato (Commission for Health Affairs of the Senate)
Japan	Ministry of Health and Welfare Ministry of Education, Science and Culture Ministry of Labor Self Defense Force Agency
Malaysia	Universities (Ministry of Education) Ministry of Health
Mexico	Interinstitutional (Ministries of Health and of Education) Commission for Human Resources Development General Direction of Education in Health of the Ministry of Health Direction of Medical Education of the Social Security Institutions (IMSS, ISSSTE, etc.) National Association of Universities and Higher Education Institutions
Netherlands	Ministry of Health Ministry of Education
Nigeria	Federal Ministry of Education Federal Ministry of Health National Universities Commission The universities

Country	Governmental Agencies
Pakistan	Federal Ministry of Health Federal Ministry of Planning Provincial Health Departments Pakistan Medical and Dental Council Universities
Poland	Ministry of Health and Social Welfare Ministry of National Education National Research Institute National Medical Centers
Russia (former USSR)	Ministry of Health Institutes of Education
Thailand	Ministry of Public Health Office of the University Affairs National Economic and Social Development Board
United States of America	State licensing agencies US Department of Education US Department of Health and Human Services (financial aid) State legislatures US Congress
Venezuela	Ministry of Education Ministry of Health

Appendix G: Selected Bibliography

The following list of references contains a few of the most important sources that readers may with to pursue in extending their understanding of the current status of medical education with respect to major issues and specific geographic areas. For the reader's convenience, the references have been classified into two broad groups: first, Issues and Topics, followed by Regions, with appropriate subcategories under each. In most cases, the references cited contain extensive bibliographies which will facilitate the in-depth study of the issue or area.

ISSUES AND TOPICS

General References and Overview

Abbett, W.S., R. G. Bridgham, and A.S. Elstein. 1982. Medical education. In *Encyclopedia of educational research*. 5th ed. New York: Free Press.

Barzansky, B., and N. Gevitz, eds. 1992. *Beyond Flexner: Medical education in the twentieth century*. Westport, CT: Greenwood Press.

Bowers, J.Z. 1978. *The impact of health services on medical education: A global view*. Report of an International Macy Conference. New York: Josiah Macy, Jr. Foundation.

‒‒‒‒‒‒‒‒‒. 1970. *Medical schools for the modern world: Report of a Macy Conference*. International Macy Conference, "How to Start a Medical School," Bellagio, Italy, 1968. Baltimore: Published for Josiah Macy, Jr. Foundation by Johns Hopkins Press.

Carlson, C., C. Martini, and M.R. Schwarz. 1990. Medical education: A global perspective. Results of the international survey of medical education.

Informational paper distributed by the American Medical Association at the Fifth World Conference on Medical Education, 24-28 October 1990.

Catley-Carlson, M. 1992. Global considerations affecting the health agenda of the 1990s. *Acad Med* 67 (7):419-424.

Curry, L., J. F. Wergin, et al. 1993. *Educating professionals*. San Francisco: Josey Bass.

Flexner, A. 1910. *Medical education in the United States and Canada*. A report to the Carnegie Foundation for the Advancement of Teaching. Bulletin no. 4. Boston, MA: Updyke.

Friedman, C.P., et al. 1983. *The new biology and medical education: Merging the biological, information, and cognitive sciences*. New York: Josiah Macy, Jr. Foundation.

McGuire, C.H., R. Foley, A. Gorr, R.W. Richards, et al., eds. 1983. *Handbook of health professions education*. San Francisco: Jossey-Bass. Contains chapters on all the topics listed below.

Mast, A. T., G. R. Schermerhorn, and J.A. Colliver. 1992. Medical education. In C. H. McGuire, section ed. *Encyclopedia of educational research,* 6th ed. New York: MacMillan.

Miller, G. 1969. Medical education. In *Encyclopedia of educational research*. 3rd ed. New York: MacMillan.

Muller, S. (Chair). 1984. Physicians for the twenty-first century: Report of the Project Panel on the General Professional Education of the Physician and College Preparation for Medicine. *J Med Educ* 59, Part 2 (November) (whole issue).

Roemer, M. 1991. *National health systems of the world:* Vol. One, The countries. New York: Oxford University Press.

Stewart, M., F. Tudiver, et al. 1992. *Tools for primary care research*. Newbury Park, CA: Sage Publications.

White, K. L. 1991. *Healing the schism: Epidemiology, medicine and the public's health*. New York: Springer-Verlag.

White, K. L., and J. Connelly, eds., 1992. *The medical school's mission and the population's health*. New York: Springer-Verlag.

Willis, D., ed. 1988. The changing character of the medical profession. *Milbank Quarterly* 66 (Supplement 2).

World Federation for Medical Education. 1988. The Edinburgh Declaration of the World Conference on Medical Education. Edinburgh, Scotland.

World Health Organization. Division of Development of Human Resources for Health. 1991. *Changing medical education: An agenda for action*. Geneva: WHO.

----------. 1990. *Achieving Health for All by the Year 2000: Midway reports of country experiences*. Ed. by E. Tarimo and A. Creese. Geneva.

----------. 1988. *World directory of medical schools*. 6th ed. Geneva.

----------, 1987. *Educational handbook for health personal*, by J.J. Guilbert. 6th Offset Publication No. 35. Geneva.

----------, 1987. *Reviewing health manpower development: A method of improving national health system*, by T. Fülöp and M.I. Roemer. Public Health Papers no. 831. Geneva.

----------, 1983. *Traditional medicine and health care coverage: A reader for health administrators and practitioners*, by R. Bannerman et al. Geneva.

----------, 1982. *International Development of Health Manpower Policy*, by T Fülöp and M.I. Roemer. WHO Offset Publication no. 61. Geneva.

----------. 1981. *Development of indicators for monitoring progress towards Health for All by the Year 2000*. Geneva.

----------. 1981. *Managerial process for national health development: Guiding principles for use in support of strategies for Health for All by the Year 2000*. Geneva.

----------. 1979. *Formulating strategies for Health for All by the Year 2000*. Geneva.

----------. 1978. *Declaration of Alma Ata on Primary Health Care*. Report of the Conference on Primary Health Care at Alma Ata, USSR, 6-12 September. Geneva.

Instructional Techniques

Barrows, H. 1988. *The tutorial process*. Springfield, IL: Southern Illinois University School of Medicine.

----------. 1985. *How to design a problem-based curriculum for the preclinical years*. New York: Springer Publishing Company.

Barrows, H., and R. Tamblyn. 1980. *Problem-based learning: An approach to medical education*. New York: Springer Publishing Company.

deVolder, M.L., and H.G. Schmidt, eds. 1984. *Tutorials in problem-based learning: New directions in teaching for the health professions*. Proceedings of the International Symposium on Problem-Based Learning, 1983. Maastricht: Van Gorcum and Co.

Douglas, K.C., M.C. Hosokawa, and F.H. Lawler. 1988. *A practical guide to clinical teaching in medicine*. New York: Springer Publishing Company.

Elstein, A.S., et al. 1978. *Medical problem solving: An analysis of clinical reasoning*. Cambridge, MA: Harvard University Press.

Foley, R. and J. Smilansky. 1980. *Teaching techniques: A handbook for health professionals*. New York: McGraw-Hill.

Lucchelli, S., ed. 1991. *Il computer nella formazione del medico* (The computer in medical education; in Italian). Franco Angeli Series, Fondazione Smith Kline.

McGaghie, W.C., et al. 1978. *Competency-based curriculum development in medical education: An introduction*. Geneva: WHO.

Wallis, B. 1988. *Problem based learning: The NewCastle Workshop*. Australia: University of NewCastle, Faculty of Medicine.

Waterman, R.E. 1988. *Clinical problem-based learning: A workbook for integrating basic and clinical science*. University of New Mexico Press.

Westberg, J., and H. Jason. 1993. *Collaborative clinical education: The foundation of effective health care.* New York: Springer Publishing Company.

Curriculum Organization and Reform

Alausa, O.K., and H.G. Schmidt. 1989. *New directions for medical education: Problem-based learning and community oriented medical education.* New York: Springer-Verlag.

Enarson, C., and F.D. Burg. 1992. An overview of reform initiatives in medical education. *JAMA* 268 (9):1141-1143.

Kantrowitz, M., et al. 1987. *Innovative tracks at established institutions for the education of health personnel: An experimental approach to change relevant to health needs.* Geneva: WHO Offset Publication no. 101.

Karl, H., J. Nystrup, and H. Walton. 1993. Medical specialization in Europe: The way forward. *Medical Education* 27 (4):299-303.

Kaufman, A. 1985. *Implementing problem-based medical education: Lessons from successful innovations.* New York: Springer Publishing Company.

Martenson, D. 1985. *Educational development in an established medical school.* Chartwell-Bratt.

Nooman, Z., H. G. Schmidt, and E.S. Ezzat, eds. 1990. *Innovation in medical education: An evaluation of its present status.* New York: Springer Publishing Company.

Porter, B., and W. Seidman. 1992. *The politics of reform in medical education and health services: The Negev Project.* New York: Springer Publishing Company.

Richards, R., T. Fülöp, et al., eds. 1987. *Innovative schools for health personnel: Report on ten schools belonging to the Network of Community-oriented Educational Institutions for Health Sciences.* Geneva: World Health Organization, Offset Publication no. 102.

Schmidt, H.G., M. Lipkin, et al., eds. 1989. *New directions for medical education: Problem-based learning and community-oriented medical education.* New York: Springer-Verlag.

Shahabudun, S., and A.B. Edariah. 1991. Managing the initial period of implementation of educational change. *Med-Teach* 13(3):205-211.

Swanson, A.G. (Principal Investigator), and M.B. Anderson (Project Director). 1993. Educating medical students: Assessing change in medical education-- The road to implementation. The ACME-TRI Report with supplements.

Association of American Medical Colleges and the Charles E. Culpeper Foundation. *Acad Med* 68(6) (Supplement).

Student and Physician Assessment

Anderson, M. B., and D. Kassebaum, eds. 1993. Proceedings of the AAMC's Consensus Conference on the Use of Standardized Patients in the Teaching and Evaluation of Clinical Skills. *Acad Med* 68 (6) (Special Issue).

Bordage, G., and G. Page. 1992. *Q4 Project Final Report 1986-1991.* Ottawa: Medical Council of Canada.

Gonella, J.S. et al (eds). 1993. Assessment measures in medical school, residency and practice: The connection. New York: Springer Publishing Co.

Harden, R.M., I.R. Hart, and H. Mulholland, eds. 1992. *Approaches to the assessment of clinical competence.* Dundee, Scotland: Center for Medical Education.

Hart, I.R., R.M. Hardin, and H.J. Walton. 1986. *Newer developments in assessing clinical competence.* Montreal, Quebec: Heal Publications, Ltd.

Hart, I.R., and R.M. Hardin. 1987. *Further developments in assessing clinical competence.* International Conference Proceedings. Montreal, Quebec: Can-Heal Publications.

Lloyd, J.S., ed. 1986. *How to evaluate residents.* Chicago: American Board of Medical Specialties.

---------. 1985. *Residency role in specialty certification.* Chicago.: American Board of Medical Specialties.

---------. 1984. *Computer applications in the evaluation of physician competence.* Chicago: American Board of Medical Specialties.

---------. 1983a. *Evaluating the skills of medical specialists.* Chicago: American Board of Medical Specialties.

---------. 1983b. *Oral examinations in medical specialty board certification.* Chicago: American Board of Medical Specialties.

---------. 1982. *Evaluation of noncognitive skills and clinical performance.* Chicago: American Board of Medical Specialties.

Monahan, T.J. 1990. State medical boards and licensing examinations. In *National Board of Medical Examiners 75th anniversary: In service to medicine.* Philadelphia: National Board of Medical Examiners.

Neufeld, V., and G. Norman. 1985. *Assessing clinical competence.* New York: Springer Publishing Company.

Sutnick, A.I., P.L. Stillman, J.J. Norcini, M. Friedman, M.B. Regan, R.G. Williams, E.K. Kachur, M.A. Haggerty, and M.P. Wilson. 1993. ECFMG assessment of clinical competence of graduates of foreign medical schools. *JAMA* 270:1041-1045.

Sutnick, A.I., L.P. Ross, and M.P. Wilson. 1992. Assessment of clinical competencies by the Foreign Medical Graduate Examination in the Medical Sciences (FMGEMS). *Teaching and Learning in Medicine* 4:150-155.

United States Medical Licensing Examinations (USMLE). USMLE Secretariat. 1992. U.S. Medical licensure statistics and current licensure requirements. American Medical Association.

Faculty and Program Evaluation

Jason, J., and J. Westberg. 1982. *Teachers and teaching in U.S. medical schools.* Norwalk, CT.: Appleton-Century-Crofts.

Katz, F.M. 1978. *Guidelines for evaluating a training programme for health personnel.* Who Offset Publication, no. 38. Geneva: WHO.

Rippey, R.M. 1981. *The Evaluation of teaching in medical schools.* Springer Series on Medical Education, Vol. 2. New York.: Springer Publishing Co.

World Health Organization. 1981. *Health programme evaluation: Guiding principles for its application in the managerial process for national health development.* Geneva: WHO.

Faculty Development

Bland, C., C. Schmitz, et al. 1990. *Successful faculty in academic medicine: Essential skills and how to acquire them.* New York: Springer Publishing Company.

Hornby, P., and P.J. Shipp, 1983. *Handbook for Organizing an HMP Workshop.* Based on Guidelines for Health Manpower Planning. Geneva: WHO.

Jacques, A., et al. Structured oral interviews for the identification of educational needs of general practitioners: Development and pilot test. *Canadian Medical Association Journal.* Forthcoming.

Miller, G. 1980. *Educating medical teachers.* Cambridge, MA: Harvard University Press.

------. 1961. *Teaching and learning in medical school.* Cambridge, MA: Harvard University Press.

Rezler, A.G., and J.A. Flaherty. 1985. *The interpersonal dimension in medical education.* New York: Springer Publishing Company.

Rubenstein, W., and Y. Talbot. 1992. *Medical teaching in ambulatory care: A practical guide.* New York: Springer Publishing Company.

Schwenk, T.L., and N. Whitman. 1984. *Residents as teachers: A guide to educational practice.* University of Utah School of Medicine.

Whitman, N., and Schwenk, T. L. 1984. *Preceptors as teachers: A guide to clinical teaching.* University of Utah School of Medicine.

REGIONS

Africa and the Middle East

Alike-Catha, A. 1990. Nigeria: Developing the primary health care system, pp. 202-212. In E. Tarimo and A. Creese, eds. *Achieving Health for all by the Year 2000: Midway reports of country experiences*. Geneva: World Health Organization.

Benatar, S.R. 1991. Medicine and health care in South Africa. *N Engl J Med* 325:30-36.

Hamilton, J.D., and O. Ogunbode. 1991. Medical education in the community: A Nigerian experience. *Lancet* 338:99-102.

Khallaf, A.G. 1990. Egypt: Winning in spite of economic problems, pp. 64-79. In E. Tarimo and A. Creese, eds. *Achieving Health For All by the Year 2000: Midway reports of country experiences*. Geneva: WHO.

Levenstein. J.H. 1988. Family medicine, medical bureaucracies and society. *S. Afr Fam Prac* 9:173-1982.

Ogunbode, O. 1991. Development of the Faculty of Health Sciences at the University of Ilorin, Nigeria. *Teaching and Learning in Medicine* 3:200-202.

Prywes, M. 1987. Coexistence: The rationale of the Beersheva experiment. *Israel Journal of Medical Science* 23:945-952.

Prywes, M., and M. Friedman. 1987. The Ben-Gurion University profile: An evaluation study. *Israel Journal of Medical Science* 23:1093-1101.

Shuval, J.T. 1992. *Social dimensions of health: The Israeli experience*. Westport: CT: Praeger.

---------. 1990. Medical manpower in Israel: Political processes and constraints. *Health Policy* 15:189-214.

Asia

Association of Higher Education of China. n.d. *Research on higher education in China*. Beijing: Association of Higher Education of China.

Fazal, E., M.G. Siddique, and N.A. Jafarey. 1985. A prospective look at the medical curriculum. *JPMA* 35:85-92.

India. Ministry of Health and Family Welfare. 1983. *The national health policy*. Government of India.

Jafarey, N.A. 1989. Some suggestions about improvement of medical education in Pakistan. *JPMA* 39:136-142.

Medical Council of India. 1992. Draft paper on revised curriculum for undergraduate medical education. New Delhi: Aiwan-e-galib Marg.

Medical Council of India. 1981. *Recommendations on graduate medical education.* New Delhi: Aiwan-e-galib Marg.

Medical Education Conference. 1986. *Proceedings of the 5th National Medical Education Conference, September 8-12, 1986.* Bangkok, Thailand: Mahidol University.

Seamic Workshop. 1982. Health manpower development in SouthEast Asia: Health for All by the Year 2000. *Proceedings of the 20th SEAMIC Workshop, Chiengmai, Thailand.* Tokyo: Seamic Workshop.

Thailand. Ministry of Public Health. 1988. *Proceedings of the First Thai Health Assembly.* September 12-15, 1988, Bangkok, Thailand.

---------National Epidemiology Board of Thailand. 1990. *The First Four Years 1987-1990.* Report of the National Epidemiology Board of Thailand. Bangkok

Zhe-Jiang Medical University. n.d. *Higher medical education in China.*

Europe

Bojan, F., P. Hajdu, and E. Belicza. 1991. Avoidable mortality: Is it an indicator of quality of medical care in Eastern European countries? *Quality Assurance in Health Care.* 3:191-203.

Czech Republic. Ministry of Health. 1990. *Reform of Health Care in the Czech Republic.*

Forgacs, J. 1991. Postgraduate and continuing education in Hungary. *Cah. Socio. Demo. Med* 31:5-14.

Ghetti, V. 1993. *Introduzione alla pedagogia medica* (Introduction to medical education; in Italian). Foundazione Smith-Kline.

---------., ed. 1991. *Il sistema sanitario europeo senza frontiere* (The European health care system without barriers; in Italian). Franco Angeli Series: Fondazione Smith Kline.

---------., ed. 1988. *Nuove tendenze nella formazione del Medico.* (New trends in medical education). Franco Angeli Editore.

Hungary. Ministry of Welfare. 1991. *Program for Reform of Health Care System in Hungary* (in Hungarian). Budapest: Government of Hungary.

Institute of Health Statistics, Prague, and Institute for Health Statistics, Bratislava. 1990. *Health services in Czechoslovakia.* Prague and Bratislava: Institutes. for Health Statistics.

Institut National de la Statistique et des Études Économiques (INSEE). 1993. *La société Française: Données sociales 1993.* INSEE.

Menu, J.P., and M. Gracia-Barbero, eds. 1991. *Health manpower education for health for all: Issues to be considered.* Fondazione Smith Kline: Franco Angeli Series.

Parkhouse, J.P., and J.P. Menu, eds. 1989. *Specialized medical education in the European Region.* Euro Reports and Studies no. 112. Copenhagen: WHO.

Raffel, N.K., and M.W. Raffel. 1988. The medical care system of Hungary. *J. Med. Pract. Manag* 4:142-149.

Ritsatakis, A. 1988. Problems related to future medical demography in the European Community. In H. Viefhues, ed., *Medical manpower in the European Community*. New York: Springer-Verlag.

Roemer, M.I., and R. Roemer. 1978. Health manpower in the socialist health care system of Poland. US Department of Health, Education, and Welfare Publ. (HRA) 78-85:1-85.

Slovak Republic. Ministry of Health. 1990. *Reform of Health Care in the Slovak Republic*.

van den Bussche, H. 1990. The history and future of physician manpower development in the Federal Republic of Germany. *Health Policy* 15:215-231.

Viefhues, H., ed. 1988. *Medical manpower in the European Community*. New York: Springer-Verlag. (Includes chapters on Belgium, Denmark, Federal Republic of Germany, France, Greece, Ireland, Italy, and the United Kingdom.)

Wojtczak, A. 1988. Aktualne problemy ksztalcenia medyczinego (Actual problems of medical education). *Probl. Szkoln. Nauk Med* 13 (1):11-21.

---------. 1982. The role of medical academies and their teaching hospitals in the regionalization of health care in Poland. In *The role of the university teaching hospital: An international perspective*, pp. 157-180. New York: Josiah Macy, Jr. Foundation.

World Health Organization. 1985. Targets for Health for All: Targets in support of the European strategy for Health for All. Copenhagen: Reg. Office for Europe.

North, South, and Central America

Anderson, M.B. 1993. Medical education in the United States and Canada revisited. *Acad Med* 68 (6):s55-s63.

Asociación Venezolana de Facultades de Medicina (AVEFAM). 1992. VIII Seminario Nacional de Educación Médica. Notas. Tucacas, Venezuela.

---------. 1987a. VII Seminario Nacional de Educación Médica. Memorias. Maracaibo, Venezuela.

---------. 1987b. Aspectos Cuantitativos y Cualitativos de la Formación de los Médicos en Venezuela. Tibaldo Garrido, Editor. Caracas, Venezuela.

---------.1978. Seminario Utilización y Formación del Médica General. Memorias. Publicación 7. Caracas.

Bennett, C.T., ed. 1993. *1994-95 medical school admission requirements, United States and Canada*. 44th ed. Washington, DC: Association of American Medical Colleges.

---------. 1992. *AAMC directory of American medical education 1992-93*. 39th ed. Washington, DC: Association of American Medical Colleges.

Bourne, C. 1989. Economic crisis in the Commonwealth Caribbean and its implications for the social services. In PAHO, ed. *Primary health care and local health systems in the Caribbean, Proceedings of the workshop on primary health care and local health care systems*. Tobago November 7-11, 1988.

Chile. Ministry of Health. 1992. *Health situation and health care in Chile*. Republic of Chile.

Jones, R.F. 1993. *American medical education: Institutions, programs and issues*. Washington, DC: Association of American Medical Colleges.

LeFranc, E.R.-M. 1989. *Structural adjustment and the health care systems in the Caribbean Region: An overview*. PAHO/WHO/CARICOM Secretariat (April).

Medina, E., and A. Kaempffer. 1988. Necisidad de médicos en Chile. *Rev. Med Chile* 116:389-394.

Narro, Robles J., et al. 1990. *Los desaffios de la educació médica en México* (Challenges in medical education in Mexico). Ed. U.N.A.M., México, D.F.

Oficina Panamericana de la Salud. 1990. *Las condiciones de salud en las Américas*. II:117-124. Publiciôn Cientifica no. 524, Oficina Panamericana de la Salud: Washington, DC.

Sherlock, P.M., and R.M. Nettleford. 1990. *The University of the West Indias: A Caribbean response to the challenge of change*. MacMillan Caribbean.

Standard, K.L. 1979. The role of the University of The West Indies in promotion of regional health services. In PAHO, ed. *Four decades of advances in health in the Commonwealth Caribbean,* pp. 133-143. Proceedings of a symposium at Bridgetown Barbados, West Indies, September 14-16, 1977. Sci. Pub. no. 383).

Universidad Central de Venezuela. 1991. *Facultadad de Medicina Informe de gestión, 1987-1990*. Tomos I y II. Caracas: Universidad Central de Venezuela.

Villalpando-Casas, J. Observaciones acerca de la educaciòn médica en Mexico: aportaciones derivadas de las investigacion educativa en una institución de salud y seguridad social. *Gac Med MEX* 124(5-6):217-227.

Villalpando-Casas, J. et.al.1988. Los estudios de especialización en medicina. (Specializing studies in medicine). Ciencia y Desarrio 110. CONACYT 79:113.

Walrond, E.R. 1988. The University of The West Indies at the Queen Elizabeth Hospital: The impact of the Faculty of Medical Sciences on health care in Barbados and the Eastern Caribbean. The Charles Duncan O'Neal Lecture. University of The West Indies.

Western Pacific

Danaraj, T.J. 1988. *Medical education in Malaysia: Development and problems*. Darul Ehsan, Selangor, Malaysia: Pelanduk Publications.

Doherty, R.L. (Chairman). 1988. *Australian medical education and workforce into the 21st century*. Report of the Committee of Inquiry into Medical Education and Medical Workforce. Canberra: Australian Government Publishing Service.

Grant. C., and H.M. Lapsley. 1987. *The Australian health care system.* Australian Studies in Health Service Administration no. 60. Kensington: University of New South Wales, School of Health Administration.

Japan. Ministry of Education, Science and Culture. n.d. *Final report of survey researchers' conference on the reform of medical education in Japan.* (In Japanese.)

Japan Society for Medical Education, ed. 1989. Medical education in Japan: Progress in its innovation 1969-1988. Japan Society for Medical Education at its twentieth anniversary. (In Japanese.)

Teacher training in Japan (International News). 1992. *Teaching and Learning in Medicine* 4(4):247-248.

Ushiba, D. 1985. Trends of medical education in Japan. *Medical Education* 19 (4):258-265.

Appendix H: Acronyms and Abbreviations Used in This Handbook

AAMC	Association of American Medical Colleges
ABEM	Associacao Brasileira de Educacao Medica
ABRASCO	Associacao Brasileira de PosGraduacao em Saude Coletiva
ACGME	Accreditation Council on Graduate Medical Education
AFS	Attestation de Formation Spécialisée)
AFSA	Attestation de Formation Spécialisée Approfondie
AIDAB	Australian International Development Assistance Bureau
AIDS	Aquired Immune Deficiency Syndrome
AIIMS	All India Institute of Medical Sciences
AKU	Aga Khan University [Pakistan]
AMA	*American* Medical Association
AMA	*Australian* Medical Association
AMC	Australian Medical Council
AMDE	Association of Medical School Deans of Europe; renamed in April 1993, Association of Medical Schools in Europe (AMSE)
AMEE	Association of Medical Education in Europe
AMEWPR	Western Pacific Association for Medial Education

AMFEM	Mexican Association of Medical Schools
AMSE	Association of Medical Schools in Europe (formerly known as AMDE, Association of Medical School Deans of Europe)
ANDEM	Agence Nationale pour le Developpement de l'Evaluation Médicale [France]
ANZME	Australian and New Zealand Association for Medical Education
ARC	Association pour la Recherche en Cancerologie [France]
ASEAN	Association of Southeast Asian Nations (Thailand, Singapore, Brunei, Indonesia, the Philippines, and Malaysia)
ASME	Association for the Study of Medical School Education
ASOFAMECH	Association of Faculties of Medicine of Chile
AUPELF	Association des Universités Partiellement ou Entièrement de Langue Française [France]
AVEFAM	Venezuelan Association of Medical Schools
AWBZ	Algemene Wet Bijzondere Ziektekosten [Netherlands]
Bac C	Baccalaureate in "hard" sciences: mathematics, physics and chemistry [France]
Bac B	Baccalaureate in biological sciences [France]
BH	Human Biology
BHU	Basic Health Unit
BMA	British Medical Association
CACMS	Committee of Canadian Medical Schools
CAME	Canadian Association for Medical Education
CAMES	Conseil Africain et Malgache de l'Enseignement Supérieur [France]
CAPES	Coordination for Further University Graduate Education (Coordenadoria de Aperfeicoamento de Pessoal de Nivel Superior) [Brazil]
CARIBSEC	Caribbean Community Secretariat
CBO	National Organization for Quality Assurance in Hospitals [Netherlands]

CCH	Caribbean Cooperation of Health
CCMRC	Commonwealth Caribbean Medical Research Council
CEA	Commissariat A l'Energie Atomique [France]
CES	Certificat d'Etudes Spéciales [France]
CFPC	College of Family Physicians of Canada
CHEW	Community Health Extension Worker [Nigeria]
CHO	Community Health Officer [Nigeria]
CHU, CHR	Hospital and University Centres [France]
CIME	Cursus Integré pour la Mobilité des Etudiants [France]
CIOMS	Council for International Organization of Medical Sciences
CMB	China Medical Board
CME	Continuing Medical Education
CMET	Center for Medical Education and Technology [India]
CMO	Chief Medical Officer [Commonwealth Caribbean]
CNCI	Centre National des Concours d'Internat
CNEM	Commission Nationale des Etudes Médicales [France]
CNESER	National Council of Higher Education and Research [France]
CNR	National Research Council [Italy]
CNRS	Centre National de la Recherche Scientifique [France]
CNU	National Council of Universities [Venezuela]
COM-SA	College of Medicine of South Africa
CONICIT	National Council of Scientific and Technological Research [Venezuela]
COPC	Community-Oriented Primary Care
COREX	Commission des Relations Extérieurs de la Conférence des Présidents d'Université [France]
CPEM	Certificat Préparatoire aux Études Médicales [France]
CPSP	College of Physicians and Surgeons Pakistan

CR	Czech Republic
CRC	Clinician Research Center
CSCT	Coopération Scientifique, Technique et du Développement
CSFR	Czech and Slovak Federative Republic
CSTD	Coopération Scientifique, Technique et du Développement [France]
DAGIC	Direction des Affaires Générales, Internationales et de la Coopération [France]
DARC Med	Développement, Approche et Reconnaissance des Différents Curriculum de Médecine
DCEM (1,2,3,4)	designates years in the undergraduate curriuculum [France]
DCH	Diploma in Child Health [Pakistan]
DEA	Diplôme d'Études Approfondés [France]
DES	Diplômes d'Études Spécialisés [France]
DESC	complementary diplomas of specialized studies [France]
DIS	Diplôme Universitaire de Spécialité [France]
DISC	Diplôme Universitaire de Spécialité Complémentaire
DM	Deutsche Marks
DNB	Diplomat of National Board [India]
DPH	Diploma in Public Health [Pakistan]
DRASS	Direction Régionale des Affaires Sanitaires et Sociales [France]
DRG	Diagnostic Related Group
DU	University Diploma [France]
ECFMG	Educational Commission for Foreign Medical Graduates
ECMS	Eastern Caribbean Medical Scheme
EEC	European Economic Community
EMA	Medical Education in the Americas
EMRO	Eastern Mediterranean Regional Office [WHO]

ENSTINET	Egyptian National Scientific and Technical Information Network
EPI	Extended Immunization Programme [Pakistan]
ERASMUS	European Community Action Scheme for the Mobility of University Students
FAO	UN Food and Agriculture Organization
FLEX	Federation Licensing Examination
FMG	Foreign Medical Graduate
FMGEMS	Foreign Medical Graduate Examination in the Medical Sciences
FMP	Family Medicine Program [Australia]
FNDCT	Fundo Nacional de Desenvolvimento Cientifico e Tecnologico [Brazil]
FRCS	Fellow of the Royal College of Surgeons
FRG	German Federal Republic
FTE	full-time equivalent
GCE	General Certificate of Education
GDP	Gross Domestic Product
GDR	German Democratic Republic
GMC	General Medical Council
GNP	Gross National Product
GP	General Practitioner
GPEP	General Professional Education of the Physician
HDR	Habilitation à Diriger les Recherches [France]
HFA	Health For All
HFCA	Health Care Financing Administration
HMD	Health Manpower Development
HMO	Health Maintenance Organization
HSC	Higher Secondary Certificate

HSMD	Health Services and Health Manpower Development
IAAME	Indian Association for the Advancement of Medical Education
ICP	Interuniversity Cooperative Programmes
ICSSR-ICMR	Indian Council for Social Science Research-Indian Council for Medical Research
IDP	Australian Universities International Development Project
IFMA	International Federation of Medical Students Associations
IIU	International Islamic University [Malaysia]
IMF	International Medical Foundation
IMSS	Instituto Mexicano del Seguro Social [Mexico]
INRA	Institut National de la Recherche Agronimique [France]
INSERM	Institut National de la Sante et de la Recherche Médicale [France]
IPASME	Institute of Social Security and Health Care of the Ministry of Education [Venezuela]
IPN	National Polytechnic Institute [Mexico]
IPSFA	The Armed Forces Institute of Social Security [Venezuela]
IRPA	Intensified Research in Priority Areas [Malaysia]
ISSSTE	Instituto de Seguridad y Servicios Sociales para los Trabajadores del Estado [Mexico]
ITTC	International Teacher Training Center
IVSS	Venezuelan Institute of Social Security
IVIC	Central University and Venezuelan Institute for Scientific Research
JAMB	Joint Admission Matriculation Board [Nigeria]
JME	Joint Matriculation Exam [Nigeria]
LCME	Liaison Committee on Medical Education
LMCC	Medical Council of Canada Qualifying Examination
LMP	Licentiate Medical Practitioner [India]

LNC	Ligue Nationale contre le Cancer [France]
LSMF	License of the State Medical Faculty [Pakistan]
MAEMHS	Malaysian Association for Education in the Medical and Health Sciences
MASA	Medical Association of South Africa
MB	Bachelor of Medicine
MBBS	Bachelor of Medicine, Bachelor of Surgery
MCAT	Medical College Admission Test
MCI	Medical Council of India
MCPE	Medical Center of Postgraduate Education [Poland]
MCQ	multiple choice question
MD	Doctor of Medicine
MHFW	Ministry of Health and Family Welfare [India]
MHPE	Master of Health Professions Education
MHSS	Ministry of Health and Social Service [Venezuela]
MMC	Malaysian Medical Coucil
MNAMS	National Academy of Medical Sciences [India]
MOH	Ministry of Health
MPH	Master of Public Health
MRC	Medical Research Council
MRCOG	Member of the Royal College of Obstetrics and Gynecology
MRCP	Member of the Royal College of Physicians
MS	Master of Surgery
MSAS	Ministry of Health and Social Service [Venezuela]
MUDr.	Medicinae Universae Doctor
MURST	Ministry of Universities and Research [Italy]
NAGER	National Geriatric Institute [Venezuela]

NBME	National Board of Medical Examiners
NDMC	National Defence Medical College [Japan]
NHS	National Health Services
NIH	National Institutes for Health
NIMR	National Institute for Medical Research
NMDC	Nigerian Medical and Dental Council
NRMP	National Resident Matching Program
NTTC	National Teacher Training Centre
NUC	National University Commission [Nigeria]
OB/Gyn	Obstetrics/Gynecology
ORS	Oral Rehydration Salts
OSCE	objective structured clinical exam
OUS	Offices of University Services
PAFAMS	Panamerican Federation of Associations of Medical Schools
PAHO	Pan American Health Organization
PBL	problem-based learning
PC2	Second Year [France]
PCB	Certificate of aptitude in Biology [France]
PCEM (1,2)	Preclinical years of the curriculum [France]
PCN	Certificate of aptitude in Physics, Chemistry, and Natural Sciences [France]
PEMEX	Petroleos Mexicanos
PHC	Primary Health Care
PLAB	Professional and Linguistic Ability Board [Pakistan]
PMDC	Pakistan Medical and Dental Council
PMU	Postgraduate Medical University [Hungary]
POS	Port of Spain Hospital

PPO	Preferred Provider Organization
PRC	People's Republic of China
PS	Permanent Secretary
QEH	Queen Elizabeth Hospital [West Indies]
RACGP	Royal Australian College of General Practitioners
RACOG	Royal Australian College of Obstetricians and Gynecologists
RBRVS	Resource-Based Relative Value Scale
RCP	Royal College of Physicians
RCPSC	Royal College of Physicians and Surgeons of Canada
RCS	Royal College of Surgeons
RHB	regional hospital board
ROME	Re-Orientation of Medical Education [India]
RRC	Residence Review Committees
RTTC	Regional Teacher Training Centers
SAMDC	South African Medical and Dental Council
SBM	Biological and Medical Sciences [France]
SR	Slovak Republic
SSC	Secondary School Certificate exam [Pakistan]
TBA	Traditional Birth Attendant [Malaysia]
TEMPUS	Trans European Mobility Programme for University Studies
TNRA	Institut National de la Recherche Agronomique [France]
UAM	Metropolitan Autonomous University [Mexico]
UCT	University of Cape Town [South Africa]
UCWI	University College of The West Indies
UFR	Unité de Formation et Recherche [France]
UG	University of Guyana
UKM	National University of Malaysia [Malaysia]

UM	University of Malaya
UN	United Nations
UNAM	National Autonomous University of Mexico
UNESCO	United Nations Educational, Scientific, and Cultural Organization
UNICEF	United Nations International Children's Emergency Fund
UREF	Université des Réseaux d'Expression Française [France]
USAID	United States Agency for International Development
USM	Science University in Penang [Malaysia]
USMLE	United States Medical Licensing Examination
USSR	Union of Soviet Socialist Republics
UT	University of Transkei
UTMB	University of Texas Medical Branch
UWI	University of the West Indies
UWIH	University (College) Hospital [West Indies]
UWO	University of Western Ontario
VA	Veterans Administration
VRAC	Faculty of Curative Medicine [Russia]
VSS	Venezuelan Institute of Social Security [Venezuela]
VTCHP	Voievodship Training Centres for Health Personnel [Poland]
VTEP	voluntary termination of employment
VWO	pre-university track [Netherlands]
WFME	World Federation for Medical Education
WHO	World Health Organization
ZOZ	Integrated Health Care Center [Poland]
ZVS	Central Bureau for the Administration of Admissions [Germany]

Index

About the Contributors

B.V. ADKOLI, MSc, MEd, serves as an Educationalist at the K.L. Wig Center for Medical Education and Technology, All India Institute of Medical Sciences. His experience relates to the application of educational technology in medical education. He is currently assisting the center in planning, designing, and conducting innovative training programs for medical teachers at the national level.

M. BROWNELL ANDERSON is Assistant Vice President, Division of Medical Student and Resident Education, at the Association of American Medical Colleges. She is responsible for staffing the AAMC's Group on Educational Affairs, an organization devoted to the development of medical education regionally and nationally. In that capacity, she serves as the primary point of referral at the AAMC for information related to curriculum innovations and student evaluation. Ms. Anderson was project director for the AAMC's recently completed ACME-TRI project, which produced *Educating Medical Students*, a report documenting the extent to which American medical schools have responded to calls for change in the medical school curriculum.

EUGENIO ARTEAGA, MD, is Associate Professor of Medicine, Department of Endocrinology, Metabolism and Nutrition in the School of Medicine, Pontificia Universidad Católica de Chile. He was a Fogarty International Fellow in Endocrinology at the University of California, San Francisco. Dr. Arteaga served from 1989-1991 as Associate Director, School of Medicine, Catholic University of Chile. His major fields of research interest are gynecologic endocrinology, bone metabolism, and menopause.

LAURA R. AZIZ, BSN, MHPE, served as a Research Specialist, Department of Medical Education, University of Illinois at Chicago (UIC) from 1990-1993. She is currently a clinical research specialist in the UIC School of Public Health and a PhD candidate in Public Health Sciences. A former Instructor/Demonstrator at the Faculty of Nursing, Cairo University, from 1985-1990 she was employed by the WHO Regional Office for the Eastern Mediterranean (EMRO), Division of Human Resources Development for Health,

Education Development and Support, where she assisted in planning, monitoring and evaluating activities related to health professions education and development in the 23 EMRO countries.

RAJA BANDARANAYAKE, MBBS, PhD, MSEd, FRACS, is Associate Professor and Director of Academic Programs in the School of Medical Education, University of New South Wales. He has 30 years experience in teaching and research in medical education and has undertaken some 60 consultancies in 22 countries. He is on two Australian postgraduate examining boards, has particular interest in curriculum development and evaluation and has written several publications on medical education. His current research project is a multidimensional evaluation of a new medical curriculum.

FERENC BOJÁN, MD, PhD, is Professor and Head of the Department of Social Medicine, University Medical School, Debrecen, Hungary, where he lectures on epidemiology, health policy, and health systems. Dr. Boján is coordinator of the European Communities Joint European Project, "Development of Medical Education for a New Public Health in Hungary," and president of the Hungarian Society for Public Health.

FRANÇOIS BONNAUD, MD, is Professor des Universités, praticien hospitalier, and Dean of the Faculty of Medicine, Limoges. Professor Bonnaud is a spécialiste d'immuno-allergologie, Specialiste de pneumonologie, and Président du Bureau de pédagogie de la Faculté de médecine de Limoges.

PETER A.J. BOUHUIJS, MA, PhD, is currently an associate professor in educational research and development at the University of Limburg in the Netherlands. He has a master's degree in experimental psychology and a doctorate in medical education. Since 1975 he has been working in the innovative Faculty of Medicine in Maastricht. He has published on various topics, including problem based learning, educational management, curriculum development, and continuing medical education. He has worked as an educational consultant in medical education in Egypt, Sudan, Thailand, the United States, Great Britain, Italy, and Canada. In 1985 he was a Fulbright Scholar at the University of Texas Medical Branch in Galveston with the late Abdul Sajid. In the Netherlands, he is editor of a Dutch journal on teaching in higher education.

L. CASSIERS is Doyen de la Faculté de Médecine, Université Catholique de Louvain. He was formerly the head of the Clinical Psychiatric Research Unit, Psychopathology-Psychiatry Group, School of Medicine, Faculty of Medicine, Université Catholique de Louvain.

J.M. CHABOT, MD, is Associate Professor in the Department of Public Health, Necker Faculty of Medicine, Paris V University. He serves as Chief Executive Officer of the National Council of Medical Board Examiners and is a Director of the Board for the Sub-Specialty "Medical Education" conducted at Paris-Necker, Paris-Dichat, and Lyon universities.

MICHAEL S. CULLEN, JP, BPharm, MCPP, MPS, MHSM, is Dean, Faculty of Health and Community Studies, University of Derby, UK, and Pharmaceutical Advisor to Southern Derbyshire Health Authority. He is active in teaching and education management. He is also active in research, and has initiated several programs at the University of Derby

HAROLD A. DRAYTON, PhD, is Director, WHO Collaborating Center for International Health and Professor, Preventive Medicine/Community Health, University of Texas Medical Branch. A founder and first Deputy Vice Chancellor of the University of Guyana, Dr. Drayton has more than 30 years' experience in tertiary-level education in the Commonwealth (English-speaking) Caribbean, including 17 years as the PAHO/WHO Caribbean Advisor on Human Resources Development for Health. From 1975-1989, he served as manager of the UNDP-funded Caribbeanwide Regional Project for the Education and Training of Health Personnel. Dr. Drayton has published widely in the field of health sciences and education. His original field of scholarship was tumor virology.

VITTORIO GHETTI, MD, a specialist in pneumonology, was trained in general surgery before becoming Medical Director of Ciba and General Director of Ciba-Geigy. Since 1979, Dr. Ghetti has been Vice President and Director of the Smith Kline Foundation of Italy, a WHO Collaborating Centre in Health Manpower Development. With the Foundazione Smith Kline he organized more than 300 workshops and more than 100 seminars on topics related to medical education. He is the editor of 80 books on related topics.

PHILLIP GODWIN, MHPEd, is a Visiting Fellow in the School of Medical Education, University of New South Wales. His professional experience has been in Nursing Education, Health Administration, Medicine and Medical Education. His current research interests include the evaluation of the hospital component of the Family Medicine Program and a health care worker project focusing on HIV/AIDS-related discrimination.

LINDA K. GUNZBURGER, PhD, is Associate Dean at Chicago Medical School. Her publications have focused on issues in continuing medical education.

NABILA HIDAYET, MD, MPH, Dr. P.H., is Professor of Preventive Medicine and Community Health, Faculty of Medicine, University of Alexandria, Egypt, where she has been active in development of innovative medical school curricula, both at her own institution and as a consultant to other regional institutions. She has been the recipient of Ford Foundation, WHO, and Fulbright fellowships, most recently to participate in the 1991 International Salzburg Seminar on New Priorities in Health Care. Dr. Hidayet is an active participant in the Network of Community-Oriented Educational Institutions for Health Sciences. Her research has focused on child survival programs and community-oriented health education and services.

TONGCHAN HONGLADAROM, MD, Dr.med., MEd, is Professor in Medical Education, Chulalongkorn University and Consultant in Medical Education to the Dean of Faculty of Medicine, Thommasat University, Thailand. He served as President (1979-1985) and Acting Dean of the Faculty of Medicine (1979), Prince of Songkla University. Dr. Hongladarom is a member of the WHO Expert Advisory Panel on Development of Human Resources for Health.

NAEEM A. JAFAREY, MBBS, is Honorary Co-Director and Professor of Pathology, National Teacher Training Center, College of Physicians and Surgeons Pakistan. He also served on several occasions as a consultant to the World Health Organization in educational development and support. His research interests are in continuing medical education and evaluation and assessment of medical students.

VÁCLAV JANOUŠEK, MD, PhD, is Professor and Vice Dean, First Medical Faculty, Charles University, Prague, and Head of the Department for Medical Education of the Postgraduate Medical and Pharmaceutical Institute, Prague. He has served as Chairman of the Czech Association for Education of Health Personnel, President of the Association of Medical Schools in Europe, member of the Advisory Board of the Association for Medical Education in Europe and Task Force CME in Europe. He is an honorary member of the Polish Academy of Medicine and is active in research and teaching in the field of medical education in which he is author and co-author of a number of papers.

ROBERT F. JONES, PhD, is Assistant Vice President for Institutional and Faculty Policy Studies at the Association of American Medical Colleges (AAMC). His specific areas of interest and responsibility encompass institutional governance and strategic planning in academic medical centers, faculty personnel policies and tenure, and space and facilities planning. He is the author or coauthor of over 25 published articles and monographs, and the editor of one book, on policies and programs in American medical education, including the Association's biennial report, *American Medical Education: Institutions, Programs, and Issues.*

SANTOSH S. KACKER, MBBS, MS, FRCS, is Director, All India Institute of Medical Sciences. He specializes in otorhinolaryngology with special interests in neuro-otology and rehabilitation of the communication handicapped. He was awarded "Padma Shri" (1986) and Jawaharlal Nehru fellowships (1987-1989) for his contributions toward the prevention of hearing impairment in children. Dr. Kacker is chairman of the Rehabilitation Council of India, Speech and Hearing section and Chair of the Committee for the development of aids for the handicapped. Recently, he has been working to introduce educational reforms in undergraduate and postgraduate medical colleges in India.

JOSÉ LAGUNA, MD, is Emeritus Professor, National Autonomous University (NAU) of Mexico School of Medicine. A former Planning Vice Minister in the Ministry of Health, Dr. Laguna served as Chairman of the Biochemistry Department, NAU School of Medicine and as the Director of the NAU School of Medicine.

JOSEPH H. LEVENSTEIN, MD, was Head of the unit of General Practice at the University of Cape Town and Chairman of the South African Academy of Family Practice/Primary Care before becoming Executive Head of the Departments of Family and Community Medicine and also Head of Family Medicine at the University of Illinois College of Medicine at Rockford in 1990. Dr. Levenstein's main areas of expertise are community-based research and education. He is a consultant to the Network of Community-Oriented Educational Institutions for Health Sciences and the World Health Organization.

OCTAVIO CASTILLO Y LÓPEZ, MD, is Dean, Popular Autonomous University of Puebla, and President of the Mexican Association of Medical Schools, Mexico.

MA XU, MD, is Director, National Center for Medical Education Development, Beijing Medical University. He is a member of the Accrediting Committee for Higher Education, National Education Committee (China) and serves on the Executive Committee of the Network of Community-Oriented Educational

Institutions for Health Sciences. Dr. Ma also serves as a consultant to the Ministry of Health and the Ministry of Higher Education.

CHRISTINE H. MCGUIRE is Professor Emerita, Department of Medical Education, University of Illinois at Chicago (UIC) College of Medicine, where she served as Associate Director and Head of Research and Evaluation from 1961-1987. She is Past National Chairman of the Group on Medical Education of the AAMC, Past President of the National Council on Measurement in Education and the Division of Professional Education of the American Educational Research Association. She is an internationally known lecturer on medical education and continues to serve as a consultant to WHO, numerous medical schools, specialty boards and examining bodies worldwide. She is best known for her research on evaluation of problem-solving and clinical judgment and for the introduction of patient management problems and other techniques in the assessment of clinical competence for which she received the John P. Hubbard Award of the National Board of Medical Examiners.

ALESSANDRO MARTIN, MD, is Senior Research Fellow at the University of Padova, Italy, Division of Gastroenterology. He is a member of the Steering Committee of the Italian Association for Medical Education. As a practicing academic gastroenterologist, he has been involved in national and international innovations in medical education at both the under- and postgraduate levels. He is the author of several articles, and chapters in books and is also the editor of books related to medical education.

GEORGE E. MILLER, MD, Professor Emeritus, University of Illinois at Chicago (UIC) College of Medicine founded the Office of Research in Medical Education, later the Center for Educational Development (CED), at UIC in 1959. CED (now the Department of Medical Education) became a WHO Collaborating Center in 1969. Dr. Miller received his medical degree from the University of Pennsylvania School of Medicine and is recognized by many as one of the "founding fathers of medical education," having instituted the Project in Medical Education at the University of Buffalo, the first sustained research and development collaboration between medical faculty members and professional educators. The author of numerous professional publications, he is perhaps best known for his seminal book, *Teaching and Learning in Medical School*. In 1985 the National Board of Medical Examiners awarded him its highest honor, the John P. Hubbard Award, for significant contributions to the pursuit of excellence in the field of evaluation in medicine. He served for 25 years as a consultant to the World Health Organization Division of Health Manpower Development.

DAVID M. MIRVIS, MD, is Professor of Preventive Medicine and Associate Dean, College of Medicine, University of Tennessee, Memphis, Tennessee. His contribution to this Handbook was written during his tenure as a Sabbatical Scholar at the JDC-Brookdale Institute, Jerusalem, Israel.

OLATOYE OGUNBODE, MD, FRCOG, is Director, WHO Collaborating Centre, and Head of the Department of Obstetrics and Gynaecology, Faculty of Health Sciences, University of Ilorin, Nigeria. He completed a term as Dean of the Faculty of Health Sciences at the University of Ilorin in 1990. Dr. Ogunbode served as Chairman of the National Association of Colleges of Medicine in 1989-1990. He has been active in the promotion of medical education throughout

Africa. His international activities include membership on the WHO Regional Task Force on Medical Education and work with the Network of Community Oriented Educational Institutions for Health Sciences, which he served as Chair from 1989-1991. He participated in the Edinburgh Conference on Medical Education of the World Federation on Medical Education and was coordinator of the Organizing Committee of the Biennial Conference of the Network, convened in Nigeria in 1991.

MOSHE PRYWES, MD, is most widely known for his role as the founding Dean of the innovative Faculty of Health Sciences at Ben Gurion University of the Negev, Beer Sheva, Israel, where he established the educational program as an integral participant in the health services system. A surgeon, Professor Prywes received his medical degree at Warsaw University. He immigrated to Israel in 1951, was an invited speaker at the first World Conference on Medical Education in 1953, and a founder of the Network of Community Oriented Educational Institutions for Health Sciences in 1979. He has been Editor-in-Chief of the *Israel Journal of Medical Sciences* since 1964. Professor Prywes has received numerous awards and honors, including the Israeli Prize in Medicine, the highest Israeli scientific distinction.

PABLO PULIDO, MD, FACP, is Executive Director of the Panamerican Federation of Associations of Medical Schools (PAFAMS) and Venezuela's interim (August 1993-February 1994) director of the Ministry of Health. He is also President of Centro Médico Docente La Trinidad, a teaching health care delivery academic center in Caracas. Dr. Pulido is a founding member of the Governing Board of the Universidad Metropolitana in Caracas and President of the Board of Trustees of Fundación Universidad Metropolitana. He has been a member of the Board of the Venezuelan Council for Scientific Research and Technology (CONICIT) and has published in areas related to analytical chemistry, biochemistry of parasites, internal medicine, tropical pathology and medical education.

ELIANA CLAUDIA RIBEIRO, MD, MPH, is Vice-Director of the Nucleous of Health Education Technology--NUTES (Núcleo de Tecnologia Educacional para a Saúde) Center of the Health Sciences, Federal University of Rio de Janeiro, where she is also an Associate Professor, lecturing at the graduate level on medical education, curricular planning, and teaching methodologies.

ROBERTO RONDÓN, M. MD, is Program Director of the Panamerican Federation of Associations of Medical Schools (PAFAMS). As a former professor of physiology and Dean of the School of Medicine of Los Andes University, he has extensive experience in medical education. As Program Director of PAFAMS, Dr. Rondón is responsible for coordinating international projects that contribute to the improvement of medical education in different counties of the Americas. He has headed various institutions of higher learning, and has published a number of scientific articles and books on health, medical education, and university affairs.

PEDRO ROSSO, MD, is Dean, Faculty of Medicine, Pontificia Universidad Católica de Chile. Dr. Rosso received his MD from the School of Medicine, University of Chile, where he also completed a fellowship in Pediatrics. He served as Director, Division of Growth and Development, Institution of Human

Nutrition at Columbia University, New York, and from 1984-1990 was Head of the Commission of Scientific Research and Director of the Center for Medical Research, School of Medicine, Catholic University of Chile. Dr. Rosso's fields of research interest include maternal nutrition, fetal growth, and maternal-fetal exchange.

EVA RYTEN, B. ès.Sc.Soc, is the Director of the Office of Research of the Association of Canadian Medical Colleges, a position she has occupied for more than 15 years. Her educational background is in statistics, political sciences, and demography. She has had a 30-year career in the study of education and educational statistics, including several years at UNESCO and the Organization for Economic Cooperation and Development in Paris. She was in charge of university statistics for the national statistical office of Canada prior to moving to the ACMC.

ABDUL W. SAJID, EdD, was Head of the University of Illinois at Chicago (UIC) Department of Medical Education and Associate Dean for Undergraduate Medical Education in the College of Medicine at the time of his death in 1992. From 1971-1982, Dr. Sajid was a faculty member in the department's predecessor, the Center for Educational Development. In 1990 he returned to UIC from the University of Texas Medical Branch in Galveston, where he was Director, Office of Educational Development/World Health Organization Collaborating Center for International Health; Professor, Preventive Medicine and Community Health; and Division Chief, International Health. He was a member of the Expert Panel Group on Health Manpower of the World Health Organization, and he served as Executive Secretary of the Governing Board of the National Council for International Health. His international teaching, consulting, and research in medical education took him to Abu Dhabi, Bahrain, Brazil, China, Egypt, Kuwait, Mexico, Pakistan, Qatar, Saudi Arabia, Sudan, Switzerland, Syria, Venezuela, and the Caribbean.

LUIZ ANTONIO SANTINI, MD, is Executive Director of the Brazilian Association of Medical Education--ABEM (Associao Brasileira de Eduçâo Medica) and Professor of Surgery, Universidade Federal Fluminense. Dr. Santini completed his residency and master's degrees in general and thoracic surgery. He is currently completing a PhD at the National School of Public Health, Oswaldo Cruz Foundation. He is a former director of the Medical School at Universidade Federal Fluminense, and also served as Vice Health Secretary of the state of Rio de Janeiro.

SHARIFAH H. SHAHABUDIN, MBBS, MHPEd., is Professor and Head, Department of Medical Education, National University of Malaysia. Dr. Shahabudin is responsible for program development and evaluation and teacher training and is currently developing distance learning programs for postgraduate and continuing education. Dr. Shahabudin's current research interest is continuing medical education, with particular emphasis on practice-linked CME.

SHRIDHAR SHARMA, MD, FRC, Psy (London), FRANZCP (Australia), is Director of a new Institute of Human Behavior and Allied Sciences in Delhi. A former Additional Director General of Health Services in the Ministry of Health, Government of India, Dr. Sharma is an eminent psychiatrist, a medical educationalist, and was the administrator responsible for medical education in

DGHS. He is the former Director of the Postgraduate Institute of Medical Education and Research, Chandigarh and Central Institute of Psychiatry, Ranchi; was Professor and Chairman in the Department of Psychiatry in Goa Medical College; and has held several national and international positions in research and professional associations. He is the author of 5 books and monographs and more than 150 research papers. Prof. Sharma has been actively involved in the field of medical education for more than three decades.

GÁBOR SZABÓ, MD, PhD, is Professor and Head of the Institute of Medical Biology, University Medical School, Debrecen, Hungary. A former dean of the same school (1973-1979), he is a lecturer on genetics, and cell and molecular biology and has been a member of the International Scientific Advisory Board of the Director General of WHO since 1988.

DAIZO USHIBA, MD, Dr.Med.Sci., is Professor Emeritus, Keio University. He formerly was Chairman of the Board of Directors of the International Medical Information Center. He is President of the Japan Society for Medical Education, Japan's first organization specializing in medical education, which he founded in 1969. He has written on trends of medical education in Japan and promotion of medical education research.

HENDRIK VAN DEN BUSSCHE was born in Belgium and received the MD degree at the Catholic University of Leuven. A German citizen since 1977, he was a Research Fellow at the Universities of Munich, Ulm and Frankfurt a. M. in the fields of medical education and medical sociology. Professor van den Bussche served as Professor of Medical Education, Interdisciplinary Center for Research and Development in Higher Education at the University of Hamburg from 1975-1992. Since January 1993 he has been Head, Unit for Health Service Services and Primary Care Research, Medical Faculty, University of Hamburg.

FELIX VARTANIAN, MD, Vice Rector and Professor, Central Institute for Advanced Medical Studies. From 1973-1980, Dr. Vartanian was in charge of the WHO program on Biological Psychiatry and Psychopharmacology, WHO, Geneva. He is a member of several national and international management organizations and editorial boards of international journals. He is the author of more than 200 publications.

REBECCA MONROE VEACH, MA, is Editor and Staff Associate, Department of Medical Education, and Assistant to the Associate Dean for Undergraduate Medical Education at the University of Illinois at Chicago College of Medicine. Her previous publications are in the field of American history, including co-editorship of a collection of essays on Abraham Lincoln and a study of the middle-size cities of Illinois.

A. VERGNENEGRE, MD, is Maître de Conference des Universités, Department of Public Health and chief of the medical information department, University Hospital, Limoges, France.

JOSÉ DE JESÚS VILLALPANDO-CASAS, MD, is a graduate of the National Autonomous University of Mexico. He has served as both an undergraduate and a postgraduate professor and is currently General Director of Education in Health for the Mexican Ministry of Health.

JOSEF VYŠOHLÍD, MD, DrSc., is Associate Professor and Consultant, Postgraduate Medical and Pharmaceutical Institute, Prague. His career has spanned nearly four decades of national and international studies, publications, and experience concerning postgraduate and continuing medical education. He spent nine years at the WHO Regional Office for Africa, where he was charged with education and training of health personnel. He is initiator/founder and former head of the Department for Medical Education at the Postgraduate Insitute, Prague; the Czech Association for Education of Health Personnel; the Research Group on Education of Health Personnel in the Czech Republic. In the field of CME, he is, among others, a co-author of the publication *Continuing Medical Education for Change*, WHO Regional Office for Europe, 1990.

MARJORIE P. WILSON, MD, has been President and CEO of the Educational Commission for Foreign Medical Graduates since 1988 and a visiting board member of the University of Pittsburgh School of Medicine since 1974. She is a member of the Robert Wood Johnson Health Policy Fellowship board, a member of the board of trustees of Analytical Services, Inc.; and a member of the National Board of Medical Examiners from 1980 to 1987 and again starting in 1989. Her research interests include the management of medical systems, especially education, research, health care leadership roles and decision making in academic medicine.

ANDRZEJ WOJTCZAK, MD, DMSc., is Professor of Medicine and Public Health and Dean, Faculty of Social Medicine, Medical Centre of Postgraduate Education, Warsaw. A former Fellow of the Rockefeller Foundation, he is an Honorary Member of the Polish Medical Alliance and serves on the Expert Panel Group of the World Health Organization. Dr. Wojtczak is Vice President of the Polish Society of Social Medicine and Public Health, a member of the Executive Committee of the Association of Medical Education of Europe and the Steering Committee of EurotransMed Leiden, a Corresponding Member of the Editorial Board of the *Journal of Public Health Policy*, and editor of *Medical World, Warsaw*. He is author of more than 250 publications and is editor of the three volume *Internal Medicine Textbook for Physicians*, a new edition of which will be published in 1994 by Polish Medical Publisher, Warsaw.